Banned Books: 2007 Resource Book

ROBERT P. DOYLE

The Giver
Lois Lowry

CAPTAIN UNDERPANTS AND THE PREPOSTEROUS PLIGHT OF THE PURPLE POTTY PEOPLE

Evil!

Horror

Laffs

THE EIGHTH EPIC NOVEL BY DAV PILKEY

TO KILL A MOCKINGBIRD
Harper Lee

Sponsored by:
AMERICAN BOOKSELLERS ASSOCIATION
AMERICAN BOOKSELLERS FOUNDATION FOR FREE EXPRESSION
AMERICAN LIBRARY ASSOCIATION
AMERICAN SOCIETY OF JOURNALISTS AND AUTHORS
ASSOCIATION OF AMERICAN PUBLISHERS
NATIONAL ASSOCIATION OF COLLEGE STORES

Endorsed by:
CENTER FOR THE BOOK IN THE LIBRARY OF CONGRESS

BANNED BOOKS AHOY!
TREASURE YOUR FREEDOM TO READ

AMERICAN LIBRARY ASSOCIATION
CHICAGO, ILLINOIS

2007 Design by Paper&Paperless, Chicago, IL

Printed on 60# Finch Opaque by Data Reproductions, Corp., Auburn Hills.

Copyright © 2007 by the American Library Association.

MAY 1 4 2009

ISBN-10: 0-8389-8425-8   ISBN-13: 978-0-8389-8425-3   ISSN: 0888-0123   LCCN: 88-659709

Table of Contents

 The following sections are available at
www.ala.org/bbooks

Books Challenged or Banned in 2006–2007

Display Ideas

First Amendment Time Line

List of Concerned National Organizations

Clip Art

the Attic

The Giving Tree

Harry Potter

Huck Finn

The Lorax

Mother Goose

The Giver

Lois Lowry

"If we don't believe in freedom of expression for people we despise, we don't believe in it at all."

—Noam Chomsky,
U.S. professor of linguistics (1928–)

The message of Banned Books Week is more than the freedom to choose or the freedom to express oneself. The essential message is that it takes more than lip service to ensure that ideas and viewpoints, popular or not, as expressed by published authors, be available to all who wish to read them.

More than simply documenting the trials and tribulations of actual or attempted bannings, over the centuries, worldwide, *Banned Books Week: Celebrating the Freedom to Read* is an opportunity to call attention to the importance of the First Amendment in a positive and proactive way. This publication is intended to encourage educational programs, including exhibits, lectures, discussions, plays, and films demonstrating the harms of censorship and the benefits of a society with a free and open flow of information.

The largest section is devoted to historical examples of censorship from 387 B.C. to 2007, and this year's edition contains two hundred new entries, ranging from *Gilgamesh: A New English Version* to *What's Eating Gilbert Grape?* All entries are books published in the English language and emphasize recent U.S. incidents involving popular titles. The verification source for each incident is listed.

The list of books challenged or removed from public and school library shelves in 2006–2007 include those by authors living and dead, with characters real and imagined, intended for audiences from young children to adults. Some are new to this list, and many are "repeat offenders." It doesn't seem to matter whether the offense is talking to God or believing in the devil, using language that's either out-of-date or too up-to-date, or something as simple as not wearing pajamas.

How It All Began

The idea of Banned Books Week emerged from the tremendously successful display of banned books in padlocked cages at the 1982 American Booksellers Association (ABA) Convention in Anaheim, California.

Later that same year, the first full week of September was chosen to coincide with the beginning of the school year, because many of the challenges occur in the school systems throughout the country. The ABA and the cosponsoring National Association of College Stores (NACS) sent out a promotional packet to their members that included a list of more than five hundred banned books, a two-color poster stating "Caution! Some People Think These Books Are Dangerous," a sample press release to send to the local media, and background information for booksellers. The American Library Association endorsed the week and publicized the event to its members.

The press—both local and national—responded enthusiastically. National coverage included a segment on NBC-TV's *Today Show*, AP and UPI wire stories, and articles and editorials in dozens of newspapers from the *New York Times* and the *Boston Globe* to the *Charlottesville, Virginia Daily Progress*. Book censorship became a front-page story for dozens of newspapers, and creators, printers, sellers, and distributors of the printed word—authors and journalists, publishers, booksellers, and librarians—became the on-camera authorities for local TV news shows. Coincidentally, Barbara Jordan's *Crisis to Crisis* series on PBS-TV featured an episode titled "Books Under Fire," which aired during the week of September 10.

During that first Banned Books Week in 1982, the most frequent questions from press and the library community across the country were, "Why was the book banned?" "Where was it banned?" "When was it banned?" "What can we do?" The list of five hundred banned books distributed by ABA and NACS didn't offer any answers—there were no annotations or explanations.

Introduction

For the next Banned Books Week in 1983, the American Library Association's Office for Intellectual Freedom prepared "A List of Books Some People Consider Dangerous," by Robert P. Doyle. The first list contained 404 titles—this year's list contains more than 1,700. Each entry offers a brief explanation of the reasons, location, and dates for the challenged, restricted, or banned titles. Then as now, the publication was intended to draw attention to the importance of the freedom to read.

Why It Matters

This freedom, not only to choose what we read, but also to select from a full array of possibilities, is firmly rooted in the First Amendment to the U.S. Constitution, which guarantees freedom of speech and freedom of the press. Although we enjoy an increasing quantity and availability of information and reading material, we must remain vigilant to assure that access to this material is preserved; would-be censors continue to threaten the freedom to read and come from all quarters and all political persuasions. Even if their motivations for restrictions are well intentioned, censors try to limit the freedom of others to choose what they read, see, or hear.

Sex, profanity, and racism remain the primary categories of objections, and most occur in schools and school libraries. Frequently, challenges are motivated by the desire to protect children. While the intent is commendable, this method of protection contains hazards far greater than exposure to the "evil" against which the protection is leveled. Supreme Court Justice William Brennan, in *Texas v. Johnson*, said, "If there is a bedrock principle underlying the First Amendment, it is that the Government may not prohibit the expression of an idea simply because society finds the idea itself offensive or disagreeable." Individuals may restrict what they themselves or their children read, but they must not call on governmental or public agencies to prevent others from reading or seeing that material.

The challenges documented in this publication are not brought by people merely expressing a point of view; rather, they represent requests that these materials be removed from schools or libraries, thus restricting access to them by others. Even when the eventual outcome allows the book to stay on the library shelves and even when the person is a lone protester, the censorship attempt is real. Someone has tried to restrict another person's ability to

choose. Challenges are as important to document as actual bannings, in which a book is removed from the shelves of a library or bookstore or from the curriculum at a school. Attempts to censor can lead to voluntary restriction of expression by those who seek to avoid controversy; in these cases, material may not be published at all or may not be purchased by a bookstore, library, or school district.

We have reason to celebrate. Due to the commitment of parents, students, librarians, teachers, and other concerned citizens, more and more challenges are unsuccessful, and the reading material remains available.

It should be noted that this bibliography is incomplete because many prohibitions against free speech and expression remain undocumented. Surveys indicate approximately 85 percent of the challenges to library materials receive no media attention and remain unreported. Moreover, this list is limited to books and does not include challenges to magazines, newspapers, films, broadcasts, plays, performances, electronic publications, or exhibits.

Caution! Some People Consider These Books Dangerous. This list includes books that have been banned or considered controversial from 387 B.C. to 2007. Browsing through this list can provide valuable ideas for preparing an exhibit or preparing for discussions, presentations, and writings.

Notable First Amendment Court Cases. This section describes some noted legal precedents concerning freedom of speech and can be used to support your programs, presentations, articles, and displays.

Quotes on the First Amendment. Summing up the value of the First Amendment can be difficult for the layperson, especially compared to these effective and memorable expressions by notable individuals! Use these quotes to illustrate your displays, provide inspiration for your celebration, include in your press materials or print on T-shirts or tote bags.

Action Guide. This section features suggested activities. From ordering lapel buttons to sponsoring a community-wide forum on censorship, creative ways to draw attention to your bookstore/library and the freedom to read are presented here. Success stories of activities from the field are included, as well as information on how to order T-shirts, books, educational materials—and even copies of the U.S. Constitution. Also included are basic public relations tips and an annotated bibliography of publications on the topic.

This year a number of resources are available at the American Library Association's Web site. For example, display ideas, a First Amendment time line, a list of concerned national organizations, and clip art are all available at http://www.ala.org/bbooks. In addition, *Books Challenged or Banned in 2006–2007* is available at http://www.ala.org/bbooks. This short list makes it easier for you to identify material that has been challenged within the past year. Reprints of the short list are available for distribution to bookstore customers and library patrons.

Indices. The three indices to the comprehensive list can help customize an exhibit or program by identifying challenged books by title, location, and category. For example, if you want to create an exhibit of books banned or challenged in your state or city, use the geographic index to find the titles. Or, if you want to have a program on children's literature or gay literature, check the topical index. Using these tools will help create an event targeted for your audience or community. Please note that the bibliography entries are numbered sequentially and the entry number (not the page number) is used in all three indices.

CAUTION! Some People Consider These Books Dangerous

e Attic

The Giving Tree

Harry Potter

The Lorax

Mother Goose

#1 *New York Times* bestselling author

JUDY BLUME

Winner of the National Book Foundation Medal for Distinguished Contribution to American Letters

Caution! Some People Consider These Books Dangerous

This "List of Books Some People Consider Dangerous" is a compilation of actual or attempted bannings, over the centuries, worldwide. All entries are books published in the English language and emphasis is on recent U.S. incidents involving popular titles. This list of books was compiled from the following sources:

1. Bald, Margaret. *Literature Suppressed on Religious Grounds, Rev. ed.* New York: Facts on File, 2006.

2. Geller, Evelyn. *Forbidden Books in American Public Libraries, 1876-1939: A Study in Cultural Change.* Westport, Conn.: Greenwood Pr., 1984.

3. Green, Jonathon. *The Encyclopedia of Censorship.* New York: Facts On File, 1990.

4. Haight, Anne Lyon, and Chandler B. Grannis. *Banned Books, 387 B.C. to 1978 A.D.*, 4th ed. New York: Bowker Co., 1978.

5. *Index on Censorship.* London: Writers and Scholars International, Ltd., published bimonthly.

6. Jones, Derek, ed. *Censorship: A World Encyclopedia. 4 vols.* Chicago: Fitzroy Dearborn, 2001.

7. Karolides, Nicholas J. *Literature Suppressed on Political Grounds, Rev. ed.* New York: Facts on File, 2006.

8. Karolides, Nicholas J., Margaret Bald, and Dawn B. Sova. *120 Banned Books: Censorship Histories of World Literature, Rev. ed.* New York: Checkmark Books, 2005.

9. *Limiting What Students Shall Read: Books and Other Learning Materials in Our Public Schools: How They Are Selected and How They Are Removed.* Report on a survey sponsored by Association of American Publishers, American Library Association, Association for Supervision and Curriculum Development. Washington, D.C.: Association of American Publishers, 1981.

10. Nelson, Randy F. "Banned in Boston and Elsewhere." In *The Almanac of American Letters.* Los Altos, Calif.: William Kaufmann, Inc., 1981.

11. *Newsletter on Intellectual Freedom.* Judith F. Krug, ed. Chicago, Ill.: American Library Association, Intellectual Freedom Committee, published bimonthly.

12. O'Neil, Robert M. *Classrooms in the Crossfire: The Rights and Interests of Students, Parents, Teachers, Administrators, Librarians, and the Community.* Bloomington, Ind.: Indiana University Press, 1981.

13. Sova, Dawn B. *Literature Suppressed on Sexual Grounds, Rev. ed.* New York: Facts on File, 2006.

14. _____. *Literature Suppressed on Social Grounds, Rev. ed.* New York: Facts on File, 2006.

15. Tebbel, John. *A History of Book Publishing in the United States.* New York: Bowker Co., 1981.

This compilation is admittedly incomplete because it is impossible to document and record all prohibitions against free speech and expression. In fact, this list is limited to books and therefore does not include prohibitions against magazines, newspapers, films, broadcasts, plays, performances, exhibits, or access to electronic resources. The professional, economic, or emotional consequences of the curtailment of an author's free expression also are not documented.

At the 1986 American Library Association (ALA) Annual Conference, the ALA Intellectual Freedom Committee adopted the following operative definitions of some terms frequently used to describe the various levels of incidents that may or may not lead to censorship. This terminology is employed by the *Newsletter on Intellectual Freedom.*

Expression of Concern: An inquiry that has judgmental overtones.

Oral Complaint: An oral challenge to the presence and/or appropriateness of the material in question.

Written Complaint: A formal, written complaint filed with the institution (library, school, etc.) challenging the presence and/or appropriateness of specific material.

Public Attack: A publicly disseminated statement challenging the value of the material, presented to the media and/or others outside the institutional organization in order to gain public support for further action.

Censorship: A change in the access status of material, made by a governing authority or its representatives. Such changes include: exclusion, restriction, removal, or age/grade level changes.

1 Abelard, Pierre. *The Letters of Abelard & Heloise.* Cooper Square. The Catholic Church condemned and burned his Introduction to Theology (1121). In 1140, he was charged with heresy, confined to a monastery, and forbidden to continue writing. Listed in the *Index Librorum Prohibitorum* (1559 and 1564). U.S. Customs lifted ban on Love Letters (1930). Source: 1, pp. 163–65; 4, p. 6; 6, pp. 2–3.

2 Abernathy, Rev. Ralph D. *And the Walls Came Tumbling Down.* Harper. Burned in protest in Denver, Colo. (1989) because it alleges that Martin Luther King, Jr. was involved with three women. E. Napolean Walton, publisher of the *Denver Cosmopolitan Advertiser*, stated, "[Abernathy] has his freedom of speech, and we have our freedom to burn it." Source: 11, Jan. 1990, p. 19.

3 Abrahams, Roger D. *African Folktales: Traditional Stories of the Black World.* Pantheon. Dallas, Tex. school administrators (1991) told teachers to rip an offending page from the school textbooks because the story, which refers to male genitals and bodily functions, didn't fit the curriculum. Instructors were also asked to avoid teaching the first two chapters of another book that dealt in part with circumcision and puberty. Source: 11, Nov. 1991, p. 197.

4 Adams, Carmen. *The Band.* Avon. Challenged, but retained, at the Madison Elementary School in Cedar Rapids, Iowa (1998). Source: 11, May 1998, pp. 87–88.

5 Adler, C. S. *Down by the River.* Coward. Removed from the Evergreen School District of Vancouver, Wash. (1983) along with twenty-nine other titles. The American Civil Liberties Union of Washington filed suit contending that the removals constituted censorship, a violation of plaintiff's rights to free speech and due process, and the acts were a violation of the state Open Meetings Act because the removal decisions were made behind closed doors. Source: 11, Nov. 1983, pp. 185–86.

6 Adler, David. *I Know I'm a Witch.* Holt. Retained on the shelves at Prairieview Elementary School in Elgin, Ill. (1998) despite a parent's complaint that the material gives children the impression that witchcraft is "fun and harmless." Source: 11, May 1998, p. 87.

7 Adler, Margo. *Drawing down the Moon.* Beacon Pr. Removed from the Kirby Junior High School in Wichita Falls, Tex. (1997) because of "Satanic" themes. Source: 11, July 1997, p. 95.

8 Adoff, Arnold, ed. *Poetry of Black America.* HarperCollins. Challenged at the Fort Walton Beach, Fla. school libraries (1996) because it "promotes violence" and contains "expletives and a reference to abortion." Source: 11, July 1996, p. 133.

9 Adoff, Arnold. *The Cabbages Are Chasing the Rabbits.* Harcourt. Challenged at the Deer Ridge, Ind. Elementary School (1992) because the book could breed intolerance for hunters in children's minds. Source: 11, May 1992, p. 94.

10 Affabee, Eric. *Wizards, Warriors & You.* Corgi. Removed from the Fairfield, Ohio elementary school libraries (1992) because of "wizardry themes." The series of books were initially challenged because they "promote violence and acceptance and involvement in occult practices." Source: 11, Sept. 1992, p. 138; Nov. 1992, p. 185.

11 Agee, Philip. *Inside the Company: CIA Diary.* Bantam; Stonehill. U.S. Customs stopped delivery of imported copies of Agee's book (1974). Source: 4, p. 99.

12 Agrippa, Henricus Cornelius. *Of the Vanitie and Uncertaintie of Artes and Sciences.* Calif. State Univ. Denounced and banned by the theological faculties of Louvain and the Sorbonne (1531). His book on the occult, *De Occulta Philosophia,* was banned in Cologne and Rome. Source: 1, pp. 222–23.

13 Aho, Jennifer S., and John W. Petras. *Learning about Sex: A Guide for Children and Their Parents.* Holt. Challenged at the Hays, Kans., Public Library (1980) and the Great Bend, R.I. Public Library (1981), but retained in both libraries. Challenged, but retained, at the Washoe County Library System in Reno, Nev. (1994) because "Nobody in their right mind would give a book like that to children on their own, except the library." Source: 11, Nov. 1980, p. 138; Nov. 1981, p. 169; Sept. 1994, p. 147; Nov. 1994, pp. 200–201.

14 Al-Shaykh, Hanan. *The Story of Zahra.* Anchor. Banned in Saudi Arabia and other Arab countries more than twenty-five years after its publication (1980) for offending religious authorities by its explicit portrayal of sexuality and its indictment of social hypocrisy in contemporary Arab society. Source: 1, p. 322.

15 **Alderman, Ellen.** *In Our Defense: The Bill of Rights in Action.* Morrow. Challenged, but retained, at the Wisconsin Rapids, Wis. high school (1998) despite two social studies teachers' objections to descriptions of violence in one chapter and explicit sexual details in another. Source: 11, Mar. 1999, p. 47.

16 **Alderson, Sue Ann, and Ann Blades.** *Ida and the Wool Smugglers.* Macmillan. Challenged in the Howard County, Md. school libraries (1991). The mother in the picture book was considered neglectful because she sent her daughter to the neighbors when she knew the smugglers were in the vicinity. Source: 11, Sept. 1991, p. 178.

17 **Alexander, Lloyd.** *The Prydain Chronicles.* Dell. Challenged as required reading at the Northbridge Mass. Middle School (1993). The complainants said that the series of fantasy novels contains religious themes that are pagan in nature and young minds would be drawn to the allure of witchcraft and black magic that runs through the books. Source: 11, Mar. 1994, p. 54.

18 _____. *The Wizard in the Tree.* Dell. After hearing impassioned pleas from parents against book banning, a Duneland School Committee in Chesterton, Ind. (1995) voted to keep the elementary school library book on the shelves. The book came under attack by a parent because a character in the story uses the words "slut" and "damn." Source: 11, Sept. 1995, p. 157.

19 **Alexander, Rae Pace.** *Young and Black in America.* Random. After the Minnesota Civil Liberties Union sued the Elk River, Minn. School Board (1983), the Board reversed its decision to restrict this title to students who have written permission from their parents. Source: 11, Sept. 1982, pp. 155–56; May 1983, p. 71; Sept. 1983, p. 153.

20 **Alinsky, Saul.** *Rules for Radicals.* Random. Challenged at the Plymouth-Canton school system in Canton, Mich. (1987) because the book holds "Lucifer or the Devil up as a role model." Source: 11, May 1987, p. 109.

21 **Allard, Harry, and James Marshall.** *The Stupids Have a Ball.* Houghton. Challenged in the

Iowa City, Iowa elementary school libraries (1993) because the book reinforces negative behavior and low self-esteem, since the Stupids rejoice in their children's behavior. Source: 11, Jan. 1994, p. 35.

22 _____. *The Stupids Step Out.* Houghton. Removed from the Silver Star Elementary School in Vancouver, Wash. (1985) because "it described families in a derogatory manner and might encourage children to disobey their parents." Challenged at the Cunningham Elementary School in Beloit, Wis. (1985) because it "encourages disrespectful language." Challenged, removed, and then returned to the shelves in the Horsham, Pa. schools (1993). The book was challenged because it "makes parents look like boobs and undermines authority." Source: 11, May 1985, p. 91; Nov. 1985, p. 204; July 1993, p. 101.

23 **Allard, Harry.** *Bumps in the Night.* Bantam. Challenged at the South Prairie Elementary School in Tillamook, Oreg. (1989) because a medium and seances are in the story. Source: 11, Jan. 1990, pp. 4–5.

24 _____. *The Stupids Die.* Houghton. Pulled from the Howard Miller Library in Zeeland, Mich. (1998) along with the three other Allard books in the series because of complaints that children shouldn't refer to anyone as "stupid." Source: 11, Sept. 1998, p. 140.

25 **Allen, Donald, ed.** *The New American Poetry, 1945–1960.* Grove. Banned for use in Aurora, Colo. High School English classes (1976) on the grounds of "immorality." Source: 11, May 1977, p. 79; 15, pp. 128–32, 238.

26 **Allende, Isabel.** *The House of the Spirits.* Knopf; Bantam. Retained in the Paso Robles, Calif. High School (1994) despite objections to accounts of sexual encounters and violence. Retained on the Stonewall Jackson High School's academically advanced reading list in Brentsville, Va. (1997) after being challenged for sexual explicitness. Challenged as obscene on the Montgomery County, Md. reading lists and school library shelves (1998). Challenged on the tenth-grade reading list at La Costa Canyon High School in Encinitas, Calif. (1999) because the work "defames" the Catholic faith and contains "pornographic passages." Retained on the summer reading lists for honors high school students at the Fairfield-Suisun Unified School District, Calif. (2000) despite objections that the book is "immoral and sexually depraved."

Challenged, but retained in the advanced English classes in Modesto, Calif. (2003). The seven-member Modesto City School Board said administrators should instead give parents more information about the books their children read, including annotations of each text. Parents can opt their children out of any assignment they find objectionable. Source: 11, Sept. 1994, p. 167; Nov. 1994, p. 201; Nov. 1997, pp. 169–70; Jan. 1998, p. 29; Mar. 1998, p. 56; May 1998, p. 70; Nov. 1999, p. 164; Nov. 2000, p. 195; Mar. 2001, p. 76; Jan. 2004, pp. 27–28.

27 **Allington, Richard.** *Once Upon A Hippo.* Scott, Foresman. Challenged, but retained in the Gwinnett County, Ga. schools (2000). A parent challenged a story in the book "The Hot Hippo, by Mwenye Hadithi because of a reference to a character called Ngai, described as the "god of everything and everywhere." Source: 11, May 2000, pp. 76–77; July 2000, p. 124.

28 **Allison, Dorothy.** *Bastard out of Carolina.* NAL. Removed from the Mt. Abram High School English classes in Salem, Maine (1996) because the language and subject matter (incest and rape) were inappropriate for fifteen-year-olds. Source: 11, Mar. 1996, p. 49; Nov. 1996, p. 196; Mar. 1997, p. 39.

29 **Alvarez, Julia.** *How the Garcia Girls Lost Their Accents.* Plume. Challenged, along with seventeen other titles in the Fairfax County, Va. elementary and secondary libraries (2002), by a group called Parents Against Bad Books in Schools. The group contends the books "contain profanity and descriptions of drug abuse, sexually explicit conduct, and torture." Retained on the Northwest Suburban High School District 214 reading list in Arlington Heights, Ill. (2006), along with eight other challenged titles. A board member, elected amid promises to bring her Christian beliefs into all board decision-making, raised the controversy based on excerpts from the books she'd found on the Internet. Source: 11, Jan. 2003, p. 10; July 2006, pp. 210–11.

30 _____. *In the Time of the Butterflies.* Algonquin; Plume. Withdrawn from inclusion at the Paul D. Schreiber High School in Port Washington, N.Y. (2000) because of a drawing of a homemade bomb. The text preceding and following the handwritten diagram does not provide details or instructions. The novel was nominated for the National Book Critics Circle Award in 1995 and named a Best Book for Young Adults by the American Library Association. Source: 11, Jan. 2001, pp. 13–14.

31 **Alyson, Sasha, ed.** *Young, Gay & Proud!* Alyson Pubns. Challenged at the public libraries of Saginaw, Mich. (1989) because the book promoted acts in violation of Michigan law and "appears to qualify as obscene material." Source: 11, May 1989, p. 78.

32 *American Heritage Dictionary.* Dell; Houghton. Removed in school libraries in Anchorage, Alaska (1976); Cedar Lake, Ind. (1976); Eldon, Mo. (1977); and Folsom, Calif. (1982) due to "objectionable language." Challenged, but retained, in the Churchill County, Nev. school libraries (1993). The controversy began after another dictionary was removed due to "objectionable language." It was removed from, and later returned to, classrooms in Washoe County, Nev. Source: 11, Sept. 1976, p. 115; Nov. 1976, p. 145; Jan. 1977, p. 7; July 1977, p. 101; Mar. 1983, p. 39; Mar. 1994, p. 71.

33 *American Jewish Yearbook.* Jewish Pubn. Banned from the 1983 Moscow International Book Fair along with more than fifty other books because it is "anti-Soviet." Source: 11, Nov. 1983, p. 201.

34 **Ames, Lee J.** *Draw 50 Monsters, Creeps, Superheroes, Demons, Dragons, Nerds, Dirts, Ghouls, Giants, Vampires, Zombies and Other Curiosa.* Doubleday. Challenged, but retained, at the Battle Creek, Mich. Elementary School library (1994) despite protests from a parent who said the book is satanic. Source: 11, Nov. 1994, p. 200.

35 **Anaya, Rudolfo A.** *Bless Me, Ultima.* TQS Pubns. Challenged at the Porterville, Calif. high schools (1992) because the book contains "many profane and obscene references, vulgar Spanish words and glorifies witchcraft and death." Retained on the Round Rock, Tex. Independent High School reading list (1996) after a challenge that the book was too violent. Removed from the Laton, Calif. Unified School District (1999) because it contains violence and profanity that might harm students. The novel is considered by many critics to be the finest work by the New Mexico writer, widely respected as one of the leading Hispanic writers in the U.S. It was chosen by teachers who thought it would be welcomed by the district's students, who are 80 percent Hispanic. Challenged at the John Jay High School in Wappingers Falls, N.Y. (2000) because the book is "full of sex and

cursing." Pulled by the Norwood, Colo. Schools' superintendent (2005) after two parents complained about profanity in the book. The superintendent confiscated all of the copies of the book and gave them to the parents, who "tossed them in the trash." The superintendent later apologized. Students organized an all-day sit-in at the school gym. President George W. Bush awarded Anaya the National Media of Arts in 2002. First Lady Laura Bush has listed the book as ninth on a list of twelve books that she highly recommends. Source: 11, Jan. 1993, p. 29; May 1996, p. 99; Sept. 1999, pp. 120–21; Mar. 2000, p. 51; Mar. 2005, p. 55.

36 **Ancona, George.** *Cuban Kids.* Marshall Cavendish. Banned in the Miami-Dade County Public Schools (2006). The picture book shows a child with a rifle and children saluting the Cuban flag with the caption, "We will be like Che!" Source: 11, Nov. 2006, p. 288.

37 **Anders, Jim.** *The Complete Idiot's Guide to Sex on the Net.* Que. Challenged, but retained, at the Will Hampton Branch of the Austin, Tex. Public Library (1999) despite complaints from at least three parents that the book is "obscene." Source: 11, Nov. 1999, p. 172.

38 **Andersen, Hans Christian.** *The Little Mermaid.* Harcourt. An edition with illustrations of bare-breasted mermaids was challenged in the Bedford, Tex. School District (1994) because it was "pornographic" and contained "satanic pictures." Source: 11, Nov. 1994, pp. 188–89.

39 **_____.** *Wonder Stories Told for Children.* Houghton. Banned in Russia by Nicholas I during the "censorship terror" (1835). Ban removed in 1849. Stamped in Illinois "For Adult Readers" to make it "impossible for children to obtain smut." Source: 4, pp. 41–42.

40 **Anderson, Christopher.** *Madonna— Unauthorized.* Dell; Simon. Challenged at the Loveland, Colo. High School library (1993) because the book has obscenities and sexual references, and one photo with Madonna posing topless. Source: 11, July 1993, p. 97.

41 **Anderson, Janice.** *The Life and Times of Renoir.* Shooting Star Pr. Restricted at the Pulaski, Pa. Elementary School library (1997) because of nude paintings in the book. Source: 11, May 1997, p. 61.

42 **Anderson, Jean.** *The Haunting of America.* Houghton. Challenged at the Sikes Elementary School media center in Lakeland, Fla. (1985) because the collection of historical ghost stories, "would lead children to believe in demons without realizing it." Source: 11, July 1985, p. 133.

43 **Anderson, Jill.** *Pumsy.* Timberline Press. The Putnam City, Okla. Elementary School counselors (1989) are forbidden to use this story of a fictional dragon because it propagates the principles of "secular humanism" and "new age religion" and that its use would "drive a wedge between children and parents." Source: 11, July 1989, p. 129.

44 **Anderson, Lee, et al.** *Windows on Our World Series.* Houghton. Removed from Alabama's list of approved texts—and from the state's classrooms—because the book promotes the "religion of secular humanism." U.S. District Court Judge W. Brevard Hand ruled on March 4, 1987, that thirty-nine history and social studies texts used in Alabama's 129 school systems "discriminate against the very concept of religion and theistic religions in particular, by omissions so serious that a student learning history from them would not be apprised of relevant facts about America's history . . . . References to religion are isolated and the integration of religion in the history of American society is ignored." The series includes: *At Home, At School*; *In Our Community*; *Ourselves and Others*; *Our Home*; *The Earth*; *America: Past and Present*; and *Around Our World*. On August 26, 1987, the U.S. Court of Appeals for the Eleventh Circuit unanimously overturned Judge Hand's decision by ruling that the information in the book was "essentially neutral in its religious content." The fact that the texts omitted references to religion was not "an advancement of secular humanism or an active hostility toward theistic religion." Source: 11, Jan. 1987, p. 6; May 1987, pp. 75, 104–7; Sept. 1987, pp. 166–67; Nov. 1987, pp. 217–18; Jan. 1988, p. 17; Mar. 1988, p. 40.

45 **Anderson, Robert, et al.** *Elements of Literature.* Holt. Retained in the Fairfax County, Va. schools (1994) despite complaints that it might "plant seeds" of violence or disobedience in students. The anthology contains stories such as Edgar Allen Poe's "The Tell-Tale Heart" and John Steinbeck's "The Pearl." Source: 11, Nov. 1994, pp. 201–2.

46 **Anderson, Sherwood.** *Dark Laughter.* Dynamic Learning Corp.; Liveright. Blacklisted in Boston, Mass. (1930). Source: 2, p. 137; 4, p. 62.

47 Andrews, V. C. *Dark Angel*. Pocket Bks. Removed from Oconee County, Ga. school libraries (1994) "due to the filthiness of the material." The school board voted unanimously at a later date to rescind its controversial book-banning order, but then rescinded that action and ordered the removal of the book. Source: 11, Sept. 1994, pp. 145–46; Nov. 1994, pp. 187–88, 200; Jan. 1995, p. 6.

48 _____. *Darkest Hour*. Pocket Bks. Removed from Oconee County, Ga. school libraries (1994) "due to the filthiness of the material." The school board voted unanimously at a later date to rescind its controversial book-banning order but then rescinded that action and ordered the removal of the book. Source: 11, Sept. 1994, pp. 145–46; Nov. 1994, pp. 187–88, 200; Jan. 1995, p. 6.

49 _____. *Dawn*. Pocket Bks. Removed from Oconee County, Ga. school libraries (1994) "due to the filthiness of the material." The school board voted unanimously at a later date to rescind its controversial book-banning order but then rescinded that action and ordered the removal of the book. Source: 11, Sept. 1994, pp. 145–46; Nov. 1994, pp. 187–88, 200; Jan. 1995, p. 6.

50 _____. *Flowers in the Attic*. Pocket Bks. Challenged at the Richmond, R.I. High School (1983) because the book contains offensive passages concerning incest and sexual intercourse. Removed from Oconee County, Ga. school libraries (1994) "due to the filthiness of the material." The school board voted unanimously at a later date to rescind its controversial book-banning order but then rescinded that action and ordered the removal of the book. Source: 11, Sept. 1983, p. 153; Jan. 1984, pp. 9–10; Sept. 1994, pp. 145–46; Nov. 1994, pp. 187–88, 200; Jan. 1995, p. 6.

51 _____. *Garden of Shadows*. Pocket Bks. Removed from Oconee County, Ga. school libraries (1994) "because the book encouraged sexual activity and the result of reading or seeing it might be 'incestuous relationships' and 'aggressive sexual behavior.'" The book was removed despite a recommendation from a committee of parents and teachers to retain it. The action stemmed from a complaint filed in May 1994 when eight other V. C. Andrews books were removed. Source: 11, Nov. 1994, p. 188; Jan. 1995, p. 6; July 1996, p. 117.

52 _____. *If There Be Thorns*. Pocket Bks. Challenged at the Richmond, R.I. High School (1983) because the book contains offensive passages concerning incest and sexual intercourse. Source: 11, Sept. 1983, p. 153; Jan. 1984, pp. 9–10.

53 _____. *My Sweet Audrina*. Poseidon; Simon & Schuster; Pocket Bks. Rejected for purchase by the Hayward, Calif. school trustees (1985) because of "rough language" and "explicit sex scenes." Challenged at the Lincoln Middle School in Pullman, Wash. (1990) because it deals with themes related to sexual violence. Removed from Oconee County, Ga. school libraries (1994) "due to the filthiness of the material." The school board voted unanimously at a later date to rescind its controversial book-banning order but then rescinded that action and ordered the removal of the book. Source: 11, July 1985, p. 111; July 1990, p. 145; Sept. 1994, pp. 145–46; Nov. 1994, pp. 187–88, 200; Jan. 1995, p. 6.

54 _____. *Petals on the Wind*. Pocket Bks. Challenged at the Richmond, R.I. High School (1983) because the book contains offensive passages concerning incest and sexual intercourse. Removed from Oconee County, Ga. school libraries (1994) "due to the filthiness of the material." The school board voted unanimously at a later date to rescind its controversial book-banning order but then rescinded that action and ordered the removal of the book. Source: 11, Sept. 1983, p. 153; Jan. 1984, pp. 9–10; Mar. 1984, p. 53; Sept. 1994, pp. 145–46; Nov. 1994, pp. 187–88, 200; Jan. 1995, p. 6.

55 _____. *Seeds of Yesterday*. Simon & Schuster; Pocket Bks.; NAL. Removed from Oconee County, Ga. school libraries (1994) "due to the filthiness of the material." The school board voted unanimously at a later date to rescind its controversial book-banning order but then rescinded that action and ordered the removal of the book. Source: 11, Sept. 1994, pp. 145–46; Nov. 1994, pp. 187–88, 200; Jan. 1995, p. 6.

56 _____. *Twilight's Child*. Pocket Bks. Removed from Oconee County, Ga. school libraries (1994) "due to the filthiness of the material." The school board voted unanimously at a later date to rescind its controversial book-banning order but then rescinded that action and ordered the removal of the book. Source: 11, Sept. 1994, pp. 145–46; Nov. 1994, pp. 187–88, 200; Jan. 1995, p. 6.

57 Andry, Andrew C., and Steven Schepp. *How Babies Are Made*. Time-Life. Moved from the children's section to the adult section of the Tampa-Hillsborough, Fla. County Public Library (1981)

15

by order of the Tampa City Council. Placed on restricted shelves at the Evergreen School District elementary school libraries in Vancouver, Wash. (1987) in accordance with the school board policy to restrict student access to sex education books in elementary school libraries. Source: 11, Jan. 1982, p. 4; May 1987, p. 87.

58 **Angelou, Maya.** *And Still I Rise.* Random. Challenged at the Northside High School library in Lafayette, La. (1982). Removed from the required reading list for Wake County High School juniors in Raleigh, N.C. (1987) because of complaints about a scene in which eight-year-old Maya is raped. Challenged at the Longview, Wash. school system (1987) because some "students could be harmed by its graphic language." Source: 11, May 1982, p. 83; May 1987, p. 91; Sept. 1987, p. 195.

59 _____. *I Know Why the Caged Bird Sings.* Bantam. Four members of the Alabama State Textbook Committee (1983) called for its rejection because Angelou's work preaches "bitterness and hatred against whites." Challenged at Mount Abram Regional High School in Strong, Maine (1988) because parents objected to a rape scene. Rejected as required reading for a gifted ninth-grade English class in Bremerton, Wash. (1990) because of the book's "graphic" description of molestation. Removed from a Banning, Calif. eighth grade class (1991) after several parents complained about explicit passages involving child molestation and rape. Challenged at the Amador Valley High School in Pleasanton, Calif. (1992) because of sexually explicit language. Temporarily banned from the Caledonia Middle School in Columbus, Miss. (1993) on the grounds that it is too sexually explicit to be read by children. Challenged in the Haines City, Fla. High School library and English curriculum (1993) because of objections to a passage that describes the author's rape when she was seven years old. Challenged in the Hooks, Tex. High School in a freshman honors history class (1993). Retained as required reading for all of Dowling High School's sophomores in Des Moines, Iowa (1994). The book became an issue after a parent objected to what he said were inappropriately explicit sexual scenes. Challenged as part of the Ponderosa High School curriculum in Castle Rock, Colo. (1994) because it is "a lurid tale of sexual perversion." Challenged at the Westwood High School in Austin, Tex. (1994) because the book is pornographic, contains profanity, and encourages premarital sex and homosexuality. The superintendent later ruled that parents must first give their children permission to be taught potentially controversial literature. Challenged

at the Carroll School in Southlake, Tex. (1995) because it was deemed "pornographic" and full of "gross evils." Challenged, but retained, on the Beech High School reading list in Hendersonville, Tenn. (1995). Challenged at the Danforth High School in Wimberley, Tex. (1995). Removed from the Southwood High School Library in Caddo Parish, La. (1995) because the book's language and content were objectionable. Eventually, the book was returned after students petitioned and demonstrated against the action. Challenged, but retained in the Volusia County, Fla. County Schools (1995). The complainants wanted the book removed because "it is sexually explicit and promotes cohabitation and rape." Challenged, but retained, on an optional reading list at the East Lawrence High School in Moulton, Ala. (1996). The book was challenged because the School Superintendent decided, "the poet's descriptions of being raped as a little girl were pornographic." Removed from the curriculum pending a review of its content at the Gilbert, Ariz. Unified School (1995). Complaining parents said the book did not represent "traditional values." Retained on the Round Rock, Tex. Independent High School reading list (1996) after a challenge that the book was too violent. Pulled from the reading list at Lakota High School in Cincinnati, Ohio (1996) because of parents' claims that its is too graphic. Removed from the high school reading list at Lakota High School in Union Township, Ohio (1997) because of Angelou's brief description of being raped at age 8 and other sexual content. Removed from the ninth-grade reading list at Richfield, Minn. High School (1997) because some parents say it is too explicit. Retained in the Mukilteo, Wash. school district's high school curriculum (1997) after objections to the work's "explicit sexual content." Challenged at the Folsom Cordova, Calif. School District (1997) because it contains sexually explicit passages. Removed from the curriculum at the Turrentine, N.C. Middle School (1997) after complaints by parents about profanity and sexual references. Challenged as an Advanced Placement English class reading assignment at the Wayne County, Ga. High School (1997) due to the novel's sexual explicitness. Removed from the ninth-grade English curriculum in Anne Arundel County, Md. (1998) by the school superintendent after parents complained the book "portrays white people as being horrible, nasty, stupid people—if a child didn't have negative feelings about white people, this could sow the seeds." Banned from the Dolores Parrott Middle School in Brooksville, Fla. school library and classrooms (1998) because of a passage in which Angelou tells of being molested and raped as an eight-year-old. Removed from the Turrentine Middle School's reading list in Alamance,

16

N.C. (1998). Returned to the Anne Arundel County, Md. approved reading list for ninth-grade English classes (1998), overriding some parents' complaints that the book is too sexually explicit. Removed from the Brooksville, Fla. eighth-grade reading list (1998) because of the book's strong sexual content. Removed from the seventh- and eighth-grade reading list at the Unity, N.H. Elementary School (1999) because the "book is too sexually explicit." Challenged on the Poolesville High School, Md. (2000) reading list due to the book's sexual content and language. Challenged as required reading for Hamilton, Mont. freshman English classes (2002). At issue are scenes in which the author explores her sexuality through intercourse as a teenager and the depiction of a rape and molestation of an 8-year-old girl; homosexuality is another theme explored in the book that has drawn criticism. Challenged, along with seventeen other titles in the Fairfax County, Va. elementary and secondary libraries (2002), by a group called Parents Against Bad Books in Schools. The group contends the books "contain profanity and descriptions of drug abuse, sexually explicit conduct, and torture." Removed as required reading in Annapolis, Md. freshman English curriculum (2006) because the book's rape scenes and other mature content are too advanced for ninth-graders. The freshman English class syllabus is sent home to parents to read at the beginning of each year. It warns them of the book's mature themes and allows parents to ask to have their children read another book instead. Retained in the Fond du Lac, Wis. High School sophomore advanced English class (2006). Parents objected to teens reading Angelou's account of being brutally raped by her mother's boyfriend and an unwanted pregnancy later in life. Parents will receive notification and be allowed to decide whether or not they approve of its use by their children, according to recommendations agreed upon by a review committee and parents who objected to the use of the book. Source: 6, p. 60; 11, Mar. 1983, p. 39; Jan. 1989, p. 8; Mar. 1989, p. 38; Nov. 1990, p. 211; Mar. 1992, p. 42; July 1992, p. 109; July 1993, p. 107; Jan. 1994, p. 34; July 1994, p. 130; Jan. 1995, pp. 11, 14; Mar. 1995, p. 56; May 1995, pp. 67, 72; Sept. 1995, pp. 158–59; Nov. 1995, pp. 183, 186–87; Jan. 1996, pp. 14, 30; Mar. 1996, pp. 47, 63; May 1996, pp. 84, 99; July 1996, p. 120; Sept. 1996, pp. 152–53; Nov. 1996, pp. 197–98; Jan. 1997, p. 26; May 1997, pp. 65–66; July 1997, p. 98; Jan. 1998, pp. 13, 14, 29; Mar. 1998, pp. 41–42; May 1998, pp. 69, 72; July 1998, p. 120; Sept. 1998, pp. 143–44; Nov. 1998, p. 182; Jan. 1999, p. 20; May 1999, p. 69; July 1999, pp. 93–94; Nov. 2000, p. 196; Nov. 2002, p. 258; Jan. 2003, p. 10; May 2006, pp. 132–33; Jan. 2007, pp. 30–31.

60 **Annas, Pamela, and Robert Rosen.** *Literature in Society: Introduction to Fiction, Poetry and Drama.* Prentice-Hall. Pulled from the senior literature class at the Hempfield, Pa. Area School District (1994) after it was determined that some passages were "vulgar." Source: 11, Jan. 1995, pp. 13–14; Mar. 1995, p. 44.

61 **Anonymous.** *Arabian Nights or The Thousand and One Nights.* U.S. Customs held up 500 sets of the translation by the French scholar Mardrus, which were imported from England (1927-31). Confiscated (1985) in Cairo, Egypt on the grounds that it contained obscene passages, which posed a threat to the country's moral fabric. The public prosecutor demanded the book, which contains stories such as "Ali Baba and the 40 Thieves" and "Aladdin and His Magic Lamp," be "burned in a public place" and said that it was the cause of "a wave of incidents of rape which the country has recently experienced." Judged inappropriate for Jewish pupils by the Israeli director of the British Consul Library in Jerusalem, Israel (1985). Source: 4, p. 28; 5, June 1985, p. 50; Aug. 1985, p. 51; Oct. 1985, p. 65; 8, pp. 317–18; 11, July 1985, p. 120.

62 **Anonymous.** *Caroline.* Blue Moon Bks. Removed from the Multnomah, Oreg. County Library (1991) because the novel contains graphic descriptions of sexual acts. Source: 11, Jan. 1992, p. 6.

63 **Anonymous.** *The Fifteen Plagues of a Maidenhead.* James Reade and Angell Carter. In 1707, James Reade and Angell Carter were prosecuted for publishing the work and charged with "obscene libel." They were acquitted after the defense counsel asserted that the court had no right to try the case because the defendants were not guilty of breaking any existing law. While the court disliked the tone and content of the book, calling it "bawdy," it acknowledged that no common law or statute existed that "could warrant an indictment against even the filthiest book." Source: 13, p. 71.

64 **Anonymous.** *Go Ask Alice.* Avon; Prentice-Hall. Removed from school libraries in Kalamazoo, Mich. (1974); Levittown, N.Y. (1975); Saginaw, Mich. (1975); Eagle Pass, Tex. (1977); Trenton, N.J. (1977); North Bergen, N.J. (1980) due to "objectionable" language and explicit sexual scenes. Challenged at the Marcellus, N.Y. School District (1975); Ogden, Utah School District (1979); Safety Harbor, St.

17

Petersburg, Fla. Middle School Library (1982) where written parental permission was required to check out the title; Osseo School District in Brooklyn Park, Minn. (1983) where a school board member found the book's language "personally offensive"; Pagosa Springs, Colo. schools (1983) because a parent objected to the "graphic language, subject matter, immoral tone, and lack of literary quality found in the book." Challenged at the Rankin County, Miss. School District (1984) because it is "profane and sexually objectionable." Challenged at the Central Gwinnett, Ga. High School library (1986) because "it encourages students to steal and take drugs." Removed from the school library shelves in Kalkaska, Mich. (1986) because the book contains "objectionable language." The Gainesville, Ga. Public Library (1986) prohibits young readers from checking out this book along with forty other books. The books, on subjects ranging from hypnosis to drug abuse to breast-feeding and sexual dysfunction, are kept in a locked room. Challenged at the King Middle School in Portland, Maine (1988). Removed from the Wall Township, N.J. Intermediate School library (1993) by the Superintendent of Schools because the book contains "inappropriate" language and "borders on pornography." Responding to an anonymous letter in 1987, the superintendent ordered the book removed from all reading lists and classroom book collections. "I thought we'd got rid of them all about five years ago," he said. Removed from an English class at Buckhannon-Upshur, W.Va. High School (1993) because of graphic language in the book. Challenged as a required reading assignment at the Johnstown, N.Y. High School (1993) because of numerous obscenities. Banned from a ninth-grade reading list at Shepherd Hill High School in Dudley, Mass. (1994) because of "gross and vulgar language and graphic description of drug use and sexual conduct." Banned from the Jonathan Alder School District in Plain City, Ohio (1995). Challenged at the Houston Junior and Senior High School in Wasilla, Alaska (1995). Removed from a supplemental reading list for sophomore English students in Warm Springs, Va. (1995) because of its "profanity and indecent situations." Confiscated by a Tiverton, R.I. middle school principal (1998), while the class was reading it. The school board later returned the book. Removed from the Aledo, Tex. Middle School library (1999) and restricted at the high school library to students with parental permission. A parent complained about the references to drug use, vulgar language, and descriptions of sex. Retained as optional reading for eighth graders at Rice Avenue Middle School in Girard, Pa. (2000). A grandmother found the book offensive because it contains "filth and smut"

that she didn't want her granddaughters reading. Source: 8, pp. 456–57; 11, Jan. 1975, p. 6; Mar. 1975, p. 41; May 1975, p. 76; July 1977, p. 100; May 1977, p. 73; May 1979, p. 49; Mar. 1980, p. 32; July 1982, p. 142; Mar. 1983, p. 52; Mar. 1984, p. 53; May 1984, p. 69; July 1986, p. 117; Sept. 1986, pp. 151–52; Nov. 1986, p. 207; Jan. 1987, p. 32; Mar. 1989, p. 39; May 1993, p. 71; July 1993, pp. 109–10; Mar. 1994, p. 54; Sept. 1994, p. 150; July 1995, p. 94; Jan. 1996, p. 12; Mar. 1996, p. 50; Sept. 1998, p. 144; Sept. 1999, pp. 119–20; May 2000, p. 92.

65 **Anonymous.** *Life: How Did It Get Here?* Jehovah's Witnesses. Challenged at the Jones Library in Amherst, Mass. (1992) because it is religious propaganda. "The book lists no authors or editors; there is no accountability for its statements." Source: 11, Sept. 1992, p. 162.

66 **Anonymous.** *Marisha II.* Blue Moon Bks. Removed from the Multnomah, Oreg. County Library (1991) because the novel contains graphic descriptions of sexual acts. Source: 11, Jan. 1992, p. 6.

67 **Anthony, Piers.** *Question Quest.* Morrow. Removed from the mandatory reading program at the Norman L. Sullivan Middle School in Bonsall, Calif. (2000) due to sexually explicit language. Source: 11, May 2000, p. 76.

68 **Apollinaire, Guillaume.** *Memoirs of a Young Rakehill.* Grove. *The Debauched Hospodar* and *Memoirs of a Young Rakehill* were seized by New Zealand Customs officers (1964). The New Zealand Indecent Publications Tribunal concluded that, "we classify the translation of two novels written by Guillaume Apollinaire as indecent unless circulation is restricted to persons professionally engaged in the study of abnormal psychology, who desire to use them for that purpose." Source: 13, p. 162.

69 **Archer, Jerome W., and A. Schwartz.** *A Reader for Writers.* McGraw-Hill. Removed from the Island Trees, N.Y. Union Free School District High School library in 1976 along with nine other titles because they were considered "immoral, anti-American, anti-Christian, or just plain filthy." Returned to the library after the U.S. Supreme Court ruling on June 25, 1982 in *Board of Education, Island Trees Union Free School District No. 26 et al. v. Pico et al.,* 457 U.S. 853 (1982). Source: 11, Nov. 1982, p. 197.

70 **Aristophanes.** *Lysistrata.* NAL; Penguin; Univ. Pr. of Virginia. U.S. Customs lifts ban (1930). In successful challenge to the Comstock Act of 1873, which empowered the Postmaster General to rule on obscenity of literature sent through the mail, Lysistrata was declared mailable. Source: 4, p. 2.

71 **Aristotle.** *The Metaphysics.* Penguin. In 1210, the bishops of the Provincial Council of Paris forbade the public or private teaching of the natural philosophy and metaphysics of Aristotle. The ban, which applied to instruction of the arts faculty of the University of Paris, was imposed under penalty of excommunication and confirmed in 1215. In 1231, Pope Gregory IX prohibited the reading of the works of Aristotle until they were purged of heresy. Source: 1, p. 205.

72 **Arms, Karen, and Pamela S. Camp.** *Biology.* Holt. Text was rejected by the superintendent of the city-county school system on the basis that it might violate a school policy forbidding the teaching of specific methods of birth control in Winston-Salem, N.C. (1980). Bowing to pressure from opponents of the textbook planned for use in a high school honors course, the Garland, Tex. Independent School District's central textbook selection committee (1985) withdrew its recommendation because the text includes "overly explicit diagrams of sexual organs, intricate discussion of sexual stimulation, and the implication of abortion as a means of birth control." Source: 11, Nov. 1980, p. 128; July 1985, p. 114.

73 **Armstrong, William Howard.** *Sounder.* Harper. Challenged, but retained, in the Rockingham County, N.C. schools (1996). A parent had problems with the use of the word "nigger" on page 21 and a reference to the main character, a black sharecropper, as "boy." Source: 11, Sept. 1996, p. 169; Nov. 1996, p. 212.

74 **Asher, Don.** *Blood Summer.* Putnam. Returned to publisher because it failed to meet literary standards in Little Rock, Ark. (1979). Source: 11, Sept. 1979, p. 104.

75 **Asimov, Isaac.** *In the Beginning: Science Faces God in the Book of Genesis.* Crown. Officials of the Christian Research Center requested San Diego, Calif. (1981) school administrators to keep this title out of all high school libraries because Asimov "subjects the Bible to merciless and unremitting destructive attack." Source: 11, Jan. 1982, p. 8.

76 **Asturias, Miguel Angel.** *The Green Pope.* Delacorte. Banned in Guatemala (1954) along with Strong Wind (1950) and The President (1946) for its exposure of the effects of American imperialism. Source: 7, pp. 467–68.

77 **Atkins, Catherine.** *When Jeff Comes Home.* Putnam. Restricted to students with parental permission in the Irving, Tex. schools (2006). The book is about a boy's recovery after being kidnapped and sexually abused by a man. The publisher recommends the book for readers thirteen and older, while *School Library Journal* suggested it for readers in grades ten and above. It was named a best book for young adults by the American Library Association in 2000. Source: 11, Mar. 2006, pp. 72–73.

78 **Atwood, Margaret.** *The Handmaid's Tale.* Fawcett; Houghton; Simon; Hall. Challenged as a book assignment at the Rancho Cotati High School in Rohnert Park, Calif. (1990) because it is too explicit for students. Challenged in the Waterloo, Iowa schools (1992) because of profanity, lurid passages about sex, and statements defamatory to minorities, God, women, and the disabled. Removed from the Chicopee, Mass. High School English class reading list (1993) because it contains profanity and sex. Challenged for use in the Richland, Wash. high school English classes (1998) along with six other titles because the "books are poor-quality literature and stress suicide, illicit sex, violence, and hopelessness." Challenged because of graphic sex., but retained on the advanced placement English list at Chamberlain High School in Tampa, Fla. (1999). Downgraded from "required" to "optional" on the summer reading list for eleventh graders in the Upper Moreland, Pa. School District (2000) due to "age-inappropriate" subject matter. Challenged, but retained in the Dripping Springs, Tex. senior Advanced Placement English courses (2001) as an optional reading assignment. Some parents were offended by the book's descriptions of sexual encounters. The Judson, Tex. school district board overruled (2006) Superintendent Ed Lyman's ban of the novel from an advanced placement English curriculum. Lyman had banned the book after a parent complained it was sexually explicit and offensive to Christians. In doing so, he overruled the recommendation of a committee of teachers, students, and parents. The committee appealed the decision to the school board. Source: 11, Jan. 1991, p. 15; July 1992, p. 126; May 1993, p. 73; Mar. 1999, p. 40; Sept. 1999, p. 121; Nov. 1999, p. 173; Sept. 2000, p. 145; July 2001, p. 174; May 2006, pp. 154–55.

79 **Auel, Jean.** *Clan of the Cave Bear.* Coronet. Challenged at the Berrien Springs, Mich. High School for use in classrooms and libraries (1988) because the novel is "vulgar, profane, and sexually explicit." Banned from the Cascade Middle School library in Eugene, Oreg. (1992) after a parent complained about a rape scene. Challenged, but retained, on the Moorpark High School recommended reading list in Simi Valley, Calif. (1993) despite objections that it contains "hard-core graphic sexual content." Source: 11, Jan. 1989, p. 28; July 1992, p. 107; Jan. 1994, p. 14; Mar. 1994, p. 70; May 1994, p. 99.

80 _____. *The Mammoth Hunters.* Bantam; Crown; Thorndike Pr. Challenged, but retained, from the Moorpark High School recommended reading list in Simi Valley, Calif. (1993) despite objections that it contains "hard-core graphic sexual content." Source: 11, Mar. 1994, p. 70; May 1994, p. 99.

81 _____. *Plains of Passage.* Bantam; Thorndike Pr. Challenged, but retained, from the Moorpark High School recommended reading list in Simi Valley, Calif. (1993) despite objections that it contains "hard-core graphic sexual content." Source: 11, Mar. 1994, p. 70; May 1994, p. 99.

82 _____. *Valley of the Horses.* Bantam; Crown. Challenged at the Bastrop, Tex. Public Library (1985) because "the book violates Texas obscenity laws." Banned from the Stroudsburg, Pa. High School library (1985) because it was "blatantly graphic, pornographic, and wholly unacceptable for a high school library." Challenged, but retained, on the Moorpark High School recommended reading list in Simi Valley, Calif. (1993) despite objections that it contains "hard-core graphic sexual content." Source: 11, May 1985, pp. 75, 79; Mar. 1986, pp. 33, 64; Jan. 1994, p. 145; Mar. 1994, p. 70; May 1994, p. 99.

83 **Avent, Sue.** *Spells, Chants and Potions.* Contemporary Perspectives. Pulled, but later placed on reserve to children with parental permission at the Forrest Elementary School library in Newport News, Va. (1992). Challenged at the Muncy, Pa. school library (1997) because of the book's "magical thinking." Source: 11, July 1992, p. 108; Sept. 1992, p. 139; May 1997, p. 61.

84 **Averroes (Ibn Rushd).** *Commentaries.* Church authorities banned his writings on the works of Aristotle between 1210 and 1277 for proposing that philosophy could claim truth outside established religious source. The ban applied to instruction at the University of Paris (1210) and in 1231, Pope Gregory IX prohibited the reading of the works of Aristotle until they were purged of heresy. Source: 1, pp. 50–51.

85 **Avi.** *The Fighting Ground.* Harper; Lippincott. Retained as part of the John Fuller School curriculum in Conway, N.H. (2000), despite a complaint by a resident calling himself a concerned Christian. Source: 11, Jan. 2001, p. 37; Mar. 2001, p. 75.

86 **Aylesworth, Thomas G.** *Servants of the Devil: A History of Witchcraft.* Addison-Wesley. Removed from the Cleveland, Okla. middle school libraries (1989) because witchcraft is a "religion" and that the First Amendment bars the teaching of religion in schools. Source: 11, July 1989, p. 128.

87 **Babbitt, Natalie.** *The Devil's Storybook.* Farrar. Returned to the Claxton, Tenn. Elementary School library (1986) shelves. The complaint against the book objected to "the total theme of the book," which makes "hell and the devil innocent and alluring." Challenged at the Chestnut Ridge Middle School in Washington Township, Pa. (2004). The complainants wanted the school district to seek parental approval before elementary- and middle-school students could check out books related to the occult. Source: 11, Mar. 1987, p. 50; May 2004, pp. 117–18.

88 _____. *The Imp in the Basket.* Chatto. Challenged as required reading in the Annville-Cleona, Pa. School District (1991) because of the story's references to demon possession. Source: 11, July 1991, p. 130.

89 **Babinski, Edward T.** *Leaving the Fold: Testimonials of Former Fundamentalists.* Prometheus Books. Challenged, but retained, at the Anderson, S.C. County Library (1995) because the book presented fundamentalism in a negative light. Source: 11, Jan. 1996, p. 30.

90 **Bach, Alice.** *When the Sky Began to Roar.* Houghton. Removed from the East Junior-Senior High School library in Lincoln, Nebr. (1987) because the book "creates despair, disrespect for parents, and a sense of hopelessness." Challenged at the Seward, Nebr. Public Library (1988) because it is "obscene." Source: 11, May 1987, p. 87; May 1988, p. 85.

91 **Bacon, Francis.** *Advancement of Learning.* Humanities; Rowman & Littlefield. All works by Bacon were banned by the Inquisition in Spain and

placed on the Sotomayor's Index (1640). Book IX of Bacon's work, dedicated to the king, was placed on the *Index Librorum Prohibitorum* in Rome, where it remained in the 1948 edition of the list. Source: 1, p. 5; 4, p. 17.

92 Bailey, Thomas A., and David M. Kennedy. *The American Pageant: A History of the Republic.* Heath. The John Birch Society's chapter in Glen Burnie, Md., condemned the textbook and demanded that it be banned in the Anne Arundel County, Md., public schools (1966). Removed (1981) from the Mississippi state-approved textbook list. Returned to the Racine, Wis. Unified School District (1984) curriculum just one week after the school board voted to ban it. Opponents of the books on the board charged that the social studies volumes contained "judgmental writing" and, in the words of one board member, "a lot more funny pictures of Republicans and nicer pictures of Democrats." Opponents also said that one text did not present an adequate analysis of the Vietnam War. Source: 7, pp. 34–36; 11, May 1981, p. 67; July 1981, p. 93; Sept. 1984, p. 158.

93 Baker, Keith. *Who Is the Beast?* Harcourt. Temporarily removed from the Marple, Pa. schools (1994) following a verbal request from a parent who said its message offended his family's religious beliefs. Source: 11, July 1994, p. 116.

94 Baldwin, James. *Another Country.* Dial; Dell. Considered obscene, the book was banned from the New Orleans, La. Public Library (1963). After a year of litigation, it was restored. Source: 4, p. 97; 8, pp. 406–7.

95 _____. *Blues for Mr. Charlie.* Doubleday. Challenged in Sioux Falls, S.Dak. (1980) because it's "pornographic" and it "tears down Christian principles." Source: 11, May 1980, p. 61.

96 _____. *Go Tell It on the Mountain.* Dell. Challenged as required reading in the Hudson Falls, N.Y. schools (1994) because the book has recurring themes of rape, masturbation, violence, and degrading treatment of women. Challenged as a ninth-grade summer reading option in Prince William County, Va. (1998) because the book "was rife with profanity and explicit sex." Source: 11, Nov. 1994, p. 190; Jan. 1995, p. 13; Mar. 1995, p. 55; Nov. 1998, p. 183.

97 _____. *If Beale Street Could Talk.* Dial; NAL. Removed from the St. Paul, Oreg. High School library (1989) because the book contains obscene language and explicit descriptions of sexual activity. Source: 11, July 1989, p. 128.

98 _____. *Tell Me How Long the Train's Been Gone.* Dial; Dell. Four members of the Alabama State Textbook Committee (1983) called for its rejection because Baldwin's work preaches "bitterness and hatred against whites." Source: 11, Mar. 1983, p. 39.

99 Balian, Lorna. *Humbug Potion: An A-B-Cipher.* Abingdon. Challenged for promoting satanism and witchcraft, but retained at the Multnomah, Oreg. County Library (1991). Source: 11, Jan. 1992, p. 6.

100 Balzac, Honore de. *Droll Stories.* French & European. All works banned in Russia (1850). Banned by Canadian Customs (1914). U.S. Customs lifts ban (1930). U.S. declares the Concord Book Catalog as obscene because it features the Balzac's work (1944). Banned in Ireland (1953) until 1967. The novel attracted the attention of censors for its excretory references and graphic sexual descriptions. Source: 4, p. 39; 6, p. 411; 12, p. 140; 13, pp. 62–63.

101 Banks, Lynne Reid. *The Indian in the Cupboard.* Avon; Doubleday. The school librarian at the Suwannee County, Fla. Elementary School (1993) routinely erased words from books deemed objectionable. In this instance, the words "heck" and "hell" were removed. Removed from the Bemidji, Minn. school district voluntary reading list and from the school library shelves (1995) because it contains subtle stereotypes inconsistent with district diversity goals. Source: 11, May 1993, pp. 69–70; Nov. 1995, p. 183.

102 _____. *Return of the Indian.* Avon; Doubleday. Removed from the Bemidji, Minn. school district voluntary reading list and from the school library shelves (1995) because it contains subtle stereotypes inconsistent with district diversity goals. Source: 11, Nov. 1995, p. 183.

103 Bannerman, Helen. *Little Black Sambo.* Putnam; Buccaneer Bks.; Greenhouse Pubs. Removed from classrooms and school library shelves by the Toronto, Ontario, Canada (1956) board of education after the board received complaints from several groups that "the popular book was a cause of mental suffering to Negroes in particular and children in general." Removed from a school library in New York City (1959) after a black resident challenged the book as racially derogatory. The book was eventually restored to library shelves. Removed from the open shelves of the Lincoln, Nebr. school system (1964) on the orders of the School Superintendent because of the inherent racism of the book. The superintendent relocated the book on the "Reserved" shelves, with a note explaining that while it was not "a part of the instructional program, it will be available to those who want to read it as optional material." Banned in Montgomery, Ala. schools (1971) because the book is "inappropriate" and "not in keeping with good human relations." The Montreal-based Canadian National Black Coalition mobilized efforts to remove the book from school and library shelves (1972). In Hamilton, Ontario, Canada, teachers ordered students to tear from school readers the pages that contained the story. The book was banned entirely in New Brunswick. Removed from the Dallas, Tex. school libraries (1972) because it "distorts a child's view of black people." Attacked in English schools and libraries (1972) because it symbolized "the kind of dangerous and obsolete books that must go." Source: 3, p. 173; 11, Apr. 1956, pp. 3–4; July 1963, p. 51; Jan. 1965, p. 12; 14, pp. 212–14.

104 **Banville, John.** *The Untouchable.* Knopf. Challenged at the Bristol, Conn. Public Library (1998) because of references to sexual relations between men and boys. Source: 11, May 1998, p. 69.

105 **Baraka, Imamu Amiri.** *The Toilet.* Grove. Expurgated at Eastern High School (1969) to eliminate all "four-letter words or vernacular." Source: 11, May 1969, p. 51.

106 **Bargar, Gary W.** *What Happened to Mr. Foster?* Clarion. Challenged at the Greenville County, S.C. Library (1982) because the novel's principle character is a homosexual. Source: 11, Jan. 1983, p. 9.

107 **Barker, Clive.** *Tapping the Vein, Book 2.* Eclipse. Removed from the Multnomah, Oreg. County Library (1991) because of its graphic violence, language, and sexual content. Source: 11, Jan. 1992, p. 6.

108 **Barnes, Djuna.** *Ryder.* St. Martin. Seized (1984) by the British Customs Office as "indecent and obscene." Source: 11, Jan. 1985, p. 16.

109 **Barth, Edna.** *Witches, Pumpkins and Grinning Ghosts.* Houghton. Challenged at the

Neely Elementary School in Gilbert, Ariz. (1992) because the book "interests little minds into accepting the devil with all of his evil works." Challenged in the Salem-Keizer, Oreg. school libraries (1992) because it would encourage children to experiment with witchcraft. Source: 11, May 1992, p. 78; July 1992, pp. 124–25.

110 **Baskin, Julia, Lindsey Newman, Sophie Pollitt-Cohen, and Courtney Toombs.** *The Notebook Girls.* Warner Bks. Challenged, but retained at the Cape May County, N.J. Library (2006). The book is comprised of the entries four New York City high-school students made in a shared journal in the aftermath of the September 11 terrorist attacks. Source: 11, Jan. 2007, p. 29.

111 **Bass, Herbert J.** *Our American Heritage.* Silver Burdett. Removed from Alabama's list of approved texts—and from the state's classrooms—because the book promotes the "religion of secular humanism." U.S. District Court Judge W. Brevard Hand ruled on March 4, 1987, that thirty-nine history and social studies texts used in Alabama's 129 school systems "discriminate against the very concept of religion and theistic religions in particular, by omissions so serious that a student learning history from them would not be apprised of relevant facts about America's history. . . . References to religion are isolated and the integration of religion in the history of American society is ignored." Other texts removed included: *History of a Free People,* by Henry W. Bragdon; *Teen Guide,* by Valerie Chamberlain; *America Is,* by Frank Freidel; *Today's Teen,* by Joan Kelly; *A History of Our American Republic,* by Glenn M. Linden; *Caring, Deciding and Growing,* by Helen McGinley; *Homemaking: Skills for Everyday Living,* by Frances Baynor Parnell; *People and Our Country,* by Norman K. Risjord; *Contemporary Living,* by Verdene Ryder; *Exploring Our Nation's History,* by Sidney Schwartz; *These United States,* by James P. Shenton; *The American Dream,* by Lew Smith; *Social Studies Series* published by Scott Foresman; and *The Rise of the American Nation,* by Lewis Paul Todd. On August 26, 1987, the U.S. Court of Appeals for the Eleventh Circuit unanimously overturned Judge Hand's decision by ruling that the information in the book was "essentially neutral in its religious content." The fact that the texts omitted references to religion was not "an advancement of secular humanism or an active hostility toward theistic religion." Source: 11, Jan. 1987, p. 6; May 1987, pp. 75, 104–7; Sept. 1987, pp. 166–67; Nov. 1987, pp. 217–18; Jan. 1988, p. 17; Mar. 1988, p. 40.

112 Baudelaire, Charles. *The Flowers of Evil.*
New Directions; Norton. Police seized all copies of
the work from the office of the publisher and the
printer (1857). Baudelaire appeared before the Sixth
Criminal Court for the "immoral passages" of the
poems and the court ruled that the body contained
"obscene and immoral passages or expression."
The court fined the author, the publisher, deprived
them of their right to vote, and ordered five poems
deleted from future editions. The French Appeals
Court lifted the ban in 1949. Source: 4, p. 46; 13,
pp. 74–75.

113 Bauer, Marion Dane, ed. *Am I Blue?:
Coming Out from the Silence.* HarperCollins.
Challenged, but retained at the Fairfield, Iowa
Middle School and High School libraries (2000)
despite objections to sexually explicit passages,
including a sexual encounter between two girls.
Source: 11, Mar. 2000, p. 62; May 2000, p. 91.

114 _____. *On My Honor.* Dell; Ticknor.
Retained at the Orchard Hill Elementary School
in Cedar Falls, Iowa (1989) after being challenged
because the 1986 Newbery Honor Book contained
"two swear words and one vulgarity." Challenged at
the Alamo Heights, Tex. School District Elementary
School (1992) because the book uses the words
"hell," "damn" and "frigging." Challenged in
fourth to sixth grade reading classes in Grove
City, Pa. (1995) because it was "depressing." The
criteria used to select the Newbery Award winning
book along with a list of other books that focus
on "divorce, death, suicide and defeat," was
contested. Source: 11, Mar. 1990, p. 47; May 1990,
p. 107; Jan. 1993, p. 13; Sept. 1995, p. 137.

115 Bauman, Robert. *The Gentleman from
Maryland: The Conscience of a Gay Conservative.*
Arbor House. Challenged at the Deschutes
County Library in Bend, Oreg. (1993) because it
"encourages and condones" homosexuality. Source:
11, Sept. 1993, pp. 158–59.

116 Bayle, Pierre. *Historical and Critical
Dictionary.* MacMillan. Burned in France (1754) and
placed by the Vatican on the Index of Forbidden
books (1757), where it remained through the first
two-thirds of the twentieth century. Source: 1, pp.
135–36.

117 Beard, Charles. *Rise of American
Civilization.* Macmillan. This Pulitzer Prize winner
was seized and destroyed by New Orleans, La.
(1937) police. Source: 15, Vol. III, p. 650.

**118 Beaumarchais, Pierre Augustin Caron
de.** *Barber of Seville.* Penguin. Forbidden to be
performed in France (1773-1775). Source: 4, p. 32.

119 _____. *Marriage of Figaro.* Penguin.
Suppressed for six years by Louis XVI at court and
in public performances on the ground of profound
immorality. The author was imprisoned in St. Lazare
(1778). Source: 4, p. 32.

120 Bechdel, Alison. *Fun Home: A Family
Tragicomic.* Houghton. Challenged, but retained
in the Marshall, Mo. Public Library (2006) despite
being deemed "pornographic" by some members
of the community. Source: 11, Nov. 2006, p. 289;
Jan. 2007, pp. 9–10; May 2007, p. 115.

121 Beck, Robert E., ed. *Literature of the
Supernatural.* McDougal, Littell. Challenged at
the Jefferson County school libraries in Lakewood,
Colo. (1986) because parents objected to many of
the stories because they "promoted the occult,
sexual promiscuity, and anti-Americanism, and that
they attacked other traditional American values."
The textbook is a collection of stories written by
such authors as Edgar Allen Poe, O. Henry, Ray
Bradbury, Dante, and Shakespeare. The Jefferson
County School Board refused to ban the book.
Source: 11, May 1986, p. 82; Sept. 1986, p. 173;
Nov. 1986, p. 224.

122 Behan, Brendan. *Borstal Boy.* Hutchinson.
Banned by the Irish Republic's Censorship of
Publications Board (1958), and later it was also
banned in both Australia and New Zealand. The
Irish Censorship Board was not required to give
any public explanation for its decisions, but it was
generally assumed that the novel was banned
because of its treatment of adolescent sexuality and
its extensive use of expletives. In fact Behan, does
not write graphically about sex and his characters
discuss the topic more than they practice it. There
can be little doubt that the book was banned
essentially because of its attempted subversion
of Irish power, structures, religious, social, and
political. Source: 6, pp. 203–4.

123 Beisner, Monika. *Secret Spells and
Curious Charms.* Farrar. Retained by the Salem-
Keizer, Oreg. School Board (1992) after complaints
that the book was a how-to book for satanism.
Source: 11, May 1992, p. 94.

124 **Belair, Richard L.** *Double Take.* Morrow. Challenged in Livingston, La. (1982) due to "objectionable" language. Source: 11, May 1982, p. 83.

125 **Bell, Alan P., and Martin S. Weinberg.** *Homosexualities: A Study of Diversity among Men and Women.* Macmillan; Simon. Challenged at the Deschutes County Library in Bend, Oreg. (1993) because it "encourages and condones" homosexuality. Source: 11, Sept. 1993, pp. 158–59.

126 **Bell, Ruth, et al.** *Changing Bodies, Changing Lives.* Random. Placed in a restrictive circulation category at the Muskego, Wis. High School library (1981). Challenged in Amherst, Wis. (1982) and the York, Maine (1982) school systems. Removed from the Sandy, Oreg. Union High School library (1984) due to "foul language and disregard for a wholesome balance about human sexuality." Challenged at the William Chrisman High School in Independence, Mo. (1984) because it is "filthy." Challenged at the Boone-Madison, W.Va. Public Library (1984). Challenged at the Gray-New Gloucester, Maine High School library (1986) because the book contains first person accounts of teenagers' sexual experiences. Challenged at the Eau Claire, Wis. Memorial High School library (1992) because of its graphic language and because the book condones abortion, homosexuality, and incest. Removed from the Kenai Peninsula Borough School District libraries in Homer, Alaska (1992) because the book was too explicit. Challenged at the Council Rock School District in Bucks County, Pa. (1994) because of passages that "undermine parental authority and depict sexual relations in explicit and vulgar language." Source: 11, July 1981, p. 92; May 1982, p. 100; July 1982, p. 124; July 1984, pp. 104, 106; Sept. 1984, p. 138; Nov. 1984, p. 186; Jan. 1985, pp. 27–28; July 1986, pp. 135–36; Sept. 1992, p. 140; Mar. 1993, p. 41; Mar. 1995, p. 44.

127 **Bellairs, John.** *The Figure in the Shadows.* Dell; Dial. Restricted at the Dysart Unified School District libraries in El Mirage, Ariz. (1990) because of two uses of profanity and because of its link to magic. Source: 11, Jan. 1991, p. 11.

128 **Belpre, Pura.** *Perez and Martina.* Warne. Challenged at the Multnomah County Library in Portland, Oreg. (1988) because the death of a mouse in the story could upset children. Source: 11, Jan. 1989, p. 3.

129 **Benchley, Peter.** *Jaws.* Bantam; Doubleday. Removed from all school libraries in Gardner, Kans. (1978) due to a sexually explicit section. Challenged at the Ogden, Utah School District (1979) and placed in a restricted circulation category. Removed from all elementary and middle school libraries in Clinton, N.C. (1980) due to "objectionable" language. Challenged in the Gwinnett County, Ga. public schools (1986) because of "obscene language." Source: 11, May 1978, p. 56; May 1979, p. 49; Sept. 1980, p. 99; Mar. 1987, p. 65.

130 **Benjamin, Carol Lea.** *The Wicked Stepdog.* Avon. Challenged by a parent at Newman Elementary School in Billings, Mont. (1994) because of objectionable language including the words "boobs," "ass," and "smoldering kisses." Despite an appeal from parents at a meeting where the offending words were emblazoned on pickets in the audience, two trustees (1994) upheld a decision not to remove the book from the district's library shelves. Source: 11, July 1994, p. 110; Sept. 1994, p. 166.

131 **Bennett, James.** *Blue Star Rapture.* Simon. Challenged, but retained on the Downers Grove, Ill. High School reading lists (1999) despite parents' complaints that the book is "obscene" and "vulgar." Source: 11, Jan. 2000, p. 28.

132 **Bentham, Jeremy.** *An Introduction to the Principles of Morals and Legislation.* Adamant Media Corp. Placed on the Index of Forbidden books (1819-1835), remaining listed through its last edition in effect until 1966. Source: 1, pp. 166–67.

133 **Berger, Melvin.** *The Supernatural: From ESP to UFOs.* John Day. Challenged, but retained, at the Cleveland, Tenn. Public Library (1993) along with seventeen other books, most of which are on sex education, AIDS awareness, and some titles on the supernatural. Source: 11, Sept. 1993, p. 146.

134 **Berger, Thomas.** *Little Big Man.* Delacorte; Fawcett; Dell. Retained on a list of supplementary texts for honor history classes at Juanita High School in Bellevue, Wash. (1986) despite claims that the book is "full of sexual material and questionable messages and should be banned." Source: 11, Sept. 1986, p. 173.

135 **Bergson, Henri.** *Creative Evolution.* Dover Pub. In 1907, the Vatican condemned "modernist" views, and in 1914, it placed Bergson's work on the Index of Forbidden books, where it remained through the last edition, published until 1966. Source: 1, pp. 62–63.

136 Berkeley, George. *Alciphron, or the Minute Philosopher.* Routledge. Placed on the Roman Index of Forbidden books. It was retained on the Index of Pope Leo XII in 1897 and remained listed through the last edition, compiled in 1948 and in print until 1996. Source: 1, p. 11.

137 Betancourt, Jeanne. *Sweet Sixteen and Never . . .* Bantam. Challenged in the Howard County, Md. schools (1991) because of the book's graphic depiction of teenage romance. Source: 11, Mar. 1992, p. 40.

138 *The Bible.* Martin Luther's translation of 1534 was burned by Papal authority in Germany in 1624. Soviet officials stated in 1926, "The section [in libraries] on religion must contain solely anti-religious books," and the Bible was not published again in the USSR until 1956. In 1952 and 1953 Fundamentalists in the U.S. attacked the Revised Standard Version because of changes in terminology. Banned in Ethiopia (1978) as "contradictory to the ongoing revolution." Translations of the Old and New Testament were banned in Turkey (1986). Challenged by an atheist "seeking to turn the tables on the religious right," but retained at the Brooklyn Center, Minn. Independent School District (1992). The challenger stated, "The lewd, indecent, and violent contents of that book are hardly suitable for young students." Challenged as "obscene and pornographic," but retained at the Noel Wien Library in Fairbanks, Alaska (1993). Challenged, but retained, in the West Shore schools near Harrisburg, Pa. (1993) despite objections that it "contains language and stories that are inappropriate for children of any age, including tales of incest and murder. There are more than three hundred examples of 'obscenities' in the book." Challenged, but retained in the Marion-Levy Public Library System (2001) in Ocala, Fla. Source: 4, pp. 3–5; 5, Sept. /Oct. 1978, p. 66; July/Aug. 1986, p. 46; 6, pp. 229–32; 8, pp. 208–12; 11, Jan. 1993, p. 8; Mar. 1993, p. 55; Mar. 1993, p. 55; July 1993, p. 123; Jan. 1994, p. 36; May 2001, p. 123.

139 Billington, Ray. *Limericks: Historical and Hysterical.* Norton. Removed, but later returned to the Tokay High School library in Lodi, Calif. (1988) because it was "really inappropriate and there ought to be better books on limericks available." Source: 11, May 1989, p. 75.

140 Bing, Leon. *Do or Die.* Harper. Challenged at the Sweetwater County Library in Green River, Wyo. (1993) because the book tells young people how to become involved in a gang. The book was retained. Source: 11, Jan. 1994, p. 14; Mar. 1994, p. 70.

141 Bird, Malcolm. *The Witch's Handbook.* Macmillan. Challenged for promoting witchcraft, but retained at the Multnomah, Oreg. County Library (1991). Source: 11, Jan. 1992, p. 6.

142 Birdseye, Tom. *Attack of the Mutant Underwear.* Puffin. Removed from the Pinellas, Fla. school district's Battle of the Books program (2006), although the book is on the Sunshine State Young Reader's Award list of books for third, fourth, and fifth-graders. Source: 11, Nov. 2006, pp. 290–91.

143 Bishop, Claire H. *The Five Chinese Brothers.* Putnam. Challenged at the Spokane, Wash. School District library (1994) because it is too violent. Challenged, but retained, at the Colton, Calif. elementary schools (1998) despite a parent's protest that it contains descriptions of violent plots to execute five brothers. Other books have been unsuccessfully challenged in recent years in the Colton School District, including John Steinbeck's *Of Mice and Men* for its use of profanity and Stephen King's *Misery* for violence. Source: 11, Jan. 1995, p. 9; Mar. 1999, p. 47.

144 Blank, Joan. *A Kid's First Book about Sex.* Down There Pr. Challenged at the Hammond, Ind. Public Library (1986) because "the book promotes immorality and promiscuity. It promotes no moral values whatsoever." Source: 11, Jan. 1987, p. 30.

145 _____. *Laugh Lines.* Grapetree Prods.; Putnam. Removed from the McKinleyville, Calif. Elementary School library (1990) for its "demeaning manner" toward individuals who read the riddles and cannot figure out the answers, rather than for its political or sexual content. Source: 11, Mar. 1991, p. 42.

146 Blatty, William P. *The Exorcist.* Bantam; Harper. Challenged at the Grinnell-Newburg, Iowa school system as "vulgar and obscene by most religious standards." Banned for use in Aurora, Colo. High School English classes (1976) on the grounds of "immorality." Source: 11, Mar. 1975, p. 41; May 1975, p. 87; May 1976, p. 70; May 1977, p. 79.

147 Block, Francesca Lia, and Suza Scalora. *The Rose and the Beast: Fairy Tales Retold.*

HarperCollins. Challenged, along with seventeen other titles in the Fairfax County, Va. elementary and secondary libraries (2002), by a group called Parents Against Bad Books in Schools. The group contends the books "contain profanity and descriptions of drug abuse, sexually explicit conduct, and torture." Source: 11, Jan. 2003, p. 10.

148 Block, Francesca Lia. *Baby Be-Bop.* HarperCollins. Removed from the Barron, Wis. School District (1998) because of the book's use of vulgar language and sexually explicit passages. The ACLU of Wisconsin filed suit against the school district on Feb. 16, 1999. The books were then returned to the library while a federal court considered the lawsuit. On October 8, 1999, it was agreed that the novel would remain available to students as part of the school district's settlement of the federal lawsuit. Removed from the mandatory reading program at the Norman L. Sullivan Middle School in Bonsall, Calif. (2000) due to sexually explicit language. Source: 8, pp. 415–16; 11, Jan. 1999, p. 9; Mar. 1999, p. 37; May 1999, p. 68; Jan. 2000, p. 28; May 2000, p. 76.

149 _____. *Girl Goddess #9: Nine Stories.* HarperCollins. Challenged, along with seventeen other titles in the Fairfax County, Va. elementary and secondary libraries (2002), by a group called Parents Against Bad Books in Schools. The group contends the books "contain profanity and descriptions of drug abuse, sexually explicit conduct, and torture." Source: 11, Jan. 2003, p. 10.

150 _____. *I Was a Teenage Fairy.* HarperCollins. Challenged, along with seventeen other titles in the Fairfax County, Va. elementary and secondary libraries (2002), by a group called Parents Against Bad Books in Schools. The group contends the books "contain profanity and descriptions of drug abuse, sexually explicit conduct, and torture." Source: 11, Jan. 2003, p. 10.

151 _____. *Witch Baby.* HarperCollins. Challenged, along with seventeen other titles in the Fairfax County, Va. elementary and secondary libraries (2002), by a group called Parents Against Bad Books in Schools. The group contends the books "contain profanity and descriptions of drug abuse, sexually explicit conduct, and torture." On March 10, 2003, the school board determined the book is suitable for elementary- and middle-school collections and placed a young-adult sticker on its spine. Source: 11, Jan. 2003, p. 10; May 2003, p. 117.

152 Bloom, Harold, ed. *Modern Critical Views: James Baldwin.* Chelsea House Pubs. Removed in the Southern Columbia School District in Elysburg, Pa. (2000) because of concerns about sexual references and foul language in a single passage. Source: 11, July 2000, p. 104.

153 Blumberg, Rhoda. *Devils and Demons.* Watts. Challenged at the Newberg, Oreg. Public Library (1988) because the book was too graphic and the topic was negative and degrading. Source: 11, Jan. 1990, pp. 4–5.

154 Blume, Judy. *Are You There God? It's Me, Margaret.* Bradbury Pr. Challenged in many libraries but removed from the Gilbert, Ariz. elementary school libraries (1980), and ordered that parental consent be required for students to check out this title from the junior high school library. Restricted in Zimmerman, Minn. (1982) to students who have written permission from their parents. Challenged in Tuscaloosa, Ala. (1982) and Fond du Lac, Wis. (1982) school systems because the book is "sexually offensive and amoral"; challenged at the Xenia, Ohio school libraries (1983) because the book "is built around just two themes: sex and anti-Christian behavior." After the Minnesota Civil Liberties Union sued the Elk River, Minn. School Board (1983), the Board reversed its decision to restrict this title to students who have written permission from their parents. Challenged as profane, immoral, and offensive, but retained in the Bozeman, Mont. school libraries (1985). Source: 9; 11, Jan. 1981, p. 9; Sept. 1982, pp. 155–56; Mar. 1983, pp. 34, 39; May 1983, p. 71; Sept. 1983, pp. 139, 153; Nov. 1983, p. 197; July 1985, p. 112.

155 _____. *Blubber.* Bradbury Pr.; Dell; Dutton. Removed from all library shelves in the Montgomery County, Md. (1980) elementary schools. Temporarily banned in Sunizona, Ariz. (1981). Challenged in the Des Moines, Iowa schools (1983) due to "objectionable" subject matter; challenged at the Smith Elementary School in Del Valle, Tex. (1983) because it contained the words "damn" and "bitch" and showed children cruelly teasing a classmate; challenged at the Xenia, Ohio school libraries (1983) because the book "undermines authority since the word 'bitch' is used in connection with a teacher"; challenged at the Akron, Ohio School District libraries (1983). Restricted at the Lindenwold, N.J. elementary school libraries (1984) because of "a problem with language." Banned, but later restricted to students with parental permission at the Peoria, Ill. School

District libraries (1984) because of its strong sexual content and language, and alleged lack of social or literary value. Removed from the Hanover, Pa. School District's elementary and secondary libraries (1984), but later placed on a "restricted shelf" at middle school libraries because the book was "indecent and inappropriate." Challenged at the Casper, Wyo. school libraries (1984). Challenged as profane, immoral, and offensive, but retained in the Bozeman, Mont. school libraries (1985). Challenged at the Muskego, Wis. Elementary School (1986) because "the characters curse and the leader of the taunting (of an overweight girl) is never punished for her cruelty." Challenged at the Perry Township, Ohio elementary school libraries (1991) because in the book, "bad is never punished. Good never comes to the fore. Evil is triumphant." Banned at Clements High School in Athens, Ala. (1998) because of objections to two uses of the word "damn" and "bitch" in the novel. The decision was later reversed. Removed from an elementary school in Arlington, Tex. (1999) because educators objected to "verbal, physical, and sexual abuse of student upon student." Source: 9; 11, May 1980, p. 51; Mar. 1982, p. 57; May 1982, p. 84; July 1982, pp. 124, 142; May 1983, pp. 73, 85–86; July 1983, p. 121; Sept. 1983, pp. 139, 153; Nov. 1983, p. 197; Nov. 1984, p. 185; Jan. 1985, pp. 8–9; Mar. 1985, pp. 33, 42, 58; July 1985, p. 112; Jan. 1987, p. 31; Mar. 1992, p. 41; July 1992, p. 124; Mar. 1999, p. 35; May 1999, p. 83; Jan. 2000, p. 8.

156 _____. ***Deenie.*** Bradbury Pr. Removed from the Utah State Library bookmobile (1980) because the book contains "the vilest sexual descriptions" and if given to "the wrong kid at the wrong time (would) ruin his life." Removed from the Gilbert, Ariz. elementary school libraries (1980), and ordered that parental consent be required for students to check out this title from the junior high school library. Challenged in Orlando, Fla. (1982); challenged in the Cotati-Rohnert Park, Calif. School District (1982) because the novel allegedly undermines parental moral values. After the Minnesota Civil Liberties Union sued the Elk River, Minn. School Board (1983), the Board reversed its decision to restrict this title to students who have written permission from their parents. Banned, but later restricted to students with parental permission at the Peoria, Ill. School District libraries (1984) because of its strong sexual content and language, and alleged lack of social or literary value. Removed from the Hanover, Pa. School District's elementary and secondary libraries (1984), but later placed on a "restricted shelf" at middle school libraries because the book was "indecent and inappropriate." Challenged at the Casper, Wyo. school libraries

(1984). Challenged as profane, immoral, and offensive, but retained in the Bozeman, Mont. school libraries (1985). Banned from district elementary school libraries in Gwinnett County, Ga. (1985) as "inappropriate." Returned to the elementary and junior high school library shelves in Clayton County, Ga. (1985) after school officials determined that the book is appropriate for young readers. Challenged by a parent in the Cornelius Elementary School library in Charlotte, N.C. (1996) due to the novel's sexual content. Challenged by a parent in the Spring Hill Elementary School District in Hernando County, Fla. (2003) due to passages that talk frankly about masturbation. The board decided to retain the title, but require students to have written parental permission to access the novel. Source: 9; 11, Nov. 1980, p. 128; Jan. 1981, p. 9; July 1982, p. 125; Sept. 1982, pp. 155–56; Jan. 1983, p. 21; May 1983, p. 71; Sept. 1983, p. 153; Jan. 1985, pp. 8–9; Mar. 1985, pp. 33, 42, 58; July 1985, p. 112; Sept. 1985, p. 151; Nov. 1985, p. 193; Jan. 1986, pp. 8–9, 21; May 1996, p. 83; Jan. 2003, pp. 8–9; Mar. 2004, pp. 48–49; May 2004, pp. 95–96.

157 _____. ***Forever.*** Bradbury Pr. Challenged at the Midvalley Junior-Senior High School in Scranton, Pa. (1982) because it contains "four-letter words and talked about masturbation, birth control, and disobedience to parents"; challenged at the Park Hill, Mo. South Junior High School library (1982) where it was housed on restricted shelves because the book promotes "the stranglehold of humanism on life in America"; challenged at the Orlando, Fla. schools (1982); the Akron, Ohio School District libraries (1983); challenged at the Howard-Suamico, Wis. High School (1983) because "it demoralizes marital sex." Challenged and eventually moved from the Holdrege, Nebr. Public Library young adult section to the adult section (1984) because the "book is pornographic and does not promote the sanctity of life, family life." Challenged at the Cedar Rapids, Iowa Public Library (1984) because it is "pornography and explores areas God didn't intend to explore outside of marriage." Placed on a restricted shelf at Patrick County, Va. School Board (1986). Challenged at the Campbell County, Wyo. school libraries (1986) because it is "pornographic" and would encourage young readers "to experiment with sexual encounters." Challenged at the Moreno Valley, Calif. Unified School District libraries (1987) because it "contains profanity, sexual situations, and themes that allegedly encourage disrespectful behavior." Challenged at the Marshwood Junior High School classroom library in Eliot, Maine (1987) because the "book does not paint a responsible role of parents";

its "cast of sex-minded teenagers is not typical of high schoolers today"; and the "pornographic sexual exploits (in the book) are unsuitable for junior high school role models." West Hernando, Fla. Middle School principal (1988) recommended that Blume's novel be removed from school library shelves because it is "inappropriate." Placed on reserve at the Herrin, Ill. Junior High School library (1992) and can be checked out only with a parent's written permission because the novel is "sexually provocative reading." Removed from the Frost Junior High School library in Schaumburg, Ill. (1993) because "it's basically a sexual 'how-to-do' book for junior high students. It glamorizes [sex] and puts ideas in their heads." Placed on the "parental permission shelf" at the Rib Lake, Wis. high school libraries (1993) after Superintendent Ray Parks filed a "request for reconsideration" because he found the book "sexually explicit." It was subsequently confiscated by the high school principal. A federal jury in Madison, Wis. awarded $394,560 to a former Rib Lake High School guidance counselor after finding that his contract was not renewed in retaliation for speaking out against the district's material selection policy. The counselor criticized the decision of the Rib Lake High School principal to restrict student access to the novel. Removed from Mediapolis, Iowa School District libraries (1994) because it "does not promote abstinence and monogamous relationships [and] lacks any aesthetic, literary, or social value." Returned to the shelves a month later but accessible only to high school students. Removed from the Fort Clarke Middle School library in Gainesville, Fla. (1995) after a science teacher objected to its sexually explicit content and a reference to marijuana. Restricted to a reserve section of the Delta High School Library in Muncie, Ind. (1995). Parents must give their permission in writing before their children can check out the book. Challenged at the Wilton, Iowa School District for junior and senior high school students (1996) because of its sexual content. Banned from middle school libraries in the Elgin, Ill. School District U46 (1997) because of sex scenes. The decision was upheld in June 1999 after an hour of emotional school board discussion. After a four-year absence, the book was returned (2002) to the shelves of the district's middle school libraries. Challenged in the Fayetteville, Ark. Middle and Junior High School libraries (2005). The complainant also submitted a list of more than fifty books, citing the books as too sexually explicit and promoting homosexuality. Source: 8, pp. 334–35; 9; 11, July 1982, pp. 124, 142; May 1982, p. 84; May 1983, pp. 85–86; Mar. 1984, p. 39; May 1984, p. 69; Mar. 1985, p. 59; Sept. 1985, p. 167; Mar. 1986, p. 39; Mar. 1987, pp. 66–67; July 1987, p. 125; Nov. 1987,

p. 239; Mar. 1988, p. 45; May 1992, p. 80; May 1993, p. 70; July 1993, pp. 98, 104–5; Sept. 1993, pp. 146–47; May 1994, pp. 83, 86; July 1994, p. 109; Mar. 1995, p. 56; July 1995, p. 93; Nov. 1995, p. 183; May 1996, p. 97; May 1997, pp. 60–61; Sept. 1999, p. 119; Mar. 2002, p. 105; May 2002, pp. 135–36; Sept. 2005, p. 215.

158 _____. **Here's to You, Rachel Robinson.** Orchard. Challenged, but retained at the Granville School library in Catskill, N.Y. (1999) despite a parent's objection to three words. Source: 11, Sept. 1999, p. 131.

159 _____. **Iggie's House.** Bradbury Pr. Challenged at the Casper, Wyo. school libraries (1984). Source: 11, Mar. 1985, p. 42.

160 _____. **It's Not the End of the World.** Bradbury Pr. Restricted at the Lindenwold, N.J. elementary school libraries (1984) because of "a problem with language." Removed from the Hanover, Pa. School District's elementary and secondary libraries (1984), but later placed on a "restricted shelf" at middle school libraries because the book was "indecent and inappropriate." Challenged at the Casper, Wyo. school libraries (1984). Challenged at the Orchard Lake Elementary School library in Burnsville, Minn. (1985). Restricted to fourth- and fifth-graders at W. C. Britt Elementary School in Gwinnett County, Ga. (1998) due to concerns about profanity. Source: 11, Nov. 1984, p. 185; Jan. 1985, p. 9; Mar. 1985, p. 42; Nov. 1985, p. 203; May 1998, pp. 69–70.

161 _____. **The One in the Middle Is the Green Kangaroo.** Bradbury Pr. Challenged at the Casper, Wyo. school libraries (1984). Source: 11, Mar. 1985, p. 42.

162 _____. **Otherwise Known as Sheila the Great.** Bradbury Pr. Challenged at the Casper, Wyo. school libraries (1984). Source: 11, Mar. 1985, p. 42.

163 _____. **Starring Sally J. Freedman as Herself.** Bradbury Pr. Removed from the Hanover, Pa. School District's elementary and secondary libraries (1984), but later placed on a "restricted shelf" at middle school libraries because the book was "indecent and inappropriate." Challenged at the Casper, Wyo. school libraries (1984). Challenged as profane, immoral, and offensive, but retained in the Bozeman, Mont. school libraries (1985). Source: 11, Jan. 1985, p. 9; Mar. 1985, p. 42; July 1985, p. 112.

164 _____. *Superfudge.* Bradbury Pr. Challenged at the Casper, Wyo. school libraries (1984). Challenged as profane, immoral, and offensive, but retained in the Bozeman, Mont. school libraries (1985). Source: 11, Mar. 1985, p. 42; July 1985, p. 112.

165 _____. *Then Again, Maybe I Won't.* Bradbury Pr. Challenged in many libraries but removed from the Gilbert, Ariz. elementary school libraries (1980), and ordered that parental consent be required for students to check out this title from the junior high school library. Challenged in Orlando, Fla. (1982); challenged in Tuscaloosa, Ala. (1982) because the book is "sexually offensive and amoral"; and challenged in the Harford County, Md. school systems (1982). After the Minnesota Civil Liberties Union sued the Elk River, Minn. School Board (1983), the Board reversed its decision to restrict this title to students who have written permission from their parents. Removed from all school library collections in St. Tammany Parish, La. (1984) because its "treatment of immorality and voyeurism do not provide for the growth of desirable attitudes," but later reinstated. Banned, but later restricted to students with parental permission at the Peoria, Ill. School District libraries (1984) because of its strong sexual content and language, and alleged lack of social or literary value. Challenged at the Casper, Wyo. school libraries (1984). Challenged as profane, immoral, and offensive, but retained in the Bozeman, Mont. school libraries (1985). Challenged in the Des Moines, Iowa elementary schools (1988) because of sexual content. Challenged at the Salem-Keizer, Oreg. School District (1989) because it is a "dismal tale of a young boy's inability to cope and his very inappropriate responses to the changes taking place in his life." Challenged at the elementary library in Tyrone, Pa. (1990) because the book deals with masturbation and erections, and that it explains how to drink whiskey, vodka, and gin. Source: 9; 11, July 1982, p. 124; Sept. 1982, pp. 155–56; May 1983, p. 71; Sept. 1983, p. 153; May 1984, p. 69; July 1984, p. 121; Jan. 1985, p. 8; Mar. 1985, pp. 33, 42, 58; July 1985, p. 112; Jan. 1990, pp. 4–5; July 1990, p. 127; Mar. 1991, p. 62.

166 _____. *Tiger Eyes.* Bradbury Pr. Removed from the Hanover, Pa. School District's elementary and secondary libraries (1984), but later placed on a "restricted shelf" at middle school libraries because the book was "indecent and inappropriate." Challenged at the Daleville, Ind. Elementary School library (1984) due to alleged sexual innuendo in the book. Challenged at the Casper, Wyo. school

libraries (1984). Pulled from the Many, La. Junior High library shelves (1999) because of descriptions of a girl's sexual encounters, getting drunk at school, and the use of profanities. Source: 11, Jan. 1985, p. 9; Mar. 1985, pp. 42, 59; Jan. 2000, p. 11.

167 **Boccaccio, Giovanni.** *The Decameron.* AMS Pr.; Johns Hopkins Univ. Pr.; Norton; Penguin. Burned and prohibited in Italy (1497, 1559). Declared to be an "obscene, lewd and lascivious book of indecent character" by a jury in Cincinnati, Ohio (1906). Seized by Detroit, Mich. police (1934), still banned in Boston, Mass. (1935). Banned in U.S. (1926-1931). Source: 6, pp. 257–58; 8, pp. 327–29; 9, p. 7; 10, p. 140.

168 **Bode, Janet, and Stan Mack.** *Heartbreak and Roses: Real Life Stories of Troubled Love.* Delacorte. Pulled from the Ouachita Parish School library in Monroe, La. (1996) because of sexual content. The Louisiana chapter of the ACLU filed a lawsuit in the federal courts on October 3, 1996, claiming that the principal and the school superintendent violated First Amendment free speech rights and also failed to follow established procedure when they removed the book. The three-year-old school library censorship case headed to court after the Ouachita Parish School Board made no decision to seek a settlement at a special meeting April 12, 1999. On August 17, 1999, the Ouachita Parish School Board agreed to return the book to the library and to develop a new book-selection policy that follows state guidelines for school media programs. Source: 11, Sept. 1996, pp. 151–52; Jan. 1997, p. 7; July 1999, p. 93; Jan. 2000, p. 27.

169 **Bode, Janet.** *View from Another Closet.* Watts. Challenged at the Niles, Mich. Community Library (1982) because the book is "a devious attempt to recruit our young people into the homosexual lifestyle." Source: 11, Jan. 1983, p. 8.

170 **Bogart, Bonnie.** *Ewoks Join the Fight.* Random. Challenged at the La Costa, Calif. Public Library (1987) because "every page except for three has some sort of violence—somebody gets knocked down or the Death Star is destroyed." Source: 11, July 1987, p. 125.

171 **Bonner, Cindy.** *Lily.* Algonquin. Removed temporarily from the Richland, Pa. Middle School Library (1994) while a "Parental Guidance" program that gives parents more control over what their children read in school is explored. A local parent complained that it was "sexually explicit" and had "no moral guidance." Source: 11, Jan. 1995, p. 8; Mar. 1995, p. 41.

172 **Booth, Jack.** *Impressions Series.* Holt. Challenged in the Oak Harbor, Wash. school system (1987) because it "undermines parental authority, is filled with morbid, frightening imagery and involves children in witchcraft and sorcery." In addition, opponents claimed, "the series promotes Eastern and other religions to the exclusion of Christianity." Challenged at the Talent Elementary School in Phoenix, Oreg. (1988) because it "promotes witchcraft and secular humanism and lacks Christian values." Temporarily banned at the Hacienda La Puente Unified School District in Hacienda Heights, Calif. (1989) because of morbid imagery. Removed from the East Whittier, Calif. School District (1989) because parents complained that some stories were evil and morbid. Challenged in the Coeur d'Alene, Idaho elementary schools (1989); Stockton, Calif. (1990); Redondo Beach, Calif. (1990); Yucaipa, Calif. (1990); Nashville, Tenn. (1990); Winters, Calif. (1990); Shingletown, Calif. (1990); Fairbanks, Alaska (1990); Wheaton, Ill. (1990); Albuquerque, N.Mex. (1990); Santa Fe, N.Mex. (1990); Campbell, Calif. (1990); Saratoga, Calif. (1990); Boise, Idaho (1990); Palatine, Ill. (1990); Barrington, Ill. (1990); Arlington Heights, Ill. (1990); Box Elder, S.Dak. (1990); Lakewood, N.Y. (1990); Newport, Oreg. (1991); Grass Valley, Calif. (1991); Gardiner, Maine (1991); Eureka, Calif. (1991); and Willard, Ohio (1991) because the series of readers "undermines absolute truth and value, teaches situational ethics and a lack of respect for authority, and curiosity in the occult." The first editions of the series were challenged because there was too much of a Canadian emphasis. Removed in the North Marion School District in Aurora, Oreg. (1991). Challenged in Frederick County, Md. schools (1992). U.S. District Court Judge William Shubb dismissed a lawsuit in California alleging that the series violated the state and federal constitutions by promoting the "religion of witchcraft and neo-paganism." U.S. District Court Judge James B. Moran dismissed a lawsuit filed against Wheaton-Warrenville, Ill. School District (1992) by parents who claimed school officials failed to implement rules allowing their children to be excluded from using the series. Source: 11, Jan. 1988, p. 13; Jan. 1989, p. 3; Jan. 1990, p. 11; Mar. 1990, p. 46; May 1990, p. 85; Sept. 1990, pp. 160–61; Nov. 1990, p. 210; Jan. 1991, pp. 14, 16, 17, 29; Mar. 1991, pp. 46–48; July 1991, pp. 107, 131–32; Sept. 1991, p. 178; Jan. 1992, p. 9; Mar. 1992, pp. 32, 45; July 1992, pp. 110–11, 117; Sept. 1992, p. 163; Jan. 1993, pp. 11, 18.

173 **Bopp, Joseph B.** *Herbie Capleenies.* Addison-Wesley. Removed from the Hermiston, Oreg. Elementary School library (1982) because of the main character's activities, which included machine-gunning his boring friends and making naked snowwomen. Source: 11, July 1982, p. 124.

174 **Borland, Hal.** *When the Legends Die.* Bantam. Removed from the Lincoln County, Wyo. High School curriculum (1995) because of "considerable obscenities." The parent complained that there were 57 swear words in 40 consecutive pages. Source: 11, July 1995, p. 100.

175 **Borten, Helen.** *Halloween.* Crowell. Challenged at the Neely Elementary School in Gilbert, Ariz. (1992) because the book shows the dark side of religion through the occult, the devil, and satanism. Source: 11, May 1992, p. 78; July 1992, p. 124.

176 **Bossert, Jill.** *Humor 2.* Madison Square Pr. Challenged at the Sno-Isle Regional Library System in Marysville, Wash. (1992) because the jokes in the book deal with adult subjects. Source: 11, Nov. 1992, p. 185.

177 **Boston Women's Health Book Collective.** *Our Bodies, Ourselves.* Simon & Schuster. Removed from high school libraries in Townshend, Vt. (1975); Pinellas County, Fla. (1975); Morgantown, W.Va. (1977), and Helena, Mont. (1978). Challenged in Amherst, Wis. (1982) due to its "pornographic" nature; Three Rivers, Mich. Public Library (1982) because it "promotes homosexuality and perversion." Challenged at the William Chrisman High School in Independence, Mo. (1984) because the book is "filthy." The controversial feminist health manual was on a bookshelf in the classroom and was the personal property of the teacher. Source: 9; 11, July 1975, p. 105; Sept. 1975, p. 138; July 1977, p. 100; Mar. 1979, p. 27; May 1982, p. 100; Mar. 1983, p. 29; July 1984, p. 106; 15, Vol. IV, p. 714.

178 **Boswell, Robert.** *Mystery Ride.* Harper; Knopf; Thorndike Pr. Expurgated by an apparent self-appointed censor at the Coquille, Oreg. Public Library (1994) along with several other books. Most were mysteries and romances in which single words and sexually explicit passages were whited out by a vandal who left either dots or solid ink pen lines where the words had been. Source: 11, Sept. 1994, p. 148.

179 Bower, William C. *The Living Bible.* Arno. Burned in Gastonia, N.C. (1981) because it is "a perverted commentary of the King James Version." Source: 11, July 1981, p. 105.

180 Bradbury, Ray. *Fahrenheit 451.* Ballantine. Expurgated at the Venado Middle School in Irvine, Calif. (1992). Students received copies of the book with scores of words—mostly "hells" and "damns"—blacked out. The novel is about book-burning and censorship. After receiving complaints from parents and being contacted by reporters, school officials said the censored copies would no longer be used. Challenged at the Conroe, Tex. Independent School District (2006) because of the following: "discussion of being drunk, smoking cigarettes, violence, 'dirty talk,' references to the Bible, and using God's name in vain." The novel went against the complainants' "religious beliefs." Source: 6, p. 279; 8, pp. 446–47; 11, July 1992, pp. 108–9; Nov. 2006, p. 293.

181 _____. *The Martian Chronicles.* Bantam. Challenged at the Haines City, Fla. High School (1982) due to several instances of profanity and the use of God's name in vain in the work. Challenged at the Newton-Conover, N.C. High School (1987) as a supplemental reading due to profanity. Challenged as required reading at the Gatlinburg-Pittman, Tenn. High School (1993) due to profanity. Pulled and replaced with a newer version at the Herbert Hoover Middle School in Edison, N.J. (1998) because a chapter contains the words "the niggers are coming." The new abridged edition of the book omits the inflammatory story, titled "Way Up in the Air." Source: 11, Jan. 1983, p. 22; May 1987, p. 103; Sept. 1993, p. 149; May 1998, pp. 71–72; July 1998, p. 109.

182 _____. *The Veldt.* Dramatic Pub. Co.; Creative Ed. Retained on the Beaverton, Oreg. School District's reading list (2006). The short story was challenged by a middle-school parent who thought its language and plot were inappropriate for students. Her biggest concern is that the story offers no consequences for the children's actions. The short story is part of Bradbury's *The Illustrated Man* anthology. It is twenty pages long and was published in 1951 as the first in the collection of eighteen science fiction stories. Source: 11, Nov. 2006, p. 319.

183 Bradford, Richard. *Red Sky at Morning.* Harper. Challenged in Omak, Wash. (1979) due to "profane language." Challenged at the Big Sky High School in Missoula, Mont. (1987) because the "language was inappropriate for freshman." Source: 11, July 1979, p. 75; July 1987, p. 150.

184 Brancato, Robin. *Winning.* Bantam. Challenged at the Greeley-Evans School District in Greeley, Colo. (1986) because the book contained "obscenities, allusions to sexual references, and promoted contempt for parents and acceptance of drug use." Source: 11, Sept. 1986, p. 171.

185 Brashler, Anne. *Getting Jesus in the Mood.* Cane Hill Pr. Challenged at the Carroll County Public Library in Westminster, Md. (1992) because the widely praised short story collection is "smutty" and contains pornography aimed at Jesus Christ. Source: 11, Sept. 1992, pp. 137–38.

186 Brautigan, Richard. *The Abortion: An Historical Romance.* Pocket Bks.; Simon & Schuster. Removed from high school library in Redding, Calif. (1978) due to "unsuitable obscene and sexual references." A California state appeals court has ruled (1989) in *Wexner v. Anderson Union High School District Board of Trustees* that the school board acted improperly when it banned this book. Source: 11, Jan. 1979, p. 11; Mar. 1989, p. 52.

187 _____. *A Confederate General from Big Sur.* Delta. Removed from high school library in Redding, Calif. (1978) due to "unsuitable obscene and sexual references." A California state appeals court has ruled (1989) in *Wexner v. Anderson Union High School District Board of Trustees* that the school board acted improperly when it banned this book. Source: 11, Jan. 1979, p. 11; Mar. 1989, p. 52.

188 _____. *The Pill vs. the Springhill Mine Disaster.* Dell. Removed from high school library in Redding, Calif. (1978) due to "unsuitable obscene and sexual references." A California state appeals court has ruled (1989) in *Wexner v. Anderson Union High School District Board of Trustees* that the school board acted improperly when it banned this book. Removed from the shelves of the Southeast Whitfield, Ga. High School library (1988) because it includes four poems that use "inappropriate" language or have sexual connotations. Source: 11, Jan. 1979, p. 11; Jan. 1989, p. 7; Mar. 1989, p. 52.

189 _____. *The Revenge of the Lawn.* Pocket Bks. Removed from high school library in Redding, Calif. (1978) due to "unsuitable obscene and sexual references." A California state appeals court has ruled (1989) in *Wexner v. Anderson Union High*

School District Board of Trustees that the school board acted improperly when it banned this book. Source: 11, Jan. 1979, p. 11; Mar. 1989, p. 52.

190 _____. *Rommel Drives on Deep into Egypt.* Delacorte; Dell. Removed from high school library in Redding, Calif. (1978) due to "unsuitable obscene and sexual references." A California state appeals court has ruled (1989) in *Wexner v. Anderson Union High School District Board of Trustees* that the school board acted improperly when it banned this book. Source: 11, Jan. 1979, p. 11; Mar. 1989, p. 52.

191 _____. *Trout Fishing in America.* Delacorte. Removed from high school library in Redding, Calif. (1978) due to "unsuitable obscene and sexual references." A California state appeals court has ruled (1989) in *Wexner v. Anderson Union High School District Board of Trustees* that the school board acted improperly when it banned this book. Source: 11, Jan. 1979, p. 11; Mar. 1989, p. 52.

192 **Bredes, Don.** *Hard Feelings.* Atheneum; Bantam. Removed from the Montello, Wis. High School library (1981). Challenged in Flat Rock, Mich. (1982) because of "objectionable" language. Source: 11, Sept. 1981, p. 126; Sept. 1982, p. 156.

193 **Briggs, Raymond.** *Father Christmas.* Coward. Removed from all elementary classrooms in Holland, Mich. (1979) after several parents complained that the work portrays Santa Claus as having a negative attitude toward Christmas. Challenged at the Albany, Oreg. Public Library (1988) because it contains cursing, drinking, and a negative image of Santa Claus. Source: 9; 11, Jan. 1980, p. 7; Jan. 1989, p. 3.

194 **Brink, Andre.** *A Dry White Season.* Morrow. Banned in South Africa in Sept. 1979. The ban was lifted in Nov. 1979, but Brink was branded a "malicious writer." Source: 5, Feb. 1980, p. 73.

195 **Bronstein, Leo.** *El Greco.* Abrams. Retained at Maldonado Elementary School in Tucson, Ariz. (1994) after being challenged by parents who objected to nudity and "pornographic," "perverted," and "morbid" themes. Source: 11, July 1994, p. 112.

196 **Brooks, Bruce.** *The Moves Make the Man.* Harper. Removed from a San Lorenzo, Calif. High School reading list (1992) after a parent complained that racist terms in the dialogue were offensive to black students. Source: 11, Sept. 1992, pp. 140–41.

197 **Brown, Claude.** *Manchild in the Promised Land.* Macmillan; NAL. Removed from high school libraries in Waukesha, Wis. (1974); Plant City, Fla. (1976); North Jackson, Ohio (1980) due to "filth and obscenity." Removed from classroom use and placed on the restricted shelf in the Baton Rouge, La. school library (1977) after Concerned Citizens and Taxpayers for Decent Books listed the book along with 64 other "offensive" works. Challenged at the Parkrose, Oreg. High School (1987) because the content is "violent, the language offensive, and women are degraded." The protestors also questioned its relevance, claiming that Parkrose students have no need to understand life in a black ghetto. Source: 8, pp. 469–70; 9; 11, May 1980, p. 51; Sept. 1987, p. 176; Nov. 1987, p. 240.

198 **Brown, Dan.** *The Da Vinci Code.* Doubleday. Banned in Egypt (2006). The culture minister told parliament, "We ban any book that insults any religion. We will confiscate this book." Parliament was debating the book at the request of several Coptic Christian members who demanded a ban because, "It's based on Zionist myth, and it contains insults towards Christ, and it insults the Christian religion and Islam." Banned in Iran (2006). Source: 11, Sept. 2006, p. 232; Jan. 2007, p. 35.

199 **Brown, Dee.** *Bury My Heart at Wounded Knee.* Holt. Removed in Wild Rose, Wis. (1974) by a district administrator because the book was "slanted" and "if there's a possibility that something might be controversial, then why not eliminate it." Source: 11, Nov. 1974, p. 145.

200 **Brown, Laurene Krasny, and Marc Brown.** *Dinosaurs Divorce.* Little. Challenged at the Rebecca Minor Elementary School in Gwinnett County, Ga. (1995) because the book could offend children whose parents are going through a divorce and create fears and anxiety in children from stable families. Source: 11, Sept. 1995, p. 157.

201 **Browne, Sir Thomas.** *Religio Medici.* Kessinger Pub. In 1645, the Catholic Church placed it on the Index of Forbidden books for its skeptical, rationalist perspective, and its allegiance to the Anglican Church. The book remained listed until 1966. Source: 1, pp. 282–83.

202 **Browning, Elizabeth Barrett.** *Aurora Leigh.* Academy. Condemned in Boston, Mass.

(1857) as "the hysterical indecencies of an erotic mind." Source: 4, p. 42.

203 Bruno, Giordano. *On the Infinite Universe and Worlds.* Greenwood Pr.; Schuman. Author imprisoned (1592-99), tried on charges of blasphemy, immoral conduct, and heresy, and executed in Rome on February 17, 1600. Placed on the Index of Forbidden Books (1603), where it remained through the last edition of the Index, in effect until 1966. Source: 8, pp. 273–75.

204 Bryant, Sara Cone. *Epaminondas and His Auntie.* Houghton. Retained, but moved from the children's section to the folk life section at the Spartanburg, S.C. County Library (1989) because "the book's drawings were stereotypical and demeaning to black people." Source: 11, Nov. 1989, pp. 236–37.

205 Budbill, David. *Bones on Black Spruce Mountain.* Bantam; Dial. Challenged at the Bennington, Vt. School District (1988) because of inappropriate language. Challenged in the Gettysburg, Pa. public schools (1993) because of offensive language. Source: 11, Mar. 1989, p. 61; Mar. 1994, p. 55.

206 Bunch, Robert. *Invisible Marijuana and Psychedelic Mushroom Gardens.* Loompanics Unlimited. Challenged at the Warrenville, Ill. Public Library (2000) because "it provides a step-by-step manual for circumventing the law." Source: 11, Mar. 2000, p. 48.

207 Bunn, Scott. *Just Hold On.* Delacorte. Banned at the Covington Junior High School in Vancouver, Wash. (1988) because the book is devoid of hope and positive role models. Source: 11, Mar. 1989, p. 61; May 1989, p. 79.

208 Bunting, Eve. *Karen Kepplewhite Is the World's Best Kisser.* Houghton; Archway. Challenged at the Little Butte Intermediate School in Eagle Point, Oreg. (1989) because the book was too mature for the elementary class students. Source: 11, Jan. 1990, pp. 4–5.

209 Burgess, Anthony. *A Clockwork Orange.* Ballantine; Norton. In 1973 a bookseller in Orem, Utah, was arrested for selling the novel. Charges were later dropped, but the bookseller was forced to close the store and relocate to another city. Removed from Aurora, Colo. high school (1976) due to "objectionable" language and from high school classrooms in Westport, Mass. (1977) because of "objectionable" language. Removed from two Anniston, Ala. high school libraries (1982), but later reinstated on a restricted basis. Source: 8, pp. 440–41; 11, May 1976, p. 70; Jan. 1977, p. 8; Mar. 1983, p. 37.

210 Burgess, Melvin. *Doing It.* Holt. Challenged in the Fayetteville, Ark. High School library (2005). The complainant also submitted a list of more than fifty books, citing the books as too sexually explicit and promoting homosexuality. Source: 11, Sept. 2005, p. 215.

211 Burroughs, Augusten. *Running with Scissors.* St. Martin. Challenged in the Howell, Mich. High School (2007) because of the book's strong sexual content. In response to a request from the president of the Livingston Organization for Values in Education, or LOVE, the county's top law enforcement official reviewed the books to see whether laws against distribution of sexually explicit materials to minors had been broken. "After reading the books in question, it is clear that the explicit passages illustrated a larger literary, artistic or political message and were not included solely to appeal to the prurient interests of minors," the county prosecutor wrote. "Whether these materials are appropriate for minors is a decision to be made by the school board, but I find that they are not in violation of the criminal laws." Source: 11, May 2007, p. 116.

212 Burroughs, Edgar Rice. *Tarzan.* Ballantine. Removed from the Los Angeles, Calif. Public Library (1929) because Tarzan was allegedly living in sin with Jane. Source: 10, p. 130.

213 Burroughs, William, and Allen Ginsberg. *The Yage Letters.* City Lights. Banned from use in Aurora, Colo. High School English classes (1976) on the grounds of "immorality." Source: 11, May 1976, p. 70; May 1977, p. 79.

214 Burroughs, William. *Naked Lunch.* Grove. Found obscene in Boston, Mass. Superior Court (1965). The Massachusetts Supreme Court (1966) cleared the novel of the charge of obscenity by a vote of 5—2, on the basis that it did indeed have redeeming social value because, however, distasteful or offensive it might be to some, it was a serious work of literature. Source: 4, p. 89; 6, pp. 388–89; 8, p. 472.

215 Buss, Fran Leeper. *Journey of the Sparrows.* Dell; Dutton. Challenged at the Carmel,

Ind. Junior High School (1994) because a parent objected to profanity and language dealing with urination, rape, violence, and sex. The parent also objected to the depiction of illegal immigration. The book was retained. Source: 11, Mar. 1995, p. 43; July 1995, p. 111.

216 Butler, William. *The Butterfly Revolution.* Ballantine. Challenged as a supplemental reading list at the Fort Scott, Kans. High School library (1987) because the book "suggested dislike of the Bible, belief in atheism, vile social habits, obscene language, and plots against adult authority." Source: 11, May 1987, p. 90.

217 Butz, Arthur R. *The Hoax of the Twentieth Century.* Inst. for Hist. Rev. Removed from the shelves of the University of Calgary library (1984) by the Royal Canadian Mounted Police. Import of the book was banned, after the university bought its copy, under a Canadian law barring import of materials considered seditious, treasonable, immoral, or indecent. Seized from the Didsbury, Alberta, Canada, Public Library (1995) and shredded. Source: 8, pp. 82–85; 11, Jan. 1985, p. 15.

218 Cabell, James Branch. *Jurgen: A Comedy of Justice.* Dover. The New York Society for the Suppression of Vice (1920) seized all plates and copies of the book and editor was charged with violating the antiobscenity provisions of the New York State Penal Code. Banned in Ireland (1953). Source: 4, p. 64; 13, pp. 126–27; 15, Vol. III, pp. 412–13.

219 Cain, James M. *Serenade.* Knopf. In 1949, after receiving complaints from patrons of the Free Public Library in Worcester, Mass., the state attorney general ordered that copies of the novel be removed from library shelves. The case appeared before the Superior Court of Suffolk County, Massachusetts, which judged the book "not obscene." The attorney general filed an appeal with the Supreme Judicial Court where, in September 1950, the novel was cleared again in a 4-3 decision in *Attorney General v. Books Named "Serenade,"* 326 Mass. 324, 94 N.E.2d 259 (1950). In presenting the majority decision, Judge Spalding write that the sexual episodes were "not portrayed in a manner that would have a 'substantial tendency to deprave or corrupt readers by inciting lascivious thoughts or arousing lustful desires.'" Source: 13, p. 210.

220 Calderone, Mary S., and James W. Ramey. *Talking with Your Child about Sex: Questions and Answers for Children from Birth to Puberty.* Morrow; Random. The Gainesville, Ga. Public Library (1986) prohibits young readers from checking out this book along with forty other books. The books, on subjects ranging from hypnosis to drug abuse to breast-feeding and sexual dysfunction, are kept in a locked room. Source: 11, July 1986, p. 117; Sept. 1986, pp. 151–52; Nov. 1986, p. 207.

221 Caldwell, Erskine. *God's Little Acre.* NAL. Sued (1933) for obscenity but acquitted. Banned in Ireland (1948), and Australia (1960), and Mass. (1950) as indecent, obscene, and impure. Source: 2, p. 148; 4, p. 83; 15, Vol. III, p. 643, Vol. IV, p. 701.

222 _____. *Tobacco Road.* NAL. Banned in Ireland (1953). Source: 4, pp. 83–84.

223 _____. *Tragic Ground.* Grosset. Boston Watch and Ward Society lodged a complaint with the police (1944), claiming the novel was "obscene" and dealt with "low life matters." Miss. E. Margaret Anderson of the Dartmouth Book Stall in Boston was arrested for her "distributing obscene material." In delivering a ruling, Judge Adlow observed to the police, "It's not for me or for you to try to establish literary tastes of the community." He stated that he found the novel to "dull," but concluded that "the judges of the Municipal Court and the members of the Police Department were not qualified to pass on the literary value of books." Source: 13, pp. 252–53.

224 Califia, Pat. *Sapphistry: The Book of Lesbian Sexuality.* Naiad Pr. Challenged as an "inappropriate" recommended text for college students at Long Beach State University, Calif. (1982). Seized and shredded (1984) by the British customs office. Source: 11, Sept. 1982, p. 158; Jan. 1985, p. 16.

225 Callen, Larry. *Just-Right Family: Cabbage Patch Kid Series.* Parker Bro. Challenged at the Rutherford County, N.C. Elementary School library (1987) because the book used ungrammatical writing. Source: 11, Nov. 1987, p. 239.

226 Calvin, John. *Civil and Canonical Law.* Forbidden by the Sorbonne in Paris (1542). Banned in England (1555). Listed as heresy in the *Index Librorum Prohibitorum* in Rome (1559 and 1564). Source: 4, p. 14.

227 Cameron, Paul. *Exposing the AIDS Scandal.* Huntington Hse. Challenged at the

34

Downers Grove, Ill. Public Library (1990) because it is factually inaccurate and promotes common fallacies related to the disease. Source: 11, Mar. 1991, p. 61.

228 Canaday, John. *The Artist as Visionary.* Metropolitan Museum of Art. Retained at Maldonado Elementary School in Tucson, Ariz. (1994) after being challenged by parents who objected to nudity and "pornographic," "perverted," and "morbid" themes. Source: 11, July 1994, p. 112.

229 _____. *Painting in Transition: Precursors of Modern Art.* Metropolitan Museum of Modern Art. Retained at Maldonado Elementary School in Tucson, Ariz. (1994) after being challenged by parents who objected to nudity and "pornographic," "perverted," and "morbid" themes. Source: 11, July 1994, p. 112.

230 Capote, Truman. *In Cold Blood: A True Account of a Multiple Murder and Its Consequences.* Modern Library; Random; Vintage; G.K. Hall; Transaction. Banned, but later reinstated after community protests at the Windsor Forest High School in Savannah, Ga. (2000). The controversy began in early 1999 when a parent complained about sex, violence, and profanity in the book that was part of an Advanced Placement English class. Source: 11, Mar. 2001, p. 76.

231 Carle, Eric. *Draw Me a Star.* Philomel Bks. This children's book dealing with the creation story was challenged in the elementary school libraries in the Edmonds, Wash. School District (1996) because the book is illustrated with highly stylized representations of a naked woman and man. Challenged, but retained in the Dorothy B. Bunce Elementary School library in Pavilion, N.Y. (1999) despite a parent's objection to a collage picture of a naked man and woman representing Adam and Eve. Source: 11, Nov. 1996, pp. 211–12; May 1999, pp. 83–84.

232 Carpenter, Edward. *Iolaus: An Anthology of Friendship.* Gale; Pagan Pr. Seized (1984) by the British Customs Office as "indecent and obscene." When first published in London in 1902, the book was not suppressed. Source: 11, Jan. 1985, p. 16.

233 Carroll, Jim. *The Basketball Diaries.* Penguin. Challenged, but retained, at the Gwinnett County, Ga. Library (1998) after the county solicitor declined to give a legal opinion on whether the book is harmful to minors. The library board had voted 2-1 to ban the book if the solicitor found the book meets the state's legal definition of harmful to minors. Source: 11, Sept. 1998, pp. 139–40; Nov. 1998, p. 191; Jan. 1999, p. 19.

234 Carroll, Lewis. *Alice's Adventures in Wonderland.* Ace; Bantam; Crown; Delacorte; Dover; NAL; Norton; Penguin; Random; St. Martin. Banned in China (1931) on the ground that "Animals should not use human language, and that it was disastrous to put animals and human beings on the same level." Source: 4, p. 49.

235 Cart, Michael. *My Father's Scar.* Simon. Challenged at the Montgomery County, Tex. Memorial Library System (2004) along with fifteen other young-adult books with gay-positive themes. The objections were posted at the Library Patrons of Texas Web site. The language describing the books is similar to that posted at the Web site of the Fairfax County, Virginia-based Parents Against Bad Books in Schools, to which Library Patrons of Texas links. Source: 11, Nov. 2004, pp. 231–32.

236 Carter, Alden R. *Sheila's Dying.* Putnam; Scholastic. Restricted to those in the eighth grade or above at the Pitman, N.J. Middle School library (1992) because the book promotes teenage stealing, drinking, profanity, and premarital sex. Source: 11, July 1992, p. 106; Jan. 1993, p. 27.

237 Carter, Forrest. *The Education of Little Tree.* Univ. of New Mex. Pr. Challenged, but retained, at the Astoria, Oreg. Elementary School (1995). The complainants wanted the book removed because it includes profanity, mentions sex, and portrays Christians as "liars, cheats and child molesters." Source: 11, Jan. 1996, p. 17; Mar. 1996, p. 64.

238 Carter, Jimmy. *Keeping Faith: Memories of a President.* Bantam. Banned from the 1983 Moscow International Book Fair along with more than fifty other books because it is "anti-Soviet." Source: 11, Nov. 1983, p. 201.

239 Carter, Judy. *The Homo Handbook: Getting in Touch with Your Inner Homo.* Fireside. Challenged in the Fayetteville, Ark. High School library (2005). The complainant also submitted a list of more than fifty books, citing the books as too sexually explicit and promoting homosexuality. Source: 11, Sept. 2005, p. 215.

240 Carus, Marianne. *What Joy Awaits You.* Open Court Pub. Co. The Utah State Textbook Commission (1988) declined to remove this elementary school book from its list of approved texts. The book contains essays by Plymouth settler John Smith and early American writer Washington Irving, which refer to Indians as "savages" and "bloodthirsty" and was branded as racist and demeaning to contemporary Indian people. Source: 11, May 1988, p. 104.

241 Casanova de Seingalt. *Memoires (History of My Life).* Harcourt. Original manuscript confined to the German publisher's safe (1820) and never published in unexpurgated form until the twentieth century. Placed on the *Index Librorum Prohibitorum* in Rome (1834). Condemned in France (1863). Banned in Ireland (1933). Seized by police in Detroit, Mich. (1934). Banned by Mussolini (1935). Source: 4, p. 31.

242 Casey, Bernie. *Look at the People.* Doubleday. Removed from the Southport, N.C. school libraries (1980) due to inappropriate words and ideas. Source: 11, Sept. 1980, p. 100.

243 Cashdan, Linda. *It's Only Love.* Thorndike Pr. Expurgated by an apparent self-appointed censor at the Coquille, Oreg. Public Library (1994) along with several other books. Most were mysteries and romances in which single words and sexually explicit passages were whited out by a vandal who left either dots or solid ink pen lines where the words had been. Source: 11, Sept. 1994, p. 148.

244 Cavendish, Richard, ed. *Man, Myth and Magic: Illustrated Encyclopedia of Mythology, Religion and the Unknown.* Marshall Cavendish. Challenged by the "God Squad," a group of three students and their parents, at the El Camino High School in Oceanside, Calif. (1986) because the book "glorified the devil and the occult." The debate evoked interest in witchcraft books in other Oceanside school libraries. Source: 11, Sept. 1986, p. 151; Nov. 1986, p. 224; Jan. 1987, p. 9.

245 Cervantes Saavedra, Miguel de. *Don Quixote.* Methuen; NAL; Norton; Random. Placed on the Index in Madrid for one sentence: "Works of charity negligently performed are of no worth." In 1981, the Chilean military junta banned the novel for supporting individual freedom and attacking authority. Source: 1, pp. 83–84; 4, p. 16.

246 Chamberlain, Wilt. *Wilt.* Warner; Macmillan. Banned from the Gaylord, Mich. Middle School library (1975) because pupils "are more interested in learning how to dribble and shoot" than in his off-court activities. Source: 9; 11, Sept. 1975, p. 138.

247 Chambers, Aidan. *Dance on My Grave: A Life and Death in Four Parts.* Bodley Head; Harper. Challenged at the Deschutes County Library in Bend, Oreg. (1993) because it "encourages and condones" homosexuality. Challenged at the Montgomery County, Tex. Memorial Library System (2004) along with fifteen other young-adult books with gay-positive themes. The objections were posted at the Library Patrons of Texas Web site. The language describing the books is similar to that posted at the Web site of the Fairfax County, Virginia-based Parents Against Bad Books in Schools, to which Library Patrons of Texas links. Source: 11, Sept. 1993, pp. 158–59; Nov. 2004, pp. 231–32.

248 Chapman, Robert L. *New Dictionary of American Slang.* Harper. Labeled and restricted at the Walled Lake School District in Commerce Township, Mich. (1994) because "This book contains words which might be offensive to the reader." Source: 11, Sept. 1994, pp. 146–47.

249 Charyn, Jerome. *Billy Budd, KGB.* Catalan Communs. Challenged at the Noel Wien Library in Fairbanks, Alaska (1992) because it was too sexually explicit and violent. Source: 11, Sept. 1992, p. 161; Nov. 1992, p. 196.

250 Chaucer, Geoffrey. *Canterbury Tales.* Bantam; Bobbs-Merrill; Doubleday; Penguin; Raintree Pubs.; NAL; Univ. of Okla. Pr. "Expurgated almost from its first appearance in America, and was still being subjected to revisions as late as 1928. Even editions available today and considered otherwise acceptable avoid some four-letter words." Removed from a senior college preparatory literature course at the Eureka, Ill. High School (1995) because some parents thought the sexual content of some of the tales was not appropriate for the students. Source: 8, pp. 426–28; 11, Nov. 1995, p. 185; Jan. 1996 p. 14; 15, Vol. II, p. 617.

251 Chbosky, Stephen. *The Perks of Being a Wallflower.* Pocket Bks. Challenged, along with seventeen other titles in the Fairfax County, Va. elementary and secondary libraries (2002), by a group called Parents Against Bad Books in Schools.

The group contends the books "contain profanity and descriptions of drug abuse, sexually explicit conduct, and torture." Removed as a reading assignment in an elective sociology course at the Massapequa, N.Y. High School (2003) because of its "offensive" content. Challenged at the Montgomery County, Tex. Memorial Library System (2004) along with fifteen other young-adult books with gay-positive themes. The objections were posted at the Library Patrons of Texas Web site. The language describing the books is similar to that posted at the Web site of the Fairfax County, Virginia-based Parents Against Bad Books in Schools, to which Library Patrons of Texas links. Retained in the Arrowhead High School curriculum in Merton, Wis. (2005). Reading the book was optional and parents could choose to have their children read something else. Arizona Superintendent of Public Instruction sent a letter (2005) to charter schools and public school principals and district superintendents asking them to make sure that the book is no longer available to minors or any other students. The book contains numerous sexual references, including a scene where a girl is forced to have oral sex with a boy during a party. Retained on the Northwest Suburban High School District 214 reading list in Arlington Heights, Ill. (2006), along with eight other challenged titles. A board member, elected amid promises to bring her Christian beliefs into all board decision-making, raised the controversy based on excerpts from the books she'd found on the Internet. Chbosky's novel, which contains references to masturbation, homosexuality, and bestiality, got the bulk of the criticism. Source: 11, Jan. 2003, p. 10; Jan. 2004, pp. 12–13; Nov. 2004, pp. 231–32; Jan. 2005, p. 11; May 2005, pp. 111–12; Jan. 2006, p. 9; July 2006, pp. 210–11.

252 Chelminski, Rudolph. *Paris.* Time-Life. Nine pages, depicting Parisian nightlife and showing pictures of nude dancers, were removed by the Indian River, Fla. County school superintendent (1981). Source: 9; 11, Mar. 1982, p. 43.

253 Chevalier, Tracy. *Girl with a Pearl Earring.* Plume; HarperCollins. Banned in Iran (2006). "The new government intends to take positive steps for reviving neglected values and considering religious teachings in the cultural field." Source: 11, Jan. 2007, p. 35.

254 Chick, Jack T. *The Big Betrayal.* Chick. Banned in Canada (1981) and challenged in New Jersey (1981) as immoral and indecent anti-Catholic literature. Source: 11, Jan. 1982, pp. 24–25.

255 Childress, Alice. *A Hero Ain't Nothin' but a Sandwich.* Avon; Coward; Putnam. Removed from Island Trees School, N.Y. Union Free District High School library in 1976 along with nine other titles because they were considered "immoral, anti-American, anti-Christian, or just plain filthy." Returned to the library after the U.S. Supreme Court ruling on June 25, 1982 in *Board of Education, Island Trees Union Free School District No. 26 et al. v. Pico et al.*, 457 U.S. 853 (1982). Removed from the San Antonio, Tex. high school libraries (1978) due to "objectionable" passages, but later reinstated after teachers filed a grievance in protest; removed from the Savannah, Ga. school libraries (1978) due to "objectionable" language. Challenged at the Lamar Elementary School library in Darlington, S.C. (1994) by a parent who stated that "offensive language in the book makes it unsuitable for any children." Challenged at the Aberdeen High School in Bel Air, Md. (1994) because the novel is "racist and vulgar." Source: 11, Sept. 1978, p. 123; Nov. 1982, p. 197; July 1978, p. 87; May 1994, p. 85; Jan. 1995, p. 12.

256 _____. *Rainbow Jordan.* Avon; Coward. Challenged at the Gwinnett County, Ga. public schools (1986) because of "foul language and sexual references." Banned from Spokane, Wash. middle schools (1998) because the book's storyline about a prostitute's daughter was "too mature." Source: 11, Mar. 1987, p. 65; July 1998, p. 110.

257 Chomsky, Noam, and Edward S. Herman. *Manufacturing Consent: The Political Economy of the Mass Media.* Pantheon. The Turkish Chief Public Prosecution Office (2006) decided to prosecute two publishers that released the book because it "degrades the Turkish identity and the Turkish Republic, and fuels hatred and discrimination among the people." The publishers could face up to six years in prison if found guilty. Source: 11, Sept. 2006, p. 234.

258 Chopin, Kate. *The Awakening.* Duffield; Oxford Univ. Pr.; Capricorn Bks.; Simon; Prometheus Bks. Retained on the Northwest Suburban High School District 214 reading list in Arlington Heights, Ill. (2006), along with eight other challenged titles. A board member, elected amid promises to bring her Christian beliefs into all board decision-making, raised the controversy based on excerpts from the books she'd found on the Internet. First published in 1899, this novel so disturbed critics and the public that it was banished for decades afterward. Source: 11, July 2006, pp. 210–11.

259 Christelow, Eileen. *Jerome and the Witchcraft Kids.* Houghton. Challenged, but retained, in the Wichita, Kans. public schools (1991) because it promotes witchcraft. Source: 11, Jan. 1992, p. 26.

260 Christensen, James C., Renwick St. James and Alan Dean Foster. *Voyage of the Basset.* Artisan. Retained in the Davis County, Utah Library (2006). The complainant objected to the book after her five-year-old son borrowed it from the children's section and showed her the illustrations it contains of topless mermaids and other partially clothed mythical creatures. The author is a retired Brigham Young University art professor and cochair of the Mormon Arts Foundation. Source: 11, Nov. 2006, p. 319.

261 Christopher, John. *The Prince in Waiting.* Macmillan. Challenged at the Canby, Oreg. junior high school library (1988) because it promotes "positive attitudes toward the occult and ridicule toward Christianity." Source: 11, May 1989, p. 78.

262 Christopher, Matt. *The Kid Who Only Hit Homers.* Little. Challenged at the Beaverton, Oreg. (1989) School District because the book mentions the occult, witchcraft, and astrology. Source: 11, Jan. 1990, pp. 4–5.

263 Chute, Carolyn. *The Beans of Egypt.* Harcourt; Warner. Challenged at the Oxford Hills High School in Paris, Maine (1996). A parent stated that, "teachers are not qualified to explore the issues of rape, incest, suicide and mental illness contained in Chute's novel." Source: 11, Nov. 1996, p. 212.

264 Clancy, Tom. *The Hunt for Red October.* Naval Inst. Pr. Removed from the Jackson County, W.Va. school libraries (1997) along with sixteen other titles. Source: 11, Jan. 1998, p. 13.

265 Clapp, Patricia C. *Witches' Children.* Penguin. Challenged at Cannon Road Elementary School library in Silver Spring, Md. (1990) because students who read it will be encouraged "to dabble with the occult." Challenged at the Howard County, Md. schools (1991) because the book was "not appropriate positive pleasurable reading for the young age group." Source: 11, Mar. 1991, p. 43; Mar. 1992, p. 40.

266 Clark, Mary Higgins. *I'll Be Seeing You.* Simon. Challenged at the Big Spring School in Carlisle, Pa. (1994). Source: 11, Mar. 1995, p. 56.

267 Clark, Walter Van Tilburg. *The Ox-Bow Incident.* NAL. Challenged in Johnston City, Ill. (1980) "because of the profanity and the use of God's name in vain." Source: 11, Sept. 1980, p. 107.

268 Clauser, Suzanne. *A Girl Named Sooner.* Hamilton; Doubleday; Avon. Removed from the Stott Elementary School library in Arvada, Colo. (1988) after a parent complained that its graphic sex scenes make it inappropriate for children. Removed by decision of the school board from the library at the Jefferson, Oreg. Middle School (1991) because of its explicit sexual content. Source: 11, July 1988, p. 119; July 1992, p. 103.

269 Clavell, James. *Shogun.* Delacorte. Challenged, along with seventeen other titles in the Fairfax County, Va. elementary and secondary libraries (2002), by a group called Parents Against Bad Books in Schools. The group contends the books "contain profanity and descriptions of drug abuse, sexually explicit conduct, and torture." Source: 11, Jan. 2003, p. 10.

270 Cleaver, Eldridge. *Soul on Ice.* Dell; McGraw-Hill. Barred (1969) from elective courses on black studies by California Superintendent of Instruction. Challenged, but retained in the Ridgefiled, Conn., senior high school ethnic studies class (1973). Challenged at the Greenwich, Conn. High School library (1975) because the book is "crime provoking and anti-American as well as obscene and pornographic;" challenged at Omak, Wash. (1979) due to "profane language." Removed from Island Trees N.Y. Union Free School District High School library in 1976 along with nine other titles because they were considered "immoral, anti-American, anti-Christian, or just plain filthy." Returned to the library after the U.S. Supreme Court ruling on June 25, 1982, in *Board of Education, Island Trees Union Free School District No. 26 et al. v. Pico et al.,* 457 U.S. 853 (1982). Source: 4, p. 100; 11, May 1975, p. 87; July 1979, p. 75; Nov. 1982, p. 197; 14, pp. 260–61.

271 Cleland, John. *Fanny Hill.* Dell; Grove. Author imprisoned (1749) on the orders of the British secretary of state on a charge of "corrupting the King's subjects." Banned in Massachusetts (1821) in the first known U.S. obscenity case. The highest court in New Jersey declared it obscene (1963). Seized in Berlin (1965), burned in Manchester, England, and Japan (1965). Source: 4, p. 29; 6, pp. 533–34; 8, pp. 330–32; 15, Vol. I, pp. 561–62, Vol. II, p. 610.

272 Clerc, Charles, and Louis Leiter, comp. *Seven Contemporary Short Novels.* Scott, Foresman. Removed from the Baker City, Oreg. High School language arts program (1999) because of two selections in the book. *The Bluest Eye*, by Toni Morrison, includes a description of a father raping his eleven-year-old daughter. *Being There*, by Jerzy Kosinski, includes descriptions of sexual relations. Source: 11, May 1999, p. 70.

273 Clinton, Cathryn. *A Stone in My Hand.* Candlewick Pr. Challenged, but retained in the Marion County Public Library System in Ocala, Fla. (2003) despite a complaint that the subject matter was too mature and the book "was written one-sidedly, specifically showing one party to be fully wrong." Reviewers noted that the book is told from a Muslim perspective and that it can be taken to be anti-Israel. An Ocala resident noted that, "this book will help further hatred of Jews, anti-Semitism, and hatred of Israel, on the part of children, that target audience." Source: 11, Nov. 2003, pp. 227–28; Jan. 2004, pp. 7–8; Mar. 2004, pp. 47–48.

274 Close, Robert S. *Love Me Sailor.* Fell. Politicians, churchmen, and civic leaders denounced the book (1945) as likely to corrupt the morals of young, and librarians publicly burned copies. Source: 6, p. 535.

275 Clutton-Brock, Juliet. *Horse.* Knopf. Challenged, but retained at the Smith Elementary School in Helena, Mont. (2004) despite a parent's concern that it "promotes evolution." Source: 11, May 2004, p. 97; July 2004, p. 157.

276 Cody, Robin. *Ricochet River.* Knopf. Retained by the West Linn-Wilsonville School Board in Wilsonville, Oreg. (2000) despite objections that the book contains explicit depictions of teenage sexual encounters without explanation of the consequences. Source: 11, Jan. 2001, p. 36.

277 Cohen, Barbara. *Unicorns in the Rain.* Atheneum. Challenged at the Jefferson County, Colo. school library (1986) because the book "puts too much emphasis on drugs and sex." Source: 11, Jan. 1987, p. 10; Mar. 1987, p. 49.

278 Cohen, Daniel. *Curses, Hexes and Spells.* Lippincott. Placed on restricted status at the Claxton, Tenn. Elementary School library (1986) because the book "contains satanic themes." Removed from the Cleveland, Okla. middle school libraries (1989) because witchcraft is a "religion" and the First Amendment bars the teaching of religion in schools. Removed from elementary school libraries in Howard County, Md. (1990) because it is virtual "how-to" manual on demon worship. Removed from the Kirby Junior High School in Wichita Falls, Tex. (1997) because of "Satanic" themes. Source: 11, Mar. 1987, p. 50; July 1989, p. 128; Jan. 1991, pp. 11–12; July 1997, p. 95.

279 _____. *Ghostly Warnings.* Cobblehill Books. Challenged, but retained at the Hastings, Nebr. Public Library (1999) along with forty other books on the topics of witches, magic, the zodiac, fortune telling, and ghost stories (most of the Dewey Decimal category 133.47). The books were called "demonic" and unsuitable for young children. Source: 11, May 1999, p. 66; July 1999, p. 104.

280 _____. *The Headless Roommate and Other Tales of Terror.* M. Evans. Restricted from fourth and fifth graders at the Old Turnpike School in Tewksbury Township, N.J. (1993) because of its violence. Source: 11, July 1993, p. 100.

281 _____. *Phantom Animals.* Putnam. Challenged, but retained at the Hastings, Nebr. Public Library (1999) along with forty other books on the topics of witches, magic, the zodiac, fortune telling, and ghost stories (most of the Dewey Decimal category 133.47). The books were called "demonic" and unsuitable for young children. Source: 11, May 1999, p. 66; July 1999, p. 104.

282 _____. *The Restless Dead: Ghostly Tales from Around the World.* Archway. Challenged at the Ochoco Elementary School in Prineville, Oreg. (1989) because the book is "totally preoccupied with the macabre, occult, and demonic activity." Source: 11, Jan. 1990, pp. 4–5.

283 _____. *Southern Fried Rat and Other Gruesome Tales.* Avon. Challenged at the Matthew Henson Middle School in Waldorf, Md. (1991) because the collection of folktales contains stories involving unusual violence, relate humorous anecdotes of drug use in school and of ways for students to cheat on exams. Source: 11, July 1991, p. 129.

284 _____. *The World's Most Famous Ghosts.* Putnam. Proposed for removal, along with more than fifty other books, from the high school library in Russell Springs, Ky. (2002) by a teachers' prayer group. Source: 11, May 2002, p. 116.

285 Cohen, Susan, and Daniel Cohen. *When Someone You Know Is Gay.* Evans. Removed from the Barron, Wis. School District (1998) because the 1992 data is outdated. The ACLU of Wisconsin filed suit against the school district on Feb. 16, 1999. The books were then returned to the library while a federal court considered the lawsuit. On October 8, 1999, it was agreed that the book would remain available to students as part of the school district's settlement of the federal lawsuit. Source: 11, Jan. 1999, p. 9; Mar. 1999, p. 37; May 1999, p. 68; Jan. 2000, p. 28.

286 Cole, Babette. *Mommy Laid An Egg.* Chronicle. Moved from the children's section to the adult section of the Camden County, Mo. Library (1998) because the book explains the birth process from conception to delivery. Source: 11, Mar. 1998, p. 40.

287 Cole, Brock. *The Goats.* Farrar. Removed from the Housel Middle School library in Prosser, Wash. (1992) because it contains a passage describing the rescue of a naked girl. Challenged at the Timberland Regional Middle School in Plaistow, N.H. (1994) because parents said it contained "offensive and inappropriate" language for seventh graders. Challenged in the Vigo County, Ind. School District classrooms and libraries (1997) because the book is "morally offensive and inappropriate for middle school students." In November 1997, the Vigo County School Corporation committee affirmed that the novel is appropriate for use by middle and high school students in classrooms and libraries. Challenged in the Londonderry, N.H. schools (2000) because "its sexuality that drive the book." The book was eventually returned to the library and curriculum. Source: 8, pp. 340–41; 11, Mar. 1993, p. 43; Jan. 1995, p. 25; Jan. 1998, p. 11; Mar. 1998, p. 55.

288 Cole, Joanna. *Asking about Sex and Growing Up.* Morrow. Challenged, but retained, in Anchorage, Alaska School District elementary school libraries (1994) after the school board voted to "retain the book despite complaints that it is inappropriate for elementary school children and teaches values opposed to those of the majority of parents." Source: 11, May 1994, p. 97.

289 _____. *Bony-Legs.* Macmillan; Scholastic. Challenged at the Jefferson County, Colo. school library (1986) because the book deals with subjects such as "witchcraft, cannibalism, and white magic." Source: 11, Mar. 1987, p. 49.

290 _____. *How You Were Born.* Morrow. Placed on restricted shelves at the Evergreen School District elementary school libraries in Vancouver, Wash. (1987) in accordance with the school board policy to restrict student access to sex education books in elementary school libraries. Source: 11, May 1987, p. 87.

291 _____. *I'm Mad at You.* Random; Collins. Placed on "restricted access" at the North Kansas City, Mo. elementary schools (1988) because "some children might not understand the book's use of humor and sarcasm." Source: 11, July 1988, p. 121; Sept. 1988, pp. 151–52.

292 _____. *A Snake's Body.* Morrow. Challenged at the Multnomah County Library in Portland, Oreg. (1988) because the photographs of a python crushing and eating a chick would upset and sadden children. Source: 11, Jan. 1990, pp. 4–5.

293 Cole, William. *Oh, That's Ridiculous!* Penguin. Challenged as inappropriate for children and kept off the Mansfield, Ohio school library shelves (1990) for over a year after a complaint against it got lost in the shuffle of a school system reorganization. It was returned to open access in January when the Board of Education voted to retain the title. Source: 11, May 1990, p. 106.

294 Collen, Lindsey. *The Rape of Sita.* Heinemann. Banned by the Mauritian government and temporarily withdrawn by its publisher after protests by Hindu fundamentalists (1993). Won a 1994 Commonwealth Writers Prize for the best book from Africa. Source: 1, pp. 277–78.

295 Collier, James Lincoln, and Christopher Collier. *Jump Ship to Freedom.* Delacorte; Dell. Removed from the Fairfax County, Va. elementary school libraries (1993) because its young black hero, a slave, questions his own intelligence, refers to himself as a "nigger," and is called that by other characters. Challenged at the Nathan Hale Middle School in Crestwood, Ill. (1996) because it "was damaging to the self-esteem of young black students." Source: 11, July 1993, pp. 102–3; Sept. 1993, p. 146; Jan. 1994, p. 13; Mar. 1997, p. 39.

296 _____. *My Brother Sam Is Dead.* Scholastic. Challenged at the Gwinnett County, Ga. school libraries (1984) because some of its characters use profanity. An abridged version with the profanity deleted has been substituted in the elementary school libraries. Removed from the curriculum of fifth grade classes in New Richmond, Ohio (1989) because the 1974 Newbery Honor Book contained the words "bastard," "goddamn," and "hell" and did not represent "acceptable ethical standards for fifth graders." Challenged in the Greenville County, S.C. Schools (1991) because the book uses the name of God and Jesus in a "vain and profane manner along with inappropriate sexual references." Challenged at the Walnut Elementary School in Emporia, Kans. (1993) by parents who said that it contained profanity and graphic violence. Removed from fifth grade classes at Bryant Ranch Elementary School in the Placentia-Yorba Linda, Calif. Unified School District (1994) because "the book is not G-rated. Offensive language is offensive language. Graphic violence is graphic violence, no matter what the context." Challenged, but retained, at the Palmyra, Pa. area schools (1994) due to profanity and violence. Challenged in the Jefferson County Public Schools in Lakewood, Colo. (1996) because of "the persistent usage of profanity" in the book, as well as references to rape, drinking, and battlefield violence. Retained in the Antioch, Calif. elementary school libraries (1996) after a parent complained about the novel's profanity and violence. Challenged at the McSwain Elementary School in Staunton, Va. (1998) because of "bad language." Challenged as a gifted fifth-grade student assignment in Tucker-Capps Elementary School in Hampton, Va. (1998) because the book uses vulgar and profane language and contains scenes of graphic violence. Challenged in the fifth-grade Oak Brook, Ill. Butler District 53 curriculum (2000) because of violence and inappropriate language. Source: 8, pp. 136–37; 11, Sept. 1983, p. 139; Mar. 1990, p. 48; July 1991, p. 129; July 1993, pp. 126–27; Sept. 1994, p. 149; Nov. 1994, p. 190; Jan. 1995, p. 26; July 1996, p. 121; Jan. 1997, p. 25; July 1998, p. 110; Mar. 1999, p. 40; Mar. 2000, p. 49.

297 _____. **War Comes to Willy Freeman.** Delacorte. Removed from the Nettleton Math and Science Magnet School in Duluth, Minn. (1994) because of objections to the book's portrayal of African American characters as demeaning, and claims that use of the word "nigger" in the text led students to use it outside the classroom. Pulled from two classes at Western Avenue School in Flossmoor, Ill. (1996) after a parent complained that the book "represents totally poor judgment, a complete lack of racial sensitivity and is totally inappropriate for fifth-graders. This book is an education in racism, a primer for developing prejudice." Source: 11, Sept. 1994, pp. 150-51; Jan. 1997, p. 9.

298 _____. **With Every Drop of Blood.** Delacorte. Challenged at the Lonnie B. Nelson Elementary School in Columbia, S.C. (1997) because passages considered racist were "inappropriate for fifth grade." Challenged in the fifth-grade Oak Brook, Ill. Butler District 53 curriculum (2000) because the book contains racial slurs. Source: 11, July 1997, p. 94; Mar. 2000, p. 49.

299 Collignon, Jeff. **Her Monster.** SoHo Pr. Removed from the Lakeview Middle School library in Greenville, S.C. (1997) by the school district administrator because the book's sexual content "is inappropriate for middle school students." Source: 11, May 1997, pp. 61–62.

300 Collins, Jackie. **Lovers and Gamblers.** Allen; Grosset; Warner. Destroyed in Beijing, China (1988) and legal authorities threatened to bring criminal charges against the publishers. Source: 11, Jan. 1989, p. 15.

301 Collins, Jim. **Unidentified Flying Objects.** Raintree. Challenged at the Escambia County, Fla. School District (1984) because the complainant claimed the book indicated that, "Ezekiel had seen a UFO when he spoke in the Bible about seeing something that looked like a wheel in the sky." Source: 11, Sept. 1984, p. 156.

302 Comfort, Alex, and Jane Comfort. **The Facts of Love.** Ballantine; Crown. Challenged in Great Bend, Kans. Public Library (1981). Challenged at the Boise, Idaho Public Library (1982). Source: 11, Nov. 1981, p. 169; Sept. 1982, p. 155.

303 Comfort, Alex. **The Joy of Sex: The Cordon Bleu Guide to Lovemaking.** Crown; Pocket Bks. Removed from the Clifton, N.J. Public Library (1996) and replaced with a dummy book made of styrofoam. The library's new policy restricts to adults any material containing "patently offensive graphic illustrations or photographs of sexual or excretory activities or contact as measured by contemporary community standards for minors." Source: 11, July 1996, pp. 118–19.

304 _____. **Joy of Sex.** Crown; Simon & Schuster. Confiscated from three bookstores by police in Lexington, Ky. (1978). Removed from the Fairhope, Ala. (1979) Public Library. Banned in Ireland (1987) to protect the young. Challenged at the Guilford Free Library, Conn. (1994), but the Board of Directors voted to reaffirm the library's circulation and book selection policies, which allow all patrons access to all library materials. Source: 4, p. 93; 11, July 1979, p. 93; May 1987, p. 110; Sept. 1994, p. 165.

305 _____. *More Joy of Sex.* Crown. Confiscated from three bookstores by police in Lexington, Ky. (1978). Removed from the Fairhope, Ala. (1979) Public Library. Restricted to patrons over 18 years of age at the Main Memorial Library in Clifton, N.J. (1996). The book is hidden behind the checkout counter and on the shelves is a dummy book jacket. The book was described as hard-core pornography by the complainant. Source: 4, p. 93; 11, July 1979, p. 93; Mar. 1996, p. 63; May 1996, p. 83.

306 Comte, Auguste. *The Course of Positive Philosophy.* Kessinger Pub. In 1869, the Catholic Church placed the third edition on the Index of Forbidden books. It was still prohibited when the last Index was compiled in 1948. Source: 1, pp. 60–61.

307 Confucius. *Analects.* Dover; Random. The first ruler of the Chin Dynasty, wishing to abolish the feudal system, consigned to the flames all books relating to the teaching of Confucius; he also buried alive hundreds of his disciples (250 B.C.). In 191 B.C., the rulers of the Han Dynasty rescinded the book-burning edict. Because the teachings of Confucius were handed down orally from master to disciple, scholars were able to reconstruct the texts from memory and from hidden manuscripts that escaped destruction. In the twentieth century, the Analects and the Confucian canon were again attacked. During the Great Proletarian Cultural Revolution of 1966-74, Mao Zedong and the leaders of the Communist Party called for a comprehensive attack on the "four old" elements within Chinese society— culture, thinking, habits and customs. During 1973-74, the Communist Party criticized Confucian thinking as promoting an ideology of exploitation, elitism, social hierarchy, and preservation of the status quo. Source: 4, p. 1; 8, pp. 205–6.

308 Conly, Jane Leslie. *Crazy Lady.* HarperCollins. Challenged at the Prospect Heights, Ill. school libraries (1996) because of "swear words." Parental notification is required at the San Jose, Calif. Unified School District (1997) for the use of the book as a supplemental reading assignment because of objectionable language. The Newbery Honor Book uses the words "damn," "hell," and "bitch" five times. Source: 11, Mar. 1996, p. 46; Mar. 1998, p. 55.

309 Connell, Vivian. *The Chinese Room.* Dial. In 1950, Middlesex County, New Jersey, prosecutor Matthew Melko collaborated with the local Committee on Objectionable Literature to produce a list of objectionable publications. Bantam Books then sued Melko in *Bantam Books v. Melko, Prosecutor of Middlesex County*, 25 N.J. Super. 292, 96 A.2d 47 (1953) for banning the book. Ultimately, the New Jersey Supreme Court granted county prosecutors the right to ban the distribution and sale of publications they found objectionable or obscene, and the court further condoned the creation of censorship committees to aid prosecutors in such actions. The decision of the high court agreed that Connell's novel was not obscene. Removed from sale, along with thirteen other books, in Fall River, Mass., (1950) as "indecent, obscene or impure, or manifestly tend to corrupt the morals of youth." Source: 13, pp. 45–46.

310 _____. *September in Quinze.* Dial; Hutchinson. Banned in Ireland (1952), after the Irish Board of Censors found the novel "obscene" and "indecent." In 1954, the novel became the subject of litigation after the British Treasury Counsel examined the novel and determined it was "obscene." Hutchinson Publishing and its director, Katherine Webb, were each fined 500 pounds. Source: 13, pp. 208–9.

311 Conner, Macet Al, and Gerry Contreras. *You and Your Family.* Bowmar. Challenged and nearly banned from the Allentown, Pa. schools (1982) because the book asked questions about the students' families, e.g., "Every family has rules. Who makes rules in your family?" Source: 11, Mar. 1983, p. 52.

312 Conniff, Richard. *The Devil's Book of Verse.* Dodd. Publication canceled by Dodd, Mead & Company (1983) because of language in the book considered "objectionable" by Thomas Nelson, Inc. of Nashville, Tenn.—Dodd, Mead's parent company. Source: 11, Nov. 1983, p. 188.

313 Conrad, Joseph. *The Nigger of the Narcissus.* Norton. Challenged in the Waukegan, Ill. School District (1984) because Conrad's work uses the word "nigger." Source: 11, July 1984, p. 105.

314 Conrad, Pam. *Holding Me Here.* Bantam. Challenged at the Lynchburg, Va. school libraries (1991) because the book contains "cursing and profane language and uses God's name" in a slanderous manner. Source: 11, Sept. 1991, p. 178.

315 Conran, Shirley. *Lace.* Simon & Schuster. Challenged at the Covington, La. Public Library (1984) as "pornographic." The complainant checked the book out after watching the TV series and found that while the TV program had been tastefully done, in the book "pornographic styling [was] unnecessary." Source: 11, July 1984, p. 103.

316 Conroy, Pat. *The Great Santini.* Bantam. Removed from the Eagan High School classroom in Burnsville, Minn. (1992). Challenged, but retained, on the Guilderland, N.Y. High School's list of approved reading materials (1993). A student filed the complaint stating that it was offensive and inappropriate for students his age. Challenged as "obscene and pornographic," but retained in the Anaheim, Calif. Union High School District (1993). Source: 11, Mar. 1993, p. 56; Sept. 1993, p. 160; Nov. 1993, pp. 192–93; Jan. 1994, p. 14.

317 _____. *The Lords of Discipline.* Bantam. Challenged in the Cobb County, Ga. schools (1992) because of passages that include profane language and describe sadomasochistic acts. Removed from an elective English course by the Westonka, Minn. School Board (1992) after parents complained about bad language and sex in the story. Banned, but later reinstated after community protests at the Windsor Forest High School in Savannah, Ga. (2000). The controversy began in early 1999 when a parent complained about sex, violence, and profanity in the book that was part of an Advanced Placement English class. Source: 11, July 1992, p. 110; Mar. 1993, p. 44; Mar. 2000, p. 63; Mar. 2001, p. 76.

318 _____. *The Prince of Tides.* Bantam; Houghton. Removed as a reading assignment for an advanced English class at the St. Andres Parish, S.C. Public School (1988) because it is "trashy pulp pornography." Following the challenge, the school board passed a resolution urging teachers to "use professional judgement and discretion in selecting works. . which. . . contain passages which most people would find abhorrent." Source: 11, May 1988, p. 89.

319 _____. *The Water Is Wide.* Bantam. Challenged in the Greenville County, S.C. schools (1991) because the book uses the name of God and Jesus in a "vain and profane manner along with inappropriate sexual references." Source: 11, July 1991, p. 130.

320 Cook, Robin. *Coma.* NAL. Removed from Big Spring High School English classes in Newville, Pa. (1992), but retained in the library. The decision came in response to complaints that the book is obscene and encourages the maltreatment of women and "radical feminism." Source: 11, Jan. 1993, p. 13; Mar. 1993, p. 44.

321 Cooke, John Peyton. *The Lake.* Avon. Challenged for having too much violence, but retained at the Multnomah, Oreg. County Library (1991). Source: 11, Jan. 1992, p. 6.

322 Cooney, Caroline. *The Terrorist.* Scholastic, Inc. Retained in Rockville, Md. (2000) on Montgomery County middle school reading lists, over objections that the book is anti-Arab. Challenged, but retained at the Franklin Middle School in Cedar Rapids, Iowa (2000) despite objections that the book negatively portrays the Islamic religion and Arabs. The book is on the Iowa Teen Award list. Source: 11, May 2000, p. 77; Jan. 2001, p. 35.

323 Cooney, Nancy H. *Sex, Sexuality and You: A Handbook for Growing Christians.* W. C. Brown. Because of its approach to abortion, the book was removed from the library shelves of the Roman Catholic chancery of Worcester, Mass. (1985), dropped from their sex education program, and is no longer used as a reference source. Source: 11, Mar. 1986, pp. 38–39.

324 Copernicus, Nicolaus. *On the Revolution of Heavenly Spheres.* Prometheus Bks. As the first person to propose the theory that the earth moves around the sun, the Catholic Church viewed the Copernican theory as a challenge to orthodoxy. In 1616, the book was placed on the Index of Forbidden books. The general prohibition against Copernicus's theories remained in effect until 1753, and his name was not removed from the Index until 1835. Source: 1, p. 248.

325 Corman, Carolyn. *Tell Me Everything.* Farrar. Removed from the Jackson County, W.Va. school libraries (1997) along with sixteen other titles. Source: 11, Jan. 1998, p. 13.

326 Cormier, Robert. *After the First Death.* Pantheon. Challenged as an assigned ninth-grade reading in the Troutdale, Oreg. schools (1989) because of the book's portrayal of teen suicide as well as the way the U.S. Army and the Palestine Liberation Organization were depicted. Challenged, but retained in the Manchester, Conn. curriculum (2000) despite charges that the book is "offensively

43

graphic in its descriptions of violence, terrorism, and suicidal thoughts." Challenged, but retained on the Liberty High School ninth-grade gifted and talented reading list in Fauquier, Va. (2000). Opponents of the book charged that it was too violent and treated suicide in a cavalier manner. Other parents cited inappropriate sexual content or gender stereotyping. Source: 11, Mar. 1990, p. 63; May 2000, p. 92; Sept. 2000, p. 145.

327 _____. *Beyond the Chocolate War.*
Knopf. Retained as optional reading for eighth graders at Rice Avenue Middle School in Girard, Pa. (2000). A grandmother found the book offensive and didn't want her granddaughters reading it. Source: 11, May 2000, p. 92.

328 _____. *The Chocolate War.* Dell;
Pantheon. Challenged and temporarily removed from the English curriculum in two Lapeer, Mich. high schools (1981) because of "offensive language and explicit descriptions of sexual situations in the book." Removed from the Liberty High School in Westminster, Md. (1982) due to the book's "foul language," portrayal of violence and degradation of schools and teachers. Challenged at the Richmond, R.I. High School (1983) because the book was deemed "pornographic" and "repulsive." Banned from the Richland Two School District middle school libraries in Columbia, S.C. (1984) due to "language problems," but later reinstated for eighth graders only. Removed from the Lake Havasu, Ariz. High School freshman reading list (1984). The school district board charged the Havasu teachers with failing to set good examples for students, fostering disrespect in the classroom, and failing to support the board. Challenged at the Cornwall, N.Y. High School (1985) because the novel is "humanistic and destructive of religious and moral beliefs and of national spirit." Banned from the Stroudsburg, Pa. High School library (1985) because it was "blatantly graphic, pornographic and wholly unacceptable for a high school library." Challenged at Barnstable High School in Hyannis, Mass. (1986) because of the novel's profanity, "obscene references to masturbation and sexual fantasies," and "ultimately because of its pessimistic ending." The novel, complainants said, fostered negative impressions of authority, of school systems, and of religious schools. Removed from the Panama City, Fla. school classrooms and libraries (1986) because of "offensive" language. Challenged at the Moreno Valley, Calif. Unified School District libraries (1987) because it "contains profanity, sexual situations, and themes that allegedly encourage disrespectful behavior." West Hernando, Fla. Middle School

principal (1988) recommended that Cormier's novel be removed from the school library shelves because it is "inappropriate." Suspended from classroom use, pending review, at the Woodsville High School in Haverhill, N.H. (1990) because the novel contains expletives, references to masturbation and sexual fantasies, and derogatory characterizations of a teacher and of religious ceremonies. Challenged as suitable curriculum material in the Harwinton and Burlington, Conn. schools (1990) because it contained profanity and subject matter that set bad examples and gave students negative views of life. Challenged at the New Milford, Conn. schools (1992) because the novel contains language, sexual references, violence, subjectivity, and negativism that are harmful to students. Challenged in the Kyrene, Ariz. elementary schools (1993) because of a masturbation scene. Returned to the Hephzibah High School tenth-grade reading list in Augusta, Ga. (1994) after the complainant said, "I don't see anything educational about that book. If they ever send a book like that home with one of my daughters again I will personally burn it and throw the ashes on the principal's desk." Challenged as required reading in the Hudson Falls, N.Y. schools (1994) because the book has recurring themes of rape, masturbation, violence, and degrading treatment of women. Challenged at the Nauset Regional Middle School in Orleans, Mass. (1995) due to profanity and sexually explicit language. Removed from the Grosse Pointe, Mich. School District library shelves (1995) because it deals with "gangs, peer pressure, and learning to make your own decisions." Challenged in the Stroudsburg, Pa. high school (1995) because it fosters disobedience. Removed from the East Stroudsburg, Pa. ninth-grade curriculum (1996) after complaints about the novel's language and content. Removed from the middle school libraries in the Riverside, Calif. Unified School District (1996) as inappropriate for seventh- and eighth-graders to read without class discussion due to mature themes, sexual situations, and smoking. Removed from the Greenville, Tex. Intermediate School library (1998) because "it contained blasphemy, profanity, and graphic sexual passages." Banned from the Broken Arrow, Okla. schools (1998) because it is the "antithesis of the district's character development curriculum." The board of education is considering forming a parent committee to review all books listed on the district's electronic bookshelf and to design a ratings system for more than four hundred titles found there. Challenged on the required reading list for ninth graders at Colton, N.Y. schools (1999) due to references to masturbation, profanity, disrespect of women, and sexual innuendo. Challenged on the York County, Va. schools reading list and in classrooms (1999 and 2000) because the book contains profanity and violence. Challenged as part of the Silverheels Middle School's supplemental reading material in South Park, Colo. (2000) because parents objected to sexually suggestive language in the book. Challenged in York County, Va. (2000) due to sexually explicit language. Challenged at the Maple Heights, Ohio School (2000) because "the book teaches immorality." Retained as optional reading for eighth graders at Rice Avenue Middle School in Girard, Pa. (2000). A grandmother found the book offensive and didn't want her granddaughters reading it. Challenged on the eighth-grade reading list of the Lancaster, Mass. School District (2000), due to the book's language and content. Challenged at a Beaver Local Board of Education meeting in Lisbon, Ohio (2001) as a "pornographic" book that should be removed from high school English classes. Challenged, but retained at the Dunedin Highland Middle School in St. Petersburg, Fla. (2001) despite objections to profanity, scenes about masturbation and sexual fantasy, and segments of the book that were considered denigrating to girls. Challenged, along with seventeen other titles in the Fairfax County, Va. elementary and secondary libraries (2002), by a group called Parents Against Bad Books in Schools. The group contends the books "contain profanity and descriptions of drug abuse, sexually explicit conduct, and torture." Challenged, but retained in the West Hartford, Conn. schools (2006). Parents of a King Philip Middle School eighth-grader thought the language, sexual content, and violence make the book PG-13. Challenged in the Wake County, N.C. schools (2006) because the book has "vulgar and sexually explicit language." Parents are getting help from Called2Action, a Christian group that says its mission is to "promote and defend our shared family and social values." Source: 9; 11, Mar. 1981, p. 48; Sept. 1982, p. 156; Sept. 1983, p. 152; Sept. 1984, p. 138; Jan. 1985, p. 10; Mar. 1985, p. 45; May 1985, p. 79; May 1986, p. 79; Nov. 1986, p. 209; July 1987, pp. 125, 126–28; Sept. 1987, pp. 168–69, Mar. 1988, p. 45; May 1990, p. 87; Mar. 1991, p. 44; May 1991, p. 90; May 1992, pp. 96–97; Jan. 1994, p. 34; July 1994, p. 130; Nov. 1994, p. 190; Jan. 1995, p. 13; Mar. 1995, p. 55; May 1995, p. 70; July 1995, p. 94; Nov. 1995, p. 184; May 1996, p. 99; July 1996, p. 82; Nov. 1996, p. 198; July 1998, p. 106; Sept. 1998, pp. 140–41; Sept. 1999, p. 122; Jan. 2000, p. 16; Mar. 2000, pp. 49, 51–52; May 2000, pp. 78, 92; Sept. 2000, pp. 144–45; Mar. 2001, pp. 43, 57; Jan. 2002, pp. 49–50; Jan. 2003, p. 10; July 2006, pp. 184–85, 187; Sept. 2006, p. 231.

329 _____. *Fade.* Delacorte; Dell. Challenged in the Campbell County, Wyo. junior high schools (1990) because of sexual and violent themes. Source: 11, Jan. 1991, p. 13; Mar. 1991, p. 62.

330 _____. *Heroes.* Delacorte. Challenged, along with seventeen other titles in the Fairfax County, Va. elementary and secondary libraries (2002), by a group called Parents Against Bad Books in Schools. The group contends the books "contain profanity and descriptions of drug abuse, sexually explicit conduct, and torture." Source: 11, Jan. 2003, p. 10.

331 _____. *I Am the Cheese.* Pantheon. Challenged at the Cornwall, N.Y. High School (1985) because the novel is "humanistic and destructive of religious and moral beliefs and of national spirit." Banned from the Bay County's four middle schools and three high schools in Panama City, Fla. (1986) because of "offensive" language. The controversy snowballed further on May 7, 1987, when the Bay County school superintendent banned 64 works of literature from classroom teaching at Bay and Mosley High Schools. After 44 parents filed a suit against the district claiming that its instructional aids policy denies constitutional rights, the Bay County School Board reinstated the books. "Banned" from Bay High School: *A Farewell to Arms*, by Ernest Hemingway; *The Great Gatsby*, by F. Scott Fitzgerald; *Intruder in the Dust*, by William Faulkner; *Lost Horizon*, by James Hilton; *Oedipus Rex*, by Sophocles; *The Red Badge of Courage*, by Stephen Crane; *A Separate Peace*, by John Knowles; *Shane*, by Jack Shaefer; *Three Comedies of American Life*, edited by Joseph Mersand. "Banned" from Mosley High School: *Adventures in English Literature*, by Patrick Murray; *After the First Death*, by Robert Cormier; *Alas, Babylon*, by Pat Frank; *Animal Farm*, by George Orwell; *Arrangement in Literature*, by Edmund J. Farrell; *The Autobiography of Benjamin Franklin*; *Best Short Stories*, edited by Raymond Harris; *Brave New World*, by Aldous Huxley; *The Call of the Wild*, by Jack London; *The Canterbury Tales*, by Geoffrey Chaucer; *The Crucible*, by Arthur Miller; *Death Be Not Proud*, by John Gunther; *Deathwatch*, by Robb White; *Desire under the Elms*, *The Emperor Jones*, and *Long Day's Journey into Night*, by Eugene O'Neill; *Exploring Life through Literature*, by Edmund J. Farrell; *Fahrenheit 451*, by Ray Bradbury; *The Fixer*, by Bernard Malamud; *Miss Julie*, by August Strindberg; *The Glass Menagerie*, by Tennessee Williams; *Great Expectations*, by Charles Dickens; *The Great Gatsby*, by F. Scott Fitzgerald; *Growing Up*, by Russell Baker; *Hamlet*, *King Lear*, *The Merchant of Venice*, and *Twelfth Night*, by William Shakespeare; *Hippolytus*, by

45

Euripides; *In Cold Blood*, by Truman Capote; *The Inferno*, by Dante; *The Little Foxes*, by Lillian Hellman; *Lord of the Flies*, by William Golding; *Major British Writers*, by G. B. Harrison; *The Man Who Came to Dinner*, by George S. Kaufman and Moss Hart; *The Mayor of Casterbridge*, by Thomas Hardy; *McTeague*, by Frank Norris; *Mister Roberts*, by Thomas O. Heggen; *The Oedipus Plays of Sophocles*; *Of Mice and Men* and *The Pearl*, by John Steinbeck; *The Old Man and the Sea*, by Ernest Hemingway; *On Baile's Strand*, by W. B. Yeats; *The Outsiders*, by S. E. Hinton; *Player Piano*, by Kurt Vonnegut; *The Prince and the Pauper*, by Mark Twain; *Prometheus Unbound*, by Percy Bysshe Shelley; *Tale Blazer Library* and *A Raisin in the Sun*, by Lorraine Hansberry; *To Kill a Mockingbird*, by Harper Lee; *Watership Down*, by Richard Adams; *Winterset*, by Maxwell Anderson; *Wuthering Heights*, by Charlotte Bronte; *The Red Badge of Courage*, by Stephen Crane; *A Separate Peace*, by John Knowles. Challenged on the seventh-grade honors English reading list at Elko, Nev. Junior High School (2004) because of the book's sexual content. Source: 8, pp. 88–93; 11, Mar. 1985, p. 45; Nov. 1986, p. 209; Mar. 1987, p. 52; July 1987, pp. 126–28; Sept. 1987, pp. 168–69; Nov. 1987, p. 224; Jan. 2005, pp. 9–10.

332 _____. *Tenderness.* Delacorte. Challenged, along with seventeen other titles in the Fairfax County, Va. elementary and secondary libraries (2002), by a group called Parents Against Bad Books in Schools. The group contends the books "contain profanity and descriptions of drug abuse, sexually explicit conduct, and torture." Source: 11, Jan. 2003, p. 10.

333 _____. *We All Fall Down.* Dell. Pulled from elementary and junior high school libraries in Stockton, Calif. (1994) after parents complained that it glorifies alcoholism and violence, contains a violent rape scene, and its characters use too much profanity. Restricted in Arlington, Tex. middle and high schools (2000) to students who have written parental permission, due to concerns over violent content. Removed from the Carver Middle School library in Leesburg, Fla. (2000) after parents complained about the book's content and language. Challenged in the Tamaqua, Pa. Area School District (2001) because the book "might not be appropriate for younger schoolmates." The school board is considering the establishment of a restricted-materials section in the district's middle-school library for books deemed objectionable. Students would need parental permission to access any title placed there. Pulled from a Baldwin, Kans.

ninth grade class (2003) by the school district superintendent because "it was clear to him it wasn't fit for his own daughter or granddaughter." The original complaint objected to fifty passages that contained profanity and sexual content. Challenged at the Cherry Hill, N.J. Public Library's young adult section (2005) by a parent claiming its "deplorable" content was unfit for young minds. The book was retained. Source: 11, Mar. 1995, p. 39; May 2000, p. 75; July 2000, p. 103; Mar. 2001, p. 54; July 2001, p. 145; Nov. 2003, p. 229; Jan. 2004, p. 12; Nov. 2005, p. 296.

334 **Corsaro, Maria, and Carole Korzeniowsky.** *Woman's Guide to a Safe Abortion.* Holt. Challenged at the Walpole, Mass. Public Library (1984) because the book is "inaccurate factually, because it is deliberately misleading and deceitful, and because its avowed purpose is to promote a behavior—killing unborn babies. . . By maintaining and displaying this material at public expense, to the public, and in particular to pregnant women who are vulnerable and may be in need of real guidance, the Walpole Public Library is promoting and abetting abortion." Source: 11, Nov. 1984, p. 184.

335 **Cory, Donald Webster.** *Homosexuality in America.* Watts. Returned to shelves of the Horry County School District middle school libraries in Conway, S.C. (1989) after an attorney advised that the 1988 state health education law did not prohibit books on homosexuality and abortion. Other titles temporarily removed include: *The Abortion Controversy* in America, by Carol Emmens; *Kids Having Kids*, by Janet Bode; and *Who They Are: The Right-to-Lifers*, by C. Paige. Source: 11, July 1989, p. 143.

336 **Cottrell, Randall.** *Wellness: Stress Management.* Dushkin Pub. Rejected as a supplemental health book in the Eagle Point, Oreg. schools (1992) because three women complained that the book cited yoga and Transcendental Meditation as ways to reduce stress, but failed to mention Christian prayer. Source: 11, Jan. 1993, p. 12.

337 **Coupe, Peter.** *The Beginner's Guide to Drawing Cartoons.* Arcturus Pub. Removed from the Meadow Ridge Elementary School library in Spokane, Wash. (1999) after a mother complained that nude cartoon characters of Adam and Eve were a bad influence on children. Source: 11, May 1999, p. 68.

338 Courtenay, Bryce. *The Power of One.* Ballantine. Retained on the Round Rock, Tex. Independent High School reading list (1996) after a challenge that the book was too violent. Source: 11, May 1996, p. 99.

339 Coville, Bruce. *Am I Blue?* HarperCollins. Challenged in the Solon, Iowa eighth-grade language arts class (2004) because the short fictional story explores a boy's confusion with his sexual identity and the gay fairy godfather who helps him overcome homophobia at school. The short story, published in *Am I Blue?: Coming out from Silence*, by Marion Dane Bauer, ed., was eventually retained. Source: 11, Jan. 2005, p. 8.

340 _____. *The Dragonslayers.* Pocket Bks. Challenged in the Berkeley County, S.C. School District (1995) because of the "witchcraft" and "deception" and because a "main character openly disobeys his parents." Source: 11, Mar. 1996, p. 63.

341 _____. *Jeremy Thatcher, Dragon Hatcher.* Harcourt. Returned to the shelves of the Fairview Elementary and Carroll, Iowa Middle School libraries (1993) after an "avalanche" of appeals overturned a Reconsideration of Instructional Materials Committee decision that the book be removed from the libraries because it "was not forthright with the message it intended to present." Source: 11, Nov. 1993, p. 191.

342 _____. *My Teacher Glows in the Dark.* Pocket Bks. Contested in the classrooms and school libraries in Palmdale, Calif. (1995) because the book includes the words "armpit farts" and "farting." Source: 11, Mar. 1996, p. 45.

343 _____. *My Teacher Is an Alien.* Pocket Bks. Challenged in the Elizabethtown, Pa. schools (1994) because it demeans teachers and parents as dumb and portrays the main character as handling a problem on her own, rather than relying on the help of others. Source: 11, Mar. 1995, p. 44.

344 Coward, Noel. *Blithe Spirit.* Grove. Challenged in the Springfield, Oreg. schools (1989) because the play encourages occult activities. Source: 11, Mar. 1990, p. 63.

345 Cox, R. David. *Student Critic.* Winthrop Publishers. Expurgated in Warsaw, Ind. (1979) to remove four pages of a story entitled "A Chip off the Old Block" because the story contains the words "damn" and "hell." Source: 11, May 1979, p. 64.

346 Cranmer, Thomas, and Others. *The Book of Common Prayer.* Oxford Univ. Pr. Cramer was responsible for the writing of most of the first Book of Common Prayer in 1549, brought into compulsory use in the Church of England by act of Parliament, and for the 1552 revision of the book. In 1533, the Catholic Queen Mary banned the use of the Prayer Book. Crammer was convicted of treason and heresy and executed. Source: 1, p. 31.

347 Crichton, Michael. *Congo.* Ballantine. Challenged as an optional text in a Yerba Buena, Calif. High School interdisciplinary course (1995) by the father of two black students who said it is part of racially discriminatory practices. The parent has filed an $8 million civil rights suit against the school district. Source: 11, Jan. 1996, p. 13.

348 Crowley, Aleister. *Magick in Theory and Practice.* Routledge. Challenged at the Dalles-Wasco, Oreg. County Public Library (1988) because the book promotes criminal activity in its depiction of human and animal sacrifice. Source: 11, Jan. 1989, p. 15.

349 Crumb, R. *The R. Crumb Coffee Table Art Book.* Little. Challenged at the Alexandrian Public Library in Mount Vernon, Ind. (1999). Source: 11, Nov. 1999, p. 171.

350 Cruse, Howard. *Stuck Rubber Baby.* Paradox Pr. Challenged at the Montgomery County, Tex. Memorial Library System (2004) along with fifteen other titles. The objections to the books, which contain young-adult fiction with gay-positive themes, were posted at the Library Patrons of Texas Web site. The language describing the books is similar to that posted at the Web site of the Fairfax County, Virginia-based Parents Against Bad Books in Schools, to which Library Patrons of Texas links. Source: 11, Nov. 2004, pp. 231–32.

351 Crutcher, Chris. *Athletic Shorts.* Dell; Greenwillow; Thorndike Pr. Challenged at the Charleston County, S.C. School library (1995) because the books deals with divorce, violence, AIDS, and homosexuality. Pulled from the elementary school collections, but retained at the middle school libraries in Anchorage, Alaska (1999). A parent challenged the book of short stories because of the book's lack of respect for parents and God, its treatment of homosexuality, and its bad language. Source: 11, July 1995, p. 94; May 1999, p. 65.

Caution! Some People Consider These Books Dangerous

352 _____. *Chinese Handcuffs.* Greenwillow. Challenged, but retained, at the Lincoln High School in Wisconsin Rapids, Wis. (1998). A parent complained about "the book's depiction of incest, rape, animal torture, teen drug use, breaking and entering, illegal use of a video camera, profanity directed to a school principal, and graphic sexual references." Source: 11, May 1998, p. 89.

353 _____. *In the Time I Get.* Dell; Greenwillow; Throndike Pr. Challenged in the Solon, Iowa eighth-grade language arts class (2004) because the short story is about a man who befriends a young man dying of AIDS. The short story, published in *Athletic Shorts*, by Chris Crutcher, was eventually retained. Source: 11, Jan. 2005, p. 8.

354 _____. *Running Loose.* Dell; Greenwillow. Challenged at the Gwinnett County, Ga. public schools (1986) because of its discussion of sex. Source: 11, Mar. 1987, p. 65.

355 _____. *Stotan!* Greenwillow. Removed from the Jackson County, W.Va. school libraries (1997) along with sixteen other titles. Source: 11, Jan. 1998, p. 13.

356 _____. *Whale Talk.* Greenwillow. Removed from all five Limestone County, Ala. high school libraries (2005) because of the book's use of profanity. Removed from the suggested reading list for a pilot English-literature curriculum by the superintendent of the South Carolina Board of Education (2005). Challenged at the Grand Ledge, Mich. High School (2005). Challenged at the Missouri Valley, Iowa High School (2007) because the book uses racial slurs and profanity. Source: 11, May 2005, p. 107; July 2005, pp. 153–54; May 2007, p. 98; 14, pp. 295–97.

357 **Cunningham, Antonia, ed.** *Guinness Book of World Records.* Bantam. Retained in the Waukesha, Wis. elementary schools (2002) despite a challenge that the book was sexually explicit. Source: 11, May 2002, p. 136.

358 **Currie, Ian.** *You Cannot Die: The Incredible Findings of a Century of Research on Death.* Methuen. Challenged at the Plymouth-Canton school system in Canton, Mich. (1987) because the book is "not only offensive to our faith, but it is a dangerous teaching to children today when the suicide rate is so high." Source: 11, May 1987, p. 110.

359 **Curry, Hayden, and Denis Clifford.** *A Legal Guide for Lesbian and Gay Couples.* Nolo Pr. Challenged at the Deschutes County Library in Bend, Oreg. (1993) because it "encourages and condones" homosexuality. Source: 11, Sept. 1993, pp. 158–59.

360 **Curtis, Christopher Paul.** *The Watsons Go to Birmingham—1963.* Bantam. Challenged in the Stafford County, Va. middle schools (2002) because a parent was offended. The book is a 1996 Newbery Honor winner and the same year was named a Coretta Scott King Honor Book. Source: 11, July 2002, pp. 154–55.

361 **Curtis, Helena.** *Biology.* Worth. San Diego, Calif. school system (1982) was threatened with a lawsuit unless the book was removed because "it treats the topic of evolution in a dogmatic manner." Source: 11, Mar. 1983, p. 40.

362 **Cusack, Isabel.** *Mr. Wheatfield's Loft.* Holt. Challenged at the Springfield, Oreg. (1988) Public Library because of profanity and the appearance of the subject of prostitution. Source: 11, Jan. 1990, pp. 4–5.

363 **Cushman, Karen.** *The Midwife's Apprentice.* Clarion. Challenged in the Newton, Kans. schools and public library (1998) because a parent thought the 1996 Newbery Award-winning book was "not appropriate for middle school students." Source: 11, July 1998, pp. 108–9.

364 **Dacey, John S.** *Adolescents Today.* Scott, Foresman. The Norwin, Pa. School Board (1985) decided to retain the textbook used in the district's tenth-grade health classes despite accusations that it is amoral, anti-family, and has a Marxist bent. A group of nineteen parents filed a federal lawsuit in March 1987. The suit charged that in the book abstaining from sex until marriage is portrayed unfavorably, birth control techniques are evaluated, and homosexuality is taught as a natural stage of sexual development. Source: 11, July 1985, p. 135; July 1987, p. 131.

365 **Dahl, Roald.** *The BFG.* Farrar. Challenged at the Amana, Iowa first-grade curriculum (1987) because the book was "too sophisticated and did not teach moral values." Source: 11, Sept. 1987, pp. 194–95.

366 _____. *Charlie and the Chocolate Factory.* Bantam; Knopf; Penguin. Removed from

48

a locked reference collection at the Boulder, Colo. Public Library (1988). The book was originally locked away because the librarian thought the book espouses a poor philosophy of life. Source: 11, Jan. 1989, p. 27.

367 _____. **The Enormous Crocodile.** Caedmon; Knopf. Challenged at the Multnomah County Library in Portland, Oreg. (1988) because of the book's sinister nature and the negative action of animals. Source: 11, Jan. 1989, p. 3.

368 _____. **George's Marvelous Medicine.** Bantam; Puffin. Challenged at the Stafford County, Va. Schools (1995) because the book "posed a safety threat because the boy in the story warms household items, such as paint thinner and soap, to make a potion." Source: 11, Sept. 1995, pp. 159–60.

369 _____. **James and the Giant Peach.** ABC-CLIO; Knopf. Challenged at the Deep Creek Elementary School in Charlotte Harbor, Fla. (1991) because it is "not appropriate reading material for young children." Challenged at the Pederson Elementary School in Altoona, Wis. (1991) because the book uses the word "ass" and parts of the book deal with wine, tobacco, and snuff. Challenged at the Morton Elementary School library in Brooksville, Fla. (1992) because the book contains a foul word and promotes drugs and whiskey. Challenged at the Stafford County, Va. Schools (1995) because the tale contains crude language and encourages children to disobey their parents and other adults. The book was removed from the classrooms and placed in the library, where access was restricted. Banned from an elementary school in Lufkin, Tex. (1999) because it contains the word "ass." Source: 11, July 1991, p. 108; Mar. 1992, p. 65; Jan. 1993, p. 27; Sept. 1995, p. 160; Jan. 2000, p. 8.

370 _____. **Matilda.** Harper; Puffin; Viking. Retained on the shelves in the Grand Rapids, Mich. school libraries (1993), but not allowed to be read in the elementary classrooms. Ten parents complained about the book, calling it offensive and "appalling in its disrespect for adult figures and children." Challenged, but retained, in the Margaret Chase Smith School library in Skowhegan, Maine (1994) after the complainant came to understand that attaching a warning label also would amount to censorship. Challenged at the Stafford County, Va. Schools (1995) because the tale contains crude language and encourages children to disobey their parents and other adults. The book was removed from the classrooms and placed in the library, where

access was restricted. Source: 11, Nov. 1993, p. 179; May 1994, p. 98; Sept. 1995, p. 160.

371 _____. **The Minipins.** Viking. Challenged at the Stafford County, Va. Schools (1995) because the tale contains crude language and encourages children to disobey their parents and other adults. The book was removed from the classrooms and placed in the library, where access was restricted. Source: 11, Sept. 1995, p. 160.

372 _____. **Revolting Rhymes.** Bantam. Challenged at the Northeast High School in Goose Lake, Iowa (1990) because of its alleged violence, the use of the word "slut," and the subject of witches. Banned in the Rockland, Mass. elementary schools (1992) after a parent complained that the book of fractured fairy tales was offensive and inappropriate for children. Challenged at the Stafford County, Va. Schools (1995) because the book spoofs nursery rhymes. Source: 11, May 1990, p. 105; Jan. 1993, p. 8; Sept. 1995, pp. 159–60.

373 _____. **Rhyme Stew.** Viking. Moved from the children's section to the adult section at the Dover, Del. Public Library (1990). The complainant called for the establishment of a national rating system similar to that of the motion picture industry that would classify books according to local community standards. Source: 11, Mar. 1991, p. 42.

374 _____. **The Witches.** Farrar; Penguin. Challenged at the Amana, Iowa first-grade curriculum because the book was "too sophisticated and did not teach moral values." Challenged at the Goose Lake, Iowa Elementary School (1990) because of its alleged violence, the use of the word "slut," the subject of witches, and the fact that "the boy who is turned into a mouse by the witches will have to stay a mouse for the rest of his life." Challenged at the Dallas, Oreg. Elementary School library (1991) because the book entices impressionable or emotionally disturbed children into becoming involved in witchcraft or the occult. Placed on a library-restricted list by the Escondido, Calif. Union Elementary School District (1992) after four parents filed complaints that it promoted the occult and was too frightening. Challenged at the La Mesa-Spring Valley, Calif. School District (1992) because it includes horrifying depictions of witches as ordinary-looking women, against whom there is no defense. Other opponents added that it promotes the religion of Wicca, or witchcraft. Challenged in the Spencer, Wis. schools (1993) because it desensitizes children to crimes related to witchcraft. Returned to the shelves of

the Escondido, Calif. Union School District school libraries (1993) after the school board lifted a partial ban. Four parents who stated the book promoted satanism filed a complaint. The district still retains bans on four books, including *Halloween ABC*, which some parents charged with promoting the occult. Challenged at Pine Forge Elementary School in the Boyertown, Pa. area (1993). Challenged, but retained, at the Battle Creek, Mich. Elementary School library (1994) despite the protests from a parent who said the book is satanic. Challenged at the Stafford County, Va. Schools (1995) because the tale contains crude language and encourages children to disobey their parents and other adults. The book was to be removed from the classrooms and placed in the library, where access could be restricted. Challenged, but retained, at the Dublin, Ohio school district (1998) despite objections that the book is "derogatory toward children and conflicts with family religious and moral beliefs." Source: 11, Sept. 1987, pp. 194–95; May 1990, p. 105; Jan. 1992, p. 26; May 1992, pp. 78–79; Nov. 1992, pp. 196–97; July 1993, p. 127; Sept. 1993, p. 157; May 1994, p. 85; Nov. 1994, p. 200; Sept. 1995, p. 160; Sept. 1998, p. 156.

375 **Dahrendorf, Ralf.** *Class and Class Conflict in Industrial Society.* Stanford Univ. Pr. Banned in South Korea (1985). Source: 5, Apr. 1986, pp. 30–33.

376 **Dakin, Edwin.** *Mrs. Eddy.* Scribner. The Christian Science Church attempted to suppress this biography of Mary Baker Eddy, the Church's founder, by demanding its withdrawal from sale. Source: 15, Vol. III, p. 418.

377 **Daldry, Jeremy.** *The Teenage Guy's Survival Guide.* Little. Restricted, but later returned to general circulation shelves with some limits on student access, based on a review committee's recommendations, at the Holt Middle School parent library in Fayetteville, Ark. (2005) despite a parent's complaint that it was sexually explicit. Source: 11, May 2005, p. 135; Sept. 2005, p. 215; Nov. 2005, pp. 295–96.

378 **Dalrymple, Douglas J., and Leonard J. Parsons.** *Marketing Management: Text and Cases.* Wiley. Seven pages of this book were expurgated at the University of Nebraska-Omaha (1981) because they contain a case study dealing with a firm that sells contraceptive devices. Source: 11, Jan. 1982, p. 19.

379 **Dalrymple, Willard.** *Sex Is for Real.* McGraw-Hill. Banned from the Brighton, Mich. (1977) High School library along with all the other sex education materials. Source: 11, Sept. 1977, p. 133.

380 **Dandicat, Edwidge.** *Krik! Krak!* Soho Pr. Challenged by a parent at the Arrowhead High School in Waukesha, Wis. (2004) as an elective reading list assignment because the book contains "sexually explicit and inappropriate material." Source: 11, Jan. 2005, p. 11.

381 **Dante Alighieri.** *The Divine Comedy.* Norton; Pocket Bks.; Random; Regnery. Burned in Florence, Italy (1497). Prohibited by Church authorities in 1581 in Lisbon, Portugal, until all copies were delivered to the Inquisition for correction. Banned in Ethiopia (1978). Source: 4, p. 6; 5, Sept./Oct. 1978, p. 66.

382 _____. *On Monarchy.* Cambridge Univ. Pr. Dante argued against papal control over secular authority and the pope condemned the book. In 1329, it was publicly burned in the marketplace of Bologna. In the sixteenth century, the Spanish Inquisition banned it, and it was listed on the Catholic Church's first Index of Forbidden books, where it remained until the nineteenth century. Source: 1, p. 234.

383 **Darwin, Charles B.** *On the Origin of Species.* Harvard Univ. Pr.; Macmillan; Modern Library; NAL; Norton; Penguin; Rowman; Ungar. Banned from Trinity College in Cambridge, UK (1859); Yugoslavia (1935); Greece (1937). In 1925, Tennessee passed a law prohibiting teachers from teaching the theory of evolution in state-supported schools. John T. Scopes, a science teacher in Dayton, volunteered to be the test case for Tennessee's anti-evolution law. The Scopes "monkey trial," eventually, was thrown out on a technicality. In 1968, the U.S. Supreme Court considered a case similar to Scopes. Susan Epperson, a high school biology teacher, challenged the constitutionality of the Arkansas Anti-Evolution Statute of 1928, which provided that teachers who used a textbook that included Darwin's theory of evolution could lose their jobs. The Supreme Court ruled that the law was unconstitutional and conflicted with the First and Fourteenth Amendments. Government power could not be used to advance religious beliefs. In the early 1980s, Arkansas and Louisiana state boards of education required the teaching of both creationism and evolution in public schools. The U.S. Supreme Court in *Edwards v. Aguillard* ruled

these laws unconstitutional in 1987 as advocating a religious doctrine and violating the establishment clause of the First Amendment. Battles about the teaching of evolution, however, still rage on, especially at the local school board level. Source: 4, p. 42; 8, pp. 276–79.

384 **Darwin, Erasmus.** *Zoonomia.* Ams Pr. Inc. Sixty-five years before his grandson Charles Darwin revolutionized biological science, Darwin formulated an evolutionary system in this treatise on animal life. Placed on the Catholic Church's Index of Forbidden books (1817), where it remained listed until 1966. Source: 1, pp. 359–60.

385 **Davis, Deborah.** *My Brother Has AIDS.* Atheneum. Challenged at the Montgomery County, Tex. Memorial Library System (2004) along with fifteen other young-adult books with gay-positive themes. The objections were posted at the Library Patrons of Texas Web site. The language describing the books is similar to that posted at the Web site of the Fairfax County, Virginia-based Parents Against Bad Books in Schools, to which Library Patrons of Texas links. Source: 11, Nov. 2004, pp. 231–32.

386 **Davis, Jenny.** *Sex Education.* Dell. Challenged at Hughes Junior High School in Bismarck, N.Dak. (1993) because it is "offensive." Source: 11, Sept. 1993, p. 145.

387 **Davis, Jim.** *Garfield: His Nine Lives.* Ballantine. Moved to the adult section of the Public Libraries of Saginaw, Mich. (1989) after patrons requested that children be denied access. Source: 11, May 1989, p. 77.

388 **Davis, Kathryn.** *The Dakotas: At the Wind's Edge.* Pinnacle Bks. Banned from sale in all Medora, N.Dak. bookstores (1983) because some Medora residents did not approve of some of Davis's fictional embellishments to the history of their town. Source: 11, July 1983, p. 123.

389 **Davis, Lindsey.** *Silver Pigs.* Crown. Challenged, along with seventeen other titles in the Fairfax County, Va. elementary and secondary libraries (2002), by a group called Parents Against Bad Books in Schools. The group contends the books "contain profanity and descriptions of drug abuse, sexually explicit conduct, and torture." Source: 11, Jan. 2003, p. 10.

390 **Davis, Terry.** *Vision Quest.* Viking. Challenged at the Mead, Wash. School District

(1984), the New Berlin, Wis. High School library (1984), and the West Milwaukee, Wis. High School library (1984) because it is "obscene." Placed on a restricted reading list by the New Berlin, Wis. School Board (1985) because it is "vulgar and not educational." Banned from the West Allis-West Milwaukee, Wis. school libraries (1986) because of its profanities. Moved from the Hughes Junior High School in Bismarck, N.Dak. (1993) to the high school because a parent considered some passages obscene, pornographic, or inappropriate for junior high students. Source: 11, July 1984, p. 101; Sept. 1984, pp. 139–40; Nov. 1984, pp. 186, 196; Jan. 1985, p. 10; Mar. 1986, p. 39; Mar. 1987, p. 51; Sept. 1993, p. 145; Nov. 1993, pp. 178–79; Jan. 1994, p. 38.

391 **Day, Doris.** *Doris Day: Her Own Story.* Morrow. Removed from two Anniston, Ala. high school libraries (1982) due to the book's "shocking" contents particularly "in light of Miss Day's All-American image," but later reinstated on a restricted basis. Source: 11, Mar. 1983, p. 37.

392 **Day, Susan, and Elizabeth McMahan.** *The Writer's Resource: Readings for Composition.* McGraw-Hill. Banned from the Jasper, Mo. schools (1991) because a character in a story used profanity and slang. Source: 11, Jan. 1992, p. 8.

393 **De Clements, Barthes.** *No Place for Me.* Viking. Challenged in the Douglas County school libraries in Castle Rock, Colo. (1991) because it introduces children to witchcraft. Source: 11, May 1991, p. 89.

394 **de Haan, Linda and Stern Nijland.** *King & King.* Tricycle Pr. Restricted to adults at the Freeman Elementary School in Wilmington, N.C. (2004) the children's book is about a prince whose true love turns out to be another prince. Moved from the children's section to the adult section at the Shelbyville-Shelby County, Ind. Public Library (2004) because the book's homosexual story was considered inappropriate by a parent. Challenged by seventy Oklahoma state legislators calling for the book to be removed from the children's section and placed in the adult section of the Metropolitan Library System in Oklahoma City, Okla. (2005). Parents of a Lexington, Mass. (2006) second-grader protested that their son's teacher read the fairy tale about gay marriage to the class without warning parents first. The book was used as part of a lesson about different types of weddings. "By presenting this kind of issue at such a young age, they're trying to indoctrinate our children," stated the parent.

The incident renewed the efforts of Waltham-based Parents' Rights Coalition to rid the state's schools of books and lessons that advance the "homosexual agenda" in public schools. U.S. District Court Judge Mark Wolf ruled February 23, 2007, that public schools are "entitled to teach anything that is reasonably related to the goals of preparing students to become engaged and productive citizens in our democracy." Wolf said the courts had decided in other cases that parents' rights to exercise their religious beliefs were not violated when their children were exposed to contrary ideas in school. Source: 11, May 2004, p. 97; July 2004, pp. 137–38; May 2005, pp. 108–9; July 2006, pp. 186–87; May 2007, pp 103–4.

395 **de Jenkins, Lyll Becerra.** *The Honorable Prison.* Dutton. Challenged at the Commodore Middle School in Bainbridge Island, Wash. (1992) as inappropriate by three parents because of violence, sexual scenes, and "lack of family values." Source: 11, May 1992, p. 84.

396 **de Schweinitz, Karl.** *Growing Up: How We Become Alive, Are Born and Grow.* Macmillan; Collier. Placed on restricted shelves at the Evergreen School District elementary school libraries in Vancouver, Wash. (1987) in accordance with the school board policy to restrict student access to sex education books in elementary school libraries. Source: 11, May 1987, p. 87.

397 **De Veaux, Alexis.** *Na-ni.* Harper. Removed from open shelves to students in grades K-2 at South Accomack Elementary Schools, Va. (1988) after the county school board agreed that it contains vulgar words ("dog turd") and improper punctuation. Source: 11, May 1988, p. 87.

398 **Dean, Roger.** *Album Cover Album.* St. Martin. Challenged at the Evergreen School District Junior High School library in Vancouver, Wash. (1987) because "of the way some of the covers represented women" citing one album cover depicting the "Statue of Liberty with bare breasts as exemplary of several photos that were pretty raw toward women." Source: 11, May 1987, p. 102.

399 **Defoe, Daniel.** *Adventures of Robinson Crusoe.* Bantam; Grosset; NAL; Norton. Placed on the Spanish Index in 1720. Source: 4, p. 25.

400 _____. *Moll Flanders.* Houghton; Modern Library; NAL; Penguin. U.S. Customs raised its ban in 1930. Source: 4, p. 25; 8, pp. 367–68.

401 _____. *Political History of the Devil.* AMS Pr.; Rowman & Littlefield. Listed on the *Index Librorum Prohibitorum* in Rome (1743), until 1966. Source: 4, p. 25.

402 _____. *Roxana.* Oxford Univ. Pr.; Viking. U.S. Customs raised its ban in 1930. Source: 4, p. 25.

403 _____. *The Shortest Way with the Dissenters.* Crowell. Burned and the author fined, imprisoned, and pilloried in London, England, in 1703. Source: 4, p. 25.

404 **Del Vecchio, John M.** *The Thirteenth Valley: A Novel.* Bantam. Banned from the Amundsen High School classrooms in Chicago, Ill. (1993) because of "explicit sexual content." Source: 11, Sept. 1993, pp. 147–48.

405 **DeLillo, Don.** *Americana.* Houghton. Removed from the Davis County, Utah Library (1980). Source: 11, Nov. 1980, p. 127.

406 **Dell, Floyd.** *Janet March.* Knopf. Banned in Boston (1923). New York Society for the Suppression of Vice lodged a formal complaint (1923) with the New York City district attorney, charging the book was "obscene." Instead of fighting the threat, the publisher, Alfred A. Knopf, promised to cease printing future copies of the book and withdrew the book. Source: 13, pp. 122–23.

407 **DeMille, Nelson.** *The Charm School.* Mass Market. Removed from the Waltham, Mass. High School summer reading list (1999) because of two sexually graphic passages. Source: 11, Jan. 2000, p. 14.

408 **Dengler, Marianna.** *A Pebble in Newcomb's Pond.* Holt. Judged unacceptable at the Thompson Junior High School in Bakersfield, Calif. (1984). Source: 11, July 1984, p. 105.

409 **Denneny, Michelle; Charles Ortlieb; and Thomas Steele.** *First Love/Last Love: New Fiction from Christopher Street.* Perigee Bks.; Putnam. Challenged at the Deschutes County Library in Bend, Oreg. (1993) because it "encourages and condones" homosexuality. Source: 11, Sept. 1993, pp. 158–59.

410 **DeSaint, Niki.** *AIDS: You Can't Catch It Holding Hands.* Lapis Pr. Challenged at the Derby,

Kans. Library (1993) because "the book didn't say abstinence is the answer and just teach it." Source: 11, July 1993, p. 124.

411 Descartes, Rene. *Discourse on Method.* Penguin. Prohibited at the University of Leiden and University of Utrecht in Netherlands (1640) because it was considered anti-Protestant. Calvinists persuaded the University of Leiden to ban Cartesian doctrine from all lectures and writings. Placed on the *Index Librorum Prohibitorum* in 1663, fourteen years after his death. Source: 6, pp. 665–66.

412 Deuker, Carl. *On the Devil's Court.* Joy Street Bks. Challenged, but retained at the Virginia Run Elementary School in Centreville, Va. (1999) despite a parent's claim that the book espouses "pro-Satanism." Source: 11, Nov. 1999, pp. 172–73.

413 Deveraux, Jude. *A Knight in Shining Armor.* Simon. Retained at the Lassen Union High School in Quincy, Calif. (1993). The book was checked out from a recreational reading library provided by the English instructor. Parents called the romance novel "obscene." Source: 11, Nov. 1993, p. 193.

414 Diagram Group. *Man's Body: An Owner's Manual.* Bantam; Paddington. Banned from the Monroe, Oreg. High School (1979) when parents complained that the reference book's portrayals of male and female anatomies were too explicit. Source: 9; 11, May 1979, p. 51.

415 _____. *Woman's Body: An Owner's Manual.* Bantam; Paddington; Pocket Bks. Banned from the Monroe, Oreg. High School (1979) when parents complained that the reference book's portrayals of male and female anatomies were too explicit. Challenged at the Evansville, Wis. High School library (1987) because the book is "filth" and it is "sick," even though it is on a restricted shelf behind the librarian's desk. Source: 9; 11, May 1979, p. 51; May 1987, p. 102.

416 Dickens, Charles. *Oliver Twist.* Airmont; Bantam; Dodd; NAL; Oxford Univ. Pr.; Penguin. A group of Jewish parents in Brooklyn, N.Y. (1949) went to court claiming that the assignment of Dickens's novel to senior high school literature classes violated the rights of their children to receive an education free of religious bias in *Rosenberg v. Board of Education of the City of New York*, 196 Misc. 542, 92 N.Y. Supp. 2d 344. The King County Supreme Court decided not to ban Dickens's work stating, "Except where a book has been maliciously written for the apparent purpose of fomenting a bigoted and intolerant hatred against a particular racial or religious group, public interest in a free and democratic society does not warrant or encourage the suppression of any book at the whim of any unduly sensitive person or group or person, merely because a character described in such book as belonging to a particular race or religion is portrayed in a derogatory or offensive manner." Removal of the book "will contribute nothing toward the diminution of anti-religious feeling," the court said. Source: 8, pp. 271–73; 12, pp. 23, 230.

417 Dickens, Frank. *Albert Herbert Hawkins—the Naughtiest Boy in the World.* Scroll Pr. Relegated to an adult shelf at the Castle Rock, Colo. elementary school libraries (1985) because it "advocates defiance of adult authority by showing misbehavior for which the protagonist goes unpunished." The Douglas County Board of Education reversed its ruling seven months later and decided the book could go back into general circulation. Source: 11, May 1985, p. 76; Sept. 1985, p. 151; Nov. 1985, p. 203.

418 _____. *Albert Herbert Hawkins and the Space Rocket.* Scroll Pr. Relegated to an adult shelf at the Castle Rock, Colo. elementary school libraries (1985) because it "advocates defiance of adult authority by showing misbehavior for which the protagonist goes unpunished," the Douglas County Board of Education reversed its ruling seven months later and decided the book could go back into general circulation. Source: 11, May 1985, p. 76; Sept. 1985, p. 151; Nov. 1985, p. 203.

419 Dickey, Eric Jerome. *The Other Woman.* Dutton. Challenged in the Fayetteville, Ark. High School library (2005). The complainant also submitted a list of more than fifty books, citing the books as too sexually explicit and promoting homosexuality. Source: 11, Sept. 2005, p. 215.

420 Dickey, James. *Deliverance.* Dell. Challenged in Montgomery County, Md. (1974) on the grounds that it employs "gutter language" and depicts "perverted acts." Burned in Drake, N.Dak. (1973), but U.S. District Court ruled that teachers should be allowed to use this title in eleventh- and twelfth-grade English classes. Moved from the Hughes Junior High School in Bismarck, N.Dak. (1993) to the High School because a parent considered some passages obscene, pornographic, or inappropriate for junior high students.

Challenged, but retained, in the Sheehan High School English curriculum in Wallingford, Conn. (1998) because the book was too "graphic and contained explicit language." After two hundred people attended a special board meeting and after listening to the teachers and "articulate" students, the board denied that request for removal. Source: 11, July 1975, p. 118; Nov. 1975, p. 174; Sept. 1993, p. 145; Nov. 1993, pp. 178–79; Jan. 1994, p. 38; July 1998, p. 120.

421 Diderot, Denis, and Jean Le Rond d'Alembert. *Encyclopedie.* French & European Pubns. Censored repeatedly during the twenty-one years of its publication. In 1759, the Catholic Church placed the first seven volume and in 1804, the entire work on the Index of Forbidden books, where it remained until 1966. Source: 1, pp. 91–94.

422 Dieckman, Ed, Jr. *The Secret of Jonestown: The Reason Why.* Noontide. Challenged at the La Grange, Ill. Public Library (1990) because it promotes "hate" for the Jewish people. "It is a Nazi book and it doesn't belong in La Grange." Source: 11, May 1990, p. 84.

423 Diehl, William. *Sharky's Machine.* Dell. Challenged at the Northside High School Library in Lafayette, La. (1982) due to "the book's treatment of drugs, prostitution, and race." Source: 11, May 1982, p. 83.

424 Donleavy, John P. *The Ginger Man.* Delacorte; Dell. Originally published by Girodias in Paris. Author expurgated that text himself to permit publication in England (1955). Source: 4, p. 97.

425 Dorner, Marjorie. *Nightmare.* Warner. Pulled from the Winona, Minn. Middle School media center and classroom libraries (1995) because of language and violence in the book. Source: 11, Jan. 1996, p. 11.

426 Dorris, Michael. *A Yellow Raft in Blue Water.* Holt; Thorndike Pr.; Warner. Challenged as required reading for freshmen in the Advanced Placement Honors English Class at Clear Lake High School in Houston, Tex. (1997). A parent described the contents as "not suggestive, not explicit, but pornographic, and in the guise of multi-cultural reading." Challenged at the Pebblebrook High School in Marietta, Ga. (1999) because of the book's profanity and explicit sexual language. Source: 11, Mar. 1998, p. 42; May 1999, p. 66.

427 Dorson, Richard M. *America in Legend: Folklore from the Colonial Period to the Present.* Pantheon. Removed from a library in Cobb County, Ga. (1977) because the book "condones draft dodging" and contains the song "Casey Jones," which includes several stanzas describing the fabled railroad engineer's sexual prowess. Source: 11, Sept. 1977, p. 133.

428 *Double Cross. Chick.* Banned in Canada (1981) and challenged in New Jersey (1981) as immoral and indecent anti-Catholic literature. Source: 11, Nov. 1981, pp. 162–63.

429 Doyle, Robert P. *Banned Books.* American Library Association. Banned from a display at Spotswood High School in Harrisonburg, Va. (1999) after a parent determined that some materials listed in the publication were inappropriate for students. Students were not required to read or even look at the publication, nor were they required to read any of the books listed in the publication. Source: 11, Jan. 2000, p. 16; Mar. 2000, pp. 39, 45.

430 Doyle, Sir Arthur Conan. *The Adventures of Sherlock Holmes.* Avon; Berkley; Harper. Banned in the USSR (1929) because of its references to occultism and spiritualism. Source: 4, p. 56.

431 Dozois, Gardner, ed. *Isaac Asimov's Skin Deep.* Berkley. Challenged in the Fairfield County, Ohio District Library (1995) because it includes profanity and explicit sex scenes. Source: 11, Nov. 1995, p. 184; Jan. 1996, p. 29.

432 Dragnich, Alex N. *Serbs and Croats: The Struggle in Yugoslavia.* Harcourt. Challenged at the Lincolnwood, Ill. Public Library (1994) because the book is "pro-Serbian and anti-Croatian." Source: 11, Mar. 1995, p. 53.

433 Dragonwagon, Crescent, and Paul Zindel. *To Take a Dare.* Bantam; Harper. Challenged at the Crook County, Oreg. Middle School library (1989) because of "excessive use of profanity." Source: 11, May 1989, p. 93.

434 Dramer, Dan. *Monsters.* Jamestown Pub. Challenged at the Jefferson County school libraries in Lakewood, Colo. (1986). The book is a junior high text of monster stories including several Greek myths on the Cyclops, the Minotaur, and Medusa, as well as stories of several modern monsters such as King Kong, Dracula, and Frankenstein's monster. The Jefferson County School Board refused to ban the book. Source: 11, May 1986, p. 82; Sept. 1986, p. 173; Nov. 1986, p. 224.

435 Draper, John William. *History of the Conflict between Religion and Science.* BiblioBazaar. First American book to be listed on the Index of Forbidden books (1876). In the last twenty years of his life, he sought to apply Charles Darwin's theories of biological evolution to human history and politics. Source: 1, pp. 137–38.

436 Draper, Sharon M., and Adam Lowenbein. *Romiette and Julio.* Simon Pulse. Challenged in the Albemarle County, Va., schools (2006), spurring a debate over the age-appropriateness of material with sexual innuendo and fictional online chat room chatter. The school board determined to move the book from the supplemental summer reading list after fifth-grade to the sixth-grade second semester curriculum. Source: 11, Jan. 2007, pp. 15–16.

437 Dreiser, Theodore. *An American Tragedy.* NAL. Banned in Boston, Mass. (1927) and burned by the Nazis in Germany (1933) because it "deals with low love affairs." Source: 2, p. 133; 4, p. 61; 6, p. 690; 8, p. 315; 15, Vol. III, pp. 404, 407.

438 _____. *Dawn.* Liveright. Banned in Ireland (1932). Source: 4, p. 61.

439 _____. *Genius.* Liveright. Banned by the New York Society for the Suppression of Vice (1916) as blasphemous and obscene. Burned by the Nazis in Germany (1933) because it "deals with low love affairs." Source: 2, p. 100; 4, p. 61; 6, p. 690; 13, pp. 84–85; 15, Vol. II, pp. 631–32.

440 _____. *Sister Carrie.* Airmont; Bantam; Bobbs-Merrill; Holt; Houghton; Penguin. Suppressed in New York City (1900). Banned in Vermont (1958). Source: 4, p. 61; 9, p. 141.

441 Driggs, John, and Stephen Finn. *Intimacy between Men.* NAL. Challenged, but retained, at the Rogers-Hough, Ark. Memorial Library (1991) because "we're headed down the road to another San Francisco community." Source: 11, Sept. 1991, pp. 151, 177.

442 Drill, Esther. *Deal with It! A Whole New Approach to Your Body, Brain, and Life as a*

Gurl. Pocket Bks. Challenged, but retained at the Marion-Levy Public Library System in Ocala, Fla. (2001). Challenged at the Montgomery County, Tex. Memorial Library System (2004) along with fifteen other young-adult books with gay-positive themes. The objections were posted at the Library Patrons of Texas Web site. The language describing the books is similar to that posted at the Web site of the Fairfax County, Virginia-based Parents Against Bad Books in Schools, to which Library Patrons of Texas links. Challenged, but retained in the Fayetteville, Ark. Public school libraries (2005). The complainant also submitted a list of more than fifty books, citing the books as too sexually explicit and promoting homosexuality. Source: 11, Nov. 2001, p. 246; Nov. 2004, pp. 231–32; Jan. 2005, pp. 5–6; May 2005, p. 135; Sept. 2005, p. 215; Nov. 2005, pp. 295–96.

443 Dumas, Alexandre. *Camille.* French & European. Banned in England (1850), France (1852); ban lifted in USSR (1958). In 1863, all of Dumas's works were placed on the Vatican's list of forbidden books, and he was identified as one of only eleven authors whose total works had been condemned by the Roman Catholic Church for emphasizing the treatment of impure love. As recently as 1948, all of Dumas's works were declared to be forbidden to Catholics throughout the world and in every translation. Source: 4, p. 48; 14, p. 74.

444 Duncan, Lois. *Daughters of Eve.* Little. Removed from the Jackson County, W.Va. school libraries (1997) along with sixteen other titles. Removed from the Fairfax County, Va. middle school libraries and classrooms (2000) because "it promotes risky behavior and violence and also seeks to prejudice young vulnerable minds on several issues." Challenged at the Lowell, Ind. Middle School (2005) because of the book's profanity and sexual content. Source: 11, Jan. 1998, p. 13; July 2000, p. 105; May 2005, pp. 109–10.

445 _____. *Don't Look behind You.* Delacorte; Dell. Challenged at the Charlestown, Ind. Middle School library (1993) because of graphic passages, sexual references, and alleged immorality in the book. Source: 11, July 1993, p. 124.

446 _____. *Killing Mr. Griffin.* Little; Dell; Scholastic. Challenged at the Sinnott Elementary School in Milpitas, Calif. (1988) because the book contained "needlessly foul" language and had no "redeeming qualities." Pulled from a Bonsall, Calif. Middle School eighth-grade reading list (1992) because of disgusting violence and profanity.

Challenged in the Shenandoah Valley, Pa. Junior-Senior High School curriculum (1995) because of violence, strong language and unflattering references to God. Challenged in a Bristol Borough, Pa., middle school for violence and language. Source: 11, July 1988, pp. 122–23; Sept. 1988, p. 179; Mar. 1993, p. 43; July 1995, p. 99; May 2000, p. 78.

447
Duong, Thu Huong. *Novel without a Name.* Morrow. Forbidden in Vietnam (1991). Duong was arrested and imprisoned without trail. She was charged with having contacts with "reactionary" foreign organizations and with having smuggled "secret documents" out of the country. Source: 6, p. 702; 8, pp. 146–47.

448
_____. *Paradise of the Blind.* Morrow. Banned in Vietnam (1988). The novel outraged Vietnamese leaders, particularly the sections describing the 1953-56 land reform campaign—its excesses and its management, its destructive effects. Party Secretary Nguyen Van Linh publicly denounced Duong as "a whore"; he issued a second banning order. The depictions of these situations and their repercussions established her leadership of the dissident movement, leading to her arrest and the banning of her works. Source: 8, pp. 151–52.

449
Durack, Mary, and Elizabeth Durack. *Kookanoo and the Kangaroo.* Lerner Pubs. Removed from Howard County, Md. (1978) because "it would be hard for primary youngsters to make the distinction between the aborigines in Australia and black children in the U.S." Source: 11, Mar. 1978, p. 30.

450
Durang, Christopher. *Laughing Wild.* Dramatists Play Service. Challenged at the Manatee County School District in Bradenton Beach, Fla. (1998) because the play contains references to Dr. Ruth Westheimer and uses several slang words for sexual acts. Source: 11, May 1998, p. 71.

451
Durant, Penny. *When Heroes Die.* Macmillan. Challenged at the Seaside, Oreg. Public Library (1993) for promoting homosexuality. Source: 11, Jan. 1994, p. 36.

452
Durrell, Lawrence. *The Black Book.* Dutton. Seized by the U.S. Customs Bureau (1961). Source: 4, p. 88.

453
Earth Science. American Book. Challenged at the Plymouth-Canton school system in Canton, Mich. (1987) because this book "teaches the theory of evolution exclusively. It completely avoids any mention of Creationism. . . The evolutionary propaganda also underminds {sic} the parental guidance and teaching the children are receiving at home and from the pulpits." Source: 11, Nov. 1981, pp. 162–63; May 1987, p. 109.

454
Eban, Abba. *My People: The History of the Jews.* Random. Banned from the 1983 Moscow International Book Fair along with more than fifty other books because it is "anti-Soviet." Source: 11, Nov. 1983, p. 201.

455
Ebert, Alan. *The Homosexual.* Macmillan. Challenged at the Niles, Mich. Community Library (1982) because "it belongs on the shelves of a porno-shop." Source: 11, Jan. 1983, p. 8.

456
Edgerton, Clyde. *The Floatplane Notebooks.* Algonquin; Ballantine. Challenged at the Carroll County High School in Hillsville, Va. (1992) because "it was wishy-washy" and "could warp a child's mind." The complainants circulated a petition demanding the firing of an English teacher and the dismissal of all school officials connected with the decision to use the novel. Source: 11, May 1992, p. 84; Sept. 1992, p. 143.

457
_____. *Walking across Egypt.* Algonquin; Hall. Removed from a Clover Hill High School class in Richmond, Va. (1997) because the book refers to African-Americans as "niggers," is punctuated with profanity, and is "unacceptable and unnecessary." Source: 11, May 1997, p. 67.

458
Ehrenreich, Barbara. *Nickel and Dimed: On (Not) Getting By in America.* Metropolitan Bks. Criticized as the book chosen for the University of North Carolina at Chapel Hill, N.C. summer reading program (2003) by Republican state lawmakers, citing a "pattern" of the university being anti-Christian. In 2002, three freshmen sued the university over its choice of *Approaching the Qur'an: The Early Revelations*, by Michael A. Sells. The Family Policy Network, a Christian group based in Virginia, filed a federal lawsuit on the students' behalf. Court later rejected the argument that the reading requirement violated the U.S. Constitution. Source: 11, Sept. 2003, p. 182.

459
Ehrlich, Max. *The Reincarnation of Peter Proud.* Bobbs-Merrill. Banned from use in Aurora, Colo. High School English classes (1976) on the grounds of "immorality." Source: 11, May 1976, p. 70; May 1977, p. 79.

56

460 Ehrlich, May. *Where It Stops, Nobody Knows.* Dial; Puffin. Removed from the Cayce-West Columbia, S.C. School District's Congaree Elementary School library (1998) because of a blasphemy and slang term for sex. Source: 11, Mar. 1999, p. 36.

461 El Saadawi, Nawal. *The Hidden Face of Eve: Women in the Arab World.* Zed Books. Prohibited from entry to many Arab countries including Egypt, where Egyptian customs and excise authorities barred it under the Importing of Foreign Goods Act. Burned in Tehran, Iran (1980), along with the publishing house. The author was imprisoned in 1981 under the Sadat regime, blacklisted from Egyptian television and radio, and the target of numerous death threats by Muslim fundamentalists. In 1993, she left Egypt, fearing for her life, and moved to the United States. Source: 8, pp. 245–47.

462 Eleveld, Mark, ed. *The Spoken Word Revolution: Slam, Hip Hop & the Poetry of a New Generation.* Sourcebooks. Challenged, but retained in the Sequim, Wash. School District (2006) despite complaints that the book contains "profanity and references to sex, drugs, and mistreatment of women that are inappropriate for young teens." Source: 11, Sept. 2006, p. 257.

463 Eliot, George. *Adam Bede.* Houghton; NAL; Penguin. Attacked as "the vile outpourings of a lewd woman's mind" and withdrawn from the British circulating libraries (1859). Source: 4, p. 45.

464 _____. *Silas Marner.* Bantam; NAL; Zodiac Pr. Banned from the Anaheim, Calif. Union High School District English classrooms (1978) according to the Anaheim Secondary Teachers Association. Source: 11, Jan. 1979, p. 6.

465 Eliot, John. *The Christian Commonwealth.* Ayer Co. Pub. Banned in Massachusetts (1661) for stating that even royal authorities owed their power to higher source. Any Massachusetts citizen who owned copies of the banned work had to "cancel or deface" them and bring them to local judges, who would then dispose of them. Source: 1, pp. 37–38.

466 Elish, Dan. *Born Too Short: The Confessions of an Eighth-Grade Basket Case.* Thorndike Pr. Banned in Carroll County, Md. schools (2005). No reason stated. Source: 11, March 2006, pp. 70–71.

467 Elliot, David. *An Alphabet for Rotten Kids.* Philomel Bks. Pulled from the Spokane, Wash. School District libraries (1999) after a parent complained its depictions of children hitting animals and destroying property gave her second-grader the wrong message. Source: 11, May 1999, p. 68.

468 Ellis, Bret Easton. *American Psycho.* Random; Simon. The Carthage, Mo. public librarian (1991) was directed first "to take the book off the shelf and keep it under the circulation desk" and then "lose it." The incident involving the novel "snowballed" and was one of the reasons why, under protest, the librarian submitted her resignation. Source: 11, Nov. 1991, p. 195.

469 Ellis, Havelock. *Studies in the Psychology of Sex.* Random. Condemned and burned in England (1898), banned from the mail by the U.S. Post Office Department unless addressed to a doctor (1941), and banned in Ireland (1953). Source: 4, pp. 56–57; 6, pp. 732–33.

470 Ellison, Ralph. *Invisible Man.* Random; Vintage. Excerpts banned in Butler, Pa. (1975); removed from the high school English reading list in St. Francis, Wis. (1975). Retained in the Yakima, Wash. schools (1994) after a five-month dispute over what advanced high school students should read in the classroom. Two parents raised concerns about profanity and images of violence and sexuality in the book and requested that it be removed from the reading list. Source: 11, July 1975, p. 105; Nov. 1994, pp. 202–3.

471 Elson, Robert T. *Prelude to World War II.* Time-Life. Challenged at the Douglas County Library in Roseburg, Oreg. (1989) because the book contains nudity and violent photos harmful to children researching the war. Source: 11, Jan. 1990, pp. 4–5.

472 Elwell, Walter A., ed. *Evangelical Commentary on the Bible.* Baker. Bk. Challenged, but retained, at the Multnomah, Oreg. County Library (1991) by a patron who believed public funds should not be expended on religious books. Source: 11, Jan. 1992, p. 6.

473 Emerson, Zack. *Echo Company.* Scholastic. Access restricted at the Marana, Ariz. Unified School District (1993) because of complaints about profanity. Source: 11, Sept. 1993, p. 143.

474 *Encyclopaedia Britannica.* Ency. Brit. Ed. Banned and then pulped in Turkey (1986) because it was a "means of separatist propaganda." Source: 3, p. 319.

475 *The Endless Quest.* TSR Hobbies. Challenged in Newton, Iowa (1985) because the books in the series contain excessive violence, destruction, witchcraft, and the occult. The titles in the series include: *The Hero of Washington Square*, *The King's Quest*, *Light on Quest Mountain*, *Spell of the Winter Wizard*, and *Under the Dragon's Wing*. Source: 11, Mar. 1986, p. 38.

476 Enger, Eldon D., et al. *Concepts in Biology.* W. C. Brown. Two pages removed from the Waltham, Mass. High School text (1980) due to their explicit nature. Source: 11, Jan. 1981, p. 10.

477 Erasmus, Desiderus. *Colloquies.* Kessinger Pub. Condemned, along with The Praise of Folly, by the Sorbonne and the Parlement of Paris (1526) for allegedly heretical sympathies with Lutheranism. All of Erasmus's works were listed in the first Index for Forbidden books established in 1559, a ban that remained until the 1930s. Source: 1, pp. 48–49.

478 Erdoes, Richard, and Alfonso Ortiz. *American Indian Myths and Legends.* Pantheon. Removed from the Anchorage, Alaska school library shelves (1997) that are accessible to students. The anthology, which contains some sexually explicit tales, was placed in special resource collections available only to teachers. Source: 11, Mar. 1998, p. 39; May 1998, pp. 70–71.

479 Escher, M. C. *The Graphic Work of M. C. Escher.* Pan/Ballentine. Retained at Maldonado Elementary School in Tucson, Ariz. (1994) after being challenged by parents who objected to nudity and "pornographic," "perverted," and "morbid" themes. Source: 11, July 1994, p. 112.

480 Escoffier, Jeffrey. *John Maynard Keynes.* Chelsea House Pubs. Removed from the Anaheim, Calif. school district (2000) because school officials said the book is too difficult for middle school students and that it could cause harassment against students seen with it. The American Civil Liberties Union (ACLU) of Southern California filed suit in *Doe v. Anaheim Union High School District* alleging that the removal is "a pretext for viewpoint-based censorship." The ACLU claims no other books have been removed from the junior high library for similar reasons, even though several, such as works by Shakespeare and Dickens, are more difficult reading. The ACLU contends that the school officials engaged in unconstitutional viewpoint discrimination by removing the book because it contains gay and lesbian material. In March 2001, the school board approved a settlement that restored the book to the high school shelves and amended the district's policy to prohibit the removal of books for subject matter involving sexual orientation, but the book will not be returned to the middle school. Source: 11, Mar. 2001, p. 53; May 2001, p. 95; July 2001, p. 173.

481 Esquivel, Laura. *Like Water for Chocolate: A Novel in Monthly Installments, with Recipes, Romances, and Home Remedies.* Doubleday. Challenged at the Arrowhead High School in Merton, Wis. (2004) as an elective reading list assignment by a parent because the book contains "sexually explicit and inappropriate material." Source: 11, Jan. 2005, p. 11.

482 Etchison, Dennis. *Cutting Edge.* Doubleday. Challenged at the Eugene, Oreg. Public Library (1988) for its language, sexual nature, and "perversity." Source: 11, Jan. 1989, p. 3.

483 Evans, Tabor. *Longarm in Virginia City.* Jove. Challenged at the Allen County Public Library in Fort Wayne, Ind. (1985) as "pornographic and objectionable." Removed from the Jordan Valley, Oreg. Union High School (1988) because it was "too sexually graphic." Challenged, but retained at the Springdale, Ark. Public Library (2001) along with all other "western" novels because the writings include "pornographic, sexual encounters." Source: 11, July 1985, pp. 111–12; Jan. 1989, p. 3; Nov. 2001, p. 277.

484 Everetts, E. *Holt Basic Readings.* Holt. Challenged at the Hawkins County school system in Church Hill, Tenn. (1983) by the Citizens Organized for Better Schools because they claim the reading series indoctrinates students in "secular humanist" beliefs. Over 400 specific objections were filed against the reading series including specific complaints against the following works included in the series: *Rumpelstiltskin*; *Cinderella*; *The Wizard of Oz*, by L. Frank Baum; Shakespeare's *Macbeth*; *Anne Frank: The Diary of a Young Girl*; readings from anthropologist Margaret Mead; science fiction writer Isaac Asimov; and fairy tale creator Hans Christian Andersen. On October 24, 1986, U.S. District Court Judge Thomas G. Hull ruled in favor of the citizens' group and that the school's use of the textbook series "burdened" the plaintiffs' First Amendment rights to exercise freedom of religion. He ordered the Hawkins County public schools to excuse fundamentalist children from reading class. On August 24, 1987, a three-judge panel of the U.S. Court of Appeals for the Sixth Circuit reversed Judge Hull's decision by ruling unanimously that public school students can be required to read and discuss the disputed books, even though parts of those books might conflict with their beliefs. The court further ruled that there was no evidence that "the conduct required of the students was forbidden by their religion." On February 22, 1988, the U.S. Supreme Court declined to consider the appeal. The denial of certiorari in the case of *Mozert v. Hawkins County* left standing the August decision by the U.S. Court of Appeals for the Sixth Circuit. Source: 11, Jan. 1984, p. 11; Mar. 1984, p. 40; May 1984, p. 79; July 1984, pp. 112–13; Jan. 1987, pp. 1, 36–38; May 1987, pp. 75, 104–7; Sept. 1987, pp. 166–67; Nov. 1987, pp. 217–18; Mar. 1988, pp. 40–41, 58; May 1988, pp. 94–95.

485 **Evslin, Bernard.** *Cerberus.* Chelsea House Pubs. Removed from the elementary school library shelves, but retained in the junior and senior high school libraries in the Francis Howell School District in St. Peters, Mo. (1990). Allegedly, the book's story line is too graphic, its titles too gruesome, and its illustrations "pornographic." (The illustrations are drawings by Michelangelo and other Masters.) The book was said to "encourage satanism." Source: 11, May 1990, p. 84; July 1990, pp. 126–27; Sept. 1990, p. 159.

486 **Eyerly, Jeannette.** *Someone to Love Me.* Lippincott. Removed from the Jackson County, W.Va. school libraries (1997) along with sixteen other titles. Source: 11, Jan. 1998, p. 13.

487 **Fanon, Frantz.** *The Wretched of the Earth.* Grove. Banned in South Korea (1985). Source: 5, April 1986, pp. 30–33.

488 **Farmer, Philip J.** *Image of the Beast.* Essex House. Challenged at the Chapmanville, W.Va. Public Library (1981) because the book puts "mental pictures in the mind [that] have no place in the library." Source: 11, Mar. 1981, p. 41.

489 **Farrell, James.** *Studs Lonigan: A Trilogy.* Avon; Vanguard. Young Lonigan (1932) was published with the notice that it was "limited to physicians, social workers, teachers, and other persons having a professional interest in the psychology of adolescence." Banned in Canada (1942); seized in Philadelphia, Pa. (1948); banned in St. Cloud, Minn. (1953) and Ireland (1953); banned in overseas libraries controlled by the U.S. Information Agency. Source: 2, p. 148; 4, p. 85.

490 _____. *A World I Never Made.* Vanguard; Constable; World; Popular Living. Tried for obscenity in the U.S. (1935) and acquitted. Banned in Milwaukee, Wis., and St. Cloud, Minn. In 1957, the U.S. Information Agency banned all of Farrell's novels from overseas libraries under its control. Source: 2, p. 159; 14, pp. 301–2; 15, Vol. III, pp. 648, 650.

491 **Fassbender, William.** *You and Your Health.* Wiley. Challenged in the Seattle, Wash. school system (1987) because of its views on substance abuse and morality, as well as promiscuity. Source: 11, July 1987, p. 131.

492 **Fast, Howard.** *Citizen Tom Paine.* Bantam; Duell; World. Banned from high school libraries in New York City (1947) because it was allegedly written by a spokesman of a totalitarian movement and because it contains incidents and expressions not desirable for children, and was improper and indecent. Accused by the House Un-American Activities Committee of writing Communist propaganda, Fast was blacklisted by the Federal Bureau of Investigation in the 1950s. Subsequently, publishers would not handle his works in the United States. Book was withdrawn (1953) from U.S. Information Agency libraries overseas. Source: 4, p. 89; 7, pp. 111–12; 15, Vol. IV, p. 700.

493 _____. *The Immigrants.* Hall. Restricted to high school students with parental permission at the Governor Morehead School in Raleigh, N.C. (1982) due to the explicit sexual scenes and vulgarities. Source: 11, Nov. 1982, p. 205.

494 _____. *Second Generation.* Hall. Restricted to high school students with parental permission at the Governor Morehead School in Raleigh, N.C. (1982) due to the explicit sexual scenes and vulgarities. Source: 11, Nov. 1982, p. 205.

495 **Faulkner, William.** *As I Lay Dying.* Random. Banned in the Graves County School District in Mayfield, Ky. (1986) because it contained "offensive and obscene passages referring to abortion and used God's name in vain." The decision was reversed a week later after intense pressure from the ACLU and considerable negative

publicity. Challenged as a required reading assignment in an advanced English class of Pulaski County High School in Somerset, Ky. (1987) because the book contains "profanity and a segment about masturbation." Challenged, but retained, in the Carroll County, Md. schools (1991). Two school board members were concerned about the book's coarse language and dialect. Banned at Central High School in Louisville, Ky. (1994) temporarily because the book uses profanity and questions the existence of God. Source: 11, Nov. 1986, p. 208; May 1987, p. 90; Mar. 1992, p. 64; Nov. 1994, p. 189.

496 _____. *The Hamlet.* Random. Banned in Ireland (1954). Source: 4, p. 77.

497 _____. *Mosquitoes.* Liveright. Seized in raid in Philadelphia, Pa. (1948); banned in Ireland (1954). Source: 4, p. 78.

498 _____. *Pylon.* Random. Blacklisted by the National Organization of Decent Literature; condemned by local censorship groups; banned in Ireland (1954). Source: 4, p. 78.

499 _____. *A Rose for Emily.* Merrill. Challenged as required reading in an honors English class at the McClintock High School in Tempe, Ariz. (1996) by a teacher on behalf of her daughter and other African-American students at the school. In May 1996, a class-action lawsuit was filed in U.S. District Court in Phoenix, alleging that the district deprived minority students of educational opportunities by requiring racially offensive literature as part of class assignments. In January 1997, a federal judge dismissed the lawsuit stating he realized that "language in the novel was offensive and hurtful to the plaintiff," but that the suit failed to prove the district violated students' civil rights or that the works were assigned with discriminatory intent. The U.S. Court of Appeals for the Ninth Circuit in San Francisco ruled that requiring public school students to read literary works that some find racially offensive is not discrimination prohibited by the equal protection clause or Title VI of the 1964 Civil Rights Act. The ruling came in the case *Monteiro v. Tempe Union High School District.* Source: 11, May 1997, p. 72; Jan. 1999, pp. 13–15.

500 _____. *Sanctuary.* Random; Vintage. In 1948, the novel, along with eight other novels, was identified as obscene in criminal proceedings in the Court of Quarter sessions in Philadelphia County, Pa. Indictments were brought by the state district

attorney against five booksellers who were charged with possessing and intending to sell the books. In *Commonwealth v. Gordon*, 66 D. & C. 101 (1949), the court determined that the novel is not obscene. Faulkner was awarded the Nobel Prize for literature in 1950. Although the novel did not go to court again, by 1954, it was again condemned as obscene by numerous local censorship groups throughout the U.S., and the National Organization of Decent Literature placed it on the disapproval list. Also in 1954, Ireland banned the novel, along with most of the author's other works, because of the language such as "son of a bitch," "whore," "slut," and "bastard" combined with the brutal violence of the story. Irish and U.S. Censors also objected to the character Ruby, who prostituted herself to obtain money to free her common-law husband from jail, to obtain legal fees and to pay their expenses. Source: 4, p. 78; 8, pp. 378–79.

501 _____. *Soldier's Pay.* Liveright. Blacklisted by the National Organization of Decent Literature; condemned by local censorship groups; banned in Ireland (1954). Source: 4, p. 78.

502 _____. *Wild Palms.* Random. Seized in raid in Philadelphia, Pa. (1948); banned in Ireland (1954). Source: 4, p. 77.

503 **Federico, Ronald.** *Sociology.* Addison-Wesley. Removed from the Florida list of approved textbooks because, as the Pro-Family Forum argued, the textbook (1982) attacks religion and promotes nudity and profanity. Source: 11, July 1982, p. 125.

504 **Feelings, Muriel.** *Jambo Means Hello: The Swahili Alphabet.* Dial; Puffin. Challenged by a school board member in the Queens, N.Y. school libraries (1994) because it "denigrate[s] white American culture, 'promotes racial separation, and discourages assimilation.'" The rest of the school board voted to retain the book. Source: 11, July 1994, pp. 110–11; Sept. 1994, p. 166.

505 **Ferguson, Alane.** *Show Me the Evidence.* Avon; Macmillan. Challenged at the Charlestown, Ind. Middle School library (1993) because of graphic passages, sexual references, and alleged immorality in the book. Source: 11, July 1993, p. 124.

506 **Ferlinghetti, Lawrence.** *Coney Island of the Mind.* New Directions. Banned for use in Aurora, Colo. High School English classes (1976) on the grounds of "immorality." Source: 11, May 1976, p. 70; May 1977, p. 79; 12, pp. 128–32, 238.

507 _____. *Starting from San Francisco.* New Directions. Banned for use in Aurora, Colo. High School English classes (1976) on the grounds of "immorality." Source: 11, May 1976, p. 70; May 1977, p. 79; 12, pp. 128–32, 238.

508 **Ferris, Jean.** *Eight Seconds.* Harcourt. Challenged at the Montgomery County, Tex. Memorial Library System (2004) along with fifteen other young-adult books with gay-positive themes. The objections were posted at the Library Patrons of Texas Web site. The language describing the books is similar to that posted at the Web site of the Fairfax County, Virginia-based Parents Against Bad Books in Schools, to which Library Patrons of Texas links. Source: 11, Nov. 2004, pp. 231–32.

509 **Fielding, Henry.** *Tom Jones.* NAL; Norton; Penguin. Banned in France (1749). Source: 4, p. 29.

510 **Fierstein, Harvey.** *The Sissy Duckling.* Simon. Challenged at the Montgomery County, Tex. Memorial Library System (2004) along with fifteen other young-adult books with gay-positive themes. The objections were posted at the Library Patrons of Texas Web site. The language describing the books is similar to that posted at the Web site of the Fairfax County, Virginia-based Parents Against Bad Books in Schools, to which Library Patrons of Texas links. Source: 11, Nov. 2004, pp. 231–32.

511 **Fitzgerald, F. Scott.** *The Great Gatsby.* Scribner. Challenged at the Baptist College in Charleston, S.C. (1987) because of "language and sexual references in the book." Source: 11, July 1987, p. 133.

512 **Fitzgerald, Frances.** *Cities on a Hill: A Journey through Contemporary American Cultures.* Simon. Challenged at the Deschutes County Library in Bend, Oreg. (1993) because it "encourages and condones" homosexuality. Source: 11, Sept. 1993, pp. 158–59.

513 **Fitzgerald, John D.** *The Great Brain.* Dial. Removed from a list of supplemental reading material for fourth graders at the Port Jervis, N.Y. schools (1992) because the novel contains a discussion of suicide. Source: 11, Nov. 1992, pp. 186–87.

514 **Fitzhugh, Louise.** *Harriet the Spy.* Harper. Challenged in the Xenia, Ohio school libraries (1983) because the book "teaches children to lie, spy, back-talk, and curse." Source: 6, pp. 832–33; 9; 11, Sept. 1983, p. 139; Nov. 1983, p. 197.

515 _____. *The Long Secret.* Harper. Challenged in the Eagle Cliffs Elementary School library in Billings, Mont. (1993) because the book is "demented" and pokes fun at religion. Source: 11, Jan. 1994, p. 36.

516 _____. *Sport.* Delacorte. Challenged at the Madison Elementary School in Cedar Rapids, Iowa (1998) due to "cuss words" and other harsh language. Source: 11, May 1998, pp. 87–88.

517 **Flaubert, Gustave.** *Madame Bovary.* Bantam; Houghton; Modern Library; NAL; Norton; Penguin. Flaubert was brought to trail in 1857 for the novel under a French law, first passed in May 1819, which aimed to suppress the exhibition, distribution, or sale of any printed matter constituting and "outrage to public and religious morality and to public decency." Placed on the *Index Librorum Prohibitorum* in Rome (1864). Banned by the National Organization of Decent Literature (1954). Source: 4, p. 47; 6, pp. 834–35; 8, pp. 362–63; 10, p. 142.

518 _____. *Novembre.* Roman. The New York Society for the Suppression of Vice charged a bookseller (1935) with selling an obscene book. The City Magistrates Court of New York City, Fourth District, Borough of Manhattan dismissed the complaint and discharged the defendant, after noting that there was not sufficient cause to hold the defendant for trail. Source: 13, pp. 174–75.

519 **Flora, James.** *Grandpa's Ghost Stories.* Macmillan. Challenged as inappropriate at the Broadwater Elementary School Library in Billings, Mont. (1994) because "[children] don't need to be allowed to read anything they want." Source: 11, May 1994, p. 84.

520 **Fogelin, Adrian.** *My Brother's Hero.* Peachtree. Removed from the Hillsborough County, Fla. fourth-grade reading list (2006), although the book is on the Sunshine State Young Reader's Award list of books for third, fourth, and fifth-graders. Source: 11, Nov. 2006, pp. 290–91.

521 **Follett, Ken.** *Eye of the Needle.* Morrow; NAL. Banned from the Marysville, Kans. high school and junior high school libraries (1993) along with five other Follett novels—*The Key to Rebecca, Lie Down with Lions, Night over Water, The Pillars of*

61

the Earth, and *Triple*—because the books were "pornographic." Later, however, the board decided to reconsider its vote, follow an established review procedure, and retain the six books. Source: 11, May 1993, pp. 70–71; Nov. 1993, p. 177; Jan. 1994, p. 35.

522 _____. ***The Hammer of Eden.*** Random; Crown; Fawcett. Challenged at the Great Falls, Mont. High School library (2000). Parents called for the review of all library books and the adoption of stricter rules to keep "obscenity" off library shelves. Source: 11, Mar. 2001, p. 54.

523 _____. ***Night over Water.*** Macmillan; Morrow; Penguin. Returned to the open shelves at the Medina, Ohio High School library (1993) despite some sexually explicit passages. The complainant then filed a police complaint against the Medina city schools, claiming the district is pandering obscenity to its students. Source: 11, May 1993, p. 86; July 1993, p. 101.

524 _____. ***Pillars of the Earth.*** Morrow; NAL. Moved to a new "reserve" section of the Chanute, Kans. school library (1994). The book came under fire because of some use of obscenity and graphic violence. Source: 11, Sept. 1994, p. 146; Mar. 1995, p. 40.

525 Ford, Michael Thomas. ***One Hundred Questions and Answers about AIDS.*** Morrow. Challenged because it encourages sexual activity, but retained in the Eau Claire, Wis. public school libraries (1993). Removed from the Jackson County, W.Va. school libraries (1997) along with sixteen other titles. Source: 11, July 1993, p. 104; Sept. 1993, p. 159; Jan. 1998, p. 13.

526 Forrest, Katherine. ***Beverly Malibu.*** Naiad Pr. Challenged, but retained, at the Oak Lawn, Ill. Public Library (1991) because the sleuth in the mystery is a lesbian. Source: 11, Nov. 1991, p. 209.

527 Forster, E. M. ***Maurice.*** Norton. Banned from the Mascenic Regional High School in New Ipswich, N.H. (1995) because it is about gays and lesbians. An English teacher was fired for refusing to remove the book. An arbitrator ruled in April 1996 that she could return to work in September without a year's back pay. The Mascenic Regional School Board is appealing the ruling. The teacher was eventually reinstated after a decision by the state's Public Employee Labor Relations Board. Source: 11, Sept. 1995, p. 166; Jan. 1996, p. 15; July 1996, pp. 130–31; Jan. 1997, p. 27.

528 Forsyth, Frederick. ***The Devil's Alternative.*** Viking. Removed from the Evergreen School District of Vancouver, Wash. (1983) along with twenty-nine other titles. The American Civil Liberties Union of Washington filed suit contending that the removals constitute censorship, a violation of plaintiff's rights to free speech and due process, and the acts are a violation of the state Open Meetings Act because the removal decisions were made behind closed doors. Source: 11, Nov. 1983, pp. 185–86.

529 Fossey, Dian. ***Gorillas in the Mist.*** Houghton. Teachers at the Westlake Middle School in Erie, Pa. (1993), using felt-tip pens, blacked out passages pertaining to masturbation and mating. Source: 11, July 1993, p. 109.

530 Fox, Mem. ***Guess What?*** Harcourt. Challenged at the Cook Memorial Library in Libertyville, Ill. (1991) because it features witches, boiling cauldrons, names of punk rockers, and a reference that could be interpreted as meaning "God is dead." Source: 11, Sept. 1991, p. 153.

531 Fox, Paula. ***The Slave Dancer.*** Bradbury Pr. Challenged, but retained, by the Fayette County, Ga. school system (1996). The 1974 Newbery Medal winner about a 13-year-old boy who is snatched from the docks of New Orleans and put on a slave ship bound for Africa. The book was considered objectionable because of language that is "insensitive and degrading." Challenged as part of the curriculum at the North Bedford County School District in Loysburg, Pa. (1998) because of the book's graphic detail and derogatory racial references. Challenged at the Shelbyville, Ky. East Middle School (2005) because the book is a too-graphic depiction of the slave trade. Source: 11, May 1996, p. 99; Mar. 1999, p. 40; May 2005, pp. 110–11.

532 France, Anatole (Jacques-Anatole Thibault). ***Penguin Island.*** Wildside Pr. Placed on the Catholic Church's Index of Forbidden books, along with all of his works. They remained on the Index until 1966. Anatole France received Nobel Prize in literature in 1921. Source: 1, p. 252.

533 Franco, Betsy, ed. ***You Hear Me?: Poems and Writings by Teenage Boys.*** Candlewick Pr. Challenged in the Houston County, Ga. public schools (2002) by a parent concerned about the book's language and topics. Source: 11, Sept. 2002, pp. 195–96.

534 Frank, Anne. *Anne Frank: The Diary of a Young Girl.* Modern Library. Challenged in Wise County, Va. (1982) due to protests of several parents who complained the book contains sexually offensive passages. Four members of the Alabama State Textbook Committee (1983) called for the rejection of this title because it is a "real downer." Removed for two months from the Baker Middle School in Corpus Christi, Tex. (1998) after two parents charged that the book was pornographic. The book was returned after students waged a letter-writing campaign to keep it, and a review committee recommended the book's retention. Source: 8, pp. 402–3; 11, Mar. 1983, p. 39; July 1998, pp. 119–20.

535 Frank, E. R. *America.* Atheneum. Challenged in the Ravenna, Ohio schools (2007) because, "What we kept finding and going over was sexual content and profanity," said the complainant. The novel has received several awards including the *New York Times* Notable Book Award. It also was a Garden State Teen Book Award nominee. Source: May 2007, p. 93.

536 _____. *Life Is Funny.* DK Ink. Pulled from the shelves of two Merced, Calif. middle-school libraries (2005) because of an "X-rated" passage describing two teens' first experience with sexual intercourse. Source: 11, May 2005, p. 107.

537 Frank, Mel, and Ed Rosenthal. *Marijuana Grower's Guide.* Red Eye Pr. Challenged at the Teton County Public Library in Jackson, Wyo. (2004) because "tax dollars are being used to purchase a how-to crime manual." Source: 11, May 2004, p. 98.

538 Frank, Pat. *Alas, Babylon.* Bantam. Challenged at the Taylorville, Ill. Junior High School (1987) because it "contains profane language." Source: 11, Sept. 1987, p. 194.

539 Franklin, Benjamin. *The Autobiography of Benjamin Franklin.* Airmont; Buccaneer Pr.; Macmillan; Norton; Random; Univ. of Tenn. Pr.; Yale Univ. Pr. "The expurgation of Benjamin Franklin seems to have increased over the years until he became in the early twentieth century one of the most censored and yet at the same time one of the most widely reprinted writers in American history. Two essays, in particular, are frequently expurgated, 'Advice on the Choice of a Mistress' and the 'Letters to the Royal Academy of Brussels.'" Source: 8, pp. 411–12; 10, p. 134; 15, Vol. II, p. 616.

540 Freedom Writers. *The Freedom Writers Diary: How a Teacher and 150 Teens Used Writing to Change Themselves and the World around Them.* Doubleday. Challenged in the Howell, Mich. High School (2007) because of the book's strong sexual content. In response to a request from the president of the Livingston Organization for Values in Education, or LOVE, the county's top law enforcement official reviewed the books to see whether laws against distribution of sexually explicit materials to minors had been broken. "After reading the books in question, it is clear that the explicit passages illustrated a larger literary, artistic or political message and were not included solely to appeal to the prurient interests of minors," the county prosecutor wrote. "Whether these materials are appropriate for minors is a decision to be made by the school board, but I find that they are not in violation of the criminal laws." The best-selling book has achieved national acclaim and was made into a recent hit movie. Source: 11, Mar. 2007, pp. 51–52; May 2007, p. 116.

541 Freud, Sigmund. *Introductory Lectures on Psychoanalysis.* Penguin. In 1934, Pope Pius XI published a statement criticizing psychoanalysis and Freud's ideas on religious belief. Freud's writings were considered off-limits to Catholics as dangerous to faith and morals according to canon law. Freud's works were censored in the Soviet Union after 1930 and were among those buried by the Nazis in 1939. Source: 1, pp. 169–70.

542 Freymann-Weyr, Garret. *My Heartbeat.* Houghton. Challenged at the Montgomery County, Tex. Memorial Library System (2004) along with fifteen other young-adult books with gay-positive themes. The objections were posted at the Library Patrons of Texas Web site. The language describing the books is similar to that posted at the Web site of the Fairfax County, Virginia-based Parents Against Bad Books in Schools, to which Library Patrons of Texas links. Source: 11, Nov. 2004, pp. 231–32.

543 Friday, Nancy. *Men in Love.* Delacorte; Dial. Temporarily placed in storage on the second floor of the Alpha Park, Ill. Library (1981) and restricted to patrons over eighteen years old unless they have written parental consent because several area residents objected to its "vulgarity." Source: 11, Jan. 1982, p. 9; May 1982, p. 100.

544 _____. *Women on Top: How Real Life Has Changed Women's Fantasies.* Pocket Bks. Removed from the Chestatee Regional Library

63

System in Gainesville, Ga. (1994) because the book on women's sexual fantasies is "pornographic and obscene" and lacks "literary merit." After months of protest and maneuvering, the library's only copy was destroyed when the child of a patron accidentally dropped it into a dishpan full of water. The book is out of print and the library does not plan to replace it. Challenged at the Chester County Library at Charlestown, Pa. (1996) because of graphic details about sex acts and fantasies. Pulled from the Gwinnett County, Ga. (1997) Public Library shelves after two residents complained about its sexually explicit content. Following four years of controversy over keeping adult-themed books from children, the board approved two new policies. One policy creates a "parental advisory" shelf of non-fiction sex and health books that extensively and explicitly depict human sex acts, either visually or verbally, or books the library staff deems are appropriate only for adults. The other policy allows parents to decide—with electronic designations on new library cards—whether their child can check out books on the parental advisory shelf. Parents also can restrict further what types of books the child can get from the library. Winniped police seized (1997) the novel from the public library. Source: 6, p. 415; 11, Nov. 1994, p. 187; Mar. 1995, p. 39; May 1995, p. 65; Nov. 1996, p. 194; Jan. 1997, p. 8; Mar. 1997, p. 49; May 1997, p. 60; Nov. 1997, p. 165.

545 **Fritz, Jean.** *Around the World in a Hundred Years: Henry the Navigator–Magellan.* Putnam. Removed from the Carroll County, Md. schools (1995) because a passage on the burning of the library in Alexandria during the fourth century said that "Christians did not believe in scholarship" and mentioned intellectual suppression by Christians. "It's a sweeping generalization and it's definitely anti-Christian." Source: 11, Nov. 1995, p. 186.

546 **Fuentes, Carlos.** *The Death of Artemio Cruz.* Farrar. Retained in the Yakima, Wash. schools (1994) after a five-month dispute over what advanced high school students should read in the classroom. Two parents had raised concerns about profanity and images of violence and sexuality in the book and requested that it be removed from the reading list. Source: 11, Nov. 1994, pp. 202–3.

547 _____. *The Old Gringo.* Farrar. Retained in the Guilford County, N.C. school media centers (1996) after a parent wanted the book removed because of its explicit language. Source: 11, Jan. 1997, p. 25.

548 **Fugard, Athol.** *Master Harold and the Boys.* Knopf; Oxford Univ. Pr. A South African order banning printed copies of the play was imposed in Dec. 1982, but was lifted temporarily a week later. Source: 5, Mar. 1983, p. 47.

549 **Gaines, Ernest J.** *The Autobiography of Miss Jane Pittman.* Bantam. Pulled from a seventh-grade class in Conroe, Tex. (1995) after complaints about racial slurs in the book. School officials later reinstated it. Challenged as an eighth-grade district-wide reading assignment in the Puyallup, Wash. schools (2006) because "racial slurs and stereotyping are used throughout the book, as well as scenes of sex, rape, and implied incest." The Puyallup School Board voted to uphold an earlier decision by a district committee requiring eighth-graders to read the novel. In explaining their vote, each board member recounted the difficulty of balancing valid concerns on each side of the debate. "It wasn't a sole issue of dealing with racism or the "n-word." "But it is our hope by giving them an explanation of the word and where it came from they'll understand it's inappropriate to use it in the future." Source: 11, Mar. 1995, p. 46; May 1995, p. 84; Jan. 2007, pp. 11–12; Mar. 2007, pp. 74–75.

550 **Gaines, Ernest.** *A Lesson before Dying.* Knopf; Vintage. Banned, but later reinstated after community protests at the Windsor Forest High School in Savannah, Ga. (2000). The controversy began in early 1999 when a parent complained about sex, violence, and profanity in the book that was part of an Advanced Placement English class. Removed from the college bookstore at Louisiana College, Pineville, La. (2004) by the college president because a love scene described in the book clashes with the school's Christian values. Source: 11, Mar. 2000, p. 63; Mar. 2001, p. 76; Mar. 2004, pp. 53–54.

551 **Galbraith, John Kenneth.** *The Affluent Society.* Houghton. Removed from the Roselle, N.J. high school library list (1972) along with *The Age of Keynes*, by Robert Lekachman, *The Struggle for Peace*, by Leonard Beaton, and *Today's Isms: Communism, Fascism, Capitalism, Socialism*, by William Ebenstein. The president of the board said, "The books were too liberal and I disagree with their points of view." Months later, after considerable public protest, the superintendent of schools placed a rush order for the books and said that they would be on the library bookshelves. Source: 7, pp. 5–7.

64

552 Galdone, Joanna. *The Tailypo: A Ghost Tale.* Houghton. Challenged at the Jefferson Terrace Elementary School library in East Baton Rouge, La. (1988) because "it is too scary" and gave the complainant's "child a nightmare." Source: 11, May 1988, p. 87.

553 Gale, Jay. *A Young Man's Guide to Sex.* Holt; Putnam. Challenged, but retained, at the Cleveland, Tenn. Public Library (1993) along with seventeen other books, most of which are on sex education, AIDS awareness, and some titles on the supernatural. Removed from the Kenai Peninsula Borough School District libraries in Homer, Alaska (1993) because it was thought to have "outdated material that could be harmful to student health." Source: 11, Sept. 1993, p. 146; Jan. 1994, p. 33.

554 Galileo, Galilei. *Dialogue Concerning the Two Chief World Systems.* Univ. of California Pr. Banned by Pope Urban VIII for heresy and breach of good faith (1633) and sentenced to prison for an indefinite period. It was not until 1824, when Canon Settele, a Roman astronomy professor, published a work on modern scientific theories, that the Roman Catholic Church finally announced its acceptance of "general opinion of modern astronomers." In the papal Index of 1835, the names of Galileo, Copernicus, and Kepler were removed. On October 31, 1992, Pope John Paul II formally rehabilitated Galileo—359 years, four months, and nine days after Galileo had been forced to recant his heresy that the earth moved around the sun. Source: 4, p. 17; 8, pp. 231–33.

555 Gallagher, I. J. *The Case of the Ancient Astronauts.* Raintree. Challenged at the Escambia County, Fla. school district (1984) because the complainant claimed the book indicated "Ezekiel had seen a UFO when he spoke in the Bible about seeing something that looked like a wheel in the sky." Source: 11, Sept. 1984, p. 156.

556 Gao Xingjian. *Fugitives.* Univ. of Chicago Pr. All works by Gao Xingjian banned in China (1989). The Chinese government denounced the awarding of the Nobel Prize in Literature (2000) to Gao, accusing the Nobel committee of being politically motivated. Source: 7, p. 184.

557 Garcia-Marquez, Gabriel. *Love in the Time of Cholera.* Knopf; Penguin; G. K. Hall. Challenged, but retained, on the Montgomery County, Md. reading lists and school library shelves (1998). A parent had complained that the book should be removed from all county schools because it contained "perverse sexual acts, adults having sex with children, and rape." Source: 11, May 1998, p. 70; July 1998, p. 119.

558 _____. *One Hundred Years of Solitude.* Avon; Harper. Purged from the book list for use at the Wasco, Calif. Union High School (1986) because the book, whose author won the 1982 Nobel Prize for literature, was "garbage being passed off as literature." Removed from the Advanced Placement English reading list at St. Johns High School in Darlington, S.C. (1990) because of profane language. Challenged for sexual explicitness, but retained on the Stonewall Jackson High School's academically advanced reading list in Brentsville, Va. (1997). Challenged on the Montgomery County, Md. reading lists and school library shelves (1998). Source: 11, July 1986, p. 119; May 1989, p. 78; Jan. 1991, p. 18; Nov. 1997, pp. 169–70; Jan. 1998, p. 29; May 1998, p. 70.

559 Garden, Nancy. *Annie on My Mind.* Farrar. Challenged at the Cedar Mill Community Library in Portland, Oreg. (1988) because the book portrays lesbian love and sex as normal. Challenged in Sedgwick, Maine (1990) by a parent when she learned that the novel was included in the seventh- and eighth-grade library. The parent objected to the lesbian relationship portrayed. The book was retained. Challenged in the Colony, Tex. Public Library (1992) because "it promotes and encourages the gay lifestyle." Challenged because it "encourages and condones" homosexuality, but retained at the Bend, Oreg. High School (1993). Challenged, but retained, at the Lapeer, Mich. West High School library (1993). Challenged at several Kansas City area schools (1993) after the books were donated by a national group that seeks to give young adults "fair, accurate, and inclusive images of lesbians and gay men"—at the Shawnee Mission School District the book was returned to general circulation; at the Olathe East High School the book was removed; protesters burned copies of the book but the Kansas City, Mo. School District kept Garden's novel on the high school shelves; in Kansas City, Kans., the school district donated the book to the city's public library; and in Lee's Summit, Mo., the superintendent removed the book. The federal district court in Kansas, later found the removal of the book unconstitutional and ordered it restored to the school district's libraries. Challenged, but retained, at the Liberty, Mo. High School library (1994). Removed from shelves of the Chanute, Kans. (1994) High School Library and access to them limited to only those students with written parental permission because of concerns about its content. Source: 8, pp. 404–6; 11, Jan. 1990, pp. 4–5; July 1992, pp. 125–26; Sept. 1993, pp. 158–59; Nov. 1993, pp. 191–92; Jan. 1994, p. 13; Mar. 1994, pp. 51–52; May 1994 p. 84; July 1994, p. 129; Sept. 1994, pp. 140–41; Mar. 1995, p. 40; Mar. 1996, p. 54.

560 _____. ***Good Moon Rising.*** Farrar. Challenged at the Montgomery County, Tex. Memorial Library System (2004) along with fifteen other young-adult books with gay-positive themes. The objections were posted at the Library Patrons of Texas Web site. The language describing the books is similar to that posted at the Web site of the Fairfax County, Virginia-based Parents Against Bad Books in Schools, to which Library Patrons of Texas links. Source: 11, Nov. 2004, pp. 231–32.

561 _____. ***Holly's Secret.*** Farrar. Challenged at the Montgomery County, Tex. Memorial Library System (2004) along with fifteen other young-adult books with gay-positive themes. The objections were posted at the Library Patrons of Texas Web site. The language describing the books is similar to that posted at the Web site of the Fairfax County, Virginia-based Parents Against Bad Books in Schools, to which Library Patrons of Texas links. Source: 11, Nov. 2004, pp. 231–32.

562 _____. ***Witches.*** Lippincott. Challenged by the "God Squad," a group of three students and their parents, at the El Camino High School in Oceanside, Calif. (1986) because the book "contains a lot of information on witch covens. This information can be easily used to form a coven." Removed from the Kirby Junior High School in Wichita Falls, Tex. (1997) because of "Satanic" themes. Source: 11, Sept. 1986, p. 151; Nov. 1986, p. 224; Jan. 1987, p. 9; July 1997, p. 95.

563 **Gardner, Benjamin Franklin.** ***Black.*** Books for Libraries Pr. Removed from the Dayton, Ohio schools (1976) after complaints that the work contained "hard-core pornography." Source: 11, Jan. 1977, p. 7.

564 **Gardner, John C.** ***Grendel.*** Knopf. Challenged at the Frederick County, Md. school system (1978) because the novel is "anti-Christian, anti-moral, full of vulgarity." Placed on a restricted list at the Wasco, Calif. High School (1986), which prohibits the novel's use in the classroom until every student in the class receives parental permission. The novel is the only book on the restricted list, and an objection by the high school principal to the "profane" nature of the novel was the catalyst that generated the restricted list policy. Challenged in the Indianapolis, Ind. schools (1986) as an accelerated English class assignment. Challenged at the Viewmont High School in Farmington, Utah (1991) because the book "was obscene and should not be required reading." Challenged, but retained, as part of the Pinelands Regional High School's English curriculum in Bass River Township, N.J. (1992) because of obscenities. Challenged in the Clayton County School District's supplemental reading list for advanced English students in Jonesboro, Ga. (1993) because the book was too violent and graphic. Challenged, but retained, on high school reading lists in the Douglas, Colo. (1997). Parents complained that the novel was too obscene and violent for high school students. The school board also declined to create a rating system for books. Source: 11, Mar. 1978, p. 39; May 1978, p. 58; May 1986, pp. 81–82; July 1986, p. 119; Jan. 1987, p. 32; May 1989, p. 87; May 1991, p. 92; Jan. 1993, p. 11; Mar. 1993, p. 56; May 1993, p. 87; May 1997, p. 78.

565 **Garrigue, Sheila.** ***Between Friends.*** Bradbury Pr. Challenged in the Des Moines, Iowa schools (1983) due to the use of the word "damn." Source: 11, May 1983, p. 73.

566 **Gassner, John, and Clive Barnes, eds.** ***Best American Plays: Sixth Series, 1963—1967.*** Crown. Challenged at the Miami, Okla. High School library (1984) because the anthology contains "The Toilet," by Leroi Jones [Imamu Amiri Baraka]. Source: 11, May 1984, p. 87.

567 **Gates, Doris.** ***Two Queens of Heaven.*** Viking. Placed on restricted shelves in the libraries of Prescott, Ariz. elementary schools (1979) because it contains two illustrations of a bare-breasted goddess. Source: 11, Jan. 1980, p. 6.

568 **Gautier, Theophile.** ***Mademoiselle de Maupin.*** French & European; Penguin. Challenged in New York City (1917) and finally cleared in 1921 after a long court fight. Banned by Nicholas I in Russia (1831-1853). Source: 4, p. 43; 15, Vol. III, p. 413.

569 **Genet, Jean.** ***Our Lady of the Flowers.*** Grove. Seized from the Birmingham, England Public Library (1957) and banned in France (1958) and Ireland (1965). The Irish Board of Censors found the novel "obscene" and "indecent," objecting particularly to the author's handling of the theme of homosexuality and brutal crime. Source: 4, p. 88; 13, pp. 178–79.

570 Genet, Jean. *The Thief's Journal.* Grove. Banned in Ireland (1961). The Irish Board of Censors found the novel "obscene" and "indecent," objecting particularly to the author's handling of the theme of homosexuality and the poetic treatment of crime. Source: 13, p. 246.

571 George, Jean Craighead. *Julie of the Wolves.* Harper. Challenged in Mexico, Mo. (1982) because of the book's "socialist, communist, evolutionary, and anti-family themes." Challenged in Littleton, Colo. (1989) school libraries because "the subject matter was better suited to older students, not sixth graders." Challenged at the Erie Elementary School in Chandler, Ariz. (1994) because the book includes a passage that some parents found inappropriate in which a man forcibly kisses his wife. The Newbery Award-winning book, depicting the experiences of an Eskimo girl, was chosen by the teacher of a third-, fourth-, and fifth-grade class for the Antarctic unit she was teaching. Challenged in the classrooms and school libraries in Palmdale, Calif. (1995) because the book describes a rape. Removed from the sixth-grade curriculum of the New Brighton Area School District in Pulaski Township, Pa. (1996) because of a graphic marital rape scene. Challenged at the Hanson Lane Elementary School in Ramona, Calif. (1996) because the award-winning book includes an attempted rape of a 13-year-old girl. Source: 11, Nov. 1982, p. 215; Sept. 1989, p. 186; Jan. 1995, p. 9; Mar. 1996, p. 45; May 1996, p. 88; Jan. 1997, p. 9.

572 Gettings, Fred. *Dictionary of Demons.* Trafalgar Square Pub. Moved out of the circulating collection of the Norwood, Ohio High School library (2000) because of concerns that the book promotes the occult. Source: 11, May 2000, p. 75.

573 Gibbon, Edward. *History of the Decline and Fall of the Roman Empire.* Modern Library. Placed on the *Index Librorum Prohibitorum* in Rome (1783) because it contradicted official church history. Source: 4, p. 33.

574 Gibran, Kahlil. *Spirits Rebellious.* Philosophical Library. The collection of short stories protesting religious and political tyranny, was publicly burned in the Beirut marketplace and suppressed by the Syrian government. Gibran was exiled from Lebanon and excommunicated from the Maronite Church. Source: 1, pp. 320–21.

575 Gibson, Walter Brown. *Complete Illustrated Book of Divination and Prophecy.* Doubleday; NAL. Challenged at the Plymouth-Canton school system in Canton, Mich. (1987) because the book deals with witchcraft. Source: 11, May 1987, p. 110; Jan. 1988, p. 11.

576 Gide, Andre. *If It Die.* Seized in New York City (1935). Police arrested the Gotham Book Mart owner for allegedly violating the New York Obscenity Statute. The City Magistrate's Court of New York City, Seventh District, Borough of Manhattan (1936) dismissed the complaint and discharged the Gotham Book Mart owner. In 1938, after Gide publicly announced his disillusionment with communism, the Soviet Union banned all of his works. In 1952, the work was placed on the *Index Librorum Prohibitorum* in Rome, on which it remained until 1966. The Irish Board of Censors banned the work in 1953 for its blatant descriptions of Gide's homosexual relations, and the ban was not lifted until the relaxing of restraints in the 1970s. Source: 4, p. 59; 13, p. 114; 15, Vol. III, p. 648.

577 Gilstrap, John. *Nathan's Run.* HarperCollins; Warner. Removed from the Annville-Cleona, Pa. Middle-High School library (1998) because "the obscene/profane language and violence in this book are of a degree that it [was] concluded to be inappropriate for a middle/high school library collection." Challenged in the Everett, Wash. School District (2000) due to sexual explicitness and violence. Source: 11, Sept. 1998, p. 141; Mar. 1999, p. 40; Sept. 2000, p. 144.

578 Ginsberg, Allen. *Collected Poetry, 1947–1980.* Harper; Viking. Removed from the Murray County High School library in Chatsworth, Ga. (1989) because "it was really gutter stuff." Challenged at the North Central High School library in Indianapolis, Ind. (1989) because explicit descriptions of homosexual acts were deemed inappropriate subject matter for high school students. Source: 11, July 1989, p. 128; Jan. 1990, p. 9; Mar. 1990, pp. 61–62.

579 _____. *Howl and Other Poems.* City Lights. Seized by U.S. Customs officials in San Francisco (1957). Prohibited in the Jacksonville, Fla. Forrest High School Advanced Placement English class (2000) because of descriptions of homosexual acts. The class syllabus warns students and parents that some people might find the reading objectionable and offers an alternative assignment. The prohibition led to the review of all materials taught in the class. Source: 4, p. 97; 6, pp. 955–56; 7, pp. 459–60; 11, Jan. 2001, p. 12.

580 _____. *Kaddish and Other Poems.*
City Lights. Banned for use in Aurora, Colo. High School English classes (1976) on the grounds of "immorality." Source: 11, May 1976, p. 70; May 1977, p. 79; 12, pp. 128–32, 238.

581 Giovanni, Nikki. *My House.* Morrow. Banned from the Waukesha, Wis. public school libraries (1975). Challenged at the West Gennessee High School in Syracuse, N.Y. (1990) because the book contains obscenities. Challenged at the Duval County, Fla. public school libraries (1992) because it contains the word "nigger" and was accused of vulgarity, racism, and sex. Source: 11, July 1975, p. 104; July 1990, p. 127; July 1992, p. 105.

582 Glasser, Ronald J. *365 Days.* Braziller. Banned, but later reinstated by a U.S. District Court ruling in Baileyville, Maine (1982). Source: 11, Mar. 1982, p. 33.

583 Glenn, Mel. *Who Killed Mr. Chippendale?: A Mystery in Poems.* Lodestar Bks. Removed from the Central School library in Huntsville, Ala. (1999) as inappropriate for fourth graders. After the book's removal, the complainant called for the formation of a group of parents to go through all the library's books, as well as monitor new books. The school's principal stated, "If a book is sexual, if it is racial, if it's violent, we'll pull it off the shelves." Source: 11, July 1999, p. 93.

584 Godchaux, Elma. *Stubborn Roots.* Macmillan. Seized and destroyed by New Orleans, La. (1937) police. Source: 15, Vol. III, p. 650.

585 Goethe, Johann Wolfgang von. *Faust.* Doubleday; Macmillan; Norton; Oxford Univ. Pr.; Penguin. Production suppressed in Berlin (1808) until certain dangerous passages concerning freedom were deleted. Franco purged Spanish libraries of all of Goethe's writings (1939). Source: 4, p. 35.

586 _____. *The Sorrows of Werther.* Ungar. Prohibited in Denmark (1776). Purged from Spanish libraries (1939) by Spanish dictator Francisco Franco. Source: 4, p. 35; 8, pp. 298–99.

587 Going, K. L. *Fat Kid Rules the World.* Putnam. Removed from the Pickens County, S.C. middle- and high-school library shelves (2007) because "the language, the sexual references, and drug use are not appropriate for middle-school students." In 2004, the book was named a Michael Printz honor book for excellence in young-adult literature by the Young Adult Library Services Association. Source: 11, May 2007, pp. 93–94.

588 Gold, Robert S., ed. *Point of Departure.* Dell. Removed from the required reading list at the North Thurston, Wash. High School (1983) because of the book's "alleged strong language and allusions to sexual conduct." The decision was later reversed. Source: 11, July 1983, p. 109; Nov. 1983, p. 187.

589 Goldfarb, Mace. *Fighters, Refugees, Immigrants: A Tale of the Hmong.* Carolrhoda Bks. Restricted to teachers only at the Des Moines, Iowa elementary schools (1988) because the book "could lead students to form a derogatory image of Southeast Asians if they are not mature enough." Source: 11, Mar. 1988, p. 46.

590 Golding, William. *Lord of the Flies.* Coward. Challenged at the Dallas, Tex. Independent School District high School libraries (1974); challenged at the Sully Buttes, S.Dak. High school (1981); challenged at Owen, N.C. High School (1981) because the book is "demoralizing inasmuch as it implies that man is little more than an animal"; challenged at the Marana, Ariz. High School (1983) as an inappropriate reading assignment. Challenged at the Olney, Tex. Independent School District (1984) because of "excessive violence and bad language." A committee of the Toronto, Ontario, Canada Board of Education ruled on June 23, 1988, that the novel is "racist and recommended that it be removed from all schools." Parents and members of the black community complained about a reference to "niggers" in the book and said it denigrates blacks. Challenged in the Waterloo, Iowa schools (1992) because of profanity, lurid passages about sex, and statements defamatory to minorities, God, women, and the disabled. Challenged, but retained on the ninth-grade accelerated English reading list in Bloomfield, N.Y. (2000). The board was still set to review *Catcher in the Rye*, by J. D. Salinger, and *A Death in the Family*, by James Agee. Source: 11, Jan. 1975, p. 6; July 1981, p. 103; Jan. 1982 p. 17; Jan. 1984, pp. 25–26; July 1984, p. 122; Sept. 1988, p. 152; July 1992, p. 126; Mar. 2000, p. 64.

591 Goode, Erich, and Richard Troiden, eds. *Sexual Deviance and Sexual Deviants.* Morrow. Destroyed by the St. Mary's, Pa. Public Library Board (1977). Source: 11, Sept. 1977, p. 100.

592 Goodwin, June. *Cry Amandla!: South African Women and the Question of Power.*

Holmes & Meier. Banned by the Directorate of Publications in Cape Town, South Africa (1984). Without giving a reason, the Directorate declared, "it will be an offense to import or distribute" the work. Source: 11, Nov. 1984, p. 197.

593 Gordimer, Nadine. *Burger's Daughter.* Penguin; Viking. Banned on July 5, 1979, in South Africa. The decision was lifted in Oct. 1979 when the government's Publication Appeal Board overruled the earlier decision of a censorship committee. Two previous novels by Gordimer also were banned but later reinstated. In 1980, Gordimer was awarded the CNA Prize, one of South Africa's highest literary awards, for the novel. She also was awarded the Nobel Prize in literature in 1991. Source: 5, Nov./Dec. 1979, p. 69; April 1980, p. 73; 8, pp. 31–32.

594 _____. *July's People.* Viking. Challenged in the honors and academic English classes in the Carlisle, Pa. schools (1993). Teachers must send parents a letter warning about the work's content and explaining that their children may read alternate selections. Retained in the Yakima, Wash. schools (1994) after a five-month dispute over what advanced high school students should read in the classroom. Two parents raised concerns about profanity and images of violence and sexuality in the book and requested that it be removed from the reading list. Source: 11, July 1993, p. 127; Nov. 1994, pp. 202–3.

595 Gordon, Sharon. *Cuba.* Benchmark Bks. Removed from all Miami-Dade County schools libraries (2006) because a parent's complaint that the book does not depict an accurate life in Cuba. The American Civil Liberties Union (ACLU) of Florida filed a lawsuit challenging the decision to remove this book and the twenty-three other titles in the same series from the district school libraries. In granting a preliminary injunction in July 2006 against the removal, Judge Alan S. Gold of U.S. District Court in Miami characterized the matter as a "First Amendment issue" and ruled in favor of the ACLU of Florida, which argued that the books were generally factual and that the board should add to its collection, rather than removing books it disagreed with. Source: 11, July 2006, p. 207; Sept. 2006, pp. 230–31; Nov. 2006, p. 288; Jan. 2007, p. 8; May 2007, pp. 91–92.

596 Gordon, Sol. *Facts about Sex: A Basic Guide.* Educational Univ. Pr. Challenged and recommended for a "parents only" section at the Concord, Ark. school library (1984) because the book "has in it terms that would be considered vulgar by any thoughtful person." Source: 11, Jan. 1985, p. 7; May 1985, p. 75; Jan. 1986, pp. 7–8.

597 _____. *You: The Teenage Survival Book.* Times Books. Removed from the Hurst-Euless-Bedford, Tex. School District libraries (1982). Source: 9; 11, May 1982, p. 84.

598 Gould, Lois. *Necessary Objects.* Random; Dell. Removed from the Hutchinson, Kans. High School library (1976) due to its explicit sexual content. Source: 11, Jan. 1977, p. 7.

599 _____. *Such Good Friends.* Random; Dell. Removed from the Hutchinson, Kans. High School library (1976) due to its explicit sexual content. Source: 11, Jan. 1977, p. 7.

600 Gould, Steven C. *Jumper.* Tor Bks. Challenged at the West Linn-Wilsonville, Oreg. School District (1995) because according to the complainant "it was inappropriate for school children to read" because of a violent scene when the book's main character escapes from a sexual attack by a group of male truck drivers. Challenged at the Plattsburgh, N.Y. schools (1995) because of vulgarity, sex, and excessive violence. Source: 11, July 1995, p. 110; Jan. 1996, p. 16.

601 Gramick, Jeannine, and Pat Furey. *The Vatican and Homosexuality: Reactions to the "Letter to the Bishops of the Catholic Church on the Pastoral Care of Homosexual Persons."* Crossroad NY. Challenged at the Deschutes County Library in Bend, Oreg. (1993) because it "encourages and condones" homosexuality. Source: 11, Sept. 1993, pp. 158–59.

602 Graves, Robert. *I, Claudius.* Random. Banned in South Africa under the Customs Act of 1955. Source: 4, p. 76.

603 Gravett, Paul. *Manga: 60 Years of Japanese Comics.* Collins Design. Removed from all branches of the San Bernardino County, Calif. Library (2006) because "there are a couple of pretty graphic scenes, especially one showing sex with a big hamster, that are not especially endearing to our community standards." Source: 11, July 2006, pp. 181–82.

604 Grawunder, Ralph, and Marion Steinmann. *Life and Health.* Random. Banned from the Boulder, Colo. Valley Board of Education's health and sex education classes (1980) attended only by students with parental permission. Challenged in the Parma, Ohio (1985) classrooms because "it preaches a religion of moral indifference." Source: 11, Jan. 1981, p. 9; Mar. 1986, p. 42.

605 Gray, Heather M., and Samantha Phillips. *Real Girl/Real World: Tools for Finding Your True Self.* Seal Pr. Challenged, but retained at the Cape May County, N.J. Library (2006). The book explores issues such as body image, emerging sexuality, and feminism. Source: 11, Jan. 2007, p. 29.

606 Green, G. Dorsey, and D. Merilee Clunis. *Lesbian Couple.* Seal Pr. Challenged at the Muscatine, Iowa Public Library (1990) because it is "wrong to promote immorality." Source: 11, Nov. 1990, p. 225.

607 Green, Jonathon, comp. *Cassell Dictionary of Slang.* Cassell. Banned in the Wake County, N.C. schools (2006) under pressure from one of a growing number of conservative Christian groups using the Internet to encourage schoolbook bans. Source: 11, Sept. 2006, p. 231.

608 Greenberg, Jerrold S., and Robert Gold. *Holt Health.* Holt. Challenged in the Garrettsville, Ohio school system (1993) because it "condones" homosexuality. Source: 11, Nov. 1993, pp. 179–80.

609 Greenburg, David. *Slugs.* Atlantic Monthly Pr. Challenged at the Evergreen, Wash. School District libraries (1984) because of its graphic descriptions of "slugs being dissected with scissors" and its verses describing the roasting, toasting, stewing, and chewing of the creatures were potentially frightening to young children. Banned from the Escondido, Calif. Elementary School District libraries (1985) as "unsuitable and should not have been allowed in the libraries in the first place." Source: 11, Sept. 1984, p. 155; July 1985, p. 111.

610 Greene, Bette. *The Drowning of Stephan Jones.* Bantam. Removed from the curriculum and school library shelves in Boling, Tex. (1993) because the book "teaches anti-Christian beliefs and condones illegal activity." The story is about two gay men who are the objects of prejudice and violence, resulting in the drowning death of one of them. Banned from the Mascenic Regional High

School in New Ipswich, N.H. (1995) because it is about gays and lesbians. An English teacher was fired for refusing to remove the book. Removed from the Barron, Wis. School District (1998) because of the book's homosexual theme. The ACLU of Wisconsin filed suit against the school district on Feb. 16, 1999. The books were then returned to the library while a federal court considered the lawsuit. On October 8, 1999, it was agreed that the book would remain available to students as part of the school district's settlement of the federal lawsuit. Banned in the Horry County, S.C. School District Board middle school libraries (2002) because the book is "educationally unsuitable and contains unacceptable language." Challenged at the Montgomery County, Tex. Memorial Library System (2004) along with fifteen other young-adult books with gay-positive themes. The objections were posted at the Library Patrons of Texas Web site. The language describing the books is similar to that posted at the Web site of the Fairfax County, Virginia-based Parents Against Bad Books in Schools, to which Library Patrons of Texas links. Source: 8, pp. 445–46; 11, Mar. 1994, p. 53; Sept. 1996, p. 166; Jan. 1996, p. 15; Jan. 1999, p. 9; Mar. 1999, p. 37; May 1999, p. 68; Jan. 2000, p. 28; Nov. 2004, pp. 231–32.

611 _____. *Summer of My German Soldier.* Bantam; Dial. Challenged as suitable curriculum material in the Harwinton and Burlington, Conn. schools (1990) because it contains profanity and subject matter that set bad examples and gives students negative views of life. Temporarily removed from an eighth-grade supplemental reading list in Cinnaminson, N.J. (1996) because it contains offensive racial stereotypes. Source: 11, Mar. 1991, p. 44; May 1991, p. 90; Jan. 1997, p. 10.

612 Greene, Constance. *Al(Exandra) the Great.* Dell; Viking. Restricted at the Lindenwold, N.J. elementary school libraries (1984) because of "a problem with language." Source: 11, Nov. 1984, p. 185.

613 _____. *Beat the Turtle Drum.* Dell; Viking. Challenged at the Orchard Lake Elementary School library in Burnsville, Minn. (1985). Source: 11, Nov. 1985, p. 203.

614 _____. *I Know You, Al.* Viking. Removed from the Hockinson, Wash. Middle School library (1984) because the book did not uphold the principles of the United States, which were "established on the moral principles of the Bible." Challenged at the Multnomah County Library in

Portland, Oreg. (1989) because of sexual references, the presentation of divorce as a fact of life, and derogatory remarks about friends. Source: 11, Sept. 1984, p. 139; Jan. 1990, pp. 4–5.

615 **Greene, Gael.** *Dr. Love.* St. Martin. Challenged at the White County Public Library in Searcy, Ark. (1983) because "it's the filthiest thing I've ever seen." Source: 11, Nov. 1983, p. 185; Jan. 1984, p. 25.

616 **Greene, Graham.** *J'Accuse: Nice, the Dark Side.* Merrimack Pub. Cir. A French court ordered (1982) the seizure of all copies of this expose of alleged corruption in Nice. The author was also ordered to pay 100 francs for each copy seized to a building developer, Daniel Guy, who is the main figure in the book. Greene told the press that the court had made no attempt to give him or his publishers advance warning about the seizure. Source: 5, Oct. 1982, p. 34.

617 **Greene, Sheppard M.** *The Boy Who Drank Too Much.* Dell. Removed from an eighth-grade literature class in the Underwood, Minn. schools (1991) because of the book's alleged sexism, and its seeming toleration of alcohol consumption by minors. Source: 11, Mar. 1992, p. 44.

618 **Griffin, John Howard.** *Black Like Me.* Houghton. In 1966, a Wisconsin man sued the local school board, claiming that the book contained obscene language for any age level. He further charged that having read the book as an assignment in English class damaged his child. The court dismissed the case. In 1967, the parent of an Arizona high school student challenged the use of the book in the classroom because of its obscene and vulgar language and the situations depicted. The school board removed the book from the classroom. Language, particularly "four-letter words," was the charge leveled in 1977 by a Pennsylvania parent and a clergyman, but the challenge was denied. An objection to the subject matter was similarly denied in a 1982 challenge in Illinois. In Missouri in 1982, the book was placed on a closed shelf when a parent challenged the book on the grounds that it was obscene and vulgar and "because of black people bring in the book." Source: 8, pp. 421–22.

619 _____. *The Devil Rides Outside.* Smith's Inc. In 1954, bookseller Alfred E. Butler was found guilty and fined for selling the novel to an undercover police officer in Detroit, Mich.

Butler appealed to the U.S. Supreme Court, which reversed the lower court's decision. In *Butler v. Michigan*, 352 U.S. 380 (1957), the court ruled unconstitutional the standards for defining obscenity that had been used for more than seventy years by U.S. federal and state censors. It declared the view that whatever corrupted the morals of youth was obscene to be an undue restriction on the freedom of speech. Source: 13, pp. 57–59.

620 **Grimm, Jacob, and Wilhelm K. Grimm, Translated by Jack Zipes.** *The Complete Fairy Tales of the Brothers Grimm.* Bantam. Restricted to sixth- through eighth-grade classrooms at the Kyrene, Ariz. elementary schools (1994) due to its excessive violence, negative portrayals of female characters, and anti-Semitic references. Source: 11, Jan. 1994, p. 34; Sept. 1994, p. 149.

621 **Grimm, Jacob.** *Hansel and Gretel.* Dial; Putnam. Challenged at the Mount Diablo, Calif. School District (1992) because it teaches children that it is acceptable to kill witches and paints witches as child-eating monsters. Source: 11, July 1992, p. 108.

622 _____. *Little Red Riding Hood.* Houghton. Banned by two California school districts—Culver City and Empire (1990)—because an illustration shows Little Red Riding Hood's basket with a bottle of wine as well as fresh bread and butter. The wine could be seen as condoning the use of alcohol. The presence of the wine bottle in the book's illustration motivated challenges by parents of students in the fifth and sixth grades in Clay County, Fla., elementary school (1990). A Bradford County, Fla. teacher initiated a complaint (1991) that the book was violent because of the actions of the wolf. The teacher questioned the appropriateness of the little girl taking wine to her grandmother and her grandmother later drinking the wine. In the same year, two teachers in Levy County, Fla., challenged the storybook for the same reason. Source: 11, July 1990, p. 128; 14, pp. 217–18.

623 _____. *Snow White.* Knopf; Little. Restricted to students with parental permission at the Duval, Fla. County public school libraries (1992) because of its graphic violence: a hunter kills a wild boar, and a wicked witch orders Snow White's heart torn out. Source: 11, July 1992, pp. 105–6.

624 **Grisham, John.** *The Client.* Doubleday. Challenged in a sixth-grade high-level reading class in Hillsborough, N.J. (1996) because of its violence and use of "curse words." Removed from the Jackson County, W.Va. school libraries (1997) along with sixteen other titles. Source: 11, July 1996, p. 122; Sept. 1996, p. 155; Jan. 1998, p. 13.

625 _____. *The Firm.* Doubleday. Removed from the Jackson County, W.Va. school libraries (1997) along with sixteen other titles. Source: 11, Jan. 1998, p. 13.

626 _____. *The Pelican Brief.* Doubleday. Removed from the Jackson County, W.Va. school libraries (1997) along with sixteen other titles. Source: 11, Jan. 1998, p. 13.

627 _____. *A Time to Kill.* Wynwood Pr. Challenged, but retained in the Fargo, N. Dak. North High School advanced English classes (2005) despite complaints about the novel's graphic rape and murder scenes. Source: 11, July 2005, p. 161; Sept. 2005, p. 239; Jan. 2006, pp. 14–15.

628 **Groening, Matt.** *The Big Book of Hell.* Random. Challenged at the Hershey, Pa. Public Library (1995) because "the entire book teaches conduct contrary to wishes of parents" and is "trash" with "no morals." A request was made to "destroy all books of a similar nature." Source: 11, Sept. 1995, p. 158.

629 **Groom, Winston.** *Forrest Gump.* Doubleday; Pocket Bks. Challenged at the Bay Point School in South Dade County, Fla. (1999) because the novel "pokes fun at blacks, makes numerous references to sex, and uses foul language inappropriate for tenth-graders." First-year teacher Michael Weiss was fired over the incident and another instructor was placed on probation. Source: 11, July 1999, p. 95.

630 **Grotius, Hugo.** *On the Law of War and Peace.* Kessinger Pub. In 1662, the States-General of Netherlands banned the book. The Spanish Inquisition condemned all of his books, and in the eighteenth century his complete works were placed on the Index of Forbidden books, where they remained until 1966. Source: 1, pp. 239–40.

631 **Gruenberg, Sidonie M.** *The Wonderful Story of How You Were Born.* Doubleday. Moved from the children's room of the Tampa-Hillsborough County, Fla. Public Library (1982) to the adult section. Source: 11, Jan. 1982, pp. 4–5.

632 **Grumbach, Jane, and Robert Emerson, eds.** *Monologues: Women II.* Drama Bks. Removed from a suggested reading list at Adams City, Colo. High School (1990) after a parent complained about obscene language in the book. Source: 11, Jan. 1991, p. 15.

633 **Guammen, David.** *To Walk the Line.* Knopf. Banned from all libraries in the Enid, Okla. public school system libraries (1974). Source: 11, Mar. 1975, p. 41.

634 **Guare, John.** *Landscape of the Body.* Dramatists Play Service. Challenged at the Manatee County School District in Bradenton Beach, Fla. (1998) because the play includes a paragraph in which a woman describes being in a pornographic movie. Source: 11, May 1998, p. 71.

635 **Guest, Judith.** *Ordinary People.* Ballantine; Hall; Viking. Temporarily banned in Enon, Ohio (1981) from junior and senior English classrooms. Challenged at the Merrimack, N.H. High School (1982) after a parent found the novel obscene and depressing. Challenged in North Salem, N.Y. (1985) as an optional summer reading book because of profanity and graphic sex scenes and because its topic—teenage suicide—was too intense for tenth graders. Challenged because it is "degrading to Christians," but retained at the Anaheim, Calif. Union High School District (1993). No longer required reading at Delta High School in Delaware, Ind. (1994) due to profanity and descriptions of sexual situations in the novel. Removed from the Faulkton, S.Dak. (1994) district classrooms. Temporarily pulled from the Lancaster, N.Y. High School curriculum (1996) because two parents contended it contains foul language, graphic references to sex, and inappropriate handling of the subject of suicide. A Lancaster student took the matter to the New York Civil Liberties Union, which sent a letter to the school board saying that it was "greatly dismayed" with the board's action. Removed, but later returned to the English classrooms and library shelves at the Fostoria, Ohio High School (1999) despite complaints about the novel's obscene language and sexual innuendos. Source: 11, Jan. 1982, p. 77; Sept. 1982, p. 170; Sept. 1985, p. 168; May 1993, pp. 86–87; Nov. 1993, pp. 192–93; Jan. 1994, p. 14; Sept. 1994, pp. 150, 152; Sept. 1996, pp. 155–56; Nov. 1996, p. 197; July 1999, p. 104.

636 _____. *Second Heaven.* NAL. Challenged in the Greenville County, S.C. schools (1991) because the book uses the name of God and

Jesus in a "vain and profane manner along with inappropriate sexual references." Source: 11, July 1991, p. 130.

637 Gunther, John. *Death Be Not Proud.* Harper. Retained by the Edgecombe County Board of Education in Tarboro, N.C. (1995) after complaints that the "book has words in it that even unsaved people would have spanked their children for saying." Source: 11, May 1995, p. 84.

638 _____. *Inside Russia Today.* Harper and Brothers. Removed from the Glenwood, Iowa, school library shelves (1970) along with eight other titles—*The Catcher in the Rye*, by J. D. Salinger; *Who's Afraid of Virginia Woolf*, by Edward Albee; *Looking Backward*, by Edward Bellamy; *The Liberal Hour*, by John Kenneth Galbraith; *Black Like Me*, by John H. Griffin; *Black Power*, by Stokley Carmichael; and an unknown title. After considerable controversy, the banned books were returned to the library shelves. Source: 7, pp. 234–35.

639 Guterson, David. *Snow Falling on Cedars.* Harcourt; Thorndike Pr.; Vintage. Challenged in the Snohomish, Wash. School District (1997) by parents who acknowledged the book's literary value, but complained that its descriptions of sexual intercourse, masturbation, and use of obscene language make it inappropriate for high school students. The book won the prestigious PEN/Faulkner award and was named 1995 book of the year by the American Booksellers Association. Pulled from the Boerne, Tex. Independent High School library and barred from the curriculum (1999) after several parents and students complained about its racial epithets and sexually graphic passages. The book was later returned to the library. Restricted by the South Kitsap, Wash. School District board (2000) after critics complained about the book's sexual content and profanity. After being approved by committees at the high school and district levels, the book was being considered for the district's approved reading list for high school students. Students are not required to read listed books of which they or their parents disapprove. Challenged, but retained in the advanced English classes in Modesto, Calif. (2003). The seven-member Modesto City School Board said administrators should instead give parents more information about the books their children read, including annotations of each text. Parents can opt their children out of any assignment they find objectionable. Source: 8, pp. 381–85; 11, Sept. 1997, p. 129; Nov. 1999, p. 163; Jan. 1999, pp. 8, 12; July 2000, p. 106; Jan. 2004, pp. 27–28.

640 Guthrie, Alfred B., Jr. *The Big Sky.* Bantam. Banned in Amarillo, Tex. (1962). Challenged in the Big Timber, Mont. schools (1991) because the book is filled with explicit, vulgar language. Source: 4, p. 82; 11, Mar. 1992, p. 44.

641 _____. *The Way West.* Houghton. Banned in Amarillo, Tex. (1962). Source: 4, p. 82.

642 Guy, Rosa. *Edith Jackson.* Viking. Removed from all school libraries collections in St. Tammany Parish, La. (1984) because its "treatment of immorality and voyeurism does not provide for the growth of desirable attitudes," but later reinstated. Source: 11, May 1984, p. 69; July 1984, p. 121.

643 _____. *The Music of Summer.* Delacorte. Removed from Adamson Middle School shelves, and Clayton, Ga.'s public libraries (1994) and placed in the young adult section for eighth graders and up because of a "really gross" sex scene. Source: 11, July 1994, p. 109.

644 Haas, Ben. *Daisy Canfield.* Pocket Bks.; Simon & Schuster. Challenged at the Covington, La. Public Library (1984) because it "had objectionable language throughout." Source: 11, July 1984, p. 103.

645 Haddix, Margaret Peterson. *Don't You Dare Read This, Mrs. Dunphrey.* Simon. Banned from the Galt Joint Union Elementary School District classrooms in Sacramento, Calif. (2003) and restricted to students with parental permission in the middle school libraries. The novel discusses parental neglect, sexual harassment at an after-school job, and other stresses experienced by the young-adult fictional character. The novel is on the ALA Best Books for Young Adults list. Source: 11, Mar. 2004, p. 52; May 2004, p. 98.

646 Haddon, Mark. *The Curious Incident of the Dog in the Night-Time.* Doubleday. Challenged at the Galveston, Tex. County Reads Day (2006) because the book could "pollute" young minds. Source: 11, March 2006, pp. 71–72.

647 Hahn, Mary Downing. *Wait Till Helen Comes.* Clarion Bks. Challenged in the Lawrence, Kans. School District curriculum (1996) because the book presents suicide as a viable, "even attractive way of dealing with family problems. Ghosts, poltergeists and other supernatural phenomena are presented as documented reality and these are capable of deadly harm to children." Source: 11, May 1996, pp. 87–88.

648 **Haislip, Barbara.** *Stars, Spells, Secrets and Sorcery.* Dell. Challenged at Nashotah, Wis. school library (1993) because the book "promotes satanism." Source: 11, May 1993, p. 86.

649 **Haldeman, Joe.** *War Year.* Holt. Removed from the Soldotna, Alaska Junior High School library (1981) because of its raw language and graphic descriptions of battlefield violence. Source: 11, July 1981, p. 91.

650 **Haley, Gail E.** *Go Away, Stay Away.* Scribner. Challenged, but retained, in the Echo Park Elementary School media center in Apple Valley, Minn. (1994). A parent filed the complaint because the story "was frightening subject matter and [I] didn't see a good lesson in [it]." Source: 11, July 1994, p. 129.

651 **Hall, Elizabeth.** *Possible Impossibilities.* Houghton. Challenged at the Sikes Elementary School media center in Lakeland, Fla. (1985) because the book "would lead children to believe ideas contrary to the teachings of the Bible." Source: 11, July 1985, p. 133.

652 **Hall, Radclyffe.** *The Well of Loneliness.* Avon. Suppressed in England (1928) as obscene. The London Sunday Express denounced it as "a challenge to every instinct of social sanity and moral decency which distinguishes Christian civilization from the corruptions of paganism." Publisher arrested in New York City (1929). Source: 4, p. 71; 6, pp. 1,019–21; 15, Vol. III, pp. 416–17.

653 **Halle, Louis J.** *Men and Nations.* Princeton. Challenged in the Jefferson County, Ky. School District (1982) because the book is a "soft sell of communism." Source: 11, Mar. 1983, p. 41.

654 **Hamilton, David.** *Age of Innocence.* Aurum Pr. Ltd. Despite pressure from protestors demanding that Barnes & Noble face child pornography charges, a prosecutor in Cobb County, Ga. (1998) declined to take the nation's largest bookstore chain to court for carrying Hamilton's book. Activists from Operation Rescue claimed the book contains children in sexually suggestive positions and should be deemed illegal. Barnes & Noble officials noted that the decision follows similar rulings by prosecutors in Texas, Maryland, Kansas, and Wisconsin. Source: 11, Jan. 1999, p. 20.

655 **Hamlin, Liz.** *I Remember Valentine.* Dutton; Pocket Bks. Challenged at the Commerce, Tex. High School library (1990) because of "pornographic" material in the book. The complainant asked that all "romance" books be removed. Source: 11, Mar. 1991, p. 43.

656 **Hanckel, Frances, and John Cunningham.** *A Way of Love, A Way of Life: A Young Person's Introduction to What It Means to Be Gay.* Lothrop. Challenged in Atlantic, Iowa (1982) because it is a "morally corrupting force"; removed from two Anniston, Ala. high school libraries (1982) but later reinstated on a restrictive basis. Challenged at the Fairbanks, Alaska North Star Borough School District libraries (1984) because schools should teach the basics, "not how to become queer dope users." Challenged at the Barron, Wis. School District (1998) because the book is about homosexuality. Source: 11, May 1982, p. 82; Mar. 1983, p. 37; Sept. 1984, pp. 137, 149–50; Jan. 1999, p. 9; Mar. 1999, p. 37.

657 **Handford, Martin.** *Where's Waldo?* Little. Challenged at the Public Libraries of Saginaw, Mich. (1989) because "on some of the pages there are dirty things." Removed from the Springs Public School library in East Hampton, N.Y. (1993) because there is a tiny drawing of a woman lying on the beach wearing a bikini bottom but no top. Source: 11, May 1989, p. 78; July 1993, p. 100.

658 **Hanigan, James P.** *Homosexuality: The Test Case for Christian Sexual Ethics.* Paulist Pr. Challenged at the Deschutes County Library in Bend, Oreg. (1993) because it "encourages and condones" homosexuality. Source: 11, Sept. 1993, pp. 158–59.

659 **Haning, Peter.** *The Satanists.* Taplinger. Challenged by the "God Squad," a group of three students and their parents, at the El Camino High School in Oceanside, Calif. (1986) because the book "glorified the devil and the occult." Source: 11, Sept. 1986, p. 151; Nov. 1986, p. 224; Jan. 1987, p. 9.

660 **Hanley, James.** *Boy.* Boriswood Ltd. Police seized the book from a lending library in Manchester (1934) and charged the librarian with distributing an "obscene publication." Impounded under British obscenity law for its graphic violence and brutal sexuality (1934). Source: 13, pp. 29–30.

661 **Hansberry, Lorraine.** *A Raisin in the Sun.* Random. Responding to criticisms from an anti-pornography organization, the Ogden, Utah School District (1979) restricted circulation of Hansberry's play. Challenged, but retained in the Normal, Ill. Community High School sophomore literature class (2004) despite objections that the play is degrading to African Americans. Source: 11, May 1979, p. 49; Sept. 2004, pp. 177–78.

662 **Harcourt, J. M.** *Upsurge.* Banned throughout Australia on 20 November 1934 when the Trade and Custom Department released its report, concluding: "This book is not without merit, though somewhat crude. But it is disfigured by some grossly indecent passages, without any excuse of being necessary." Source: 6, pp. 1,028–29.

663 **Hardin, Garrett.** *Population, Evolution and Birth Control.* Freeman. The Brighton, Mich. School Board (1977) voted to remove all sex education books from the high school library. Source: 11, Sept. 1977, p. 133.

664 **Hardy, Thomas.** *Jude the Obscure.* Airmont; Bantam; Bobbs-Merrill; Houghton; NAL; Norton; St. Martin. Banned by Bristol, England circulating libraries (1896). Source: 4, p. 51; 8, pp. 349–51.

665 _____. *Tess of the D'Urbervilles.* Bantam; Houghton; NAL; Norton; Penguin; St. Martin. Banned by Mudie's and Smith's circulating libraries (1891) and the novel was also object of banning by the Watch and Ward Society in Boston, Mass., which charged that the novel contained illicit sexuality and immorality. The society forced Boston booksellers to agree that they would not advertise or sell the novel, and most adhered to the request. Banned by the Bristol, England circulating libraries (1896). Source: 4, p. 51; 13, pp. 242–43.

666 **Harington, Donald.** *Lightning Bug.* Harcourt. Challenged at the Rogers-Hough Ark. Memorial Library (1991) because the book uses language "very descriptive of. . . perverted sex." Source: 11, Sept. 1991, p. 151.

667 **Harkness, John, and David Helgren, eds.** *Populations.* Globe Book Co. Removed from the Palmyra, N.J. School District's science curriculum (1994) after nearly three hours of passionate debate between parents who believed the book presented only one side of how world overpopulation should be addressed and teachers who found it an integral part of the class curriculum. Source: 11, Mar. 1995, p. 45.

668 **Harlan, Elizabeth.** *Footfalls.* Atheneum; Ballantine. Challenged at the Obsidian Junior High School in Redmond, Oreg. (1988) for its profanity and sexual content. Source: 11, Jan. 1989, p. 3.

669 **Harris, E. Lynn.** *And This Too Shall Pass.* Doubleday. Challenged, but retained, at the Central High School in Louisville, Ky. (1998) despite claims the book describes homosexual acts in a positive light. Source: 11, Mar. 1998, p. 55; May 1998, p. 71.

670 _____. *Invisible Life.* Anchor; Consortium. Challenged, but retained, at the Central High School in Louisville, Ky. (1998) despite claims the book is pornographic and a recruitment tool for the gay community. Source: 11, Mar. 1998, p. 55; May 1998, p. 71.

671 _____. *Just As I Am.* Anchor; Doubleday. Challenged, but retained, at the Central High School in Louisville, Ky. (1998) despite claims the book describes homosexual acts in a positive light. Source: 11, Mar. 1998, p. 55; May 1998, p. 71.

672 **Harris, Frank.** *My Life and Loves.* Grove. Banned in England (1922); imports banned in the U.S. and frequently destroyed by U.S. Customs (1922-1956). Source: 4, p. 54; 13, pp. 170–71; 15, Vol. III, p. 415.

673 **Harris, Raymond, ed.** *Best Selling Chapters.* Jamestown Pubs. Challenged, but retained, in a sixth-grade literature class at Hichborn Middle School in Howland, Nebr. (1993). The challenge was directed at the Ray Bradbury story, "A Sound of Thunder," which contains "offensive" language. Challenged in the Keene, N.H. Middle School (1993) because of some of the language and subject matter in the textbook, specifically in passages from John Steinbeck's *Of Mice and Men*; *To Kill a Mockingbird*, by Harper Lee; and *A Day No Pigs Would Die*, by Robert Newton Peck. The complainant objected to expressions such as "crazy bastard," "hell" and "damn," "Jesus Christ," and "God Almighty." Source: 11, Sept. 1993, p. 160; Jan. 1994, p. 15.

674 _____. *Best Short Stories, Middle Level.* Jamestown Pubs. Challenged, but retained, in a sixth-grade literature class at Hichborn Middle

School in Howland, Nebr. (1993). The challenge was directed at the Ray Bradbury story, "A Sound of Thunder," which contains "offensive" language. Source: 11, Sept. 1993, p. 160.

675 Harris, Robie H. *It's Perfectly Normal: A Book about Changing Bodies, Growing Up, Sex, and Sexual Health.* Candlewick Pr. Challenged at the Provo, Utah Library (1996) because it contains discussions of intercourse, masturbation, and homosexuality. Removed from the Clover Park, Wash. School District library shelves (1996) because parents charged that it was too graphic and could foster more questions than it answers. Challenged at the Chester County, Pa. Library (1996) because the "book is an act of encouragement for children to begin desiring sexual gratification . . . and is a clear example of child pornography." Challenged, but retained, in the children's section of the Mexico-Audrain County, Mo. Library (1997). A Baptist minister complained not only about this title, but also about other "material concerning family sensitive issues, such as sexuality, the death of a loved one, or the birth process." Challenged, but retained, at the Fargo, N.Dak. Public Library (1997). The statement requesting the book's removal cited the book as "too explicit, pornographic, and too easily accessible to children." Challenged, but retained at the Auburn-Placer County, Calif. Library (1999) because of sexually explicit material. Challenged in the Holland, Mass. Public Library (2000) due to its sexually explicit content. The book was moved from the children's to the adult section of the library. Challenged at the Marion County, Fla. Public Library (2001). Critics called the book pornographic and demanded it be permanently removed from the library or placed in a special restricted-access area. Restricted to elementary school pupils with parental permission at the Anchorage, Alaska (2001) due to objections to the book's "value statements" and because "marriage is mentioned once in the whole book, while homosexual relationships are allocated an entire section." Challenged, but retained in the Montgomery County, Tex. library system (2002) after a conservative Christian group, the Republican Leadership Council, characterized the book as "vulgar" and trying "to minimize or even negate that homosexuality is a problem." Relocated from the young adult to the adult section of the Fort Bend County Libraries in Richmond, Tex. (2003). The same title was recently moved to the restricted section of the Fort Bend School District's media centers after a resident sent an e-mail message to the superintendent expressing concern about the book's content. The Spirit of Freedom Republican Women's Club petitioned the superintendent

to have it, along with *It's So Amazing*, moved because they contain "frontal nudity and discussion of homosexual relationships and abortion." Challenged, but retained at the Holt Middle School parent library in Fayetteville, Ark. (2005) despite a parent's complaint that it was sexually explicit. Source: 8, pp. 346–48; 11, Sept. 1996, p. 152; Jan. 1997, p. 8; Mar. 1997, p. 49; Nov. 1997, p. 181; Jan. 1998, p. 27; Nov. 1999, p. 171; Sept. 2000, p. 143; Mar. 2001, p. 54; Nov. 2001, pp. 247, 278; Jan. 2002, p. 13; Nov. 2002, pp. 256–57; Jan. 2003, p. 33; Jan. 2004, p. 9; May 2005, p. 135; Sept. 2005, p. 215; Nov. 2005, pp. 295–96.

676 _____. *It's So Amazing.* Candlewick Pr. Relocated from the young adult to the adult section of the Fort Bend County Libraries in Richmond, Tex. (2003). The same title was recently moved to the restricted section of the Fort Bend School District's media centers after a resident sent an e-mail message to the superintendent expressing concern about the book's content. The Spirit of Freedom Republican Women's Club petitioned the superintendent to have it, along with *It's Perfectly Normal: A Book about Changing Bodies, Growing Up, Sex, and Sexual Health,* moved because they contain "frontal nudity and discussion of homosexual relationships and abortion." Restricted, but later returned to general circulation shelves with some limits on student access, based on a review committee's recommendations, at the Holt Middle School parent library in Fayetteville, Ark. (2005) despite a parent's complaint that it was sexually explicit. Relocated to the reference section of the Northern Hills Elementary school media center in Onalaska, Wis. (2005) because a parent complained about its frank yet kid-friendly discussion of reproduction topics, including sexual intercourse, masturbation, abortion, and homosexuality. Source: 11, Jan. 2004, p. 9; May 2005, p. 135; Sept. 2005, p. 215; Nov. 2005, pp. 281–82, 295–96.

677 Hart, Jack. *Gay Sex: Manual for Men Who Love Men.* Alyson Pubns. Challenged at the Fort Vancouver, Wash. Regional Library (1993) when a group of citizens asked the Goldendale City Council to establish more restrictive criteria for sexually explicit material. Source: 11, July 1993, p. 103.

678 Hartinger, Brent. *Geography Club.* HarperTempest. Withdrawn from Curtis Junior High and Curtis Senior High school libraries (2005) after a University Place, Wash. couple with children in both schools filed a written complaint. They wrote that the book could result in a "casual and loose approach to sex," encourage use of Internet porn, and the physical meeting of people through chat rooms. Source: 11, Jan. 2006, pp. 12–13; March 2006, p. 73.

679 Hartley, William H., *and William S.* Vincent. American Civics. Harcourt. Challenged in Mahwah, N.J. (1976) by several local residents and a school trustee who argued that it "promotes socialized medicine and considers government a big machine with the people having no voice." The deciding vote on the issue was split, 4—4, in effect denying the use of the textbook for ninth grade. Source: 7, p. 30.

680 Harwood, Richard. *Did Six Million Really Die?* Historical Review Pr. Canadian law bars the import of materials considered seditious, treasonable, immoral, or indecent; so-called hate crime is included in these categories. Ernest Zundel, the publisher, was charged under S.181 of Canada's Criminal Code with "publishing false news" and was tried in 1985 for publishing a booklet that denies the official accounts of Nazis exterminating Jews in wartime prison camps. The case worked its way in the Canadian courts and ruling in 1992 (*R. v. Zundel*), the Supreme Court in a 4-3 decision held that section 181 of the Criminal Code was indeed unconstitutional as a violation of the right of freedom of expression guarantees. The code requires the expression to be nonviolent; the court found the novel to be nonviolent. Thus, Zundel was acquitted. Publishing or distributing neo-Nazis or Holocaust-denial literature is illegal in Germany. Zundel was convicted during the 1991 visit to Germany for inciting racial hatred. Source: 7, pp. 149–50.

681 Hashak, Israel. *Jewish History, Jewish Religion.* Westview. Challenged at the Milford, Mass. Library (1995) because it is anti-Semitic. Source: 11, May 1995, p. 66.

682 Haskins, Jim. *Voodoo and Hoodoo.* Madison Bks.; Original Pubns. Banned at the Clearwood Junior High School library in Slidell, La. (1992) because the book included "recipes" for spells. U.S. District Court Judge Patrick Carr ruled on October 6, 1994, that the St. Tammany Parish School Board couldn't ban the book solely because members do not approve of its content. A week later, the board voted 8-5 to appeal the judgment. The school board appealed the decision to the U.S. Court of Appeals for the Fifth Circuit. On April 1, 1996, the St. Tammany Parish School Board, however, ended the four-year attempt to ban the book by returning it to the library. Under

the agreement, it will be available only with written parental permission to students in eighth grade or above. Momentum for a settlement occurred after two board members who fought to ban the book left the board in 1994. Additionally, the board's insurer indicated that it might not foot the bill if the board continued to fight the suit. Source: 11, July 1992, p. 106; Sept. 1992, p. 137; Jan. 1993, p. 23; Mar. 1993, p. 41; Jan. 1995, pp. 19–20; Sept. 1995, p. 153; July 1996, p. 134.

683 Hastings, Selina. *Sir Gawain and the Loathly Lady.* Lothrop; Macmillan. Challenged at the public libraries of Saginaw, Mich. (1989). The complainant requested the library to "white out the swearing" which appears on page 16 of the book. The objectionable words were "God Damn You." Challenged at the elementary school libraries in Antigo, Wis. (1992) because a parent objected to a reference to the Loathly Lady as a "hell-hag" and to another passage in which the Black Knight suggests that King Arthur "roast in hell." Source: 11, May 1989, p. 77; Jan. 1993, p. 28.

684 Haugaard, Erick C. *The Samurai's Tale.* Houghton. Challenged at the Wilsona School District in Lake Los Angeles, Calif. (1995) because of violence and references to Buddha and ritual suicide. Source: 11, Jan. 1996, p. 13.

685 Hautzig, Deborah. *Hey Dollface.* Greenwillow. Challenged at the Bend, Oreg. High School (1993) because it "encourages and condones" homosexuality. Challenged at the Montgomery County, Tex. Memorial Library System (2004) along with fifteen other young-adult books with gay-positive themes. The objections were posted at the Library Patrons of Texas Web site. The language describing the books is similar to that posted at the Web site of the Fairfax County, Virginia-based Parents Against Bad Books in Schools, to which Library Patrons of Texas links. Source: 11, Sept. 1993, pp. 158–59; Nov. 2004, pp. 231–32.

686 Hawes, Hampton. *Raise Up Off Me.* Coward. Challenged at the King High School in Corpus Christi, Tex. (1989) because the book contains "vulgar language and descriptions of abnormal sexual activity." Source: 11, Jan. 1990, p. 32.

687 Hawthorne, Nathaniel. *The Scarlet Letter.* Bantam; Dell; Dodd; Holt; Houghton; Modern Library; NAL; Norton. Subject of savage attacks by moralists in 1852. The National Board of

Censorship forced the producers of the film version to change a few things; for one, Hester has to get married. Challenged in Michigan high school English classes (1961) by parents claiming that it was "pornographic and obscene." They demanded that the book be taken out of the curriculum, but the request was denied. Challenged again in Michigan a parent and principal objecting to the inclusion of the novel in the high school curriculum (1977) because it dealt with a clergyman's "involvement in fornication." The book was removed from the classroom use and from the recommended reading list. That same year, a parent in Missouri condemned the book for its use of "4-letter words" and "other undesirable content" and demanded its removal from the high school library. The school librarian recognized that the parent had not read the book because no obscenities appeared in the novel, and she convinced the parent of his error. The book was retained. Banned from the Lindale, Tex. Advanced Placement English reading list (1996) because the book "conflicted with the values of the community." Challenged, but retained in the sophomore curriculum at West Middlesex, Pa. High School (1999). Source: 8, pp. 480–81; 9, p. 142; 11, Nov. 1996, p. 199; July 1999, p. 105; 15, Vol. I, p. 562.

688 **_____. *Young Goodman Brown and Other Short Stories.*** Dover. Challenged at the Copenhagen, N.Y. Central School (1992) because the story may give children the wrong message about witchcraft. Source: 11, Jan. 1993, p. 12.

689 Hayden, Penny. *Confidence.* Bantam; Doubleday. Expurgated by an apparent self-appointed censor at the Coquille, Oreg. Public Library (1994) along with several other books. Most were mysteries and romances in which single words and sexually explicit passages were whited out by a vandal who left either dots or solid ink pen lines where the words had been. Source: 11, Sept. 1994, p. 148.

690 Hedayat, Sadegh. *The Blind Owl.* Grove Pr. The widely acclaimed Iranian classic, written in the 1930s, was banned in Iran (2006). "The new government intends to take positive steps for reviving neglected values and considering religious teachings in the cultural field." Source: 11, Jan. 2007, p. 35.

691 Hedderwick, Mairi. *Katie Morag and the Tiresome Ted.* Little. Challenged at the public libraries of Saginaw, Mich. (1989) because on the last page of the story "the mother's sweater is open to fully expose her breast." The library was asked to cover the drawing with a marker. Source: 11, May 1989, p. 77.

692 Hedges, Peter. *What's Eating Gilbert Grape.* Simon. Banned by the superintendent at the Carroll, Iowa High School (2006) because of parental concerns about an oral sex scene. In response, students started an Internet protest on the social network Facebook. Hundreds joined the group— "Un-ban Gilbert Grape! Censorship is Wrong"—and organizers say they plan to collect signatures calling for a formal review. "Parents were already notified of its content, and had to sign a permission slip for their child to read it." Later, the Carroll school board voted to overturn Superintendent Rob Cordes' decision to ban the book from the high school's literature-to-film class. The author said, "The district shouldn't let those larger themes be obscured by the relatively few pages with sexual content that he intended to drive plot." Source: 11, Jan. 2007, pp. 12–13; Mar. 2007, p. 73.

693 Hegi, Ursula. *Stones from the River.* Scribner; Simon. Banned, but later reinstated after community protests at the Windsor Forest High School in Savannah, Ga. (2000). The controversy began in early 1999 when a parent complained about sex, violence, and profanity in the book that was part of an Advanced Placement English class. Source: 11, Mar. 2000, p. 63; Mar. 2001, p. 76.

694 Heidish, Marcy. *Woman Called Moses.* Bantam; Houghton. Removed by a patron at the Wilmington, N.C. school library (1992) because of strong language. Source: 11, July 1992, p. 107.

695 Heinlein, Robert. *Stranger in a Strange Land.* Putnam. Challenged, but retained in the South Texas Independent School District in Mercedes, Tex. (2003). Parents objected to the adult themes—sexuality, drugs, and suicide—found in the 1962 Hugo Award-winning novel. Heinlein's book was part of the summer Science Academy curriculum. The board voted to give parents more control over their childrens' choices by requiring principals to automatically offer an alternative to a challenged book. Source: 11, Nov. 2003, pp. 249–50.

696 Heller, Joseph. *Catch-22.* Modern Library; Simon & Schuster. Banned in Strongsville, Ohio (1972), but school board's action was overturned in 1976 by a U.S. District Court in *Minarcini v. Strongsville City School District*, 541 F.2d 577 (6th Cir. 1976). Challenged at the Dallas, Tex.

Independent School District high school libraries (1974); in Snoqualmie, Wash. (1979) because of its several references to women as "whores." Source: 4, p. 96; 8, pp. 433–34; 11, Jan. 1975, p. 6; July 1979, p. 85; 12, pp. 145–48.

697 _____. *Good as Gold.* Pocket Bks. Banned on June 28, 1979, in South Africa. The government's censorship authorities gave no reason. Source: 5, Nov. /Dec. 1979, p. 69.

698 _____. *Something Happened.* Ballantine; Knopf. Banned in South Africa (1974). The government's censorship authorities gave no reason. Source: 5, Nov. /Dec. 1979, p. 69.

699 **Helms, Tom.** *Against All Odds.* Crowell. Removed from the Evergreen School District of Vancouver, Wash. (1983) along with twenty-nine other titles. The American Civil Liberties Union of Washington filed suit contending that the removals constitute censorship, a violation of plaintiff's rights to free speech and due process, and the acts are a violation of the state Open Meetings Act because the removal decisions were made behind closed doors. Source: 11, Nov. 1983, pp. 185–86.

700 **Helper, Hinton Rowan.** *The Impending Crisis of the South: How to Meet It.* Burdick Brothers. Published in 1857, the author suggested the elimination of slavery and book was banned in most Southern states. In North Carolina, the Reverend Daniel Worth had to stand trial for owning the text, and in Arkansas three men were hanged for owning the book. Source: 9, p. 131.

701 **Helvetius, Claude-Adrien.** *De L'Esprit.* Kessinger Pub. Condemned as atheistic, materialistic, sacrilegious, immoral, and subversive, the epitome of all the dangerous philosophical trends of the age. Banned by the archbishop of Paris (1758), the pope (1759), the Parlement of Paris (1759), and the Sorbonne (1759), the book became an underground best seller. Source: 1, pp. 71–72.

702 **Hemingway, Ernest.** *Across the River and into the Trees.* Scribner. Banned in Ireland (1953) and South Africa (1956) as "objectionable and obscene." Source: 4, p. 80.

703 _____. *A Farewell to Arms.* Scribner. The June 1929 issue of Scribner's Magazine, which ran Hemingway's novel, was banned in Boston, Mass. (1929). Banned in Italy (1929) because of its painfully accurate account of the Italian retreat from Caporetto, Italy; banned in Ireland (1939);

challenged at the Dallas, Tex. Independent School District high school libraries (1974); challenged at the Vernon-Verona-Sherill, N.Y. School District (1980) as a "sex novel"; burned by the Nazis in Germany (1933). Source: 2, p. 137; 4, pp. 79–80; 11, Jan. 1975, pp. 6–7; May 1980, p. 62.

704 _____. *For Whom the Bell Tolls.* Scribner. Declared nonmailable by the U.S. Post Office (1940). On Feb. 21, 1973, eleven Turkish book publishers went on trial before an Istanbul martial law tribunal on charges of publishing, possessing, and selling books in violation of an order of the Istanbul martial law command. They faced possible sentences of between one month's and six month's imprisonment "for spreading propaganda unfavorable to the state" and the confiscation of their books. Eight booksellers also were on trial with the publishers on the same charge involving For Whom the Bell Tolls. Source: 4, p. 80; 5, Summer 1973, xii.

705 _____. *The Killers.* Macmillan. Challenged, but retained, in the Bridgeport, Conn. public schools (1995). The short story, published in 1927, repeatedly uses the word "nigger." It was not part of the curriculum, but was chosen by a teacher as part of a unit on violence in literature. Source: 11, Jan. 1996, p. 30.

706 _____. *The Sun Also Rises.* Scribner. Banned in Boston, Mass. (1930), Ireland (1953), Riverside, Calif. (1960), and San Jose, Calif. (1960). Burned in Nazi bonfires (1933). Source: 4, pp. 79–80; 14, pp. 272–73.

707 _____. *To Have and Have Not.* Scribner. Banned in Detroit, Mich. (1938) and distribution forbidden in Queens, N.Y. (1938). Source: 4, pp. 79–80; 14, pp. 274–75; 15, Vol. III, p. 652.

708 **Hendrix, Harville.** *Keeping the Love You Find: A Guide for Singles.* Pocket Bks. Pulled from the Staples-Motley, Minn. High School health classes (1995) because its sexual subject matter was deemed inappropriate for freshmen and sophomores. The book was not a textbook or required reading, but a resource. Source: 11, May 1995, p. 70.

709 **Henege, Thomas.** *Skim.* Dodd. Publication canceled by Dodd, Mead & Company (1983) because of language in the book considered "objectionable" by Thomas Nelson, Inc. of Nashville, Tenn.—Dodd, Mead's parent company. Source: 11, Nov. 1983, p. 188.

710 **Hentoff, Nat.** *The Day They Came to Arrest the Book.* Dell. Challenged in the Albemarle County schools in Charlottesville, Va. (1990) because it offers an inflammatory challenge to authoritarian roles. Source: 11, Jan. 1991, p. 18.

711 **Herbert, Frank.** *Soul Catcher.* Ace Bks. Challenged, but retained, at the Lake Washington School District in Kirkland, Wash. (1993) despite objections there is "a very explicit sex scene," it is "a mockery of Christianity," and "very much anti-God." Source: 11, Jan. 1994, p. 16; Mar. 1994, p. 71.

712 **Herge.** *Tintin in America.* Little. Removed from the Spokane, Wash. School District libraries (1995) as racially demeaning and insulting. Source: 11, Jan. 1996, p. 12.

713 **Herman, Victor.** *Coming Out of the Ice.* Harcourt. Restricted to seniors at the Mount Baker High School in Bellingham, Wash. (1998). In addition, before the book is assigned, parents will get a summary of its plot, along with a description of the graphic passages that led one parent to ask that the book be pulled from the high school's curriculum. Source: 11, July 1998, p. 110.

714 **Hermes, Patricia.** *Solitary Secret.* Harcourt. Moved from the library at Parker, Colo. Junior High School (1988) to the senior high school because of its graphic detail of sex. Source: 11, Mar. 1988, p. 45.

715 **Heron, Ann.** *How Would You Feel If Your Dad Was Gay?* Alyson Pubns. Challenged at the Mesa, Ariz. Public Library (1993) because it "is vile, sick and goes against every law and constitution." Retained at the Dayton and Montgomery County, Ohio Public Library (1993). Challenged, but retained, in the Oak Bluffs, Mass. school library (1994). Though the parent leading the protest stated that "The subject matter . . . is obscene and vulgar and the message is that homosexuality is okay," the selection review committee voted unanimously to keep the book. Source: 11, Jan. 1994, p. 34; Mar. 1994, p. 69; May 1994, p. 98.

716 _____. *One Teenager in Ten: Testimony by Gay and Lesbian Youth.* Alyson Pubns. Challenged at the Deschutes County Library in Bend, Oreg. (1993) because it "encourages and condones" homosexuality. Retained at the Estes Park, Colo. Public Library (1994) after challenges to the book for its graphic content. Source: 11, Sept. 1993, pp. 158–59; Sept. 1994, p. 165.

717 _____. *Two Teenagers in Twenty.* Alyson Pubns. Removed from the Barron, Wis. School District (1998) because of the book's homosexual theme and because it contains outdated information about AIDS. The ACLU of Wisconsin filed suit against the school district on Feb. 16, 1999. The book was then returned to the library while a federal court considered the lawsuit. On October 8, 1999, it was agreed that the book would remain available to students as part of the school district's settlement of the federal lawsuit. Source: 11, Jan. 1999, p. 9; Mar. 1999, p. 37; May 1999, p. 68; Jan. 2000, p. 28.

718 **Herron, Carolivia.** *Nappy Hair.* Knopf; Dragonfly. Challenged in Brooklyn, N.Y. (1998) because it was considered racially insensitive. Source: 11, Jan. 1999, p. 10; Mar. 1999, p. 25.

719 **Herzberg, Max J.** *Myths and Their Meanings.* Allyn & Bacon. Challenged in the Woodland Park, Colo. High School (1992) because the stories about mythological figures like Zeus and Apollo threaten Western civilization's foundations. Source: 11, May 1992, p. 82.

720 **Hesse, Hermann.** *Steppenwolf.* Holt. Forbidden by Hitler in Germany (1943-44) for its "lewd lustfulness." Challenged at the Glenwood Springs, Colo. High School library (1982) due to book's references to lesbianism, hermaphroditism, sexual perversion, drug use, murder, and insanity. Source: 9; 11, Sept. 1982, p. 169; 14, pp. 263–64.

721 **Hewitt, Kathryn.** *Two by Two: The Untold Story.* Harcourt. Challenged at the Hubbard, Ohio Public Library (1991) because the book alters the story of Noah's Ark, making it secular and confusing to children. Source: 11, Sept. 1991, p. 153.

722 **Hill, Douglas Arthur.** *Witches and Magic-Makers.* Knopf. Challenged, but retained at the Hastings, Nebr. Public Library (1999) along with forty other books on the topics of witches, magic, the zodiac, fortune telling, and ghost stories (most of the Dewey Decimal category 133.47). The books were called "demonic" and unsuitable for young children. Source: 11, May 1999, p. 66; July 1999, p. 104.

723 **Hinton, S. E.** *The Outsiders.* Dell; Viking. Challenged on an eighth-grade reading list in the South Milwaukee, Wis. schools (1986) because "drug and alcohol abuse was common" in the novel and "virtually all the characters were from broken homes." Challenged at the Boone, Iowa

School District (1992) because the book glamorizes smoking and drinking and uses excessive violence and obscenities. Challenged at the George Washington Middle School in Eleanor, W.Va. (2000) due to objections to the focus on gangs and gang fights. Source: 11, Jan. 1987, p. 13; Nov. 1992, p. 199; July 2000, p. 106.

724 _____. **Rumble Fish.** Delacorte; Dell. Challenged at the Poca Middle School in Charleston, W.Va. (1991) because the book is "too frank." Source: 11, Jan. 1992, p. 9.

725 _____. **Tex.** Dell. Challenged due to foul language and violence, but retained at Campbell Middle School in Daytona Beach, Fla. (1995). Restricted by the Central Dauphin school board in Harrisburg, Pa. (2000) due to graphic language. Source: 11, May 1995, pp. 69–70; July 1995, pp. 110–11; Sept. 2000, p. 144.

726 _____. **That Was Then, This Is Now.** Dell; Viking. Challenged at the Pagosa Springs, Colo. schools (1983) because a parent objected to the "graphic language, subject matter, 'immoral tone,' and lack of literary quality." Challenged on an eighth-grade reading list in the South Milwaukee, Wis. schools (1986) because "drug and alcohol abuse was common" and "virtually all the characters were from broken homes." Challenged at the Poca Middle School in Charleston, W.Va. (1991) because the book is "too frank." Source: 9; 11, Mar. 1984, p. 53; Jan. 1987, p. 13; Jan. 1992, p. 9.

727 **Hitchcock, Alfred.** **Alfred Hitchcock's Witches Brew.** Random. Challenged at the Fond du Lac, Wis. school system (1982) because the anthology contains stories about magic, witchcraft, and the supernatural. Source: 11, Mar. 1983, p. 39.

728 **Hite, Shere.** **The Hite Report on Male Sexuality.** Knopf. Challenged at the Southern Pine, N.C. Public Library (1983) because it is inappropriate "for the development of moral character in children or anyone for that matter." Source: 11, May 1983, p. 85.

729 **Hitler, Adolf.** **Mein Kampf.** Houghton. Banned in Palestine (1937), Czechoslovakia (1932) for its fierce militaristic doctrines. Banned from the 158 Stars and Stripes bookstores in West Germany. Since all Nazi literature has been banned in West Germany for decades, the circulation manager for the U.S. government chain stated, "we're guests in Germany, and I think we should show certain

respect to our hosts." The publisher of the first unabridged Czech edition received a three-year suspended sentence for promoting Nazism. Czech police seized some 300 copies of the book. Source: 4, p. 72; 8, pp. 130–34; 11, Jan. 1989, p. 14; Mar. 2001, p. 62.

730 **Hobbes, Thomas.** **Leviathan.** Penguin. Placed on the Catholic Church's Index of Forbidden books (1703) and banned in Holland because of its frank materialism. He was forbidden thereafter by the English government from publishing his philosophic opinion. His complete works were listed on the Roman Index until 1966. Source: 1, pp. 187–88.

731 **Hobson, Laura Z.** **Gentleman's Agreement.** Simon. Banned from reading lists at DeWitt Clinton High School, Bronx, N.Y. (1948), by the high school principal "on the grounds that it makes light of extramarital relations." After considerable protest, the board of superintendents reversed the ban eight months later. Source: 14, pp. 154–55.

732 **Hodges, Hollis.** **Don't Tell Me Your Name.** Avon; Crown. Relegated to the restricted shelf at the Covington Junior High School Library in Vancouver, Wash. (1985), the Evergreen School Board reversed its earlier ruling and decided to keep the novel despite parents' contention it is sexually explicit and inappropriate for junior high readers. Source: 11, July 1985, p. 133; Nov. 1985, pp. 203–4; July 1986, p. 118.

733 **Hogan, William.** **The Quartzsite Trip.** Avon. Challenged at Vancouver, Wash. Pacific Junior High School library (1985) because "the subject matter was too adult for junior high school students." Placed in a collection for teacher use only in the Lincoln, Nebr. East High School library (1987) after a complaint was filed by a teacher. Source: 11, May 1985, p. 91; July 1985, p. 134; Nov. 1987, p. 225.

734 **Hoke, Helen.** **Witches, Witches, Witches.** Watts. Challenged at the Smith Valley, Nev. school libraries (1988) because the book "is replete with scenes of intrusion, oppression, cannibalism, abduction, transformation, incantations, deceptions, threats, and sexism." Source: 11, July 1988, pp. 121–22; Sept. 1988, p. 178.

735 **Holland, Margaret, and Craig McKee.** **The Unicorn Who Had No Horn.** Willowsip Pr. Challenged at the Cornell, Wis. Elementary School

library (1991) because it allegedly promotes "New Age religion" and includes content related to witchcraft and the occult. Source: 11, Jan. 1992, p. 6; Mar. 1992, p. 63.

736 **Holliday, Laurel.** *Children in the Holocaust and World War II: Their Secret Diaries.* Pocket Bks. Limited to students in the seventh grade or higher at the Canal Winchester Middle School in Columbus, Ohio (1999) because of references to sex, a self-induced abortion, and drug use. Source: 11, July 1999, p. 94; Nov. 1999, pp. 171–72.

737 **Homer.** *The Odyssey.* Airmont; Doubleday; Harper; Macmillan; NAL; Oxford Univ. Pr.; Penguin. Plato suggested expurgating Homer for immature readers (387 B.C.) and Caligula tried to suppress it because it expressed Greek ideals of freedom (35). Source: 4, p. 1.

738 **Homes, A. M.** *Jack.* Vintage. Placed on the Spindale, N.C. school library's (1996) reserve shelf. This meant parental permission was required for a student to check it out. A parent did not find the novel "proper to be in the library due to the language." Challenged in the Barron, Wis. School District (1998). Source: 11, Nov. 1996, pp. 193–94; Jan. 1999, p. 9.

739 **Hoobler, Dorothy, and Thomas Hoobler.** *Nelson and Winnie Mandela.* Watts. Challenged at the Hillsboro, Oreg. Public Library (1988) by a patron who charged that the Mandelas and the African National Congress are Communist-backed and advocate violence. After being reviewed, the book was retained in the library's collection. Source: 7, p. 361; 11, Jan. 1989, p. 3.

740 **Hotze, Sollace.** *A Circle Unbroken.* Houghton. Challenged at Cary, Ill. Junior High School (1994) because references in the book to sex are too explicit for seventh and eighth graders; retained by school board vote. Source: 11, May 1994, p. 83; July 1994, pp. 128–29.

741 **Howe, Norma.** *God, the Universe and Hot Fudge Sundaes.* Houghton. Challenged at the Canby, Oreg. Junior High School library (1988) because the book "pushes several items of the humanist agenda: death education, anti-God, pro-evolution, anti-Bible, anti-Christian, and logic over faith." Source: 11, May 1989, p. 78.

742 **Hoyt, Olga.** *Demons, Devils and Djinn.* Abelard-Schuman. Challenged at Elkhorn Middle

School in Frankfort, Ky. (1990) because "it describes devil worship." Source: 11, May 1990, p. 84; July 1990, p. 145.

743 **Hubbard, L. Ron.** *Mission Earth.* Bridge Pubns. Inc. Challenged at the Dalton, Ga. Regional Library System (1990) because of "repeated passages involving chronic masochism, child abuse, homosexuality, necromancy, bloody murder, and other things that are anti-social, perverted, and anti-everything." Source: 11, July 1990, p. 125.

744 **Huegel, Kelly.** *GLBTQ: The Survival Guide for Queer and Questioning Teens.* Free Spirit Pub. Challenged in the Fayetteville, Ark. High School library (2005). The complainant also submitted a list of more than fifty books, citing the books as too sexually explicit and promoting homosexuality. Source: 11, Sept. 2005, p. 215.

745 **Hughes, Langston.** *The Best Short Stories by Negro Writers.* Little. Removed from the Island Trees, N.Y. Union Free District High School library in 1976 along with nine other titles because they were considered "immoral, anti-American, anti-Christian, or just plain filthy"; returned to the library after the U.S. Supreme Court ruling on June 25, 1982, in *Board of Education, Island Trees Union Free School District No. 26 et al. v. Pico et al.,* 457 U.S. 853 (1982). Source: 11, Nov. 1982, p. 197.

746 **Hughes, Tracy, ed.** *Everything You Need to Know about Teen Pregnancy.* Rosen. Challenged, but retained, at the Cleveland, Tenn. Public Library (1993) along with seventeen other books, most of which are on sex education, AIDS awareness, and some titles on the supernatural. Source: 11, Sept. 1993, p. 146.

747 **Hugo, Victor.** *Hernani.* French & European; Larousse. Banned by Nicholas I in Russia (1850). Source: 4, p. 41.

748 _____. *Les Miserables.* Dodd; Fawcett; Penguin. Listed in the *Index Librorum Prohibitorum* in Rome from 1864-1959; voted out of a library by a Philadelphia, Pa. (1904) because it mentioned a grisette. Source: 2, p. 92; 4, p. 41.

749 _____. *Notre Dame de Paris.* Penguin. Banned by Nicholas I in Russia (1850). Listed in the *Index Librorum Prohibitorum* in Rome from 1864-1959. Source: 4, p. 41.

750 Hull, Eleanor. *Alice with the Golden Hair.* Atheneum. Removed, but later reinstated at the Pine Middle School library in Gibsonia, Pa. (1990) because of its adult language. Source: 11, Nov. 1990, pp. 209–10; Jan. 1991, pp. 28–29.

751 Hume, David. *On Religion.* Collins; World Pub. Co. In 1827, all of his historical and philosophical works were placed on the Index of Forbidden books, where they remained until 1966. Banned in Turkey (1986). Source: 1, pp. 77–78; 5, July/Aug. 1986, p. 46.

752 Humphrey, Derek. *Final Exit.* Hemlock Soc. Challenged at the Cook Memorial Library in Libertyville, Ill. (1991) because the book "diminishes the value of the elderly and encourages breaking the law by assisting homicide and drug abuse." Banned in Australia (1992). After an appeal by the book distributors, in June 1992, the Australian Film and Literature Board of Review reversed the decision of the censors and classified the book as Category I—Restricted. Under this designation, the book must be sealed in plastic and cannot be sold to anyone under the age of 18. That same year, New Zealand customs officials were ordered to seize all copies of the book coming into the country and to hold them until the Office of Indecent Publications could review the suitability of the work. After careful review, the censors determined that the book would be permitted unrestricted entry. In Britain, because assisted suicide is against the law, publisher will not publish the work. Source: 8, p. 454; 11, Jan. 1992, p. 25.

753 Hunter, Evan. *The Chisholms.* Harper. A Livermore Valley, Calif. Unified School District book selection committee (1981) voted to remove this title from the Granada High School library due to poor literary quality, gratuitous violence, as well as explicitly sexual passages. Source: 11, Jan. 1982, p. 8.

754 Hurston, Zora Neale. *Their Eyes Were Watching God.* Chelsea House Pubs., Negro Univ. Pr., Univ. of Ill. Pr. Challenged for sexual explicitness, but retained on the Stonewall Jackson High School's academically advanced reading list in Brentsville, Va. (1997). A parent objected to the novel's language and sexual explicitness. Source: 11, Nov. 1997, pp. 169–70; Jan. 1998, p. 29.

755 Hurwin, Davida. *Time for Dancing.* Puffin. Challenged, along with seventeen other titles in the Fairfax County, Va. elementary and secondary libraries (2002), by a group called Parents Against Bad Books in Schools. The group contends the books "contain profanity and descriptions of drug abuse, sexually explicit conduct, and torture." Source: 11, Jan. 2003, p. 10.

756 Hus, Jan. *De Ecclesia.* Greenwood Pr. His work denied the pope's infallibility and proposed that the state should supervise the church. Put on trail at the church Council of Constance, Germany, he was convicted of heresy. His books destroyed, and he was burned at the stake (1415). Source: 1, pp. 66–67.

757 Hutchins, Maude. *A Diary of Love.* Greenwood. Banned by the Chicago, Ill. Police Bureau of Censorship in 1950 because the book was "so candidly filthy in spots as to constitute a menace to public morals." Source: 15, Vol. IV, p. 710.

758 Huxley, Aldous. *Antic Hay.* Harper; Bantam; Modern Library. Banned on grounds of obscenity in Boston, Mass. (1930). A Baltimore, Md. (1952) teacher was dismissed for assigning Huxley's novel to his senior literature class. The teacher's unsuccessful quest for vindication is reported in *Parker v. Board of Education*, 237 F.Supp. 222 (D. Md.). Source: 4, p. 75; 12, pp. 23, 230.

759 _____. *Brave New World.* Harper. Banned in Ireland (1932). Removed from classroom in Miller, Mo. (1980) and challenged frequently throughout the U.S. Challenged as required reading at the Yukon, Okla. High School (1988) because of "the book's language and moral content." Challenged as required reading in the Corona-Norco, Calif. Unified School District (1993) because it is "centered around negative activity." The book was retained, and teachers selected alternatives if students object to Huxley's novel. Removed from the Foley, Ala. High School library (2000) pending review, because a parent complained that its characters showed contempt for religion, marriage and the family. The parent complained to the school and to Alabama Governor Don Siegelman. Challenged, but retained in the South Texas Independent School District in Mercedes, Tex. (2003). Parents objected to the adult themes—sexuality, drugs, and suicide—found in the novel. Huxley's book was part of the summer Science Academy curriculum. The board voted to give parents more control over their childrens' choices by requiring principals to automatically offer an alternative to a challenged book. Source: 4, p. 75; 5; 8, pp. 424–25; 11, May 1980, p. 52; July 1988, p. 140; Jan. 1994, p. 14; Mar. 1994, p. 70; Nov. 2000, p. 193; Jan. 2001, p. 11; Nov. 2003, pp. 249–50.

760 _____. **The Doors of Perception.** Harper. Challenged at the Oconto, Wis. Unified School District (1980) because it "glorifies the use of drugs." Source: 11, Mar. 1981, p. 41.

761 _____. **Eyeless in Gaza.** Harper. Banned in Ireland (1926-1953). Source: 4, p. 75.

762 _____. **Point Counter Point.** Harper. Banned in Ireland (1930) on the grounds of offending public morals. The ban was not revoked until 1970. Source: 4, p. 75; 13, p. 194.

763 **Hyde, Margaret O., and Elizabeth Forsyth. Know about AIDS.** Walker. Challenged, but retained, at the Cleveland, Tenn. Public Library (1993) along with seventeen other books, most of which are on sex education, AIDS awareness, and some titles on the supernatural. Source: 11, Sept. 1993, p. 146.

764 **Ibsen, Henrik. A Doll's House.** Penguin. Four members of the Alabama State Textbook Committee (1983) called for the rejection of Ibsen's work because it propagates feminist views. Source: 11, Mar. 1983, p. 39.

765 _____. **An Enemy of the People.** Penguin. Works purged by Franco government (1939); works formerly banned reported to be extremely popular in USSR (1938). Source: 4, p. 48.

766 _____. **Four Great Plays by Ibsen.** NAL. Challenged, but retained, in the Carroll County, Md. schools (1991). Two school board members were concerned about the play, Ghosts, which deals with venereal disease, incest, and suicide. Source: 11, Mar. 1992, p. 64.

767 _____. **Ghosts.** Beekman; Dutton. Banned in England (1892); purged by the Franco government (1939). Ban lifted in USSR (1958). Source: 4, p. 48.

768 **Illustrated Encyclopedia of Family Health.** Marshall Cavendish. Removed from the library at Sage Valley Junior High School in Gillette, Wy. (1986) after a resident said the book contained photographs that were "very nude and very explicit." Challenged in an intermediate school library in Beaverton, Oreg. (1991) because of explicit line drawings of sexual intercourse positions and removed from the library, but maintained for staff use only. Source: 11, July 1986, p. 118; July 1992, p. 103.

769 **Irving, John. A Prayer for Owen Meany.** Ballantine; Morrow. Pulled from the Boiling Springs High School senior literature class in Carlisle, Pa. (1992) after several complaints from parents about its content and language. Challenged in the Kanawha County, W.Va. high schools (2000) as "pornographic, offensive and vulgar." The novel is on the county book list for suggested reading material for the eleventh and twelfth grades. Source: 11, July 1992, p. 112; Sept. 1992, p. 142; July 2000, p. 106.

770 **Isay, Richard. Being Homosexual: Gay Men and Their Development.** Avon; Farrar. Challenged at the Deschutes County Library in Bend, Oreg. (1993) because it "encourages and condones" homosexuality. Source: 11, Sept. 1993, pp. 158–59.

771 **Isensee, Rick. Love Between Men.** Prentice-Hall; Alyson Pubns. Challenged at the Chester County Library at Charlestown, Pa. (1996) because it was "pornographic and smutty." Source: 11, Nov. 1996, p. 194.

772 **Ives, Vernon. Russia.** Holiday. Removed from library shelves at Proctor and New Hartford, N.Y. high schools (1955) on the advice of a textbook commission of the New York Education Department. According to the commission, the book, while not seditious or disloyal, contained passages "that are either untrue or almost certain to evoke untrue inferences." Banned by the Avoyelles Parish school board in Marksville, La., (1966) because the book was "pro-Russian in comparing Russia to the United States." Source: 7, pp. 435–36.

773 **Izzi, John. Metrication, American Style.** Phi Delta Kappa Ed. Banned at the Toll Gate High School in Warwick, R.I. (1985) because it is "discriminatory toward women." Source: 11, July 1985, p. 114.

774 **Jackson, Jesse. Call Me Charley.** Harper. Parents of a black fourth-grade student filed suit against Grand Blanc, Mich. school officials (1979) after a teacher read this title to their son's class. The work includes a white character who calls a black youth "Sambo," "nigger," and "coon." Source: 11, Mar. 1979, p. 38.

775 **Jackson, Shirley. The Lottery.** Ency. Brit.; Farrar; Popular Library. The film version of Jackson's short story was banned in Forest Lake, Minn. but

reinstated by U.S. District Court judge (1981). Source: 9; 11, July 1981, p. 88.

776 Jacobs, Anita. *Where Has Deedie Wooster Been All These Years?* Delacorte. Removed from the Hockinson, Wash. Middle School library (1984) because it is "garbage" and the novel's discussion of a young girl's first menstrual cycle is particularly objectionable. Source: 11, Sept. 1984, p. 138.

777 Jagendorf, Moritz A. *Tales of Mystery: Folk Tales from Around the World.* Silver Burdett. Removed to a locked closet in the superintendent's office in Banner County, Nebr. (1992) because the book "has to do with a lot of negative things and might not be good for someone with low self-esteem or suicide tendencies." Source: 11, May 1992, p. 80.

778 Jaivin, Linda. *Eat Me.* Broadway Bks. Removed from the Marion County Public Library in Ocala, Fla. (2003). The library director noted that the Australian bestseller was removed because the library lacks a designated erotica collection, and the novel met only three of seventeen criteria used to evaluate books for acquisition. The Marion County Public Library Advisory Board recommended that the library director retain the novel. The board's vote was only a suggestion and the final decision went back to the library director. In Feb. 2004, the director reversed her earlier decision, reinstated the novel, and stated that her personal dislike for the book overshadowed her objectivity and adherence to policy. Source: 11, Jan. 2004, pp. 7–8; Mar. 2004, pp. 47–48; May 2004, pp. 115–16; Sept. 2004, pp. 175–76.

779 Jakes, John. *Bastard.* Jove. Removed from the Montour, Pa. High School library (1976). Source: 11, Nov. 1976, pp. 143–44.

780 James, Henry. *Turn of the Screw.* Tor Bks. Challenged at the St. Johns County Schools in St. Augustine, Fla. (1995). Source: 11, Jan. 1996, p. 14.

781 James, Norah C. *Sleeveless Errand.* Scholaris Pr. Police seized copies at the premises of Scholaris Press (1929) and the director of public prosecution cited the "obscene" language used by the characters as evidence of its "shocking depravity." The magistrate ruled in favor of the prosecution and granted the destruction order, stating that the novel suggested "thoughts of the most impure character" to readers of all ages. Source: 13, p. 223.

782 Jameson, Jenna and Neil Strauss. *How to Make Love Like A Porn Star: A Cautionary Tale.* Regan Books. Houston, Tex. mayor ordered city librarians (2005) to keep the book behind the counter. After committee review, the autobiography, which spent six weeks on the *New York Times* bestseller list, was returned to the open shelves. Source: 11, Mar. 2005, pp. 55–56; May 2005, pp. 131–32.

783 Jay, Carla, and Allen Young. *The Gay Report.* Summit. Challenged at the Niles, Mich. Community Library (1982). Source: 11, Jan. 1983, p. 8.

784 Jefferson, Thomas. *A Summary View of the Rights of British America.* John Dunlap. Banned for political reasons in Russia under Czar Nicholas I (1833). Source: 7, p. 476.

785 Jenness, Aylette. *Families: A Celebration of Diversity, Commitment and Love.* Houghton. Temporarily removed, but later reinstated, at the Winfield, Ill. Public Library (1990) because of objections to two of the stories. One involves a gay couple that adopted a baby at birth and the other involves a lesbian couple that raises one of the couple's children. Source: 11, Mar. 1991, p. 61.

786 Jennings, Gary. *Black Magic, White Magic.* Dell; Dial; Hart-Davis. Retained at the Ector County, Tex. school library (1989) after being challenged because the book might lure children into the occult. Source: 11, Jan. 1990, p. 9; May 1990, p. 107.

787 Jennings, Kevin, ed. *Becoming Visible: A Reader in Gay and Lesbian History for High School and College Students.* Alyson Pubns. Banned from the two high school libraries in Mehlville, Mo. (1996) by order of the superintendent. The donated book was removed because it "does not meet the needs of the curriculum." Source: 11, May 1996, pp. 82–83.

788 Jeschke, Susan. *The Devil Did It.* Holt. Challenged at the elementary school libraries in Howard County, Md. (1990) because it shows the devil as "a benign or friendly force." Source: 11, Jan. 1991, p. 12.

789 Jewkes, Wilfred Thomas. *The Perilous Journey.* Harcourt. Pulled from the curriculum of the Baltimore County, Md. school system (1989) because a three-page retelling of an African-

American folk legend was considered racially insensitive. The offensive story was "All God's Chillen Had Wings." Source: 11, Jan. 1990, p. 11.

790 **Jimenez, Carlos M.** *The Mexican-American Heritage.* TQS Pubs. Challenged in the Santa Barbara, Calif. schools (1996) because the book promotes "Mexican nationalism." Source: 11, May 1996, p. 98.

791 **Johnson, Earvin (Magic).** *What You Can Do to Avoid AIDS.* Times Books. Removed from the Horace Greeley High School in Chappaqua, N.Y. (1996) because a group of parents complained that the basketball player's written description of oral and anal sex were inappropriate for 14- and 15-year-olds. Johnson's book is endorsed by the American Medical Association and the Children's Defense Fund. Source: 11, May 1996, p. 88; July 1996, p. 119.

792 **Johnson, Eric W.** *Love and Sex and Growing Up.* Bantam. Challenged, but retained, at the Cleveland, Tenn. Public Library (1993) along with seventeen other books, most of which are on sex education, AIDS awareness, and some titles on the supernatural. Source: 11, Sept. 1993, p. 146.

793 _____. *Love and Sex in Plain Language.* Lippincott/Harper; Bantam. Moved from the children's room of the Tampa-Hillsborough County, Fla. Public Library (1982). Challenged in the Williamsport, Pa. schools (1988) because of allegedly inaccurate and misleading information in the book. Source: 11, Jan. 1982, pp. 4–5; May 1988, p. 104.

794 _____. *Sex: Telling It Straight.* Bantam; Lippincott. Placed on restricted shelves at the Evergreen School District elementary school libraries in Vancouver, Wash. (1987) in accordance with the school board policy to restrict student access to sex education books in elementary school libraries. Source: 11, May 1987, p. 87.

795 **Johnson, Julie.** *Adam & Eve & Pinch Me.* Little. Challenged at the Greenville, S.C. middle school libraries (1997) because the book uses objectionable language like "damn" and "jerk-ass." Source: 11, Sept. 1997, p. 126.

796 **Johnson, Sam, et al.** *Beavis and Butt-Head Ensucklopedia.* MTV Books; Pocket Bks. Challenged at the Salt Lake County, Utah Public Library (1995) by a parent because it has "no literary value whatsoever. It was totally perverse garbage, trash. I consider it pornography." The complainant requested the removal of all Beavis and Butt-Head materials, including seven cassettes, seven CDs, and two copies of *MTV's Beavis and Butt-Head Experience.* Source: 11, May 1995, pp. 67–68.

797 **Jonas, Ann.** *Aardvarks Disembark.* Greenwillow. Challenged at the Hubbard, Ohio Public Library (1991) because the book alters the story of Noah's Ark, making it secular and confusing to children. Source: 11, Sept. 1991, p. 153.

798 **Jones, Clinton R.** *Understanding Gay Relatives and Friends.* Seabury Pr. Challenged at the Elkhart, Ind. Public Library (1982) because it attempts to "get people to accept the homosexual lifestyle, like there is nothing wrong with it." Source: 11, Mar. 1983, p. 56.

799 **Jones, James.** *From Here to Eternity.* Dell; Dial. Won the National Book Award (1951). Banned in Holyoke and Springfield, Mass. and in Denver, Colo. (1951). Banned from the mails in 1955 by the New York City post office. In 1956, the prosecuting attorney in Port Huron, St. Clair County, Mich., ordered booksellers and distributors to cease displaying and selling all books that appeared on the disapproved list of the National Organization for Decent Literature, a Catholic censorship group founded in 1938. Source: 4, p. 94; 13, pp. 82–83.

800 **Jong, Erica.** *Fear of Flying.* Holt. Challenged in Terre Haute, Ind. (1982) as optional reading in an elective course for junior and senior high school students. Source: 11, May 1982, p. 86.

801 **Jordan, June.** *Living Room.* Thunder's Mouth. Banned from the Baldwin, Mich. High School library (1990) because it contains profanity and racial slurs. Source: 11, Jan. 1991, p. 12.

802 **Josephs, Rebecca.** *Early Disorders.* Fawcett; Farrar. Challenged at the Mukwonago, Wis. High School (1988) because the book's "portrayal of anorexia nervosa was not factual and the account of a girl's life, thoughts, and emotions used pornographic language and made fun of religion." Source: 11, May 1988, p. 104.

803 **Joyce, James.** *Dubliners.* Modern Library; Penguin. Destroyed by printer because he found passages objectionable (1912). Source: 4, p. 65.

804 _____. ***Exiles.*** Penguin. Banned in Turkey (1986). Source: 5, July/Aug. 1986, p. 46.

805 _____. ***Ulysses.*** Farrar; Modern Library; Random/Vintage. Burned in U.S. (1918), Ireland (1922), Canada (1922), England (1923) and banned in England (1929). In *United States v. One Book Entitled "Ulysses,"* 5 F.Supp. 182 (S.D.N.Y. 1993), later affirmed in *United States v. One Book Entitled "Ulysses,"* 72 F.2d 705 (2d Cir. 1934), the U.S. courts established the possibility of a defense of literary merit against the charges of obscenity. Source: 4, pp. 65–66; 6, p. 412; 8, pp. 391–92; 15, Vol. III, pp. 411–12, 557–58, 645.

806 Jukes, Mavis. ***The Guy Book: An Owner's Manual.*** Crown Pub. Challenged in the Lockwood, Mont. Middle School library (2006) by parents who objected to what they believe to be misleading, sexually explicit material in the book. The book was retained. The challenge came on the heels of a December decision by the board to pull three books from the middle-school library. Those books were *The Vanishing Hitchhiker: American Urban Legends,* by Jan Brunvand, and *Urban Legends* and *Alligators in the Sewer,* both by Thomas Craughwell. The same parent brought those titles—and their content—to the attention of the librarian and superintendent. Source: 11, May 2006, pp. 129–30.

807 _____. ***It's a Girl Thing: How to Stay Healthy, Safe and in Charge.*** Knopf. Written parental permission is required to see the book at the Palm Beach, Fla. elementary and middle schools (1999) because of concerns that the book—written for preteen girls—is more explicit than some parents would find acceptable. Source: 11, May 1999, p. 66.

808 Julian, Cloyd J., and Nancy S. Simon. ***Family Life and Human Sexuality.*** Holt. Challenged as a supplemental text in an elective course in the Omaha, Nebr. School District (1987) because the book promotes "Planned Parenthood, abortion, and artificial methods of birth control." The book was adopted after the course's previous text, *Finding My Way,* by Andrew Riker, was replaced because it was considered too controversial. Source: 11, Nov. 1987, p. 225.

809 Juster, Norton. ***The Phantom Tollbooth.*** Collins; Knopf; Penguin; Random; Scholastic. Removed from a locked reference collection at the Boulder, Colo. Public Library (1988). The book was originally locked away because the librarian considered it a poor fantasy. Source: 11, Jan. 1989, p. 27.

810 Kallen, Stuart A. ***Ghastly Ghost Stories.*** Abdo & Dghtrs. Challenged, but retained, in the Warrensburg-Latham, Ill. school library (1992) because the series of seven books are "possibly harmful to a child's psychological development." Source: 11, Jan. 1993, p. 7; Mar. 1993, p. 41.

811 _____. ***Vampires, Werewolves and Zombies.*** Abdo & Dghtrs. Challenged, but retained, at the Cleveland, Tenn. Public Library (1993) along with seventeen other books, most of which are on sex education, AIDS awareness, and some titles on the supernatural. Source: 11, Sept. 1993, p. 146.

812 Kane, William M., and Mary Bronson Merki. ***Human Sexuality: Relationships and Responsibilities.*** Glencoe. Challenged at the Bremerton, Wash. schools (1992) because it allegedly is "based on fraudulent research, stresses homosexuality, and is inappropriate for teenagers." Source: 11, July 1992, p. 112.

813 Kane, William; Peggy Blake; and Robert Frye. ***Understanding Health.*** Random. Challenged in Jefferson County, Ky. (1983) because it contains a chapter on sex education, which includes slang sexual terminology. Banned from the curriculum at the Oak Hills, Ohio High School (1983) because the book discusses abortion, premarital sex, and euthanasia. Source: 11, Sept. 1983, p. 142; Nov. 1983, p. 186; July 1984, p. 107; Sept. 1984, p. 157.

814 Kant, Immanuel. ***The Critique of Pure Reason.*** St. Martin. Placed on the Roman Index until the 20th century. Prohibited in the Soviet Union (1928) along with all of Kant's writings, presumably because the metaphysical and transcendental themes of Kant's works were thought to conflict with Marxist-Leninist ideology. All of Kant's works were purged from libraries of Spain under the Franco dictatorship in 1939. Source: 3, p. 163; 4, p. 31; 8, p. 288.

815 _____. ***Religion within the Boundaries of Pure Reason.*** Continuum. Banned by the Lutheran church because, "Our sacred person you have with your so-called philosophy attempted to bring into contempt. . . and you have at the same time assailed the truth of the Scriptures and the foundations of Creed beliefs. . . We order that henceforth you shall employ your talents to better purpose and that you shall keep silence on matters which are outside of your proper functions." Prohibited in the Soviet Union (1928) along with all of Kant's writings, presumably because the metaphysical and transcendental themes of Kant's works were thought to conflict with Marxist-Leninist ideology. All of Kant's works were purged from libraries of Spain under the Franco dictatorship in 1939. Source: 3, p. 163; 8, pp. 286–88.

816 Kantor, MacKinlay. *Andersonville.* NAL. Banned from the four Amarillo, Tex. High schools and at Amarillo College (1962) because its political ideas and that its author was cited by the House Un-American Activities Committee. Withdrawn from the eleventh grade reading list at the Whitehall, Mich. High School (1963) because the book "wasn't fit for high school students." Challenged, but retained in Amherst, Ohio high school (1967) despite claims the book is "filth." Challenged in Rock County, Wis. (1969). Challenged, but retained in the Buncombe County, N.C. schools (1973 and 1981) despite claims the book was unsuitable for school libraries because it contains objectionable language. Source: 4, pp. 11–12; 8, pp. 10–12.

817 Kauffmann, Stanley. *The Philanderer.* Simon. Condemned by legal authorities on the Isle of Man (1953) after police received a complaint that a person could obtain the book at Boots' Library. The novel's trial was influential in changing the obscenity law in England, a change motivated largely by the summation of Mr. Justice Sable, who presided over the trial in the Queen's Bench Division in the Old Bailey. Sable warned that if criminal law were to be driven too far in the desire to stamp out the "bawdy muck," there existed a risk of a revolt, "a demand for a change in the law, so that the pendulum may swing to far the other way and allow to creep in things that at the moment we can keep out." The decision was not binding on future cases because it was not a court of appeal judgment, and Customs and postal authorities continued to seize books in transit, but this case set the stage for change in English obscenity laws. Source: 13, pp. 190–91.

818 Kaufman, Joe. *How We Are Born, How We Grow, How Our Bodies Work, and How We Learn.* Golden Pr. Removed from circulation collection, and now available only as a reference book, at the Old Kings Elementary School in Bunnell, Fla. (1991) because two pages on the reproductive process were found objectionable. Source: 11, Mar. 1992, p. 40.

819 Kaufman, Sue. *Falling Bodies.* Doubleday. Challenged in Terre Haute, Ind. (1982) as optional reading in an elective course for junior and senior high school students. Source: 11, May 1982, p. 86.

820 Kaysen, Susanna. *Girl, Interrupted.* Vintage. Removed temporarily from the curriculum, pending its review, from the Orono, Maine High School (2006) after a parent complained about strong language and vivid descriptions. Movie stars Angelina Jolie and Winona Ryder brought the book into the limelight when they starred in the 2000 film version. Source: 11, March 2006, pp. 73–74.

821 Kazan, Elia. *Acts of Love.* Knopf; Warner. Removed from the Utah State Library bookmobile (1980). Source: 11, Nov. 1980, p. 128.

822 Kazantzakis, Nikos. *The Last Temptation of Christ.* Simon & Schuster. The author was excommunicated in 1954 from the Eastern Orthodox Church. The same year the novel was also placed on the Roman Catholic Church's Index of Forbidden Books. Challenged in Long Beach, Calif. (1962-1965). Banned in Singapore (1988) as a result of pressure from fundamentalist Christians. Challenged, but retained, at the Sussex County Community College in Newton, N.J. (1998) despite an employee's charges that the book is "totally offensive" and "an outrage and insult to every Christian in the world." Source: 4, p. 68; 8, pp. 260–61; 11, Mar. 1999, p. 47.

823 Keable, Robert. *Simon Called Peter.* Dutton. The Boston Watch and Ward Society brought charges against Edith Law of Arlington, Mass., the owner of a Boston rental library, who was convicted in the Cambridge District Court in October 1922 and fined $100 for stocking the novel in her rental library. In an appeal, Judge Stone suspended the fine but warned Law that she faced a jail sentence if she were ever again convicted in an obscenity case. The case drew particular attention because the novel had been a best seller for more than a year. The New York Society for the Suppression of Vice tried without success to have the book banned (1922), but the courts refused to hear the complaint. Source: 13, pp. 219–20.

824 Keefer, Edward C., ed. *Foreign Relations of the United States 1964-68, Volume XXVI, Indonesia, Malaysia-Singapore, Philippines.* U.S. State Department. The U.S. government recalled all copies of this U.S. State Department history book from hundreds of libraries in the U.S. and abroad (2001) because it details the U.S. role in Indonesia's deadly purge of communists in the 1960s. The prestigious series, which began in 1861, is often embattled. For example, the history dealing with Greece, Cyprus, and Turkey was printed in February 2000, but is locked up at the Government Printing Office under the label: "Embargo: This publication cannot be released." Officials declined to say why. Source: 11, Nov. 2001, pp. 245–46.

825 Keehn, Sally. *I Am Regina.* Philomel Bks. Challenged as optional fifth-grade reading at the Orland Park, Ill. School District 135 (1996) because the book uses unflattering stereotypes to depict Native Americans and uses the word "squaw," which was offensive. Source: 11, Jan. 1997, p. 10.

826 Keeping, Charles. *Through the Window.* Oxford Univ. Pr.; Watts; Weston Woods. Challenged at the Cedar Rapids, Iowa Public Library (1985) because "the harsh realities of life it depicts are not suitable for young readers." Source: 11, Sept. 1985, p. 167.

827 Kehret, Peg. *Abduction!* Dutton. Challenged, but retained at the two Apple Valley, Mass. middle- and eight elementary-school libraries (2006) despite the complaint that the book was too violent. Source: 11, July 2006, p. 208.

828 Kellerman, Faye. *Milk and Honey.* Morrow. Challenged at the Rogers-Hough, Ark. Memorial Library (1991) because of "sacrilegious language." Source: 11, Sept. 1991, p. 151.

829 Kelley, Leo P. *Night of Fire and Blood.* Childrens Pr. Found unsuitable for younger children in Aurora, Colo. (1984) because it deals with "violence and self-mutilation." Source: 11, May 1984, p. 69.

830 Kellogg, Marjorie. *Tell Me That You Love Me, Junie Moon.* Farrar. Challenged at the Frederick County, Md. school system (1978) because it teaches that, "it's all right to do things against society's rules." Source: 11, Mar. 1978, p. 39; May 1978, p. 58.

831 Kellogg, Steven. *Pinkerton, Behave!* Dial. Challenged, but retained at the Elm Tree Elementary School library in Benton, Ark. (2000) despite the objections to a character in the book holding a gun. Challenged, but retained at the Evanston, Ill. Public Library (2004) despite complaints that the image of a masked burglar pointing a gun at woman is too violent for young

readers. Source: 11, Jan. 2001, p. 35; July 2004, p. 157; Nov. 2004, pp. 255–56.

832 Kenan, Randall. *James Baldwin.* Chelsea House Pubs. Removed from the Anaheim, Calif. school district (2000) because school officials said the book is too difficult for middle school students and that it could cause harassment against students seen with it. The American Civil Liberties Union (ACLU) of Southern California filed suit in *Doe v. Anaheim Union High School District* alleging that the removal is "a pretext for viewpoint-based censorship." The ACLU claims no other books have been removed from the junior high library for similar reasons, even though several, such as works by Shakespeare and Dickens, are more difficult reading. The ACLU contends that the school officials engaged in unconstitutional viewpoint discrimination by removing the book because it contains gay and lesbian material. In March 2001, the school board approved a settlement that restored the book to the high school shelves and amended the district's policy to prohibit the removal of books for subject matter involving sexual orientation, but the book will not be returned to the middle school. Source: 11, Mar. 2001, p. 53; May 2001, p. 95; July 2001, p. 173.

833 Kennedy, X. J. *Literature: Introduction to Fiction, Poetry and Drama.* Harper. Challenged in the Ojai, Calif. schools (1993) because selections contained foul language and blasphemy, and they glamorize sexual misconduct. Source: 11, Jan. 1994, p. 37.

834 Kepler, Johannes. *The New Astronomy.* Oxford Univ. Pr. Banned by the Vatican under a general prohibition on reading or teaching heliocentric theory (1619). The ban on his theories remained in effect until 1753. Source: 1, pp. 212–13.

835 Kerr, M. E. *Dinky Hocker Shoots Smack.* Dell; Harper. Removed from Kent, Wash. elementary school libraries (1977) because of complaints about "vulgarity" and "defamation of the word of God in the work." Challenged, but retained, at the Merritt Brown Middle School library in Panama City, Fla. (1998) despite a parent's concern that passages are "sacrilegious and morally subversive." Source: 9; 11, Mar. 1977, p. 36; Sept. 1998, p. 139.

836 _____. *Gentle Hands.* Bantam; Harper. Challenged at the Lake Braddock, Va. Secondary School (1983) because the book is "anti-Semitic"

and "glamorizes drug abuse and makes drugs 'tempting' to teenagers." Source: 11, July 1983, p. 109; Nov. 1983, p. 187; Mar. 1984, p. 53.

837 **Kesey, Ken.** *One Flew over the Cuckoo's Nest.* NAL; Penguin; Viking. Challenged in the Greeley, Colo. Public school district (1971) as a non-required American Culture reading. In 1974, five residents of Strongsville, Ohio, sued the board of education to remove the novel. Labeling it "pornographic," they charged the novel "glorifies criminal activity, has a tendency to corrupt juveniles and contains descriptions of bestiality, bizarre violence, and torture, dismemberment, death, and human elimination." Removed from public school libraries in Randolph, N.Y., and Alton, Okla. (1975). Removed from the required reading list in Westport, Mass. (1977). Banned from the St. Anthony, Idaho Freemont High School classrooms (1978) and the instructor fired—*Fogarty v. Atchley.* Challenged at the Merrimack, N.H. High School (1982). Challenged as part of the curriculum in an Aberdeen, Wash. High School honors English class (1986) because the book promotes "secular humanism." The school board voted to retain the title. Challenged in the Placentia-Yorba Linda, Calif. Unified School District (2000) after complaints by parents stated that teachers "can choose the best books, but they keep choosing this garbage over and over again." Source: 8, pp. 478–79; 11, Jan. 1977, p. 8; May 1978, p. 57; July 1978, pp. 96, 100; Sept. 1982, p. 170; 12, pp. 104–11, 229; Nov. 1986, p. 225; Mar. 2001, p. 55; 15, Vol. IV, p. 714.

838 _____. *Sometimes a Great Notion.* Penguin. Challenged for use in Richland, Wash. high school English classes (1998) along with six other titles because the "books are poor-quality literature and stress suicide, illicit sex, violence, and hopelessness." Source: 11, Mar. 1999, p. 40.

839 **Kessel, Joyce K.** *Halloween.* Carolrhoda Bks.; Lerner Pubs. Challenged at the Neely Elementary School in Gilbert, Ariz. (1992) because the book shows the dark side of religion through the occult, the devil, and satanism. Source: 11, May 1992, p. 78; July 1992, p. 124.

840 **Keyes, Daniel.** *Flowers for Algernon.* Bantam; Harcourt. Banned from the Plant City, Fla. (1976) and Emporium, Pa. (1977) public schools because of references to sex; banned from the Glen Rose, Ark. High School library (1981); challenged at the Oberlin, Ohio High School (1983) because several pages of the novel detail a sexual encounter of the protagonist. Challenged

as a required reading at the Glenrock, Wyo. High School (1984) because several "explicit love scenes were distasteful." Challenged at the Charlotte-Mecklenburg, N.C. schools (1986) as a tenth-grade supplemental reading because it is "pornographic." Challenged, but retained, in the Yorktown, Va. schools (1996). A parent complained about the profanity and references to sex and drinking in the novel. Removed from the ninth-grade curriculum by the Rabun, Ga. County Board of Education (1997) because it was "inappropriate" for the ninth grade. Source: 11, July 1976, p. 85; May 1977, p. 73; July 1981, p. 91; Jan. 1984, p. 26; July 1984, p. 122; Jan. 1987, p. 12; Mar. 1987, p. 54; May 1987, p. 103; July 1987, p. 150; May 1996, p. 100; July 1997, p. 97.

841 **Kidd, Flora.** *Between Pride and Passion.* Harlequin. More than fifty Harlequin romances donated by Glide, Oreg. residents were threatened with removal from the high school library (1984) because "teenagers already have trouble with their emotions without being stimulated by poorly written books." Source: 11, July 1984, p. 104.

842 **Kilgore, Kathleen.** *The Wolfman of Beacon Hill.* Little. Challenged at the Pilot Butte Junior High School in Bend, Oreg. (1989) because the material does not enlighten, uplift, or encourage character-building traits. Source: 11, Jan. 1990, pp. 4–5.

843 **Killingsworth, Monte.** *Eli's Songs.* Macmillan. Challenged in the Rural Dell School District in Molalla, Oreg. (1992) because the book is "anti-local," has "logger-bashing" sentiments and an "ecological slant." Source: 11, July 1992, pp. 124–25.

844 **Kincaid, Jamaica.** *Lucy.* Farrar; NAL; Hall. Challenged at the West Chester, Pa. schools (1994) as "most pornographic." The book was changed from required to optional reading. Source: 11, Jan. 1995, p. 25; Mar. 1995, p. 45; May 1995, p. 71.

845 **Kincaid, James Russell.** *Erotic Innocence: The Culture of Child Molesting.* Duke Univ. Pr. Challenged, but retained in the Montgomery County, Tex. library system (2002) after a conservative Christian group, the Republican Leadership Council, characterized the book as "helping to lay the groundwork for a culture of child molesters and homosexuals." Source: 11, Jan. 2003, p. 33.

846 **King, Frederick; Herbert Rudman; and Doris Leavell.** *Understanding the Social*

Sciences. Laidlaw. Removed from Alabama's list of approved texts—and from the state's classrooms—because the book promotes the "religion of secular humanism." U.S. District Court Judge W. Brevard Hand ruled on March 4, 1987, that thirty-nine history and social studies texts used in Alabama's 129 school systems "discriminate against the very concept of religion and theistic religions in particular, by omissions so serious that a student learning history from them would not be apprised of relevant facts about America's history. . . . References to religion are isolated and the integration of religion in the history of American society is ignored." The series includes: *Understanding People; Understanding Families; Understanding Communities; Understanding Religions of the World; Understanding Our Country;* and *Understanding the World.* On August 26, 1987, the U.S. Court of Appeals for the Eleventh Circuit unanimously overturned Judge Hand's decision by ruling that the information in the book was "essentially neutral in its religious content." The fact that the texts omitted references to religion was not "an advancement of secular humanism or an active hostility toward theistic religion." Source: 11, Jan. 1987, p. 6; May 1987, pp. 75, 104–7; Sept. 1987, pp. 166–67; Nov. 1987, pp. 217–18; Jan. 1988, p. 17; Mar. 1988, p. 40.

847 **King, Larry. *Tell It to the King.*** Putnam; Thorndike Pr. Challenged at the Public Libraries of Saginaw, Mich. (1989) because it is "an insult to one's intelligence" and contains foul language. Source: 11, May 1989, p. 77.

848 **King, Stephen. *The Bachman Books.*** NAL. Removed from the West Lyon Community School library in Larchwood, Iowa (1987) because "it does not meet the standards of the community." Source: 11, May 1987, p. 86; July 1987, p. 125.

849 _____. ***Carrie.*** Doubleday. Challenged at the Clark High School library in Las Vegas, Nev. (1975) because it is "trash." Placed in special closed shelf at the Vergennes, Vt. Union High School library (1978) because it could "harm" students, particularly "younger girls." Removed from the West Lyon Community School library in Larchwood, Iowa (1987) because "it does not meet the standards of the community." Banned from the Altmar-Parish-Williamstown, N.Y. district libraries (1991). Challenged, along with eight other Stephen King novels, in Bismarck, N.Dak. (1994) by a local minister and a school board member, because of "age appropriateness." Challenged by a parent, and currently under review, at the Boyertown, Pa. Junior

High East library (1994). The parent "objected to the book's language, its violence, and its sexual descriptions, as well as what she described as a 'Satanic killing' sequence." Source: 11, Jan. 1979, p. 6; May 1987, p. 86; July 1987, p. 125; Mar. 1992, p. 40; May 1994, pp. 84–85.

850 _____. ***Christine.*** NAL; Viking. The Washington County, Ala. Board of Education (1985) voted unanimously to ban the novel from all county school libraries because the book contains "unacceptable language" and is "pornographic." Removed from the West Lyon Community School library in Larchwood, Iowa (1987) because "it does not meet the standards of the community." Removed from the Washington Middle School library in Meriden, Conn. (1989) after a parent complained about offensive passages. Removed from the Livingston, Mont. Middle School library (1990) because it was deemed not "suitable for intended audience," owing to violence, explicit sex, and inappropriate language. Challenged at the Webber Township High School library in Bluford, Ill. (1993) along with all other King novels. Challenged, along with eight other Stephen King novels, in Bismarck, N.Dak. (1994) by a local minister and a school board member, because of "age appropriateness." Source: 11, Jan. 1986, p. 7; May 1987, p. 86; July 1987, p. 125; May 1989, p. 75; Jan. 1991, p. 12; July 1993, p. 124; May 1994, pp. 84–85.

851 _____. ***Cujo.*** NAL; Viking. Challenged at the Rankin County, Miss. School District (1984) because it is "profane and sexually objectionable." Removed from the shelves of the Bradford, N.Y. school library (1985) "because it was a bunch of garbage." Rejected for purchase by the Hayward, Calif. school trustees (1985) because of "rough language" and "explicit sex scenes." The Washington County, Ala. Board of Education (1985) voted unanimously to ban the novel from all county school libraries because the book contains "unacceptable language" and is "pornographic." Removed from a high school library in Durand, Wis. (1987) pending review by a nine-member panel of school personnel and community members. Challenged, but retained at a South Portland, Maine middle school (1992) despite complaints of "profanity" and sexual references. Challenged from Sparta, Ill. schools (1992). The school board honored the parents' request to bar their children from using the book, but refused to ban the book. Challenged, along with eight other Stephen King novels, in Bismarck, N.Dak. (1994) by a local minister and a school board member, because of "age appropriateness." Removed at the Crook

91

County High School in Prineville, Oreg. (1998) because it contains "profanity, sexual content, and other factors." The parent also requested that all books by Stephen King be removed from the school because, "I object to any book written by Stephen King as he writes horror fiction, which has no value." Three other King books are under review: *The Running Man*, *Bachman Books*, and *The Green Mile, Part 1*. Challenged at the West Hernando Middle School in Brooksville, Fla. (1998) because of the book's sexually explicit scenes and language. Source: 8, pp. 442–44; 11, May 1984, p. 69; Jan. 1985, p. 8; May 1985, pp. 75, 77; July 1985, p. 111; Jan. 1986, p. 7; Nov. 1987, p. 226; May 1994, pp. 84–85; July 1998, p. 110; Jan. 1999, p. 7.

852 _____. ***The Dark Half.*** NAL; Viking: G. K. Hall. Retained in the Roseburg, Oreg. High School library (1994) despite a parent's complaint that the book contains "extreme, bloodthirsty violence." Banned, but later reinstated in the Stanley-Boyd, Wis. School District high school library (1998) despite a parent's objection to the "profane" language in the first chapter. The school board enacted a new policy that allows parents to call the school librarian and restrict their children's access to certain books or authors. Source: 11, Sept. 1994, pp. 166–67; Jan. 1999, p. 9; Mar. 1999, p. 37.

853 _____. ***The Dead Zone.*** Doubleday. Removed from the West Lyon Community School library in Larchwood, Iowa (1987) because "it does not meet the standards of the community." Restricted to high school students with parental permission at the Duval County, Fla. school system (1992) because of "filthy language" in the book. Banned in the Peru, Ind. school system (1992) along with *Cujo* and *Christine* because the books are "filthy." Challenged, along with eight other Stephen King novels, in Bismarck, N.Dak. (1994) by a local minister and a school board member, because of "age appropriateness." Source: 11, May 1987, p. 86; July 1987, p. 125; May 1992, pp. 79, 80; July 1992, pp. 105, 106; May 1994, pp. 84–85.

854 _____. ***Different Seasons.*** Doubleday. Removed from the West Lyon Community School library in Larchwood, Iowa (1987) because "it does not meet the standards of the community." Removed from the Washington Middle School library in Meriden, Conn. (1989) after a parent complained about offensive passages. Challenged at the Eagan High School in Burnsville, Minn. (1992). Accessible to West Hernando Middle School library students in Brooksville, Fla. (2001) only if they have a signed and verified permission slip from their parents. A student was offended by references to

oral sex and prison rape scenes in the short story "Rita Hayworth and Shawshank Redemption," the basis for the 1994 movie *The Shawshank Redemption*. Source: 11, May 1987, p. 86; July 1987, p. 125; May 1989, p. 75; Mar. 1993, p. 56; Jan. 2002, p. 15.

855 _____. ***The Drawing of the Three.*** NAL. Challenged, along with eight other Stephen King novels, in Bismarck, N.Dak. (1994) by a local minister and a school board member, because of "age appropriateness." Source: 11, May 1994, pp. 84–85.

856 _____. ***The Eyes of the Dragon.*** NAL. Challenged, along with eight other Stephen King novels, in Bismarck, N.Dak. (1994) by a local minister and a school board member, because of "age appropriateness." Source: 11, May 1994, pp. 84–85.

857 _____. ***Firestarter.*** Viking. Challenged at the Campbell County, Wyo. School System (1983-1984) because of its alleged "graphic descriptions of sexual acts, vulgar language, and violence." Removed from the Washington Middle School library in Meriden, Conn. (1989) after a parent complained about offensive passages. Source: 11, Mar. 1984, p. 39; May 1989, p. 75.

858 _____. ***Four Past Midnight.*** NAL. Challenged at the Sparta, Ill. High School library (1992), along with all other King novels, due to violence, sex, and explicit language. Source: 11, July 1992, p. 106.

859 _____. ***Gerald's Game.*** Viking. Removed from Columbia High School in Lake City, Fla. (1998) because of the book's portrayal of graphic violence and lewd sexual conduct. A parent threatened to take legal action against the school system if the school did not decide to remove all "offensive" library books. Source: 11, Jan. 1999, pp. 7–8.

860 _____. ***It.*** Viking. Challenged in the Lincoln, Nebr. school libraries (1987) because of the novel's "corruptive, obscene nature." Placed on a "closed shelf" at the Franklinville, N.Y. Central High School library (1992) because of explicit sexual acts, violence, and profane language. Students will need parental permission to check it out. Source: 11, Nov. 1987, p. 225; Mar. 1993, p. 41.

861 _____. ***Night Shift.*** Doubleday. Removed from the West Lyon Community School library in Larchwood, Iowa (1987) because "it does not meet

the standards of the community." Removed from the Green Bay, Wis. School District classrooms (1988) because the book contains a short story entitled "Children of the Corn," which "teaches about the occult and rebellion by children and makes a mockery of Christianity." The book was returned, however, after questions were raised by school board members about the administrative decision to ban the book. Source: 11, May 1987, p. 86; July 1987, p. 125; Jan. 1989, p. 11; Mar. 1989, p. 44.

862 _____. *Pet Sematary.* NAL. Challenged, along with eight other Stephen King novels, in Bismarck, N.Dak. (1994) by a local minister and a school board member, because of "age appropriateness." Source: 11, May 1994, pp. 84–85.

863 _____. *'Salem's Lot.* Doubleday; NAL. Banned from the Cleveland, Tex. Independent High School English classes (1986) overruling a review committee's recommendation, even after teachers already had inked out objectionable words with a felt-tip marker. A single copy is available in the restricted section of the high school library to students who have a permission slip signed by their parents. Banned from the Goochard, Vt. High School library (1988) because of sexually explicit language. Source: 11, Jan. 1987, p. 12; Mar. 1987, pp. 54–55; Sept. 1988, p. 152.

864 _____. *The Shining.* Doubleday. Challenged at the Campbell County, Wyo. School System (1983) because "the story contains violence, demonic possession and ridicules the Christian religion." The novel is now available to all students in grades seven through twelve, at the discretion of district librarians. Removed from the Evergreen School District's four junior high school libraries in Vancouver, Wash. (1986) because the book's "descriptive foul language" made it unsuitable for teenagers. Removed from the Livingston, Mont. Middle School library (1990) because it was deemed not "suitable for intended audience," owing to violence, explicit sex, and inappropriate language. Challenged, along with eight other Stephen King novels, in Bismarck, N.Dak. (1994) by a local minister and a school board member, because of "age appropriateness." Source: 11, Jan. 1984, p. 10; Mar. 1984, p. 39; May 1986, p. 81; July 1987, p. 125; Jan. 1991, p. 12; May 1994, pp. 84–85.

865 _____. *The Skeleton Crew.* NAL. Challenged at the Salmon, Idaho High School library (1993) because of graphic street language about homosexuality, among other reasons. Source: 11, July 1993, p. 124.

866 _____. *The Stand.* Doubleday; NAL. Restricted to ninth grade students with parental consent at the Whitford Intermediate School in Beaverton, Oreg. (1989) because of "sexual language, casual sex, and violence." Source: 11, Jan. 1990, pp. 4–5.

867 _____. *The Talisman.* Viking. Challenged at the Salmon, Idaho High School library (1993) because of graphic street language about homosexuality, among other reasons. Source: 11, July 1993, p. 124.

868 _____. *Thinner.* NAL. Challenged, along with eight other Stephen King novels, in Bismarck, N.Dak. (1994) by a local minister and a school board member, because of "age appropriateness." Source: 11, May 1994, pp. 84–85.

869 _____. *The Tommyknockers.* NAL. Restricted to high school students with parental permission at the Duval County, Fla. school system (1992) because of "filthy language" in the book and "it's extremely graphic." Source: 11, May 1992, p. 79; July 1992, p. 105.

870 **Kingsolver, Barbara.** *The Bean Trees.* Harper. Temporarily restricted in the Yorkville, Ill. schools (1998) because it is "obscene, coarse, disgusting, and irreverent." Source: 11, July 1998, p. 108; Sept. 1998, p. 156.

871 **Kingston, Jeremy.** *Witches and Witchcraft.* Aldus Bks. Removed from the Duerson-Oldham County Public Library in LaGrange, Ky. (1987) because "young or immature minds may become intrigued by Satan as a result of reading the book." Source: 11, Sept. 1987, p. 174.

872 **Kinsey, Alfred.** *Sexual Behavior in the Human Female.* Saunders. Banned in South Africa (1953), Ireland (1953), and in U.S. Army post exchanges in Europe as having "no worthwhile interest for soldiers." Source: 4, p. 75.

873 _____. *Sexual Behavior in the Human Male.* Saunders. Banned in South Africa (1953), Ireland (1953), and in U.S. Army post exchanges in Europe as having "no worthwhile interest for soldiers." Source: 4, p. 75.

874 **Kipling, Rudyard.** *Drums of the Fore and Aft.* Doubleday. Removed from the Sunday school library of the Crawfordsville, Ind. (1899) First

Methodist Episcopal Church because a parishioner complained that it was "fairly reeking with profanity, and the most outrageous slang." Source: 15, Vol. II, p. 624.

875 _____. *The Elephant's Child.*
Checkboard; Dutton; Harcourt; Interlink; Knopf; Prentice-Hall; Warne. Challenged in the Davenport, Iowa Community School District (1993) because the book is "99 percent" violent. Throughout the book, when the main character, an elephant child, asks a question, he receives a spanking instead of answers. Source: 11, July 1993, p. 99.

876 _____. *Just So Stories.* Macmillan; Penguin; Viking. Challenged at the Hardin Park Elementary School library in Watauga County, N.C. (1990) because the word "nigger" appears in the story "How the Leopard Got Its Spots." Source: 11, July 1990, p. 145.

877 **Kirk, Marshall, and Hunter Madison.** *After the Ball: How America Will Conquer Its Hatred and Fear of Homosexuals in the '90s.* NAL. Challenged at the Deschutes County Library in Bend, Oreg. (1993) because it "encourages and condones" homosexuality. Source: 11, Sept. 1993, pp. 158–59.

878 **Kirkwood, James.** *There Must Be a Pony!* A Novel. Avon. Seized (1984) by the British customs office as "indecent and obscene." Source: 11, Jan. 1985, p. 16.

879 **Kittredge, Mary.** *Teens with AIDS Speak Out.* Simon. Challenged, but retained, at the Cleveland, Tenn. Public Library (1993) along with seventeen other books, most of which are on sex education, AIDS awareness, and some titles on the supernatural. Source: 11, Sept. 1993, p. 146.

880 **Kitzinger, Sheila.** *Being Born.* Putnam. Challenged at the Lakeview, Oreg. school libraries (1991) because the complainant's son asked, "rather pointed questions" about childbirth. Challenged, but retained, at the Washoe County Library System in Reno, Nev. (1994) because "Nobody in their right mind would give a book like that to children on their own, except the library." Source: 11, Nov. 1991, p. 209; Sept. 1994, p. 147; Nov. 1994, pp. 200–01.

881 **Klause, Annette Curtis.** *Blood and Chocolate.* Delacorte. Temporarily pulled from the LaPorte, Tex. Independent School District school library shelves (2001) until the district can review

and possibly amend its selection policies. Source: 11, Nov. 2001, p. 247.

882 **Klein, Aaron.** *Science and the Supernatural.* Doubleday. Challenged, but retained, at the Cleveland, Tenn. Public Library (1993) along with seventeen other books, most of which are on sex education, AIDS awareness, and some titles on the supernatural. Source: 11, Sept. 1993, p. 146.

883 **Klein, Norma.** *Angel Face.* Fawcett; Viking. Challenged at the Commerce, Tex. High School library (1990) because of "pornographic" material in the book. The complainant asked that all "romance" books be removed. Source: 11, Mar. 1991, p. 43.

884 _____. *Beginners' Love.* Hillside Bks. Challenged, but retained in the Chester, S.C. High School library (1999) with the provision that parents can instruct the school not to let their own children borrow it. The book's graphic description of sex, discussions of abortion, and the character's use of marijuana were considered objectionable by some parents. South Carolina Attorney General Charlie Condon ruled that the school board could reasonably conclude that the novel was "pervasively vulgar" and "educationally unsuitable" and, thus, removal by the board would not violate the First Amendment. Source: 11, Mar. 1999, p. 36; Nov. 1999, p. 163.

885 _____. *Confessions of an Only Child.* Bradbury Pr. Challenged, but retained, in a Gwinnett County, Ga. Elementary School library (1985) because "the use of a profanity by the lead character's father during a single episode destroyed the entire book." Source: 11, Mar. 1986, p. 57; Mar. 1986, p. 57; July 1986, p. 135.

886 _____. *Family Secrets.* Fawcett. Removed from the Howard County, Md. middle school media centers (1991) because the book's "constant reference to the sex act" and "inappropriate foul language." Source: 11, Mar. 1992, p. 40.

887 _____. *Give Me One Good Reason.* Avon. Challenged at the Widefield, Colo. School District (1984) because the book is "filled with promiscuity, homosexuality, abortion, and profanity." Source: 11, May 1984, p. 69.

888 _____. *Honey of a Chimp.* Pantheon. Removed from the Hanover, Pa. School District's elementary and secondary libraries (1984), but later

placed on a "restricted shelf" at middle school libraries, because the book contained "strong sexual content, bias to liberal values and morals, and indecent language. The material condones certain values, attitudes, and behaviors." Source: 11, Jan. 1985, p. 9.

889 _____. *It's Not What You Expect.* Avon. Removed from all the Montgomery County, Md. elementary school libraries (1980). Source: 11, May 1980, p. 51.

890 _____. *It's OK If You Don't Love Me.* Dial; Fawcett. Banned in Hayward County, Calif. (1981) because of the book's sexually explicit passages and "rough language." Removed from the shelves of the Widefield, Colo. High School library (1983) because it portrays "sex as the only thing on young people's minds." Removed from the Vancouver, Wash. School District (1984) due to its sexual passages, but later reinstated at the high school level libraries. Source: 11, Mar. 1982, p. 44; May 1983, p. 71; July 1984, p. 104.

891 _____. *Just Friends.* Fawcett. Challenged at the Hamden, Conn. Middle School (1994) because it is "nothing more than pornographic smut." Banned at, but later returned to, the Cameron, Mo. High School library (1998) after student complaints. The book was initially challenged because it was "too explicit and did not link actions to consequences." Removed from the mandatory reading program at the Norman L. Sullivan Middle School in Bonsall, Calif. (2000) due to sexually explicit language. Source: 11, Nov. 1994, p. 189; July 1998, p. 119; May 2000, p. 76.

892 _____. *Love Is One of the Choices.* Dial. Removed from the Evergreen School District of Vancouver, Wash. (1983) along with twenty-nine other titles. The American Civil Liberties Union of Washington filed suit contending that the removals constitute censorship, a violation of plaintiff's rights to free speech and due process, and the acts are a violation of the state Open Meetings Act because the removal decisions were made behind closed doors. Source: 11, Nov. 1983, pp. 185–86.

893 _____. *Mom, the Wolf Man and Me.* Pantheon. Challenged at the Orlando, Fla. (1980) due to its "objectionable" subject matter. Source: 11, Mar. 1981, p. 47.

894 _____. *My Life as a Body.* Fawcett;

Knopf. Challenged at the Douglas County Library in Roseburg, Oreg. (1989) because the book condones homosexuality and premarital sex. Challenged for being too explicit, but retained at the Multnomah, Oreg. County Library (1991). Source: 11, Jan. 1990, pp. 4–5; Jan. 1992, p. 6.

895 _____. *Naomi in the Middle.* Dial; Pocket/Archway. Restricted in Brockport, N.Y. (1977) to students with parental permission. Banned in Monroe, La. (1980) because "it is certainly not our intention to have objectionable materials on library shelves." Challenged at the Orlando, Fla. Public Library (1980). Challenged at the Charlotte, N.C. public library system (1986) because the book "is a perfect picture of secular humanism." Challenged at the Napa, Calif. City-County Library (1992) because of sexually explicit language. Challenged at the Mesa, Ariz. Public Libraries (1995) because of four pages of inappropriate material describing human sexual anatomy and how babies are conceived. Source: 11, Nov. 1977, p. 155; July 1980, p. 76; Mar. 1981, p. 47; Jan. 1987, p. 31; July 1992, p. 105; July 1995, p. 109.

896 _____. *The Queen of the What Ifs.* Fawcett; Knopf. Pulled from the Monte Vista Middle School library in Tracy, Calif. (1989) after two parents complained that its sexual content made the book inappropriate for middle school students. About a half dozen other titles also were removed and the parents have indicated a desire to review all books ordered for the library. Source: 11, May 1989, p. 75.

897 _____. *Sunshine.* Avon; Holt. Removed from the East Baton Rouge Parish, La. (1975) after the parents of a student said they found the language and content of the book offensive. Source: 11, July 1975, p. 104.

898 _____. *That's My Baby.* Viking. Banned at, but later returned to, the Cameron, Mo. High School library (1998) after student complaints. The book was initially challenged because it was "too explicit and did not link actions to consequences." Source: 11, July 1998, p. 119.

899 _____. *What It's All About.* Dial. Challenged at the Dubuque, Iowa Community School District (1984) because "it condones and even endorses immoral behavior because it contains profanity, nudity, sexual relationships outside of marriage and an excessive number of people who are divorced." Source: 11, Sept. 1984, p. 155.

900 **Klein, Stanley.** *Steck-Vaughn Social Studies.* Steck. Removed from Alabama's list of approved texts—and from the state's classrooms —because the book promotes the "religion of secular humanism." U.S. District Court Judge W. Brevard Hand ruled on March 4, 1987, that thirty-nine history and social studies texts used in Alabama's 129 school systems "discriminate against the very concept of religion and theistic religions in particular, by omissions so serious that a student learning history from them would not be apprised of relevant facts about America's history. . . . References to religion are isolated and the integration of religion in the history of American society is ignored." The series includes: *Our Family; Our Neighbors; Our Communities; Our Country Today; Our Country's History*; and *Our World Today*. On August 26, 1987, the U.S. Court of Appeals for the Eleventh Circuit unanimously overturned Judge Hand's decision by ruling that the information in the book was "essentially neutral in its religious content." The fact that the texts omitted references to religion was not "an advancement of secular humanism or an active hostility toward theistic religion." Source: 11, Jan. 1987, p. 6; May 1987, pp. 75, 104–7; Sept. 1987, pp. 166–67; Nov. 1987, pp. 217–18; Jan. 1988, p. 17; Mar. 1988, p. 40.

901 **Knott, Blanche.** *Truly Tasteless Jokes.* Ballantine. Removed from open display at the Casa Grande, Ariz. Public Library (1988) and restricted to adult use only with proof of age before checking the book out or even looking at it. Source: 11, Jan. 1989, p. 7.

902 **Knowles, John.** *A Separate Peace.* Bantam; Dell; Macmillan. Challenged in Vernon-Verona-Sherill, N.Y. School District (1980) as a "filthy, trashy sex novel." Challenged at the Fannett-Metal High School in Shippensburg, Pa. (1985) because of its allegedly offensive language. Challenged as appropriate for high school reading lists in the Shelby County, Tenn. school system (1989) because the novel contained "offensive language." Challenged, but retained the Champaign, Ill., high school English classes (1991) despite claims that "unsuitable language" made it inappropriate. Challenged by the parent of a high school student in Troy, Ill., (1991) citing profanity and negative attitudes. Students were offered alternative assignments while the school board took the matter under advisement, but no further action was taken on the complaint. Challenged at the McDowell County, N.C. schools (1996) because of "graphic language." Source: 11, May 1980, p. 62; Nov. 1985, p. 204; Jan. 1990, pp. 11–12; Jan. 1997, p. 11; 14, pp. 256–57.

903 **Knowlton, Charles.** *Fruits of Philosophy: The Private Companion of Married Couples.* Watson. The author was brought to trail in Taunton, Massachusetts, and charged with distributing "obscene material," then filed $50 and court costs. In December 1832, Knowlton was found guilty of distributing his book and sentenced to three months of hard labor in the Cambridge House of Corrections. Knowlton appeared in court of Greenfield, Mass., three different times, but the case was finally dismissed because the jury in all three trials could not come to a decision. The book was also challenged in British courts (1877) and eventually the defendants recovered their stock of books, stamped in red "Recovered from Police" and sold them. Source: 14, pp. 148–50.

904 **Knudsen, Eric.** *Teller of Tales.* Mutual Pub. Co. Challenged in the Columbia County, Ga. school libraries (1992) because the biography of Hans Christian Andersen contains the phrase "go to hell." Source: 11, Nov. 1992, p. 197.

905 **Koertge, Ronald.** *The Arizona Kid.* Avon; Little. Challenged because it "encourages and condones" homosexuality, but retained at the Bend, Oreg. High School (1993). Pulled from and later restored to the seventh-grade English classroom at Minnetonka, Minn. Middle School West (1994) after a parent found the content inappropriate for twelve- and thirteen-year-olds. Source: 11, Sept. 1993, pp. 158–59; Nov. 1993, p. 192; July 1994, p. 114; Sept. 1994, p. 166.

906 **_____.** *Where the Kissing Never Stops.* Atlantic Monthly Pr. Retained as optional reading for eighth graders at Rice Avenue Middle School in Girard, Pa. (2000). A grandmother found the book offensive and didn't want her granddaughters reading it. Source: 11, May 2000, p. 92.

907 **Koontz, Dean R.** *Funhouse.* Berkley. Removed from the South Brunswick Middle School Library in Boiling Spring Lakes, N.C. (1995) by a patron because the book "contains material on orgies, rape, and lesbianism. There is also blasphemy and the book promotes domestic violence and alcohol abuse." The book was donated by the Lions Club in a book drive. Source: 11, Nov. 1995, pp. 183–84; Jan. 1996, p. 11.

908 **_____.** *Night Chills.* Atheneum. Challenged at the Mountain View High School in Bend, Oreg. (1992) because it contains "explicit" sexual incidents. Source: 11, Jan. 1993, p. 9.

909 _____. *The Voice of the Night.*
Doubleday; Thorndike Pr. Challenged as extra
reading material at Westcott Junior High School
in Westbrook, Maine (2000) because the novel
describes people having sex and the mutilation of
animals and people. Source: 11, Mar. 2000, p. 50.

910 _____. *Watchers.* Putnam. Removed from
the Hickory High School curriculum in Sharon, Pa.
(1996) by the superintendent because the language
was offensive. Source: 11, Mar. 1997, p. 50.

911 Kopay, David, and Perry D. Young.
*The David Kopay Story: An Extraordinary
Self-Revelation.* Fine. Challenged because it
"encourages and condones" homosexuality, but
retained at the Bend, Oreg. High School (1993).
Source: 11, Sept. 1993, pp. 158–59; Nov. 1993,
p. 192.

912 *The Koran.* Penguin; Tahrike Tarsile; Quran.
Ban lifted by the Spanish Index (1790). Restricted
to students of history in USSR (1926). In 1995, a
Malay translation was banned by the government of
Malaysia. The banning was part of an official policy
aimed at outlawing "deviant" Islamic sects. In China
during the Cultural Revolution of the 1960s and
1970s, study of the *Koran* was forbidden and its
reading in mosques prohibited. In 1986 in Ethiopia,
under the socialist military government, it was
reported that copies of the *Koran* were destroyed
or confiscated by the army, Koranic schools and
mosques were closed or razed, Muslims were
prohibited from praying and some were ordered to
Christianity and burn the *Koran*. Source: 4, p. 5; 8,
pp. 251–53.

913 Kornblum, William, and Joseph Julian.
Social Problems. Prentice-Hall. Reinstated at
the Anadarko, Okla. Public Schools (1993) after
a textbook review committee recommendation.
A minister who complained about the book's
references to homosexuality, lesbians, and child
molesters challenged the text. Source: 11, Sept.
1993, p. 160.

914 Kosinski, Jerzy. *Being There.* Bantam.
Challenged as a reading assignment for an
eleventh-grade English class at Crete, Nebr.
High School (1989). Reinstated after being
removed from the Mifflinburg, Pa. High School
(1989) because the book's main character has a
homosexual experience. Challenged as required
reading in a senior advanced English course in
Davenport, Iowa (1993) because of a description of
masturbation. Challenged on the curricular reading
list at Pomperaug High School in Southbury, Conn.
(1995) because sexually explicit passages are not
appropriate high school reading. Source: 11, May
1989, pp. 79, 93; July 1993, p. 105; July 1995, p. 98.

**915 Kotzwinkle, William, and Glenn
Murray.** *Walter the Farting Dog.* Frog, Ltd.
Challenged, but retained on the library shelves
of the West Salem, Wis. Elementary School (2004)
despite the book's use of the word "fart" and
"farting" twenty-four times. Source: 11, May 2004,
p. 118; July 2004, p. 138.

916 Kotzwinkle, William. *Nightbook.* Avon.
Challenged at the Huron, S.Dak. Public Library
(1980) because "there's not a page in [the book] fit
to be read by anyone." Source: 11, July 1980, p. 84.

917 Kovic, Ron. *Born on the Fourth of July.*
McGraw-Hill. Placed on a closed shelf in Maryland
(1982) after a parent objected to the book as un-
American, finding fault also with its language and
its display of sex. Source: 7, 64.

918 Krantz, Judith. *Mistral's Daughter.*
Bantam. Banned from the Stroudsburg, Pa. High
School library (1985) because it was "blatantly
graphic, pornographic, and wholly unacceptable for
a high school library." Source: 11, May 1985, p. 79.

919 Kroeker, Gary. *The Magi.* Erica House
Bk. Pub. Banned at the Los Altos High School in
Hacienda Heights, Calif. (1998) because the novel
was "too racy." The author is an English teacher at
the school. Source: 11, July 1998, p. 104; Mar. 1999,
p. 35.

920 Kroll, Ken. *Enabling Romance: A Guide to
Love, Sex and Relationships for the Disabled.* First
Woodline House. Removed from the Clifton, N.J.
Public Library (1996) and replaced with a dummy
book made of styrofoam. The library's new policy
restricts to adults any material containing "patently
offensive graphic illustrations or photographs
of sexual or excretory activities or contact as
measured by contemporary community standards
for minors." Source: 11, July 1996, pp. 118–19.

921 Kropp, Paul. *Wilted.* Coward. Banned
from the Evergreen School District libraries in
Vancouver, Oreg. (1983) because the "sexual scenes
were a bit much for elementary schools." Source:
11, Sept. 1983, p. 139.

922 Kung, Hans. *Infallible? An Inquiry.* Doubleday. In 1979, the Vatican withdrew the Swiss priest and prominent Catholic theologian's permission to teach in the name of the church and prohibited Catholic institutions from employing him. Source: 8, pp. 249–50.

923 Kushner, Ellen. *Mystery of the Secret Room.* Bantam. Challenged at the Berkeley County, S.C. school libraries (1992) because the book teaches witchcraft. Source: 11, July 1992, p. 108.

924 Kuskin, Karla. *The Dallas Titans Get Ready for Bed.* Harper. Challenged at the Douglas County Library in Roseburg, Oreg. (1989) because children are not ready for illustrations and conversation about jockstraps. Source: 11, Jan. 1990, pp. 4–5.

925 Lader, Lawrence. *Foolproof Birth Control.* Beacon Pr. Banned from the Brighton, Mich. High School library (1977) along with all other sex education materials. Source: 11, Sept. 1977, p. 133.

926 Laine, James W. *Shivaji: Hindu King in Islamic India.* Oxford Univ. Pr. In 2003, Hindu fundamentalists, contending that he had insulted the reputation of Shivaji, the seventeenth century century Hindu king and warrior, ransacked the institute in Pune, India, where he had conducted research for his book. The book was banned in Maharashtra State in India, which brought criminal charges against Laine and his publisher and threatened to extradite him to India. A high court in Bombay stayed the criminal charges against him. Source: 1, pp. 303–5.

927 Laing, Frederick. *Tales from Scandinavia.* Silver Burdett. Removed to a locked closet in the superintendent's office in Banner County, Nebr. (1992) because the book "has to do with a lot of negative things and might not be good for someone with low self-esteem or suicide tendencies." Source: 11, May 1992, p. 80.

928 Landis, James David. *The Sisters Impossible.* Knopf. Removed from the Sallisaw, Okla. school libraries (1985) due to offensive language. Later, returned to the shelves of the Eastside Elementary School library in Sallisaw, Okla. (1986) after the school board agreed to an out-of-court settlement with a group of parents who filed a suit to reverse the board's 1985 decision to ban the book. The book was originally banned because it uses "hell" seven times and the words "fart" and "bullshit" once each in its 169 pages. Challenged in the Fairbanks, Alaska school libraries (1988) because off "the language in the book and to a scene in which aspiring young ballerinas danced naked in a dressing room before class." Challenged because of objectionable language, but retained at the J. G. Dyer Elementary School library in Gwinnett County, Ga. (1997). Source: 11, July 1985, p. 112; Mar. 1986, pp. 60, 65–66; July 1986, p. 136; Mar. 1988, p. 71; July 1997, p. 109; Sept. 1997, p. 148.

929 Langley, Andrew. *100 Greatest Tyrants.* Grolier. Challenged at the Mount Isa, Queensland, Australia, high school (2006) by a legislator who described the book as offensive and inappropriate for history studies in any Australian school. The school principal refused to remove the book from the library, describing it as a useful resource for generating debate and critical-thinking skills among students. Source: 11, Jan. 2007, pp. 33–34.

930 Langton, Jane. *The Fragile Flag.* Harper. Challenged at the Jefferson County, Colo. school library (1986) because the book portrays the U.S. government as "shallow" and "manipulative," and "lacking in intelligence and responsibility." Source: 11, Jan. 1987, p. 29; Mar. 1987, p. 49.

931 LaPlace, John. *Health.* Prentice-Hall. Banned from senior high school classrooms in the Diocese of Buffalo, N.Y. (1981). Challenged at the Randolph, N.J. High School (1984) by a group of parents and clergy who say "the textbook is too liberal and should be replaced or supplemented by a more traditional book." Source: 11, Jan. 1981, p. 10; July 1984, p. 106.

932 Larrick, Nancy, and Eve Merriam. *Male and Female under 18.* Prentice-Hall. Banned by the Chelsea, Mass. School Board (1977) from the high school library because of objections to one poem by a teenage girl. The banning was reversed by a U.S. District Court ruling in *Right to Read Defense Committee v. School Committee of the City of Chelsea*, 454 F.Supp. 703 (D. Mass. 1978). Source: 4, p. 104; 12, pp. 12–14, 148–53, 229, 239.

933 Larson, Rodger. *What I Know Now.* Holt. Challenged at the Montgomery County, Tex. Memorial Library System (2004) along with fifteen other young-adult books with gay-positive themes. The objections were posted at the Library Patrons of Texas Web site. The language describing the books is similar to that posted at the Web site of the Fairfax County, Virginia-based Parents Against Bad Books in Schools, to which Library Patrons of Texas links. Source: 11, Nov. 2004, pp. 231–32.

934 **Laurence, Margaret.** *Christmas Birthday Story.* Knopf. Challenged at the York, Maine school system (1982). Source: 11, July 1982, p. 124.

935 _____. *A Jest of God.* Knopf. Challenged at the Peterborough, Ontario County, Canada schools (1984) after a resolution from the nearby Burleigh-Anstruther municipal council asked that the books be reviewed for their moral content. Source: 11, Mar. 1985, p. 45.

936 _____. *The Stone Angel.* Bantam. Challenged at the Peterborough, Ontario County, Canada schools (1984) after a resolution from the nearby Burleigh-Anstruther municipal council asked that the books be reviewed for their moral content. Source: 11, Mar. 1985, p. 45.

937 **Lawrence, D. H.** *Collected Paintings.* Banned by U.S. Customs (1929). Source: 10, p. 142; 15, Vol. III, p. 414.

938 _____. *Lady Chatterley's Lover.* Bantam; Grove; NAL; Random. Banned by U.S. Customs (1929), banned in Ireland (1932), Poland (1932), Australia (1959), Japan (1959), India (1959), and Canada (1960-1962). Dissemination of Lawrence's novel has been stopped in China (1987) because the book "will corrupt the minds of young people and is also against the Chinese tradition." Source: 2, p. 137; 4, pp. 69–70; 6, pp. 1,382–86; 8, pp. 354–57; 11, July 1987, pp. 135–36; 15, Vol. III, pp. 407, 414.

939 _____. *Paintings of D.* H. Lawrence. Cory, Adams & McKay. Barred by U.S. Customs (1929). Source: 4, p. 69.

940 _____. *Pansies.* Penguin. Seized by postal authorities (1928) in England and was substantially altered prior to its republication in 1929. Source: 3, p. 170; 13, pp. 184–85.

941 _____. *The Rainbow.* Penguin; Modern Library/ Random; Viking. Ordered destroyed by the British magistrate's court (1915). Source: 2, p. 100; 4, p. 69; 13, pp. 198–99.

942 _____. *Sons and Lovers.* Penguin; Modern Library/Random; Viking. In 1961, an Oklahoma City group called Mothers United for Decency hired a trailer, dubbed it "smutmobile," and displayed books deemed objectionable, including Lawrence's novel. Source: 4, p. 119.

943 _____. *Women in Love.* Penguin/Viking. Seized by John Summers of the New York Society for the Suppression of Vice and declared obscene (1922). Source: 8, p. 394; 11, p. 142; 15, Vol. III, p. 415.

944 **Lawrence, Jerome, and Robert E. Lee.** *Inherit the Wind.* Dramatists Play Service. Challenged, but retained, at the Lakewood, Ohio High School (1997). The book was challenged by parents who objected to what they called the play's allegedly anti-religious nature. Source: 11, May 1997, p. 79.

945 **Lawrence, Margaret.** *The Diviners.* Bantam; Univ. Chicago Pr. Challenged at the Peterborough, Ontario, Canada County schools (1984) after a resolution from the nearby Burleigh-Anstruther municipal council asked that the books be reviewed for their moral content. Removed from the summer reading list for the Clark, N.J. School District's seventh graders (1997) because of detailed descriptions of sexual intercourse. A group called Parents Against Pornographic Adult Literature was formed to ensure reading lists are correctly oriented and reviewed for Clark students. Source: 11, Mar. 1985, p. 45; Nov. 1997, p. 169.

946 **Lawson, Robert.** *They Were Strong and Good.* Viking. Challenged because the novel "glorifies slavery and racism," but retained at the Multnomah, Oreg. County Library (1991). Source: 11, Jan. 1992, p. 6.

947 **Leach, Maria.** *Whistle in the Graveyard: Folktales to Chill Your Bones.* Puffin. Challenged at the Neely Elementary School in Gilbert, Ariz. (1992) because the book shows the dark side of religion through the occult, the devil, and satanism. Source: 11, May 1992, p. 78; July 1992, p. 124.

948 **Lebert, Benjamin.** *Crazy.* Knopf. Removed from the Canyon Vista Middle School in Round Rock, Tex. (2003) by the principal who decided a parent was correct in being concerned about the book's availability. The parent called the book "vulgar; it talked about parts of the body." There was free use of the 'F-word' and several 'C-words.'

The book was taken off the shelf at the district's other junior high school library. Source: 11, Nov. 2003, p. 229.

949 **Lederer, William J., and Eugene Burdick.** *The Ugly American.* Norton. In 1953, Senator Joe McCarthy led an investigation of the Overseas Library Program. In response to the investigation, "no material by any controversial persons, Communists, fellow travelers, etc. will be used' by the U.S. overseas libraries. The novel was temporarily censored by George A. Allen, director of the U.S. Information Agency, the federal agency responsible for U.S. overseas libraries (1958), because the book "would not be in the interest of the United States." In December 1958, Allen changed his mind. Senator J. W. Fullbright criticized the novel from the Senate floor in 1959. He was upset by the portrayal of American overseas as "boobs or worse," while Russian diplomats were portrayed as "talented, dedicated servants of communism." In 1963 survey by the Wisconsin English Department chairpersons and school administrators, a Wisconsin teacher and a group of parents objected to the novel because of its critical pictures of Americans abroad. Other have been critical of the novel based on its "filthy language and reference to sex" and its profane and vile language. Source: 8, pp. 180–81.

950 **Lee, Harper.** *To Kill a Mockingbird.* Lippincott/Harper; Popular Library. Challenged in Eden Valley, Minn. (1977) and temporarily banned due to words "damn" and "whore lady" used in the novel. Challenged in the Vernon-Verona-Sherill, N.Y. School District (1980) as a "filthy, trashy novel." Challenged at the Warren, Ind. Township schools (1981) because the book does "psychological damage to the positive integration process " and "represents institutionalized racism under the guise of 'good literature.'" After unsuccessfully banning Lee's novel, three black parents resigned from the township human relations advisory council. Challenged in the Waukegan, Ill. School District (1984) because the novel uses the word "nigger." Challenged in the Kansas City, Mo. junior high schools (1985). Challenged at the Park Hill, Mo. Junior High School (1985) because the novel "contains profanity and racial slurs." Retained on a supplemental eighth-grade reading list in the Casa Grande, Ariz. Elementary School District (1985), despite the protests by black parents and the National Association for the Advancement of Colored People who charged the book was unfit for junior high use. Challenged at the Santa Cruz, Calif. Schools (1995) because of its racial themes.

Removed from the Southwood High School Library in Caddo Parish, La. (1995) because the book's language and content were objectionable. Challenged at the Moss Point, Miss. School District (1996) because the novel contains a racial epithet. Banned from the Lindale, Tex. Advanced Placement English reading list (1996) because the book "conflicted with the values of the community." Challenged by a Glynn County, Ga. (2001) School Board member because of profanity. The novel was retained. Returned to the freshmen reading list at Muskogee, Okla. High School (2001) despite complaints over the years from black students and parents about racial slurs in the text. Challenged, but retained in the Normal, Ill. Community High School sophomore literature class (2004) despite concerns the novel is degrading to African Americans. Challenged at the Stanford Middle School in Durham, N.C. (2004) because the 1961 Pulitzer Prize-winning novel uses the word "nigger." Challenged at the Brentwood, Tenn. Middle School (2006) because the book contains "profanity" and "contains adult themes such as sexual intercourse, rape, and incest." The complainants also contend that the book's use of racial slurs promotes "racial hatred, racial division, racial separation, and promotes white supremacy." Source: 8, p. 483; 11, Mar. 1978, p. 31; May 1980, p. 62; Mar. 1982, p. 47; July 1984, p. 105; May 1985, p. 80; July 1985, p. 134; Mar. 1986, pp. 57–58; May 1995, p. 68; Nov. 1995, p. 183; Nov. 1996, pp. 196–97, 199; Nov. 2001, pp. 277–78; Jan. 2002, p. 50; Jan. 2004, p. 11; May 2004, pp. 98–99; March 2006, p. 74.

951 **Lee, Joanna.** *I Want to Keep My Baby.* NAL. Removed from the Morehead High School library in Rockingham County, N.C. (1994) because of "antireligious sentiments—the girl's comment that her boyfriend was 'her God'—and sexual situations." After a three-hour public debate, the Rockingham County School Board later reversed its previous ban against the book. Source: 11, Sept. 1994, p. 148; Nov. 1994, p. 201.

952 **Legman, Gershon, ed.** *The Limerick: 1,700 Examples with Notes, Variants and Index.* Carol Pub. Group. Challenged at the Oak Lawn, Ill. Public Library (1991) because the book contains bawdy limericks with explicit sexual references. Source: 11, Nov. 1991, p. 209; Jan. 1992, p. 26.

953 **LeGuin, Ursula K.** *A Fisherman of the Inland Sea.* HarperPrism. Removed from the West Brazoria, Tex. Junior High School library (2006) because of inappropriate language. Books on "sensitive topics such as death, suicide, physical or sexual abuse, and teenage dating relationships" were moved to a restricted "young-adult" section from which students can borrow only with written parental permission. Source: 11, Nov. 2006, pp. 289–90.

954 _____. *Lathe of Heaven.* Avon. Challenged on a Washougal, Wash. High School reading list (1984) because it contained "profuse profanity." Source: 11, Sept. 1984, p. 157.

955 **Lehrman, Robert.** *Juggling.* Harper. Challenged at Woodbury, Minn. Library (1990). The book is about the life and sexual encounters of a teenage soccer player. Source: 11, July 1990, p. 145.

956 **L'Engle, Madeleine C.** *Many Waters.* Farrar; Dell. Challenged at the Hubbard, Ohio Library (1991) because the book alters the story of Noah's Ark, making it secular and confusing children. Source: 11, Sept. 1991, p. 153.

957 _____. *A Wrinkle in Time.* Dell. Challenged, but retained on the media center shelves of the Polk City, Fla. Elementary School (1985). A student's parent filed the complaint, contending the story promoted witchcraft, crystal balls, and demons. Challenged in the Anniston, Ala. schools (1990) because the book sends a mixed signal to children about good and evil. The complainant also objected to listing the name of Jesus Christ together with the names of great artists, philosophers, scientists, and religious leaders when referring to defenders of Earth against evil. Challenged, but retained, by the Catawba County School Board in Newton, N.C. (1996). A parent requested the book be pulled from the school libraries because it allegedly undermines religious beliefs. Source: 11, July 1985, p. 133; Mar. 1991, p. 62; May 1996, pp. 97–98.

958 **Lenin, Vladimir I.** *Declaration of Independence.* Banned in Oklahoma City, Okla. (1940). Bookstore owners were sentenced to ten years in prison and fined $5,000.00 for selling Lenin's work (1940). Source: 4, p. 60; 10, p. 142.

959 _____. *The State and Revolution.* China Books; International Publishing. Lenin has been censored so often and by so many that it is difficult to catalog all the challenges. Seized as obscene in Boston, Mass. (1927); seized as subversive in Hungary (1927); burned In Munich, Germany (1933); in Providence, R.I. (1954) postal authorities

attempted to withhold from delivery to Brown University 75 copies of this "subversive" title. Banned in Grenada (1989) along with eighty-five other titles. Source: 4, p. 60; 7, pp. 461–63.

960 _____. *United States Constitution.* Banned in Oklahoma City, Okla. (1940). Source: 4, p. 60.

961 **Letts, Billie.** *Where the Heart Is.* G. K. Hall; Warner. Challenged in the Tamaqua, Pa. Area School District (2001) because the book "might not be appropriate for younger schoolmates." The school board is considering the establishment of a restricted-materials section in the district's middle-school library for books deemed objectionable. Students would need parental permission to access any title placed there. Retained in the Natrona County, Wyo. School District (2002) after being challenged for graphic violence, obscene language, and drug use. Source: 11, Mar. 2001, p. 54; July 2001, p. 145; Sept. 2002, p. 223.

962 **Levenkron, Steven.** *The Best Little Girl in the World.* Contemporary Books. Retained as optional reading for eighth graders at Rice Avenue Middle School in Girard, Pa. (2000). A grandmother found the book offensive and didn't want her granddaughters reading it. Source: 11, May 2000, p. 92.

963 **Levin, Ira.** *Rosemary's Baby.* Dell; Random. Removed from the required reading list in Westport, Mass. (1977); banned from use in Aurora, Colo. High School English classes (1976) on the grounds of "immorality." Source: 11, Jan. 1977, p. 8; May 1977, p. 79.

964 _____. *Stepford Wives.* Random. Prohibited for use in the Warsaw, Ind. schools (1979) because of its "questionable nature" and because it might offend someone in the community. Source: 11, Mar. 1980, p. 40.

965 **Levine, Ellen.** *I Hate English.* Scholastic. Challenged by a school board member in the Queens, N.Y. school libraries (1994) because "The book says what a burden it is they have to learn English. They should just learn English and don't complain about it." The rest of the school board voted to retain the book. Source: 11, July 1994, pp. 110–11; Sept. 1994, p. 166.

966 **Levitt, Steven D., and Stephen J. Dubner.** *Freakonomics: A Rogue Economist Explores the Hidden Side of Everything.* Morrow.

Retained on the Northwest Suburban High School District 214 reading list in Arlington Heights, Ill. (2006), along with eight other challenged titles. A board member, elected amid promises to bring her Christian beliefs into all board decision-making, raised the controversy based on excerpts from the books she'd found on the Internet. Source: 11, July 2006, pp. 210–11.

967 Levoy, Myron. *Alan and Naomi.* Dell; Harper. Challenged in Gwinnett County, Ga. (1981) because of objections to the book's language ("hell" and "damn") and mature subject matter. Challenged, but retained, in the Carroll County, Md. schools (1991). Two school board members were concerned about the "sad ending" and "poor" portrayal of Jews. Source: 11, Nov. 1981, p. 168; Mar. 1992, p. 64.

968 Levy, Edward. *Came a Spider.* Arbor House. Removed and later returned to the shelves of the Freeman High School library in Spokane, Wash. (1986) because it contained a two-page description of teenagers engaged in sexual intercourse. Source: 11, May 1986, pp. 80–81.

969 Lewin, Esther. *Random House Thesaurus of Slang.* Random. Placed on a limited access shelf at the Floyd Light Middle School library in Portland, Oreg. (1992). Source: 11, May 1992, p. 81.

970 Lewis, C. S. *The Lion, the Witch and the Wardrobe.* Macmillan. Challenged in the Howard County, Md. school system (1990) because it depicts "graphic violence, mysticism, and gore." Source: 11, Jan. 1991, p. 28.

971 Lewis, Richard, comp. *There Are Two Lives: Poems by Children of Japan.* Simon & Schuster. Despite being on the library's open shelves for 25 years, this book is now restricted to students with parental permission at the Annville-Cleona, Pa. Elementary School library (1999) because an anonymous parent "objected to the entire book." Source: 11, May 1999, pp. 66–67.

972 Lewis, Sinclair. *Cass Timberlane.* Woodhill. Banned in Ireland (1953), in East Berlin (1954). Source: 4, p. 70.

973 _____. *Elmer Gantry.* NAL. Banned in Boston, Mass. (1927); Camden, N.J. (1927); Glasgow, Scotland (1927); Ireland (1931), as "offensive to public morals." The ban in Ireland was upheld in 1953. U.S. Post Office banned any catalog listing of this title (1931). The novel was singled out by censors because of the sexual adventures of its title character and for the language that frequently peppers his personal conversation. Source: 2, p. 133; 4, pp. 70–71; 14, pp. 126–27; 15, Vol. III, pp. 404–5.

974 _____. *It Can't Happen Here.* Doubleday. Banned in Germany (1937). In 1954, all of Sinclair Lewis's books were banned in East Berlin. Source: 7, pp. 266–67.

975 _____. *Kingsblood Royal.* Grosset; Random; Popular Library. In New York City, the Society for the Suppression of Vice sought to prevent sales of the book after complaints arose about the suggested sexual content of the novel. The society's efforts to bring charges against the book were fruitless, and only a few booksellers agreed to remove the novel from their stock. Removed from Illinois libraries (1953) on a mother's complaint that her daughter had borrowed a book that was offensive. Banned in Ireland (1953) for the use of the term nigger and the "suggestive sexuality." Source: 4, p. 71; 14, pp. 203–4.

976 Leyland, Winston, ed. *My Deep Dark Pain Is Love: A Collection of Latin American Gay Fiction.* Gay Sunshine. Seized and shredded (1984) by the British Customs Office. Source: 11, Jan. 1985, p. 16.

977 _____. *Now the Volcano: An Anthology of Latin American Gay Literature.* Gay Sunshine. Seized and shredded (1984) by the British Customs Office. Source: 11, Jan. 1985, p. 16.

978 Li, Hongzhi. *Zhuan Falun: The Complete Teachings of Falun Gong.* Fair Winds Pr. In 1996, the Chinese government's Press and Publications Administration issued a notice banning five Falun Gong publications for propagating ignorance and superstition. On July 22, 1999, the government declared that Falun Gong, as an "evil cult" that advocated superstition and jeopardized social stability, was now an illegal organization. It was prohibited "to distribute books, video/audio tapes or any other materials that propagate Falun Dafa (Falun Gong)" and thousands of people were sent to labor camps, psychiatric wards, or prisons. Source: 8, pp. 308–10.

979 Lieberman, Gail. *Sex and Birth Control: A Guide for the Young.* Crowell; Harper. Challenged at the Cleveland, Tenn. Public Library (1993) along with seventeen other books, most of which are on sex education, AIDS awareness, and some titles on the supernatural. Source: 11, Sept. 1993, p. 146.

980 **Lightner, A. M. *Gods or Demons?*** Fourwinds Pr. Challenged at the Canby, Oreg. Junior High School library (1988) because the book "promotes a secular-humanistic belief in evolution and portrays the 'Bible as myth.'" Source: 11, May 1989, p. 78.

981 **Lindgren, Astrid. *The Children on Troublemaker Street.*** Macmillan. Challenged at the Sweetwater County Library in Green River, Wyo. (1992) because of concerns about how it depicts the "almost swearing of a 4-year-old-child." Source: 11, July 1992, p. 126.

982 **_____. *The Runaway Sleigh Ride.*** Viking. Challenged in the Kokomo-Howard County, Ind. Public Library (1995) because it makes "light of a drinking situation." The book is by the author of the Pippi Longstocking series. Removed, but later returned to the Enfield, Conn. elementary school libraries (1999) despite a parent's objection to passages in which characters sing songs praising drinking. Source: 11, Mar. 1996, p. 46; May 1999, pp. 65–66; July 1999, p. 104.

983 **Lingeman, Richard R. *Drugs from A to Z: A Dictionary.*** McGraw-Hill. Challenged, but retained, in the Des Moines, Iowa school libraries (1986) because the book "not only gives definitions of drugs but also tells how and what to use to get a cheap high—which could be lethal." Source: 11, July 1986, p. 135.

984 **Lion, Elizabeth M. *Human Sexuality in Nursing Process.*** Wiley. President of the National Black Nurses Association called (1982) on nursing schools to boycott this text because it contains material that is "offensive and insensitive" to blacks. Source: 11, Jan. 1983, p. 23.

985 **Lionni, Leo. *In the Rabbit's Garden.*** Pantheon. Challenged at the Naas Elementary School library in Boring, Oreg. (1986) because the story about two rabbits living in a lush garden paradise made a mockery of the Bible's tale of Adam and Eve. Unlike the story of Adam and Eve, Lionni rewards his bunnies for eating the forbidden fruit by allowing them to live happily ever after. Source: 11, Mar. 1987, p. 66.

986 **Lipke, Jean C. *Conception and Contraception.*** Lerner Pubs. The Brighton, Mich.

School Board (1977) voted to remove all sex education books from the high school library. Source: 11, Sept. 1977, p. 133.

987 **Lipsyte, Robert. *The Contender.*** Bantam; Harper. Challenged as a summer youth program reading assignment in Chattanooga, Tenn. (1989) because "it sounds like pretty explicit stuff." Source: 11, Nov. 1989, p. 162.

988 **_____. *One Fat Summer.*** Harper. Challenged at the Greenville, S.C. middle school libraries (1997) because the book includes a passage on masturbation. Removed from the required reading list at the Jonas E. Salk Middle School in Levittown, N.Y. (1997) because it was "sexually explicit and full of violence." The book was a *New York Times* Outstanding Children's Book of 1977. Pulled from Rock Crusher Elementary School in Crystal River, Fla. (1999) after a parent complained that it contains derogatory terms for African-Americans, Jews, and Italians and describes a male character masturbating. Pulled from the Ansonia, Conn. Public Library local schools' display (2004) following a parental complaint about a paragraph describing the masturbation fantasy of a teenage boy. Source: 11, Sept. 1997, pp. 126–28; Jan. 2000, p. 11; Nov. 2004, p. 229.

989 **Llywelyn, Morgan. *Druids.*** Morrow. Removed from middle school libraries in Fairfax County, Va. (2001) due to its depictions of oral sex and rape. Source: 11, Sept. 2000, pp. 145–46; May 2001, p. 96.

990 **Locke, John. *An Essay Concerning Human Understanding.*** Dover; Oxford Univ. Pr.; NAL. Placed on the *Index Librorum Prohibitorum* in Rome (1700), where it remained until 1996. Prohibited reading at Oxford (1701). A Latin version was permitted only on the proviso that "no tutors were to read with their students this essential investigation into the basis of knowledge." Source: 1, pp. 96–97; 3, p. 174; 4, p. 24.

991 **Locker, Sari. *Sari Says: The Real Dirt on Everything from Sex to School.*** Harper. Removed from the shelves at the James Kennedy Public Library in Dyersville, Iowa (2002) because it deals with sexual issues. Source: 11, Sept. 2002, p. 196; Nov. 2002, pp. 255–56.

992 **Lockridge, Ross, Jr. *Raintree Country.*** Pan Macmillan. Attacked in New York City (1953) as "1066 pages of rank obscenity, blasphemy and

sacrilege . . . inimical to faith and morals [and] within the prohibition of the Catholic Index." Source: 15, Vol. IV, p. 709.

993 **Loewen, James W., and Charles Sallis, eds.** *Mississippi: Conflict and Change.* Pantheon. Rejected from use in the Mississippi public schools because the textbook stressed black history too much. A U.S. District Court ruled that the criteria used for rejecting this text were not justifiable in *Loewen v. Turnipsend*, 488 F.Supp. 1138 (N. D. Miss. 1980). Source: 11, July 1980, p. 86; 12, pp. 167–71, 239.

994 **Lofting, Hugh John.** *Doctor Dolittle.* Lippincott; Dell. Expurgated in the 1960s by J. B. Lippincott Company in the effort to make the books conform to the changing sensibilities of a world that was beginning "to coalesce into one international, multiracial society." The 1988 version of the Dr. Dolittle books, published by Dell Publishing, was the result of radical censoring by two editors at Dell and by Christopher Lofting, the author's son. Source: 14, pp. 111–12.

995 **Logan, Daniel.** *America Bewitched: The Rise of Black Magic and Spiritism.* Morrow. Challenged by the "God Squad," a group of three students and their parents, at the El Camino High School in Oceanside, Calif. (1986) because the book "glorified the devil and the occult." Source: 11, Sept. 1986, p. 151; Nov. 1986, p. 224; Jan. 1987, p. 9.

996 **Logan, Jake.** *Slocum Series.* Berkley. Challenged, but retained at the Springdale, Ark. Public Library (2001) along with all other "western" novels because the writings include "pornographic, sexual encounters." Source: 11, Nov. 2001, p. 277.

997 **London, Jack.** *The Call of the Wild.* Ace; Bantam; Grosset; Macmillan; NAL; Penguin; Pocket Bks.; Raintree; Tempo. Banned in Italy (1929), Yugoslavia (1929), and burned in Nazi bonfires (1933). Source: 4, p. 63.

998 **Longstreet, Stephen, ed.** *The Drawings of Renoir.* Borden. Retained at Maldonado Elementary School in Tucson, Ariz. (1994) after being challenged by parents who objected to nudity and "pornographic," "perverted," and "morbid" themes. Source: 11, July 1994, p. 112.

999 **Lopez, Tiffany Ana.** *Growing Up Chicana/o: An Anthology.* Morrow. Challenged, along with seventeen other titles in the Fairfax

County, Va. elementary and secondary libraries (2002), by a group called Parents Against Bad Books in Schools. The group contends the books "contain profanity and descriptions of drug abuse, sexually explicit conduct, and torture." Source: 11, Jan. 2003, p. 10.

1000 **Louys, Pierre.** *Aphrodite.* AMS Pr. Banned by U.S. Customs Department (1929) as lascivious, corrupting, and obscene. In 1930 a New York book dealer, E. B. Marks, was fined $250 for possessing a copy of *Aphrodite* in contravention of the state laws on obscene publications. In 1935, an attempt was made to import the publication into America. This was banned, although the authorities overlooked a 49-cent edition, openly advertised in the *New York Times* Book Review and apparently, despite postal regulations, available through the mail. Source: 3, p. 176; 4, p. 60.

1001 _____. *The Songs of Bilitis.* William Godwin; Capricorn Bks. Banned by U.S. Customs Department (1929) as lascivious, corrupting, and obscene. Source: 4, p. 60.

1002 _____. *The Twilight of the Nymphs.* Fortune Pr. Banned by U.S. Customs Department (1929) as lascivious, corrupting, and obscene. Source: 4, p. 60.

1003 **Lowen, Paul.** *Butterfly.* Blue Moon Bks.; St. Martin. Challenged at the Tigard, Oreg. Public Library (1988) because of explicit sex and extreme physical and psychological cruelty. Source: 11, Jan. 1990, pp. 4–5.

1004 **Lowry, Lois.** *Anastasia Again!* ABC-Clio. Removed from the Lake Wales, Fla. elementary school library (2005) because of a complaint that the book's references to beer, Playboy magazine, and Anastasia making light of wanting to kill herself were inappropriate for children. Source: 11, May 2005, p. 107.

1005 _____. *Anastasia at Your Service.* Houghton; Dell. Challenged at the Casper, Wyo. school libraries (1984). Source: 11, Mar. 1985, p. 42.

1006 _____. *Anastasia Krupnik.* Bantam; Houghton. Removed by the school's principal, and later returned to the Roosevelt Elementary School library in Tulare, Calif. (1986) with the word "shit" whited out. Challenged, but retained, in the Wichita, Kans. public schools (1991) because it was offensive. Removed from, but later returned to, the Stevens Point, Wis. Area School elementary recommended reading list (1992) due to the book's profanity and occasional references to underage drinking. Removed from the Cayce-West Columbia, S.C. School District's Congaree Elementary School library (1998) because of Lowry's use of a vulgarity for human waste, as well as the use of a slang term for sex. Source: 11, Mar. 1987, p. 49; Jan. 1992, p. 26; Mar. 1993, p. 45; May 1993, p. 87; Mar. 1999, p. 36.

1007 _____. *Autumn Street.* Houghton. Challenged at the Casper, Wyo. school libraries (1984). Source: 11, Mar. 1985, p. 42.

1008 _____. *Find a Stranger, Say Good-bye.* Houghton. Challenged at the Casper, Wyo. school libraries (1984). Source: 11, Mar. 1985, p. 42.

1009 _____. *The Giver.* Dell; Houghton. Temporarily banned from classes by the Bonita Unified School District in La Verne and San Dimas, Calif. (1994) after four parents complained that violent and sexual passages were inappropriate for children. Restricted to students with parental permission at the Columbia Falls, Mont. school system (1995) because of the book's treatment of themes of infanticide and euthanasia. Challenged at the Lakota High School in Cincinnati, Ohio (1996). Challenged at the Troy Intermediate School in Avon Lake, Ohio (1999) as an "optional" reading choice for sixth-grade students. A pastor objected to the books "mature themes"—suicide, sexuality, and euthanasia. Challenged, but retained at a Lake Butler, Fla. public middle school (1999). A parent complained because the issues of infanticide and sexual awakening are discussed in the book. Challenged as a suggested reading for eighth-grade students in Blue Springs, Mo. (2003). Parents called the book "lewd" and "twisted" and pleaded for it to be tossed out of the district. The book was reviewed by two committees and recommended for retention, but the controversy continues in 2005. Challenged, but retained at the Seaman, Kans. Unified School District 345 elementary school library (2006). Source: 11, Mar. 1995, p. 42; Jan. 1996, p. 11; Nov. 1996, p. 198; May 1999, p. 70; Jan. 2000, p. 13; Mar. 2005, pp. 57–58; May 2006, p. 153.

1010 _____. *The One Hundredth Thing about Caroline.* Houghton. Challenged at the Casper, Wyo. school libraries (1984). Source: 11, Mar. 1985, p. 42.

1011 _____. *A Summer to Die.* Houghton. Challenged at the Casper, Wyo. school libraries (1984). Source: 11, Mar. 1985, p. 42.

1012 _____. *Taking Care of Terrific.* Houghton. Challenged at the Casper, Wyo. school libraries (1984). Source: 11, Mar. 1985, p. 42.

1013 Ludlum, Robert. *The Matarese Circle.* R. Marek. Restricted at the Pierce, Nebr. High School (1983) to students with parental consent because the book contains unnecessarily rough language and sexual descriptions. Source: 11, May 1983, p. 72.

1014 Ludwig, Coy L. *Maxfield Parrish.* Watson-Guptill. Retained at Maldonado Elementary School in Tucson, Ariz. (1994) after being challenged by parents who objected to nudity and "pornographic," "perverted," and "morbid" themes. Source: 11, July 1994, p. 112.

1015 Lund, Doris. *Eric.* Dell; Harper. Pulled from Lexington, N.C. Middle School (1994) classrooms because of the intense way in which it addresses death. Source: 11, July 1994, p. 115.

1016 Luther, Martin. *Address to the German Nobility.* Concordia; Doubleday. Luther's books were burned in Louvain and Liege in October 1520 and the following months in Cologne and Mainz. Prohibited by edicts of the Emperor and the Pope (1521). Censorship of Luther's writing was pervasive throughout Europe. His work and those of his disciples were destroyed and banned in England, France, Spain, and the Netherlands. Luther's works remained on the Vatican's Index of Forbidden Books until 1930. They were still prohibited, however, according to the church's canon law barring Catholics under penalty of mortal sin from reading books "which propound or defend heresy or schism." Source: 4, pp. 11–12; 8, pp. 267–69.

1017 _____. *Works.* Concordia; Doubleday. Luther's books were burned in Louvain and Liege in October 1520 and the following months in Cologne and Mainz. Prohibited by edicts of the Emperor and the Pope (1521). Censorship of Luther's writing was pervasive throughout Europe. His work and those of his disciples were destroyed and banned in England, France, Spain, and the Netherlands. Luther's works remained on the Vatican's Index of Forbidden Books until 1930. They were still prohibited, however, according to the church's canon law barring Catholics under penalty of mortal sin from reading books "which propound or defend heresy or schism." Source: 4, pp. 11–12; 8, pp. 267–69.

105

1018 Lynch, Chris. *Extreme Elvin.*
HarperCollins. Removed from the Crawford County, Ga. Middle School library (2003) because the book deals with complex issues teenagers confront. Source: 11, Jan. 2004, p. 9.

1019 _____. *The Iceman.* Harper. Removed from the Carroll Middle School Library in Southlake, Tex. (1995) because of "profanity" and it "was not highly recommended for its literary value." Challenged at the Haysville, Kans. Middle School library (1996) when a parent counted 36 places where profanity was used in the book. Challenged on the summer reading list at the Windsor Locks, Conn. Middle School (1998) because of the book's language and the main character's violent behavior. The superintendent proposed a plan to segregate "controversial" materials in the library and require parental permission to read them. Removed from the Medford, Wis. Middle School library (1999) because of foul language and the opinion that it was not "inspiring." Source: 11, May 1995, p. 67; Mar. 1997, p. 49; Jan. 1999, p. 7; May 1999, p. 69.

1020 Maas, Peter. *Serpico.* Viking. Challenged in the Zimmerman, Minn. School District high school libraries (1982). Maas's book was available to students under 18 only with parental permission. Source: 11, Sept. 1982, p. 156.

1021 _____. *The Valachi Papers.* Putnam; Bantam. U.S. Department of Justice sued author to restrain the book's publication (1966). Source: 4, p. 99.

1022 Machiavelli, Niccolo. *Discourses.*
Bantam; Penguin; Routledge & Paul. Placed in the *Index Librorum Prohibitorum* in Rome (1555). Source: 4, p. 9.

1023 _____. *The Prince.* Bantam; NAL; Penguin. Placed in the *Index Librorum Prohibitorum* in Rome (1555). Source: 4, pp. 9–10; 10, pp. 156–57.

1024 Mackler, Carolyn. *The Earth, My Butt, and Other Big Round Things.* Candlewick Pr. Banned by the Carroll County Superintendent in Westminster, Md. (2006), but after protests from students, librarians, national organizations, and the publisher, the book was returned to the high school libraries, but not middle schools. The superintendent objected to the book's use of profanity and its sexual references. The book was named the 2004 Michael L. Printz Honor Book, the American Library Association Best Book for Young Adults, and the International Reading Association's 2005 Young Adults' Choice, among other accolades. Source: 11, Mar. 2006, pp. 70–71.

1025 _____. *Love and Other Four Letter Words.* Delacorte. Removed from the Lincoln Junior High School in Naperville, Ill. (2001) because in addition to swear words and discussions about "getting wasted," the book contains graphic passages about masturbation and sexual intercourse. Source: 11, Jan. 2002, pp. 15–16.

1026 _____. *Vegan Virgin Valentine.* Candlewick Pr. Challenged in the Mandarin High School library in Jacksonville, Fla. (2007) because of inappropriate language. Source: 11, May 2007, p. 91.

1027 Madaras, Lynda, and Dane Saavedra. *What's Happening to My Body? Book for Boys: A Growing-up Guide for Parents & Sons.* Newmarket. Challenged at the Mt. Morris, Ill. School District seventh grade class (1986) because it is written from a "permissive point of view." Challenged, but retained, at the Cleveland, Tenn. Public Library (1993) along with seventeen other books, most of which are on sex education, AIDS awareness, and some titles on the supernatural. Challenged in the Kenai Peninsula Borough schools in Homer, Alaska (1993) because of objections to the way masturbation and homosexuality were presented and to slang words used to describe sexual methods as well as the male anatomy. Missing from the Northside Intermediate School library in Milton, Wis. (1994) after a parent complained, "I don't think my ten-year-old son, or anyone's, needs to know that stuff." Challenged, but retained, at the Washoe County Library System in Reno, Nev. (1994) because "nobody in their right mind would give a book like that to children on their own, except the library." Removed from the media center at Denn John Junior Middle School in Kissimmee, Fla. (1997) because it describes inappropriate subjects like group masturbation. The book is accessible to parents only through the guidance office. Source: 11, Mar. 1987, p. 53; July 1987, pp. 149–50; Sept. 1993, p. 146; Jan. 1994, p. 33; July 1994, pp. 111–12; Sept. 1994, p. 147; Nov. 1994, pp. 200–201; Nov. 1997, p. 167.

1028 Madaras, Lynda, and Area Madaras. *What's Happening to My Body? Book for Girls: A Growing-up Guide for Parents & Daughters.* Newmarket. Challenged at the Mt. Morris, Ill. School District seventh grade class (1986) because it is written from a "permissive point of view."

Challenged, but retained, at the Cleveland, Tenn. Public Library (1993) along with seventeen other books, most of which are on sex education, AIDS awareness, and some titles on the supernatural. Removed from the media center at the Denn Junior Middle School in Kissimmee, Fla. (1997) because it describes inappropriate subjects like group masturbation. The book is accessible to parents only through the guidance office. Challenged at the Crescent Harbor Elementary School library in Oak Harbor, Wash. (1998) because of the book's frankness and use of slang terminology for body parts and sexual acts. H. W. Wilson's *Children's Catalogue* recommends the book for children from 9 to 15 and the book is also featured on Disney's "Parent Express" Web site. Source: 11, Mar. 1987, p. 53; July 1987, pp. 149–50; Sept. 1993, p. 146; Nov. 1997, p. 167; Sept. 1998, pp. 141–42.

1029 **Madaras, Lynda.** *Lynda Madaras Talks to Teens about AIDS: An Essential Guide for Parents, Teachers & Young People.* Newmarket. Challenged, but retained, at the Cleveland, Tenn. Public Library (1993) along with seventeen other books, most of which are on sex education, AIDS awareness, and some titles on the supernatural. Source: 11, Sept. 1993, p. 146.

1030 **Madden, David.** *The Suicide's Wife.* Avon; Bobbs-Merrill. Challenged at the Covington, La. Public Library (1984) because it was "just too immorally written all the way through." Source: 11, July 1984, p. 103.

1031 **Madonna.** *Sex.* Warner. The mylar-wrapped, spiral-bound book of photographs of the exhibitionist pop star Madonna in revealing and erotic poses raised challenges across the country soon after its release in Oct. 1992. In several cities, political leaders exerted pressure on libraries not to acquire or to restrict circulation of the book. In Houston, Tex. (1992) a group called Citizens Against Pornography (CAP) mobilized efforts to have the book removed. The public library agreed to keep the book, but not allow it to circulate and to restrict in-library access to adults only. In Mesa, Ariz. (1992), the mayor ordered the library not to shelve the book. In Austin, Tex. (1992), the county attorney told the library that to make the book available to minors in any way was illegal. The Pikes Peak Library in Colorado Springs, Colo. (1992) and the St. Louis, Mo. Public Library (1992) cancelled the library's order after citizen protest. In Nebraska, the Omaha Public Library (1992) did not plan to buy the book, but six of seven City Council members asked the library to remove it from any potential acquisitions list. The book was challenged at the Champaign, Ill. Public Library (1992) and in Ingham County, Mich. the library board (1992) declined to ban the controversial book. In the public libraries of Manchester, Conn., South Bend, Ind. and Topeka and Shawnee, Kans. (1992), and Spokane, Wash. (1993) the book was challenged. The Downers Grove, Ill. Public Library (1993) retained the book, but at the Naperville, Ill. Public Library (1993) it is excluded. Challenged at the Beloit, Wis. Public Library (1993), along with other adult literature, after complaints that minors were perusing the book's photographs of erotic poses and skimpy outfits. Banned in Ireland (1992). Source: 6, p. 1,211; 11, Jan. 1993, pp. 1, 31–33; Mar. 1993, pp. 37–38; May 1993, pp. 65–66; July 1993, p. 104; Nov. 1993, p. 179.

1032 **Magnus, Erica.** *The Boy and the Devil.* Carolrhoda. Challenged at the Science Hill, Ky. Elementary School library (1987) because the book "hints of a satanic cult" since "there's no way a person can outwit the devil without God's help and nowhere is God mentioned in the book." Source: 11, May 1987, p. 86; July 1987, pp. 147–48.

1033 **Mah, Adeline Yen.** *A Thousand Pieces of Gold: My Discovery of China's Character in the History and Meaning of Its Proverbs.* HarperCollins. Challenged, along with seventeen other titles in the Fairfax County, Va. elementary and secondary libraries (2002), by a group called Parents Against Bad Books in Schools. The group contends the books "contain profanity and descriptions of drug abuse, sexually explicit conduct, and torture." Source: 11, Jan. 2003, p. 10.

1034 **Mahfouz, Naguib.** *Children of the Alley.* Three Continents Pr. Banned by Cairo's Al-Azhar University (1959), condemning it as "blasphemous," and calling the author a heretic for causing offense to the prophets of Islam and for misrepresenting the character of Muhammad. In 1988, Mahfouz won the Nobel Prize and fundamentalist renewed their attacks, fearing that the prize would be used as a pretext to remove the book from the proscribed list. In October 1994, Mahfouz was stabbed several times in the neck as he sat in a car outside his Cairo home. A few weeks after the attack, the novel was published in the Egyptian press for the first time in 35 years. As of mid-1997, however, the novel has not been published in book form in Egypt. Source: 8, pp. 219–20.

1035 **Mailer, Norman.** *Ancient Evenings.* Little. Rejected for purchase by the Hayward, Calif. school trustees (1985) because of "rough language" and "explicit sex scenes." Source: 11, July 1985, p. 111.

1036 _____. *The Naked and the Dead.* Holt; NAL. Banned in Canada (1949) and Australia (1949). Source: 4, p. 96; 6, p. 412.

1037 _____. *Why Are We in Vietnam?* Putnam. In Huntsville, Ala., the assistant city attorney requested that the novel be removed from the public library shelves (1967). After considerable controversy, the book was eventually returned to the public library shelves. Source: 7, pp. 529–30.

1038 **Maimonides.** *The Guide of the Perplexed.* Univ. of Chicago Pr.; Dover; Peter Smith; Shalom. Condemned by his orthodox opponents as heresy. Copies of the publication were burned (1200) when discovered, it was barred from Jewish homes, and anyone reading it was excommunicated; the work was still facing bans in the 19th century. Orthodox Jewish opponents objected to Maimonides's sympathy for Aristotelian thought, which was considered fundamentally incompatible with Hebrew tradition. Maimonides was probably the first Jewish author to have his works burned. Source: 3, p. 29; 8, pp. 237–38.

1039 **Malamud, Bernard.** *The Fixer.* Dell; Farrar; Pocket Bks. Banned from use in Aurora, Colo. High School English classes (1976); removed from the Island Trees, N.Y. Union Free School District High School library in 1976 along with nine other titles because they were considered "immoral, anti-American, anti-Christian, or just plain filthy." Returned to the library after the U.S. Supreme Court ruling on June 25, 1982, in *Board of Education, Island Trees Union Free School District No. 26 et al. v. Pico et al.,* 457 U.S. 853 (1982). Source: 11, May 1977, p. 79; Nov. 1982, p. 197.

1040 **Malcolm X, and Alex Haley.** *The Autobiography of Malcolm X.* Ballantine. Challenged in the Duval County, Fla. public schools (1993) because the slain Black Muslim leader advocated anti-white racism and violence. Restricted at the Jacksonville, Fla. middle school libraries (1994) because it presents a racist view of white people and is a "how-to manual" for crime. Source: 11, Sept. 1993, p. 147; May 1994, p. 83.

1041 **Maloney, Ray.** *The Impact Zone.* Delacorte; Dell. Challenged at the Multnomah County Library in Portland, Oreg. (1989) because of profanity and sexual references. Source: 11, Jan. 1990, pp. 4–5.

1042 **Malory, Sir Thomas.** *Le Morte D'Arthur.* Scribner; Collier; Penguin. Challenged as a required reading assignment at the Pulaski County High School in Somerset, Ky. (1987) because it is "junk." Source: 11, May 1987, p. 90.

1043 **Manchester, William Raymond.** *The Glory and the Dream.* Little. Challenged at the Conway, Ark. High School (1989) as having inappropriate sexual and racial content. Source: 11, July 1989, p. 129; Sept. 1989, p. 186.

1044 **Mandela, Nelson.** *The Struggle Is My Life.* Int. Defense and Aid Fund for Southern Africa. Banned in South Africa. The ban was lifted (1990) after Mandela was released from prison. Confiscated in Grenada (1988-89). Source: 7, pp. 471–72.

1045 **Mandeville, Bernard.** *The Fable of the Bees.* Penguin. Presented twice by an English grand jury for blasphemy (1723 and 1728), and in France it was ordered burned. The Vatican listed it on the Index of Forbidden books, where it remained until 1966. Source: 1, pp. 104–6.

1046 **Manes, Stephen.** *Slim Down Camp.* Bantam; Houghton. Challenged at the Des Plaines, Ill. Public Library (1992) because it contains "repeated profanity and immoral situations." Source: 11, May 1992, p. 79.

1047 **Manet, Edouard.** *Manet.* Abrams. Retained at Maldonado Elementary School in Tucson, Ariz. (1994) after being challenged by parents who objected to nudity and "pornographic," "perverted," and "morbid" themes. Source: 11, July 1994, p. 112.

1048 **Mann, Patrick.** *Dog Day Afternoon.* Delacorte. Placed in a special closed shelf at the Vergennes, Vt. Union High School library (1978). Decision upheld in *Bicknell v. Vergennes Union High School Board,* 475 F.Supp. 615 (D. Vt. 1979), 638 F. 2d 438 (2d Cir. 1980). Source: 11, Jan. 1979, p. 6; 12, pp. 151, 239; 14, pp. 113–15; 15, Vol IV, p. 715.

1049 **Manson, Marilyn.** *The Long, Hard Road out of Hell.* Regan. Challenged because of explicit references to sex, violence, and the occult, but retained at the West Chicago, Ill. Public Library (1998). Source: 11, Jan. 1999, p. 19.

1050 **Maple, Eric.** *Devils and Demons.* Pan; Kingfisher; Rouke. Challenged at the Essrig

Elementary School in Carrollwood, Fla. (1988) because the book contains a pledge to Satan. Source: 11, Jan. 1989, p. 7.

1051 Mapplethorpe, Robert.
Mapplethorpe. Jonathan Cape. Seized by police from the University of Central England library in Birmingham, U.K. (1998). Lawyers acting for the Crown Prosecution Service decided parts of it were likely to "deprave or corrupt" under the 1959 Obscene Publications Act, and advised the police that they had grounds to ask the university to destroy it. The university and publisher have refused to destroy the book. The Crown Prosecution Service concluded that there was insufficient evidence to expect a conviction. Source: 11, May 1998, p. 75; Mar. 1999, p. 48.

1052 Maraini, Fosco. *Tokyo.* Time-Life.
Challenged at the Cherry River Elementary School library in Richwood, W.Va. (1983) because the book includes a photograph of the backsides of nude Japanese men in a public bath. Source: 11, July 1983, p. 122.

1053 Marchetti, Victor, and John D.
Marks. *The CIA and the Cult of Intelligence.* Dell; Knopf. The Central Intelligence Agency obtained a U.S. Court injunction against its publication (1972). Towards the close of its 1974-1975 term the U.S. Supreme Court declined for the second time to review an appeal by the authors, thus upholding the CIA's right to enforce its secrecy agreement with Marchetti, a former employee, and required him to submit material before publication. Source: 4, p. 100; 5, Spring 1976, pp. 88–89.

1054 Marcus, Eric. *Is It a Choice? Answers to Three Hundred of the Most Frequently Asked Questions about Gays and Lesbians.* Harper.
Challenged at the Indianola, Iowa Public Library (1993) because it was not "of much concern to the Christian-believing people of this community." The book is about homosexuality. Source: 11, Jan. 1994, p. 35.

1055 Marcus, Eric. *The Male Couple's Guide to Living Together: What Gay Men Should Know about Living with Each Other and Coping in a Straight World.* Harper. Challenged at the Muscatine, Iowa Public Library (1990) because it is "wrong to promote immorality." Source: 11, Nov. 1990, p. 225.

1056 Marianna. *Miss Flora McFlimsey's Easter Bonnet.* Lothrop. Challenged at the Troy,

Mich. Public Library (1991) because it contained an offensive and unflattering illustration of a black doll. Source: 11, Jan. 1992, p. 26.

1057 Mariels, Elaine Nicpon. *Human Anatomy and Physiology.* Scott Foresman/Addison-Wesley. Challenged, but retained, in the Escambia County, Fla. schools (1998) because of pictures showing a vaginal birth, vaginal warts caused by herpes, and a self-examination for breast cancer. Source: 11, July 1998, p. 107.

1058 Marsden, John. *Letters from the Inside.* Houghton. Challenged, but retained, as required reading for the Youngstown, Ohio State University English Festival (1997) because the book contains the "F-word." Source: 11, May 1997, p. 66.

1059 Martin, Tony. *The Jewish Onslaught: Despatches from the Wellesley Battlefront.* Majority Pr. Criticized at the Enoch Pratt Free Library in Baltimore, Md. (1994) because the book accuses Jews of masterminding the slave trade and blocking the advance of African Americans. "There's no reason for our public library to spend shrinking public funds to promote the circulation of such hatred." Source: 11, Sept. 1994, p. 146.

1060 Martin, W. K. *Marlene Dietrich.* Chelsea House Pubs. Removed from the Anaheim, Calif. school district (2000) because school officials said the book is too difficult for middle school students and that it could cause harassment against students seen with it. The American Civil Liberties Union (ACLU) of Southern California filed suit in *Doe v. Anaheim Union High School District* alleging that the removal is "a pretext for viewpoint-based censorship." The ACLU claims no other books have been removed from the junior high library for similar reasons, even though several, such as works by Shakespeare and Dickens, are more difficult reading. The ACLU contends that the school officials engaged in unconstitutional viewpoint discrimination by removing the book because it contains gay and lesbian material. In March 2001, the school board approved a settlement that restored the book to the high school shelves and amended the district's policy to prohibit the removal of books for subject matter involving sexual orientation, but the book will not be returned to the middle school. Source: 11, Mar. 2001, p. 53; May 2001, p. 95; July 2001, p. 173.

1061 Martinac, Paula. *k. d. lang.* Chelsea House Pubs. Removed from the Anaheim, Calif. school district (2000) because school officials said

the book is too difficult for middle school students and that it could cause harassment against students seen with it. The American Civil Liberties Union (ACLU) of Southern California filed suit in *Doe v. Anaheim Union High School District* alleging that the removal is "a pretext for viewpoint-based censorship." The ACLU claims no other books have been removed from the junior high library for similar reasons, even though several, such as works by Shakespeare and Dickens, are more difficult reading. The ACLU contends that the school officials engaged in unconstitutional viewpoint discrimination by removing the book because it contains gay and lesbian material. In March 2001, the school board approved a settlement that restored the book to the high school shelves and amended the district's policy to prohibit the removal of books for subject matter involving sexual orientation, but the book will not be returned to the middle school. Source: 11, Mar. 2001, p. 53; May 2001, p. 95; July 2001, p. 173.

1062 **Marx, Karl, and Friedrich Engels.** *German Ideology.* Intl. Pubs. Co. Banned in South Korea (1985). East Germany rewrote or expurgated all of Marx's writing in 1953. The Soviet Union began fairly heavy editing of Marx's writings in the 1960s, often altering works to more fully support the positions held by the Communist Party. Marx's texts were included on the South African Index of Objectionable Literature (1974). Marx's works were removed from the list in 1991. Source: 5, Apr. 1986, pp. 30–33; 7, pp. 127–29.

1063 **Marx, Karl.** *Capital.* Imported Publishers; Random; Regnery. Prohibited reading in China (1929) and challenged at the Boston, Mass. Public Library (1950-1953) because of the book's communistic message. Restricted at Marquette University in Milwaukee, Wis. (1953). Instructors submitted the names of students who borrowed the book; the list was subsequently turned over to the archbishop. Removed from the Brooksfield, Fla. Public library (1953) because they were "communist propaganda." East Germany rewrote or expurgated all of Marx's writing in 1953. The Soviet Union began fairly heavy editing of Marx's writings in the 1960s, often altering works to more fully support the positions held by the Communist Party. Marx's texts were included on the South African Index of Objectionable Literature (1974). Marx's works were removed from the list in 1991. In South Korea, where communism is illegal, the government sued the publisher in court, charging a violation of South Korea's National Security Law. Source: 4, pp. 44–45; 7, pp. 127–29.

1064 **_____.** *The Communist Manifesto.* Intl. Pub. Co. Prohibited in Germany (1878), in China (1929), challenged at the Boston, Mass. Public Library (1950-1953) because of the book's communistic message. East Germany rewrote or expurgated all of Marx's writing in 1953. The Soviet Union began fairly heavy editing of Marx's writings in the 1960s, often altering works to more fully support the positions held by the Communist Party. Marx's texts were included on the South African Index of Objectionable Literature (1974). Marx's works were removed from the list in 1991. In South Korea, where communism is illegal, the government sued the publisher in court, charging a violation of South Korea's National Security Law. Source: 4, pp. 44–45; 7, pp. 127–29; 8, pp. 122–25.

1065 **Masland, Robert P. Jr., ed., and David Estridge, ex. ed.** *What Teenagers Want to Know about Sex: Questions and Answers.* Little. Challenged in the Kenai Peninsula Borough schools in Homer, Alaska (1993) because it presents "sexual relations in an amoral light." Source: 11, Jan. 1994, pp. 33–34.

1066 **Mason, Bobbie Ann.** *In Country.* Harper. Recalled as supplemental reading in two college preparatory English classes at the Charlton County High School in Folkston, Ga. (1994). All of the parents of the forty-eight students in the classes had given permission for their children to read the book. But it was removed from their hands in May after one of those parents complained it included profanity. Challenged at the West Chester, Pa. schools (1994) as "most pornographic." Source: 11, Sept. 1994, p. 150; Jan. 1995, p. 25; Mar. 1995, p. 45; July 1995, p. 99.

1067 **Masters, Edgar Lee.** *Spoon River Anthology.* Buccaneer Bks.; Macmillan. Several students brought suit against the Scioto-Darby School District in Willard, Ohio (1974) for removing two pages because the poems were "inappropriate" and their language might be offensive to some. The case was dismissed in *Kramer v. Scioto-Darby City School District*, Civil Action 72-406, Southern District of Ohio, Mar. 8, 1974. Source: 12, pp. 133–34, 238.

1068 **Mathabane, Mark.** *Kaffir Boy.* NAL. Challenged at the Amador High School in Sutter Creek, Calif. (1993) and Manasquan, N.J. schools (1993) because of a brief but graphic passage involving homosexuality. Temporarily pulled from the Greensboro, N.C. high school libraries (1996)

after a resident sent letters to school board members and some administrators charging that the book could encourage young people to sexually assault children. Challenged as part of the sophomore curriculum at the Lewis S. Mills High School (1996) in Burlington, Conn. because of brutal and graphic language. Challenged, but retained, on a core reading list for high school sophomores, at the Lincoln Unified School District in Stockton, Calif. (1997). Some parents referred to the book as "pornographic and racially insensitive." Removed from a Federal Hocking High School English class in Athens, Ohio (1999) because it contains a sexually graphic passage that some have deemed offensive. Kearsley, Mich. school officials (2000) deleted six sentences describing a homosexual molestation scene in the book after some parents found it offensive. Removed from sophomore reading list at Armijo High School in Fairfield, Calif. (2000) due to its sexual content. Retained at the East Union High School in Manteca, Calif. (2006) senior English class. The controversial autobiography was challenged as inappropriate because a passage uses the words "penis" and "anus" to describe a scene in which a group of young boys are about to prostitute themselves to a group of men for food. Source: 11, Jan. 1994, pp. 15, 38; July 1996, p. 119; Mar. 1997, p. 38; May 1997, p. 62; July 1997, pp. 109–10; May 1999, p. 70; Mar. 2000, p. 50; Nov. 2000, p. 195; July 2006, pp. 209–10.

1069 **Matthiessen, Peter.** *In the Spirit of Crazy Horse.* Viking. South Dakota Governor William J. Janklow named three South Dakota bookstores in a $20-million libel suit because the bookstores refused to stop selling Matthiessen's book. A Sioux Falls judge ruled on June 18, 1984 that Matthiessen's work is not defamatory and threw out the case. Source: 6, pp. 1,555–56; 8, pp. 100–105; 11, July 1983, p. 112; Jan. 1984, p. 18; May 1984, p. 75; July 1984, p. 116; Sept. 1984, p. 148.

1070 **May, Julian.** *A New Baby Comes.* Creative Ed. Soc. Placed on restricted shelves at the Evergreen School District elementary school libraries in Vancouver, Wash. (1987) in accordance with the school board policy to restrict student access to sex education books in elementary school libraries. Source: 11, May 1987, p. 87.

1071 **Mayer, Mercer.** *Liza Lou & the Yellow Belly Swamp.* Macmillan. Challenged at the Douglas County Library in Roseburg, Oreg. (1988) because of scary pictures and references to boiling children. Source: 11, Jan. 1990, pp. 4–5.

1072 **Mayer, Mercer.** *A Special Trick.* Dial. Challenged at the Coburg Elementary School in Eugene, Oreg. (1992) for allegedly satanic art. The book was retained, but the school principal removed an accompanying audiotape that encourages children to look closely at the artwork. Source: 11, July 1992, p. 103.

1073 **Mayle, Peter.** *What's Happening to Me? The Answers to Some of the World's Most Embarrassing Questions.* Carol Pub. Group; Stuart. Challenged and eventually moved from the Henderson, Nev. Public Library (1983) children's section to the adult shelves because the book is "too sexually explicit and unsuitable for children." Challenged, but retained, at the Cleveland, Tenn. Public Library (1993) along with seventeen other books, most of which are on sex education, AIDS awareness, and some titles on the supernatural. Source: 11, Mar. 1984, p. 39; May 1984, p. 71; Sept. 1993, p. 146.

1074 _____. *Where Did I Come From?* Stuart. Banned from elementary classrooms in Hamden, Conn. (1980) because it was judged not appropriate. Challenged at the Washoe County Library System in Reno, Nev. (1994) because "Nobody in their right mind would give a book like that to children on their own, except a library." Source: 11, Mar. 1980, p. 32; Sept. 1994, p. 147.

1075 **Mazer, Harry.** *I Love You, Stupid.* Crowell. Banned from Des Moines, Iowa junior high school libraries (1982) after a parent's complaint that the book was "morally inappropriate." Removed from the Evergreen School District of Vancouver, Wash. (1983) along with twenty-nine other titles. The American Civil Liberties Union of Washington has filed suit contending that the removals constitute censorship, a violation of plaintiff's rights to free speech and due process, and the acts are a violation of the state Open Meetings Act because the removal decisions were made behind closed doors. Source: 11, Sept. 1982, p. 155; Nov. 1983, pp. 185–86.

1076 _____. *The Last Mission.* Dell. Challenged at the Pequannock Valley Middle School in Pompton Plains, N.J. (1984) because of its "language." Moved from the Alexander Middle School library to the Nekoosa, Wis. High School library (1986) because of "profanity" in the book. Banned, but later reinstated in the Carroll Middle School Library in Southlake, Tex. (1995). In the original complaint, a parent requested its removal

111

because of excessive profanity. Challenged, but retained at the Auburn-Placer County, Calif. Library (1999) because of sexually explicit material. Source: 11, Nov. 1984, p. 185; Mar. 1985, p. 59; Jan. 1987, p. 10; May 1995, p. 67; July 1995, p. 95; Sept. 1995, p. 159; Nov. 1999, p. 171.

1077 _____. **Snow Bound.** Dell; Peter Smith. Challenged at the Stoughton, Wis. middle school reading program (1987) because the book includes "several profane oaths invoking the deity, two four-letter words for bodily wastes, and the term 'crazy bitch' and 'stupid female.'" Source: 11, May 1987, p. 103.

1078 **Mazer, Norma Fox. Out of Control.** Avon; Morrow; Thorndike Pr. Banned at the Cooper Middle School Library in Putnam City, Okla. (1995) because of language "inappropriate for that age level." Challenged also at the Oklahoma City, Okla. Metropolitan Library System (1995), but retained. Source: 11, July 1995, p. 94.

1079 _____. **Saturday, the Twelfth of October.** Delacorte; Dell; Dial. Removed from the seventh-grade classroom in Chester, Vt. (1977) after a parent described the book as "filthy." Source: 11, Mar. 1978, p. 31.

1080 _____. **Up in Seth's Room.** Delacorte. Removed from the Campbell County, Wyo. School District libraries and classrooms (1982). After complaints of three district media specialists about the "illegitimately constituted" review committee, however, the book was reinstated. Source: 11, Mar. 1983, p. 51.

1081 **McAlpine, Helen, and William McAlpine. Japanese Tales and Legends.** Oxford Univ. Pr. Challenged at the Wilsona School District in Lake Los Angeles, Calif. (1995) because of depictions of violence and references to Buddha and ritual suicide. Source: 11, Jan. 1996, p. 13.

1082 **McBain, Ed. Alice in Jeopardy.** Pocket. Challenged at the Sno-Isle Libraries in Arlington, Wash. (2006) because of "curse words and graphic sex scenes." Source: 11, Jan. 2007, p. 11.

1083 **McBride, Will, and Helga Fleischhauer-Hardt. Show Me!** St. Martin. Publisher prosecuted on obscenity charges in Massachusetts (1975), New Hampshire (1976), Oklahoma (1976), and Toronto, Ontario, Canada (1976). In all four cases, the judges ruled as a matter

of law that the title was not obscene. Frequently challenged in libraries across the country, e.g., at the Stanislaus County, Calif. library (1984), and the San Jose, Calif. library (1984) because the book "condones child molestation or child pornography." Less than two weeks later, the copy of the book was reported lost by the borrower, a member of the Turlock Action Committee, which organized the movement to ban the book. Challenged at the Seattle, Wash. Public Library (1985) because "it is inappropriate for the library collection." Challenged at the Alameda County, Calif. Library (1986) because "we are giving the pedophile a platform on which to stand" and placed on restrictive shelves in three branches. Challenged at the Steele Memorial Library in Elmira, N.Y. (1986) because it "promotes masturbation, sex between young people, and incest." Source: 11, Nov. 1984, pp. 183, 195; Jan. 1985, pp. 7, 27; May 1985, p. 79; July 1985, pp. 112–13; Mar. 1986, p. 37; May 1986, p. 97; Jan. 1987, pp. 29–31.

1084 **McCall, Don. Jack the Bear.** Fawcett. Removed from the Monticello, Iowa school library (1978) due to "objectionable" language. Source: 11, May 1978, p. 56.

1085 **McCammon, Robert. Boy's Life.** Pocket Bks.; Thorndike Pr. Challenged as required reading in the Hudson Falls, N.Y. schools (1994) because the book has recurring themes of rape, masturbation, violence, and degrading treatment of women. Source: 11, Nov. 1994, p. 190; Jan. 1995, p. 13; Mar. 1995, p. 55.

1086 **McCammon, Robert. Mystery Walk.** Pocket Bks. Challenged in the Salem-Keizer, Oreg. school libraries (1992) because "it is full of violence and profanity." Source: 11, July 1992, p. 125.

1087 **McCarthy, Mary. The Group.** Harcourt. Banned in Ireland on January 21, 1964. The Irish Board of Censors found the work "obscene" and "indecent," objecting particularly to the author's handling of the characters' sexuality, suggestions of homosexuality and "promiscuity." The work was officially banned from sale in Ireland until 1967. Placed on its "Publication Restricted or Prohibited" list (1964) by New Zealand Customs. Faced with public disapproval, the comptroller of Customs lifting the prohibition. Challenged in Terre Haute, Ind. (1982) as an optional reading in an elective English course for junior and senior high school students. Source: 8, pp. 343–44; 11, May 1982, p. 86.

1088 **McCoy, Kathy, and Charles Wibbelsman.** *The New Teenage Body Book.* Body Pr. Withdrawn as a textbook, but retained as a "classroom resource," in the ninth-grade health classes in Pembroke, Mass. (1990) because it is "obscene." Parents have asked that the abstinence-based sex education program Sex Respect be substituted. Complainant wants school officials indicted for distributing obscene materials to children. Source: 11, Jan. 1991, p. 17; Mar. 1991, p. 44; Jan. 1992, p. 8.

1089 **McCuen, Gary E., and David L. Bender.** *The Sexual Revolution.* Greenhaven. Banned from the Brighton, Mich. High School library (1977) along with all other sex education materials. Source: 11, Sept. 1977, p. 133.

1090 **McCullers, Carson.** *Member of the Wedding.* Houghton. Challenged in the Tamaqua, Pa. Area School District (2001) because the book "might not be appropriate for younger schoolmates." The school board is considering the establishment of a restricted-materials section in the district's middle-school library for books deemed objectionable. Students would need parental permission to access any title placed there. Source: 11, Mar. 2001, p. 54; July 2001, p. 145.

1091 **McCunn, Ruthanne Lum.** *Thousand Pieces of Gold.* Design Enterprises. Removed from elementary school library shelves in Sonoma County, Calif. (1984) because certain passages were too "sexually explicit." Challenged at the Commodore Middle School in Bainbridge Island, Wash. (1992) as inappropriate by three parents because of violence, sexual scenes, and "lack of family values." Rejected as an addition to a core literature list by the Amador County, Calif. (1994) Unified School District because "it makes America look bad." Source: 11, Sept. 1984, p. 137; May 1992, p. 84; July 1994, p. 109.

1092 **McDermott, Beverly Brodsky.** *The Golem: A Jewish Legend.* Lippincott. A first grade teacher asked the Newburgh, N.Y. school officials (1993) to ban this Caldecott Award-winning children's book about the persecution of Jews in sixteenth-century Prague. The teacher objected to the strong language and threatening artwork that children might not understand. Source: 11, Nov. 1993, p. 178.

1093 **McFarland, Philip J., et al.** *Themes in World Literature.* Houghton. Challenged at the Tempe Union High School District in Mesa, Ariz. (1995). The story, "A Rose for Emily," by William Faulkner was objectionable because it uses the word "nigger" six times as well as other demeaning phrases. Source: 11, Jan. 1996, p. 13; May 1996, p. 98.

1094 **McGahern, John.** *The Dark.* Penguin. Banned in Ireland (1965). No detailed official statement was required to be made available for the historical record, but it was assumed the novel was banned on the basis of several passages that dealt with the central character's discovery of his sexuality. Source: 6, pp. 1,480–81.

1095 **McHargue, Georgess.** *Meet the Werewolf.* Harper. Challenged at the Evergreen School District in Vancouver, Oreg. (1983) because the book was "full of comments about becoming a werewolf, use of opium, and pacts with the devil." Challenged because the book would lead children to believe ideas contrary to the teachings of the Bible, but retained by the Sikes Elementary School media center in Lakeland, Fla. (1985). Challenged at the Barringer Road Elementary School in Ilion, N.Y. (1992) because the book's passages on the occult were objectionable. Source: 11, Sept. 1983, p. 139; July 1985, p. 133; Jan. 1993, p. 9.

1096 **McHugh, Vincent.** *The Blue Hen's Chicken.* Random. Confiscated in New York City (1947) because the poetry book contained a part titled "Suite from Catullus," eight short poems that were variations on a theme of the Roman poet. Source: 15, Vol. IV, p. 699.

1097 **McKay, Susan.** *Living Law.* Scholastic and Constitutional Rights Foundation. Removed (1981) from the Mississippi state-approved textbook list because of complaints that the book "undermines" the values parents teach at home. Source: 11, May 1981, p. 67; July 1981, p. 93.

1098 **McKissack, Patricia.** *Mirandy and Brother Wind.* Knopf. Challenged at the Glen Springs Elementary School in Gainesville, Fla. (1991) because of the book's use of black dialect. Source: 11, July 1991, p. 129.

1099 **McMillan, Rosalyn.** *Knowing.* Warner. Challenged, but retained at the Cumberland County Library in Fayetteville, N.C. (1999) despite a complaint that the book contains profanity. In addition, the complainant suggested that the library move sexually explicit materials, as well as ones about homosexuality, into an adult section and establish a review committee to screen materials. Source: 11, July 1999, p. 94; Jan. 2000, pp. 27–28.

1100 **Medved, Michael.** *Hollywood vs. America: Popular Culture and the War against Traditional Values.* HarperCollins. Withdrawn from the freshman curriculum at Greencastle, Ind. High School (1997) because of the graphic language in Medved's work, especially the chapter devoted to popular music. Source: 11, July 1997, p. 98.

1101 **Meeks, Linda, and Philip Heit.** *Your Relationship.* Merill Pub. Challenged in the Barrington, Ill. School District (1990) because the book has a chapter on incest that creates "ugly imagery for innocent minds." Source: 11, Jan. 1991, p. 29.

1102 **Melville, Herman.** *Moby Dick.* Modern Library. Banned from the Advanced Placement English reading list at the Lindale, Tex. schools (1996) because it "conflicts with the values of the community." Source: 11, Nov. 1996, p. 199.

1103 **Meretzky, Eric.** *Zork: The Malifestro Quest.* Tor Bks. Challenged at the Jeffers Elementary School in Spring Lake, Mich. (1990) because it "is a disgrace to the Lord and to the Spring Lake school system." Source: 11, May 1990, p. 84; July 1990, p. 145.

1104 **Meriwether, Louise.** *Daddy Was a Numbers Runner.* Jove. Removed from all Oakland, Calif. (1977) junior high school libraries and its use restricted in senior high schools, following a complaint about the book's explicit depiction of ghetto life. Source: 11, May 1977, p. 71.

1105 **Mernissi, Fatima.** *The Veil and the Male Elite: A Feminist Interpretation of Women's Rights in Islam.* Addison-Wesley. Banned in Morocco, Saudia Arabia, and Syria (1991). Authorities regarded as particularly threatening Mernissi's contention that the sacred texts were manipulated as political weapons and that commonly accepted hadith are based on falsehood. Saudia Arabia is ruled by Muslim religious law, or sharia, which encompasses the hadith. Moroccan legal family coeds at the time were also based on sharia. In 2003, the book was translated for the first time into Farsi and published in Iran by Ney Publications. In August 2003, its translator, publisher, and the Iranian official who authorized the book's publication were convicted by the Criminal Court of Tehran of "insulting and

undermining the holy tenets of Islam," "sullying the person of the Prophet Muhammad," and "distorting Islamic history" by "publishing false, slanderous, and fabricated texts." The court also ordered that copies of Mernissi's book be shredded. Source: 8, pp. 305–6.

1106 **Merriam-Webster Editorial Staff.** *Merriam-Webster Collegiate Dictionary.* Merriam-Webster. Removed from classrooms in Carlsbad, N. Mex. schools (1982) because the dictionary defines "obscene" words. Challenged in the Upper Pittsgrove Township, N.J. schools (1989) because the definition of sexual intercourse was objectionable. Challenged, but the 1,100 copies of the dictionary were returned to the Sparks, Nev. Elementary School classrooms (1993). A sixth-grade teacher objected to the book because it includes obscene words. Source: 11, Nov. 1982, p. 206; Jan. 1990, p. 11; Jan. 1994, p. 37.

1107 **Merriam, Eve.** *Halloween ABC.* Macmillan. Challenged at the Douglas County Library in Roseburg, Oreg. (1989) because the book encourages devil worshipping. Challenged at the Howard County, Md. school libraries (1991) because "there should be an effort to tone down Halloween and there should not be books about it in the schools." Challenged in the Wichita, Kans. public schools (1991) because it is "satanic and disgusting." Challenged at the Acres Green Elementary School in Douglas County, Colo. (1992). Challenged and retained, but will be shelved with other works generally available only to older students and won't be used in future Halloween displays at the Federal Way School District in Seattle, Wash. (1992). The compromise was for a group of parents who objected to the book's satanic references. Challenged, but retained in the Othello, Wash. elementary school libraries (1993) because the book "promotes violent criminal and deviant behavior." Challenged, but retained at the Ennis, Texas Public Library (1993). Challenged in the Cameron Elementary School library in Rice Lake, Wis. (1993) because the "poems promote satanism, murder, and suicide." The book was retained. Challenged in the Spokane, Wash. School District library (1994) by a father who found the poems morbid and satanic. In particular, the parent disapproved of one poem, which "appears to be a chant calling forth the Devil." Challenged in the Sandwich, Mass. Public Library (1995) because it is "too violent for young children." Challenged, but retained in the Wellsville, N.Y. elementary school library (2000) despite complaints the book promotes violence. Source: 11, Jan. 1990, pp. 4–5;

Sept. 1991, p. 178; Jan. 1992, p. 26; May 1992, p. 94; Mar. 1993, p. 43; July 1993, pp. 103–4; Sept. 1993, p. 159; Jan. 1994, pp. 13–14; Mar. 1994, pp. 69–70; Jan. 1995, p. 9; Mar. 1995, p. 41; Sept. 1995, p. 158; Mar. 2001, p. 75.

1108 _____. *The Inner City Mother Goose.* Simon & Schuster/Touchstone. An Erie County, N.Y. judge (1972) called for a grand jury investigation of this satirical book of adult nursery rhymes, alleging it taught crime; similar controversies were reported in Baltimore, Md.; Minneapolis, Minn.; San Francisco, Calif. Removed from the Whitney Point, N.Y. middle school library (2000) after a parent complained about its language and content. Source: 4, p. 91; 11, July 2000, p. 104.

1109 Merrick, Gordon. *One for the Gods.* Avon. Seized (1984) by the British Customs Office. Source: 11, Jan. 1985, p. 26.

1110 Metalious, Grace. *Peyton Place.* Simon & Schuster. In 1957, the city of Knoxville, Tenn., activated a city ordinance that permitted the Knoxville City Board of Review to suppress any publication that it considered to be obscene. The target was Metalious' novel; local dealers were forbidden to sell it. When one indignant newsstand owner tested the ordinance, it was ruled unconstitutional. Banned in Ireland as "obscene" and "indecent" from 1958 until the introduction of the Censorship of Publications Bill in 1967. Temporary ban lifted in Canada (1958). The novel was one of several paperbacks considered objectionable for sale to youths under 18 in *State v. Settle*, 156 A.2d 921 (R.I. 1959). In 1959, the Rhode Island Commission to Encourage Morality in Youth brought action against Bantam and three other New York paperback publishers. The Rhode Island Superior Court upheld the decision, which was later reversed by the U.S Supreme Court in *Bantam Books, Inc. et al., v. Joseph A. Sullivan, et al.* Source: 4, p. 97; 8, pp. 373–74.

1111 Meyer, Michael, ed. *Bedford Introduction to Literature.* St. Martin. The Paxon School for Advanced Studies in Jacksonville, Fla. (2000) principal authorized teachers to cut out the play Angels in America from the textbook. The Duval County School Board first banned the play three years ago after learning that it was being used in a class at Douglas Anderson School of the Arts. The play is the first half of Tony Kushner's work depicting the United States in the 1980s as the AIDS epidemic began to spread. It won the 1993 Pulitzer Prize for drama and several Tony awards, including best play. Source: 11, Mar. 2001, p. 56.

1112 Mezrich, Ben. *Bringing Down the House: The Inside Story of Six M.I.T. Students Who Took Vegas for Millions.* Arrow; Free Press. Challenged in the Beaverton, Oreg. schools as supplemental reading (2004) because it contains profanity and abundant references to prostitution and gambling. In 2004, the book was number eighteen on *The New York Times*'s paperback nonfiction best-seller list. Source: 11, Mar. 2005, pp. 58–59.

1113 Mill, John Stuart. *Social Philosophy.* Listed on the *Index Librorum Prohibitorum* in Rome (1856) until 1966. Source: 4, p. 42.

1114 _____. *System of Logic.* Univ. of Toronto Pr. Listed on the *Index Librorum Prohibitorum* in Rome (1856). Source: 4, p. 42.

1115 Millard, Anne, and Patricia Vanags. *The Usborne Book of World History.* EDC Pubs. Restricted to teachers only in the Gwinnett County, Ga. schools (1998) after objections to nude drawings depicting life in ancient civilizations. Complainants also objected to *The Usborne Time Traveler Books* (Pharaohs and Pyramids), by Tony Allan. Source: 11, Sept. 1998, pp. 143–44.

1116 Miller, Arthur. *The Crucible.* Penguin. Challenged at the Cumberland Valley High School, Harrisburg, Pa. (1982) because the play contains "sick words from the mouths of demon-possessed people. It should be wiped out of the schools or the school board should use them to fuel the fire of hell." Challenged as a required reading assignment at the Pulaski County High School in Somerset, Ky. (1987) because it is "junk." Challenged, but retained in the sophomore curriculum at West Middlesex, Pa. High School (1999). Source: 11, Mar. 1983, pp. 52–53; May 1987, p. 90; July 1999, p. 105.

1117 _____. *Death of a Salesman.* Penguin; Viking. Challenged at the Dallas, Tex. Independent School District high school libraries (1974); banned from English classes at Spring Valley Community High School in French Lick, Ind. (1981) because the play contains the words "goddamn," "son of a bitch," and "bastard." Challenged as a required reading assignment at the Pulaski County High School in Sinking Valley, Ky. (1987) because it is "junk." Challenged, but retained, at Egyptian High School in Tamms, Ill. (1997). The play was considered offensive by some because of "profanity." Source: 11, July 1975, pp. 6–7; May 1981, p. 68; May 1987, p. 90; May 1997, p. 78.

1118 Miller, Deborah A., and Alex Waigandt. *Coping with Your Sexual Orientation.* Rosen. Moved from the Chestnut Ridge Middle School library in Washington Township, N.J. (1994) because school administrators have been accused of "indoctrinating children in the gay lifestyle." Source: 11, Sept. 1994, p. 148.

1119 Miller, Henry. *Opus Pistorum.* Grove Pr. Removed from the Cumberland County, N.C. library system (1993) because it lacks "serious literary or artistic merit for this library's collection." Source: 11, Mar. 1993, p. 42.

1120 _____. *Sexus.* Grove. Banned in France (1950); in Norway (1956). Source: 4, p. 74.

1121 _____. *Tropic of Cancer.* Grove. Banned from U.S. Customs (1934). The U.S. Supreme Court found the novel not obscene (1964). Banned in Turkey (1986). Source: 4, p. 74; 5, July/ Aug. 1986, p. 46; 6, pp. 1,597–98; 8, pp. 387–89.

1122 _____. *Tropic of Capricorn.* Grove. Ban upheld by U.S. Court of Appeals in San Francisco (1953). An appeals court in Istanbul, Turkey, authorized a public burning (1989) of Miller's 1939 novel as sexually exploitative. Source: 4, p. 74; 6, pp. 1,597–98; 8, pp. 387–89; 11, May 1989, p. 90.

1123 Miller, Jim, ed. *The Rolling Stone Illustrated History of Rock and Roll.* Random. Challenged in Jefferson County, Ky. (1982) because it "will cause our children to become immoral and indecent." Source: 11, Mar. 1983, p. 41.

1124 Milton, John. *Paradise Lost.* Airmont; Holt; Modern Library/Random; NAL; Norton. Listed on the *Index Librorum Prohibitorum* in Rome (1758). Source: 4, p. 22.

1125 Mishima, Yukio. *The Sound of Waves.* Putnam. Challenged, but retained, at the Lake Washington School District in Kirkland, Wash. (1993), despite objections that it is "crude, vulgar, degrading to women, seductive, enticing, and suggestive." Challenged in the Newark, Calif. Unified School District (2001) because the book is sexually explicit. Source: 11, Jan. 1994, p. 16; Mar. 1994, p. 71; Mar. 2001, p. 55.

1126 Mitchell, Margaret. *Gone with the Wind.* Avon; Macmillan. Banned from the Anaheim, Calif. Union High School District English classrooms (1978) according to the Anaheim Secondary Teachers Association. Challenged in the Waukegan, Ill. School District (1984) because the novel uses the word "nigger." Source: 11, Jan. 1979, p. 6; July 1984, p. 105.

1127 Mitchell, Stephen. *Gilgamesh: A New English Version.* Free Pr. Challenged in the Clearview Regional High School in Harrison Township, N.J. (2006) because the modern translation of one of the oldest known pieces of literature was considered sexually descriptive and unnecessarily explicit. The work itself dates back to about 1700 B.C., some one thousand years before the writings of Homer. Source: 11, Jan. 2007, p. 10.

1128 Mochizuki, Ken. *Baseball Saved Us.* Lee & Low Bks. Challenged, but retained on the second-grade reading list in the New Milford, Conn. schools (2006) despite the fact the word "Jap" is used to taunt the main character in the book. The children's story is about the World War II Japanese-American internment. Source: 11, July 2006, pp. 183–84.

1129 Moe, Barbara A. *Everything You Need to Know about Sexual Abstinence.* Rosen. Pulled from the Ouachita Parish School library in Monroe, La. (1996) because of sexual content. The Louisiana chapter of the ACLU filed a lawsuit in the federal courts on October 3, 1996, claiming that the principal and the school superintendent violated First Amendment free speech rights and also failed to follow established procedure when they removed the book. The three-year-old school library censorship case headed to court after the Ouachita Parish School Board made no decision to seek a settlement at a special meeting April 12, 1999. On August 17, 1999, the Ouachita Parish School Board agreed to return the book to the library and to develop a new book-selection policy that follows state guidelines for school media programs. Source: 11, Sept. 1996, pp. 151–52; Jan. 1997, p. 7; July 1999, p. 93; Jan. 2000, p. 27.

1130 Mohr, Richard D. *A More Perfect Union: Why Straight America Must Stand Up for Gay Rights.* Beacon Pr. Challenged, but retained, at the Belfast, Maine Free Library (1996) because "homosexuality destroys marriages and families; it destroys the good health of the individual and the innocent are infected by it." Source: 11, May 1996, p. 97.

1131 Momaday, N. Scott. *House Made of Dawn.* Harper; NAL; Penguin. Challenged at the Reynolds High School in Troutdale, Oreg. (1989)

because two pages of the 1969 Pulitzer Prize winner were sexually explicit. Retained on the Round Rock, Tex. Independent High School reading list (1996) after a challenge that the book was too violent. Source: 11, Jan. 1990, p. 32; May 1996, p. 99.

1132 Montaigne, Michel de. *Essays.* AMS Pr.; French & European; Gordon Pr.; Stanford Univ. Pr. His book was confiscated on a trip to Rome, and a papal censor ordered revisions (1580-81). The Spanish Inquisition condemned it (1640). Sections banned in France (1595), listed on the *Index Librorum Prohibitorum* in Rome (1676), where it remained for almost 300 years. Source: 1, pp. 98–100; 4, p. 15; 8, pp. 234–36.

1133 Moore, George. *Esther Waters.* Dent. Excluded from British circulating libraries in 1894, as both Mudie's Library and Smith's Library refused to stock it, viewing it as too risqué because the main character suffers as the result of her one sexual indiscretion, but she does not die, and because of the candid manner in which her situation is presented. Source: 14, pp. 132–33.

1134 Morgan, Melissa J. *TTYL.* Grosset & Dunlap. Challenged at the William Floyd Middle School library in Mastic, N.Y. (2007) because the book includes "curse words, crude references to the male and female anatomy, sex acts and adult situations like drinking alcohol and flirtation with a teacher that almost goes too far." A spokesman for the William Floyd School District said the book will remain in the library, and that the book is very popular with students across the country. The spokesperson also said unlike many books that young people read, the book deals with controversial subjects without glorifying negative behaviors. Source: 11, May 2007, p. 92.

1135 Morris, Desmond. *The Naked Ape.* Dell; McGraw-Hill. Removed from the Island Trees, N.Y. Union Free School District High School library in 1976 along with nine other titles because they were considered "immoral, anti-American, anti-Christian, or just plain filthy." Returned to the library after the U.S. Supreme Court ruling on June 25, 1982, in *Board of Education, Island Trees Union Free School District No. 26 et al. v. Pico et al.,* 457 U.S. 853 (1982). Reinstated after being removed from the Mifflinburg, Pa. High School (1989) because the book includes material on human sexuality that is "explicit, almost manual description of what some would refer to as deviant sexual relations." Source: 11, Nov. 1982, p. 197; May 1989, p. 93.

1136 Morrison, Lillian. *Remember Me When This You See.* Crowell; Scholastic. Challenged at the Gwinnett County, Ga. Elementary School library (1986) because a line from the poetry book – "Don't make love in a potato field/Potatoes have eyes" – was objectionable. Source: 11, Mar. 1987, p. 65.

1137 Morrison, Toni. *Beloved.* Knopf; NAL. Challenged at the St. Johns County Schools in St. Augustine, Fla. (1995). Retained on the Round Rock, Tex. Independent High School reading list (1996) after a challenge that the book was too violent. Challenged by a member of the Madawaska, Maine School Committee (1997) because of the book's language. The 1987 Pulitzer Prize winning novel has been required reading for the Advanced Placement English class for six years. Challenged in the Sarasota County, Fla. schools (1998) because of sexual material. Challenged in the Wake County, N.C. schools (2006) because the book has "vulgar and sexually explicit language." Parents are getting help from Called2Action, a Christian group that says its mission is to "promote and defend our shared family and social values." Retained on the Northwest Suburban High School District 214 reading list in Arlington Heights, Ill. (2006), along with eight other challenged titles. A board member, elected amid promises to bring her Christian beliefs into all board decision-making, raised the controversy based on excerpts from the books she'd found on the Internet. Pulled from the senior Advanced Placement English class at Eastern High School in Louisville, Ky. (2007) because two parents complained that the Pulitzer Prize-winning novel about antebellum slavery depicted the inappropriate topics of bestiality, racism, and sex. Source: 11, Jan. 1996, p. 14; May 1996, p. 99; Jan. 1998, p. 14; July 1998, p. 120; July 2006, pp. 210–11; May 2007, pp. 98, 121.

1138 _____. *The Bluest Eye.* NAL. Pulled from an eleventh grade classroom at Lathrop High School in Fairbanks, Alaska (1994) by school administrators because "It was a very controversial book; it contains lots of very graphic descriptions and lots of disturbing language." Challenged at the West Chester, Pa. schools (1994) as "most pornographic." Banned from the Morrisville, Pa. Borough High School English curriculum (1994) after complaints about its sexual content and objectionable language. Challenged at the St. Johns County Schools in St. Augustine, Fla. (1995). Challenged on the optional summer reading list at the Lynn, Mass. schools (1995) because of the book's sexual content. Challenged on Montgomery County, Md. reading lists and school library shelves

(1998). Removed from the reading list for ninth- and tenth-graders at Stevens High School in Claremont, N.H. (1999) because of a parent's complaint about the book's sexual content. Challenged, but retained at the Kern High School District in Bakersfield, Calif. (2003) despite complaints of the book's sexually explicit material. Banned from the Littleton, Colo. curriculum and library shelves (2005) after complaints about its explicit sex, including the rape of an eleven-year-old girl by her father. Challenged in the Howell, Mich. High School (2007) because of obscenities and strong sexual content. In response to a request from the president of the Livingston Organization for Values in Education, or LOVE, the county's top law enforcement official reviewed the books to see whether laws against distribution of sexually explicit materials to minors had been broken. "After reading the books in question, it is clear that the explicit passages illustrated a larger literary, artistic or political message and were not included solely to appeal to the prurient interests of minors," the county prosecutor wrote. "Whether these materials are appropriate for minors is a decision to be made by the school board, but I find that they are not in violation of the criminal laws." Source: 8, p. 321; 11, May 1994, p. 86; Jan. 1995, p. 25; Mar. 1995, pp. 44–45; May 1995, p. 71; July 1995, p. 98; Jan. 1996, p. 14; May 1998, p. 70; Sept. 1999, pp. 121–22; Mar. 2004, pp. 50–51; May 2004, pp. 118–19; Jan. 2006, p. 13; Mar. 2007, pp. 51–52; May 2007, p. 116.

1139 _____. *Song of Solomon.* Knopf; NAL. Challenged, but retained, in the Columbus, Ohio schools (1993). The complainant believed that the book contains language degrading to blacks, and is sexually explicit. Removed from required reading lists and library shelves in the Richmond County, Ga. School District (1994) after a parent complained that passages from the book were "filthy and inappropriate." Challenged at the St. Johns County Schools in St. Augustine, Fla. (1995). Removed from the St. Mary's County, Md. schools' approved text list (1998) by the school superintendent overruling a faculty committee recommendation. Complainants referred to the novel as "filth," "trash," and "repulsive." Source: 11, July 1993, p. 108; Sept. 1993, p. 160; May 1994, p. 86; Jan. 1996, p. 14; Mar. 1998, p. 42.

1140 _____. *Sula.* Knopf. Challenged on the Poolesville High School, Md. (2000) reading list because of the book's sexual content and language. On Oct. 5, 2000, Montgomery County Circuit Court Judge Paul McGuckian dismissed the bid to ban the work from the curriculum. The school, however, decided to remove the book from the summer reading list. Source: 11, Nov. 2000, p. 196; Jan. 2001, pp. 36–37.

1141 Mosca, Frank. *All-American Boy.* Alyson Pubns. Challenged at several Kansas City area schools (1993) after the books were donated by a national group that seeks to give young adults "fair, accurate and inclusive images of lesbians and gay men"—at the Shawnee Mission School District the book was returned to general circulation; at the Olathe East High School the book was removed; protesters burned copies of the book but the Kansas City, Mo. School District kept Mosca's novel on the high school shelves; in Kansas City, Kans., the school district donated the book to the city's public library; and in Lee's Summit, Mo. the superintendent removed the book. Source: 11, Mar. 1994, pp. 51–52; May 1994, p. 84.

1142 *Mother Goose: Old Nursery Rhymes.* Arthur Rackham, illustrator. Durst. Challenged at the Dade County, Fla. Public Library (1983) by a Miami Metro Commissioner because the anthology of nursery rhymes contains the following anti-Semitic verse: "Jack sold his gold egg/to a rogue of a Jew/who cheated him out of/half of his due." Source: 11, July 1983, p. 107; Jan. 1984, p. 25.

1143 Mowat, Farley. *And No Birds Sang.* Bantam. Challenged in the Northwestern Middle School library, Springfield, Ohio (1994) because of "improper language." Source: 11, July 1994, p. 111.

1144 _____. *Never Cry Wolf.* Bantam; Little. Removed from the Panama City, Fla. school classrooms and libraries (1987) because of "offensive" language. Source: 11, July 1987, pp. 126–28; Sept. 1987, pp. 168–69.

1145 _____. *Woman in the Mists: The Story of Dian Fossey & the Mountain Gorillas of Africa.* Warner. Removed from a required reading list in the Omaha, Nebr. public schools (1991) because the book has racial slurs, passages degrading to women, profanity, and a long discussion of the aftermath of Fossey's abortion. Source: 11, Mar. 1992, p. 44.

1146 Muller, Gilbert H., and Harvey S. Wiener, comps. *The Short Prose Reader.* McGraw-Hill. Challenged at the Cecil County Board of Education in Elkton, Md. (1994). Many deemed the text controversial because it included essays dealing with issues of abortion, gay rights, alcohol, and sex education. Source: 11, Mar. 1995, p. 55.

1147 Mungo, Raymond. *Liberace.* Chelsea House Pubs. Removed from the Anaheim, Calif. school district (2000) because school officials said the book is too difficult for middle school students and that it could cause harassment against students seen with it. The American Civil Liberties Union (ACLU) of Southern California filed suit in *Doe v. Anaheim Union High School District* alleging that the removal is "a pretext for viewpoint-based censorship." The ACLU claims no other books have been removed from the junior high library for similar reasons, even though several, such as works by Shakespeare and Dickens, are more difficult reading. The ACLU contends that the school officials engaged in unconstitutional viewpoint discrimination by removing the book because it contains gay and lesbian material. In March 2001, the school board approved a settlement that restored the book to the high school shelves and amended the district's policy to prohibit the removal of books for subject matter involving sexual orientation, but the book will not be returned to the middle school. Source: 11, Mar. 2001, p. 53; May 2001, p. 95; July 2001, p. 173.

1148 Murdoch, Iris. *The Nice and the Good.* Penguin. Banned in South Africa (1977). Source: 5, Nov./Dec. 1977, p. 68.

1149 Murphy, Barbara Beasley. *Home Free.* Delacorte; Dell. Retained at the Hillcrest School library in East Ramapo, N.J. (1988), but the book will not be lent to a fourth or fifth grader who is not deemed an "advanced reader or critical thinker" by a parent, teacher, or librarian. The book contains the word "nigger." Source: 11, May 1988, p. 86.

1150 _____. *No Place to Run.* Archway. Removed from two Anniston, Ala. high school libraries (1982) due to "the curse words and using the Lord's name in vain," but later reinstated on a restricted basis. Source: 11, Mar. 1983, p. 37.

1151 Murray, William. *Tip on a Dead Crab.* Dodd. Publication canceled by Dodd, Mead & Company (1983) because of language in the book considered "objectionable" by Thomas Nelson, Inc. of Nashville, Tenn.—Dodd, Mead's parent company. Source: 11, Nov. 1983, p. 188.

1152 Myers, Lawrence W. *Improvised Radio Jamming Techniques.* Paladin Pr. Challenged for promoting illegal actions, but retained at the Multnomah, Oreg. County Library (1991). Source: 11, Jan. 1992, p. 6.

1153 Myers, Walter Dean. *Fallen Angels.* Scholastic. Challenged in the Bluffton, Ohio schools (1990) because of its use of profane language. Restricted as supplemental classroom reading material at the Jackson County, Ga. High School (1992) because of undesirable language and sensitive material. Challenged at the West Chester, Pa. schools (1994). Removed from a twelfth-grade English class in Middleburg Heights, Ohio (1995) after a parent complained of its sexually explicit language. The novel won the Coretta Scott King Award and was named Best Book of 1988 by *School Library Journal*. Challenged, but retained at the Lakewood, Ohio High School (1997). The book was challenged by parents who objected to the novel's violence and vulgar language. Removed from the Laton, Calif. Unified School District (1999) because the novel about the Vietnam War contains violence and profanity. Removed as required reading in the Livonia, Mich. public schools (1999) because it contains "too many swear words." Challenged, but retained in the Arlington, Tex. school district's junior high school libraries (2000) despite a parent's complaint that the book's content was too strong for younger students. Challenged, along with seventeen other titles in the Fairfax County, Va. elementary and secondary libraries (2002), by a group called Parents Against Bad Books in Schools. The group contends the books "contain profanity and descriptions of drug abuse, sexually explicit conduct, and torture." Banned from the George County, Miss. schools (2002) because of profanity. Banned at the Franklin Central High School in Indianapolis, Ind. (2003) because of concerns about the book's profanity. The book was assigned in English classes for sophomores. Removed from the Blue Valley School District's high school curriculum in Overland Park, Kans. (2005). The book was challenged by parents and community members along with thirteen other titles. Retained on the Northwest Suburban High School District 214 reading list in Arlington Heights, Ill. (2006), along with eight other challenged titles. A board member, elected amid promises to bring her Christian beliefs into all board decision-making, raised the controversy based on excerpts from the books she'd found on the Internet. Source: 8, pp. 451–53; 11, Nov. 1990, p. 211; Sept. 1992, p. 142; Jan. 1995, p. 25; Mar. 1996, p. 49; May 1996, p. 79; Nov. 1999, pp. 164–65; Jan. 2001, p. 36; Jan. 2003, p. 10; Mar. 2003, p. 55; Jan. 2004, pp. 11–12; Nov. 2005, pp. 282–83; July 2006, pp. 210–11.

1154 _____. *Fast Sam, Cool Clyde and Stuff.* Viking. Challenged by an elementary school administrator in Akron, Ohio (1983). Source: 9; 11, May 1983, p. 86.

119

1155 _____. *Hoops.* Dell. Challenged in Littleton, Colo. (1989) school libraries because the book "endorses" drinking, stealing, and homosexuality, uses offensive words, and contains a sex scene. Challenged but retained in Vanlue, Ohio (2000) High School English classes despite objections that the book is evil and depicts drugs, alcohol, and sex. Source: 11, Sept. 1989, p. 186; July 2000, p. 125.

1156 _____. *Young Martin's Promise.* Raintree. Challenged by a school board member in the Queens, N.Y. school libraries (1994) because King "was a leftist hoodlum with significant Communist ties. King was a hypocritical adulterer." The rest of the school board voted to retain the book. Source: 11, July 1994, pp. 110–11; Sept. 1994, p. 166.

1157 **Myrer, Anton.** *A Green Desire.* Avon. Banned from the Stroudsburg, Pa. High School library (1985) because it was "blatantly graphic, pornographic and wholly unacceptable for a high school library." Source: 11, May 1985, p. 79.

1158 **Nabokov, Vladimir.** *Lolita.* Berkley; McGraw-Hill; Putnam. Banned as obscene in France (1956-1959), in England (1955-59), in Argentina (1959), and in New Zealand (1960). The South African Directorate of Publications announced on Nov. 27, 1982, that the novel had been taken off the banned list, eight years after a request for permission to market the novel in paperback had been refused. Challenged at the Marion-Levy Public Library System in Ocala, Fla. (2006). The Marion County commissioners voted to have the county attorney review the novel that addresses the themes of pedophilia and incest, to determine if it meets the state law's definition of "unsuitable for minors." Source: 4, p. 81; 5, Apr. 1983, p. 47; 8, pp. 359–60; 11, Mar. 2006, pp. 69–70; Nov. 2006, p. 317.

1159 **Nasrin, Taslima.** *Lajja (Shame).* Penguin. Banned in Bangladesh (1993) on the grounds that it had "created misunderstanding among communities." A fatwa, or death decree, was issued by a mullah, or Muslim cleric, of the Council of Soldiers of Islam, a militant group based in Sylhet, Bangladesh. The author fled to Stockholm, Sweden, and remained in exile in Europe and the United States. Source: 8, pp. 255–58.

1160 **National Register Publishing Co. Staff.** *Official Catholic Directory.* National Register Publishing Co. Challenged by a patron who believed public funds should not be expended on religious books, but retained at the Multnomah, Oreg. County Library (1991). Source: 11, Jan. 1992, p. 6.

1161 **Naylor, Phyllis Reynolds.** *Achingly Alice.* Atheneum. Banned from the Webb City, Mo. school library (2002) because the book promotes homosexuality and discusses issues "best left to parents." Source: 11, Nov. 2002, p. 256.

1162 _____. *The Agony of Alice.* Atheneum. Challenged, but retained at the Franklin Sherman Elementary School library and on the Fairfax County, Va. approved reading list (2000). The book, however, is limited in its classroom use to small discussion groups for girls only. Source: 11, Mar. 2000, p. 62.

1163 _____. *Alice in Lace.* Atheneum. Banned from the Webb City, Mo. school library (2002) because the book promotes homosexuality and discusses issues "best left to parents." Source: 11, Nov. 2002, p. 256.

1164 _____. *Alice on the Outside.* Atheneum. Available with parental permission in the librarian's office at Shelbyville, Ky. East Middle School (2005) because the book is "too sexually explicit" for middle-school students. Source: 11, May 2005, p. 108; July 2005, pp. 185–86.

1165 _____. *Alice the Brave.* Atheneum. Challenged in the Mesquite, Tex. Pirrung Elementary School library (2004) due to sexual references. Source: 11, Nov. 2004, p. 231.

1166 _____. *Alice, In Between.* Atheneum. Removed from the Monroe, Conn. sixth-grade required reading list (1998) after some parents called attention to the book's sexual content. The series of books by the Newbery Award-winning children's author includes *The Agony of Alice* and *Outrageously Alice.* Source: 11, Nov. 1998, p. 182.

1167 _____. *All But Alice.* Atheneum. Restricted to students with parental permission at the Monroe Elementary School library in Thorndike, Maine (1997). Removed from the District 196 elementary school libraries in Rosemount-Apple Valley-Eagan, Minn. (1997) because of a brief passage in which the seventh-grade heroine discusses sexually oriented rock lyrics with her father and older brother; the school board considered the book inappropriate for the ages of the students. Source: 11, Sept. 1997, pp. 126, 148; Nov. 1997, p. 166.

1168 _____. *The Fear Place.* Atheneum. Challenged at the Madison Elementary School in Cedar Rapids, Iowa (1998). A review committee asked that the book carry a warning about objectionable language and that teachers consider notifying parents if they are going to use the book in class. Source: 11, May 1998, pp. 87–88.

1169 _____. *The Grooming of Alice.* Atheneum. Banned from the Webb City, Mo. school library (2002) because the book promotes homosexuality and discusses issues "best left to parents." Source: 11, Nov. 2002, p. 256.

1170 _____. *Reluctantly Alice.* Atheneum. Challenged in the Wake County, N.C. schools (2006). Parents are getting help from Called2Action, a Christian group that says its mission is to "promote and defend our shared family and social values." Source: 11, Sept. 2006, p. 231.

1171 _____. *Send No Blessings.* Puffin; Macmillan. Challenged at the Cedar Valley Elementary School in Kent, Wash. (1993) because parents claimed the book condones child molestation and promiscuity. Source: 11, Mar. 1993, p. 55.

1172 _____. *Witch Herself.* Atheneum; Dell. Retained at the Ector County, Tex. school library (1989) after being challenged because the book might lure children into the occult. Source: 11, Jan. 1990, p. 9; May 1990, p. 107.

1173 _____. *Witch Water.* Atheneum; Dell. Retained at the Ector County, Tex. school library (1989) after being challenged because the book might lure children into the occult. Source: 11, Jan. 1990, p. 9; May 1990, p. 107.

1174 _____. *Witch's Sister.* Atheneum; Dell. Challenged at the Multnomah County Library in Portland, Oreg. (1988) because the occult topic could be frightening and traumatic for children. Retained at the Ector County, Tex. school library (1989) after being challenged because the book might lure children into the occult. Source: 11, Jan. 1989, p. 3; Jan. 1990, p. 9; May 1990, p. 107.

1175 **Nehring, James.** *Why Do We Gotta Do This Stuff, Mr. Nehring?* M. Evans. Challenged, but retained, by the Pocatello, Idaho Library Board (1994) which refused to remove or label books that contain obscene language. Source: 11, May 1994, pp. 97–98.

1176 **Nelson, O. T.** *The Girl Who Owned a City.* Runestone Pr.; Lerner Pubs. Challenged in the Fort Fairfield, Maine schools (2000) because the book promotes violence, including explaining how to make a Molotov cocktail. Source: 11, July 2000, p. 104.

1177 **Nelson, Theresa.** *Earthshine.* Orchard. Challenged, but retained, in the Anchorage, Alaska school libraries (1997). Parents of a student wanted the book removed from all public school libraries because "it contains profanity and deals with subjects like homosexuality, abortion, and children running away from home." Source: 11, May 1997, p. 77.

1178 **Neufeld, John.** *Freddy's Book.* Ballantine; Random. Removed from the elementary school library in Spring Valley, Ill. (1977) after a parent complained about the book's theme. Challenged, but retained, at the Lake Fenton, Mich. Elementary School library (1989) because of the book's descriptions of male and female genitalia, menstruation, erections, sexual intercourse, and wet dreams. The book was, however, placed on a restricted shelf and requires parents to check the book out. Partly as a result of the controversy, all of the district's library books were slated to be reviewed by a four-member committee consisting of a parent, teacher, librarian, and district administrator. Source: 11, Jan. 1978, p. 6; Jan. 1990, p. 9.

1179 **Neville, Henry.** *Isle of Pines.* Allen Banks and Charles Harper at the Flower-Deluice near Cripplegate Church. Banned the year of its publication (1668) after authorities in the Massachusetts colony discovered it while searching for unlicensed material on the premise of the only two printers in the colony. Source: 13, p. 116.

1180 **Newman, Leslea.** *Gloria Goes to Gay Pride.* Alyson Pubns. Removed from the Brooklyn, N.Y. School District's curriculum (1992) because the school board objected to words that were "age inappropriate." Retained at the Dayton and Montgomery County, Ohio Public Library (1993). Challenged at the Chandler, Ariz. Public Library (1994) because the book is a "skillful presentation to the young child about lesbianism/homosexuality." Source: 11, May 1992, p. 83; Mar. 1994, p. 69; July 1994, p. 128; Nov. 1994, p. 187.

1181 _____. *Heather Has Two Mommies.* Alyson Pubns. Removed from the Brooklyn, N.Y. School District's curriculum (1992) because the school board objected to words that were "age inappropriate." Challenged in Fayetteville, N.C. (1992). Moved from the children's section to the adult section in Elizabethtown, N.C. library (1993) because it "promotes a dangerous and ungodly lifestyle from which children must be protected." Moved from the children's section to the young adult section at the Chestatee Regional Library System in Gainesville, Ga. (1993). Three area legislators wanted the book removed and said, "We could put together a resolution to amend the Georgia state constitution to say that tax dollars cannot be used to promote homosexuality, pedophilia, or sado-masochism." Moved from the children's section to the adult section at the Mercer County Library System in Lawrence, N.J. (1993). Challenged at the North Brunswick, N.J. Public Library (1993), the Cumberland County Public, N.C. Library (1993) and Wicomico County Free Library in Salisbury, Md. (1993). Challenged at the Mesa, Ariz. Public Library (1993) because it "is vile, sick, and goes against every law and constitution." Retained at the Dayton and Montgomery County, Ohio Public Library (1993). Challenged, but retained, in the Oak Bluffs, Mass. school library (1994). Though the parent leading the protest stated, "The subject matter . . . is obscene and vulgar and the message is that homosexuality is okay," the selection review committee voted unanimously to keep the book. Removed by officials at the Cottage Grove, Oreg. (1994) Lane County Head Start Center. Challenged at the Chandler, Ariz. Public Library (1994) because the book is a "skillful presentation to the young child about lesbianism/homosexuality." Challenged at the Wichita Falls, Tex. Public Library (1998). The deacon body of the First Baptist Church requested that any literature that promotes or sanctions a homosexual lifestyle be removed. The Wichita Falls City Council established a policy that allows library cardholders who collect 300 signatures to have children's books moved to an adult portion of the library. U.S. District Court Judge Jerry Buchmeyer struck down the library resolution as unconstitutional and the books were returned. Challenged, but retained in the juvenile non-fiction section of the Nampa, Idaho Public Library (1999). Source: 11, May 1992, p. 83; Jan. 1993, pp. 9, 28; May 1993, p. 71; July 1993, pp. 100–101, 126; Sept. 1993, pp. 143–44; Nov. 1993, pp. 177–78; Jan. 1994, pp. 13, 34–35; Mar. 1994, p. 69; May 1994, p. 98; July 1994, pp. 110, 115; Sept. 1994, pp. 147–48, 166; Nov. 1994, p. 187; July 1998, pp. 106–7; Jan. 1999, pp. 8–9; Mar. 1999, p. 36: May 1999, p. 67; Sept. 1999, p. 131; Nov. 1999, p. 172; Nov. 2000, pp. 201–2.

1182 **Newton, Michael.** *The Encyclopedia of Serial Killers.* Facts on File. Challenged and

retained in the Hillsborough County, Fla. School District (2002) over a parent's objections to the book's "gruesome details." Source: 11, July 2002, p. 179.

1183 **Nichols, John.** *The Milagro Beanfield War.* Holt. Pulled from a junior English class at the Shawnee High School in Lima, Ohio (1999) because it contained offensive material, including sex and violence. Source: 11, July 1999, p. 97.

1184 **Nix, Garth.** *Shade's Children.* HarperCollins. Challenged, but retained at the Transit Middle School library in Williamsville, N. Y. (2001) after objections that the book "is vulgar, obscene, and educationally unsuitable." Source: 11, May 2001, p. 124.

1185 **Noel, Janet.** *The Human Body.* Grosset. The York, Maine Middle School review committee (1982) voted unanimously to remove the book from the library "because of the inappropriateness of written and pictorial material." After a backlash from anti-censorship parents, the book was moved from the middle school library to the junior high library for use by seventh and eighth graders. Source: 11, July 1982, pp. 123–24.

1186 **Norstog, Knut J., and Andrew J. Meyerriecks.** *Biology.* Merrill. A Sallisaw, Okla. Senior High School biology teacher (1986) removed pages 467-76 from the textbook because they were "irrelevant" to the school's curriculum requirements. The pages contained information on reproduction and birth control. The teacher said he was "trying to circumvent a problem, rather than create one, when students were forced to take the books parents might find objectionable into their homes." Source: 11, July 1986, p. 121.

1187 **Nunokawa, Jeff.** *Oscar Wilde.* Chelsea House Pubs. Removed from the Anaheim, Calif. school district (2000) because school officials said the book is too difficult for middle school students and that it could cause harassment against students seen with it. The American Civil Liberties Union (ACLU) of Southern California filed suit in *Doe v. Anaheim Union High School District* alleging that the removal is "a pretext for viewpoint-based censorship." The ACLU claims no other books have been removed from the junior high library for similar reasons, even though several, such as works by Shakespeare and Dickens, are more difficult reading. The ACLU contends that the school officials engaged in unconstitutional viewpoint discrimination by removing the book because it contains gay and lesbian material. In March 2001, the school board approved a settlement that restored the book to the high school shelves and amended the district's policy to prohibit the removal of books for subject matter involving sexual orientation, but the book will not be returned to the middle school. Source: 11, Mar. 2001, p. 53; May 2001, p. 95; July 2001, p. 173.

1188 Nye, Robert. *Beowulf, a New Telling.* Hill and Wang. Challenged, but retained, in the Hood River County, Oreg. schools (1998). A parent complained that the book was "inappropriate for middle school students because of the evil intentions of its characters, graphic descriptions of gore and mutilations, and descriptions of monstrous characters." Source: 11, July 1998, p. 121.

1189 Oates, Joyce Carol. *Where Are You Going, Where Have You Been?* Fawcett. Challenged in the Tyrone, Pa. schools (1990) because of its use of profane language. Source: 11, Mar. 1991, pp. 61–62.

1190 Oates, Stephen. *Portrait of America, Vol. II.* Houghton. Returned to the Racine, Wis. Unified School District (1984) curriculum just one week after the school board voted to ban it. Opponents of the books on the board charged that the social studies volumes contained "judgmental writing" and, in the words of one board member, "a lot more funny pictures of Republicans and nicer pictures of Democrats." Opponents also said that one text did not present an adequate analysis of the Vietnam War. Source: 11, Sept. 1984, p. 158.

1191 O'Brien, Edna. *August Is a Wicked Month.* Penguin. All novels published by Edna O'Brien during the 1960s were banned in Ireland by the Censorship of Publications Board: *The Country Girls* (1960); *The Lonely Girl* (1962) and its reprint *Girl with Green Eyes* (1964); *Girls in Their Married Bliss* (1964); *August Is a Wicked Month* (1965), which was also banned in Australia, Rhodesia, and South Africa. O'Brien's work gained notoriety in Ireland in the 1960s because of its detailed exploration of female sexuality. Source: 6, pp. 1,749–50.

1192 O'Brien, Kate. *The Land of the Spices.* Virago Pr. In Spain, her travel book, Farewell Spain (1937) was banned because it was criticized the Franco regime; O'Brien was barred from entering the country until 1957. In Ireland, two of her novels, *Mary Lavelle* (1936) and *The Land of Spices* (1941), were banned by the Censorship of Publications Board. The impact of the banning was considerable. In the short term, it drew attention to the extremes to which the Censorship Board went in recommending books to be banned, particularly those by Irish authors. In the long term, the 1942 Irish Senate debate initiated the discussions that led to the creation of a Censorship of Publications Appeal Board in 1946. Source: 6, pp. 1,750–51.

1193 O'Brien, Sharon. *Willa Cather.* Chelsea House Pubs. Removed from the Anaheim, Calif. school district (2000) because school officials said the book is too difficult for middle school students and that it could cause harassment against students seen with it. The American Civil Liberties Union (ACLU) of Southern California filed suit in *Doe v. Anaheim Union High School District* alleging that the removal is "a pretext for viewpoint-based censorship." The ACLU claims no other books have been removed from the junior high library for similar reasons, even though several, such as works by Shakespeare and Dickens, are more difficult reading. The ACLU contends that the school officials engaged in unconstitutional viewpoint discrimination by removing the book because it contains gay and lesbian material. In March 2001, the school board approved a settlement that restored the book to the high school shelves and amended the district's policy to prohibit the removal of books for subject matter involving sexual orientation, but the book will not be returned to the middle school. Source: 11, Mar. 2001, p. 53; May 2001, p. 95; July 2001, p. 173.

1194 O'Brien, Tim. *In the Lake of the Woods.* Houghton. Challenged for use in the Richland, Wash. high school English classes (1998) along with six other titles because the "books are poor-quality literature and stress suicide, illicit sex, violence, and hopelessness." Source: 11, Mar. 1999, p. 40.

1195 _____. *The Things They Carried.* Broadway Bks.; Houghton. Determined unsuitable suitable for classroom reading in Waukesha, Wis., (1992) because of "anti-American attitudes, offensive language, political bias, and disturbing fiction." Challenged, but retained at the Pennridge, Pa. high school (2000) despite a protest of the book's strong language. O'Brien was a finalist for the 1990 Pulitzer Prize and the National Book Critics Circle Award. Banned from the George County, Miss. schools (2002) because of profanity. Retained on the Northwest Suburban High School District 214 reading list in Arlington Heights, Ill. (2006), along with eight other challenged titles. A board member, elected amid promises to bring her

Christian beliefs into all board decision-making, raised the controversy based on excerpts from the books she'd found on the Internet. Source: 11, Jan. 2001, p. 37; Mar. 2003, p. 55; July 2006, pp. 210–11.

1196 O'Connor, Flannery. *The Complete Stories.* Noonday Pr. Prohibited at the Opelousas, La. Catholic High School (2000) by Bishop Edward J. O'Donnell of Lafayette, La. along with any "similar book." Some parents protested when they saw the word "nigger" in the collection of short stories assigned for the summer reading of students after their junior year. Source: 11, Jan. 2001, p. 13.

1197 O'Connor, Frank. *Dutch Interior.* Knopf. Banned in Ireland (1940). The Irish Republic's Censorship Board was not required to state publicly why it banned individual books as "indecent or obscene," but it was widely believed that O'Connor's novel and short stories were so treated primarily because of their critique of the Irish Catholic middle class. Source: 6, pp. 1,757–58.

1198 O'Connor, Jane. *Just Good Friends.* Dell; Harper. Removed from the Jefferson Magnet Arts Library, and transferred to a middle school in Eugene, Oreg. (1988) because of the book's sexual references. Source: 11, Jan. 1989, p. 3.

1199 _____. *Lu Lu and the Witch Baby.* Harper. Challenged at the Dakota, Ill. Primary School (1991) because it "promotes lying and witchcraft." Source: 11, May 1991, p. 89.

1200 O'Donnell, E. P. *Green Margins.* Houghton. Seized and destroyed by New Orleans, La. (1937) police. Source: 15, Vol. III, p. 650.

1201 O'Faolain, Sean. *Midsummer Night Madness and Other Stories.* Viking. Banned in Ireland (1932). His second novel, *Bird Alone*, was published and banned in Ireland (1936). The ban remained in force until 1947, when the newly established appeal board revoked it. Source: 6, pp. 1,761–62.

1202 O'Hara, Frank. *Lunch Poems.* City Lights. Banned for use in Aurora, Colo. High School English classes (1976) on the grounds of "immorality." Source: 11, May 1977, p. 79.

1203 O'Hara, John. *Appointment in Samarra.* Random. Declared not mailable by the U.S. Department of Post Office (1941) because of "obscene Language." The novel remained on the U.S. Post Office's index of banned books through the mid-1950s. The novel also attracted the attention of the National Organization for Decent Literature (NODL), a Roman Catholic organization that identified "objectionable" literature and advised members against reading "offensive" and "objectionable" novels. In 1953, NODL found the novel to be "objectionable" and placed in on their list of blacklisted books. The list was then sent to cooperating book dealers who agreed to remove the book from their racks. As a result, the novel was banned from sale in St. Cloud, Minn.; Port Huron and Detroit, Mich. Sales were limited in numerous other cities, through the efforts of local chapters, until the demise of the organization in the late 1950s. Source: 4, p. 86; 8, pp. 409–10.

1204 _____. *Ten North Frederick.* Random. Banned by Police Commissioner in Detroit, Mich. (1957), a series of local bans and seizures spread over a two-year period (1957-1958). Source: 4, pp. 86–87.

1205 O'Hara, Mary. *My Friend Flicka.* Harper; Lippincott. Pulled from fifth- and sixth-grade optional reading lists in Clay County, Fla. schools (1990) because the book uses the word "bitch" to refer to a female dog, as well as the word "damn." Source: 11, Jan. 1991, p. 16.

1206 O'Huigin, Sean. *Scary Poems for Rotten Kids.* Black Moss Pr. Challenged in the Livonia, Mich. schools (1990) because the poems frightened first-grade children. Source: 11, Mar. 1991, p. 62.

1207 O'Keeffe, Georgia. *Georgia O'Keeffe.* Viking. Retained at Maldonado Elementary School in Tucson, Ariz. (1994) after being challenged by parents who objected to nudity and "pornographic," "perverted," and "morbid" themes. Source: 11, July 1994, p. 112.

1208 *The Old Farmer's Almanac.* Yankee Bks. During World War II, according to Robb Sagendorph, the U.S. Army temporarily banned the publication on the grounds that its weather forecasts aided the enemy. Source: 6, p. 45.

1209 O'Malley, Kevin, illus. *Froggy Went A-Courtin'.* Stewart, Tabori and Chang. Restricted at the Baltimore County, Md. school libraries (1996) because of Froggy's nefarious activities including burning money, and speeding away from the cat police, as well as robbery and smoking. The book is to be kept in restricted areas of the libraries where only parents and teachers will be allowed to check it out and read it to children. Source: 11, Jan. 1997, p. 7; Mar. 1997, p. 35.

1210 **Opie, Iona Archibald, and Peter Opie, eds.** *I Saw Esau: The Schoolchild's Pocket Book.* Candlewick Pr. Challenged at the Cedar Grove Elementary School in Murfreesboro, Tenn. (2007). The complainant stated, "I understand that it is a book of poetry, but there is a fine line between poetry art and porn and this book's illustrations are absolutely offensive in every way." The book is a collection of schoolyard jokes, riddles, insults and jump-rope rhymes and is illustrated by Maurice Sendak. Source: 11, May 2007, p. 94.

1211 **Oppenheim, Irene.** *Living Today.* Bennett. Returned to the Racine, Wis. Unified School District (1984) curriculum just one week after the school board voted to ban it. The home economics text was criticized for encouraging premarital sex and advocating that unmarried couples live together. Source: 11, Sept. 1984, p. 158.

1212 **Orenstein, Peggy.** *Schoolgirls: Young Women, Self-esteem and the Confidence Gap.* Doubleday. Challenged in Courtland, Ohio High School (1996) because of its "rotten, filthy language." The teacher offered the parents a black marker with which to delete offending passages, but the parents wanted it banned. The school board voted to continue the book. Source: 11, Mar. 1997, p. 50.

1213 **Orgel, Doris.** *The Devil in Vienna.* Dial; Puffin. Challenged, but retained at the Grant Wood Elementary School media center in Cedar Rapids, Iowa (2000) despite objections to the book's inclusion of a brief incident of an old man exposing himself to a six-year-old girl. Source: 11, Mar. 2000, p. 61.

1214 **Ortiz, Victoria.** *The Land and People of Cuba.* Lippincott. Removed from the Rockaway Junior High School, Miami, Fla. school library (1974) by the principal because the book "was anti-American propaganda favoring the pro-Castro viewpoint." The book was also rejected by Dade County's public libraries (1974). Source: 7, pp. 294–95.

1215 **Orwell, George.** *1984.* Harcourt. Challenged in the Jackson County, Fla. (1981)

because Orwell's novel is "pro-communist and contained explicit sexual matter." Source: 8, pp. 141–42; 9; 11, May 1981, p. 73.

1216 _____. *Animal Farm.* Harcourt. Banned from Bay County's four middle schools and three high schools in Panama City, Fla. (1987) by the Bay County school superintendent. After 44 parents filed a suit against the district claiming that its instructional aids policy denies constitutional rights, the Bay County School Board reinstated the book, along with 64 others banned. A survey of censorship challenges in the schools, conducted in DeKalb County, Ga. (1982) for the period 1979 to 1982, revealed that the novel had been objected to for its political theories. The New York State English Council's Committee on Defenses Against Censorship conducted a comparable study in New York State English classrooms in 1968. Its findings identified the novel on its list of "problem books;" the reason cited was that "Orwell was a communist." A 1963 Wisconsin survey revealed that the John Birch Society had challenged the novel's use; it objected to the words "masses will revolt." Suppressed from being displayed at the 1977 Moscow international book fair. Banned in 2002 from schools in the United Arab Emirates, along with 125 others. The Ministry of Education banned it on the grounds that it contained a written or illustrated material that contradicts Islamic and Arab values—in this text, pictures of alcoholic drinks, pigs, and other "indecent images." Source: 8, pp. 15–16.

1217 **Ostrovsky, Victor, and Claire Hoy.** *By Way of Deception: The Making and Unmaking of a Mossad Officer.* Bloomsbury; St. Martin. The government of Israel initiated the challenges through lawsuits seeking to block publication. The Israelis won a court order in Toronto, Ontario, Canada (1990), that blocked publication. Israel's request was based on its claim that the book "would disseminate confidential information and that this information could endanger the lives of various people in the employ of the State of Israel and would be detrimental to the State of Israel." The New York Supreme Court found the Israeli claims of endangered lives "groundless" and that the "heavy presumption against a prior restraint on publication" had not been overcome. Following this ruling, the Israeli government withdrew its lawsuit in Canada. Source: 7, p. 84.

1218 **Ovid.** *The Art of Love.* Harvard Univ. Pr.; Indiana Univ. Pr.; Oxford Univ. Pr. Emperor Augustus banished the author (8 A.D.); book burned in Florence (1497) and barred by U.S. Customs (1929). Proscribed in the Tridentine Index of 1564, and in England in 1599 a translation by the poet Christopher Marlowe was burned at Stationer's Hall on the orders of the archbishop of Canterbury, on account of its immorality. Source: 3, p. 224; 4, p. 2; 6, pp. 1,787–88; 8, p. 320.

1219 _____. *Elegies.* Liveright. Burned in Florence (1497) and in England (1599). Source: 4, p. 2.

1220 Oxenbury, Helen. *Tiny Tim: Verses for Children.* Delacorte. Challenged at the Cherry Hill, N.J. Elementary School (1987) because the book is too violent. One rhyme reads: "I had a little brother, his name is Tiny Tim. I put him in the bathtub to teach him how to swim. He drank up all the water. He ate up all the soap. He died last night with a bubble in his throat." In another rhyme, a man "who had a face made out of cake" was baked in an oven and exploded. Source: 11, July 1987, p. 149.

1221 Packer, Kenneth L., and Jeannine Bower. *Let's Talk about Health.* Sebco. Challenged at the Salem-Keizer, Oreg. School District (1986) because of the book's handling of issues such as dating, premarital sex, homosexuality, and masturbation. Source: 11, May 1986, p. 84.

1222 Paine, Thomas. *The Age of Reason.* Bobbs-Merrill; Citadel. Author and publisher imprisoned in France (1792), prosecuted in England (1797), and Richard Carlile was prosecuted for publishing the works of Paine, was fined 1,000 pounds and imprisoned for two years in England (1819). But because Paine never hesitated to speak his mind, by the end of his life he had become an outcast in America, England, and France. Although he spent his final years in America, he was ostracized and shunned as an atheist and as a traitor to the cause of freedom. He survived a murder attempt, was stripped of his right to vote, and labeled a blasphemer. Source: 2, p. 7; 4, pp. 33–34; 8, pp. 202–3.

1223 _____. *The Rights of Man.* Citadel; Penguin. Author and publisher imprisoned in France (1792), prosecuted in England (1797), and Richard Carlile was prosecuted for publishing the works of Paine, was fined 1,000 pounds and imprisoned for two years in England (1819). But because Paine never hesitated to speak his mind, by the end of his life he had become an outcast in America, England, and France. Although he spent his final years in America, he was ostracized and shunned as an

atheist and as a traitor to the cause of freedom. He survived a murder attempt, was stripped of his right to vote, and labeled a blasphemer. Source: 4, pp. 33–34; 8, pp. 160–62.

1224 Palahniuk, Chuck. *Choke: A Novel.* Doubleday. Challenged in the Fayetteville, Ark. High School library (2005). The complainant also submitted a list of more than fifty books, citing the books as too sexually explicit and promoting homosexuality. Source: 11, Sept. 2005, p. 215.

1225 Parish, James Robert. *Whoopi Goldberg: Her Journey from Poverty to Mega-Stardom.* Carol Pub. Group. Challenged in the Muskego-Norway, Wis. School District (2000) because it contains vulgar language. Source: 11, July 2000, p. 105; Nov. 2000, p. 216.

1226 Park, Barbara. *Junie B. Jones and Some Sneaky, Peeky Spying.* Random. Challenged in the Wake County, N.C. schools (2006). Parents are getting help from Called2Action, a Christian group that says its mission is to "promote and defend our shared family and social values." Source: 11, Sept. 2006, p. 231.

1227 _____. *Junie B. Jones and the Stupid Smelly Bus.* Random; Turtleback. Challenged, but retained, in the second-grade reading curriculum at the Harmony Township, N.J. school (1998). A parent complained that the book sends a message to children that extreme emotions such as hate are fine, and that the book never resolves any of the issues it raises or points out that there are ways to handle negative emotions constructively. Source: 11, Nov. 1998, pp. 191–92.

1228 _____. *Mick Harte Was Here.* Knopf. Challenged, but retained, at the Liberty Middle School Library in Seneca, S.C. (1998) after a seventh grader's grandmother complained to school officials. Challenged, but retained at the Centennial Elementary School library in Fargo, N. Dak. (2004) after parents complained to school officials that the book contains themes and language inappropriate for elementary students. Source: 11, May 1998, p. 70; Nov. 2004, pp. 229–30; Jan. 2005, p. 27; May 2005, p. 131.

1229 Parker, Stephen. *Life before Birth: The Story of the First Nine Months.* Cambridge Univ. Pr. Placed on restricted shelves at the Evergreen School District elementary school libraries in Vancouver, Wash. (1987) in accordance with the school board policy to restrict student access to sex education books in elementary school libraries. Source: 11, May 1987, p. 87.

1230 Parks, Gordon. *The Learning Tree.* Fawcett; Harper. Temporarily banned from the junior high school in Cheyenne, Wyo. (1976); Citizens United for Responsible Education demanded that Park's novel be removed from the Montgomery County, Md. school system (1978); challenged at the Westerly, R.I. High School (1979); subject of a court challenge by the Moral Majority of Washington State in Mead, Wash. (1982) because it includes "objectionable material, swearing, obscene language, explicit detail of premarital sexual intercourse, other lewd behavior, specific blasphemies against Jesus Christ and excessive violence and murder." The case was dismissed by U.S. District Court Judge Robert McNichols. Removed from, and then restored to, a Suwannee, Fla. High School library (1991) because the book is "indecent." Challenged at the Eagan High School in Burnsville, Minn. (1992) on the grounds that it contains vulgar and sexually explicit language, and descriptions of violent acts. Challenged on the summer reading list at LeFlore High School in Mobile, Ala. (2006) because the author frequently used inappropriate words, such as "nigga," "bitch," "bastard," and "ass." Source: 9; 11, July 1976, p. 68; Sept. 1978, p. 123; May 1979, p. 59; Nov. 1982, p. 212; Jan. 1992, p. 25; Mar. 1993, p. 56; Nov. 2006, p. 290.

1231 Parsipur, Shahrnush. *Touba and the Meaning of Night.* Noghreh Pub.; Feminist Pr. at CUNY. Banned in Iran (1989) because of the novel's controversial depiction of women. The main character's exploration of orthodox religion, Sufism, nationalism, and other forms of thoughts did not sit comfortably with the Islamic Republic. In addition to the novel's content, Parsipur's writing style blurs the boundaries between reality and fiction. Imprisoned both by the shah's security agency and later the Islamic Republic, the author sought political refugee status and moved to the United States in 1994. A critically acclaimed bestseller in Iran, the novel, like all of the author's books of fiction and memoir remains banned. Source: 1, pp. 353–54.

1232 _____. *Women without Men: A Novel of Modern Iran.* Noghreh Pub.; Feminist Pr. at CUNY. Banned in Iran (1989) as "un-Islamic" because of its treatment of the themes of virginity, rape, prostitution, failed marriage, and references to Western culture. The novella proved to be far too radical in its critique of male patriarchy, and while

it brought Parsipur success, it also prompted the government to arrest her. Mohammad Reza Aslani, the publisher and owner of Noghreh Publishing, was also arrested, and his publishing house was immediately closed down. In 1994, Parsipur sought political refugee status and moved to the United States. Source: 1, pp. 353–54.

1233 Parsons, Alexander. *Leaving Disneyland.* Thomas Dunne Bks. Banned in Carroll County, Md. schools (2005). No reason stated. Source: 11, March 2006, pp. 70–71.

1234 Partridge, Eric. *Dictionary of Slang and Unconventional English.* Macmillan. Challenged in Pinellas County, Fla. (1973) due to profanity. Source: 11, Mar. 1974, p. 32.

1235 Pascal, Blaise. *Pensees.* Penguin. Placed on the *Index Librorum Prohibitorum* in Rome (1789). Source: 4, p. 24.

1236 _____. *The Provincial Letters.* Penguin. Burned in France for its alleged anti-religiosity in 1657. Louis XIV ordered in 1660 that it "be torn up and burned. . . at the hands of the High Executioner, fulfillment of which is to be certified to His Majesty within the week; and that meanwhile all printers, booksellers, vendors and others, of whatever rank and station, are explicitly prohibited from printing selling, and distributing, and even from having in their possession the said book. . . under the pain of public, exemplary punishment." Pascal's work remained on the Roman Index until 1966. Source: 3, p. 229.

1237 Pascal, Francine. *Hanging Out with Cici.* Archway; Dell; Viking. Challenged at the Greeley-Evans School District in Greeley, Colo. (1986) because the book contained "obscenities, allusions to sexual references, and promoted contempt for parents and acceptance of drug use." Source: 11, Sept. 1986, p. 171.

1238 Pasternak, Boris Leonidovich. *Doctor Zhivago.* Ballantine; NAL; Pantheon. Moscow condemned the book (1958), refused to publish it, and vilified the author. Source: 4, p. 73; 6, pp. 1,823–24; 8, pp. 44–45.

1239 Paterson, Katherine. *Bridge to Terabithia.* Crowell. The Newbery Award-winning book was challenged as sixth-grade recommended reading in the Lincoln, Nebr. schools (1986) because it contains "profanity" including the phrase "Oh,

Lord" and "Lord" used as an expletive. Challenged as suitable curriculum material in the Harwinton and Burlington, Conn. schools (1990) because it contains language and subject matter that set bad examples and give students negative views of life. Challenged at the Apple Valley, Calif. Unified School District (1992) because of vulgar language. Challenged at the Mechanicsburg, Pa. Area School District (1992) because of profanity and references to witchcraft. Challenged and retained in the libraries, but will not be required reading, at the Cleburne, Tex. Independent School district (1992) because of profane language. A challenge to this Newbery Award-winning book in Oskaloosa, Kans. (1993) led to the enactment of a new policy that requires teachers to examine their required material for profanities. Teachers will list each profanity and the number of times it was used in the book, and forward the list to parents, who will be asked to give written permission for their children to read the material. Challenged in the Gettysburg, Pa. public schools (1993) because of offensive language. Challenged at the Medway, Maine schools (1995) because the book uses "swear words." Removed from the fifth-grade classrooms of the New Brighton Area School District in Pulaski Township, Pa. (1996) due to "profanity, disrespect of adults, and an elaborate fantasy world they felt might lead to confusion." Challenged in the middle school curriculum in Cromwell, Conn. (2002) due to concern that it promotes witchcraft and violence. Source: 11, Mar. 1987, p. 67; Mar. 1991, p. 44; May 1992, p. 95; Sept. 1992, pp. 162–63; Nov. 1992, p. 198; Mar. 1993, p. 45; July 1993, pp. 105–6; Mar. 1994, p. 55; July 1995, p. 97; May 1996, p. 88; Sept. 2002, p. 197; Nov. 2002, pp. 257–58.

1240 _____. *The Great Gilly Hopkins.* Harper. Challenged at the Lowell Elementary School in Salina, Kans. (1983) because the book used the words "God," "damn" and "hell" offensively. Challenged at the Orchard Lake Elementary School library in Burnsville, Minn. (1985) because "the book took the Lord's name in vain" and had "over forty instances of profanity." Challenged at the Jefferson County, Colo. elementary schools (1988) because "Gilly's friends lie and steal, and there are no repercussions. Christians are portrayed as being dumb and stupid." Pulled from, but later restored to, the language arts curriculum at four Cheshire, Conn. elementary schools (1991) because the book is "filled with profanity, blasphemy and obscenities, and gutter language." Challenged at the Alamo Heights, Tex. School District elementary schools (1992) because it contains the words "hell" and "damn." Challenged at the Walnut Elementary School in Emporia, Kans. (1993) by parents who

said that it contains profanity and graphic violence. Challenged due to explicit language, but retained in the Lander County, Nev. School District (1997). Source: 11, July 1983, p. 121; Nov. 1985, p. 203; Mar. 1988, p. 45; Mar. 1992, p. 42; May 1992, p. 96; July 1992, pp. 109–10; Jan. 1993, p. 13; July 1993, pp. 126–27; Mar. 1998, p. 56.

1241 _____. *Jacob Have I Loved.* Avon; Cromwell; Random. Challenged at the Bernardsville, N.J. schools (1989) as unsuitable for a sixth-grade reading class. The Newbery award-winning book was offensive to several parents on moral and religious grounds. Challenged in the Gettysburg, Pa. public schools (1993) because of offensive language. Source: 11, Jan. 1990, p. 33; Mar. 1994, p. 55.

1242 **Paterson, Thomas.** *American Foreign Policy, Vol. II.* Heath. Returned to the Racine, Wis. Unified School District (1984) curriculum just one week after the school board voted to ban it. Opponents of the books on the board charged that the social studies volumes contained "judgmental writing" and, in the words of one board member, "a lot more funny pictures of Republicans and nicer pictures of Democrats." Opponents also said that one text did not present an adequate analysis of the Vietnam War. Source: 11, Sept. 1984, p. 158.

1243 **Patrick, John, and Carol Berkin.** *The History of the American Nation.* Macmillan; Collier. Challenged at the Amherst-Pelham, Mass. Regional Junior High School (1987) by a group of parents who charge that, among other things, it is sexist and distorts the history of minorities. Source: 11, Jan. 1988, p. 11.

1244 **Patterson, Lillie.** *Halloween.* Garrard. Challenged at the Neely Elementary School in Gilbert, Ariz. (1992) because the book shows the dark side of religion through the occult, the devil, and satanism. Source: 11, May 1992, p. 78; July 1992, p. 124.

1245 **Paulsen, Gary.** *The Foxman.* Viking; Puffin. Challenged at Cary, Ill., Junior High School (1994) because references in the book to sex are too explicit for seventh and eighth graders; retained by a school board vote. Source: 11, May 1994, p. 83; July 1994, pp. 128–29.

1246 _____. *Harris and Me.* Harcourt. Challenged due to explicit language, but retained in the Lander County, Nev. School District (1997). Source: 11, Mar. 1998, p. 56.

1247 _____. *Nightjohn.* Delacorte. Challenged as a seventh-grade summer reading option in Prince William County, Va. (1998) because the book "was rife with profanity and explicit sex." Source: 11, Nov. 1998, p. 183.

1248 **Paulsen, Gary.** *Zero to Sixty: The Motorcycle Journey of a Lifetime.* Harvest Bks. Removed from the West Brazoria, Tex. Junior High School library (2006) because of depictions of sex acts and profanity. Books on "sensitive topics such as death, suicide, physical or sexual abuse, and teenage dating relationships" were moved to a restricted "young-adult" section from which students can borrow only with written parental permission. Source: 11, Nov. 2006, pp. 289–90.

1249 **Peck, M. Scott.** *The Road Less Traveled.* Touchstone Bks. Removed from the college bookstore at Louisiana College, Pineville, La. (2003), by the college president because "profane language in the book clashes with the school's Christian values." Source: 11, Mar. 2004, pp. 53–54.

1250 **Peck, Robert Newton.** *A Day No Pigs Would Die.* ABC-CLIO; Dell; Knopf. Challenged in Jefferson County, Colo. school libraries (1988) because "it is bigoted against Baptists and women and depicts violence, hatred, animal cruelty, and murder." Challenged as suitable curriculum material in the Harwinton and Burlington, Conn. schools (1990) because it contains language and subject matter that set bad examples and give students negative views of life. Challenged at the Sherwood Elementary School in Melbourne, Fla. (1993) because the book could give the "impression that rape and violence are acceptable." The comment was made in reference to a descriptive passage about a boar mating a sow in the barnyard. Challenged, but retained, on the shelves at Waupaca, Wis. school libraries (1994) after a parent "objected to graphic passages dealing with sexuality in the book." Removed from seventh-grade classes at Payson, Utah Middle School (1994) after several parents "had problems with language, with animal breeding, and with a scene that involves an infant grave exhumation." Challenged at the Pawhuska, Okla. middle school (1995) because the book uses bad language, gives "gory" details of mating, and lacks religious values. Pulled from an Anderson, S.C. middle school library (1995) because of the "gory" descriptions of two pigs mating, a pig being slaughtered, and a cow giving birth. Challenged at the Anderson, Mo. Junior High School (1996) because of its content. Banned

from the St. Lawrence School in Utica, Mich. (1997) because of a passage involving pig breeding. The teacher quit her job over the banning of the novel. Source: 11, May 1988, p. 85; July 1988, pp. 119–20, 139; Sept. 1988, pp. 151, 177; Mar. 1991, p. 44; May 1991, p. 90; July 1993, pp. 97–98; May 1994, pp. 98–99; July 1994, pp. 117, 129; July 1995, p. 98; Mar. 1996, p. 46; Jan. 1997, p. 10; May 1997, p. 64.

1251 _____. *Soup.* Dell; Knopf. Challenged as a fourth-grade reading assignment at the Woodbridge, N.J. (1992) schools because of objectionable language and because "it teaches children how to lie, manipulate, steal, and cheat." Source: 11, Jan. 1993, p. 12.

1252 _____. *Trig.* Little. Challenged at the Cunningham Elementary School in Beloit, Wis. (1985) because the book "encourages disrespectful language." Source: 11, July 1985, p. 134.

1253 **Pell, Derek.** *Doktor Bey's Suicide Guidebook.* Avon. Placed "on reserve" at the Prairie High School library in Cedar Rapids, Iowa (1986) because the book "could push a classmate contemplating suicide over the edge." Source: 11, Sept. 1986, p. 152.

1254 **Pelzer, Dave.** *A Child Called It.* Health Communications; Omaha Pr. Pub. Co. Removed from the Sussex, Del. Central Middle School (2000) until the committee completes its review because of the book's profanity and violence. Source: 11, July 2000, p. 105.

1255 **Penney, Alexandra.** *How to Make Love to a Man...Safely.* Crown. Former Weslaco, Tex. (1995) librarian filed a federal lawsuit charging that she was fired for publicly discussing that city's efforts to ban Penney's work from the library. Source: 11, Sept. 1995, p. 155.

1256 **Perkins, Al.** *Don and Donna Go to Bat.* Beginner Bks. Returned to Shaftsbury, Vt. Elementary School library (1987). The complainant stated that children should not be exposed to "sexist attitudes in the story." Source: 11, Sept. 1987, p. 194.

1257 **Perry, Shawn, ed.** *Words of Conscience: Religious Statements of Conscientious Objectors.* National Interreligious Service Board for Conscientious Objectors. Access restricted in Coleman, Wis. (1982) due to the book's alleged political overtones. Source: 11, July 1982, p. 126.

129

1258 Perry, Troy. *The Lord Is My Shepherd and He Knows I'm Gay.* Dell. Challenged at the Niles, Mich. Community Library (1982) because of the book's "pornographic" nature. Source: 11, Jan. 1983, p. 8.

1259 Peters, Lisa Westberg. *Our Family Tree: An Evolution Story.* Harcourt. Retained in the Seaman, Kans. Unified School District 345 elementary school library (2006). Objections were raised because the book is about the scientific theory of evolution. Source: 11, May 2006, p. 153.

1260 Petronius, Gaius. *Satyricon.* NAL; Penguin. The New York Society for the Suppression of Vice went to court (1921) and case was dismissed twice in 1922. Ordered destroyed by the police court of the City of Westminster in London (1934). Source: 4, p. 3; 13, pp. 206–7.

1261 Pettit, Mark. *A Need to Kill.* Media Pub. Challenged in the Lincoln, Nebr. middle school libraries (1998). The book is about an executed child-killer and contains passages concerning murder, masturbation, and perverse sex, considered inappropriate for junior high. Source: 11, July 1998, p. 106.

1262 Pfeiffer, Susan. *About David.* Dell; Delacorte. Challenged at the Bay County's four middle schools and three high schools in Panama City, Fla. (1986) because it contains "profanity and sexual explicit passages." Source: 11, Nov. 1986, p. 209.

1263 Pierce, Ruth I. *Single and Pregnant.* Beacon Pr. Challenged and recommended for a "parents only" section at the Concord, Ark. school library (1984) because the author had "little to say that would discourage premarital sex." Source: 11, Jan. 1985, p. 7; May 1985, p. 75; Jan. 1986, pp. 7–8.

1264 Pierce, Tamara. *Alanna: Song of the Lioness, Book One.* Knopf. Removed by a library staff member, but later returned to the shelves of the David Hill Elementary School in Hillsboro, Oreg. (1989) because of sexual references and the use of an amulet to prevent pregnancy. Source: 11, Jan. 1990, pp. 4–5.

1265 _____. *In the Hand of the Goddess: Song of the Lioness, Book Two.* Macmillan. Removed by a library staff member, but later returned to the shelves of the David Hill Elementary School in Hillsboro, Oreg. (1989) because of sexual references and use of an amulet to prevent pregnancy. Source: 11, Jan. 1990, pp. 4–5.

1266 _____. *The Woman Who Rides Like a Man: Song of the Lioness, Book Three.* Macmillan. Removed by a library staff member, but later returned to the shelves of the David Hill Elementary School in Hillsboro, Oreg. (1989) because of sexual references and the use of an amulet to prevent pregnancy. Source: 11, Jan. 1990, pp. 4–5.

1267 Pike, Christopher. *Bury Me Deep.* Archway. Removed from the Nampa, Idaho West Middle School (2000) due to its violence and sexual content. Source: 11, May 2000, p. 74.

1268 _____. *Chain Letter 2.* Flare. Removed from the Nampa, Idaho West Middle School (2000) due to its violence and sexual content. Source: 11, May 2000, p. 74.

1269 _____. *Die Softly.* Archway. Removed from Escondido, Calif. middle school libraries (1999) along with 24 other novels by the best-selling author. Passages deemed offensive made references to whiskey drinking, bribery, sex, and a nightmare about dismemberment. Source: 11, July 1998, p. 104; Nov. 1999, p. 161.

1270 _____. *Final Friends: The Party.* Pocket Bks. Recommended for removal from Escondido, Calif. middle school libraries (1998) because the book is "vulgar and unsuitable." Source: 11, July 1998, p. 104.

1271 _____. *The Graduation: Final Friends Book 3.* Pocket Bks. Challenged at the Weatherly, Pa. Area Middle School library (1992) because parents were upset by passages in the book dealing with depression, suicide, and contraception. Source: 11, May 1992, p. 81; July 1992, p. 125.

1272 _____. *Last Act.* Archway. Removed from the Nampa, Idaho South Middle School (2000) due to its violence and sexual content. Source: 11, May 2000, p. 74.

1273 _____. *The Listeners.* Tor Bks. Removed from the Nampa, Idaho West Middle School (2000) due to its violence and sexual content. Source: 11, May 2000, p. 74.

1274 _____. *The Lost Mind.* Pocket Bks. Removed from the Nampa, Idaho West Middle School (2000) due to its violence and sexual content. Source: 11, May 2000, p. 74.

1275 _____. *The Midnight Club.* Pocket Bks. Removed from the Nampa, Idaho West Middle School (2000) due to its violence and sexual content. Source: 11, May 2000, p. 74.

1276 _____. *Remember Me 3.* Pocket Bks. Removed from the Nampa, Idaho West Middle School (2000) due to its violence and sexual content. Source: 11, May 2000, p. 74.

1277 _____. *Remember Me.* Pocket Bks. Removed from the Liberty Middle School library in Seneca, S.C. (1998) after a seventh-grader's grandmother complained to school officials. Source: 11, May 1998, p. 70.

1278 _____. *Road to Nowhere.* Archway; Turtleback. Recommended for removal from Escondido, Calif. middle school libraries (1998) because the book is "vulgar and unsuitable." Source: 11, July 1998, p. 104.

1279 _____. *The Star Group.* Archway. Removed from the Nampa, Idaho West Middle School (2000) due to its violence and sexual content. Source: 11, May 2000, p. 74.

1280 _____. *Witch.* Archway. Removed from the Nampa, Idaho West Middle School (2000) due to its violence and sexual content. Source: 11, May 2000, p. 74.

1281 **Pilkey, Dav.** *Adventures of Captain Underpants.* Blue Sky Pr. Removed from the Maple Hill School in Naugatuck, Conn. (2000) due to concerns that it caused unruly behavior among children. Source: 8, p. 430; 11, May 2000, p. 73.

1282 _____. *The Adventures of Super Diaper Baby.* Blue Sky Pr. Challenged, but retained in the Riverside, Calif. Unified School District classrooms and libraries (2003), despite a complaint of the book's "inappropriate" scatological storyline. Source: 8, p. 431; 11, Sept. 2003, p. 201.

1283 _____. *Captain Underpants and the Invasion of the Incredibly Naughty Cafeteria Ladies from Outer Space (and the Subsequent Assault of Equally Evil Lunchroom Zombie Nerds).* Blue Sky Pr. Challenged, but retained at the Orfordville, Wis. Elementary School library (2000). A parent charged that the book taught students to be disrespectful, not to obey authority, not to obey the law, including God's law, improper spelling, to make excuses and lie to escape responsibility, to make fun of what people wear, and poor nutrition. Source: 11, Mar. 2000, p. 62.

1284 _____. *Captain Underpants and the Perilous Plot of Professor Poopypants.* Scholastic. Removed from the Hope-Page, Tex. Consolidated School District (2002) because a parent "didn't care for the language. I didn't care for the innuendo." The board approved a policy requiring that the consolidated school board approve all library purchases and allowing them to reject materials "that label or characterize undeserving individuals in a derogatory manner." Source: 8, p. 430.

1285 **Pinkwater, Daniel.** *The Devil in the Drain.* Dutton. Challenged in the Galesville-Ettrick, Wis. School District (1987). Source: 11, Nov. 1987, p. 226.

1286 **Pipher, Mary.** *Reviving Ophelia.* Putnam. Challenged for use in the Richland, Wash. high school English classes (1998) along with six other titles because the "books are poor-quality literature and stress suicide, illicit sex, violence, and hopelessness." Source: 11, Mar. 1999, p. 40.

1287 **Plante, David.** *The Catholic.* Atheneum; Chatto. Banned in South Africa (1986). Source: 5, June 1986, p. 41.

1288 **Plath, Sylvia.** *The Bell Jar.* Bantam; Harper. Prohibited for use in the Warsaw, Ind. schools (1979). Challenged in Edwardsville, Ill. (1981) when three hundred residents signed a petition against Plath's novel because it contains sexual material and advocates an "objectionable" philosophy of life. Challenged for use in the Richland, Wash. high school English classes (1998) along with six other titles because the "books are poor-quality literature and stress suicide, illicit sex, violence, and hopelessness." Source: 8, pp. 418–19; 11, Mar. 1980, p. 40; July 1981, p. 102; Mar. 1999, p. 40.

1289 **Platt, Kin.** *Head Man.* Greenwillow; Dell. The Anaconda, Mo. School Board (1982) handed school principal Patrick Meloy a list of thirty-four restricted titles including Platt's book and gave him authority to censor or destroy any book he believes is "pornographic." Challenged at the Elkader, Iowa Central High School library (1983) because the book's description of the Los Angeles ghetto by a youth gang leader contains "street talk and four-letter words offensive to Elkader residents." Challenged at the Rankin County, Miss. School District (1984) because it is "profane and sexually objectionable." Source: 11, Mar. 1983, p. 41; July 1983, p. 121; May 1984, p. 70; Jan. 1985, p. 8.

1290 **Pollan, Michael.** *The Botany of Desire: A Plant's-Eye View of the World.* Random. Retained on the Buffalo Grove, Ill. High School (2006), along with eight other challenged titles. A board member, elected amid promises to bring her Christian beliefs into all board decision-making, raised the controversy based on excerpts from the books she'd found on the Internet. Source: 11, July 2006, pp. 210–11.

1291 **Pomeroy, Wardell B.** *Boys and Sex.* Delacorte. Challenged at the Santa Fe, N.Mex. High School library (1983) by a school librarian because of its "sordid, suggestive, permissive type of approach." Removed from two middle school libraries in the Greece, N.Y. (1988) because the book "promotes prostitution, promiscuity, homosexuality, and bestiality." Pulled from the Black River Falls, Wis. Middle School library (1990) because the book "dealt with bestiality, masturbation and homosexuality, and endorsed pre-adolescent and premarital sex." Pulled from the Rangely, Colo. Middle School library shelves (1994). Challenged in the Charlotte, N.C. Public Library (2000) because of its sexual content. Source: 11, May 1983, p. 85; July 1988, p. 121; Sept. 1988, p. 178; May 1991, p. 75; May 1994, p. 83; Sept. 2000, p. 143.

1292 _____. *Girls and Sex.* Delacorte. Challenged at the Santa Fe, N.Mex. High School library (1983) by a school librarian because of its "sordid, suggestive, permissive type of approach." Pulled from the Black River Falls, Wis. Middle School library (1990) because the book "dealt with bestiality, masturbation and homosexuality, and endorsed pre-adolescent and premarital sex." Pulled from the Rangely, Colo. Middle School library shelves (1994). Challenged in the Charlotte, N.C. Public Library (2000) because of its sexual content. Source: 11, May 1983, p. 85; May 1991, p. 75; May 1994, p. 83; Sept. 2000, p. 143.

1293 **Ponce, Charles.** *The Game of Wizards.* Penguin. Challenged by the "God Squad," a group of three students and their parents,

at the El Camino High School in Oceanside, Calif. (1986) because the Chinese yin and yang symbol is drawn on page 95. The complainant wrote, "This is the symbol of Confucianism and represents reincarnation. This book also deals with transcendental meditation." Source: 11, Sept. 1986, p. 151; Nov. 1986, p. 224; Jan. 1987, p. 9.

1294 **Portal, Colette.** *The Beauty of Birth.* Knopf. Moved from the children's room of the Tampa-Hillsborough County, Fla. Public Library (1982) to the adult section. Source: 11, Jan. 1982, pp. 4–5.

1295 **Porter, Jean Stratton.** *Her Father's Daughter.* Am. Repr.-Rivercity Pr. Removed from the Clatskanie, Oreg. Library District (1991) because of alleged bigotry against the Japanese. Source: 11, July 1992, p. 103.

1296 **Potok, Chaim.** *My Name Is Asher Lev.* Knopf. Banned from the 1983 Moscow International Book Fair along with more than fifty other books because it is "anti-Soviet." Source: 11, Nov. 1983, p. 201.

1297 **Prelutsky, Jack.** *The Headless Horseman Rides Tonight and Other Poems to Trouble Your Sleep.* Greenwillow. Challenged at the Victor Elementary School media center in Rochester, N.Y. (1982) because it "was too frightening for young children to read." Source: 11, July 1982, p. 142.

1298 _____. *Nightmares: Poems to Trouble Your Sleep.* Greenwillow. Placed in the professional reading section of the Kirkland, Wash. district libraries (1979) where it would be unavailable to students without a teacher's permission. Challenged at the Paul E. Culley Elementary School in Las Vegas, Nev. (1987) because the poems were too frightening for small children. Placed in a "reserved" section at Little Butte Intermediate School in Eagle Point, Oreg. (1988) because the book could "disturb a child's sleep and offered no learning experience." Removed from the Berkeley County, S.C. schools (1993) that include fourth graders and younger children due to violent passages. Removed from the Eau Claire, Wis. elementary school libraries (1993) because the poems "graphically describe violent acts against children that would be criminal activity if acted out." Source: 11, Sept. 1979, p. 104; Jan. 1988, p. 32; Jan. 1989, p. 3; Sept. 1993, pp. 148–49; Mar. 1994, p. 53.

1299 _____. *Rolling Harvey down the Hill.* Greenwillow. Challenged at the Consolidated

School library in New Fairfield, Conn. (1989) because the book of children's verses is "repulsive" and against the country's "moral fiber." Source: 11, July 1989, p. 127.

1300 Pressfield, Steven. *Gates of Fire.* Doubleday. Retained in the Fairfax County, Va. Public Schools (2002) after being challenged for "too much profanity." Source: 11, July 2002, p. 179.

1301 Preston, Richard. *The Hot Zone.* Wheeler Pub.; Anchor Bks. Challenged for use in the Richland, Wash. high school English classes (1998) along with six other titles because the "books are poor-quality literature and stress suicide, illicit sex, violence, and hopelessness." Source: 11, Mar. 1999, p. 40.

1302 Price, Richard. *Bloodbrothers.* Houghton. Banned from the Stroudsburg, Pa. High School library (1985) because it was "blatantly graphic, pornographic, and wholly unacceptable for a high school library." Source: 11, May 1985, p. 79.

1303 Price, Richard. *Wanderers.* Houghton. Banned from the Vergennes, Vt. Union High School library (1978). Decision upheld in *Bicknell v. Vergennes Union High School Board*, 475 F.Supp. 615 (D. Vt. 1979), 638 F. 2d 438 (2d Cir. 1980). Source: 11, Jan. 1979, p. 6; 12, pp. 151, 239; 15, Vol. IV, p. 715.

1304 Price, Susan. *The Devil's Piper.* Faber; Greenwillow. Challenged at the Canby, Oreg. Junior High School library (1988) because it "could encourage young minds to pursue occult, suicide, or adopt ill attitudes." Source: 11, May 1989, p. 78.

1305 Proulx, Annie. *Brokeback Mountain.* Scribner. Retained at St. Andrew's Episcopal School in Austin, Tex. (2005). The private school returned a three million dollar donation rather than submit to the donor's request that the short story be removed from the school's list of optional reading for twelfth graders. Source: 11, Jan. 2006, p. 37.

1306 Pullman, Phillip. *The Broken Bridge.* Knopf. Removed from the Jackson County, W.Va. school libraries (1997) along with sixteen other titles. Source: 11, Jan. 1998, p. 13.

1307 Purdy, Candace, and Stan Kendziorski. *Understanding Your Sexuality.* Scott, Foresman. Challenged at the York,

Maine school system (1982). Challenged at the Chambersburg, Pa. Area Senior High School health class (1984) because "the Christian child must go to school and be subjected to the immoral teachings of this book." Source: 11, July 1982, p. 124; Jan. 1985, pp. 11–12.

1308 Puzo, Mario. *The Godfather.* NAL; Putnam. Challenged at the Grinnell-Newburg, Iowa school system (1975) because the book is "vulgar and obscene by most religious standards." Source: 9; 11, Mar. 1975, p. 41; May 1975, p. 87.

1309 Pyle, Howard. *King Stork.* Little. Challenged at the public libraries of Saginaw, Mich. (1989) because it "would encourage boys beating girls when the drummer beats the enchantress with a switch until she becomes a 'good' princess." Unavailable to children unless they have written permission from their parents to check out the book or to read it in the library at the Sandstone Elementary School library in Billings, Mont. (1993). The objections to the near hundred-year-old book included a scene in which a husband beat his witchy wife into submission and illustrations from the 1973 edition of a princess in revealing clothing. Source: 11, May 1989, p. 77; July 1993, p. 99.

1310 Pynchon, William. *The Meritorius Price of Our Redemption.* First book publicly burned in the United States, where the Massachusetts Colony authorities destroyed it in 1650. Although Pynchon was one of the founders of the colony, and a signatory to its charter, his book proved so contentious in its criticism of the puritan orthodoxy that dominated the theological attitudes of the colony, that after it had been read by the General Council, it was condemned to be burned by the common executioner in the Market Place. Pynchon himself was publicly censured and escaped further punishment only by sailing back to England. Source: 3, pp. 247–48.

1311 Quinlan, Patricia. *Tiger Flowers.* Dial. Challenged, but retained on the library shelves of a Dallas-Fort Worth-area elementary school (1999). The children's book is about a boy whose uncle dies from AIDS. Source: 11, Nov. 1999, p. 172.

1312 Rabelais, Francois. *Gargantua & Pantagruel.* Penguin. Blacklisted by French Parliament (1533); censored by the Sorbonne (1552); banned by Henry II (1554), listed on the *Index Librorum Prohibitorum* in Rome (1564); U.S. Customs Department lifted ban (1930) and banned in South Africa (1938). In 1951, city and county law enforcement officers obtained a warrant and raided the Dubuque, Iowa Public Library, where they seized the novel as obscene. The book was later returned to library shelves, as "restricted" material. Source: 4, p. 14; 6, pp. 2,003–4; 14, pp. 151–52.

1313 Radishchev, Alkeksandr Nikolaevich. *A Journey from St. Petersburg to Moscow.* Harvard Univ. Pr. Catherine II the Great issued orders for the book to be confiscated from sale and the whole edition destroyed (1790) because the book "is trying in every possible way to break down respect for authority and for the authorities, to stir up in the people indignation against their superiors and against the government." Radishchev was quickly arrested and condemned to death; his sentence was later commuted to an exile in Siberia. After almost six years in exile, Catherine having died, her successor Paul I issued orders for many in disfavor during his mother's resign, including Radishchev to be released. Alexander I, the next czar, granted him full pardon in 1801. Source: 7, pp. 275–77.

1314 Radlauer, Ruth, and Ed Radlauer. *Chopper Cycle.* Watts. Challenged at the Morrish Elementary School in Swartz Creek, Mich. (1982) because of its negative approach to law enforcement. Source: 11, Nov. 1982, p. 215.

1315 Rampling, Anne. *Belinda.* Arbor House. Challenged at the Multnomah County Library in Portland, Oreg. (1988) because of its sexual nature. Source: 11, Jan. 1989, p. 3.

1316 Randal, Jonathan C. *After Such Knowledge, What Forgiveness?—My Encounters with Kurdistan.* Farrar; Aresta. Confiscated by order of a Turkish state security court (2002). The Istanbul State Security Court sentenced the publisher to six months in jail but converted the sentence to a fine of $500. The book remained banned after the trail. The International Freedom to Publish Committee selected the publisher as the 2005 recipient of the Jeri Laber International Freedom to Publish Award. He was recognized for his long commitment to Kurdish writings in the face of great political obstacles—and personal peril— over the past decades. Source: 7, pp. 13–14.

1317 Randall, Dudley. *Black Poets.* Bantam. Banned for use in English classrooms at the Tinley Park, Ill. High School (1982) because the book "extols murder, rape, theft, incest, sodomy, and other acts." Source: 11, Mar. 1983, p. 40.

1318 Randolph, Vance, comp. *Pissing in the Snow and Other Ozark Folktales.* Univ. of Ill. Pr.; Avon. Challenged at the Rogers-Hough, Ark. Memorial Library (1988) because the book is "vulgar and obscene." Source: 11, July 1988, p. 119.

1319 Rapp, Adam. *The Buffalo Tree.* HarperCollins. Banned from the Muhlenberg, Pa. High School (2005). Several months later the board reversed that decision and determined that a reading list be made available to parents including a rating system, plot summaries of all assigned books, and the identification of any potentially objectionable content. Source: 11, July 2005, pp. 161–62; 13, pp. 32–34.

1320 Raucher, Herman. *Summer of '42.* Dell. Challenged at the Grinnell-Newburg, Iowa (1975) school system as "vulgar and obscene by most religious standards." Removed from the reading list of an elective English course at Pulaski County, Ky. (1978) High School after a parent complained about "four-letter language" in the work. Source: 9; 11, Mar. 1975, p. 41; May 1975, p. 87; Mar. 1979, p. 27.

1321 Ray, Ron. *Gays in or out of the Military.* Brassey's. Pulled from the Ouachita Parish School library in Monroe, La. (1996) because of sexual content. The Louisiana chapter of the ACLU filed a lawsuit in the federal courts on October 3, 1996, claiming that the principal and the school superintendent violated First Amendment free speech rights and also failed to follow established procedure when they removed the book. The three-year-old school library censorship case headed to court after the Ouachita Parish School Board made no decision to seek a settlement at a special meeting April 12, 1999. On August 17, 1999, the Ouachita Parish School Board agreed to return the book to the library and to develop a new book-selection policy that follows state guidelines for school media programs. Source: 11, Sept. 1996, pp. 151–52; Jan. 1997, p. 7; July 1999, p. 93; Jan. 2000, p. 27.

1322 Reavin, Sam. *The Hunters Are Coming.* Putnam. Challenged at the Cousens Memorial School library in Lyman, Maine (1999) because the book portrays hunters in a negative light. Source: 11, May 1999, p. 83.

1323 Reddin, Keith. *Life and Limb.* Dramatists Play Service. Challenged at the Manatee County school district in Bradenton Beach, Fla. (1998) because the play contains references to pornographic magazines, most of them fictional. Source: 11, May 1998, p. 71.

1324 Reed, Rick. *Obsessed.* Dell. Permanently removed from the East Coweta County, Ga. High School library (1996) because of several sexually and violently graphic passages. Source: 11, Jan. 1997, p. 7; Mar. 1997, p. 35.

1325 Reiss, Johanna. *The Upstairs Room.* Bantam; Harper. Removed from the required reading list for fourth graders at Liberty, Ind. Elementary School (1993). The Newbery Honor Book about a girl in Holland hiding from the Nazis during World War II was investigated because of profanity. Challenged as assigned reading for sixth-grade students in Sanford, Maine (1996) because of profanity. Source: 11, July 1993, p. 105; July 1996, p. 118.

1326 Remarque, Erich Maria. *All Quiet on the Western Front.* Fawcett; Little. Banned in Boston, Mass. (1929) on grounds of obscenity; seized by U.S. Customs in Chicago, Ill. (1929); Austrian soldiers forbidden to read it (1929); barred from Czech military libraries by the war department (1929); banned in Thuringia, Germany (1930); banned in Italy because of the book's anti-war propaganda (1933); and consigned to the Nazi bonfires (1933). Source: 2, pp. 137, 139; 4, pp. 6–7; 15, Vol. III, pp. 417–18.

1327 _____. *The Road Back.* Avon; Grosset; Little; Putnam. Banned in Ireland (1931). Source: 4, p. 81.

1328 Renan, Ernest. *Life of Jesus.* Prometheus Bks. Condemned by the Catholic Church and placed on the Index of Forbidden books (1897), along with nineteen other works by Renan, and remained listed until 1966. The biography was the first to use modern historical methods to recount the life of Jesus. Source: 1, pp. 190–92.

1329 Rench, Janice E. *Understanding Sexual Identity: A Book for Gay Teens & Their Friends.* Lerner Pubs. Pulled from the Rangely, Colo. Middle School library shelves (1994). Moved from the Chestnut Ridge Middle School library to the guidance center in Washington Township, N.J. (1994) because school administrators have been accused of "indoctrinating children in the gay lifestyle." Restricted to students with parental permission at the Brownsville, Pa. Area High School District Library (1997) because a parent complained the book contains references to gays and lesbians. The controversy prompted the Greater Pittsburgh chapter of the ACLU to write to the school district saying it would challenge in court any effort to ban the book from the high school library because of its references to homosexuality. The book's author offered to donate three copies to the high school, since the library's copy was never returned. Source: 11, May 1994, p. 83; Sept. 1994, p. 148; Sept. 1997, p. 126; Nov. 1997, p. 181; Jan. 1998, p. 11.

1330 Rennison, Louise. *Knocked Out by My Nunga-Nungas: Further, Further Confessions of Georgia Nicolson.* HarperCollins. Challenged at the Oregon, Wis. Middle School (2002) by a parent who was particularly offended by a passage in which a boy touches a girl's breast. Source: 11, Jan. 2003, p. 10.

1331 _____. *On the Bright Side, I'm Now the Girlfriend of a Sex God: Further Confessions of Georgia Nicolson.* Avon. Retained in the Bozeman, Mont. School District's middle-school libraries (2005) despite a complaint that an unstable person seeing a girl reading the book might think from the title that the girl is promiscuous and stalk her. Source: 11, Mar. 2005, p. 74.

1332 Reuben, David. *Everything You Always Wanted to Know about Sex, but Were Afraid to Ask.* Bantam. Challenged at the William Chrisman High School in Independence, Mo. (1984) because the book is "filthy." The Reuben's work was on a bookshelf in the classroom and was the personal property of the teacher. Source: 11, July 1984, p. 106.

1333 Revesz, Therese Ruth. *Witches.* Contemporary Perspective. Pulled, but later placed on reserve to children with parental permission at the Forrest Elementary School library in Hampton, Va. (1992). Source: 11, July 1992, p. 108; Sept. 1992, p. 139.

1334 Reynolds, Marilyn. *Detour for Emmy.* Morning Glory Pr. Removed from Dysart Unified School District libraries, Dysart, Ariz., (2000) for its portrayal of teenage pregnancy. Challenged in the Action Middle School library in Granbury, Tex. (2005) because it "talks very vividly about sexual encounters of a fifteen-year-old." The book was cited as one of the American Library Association's Best Books for Young Adults in 1993. Source: 11, May 2000, p. 73; Nov. 2005, pp. 280–81; Jan. 2006, pp. 10–11.

1335 Rhyne, Nancy. *Murder in the Carolinas.* Blair. Removed from the Berkeley County, S.C. elementary and middle school libraries (1992) because the book—real-life stories of South

135

Carolina murders based on newspaper accounts—contained descriptions of actual murders that were too graphic for young readers. Source: 11, July 1992, pp. 107–8.

1336 Richards, Arlene K., and Irene Willis. *What to Do If You or Someone You Know Is under 18 and Pregnant.* Lothrop. Challenged at the Racine, Wis. Unified School District libraries (1991) because the book uses street language to describe sexual intercourse and contraceptives, contains "sexually suggestive and provocative" language, and "promotes teenage sexual promiscuity." Source: 11, Jan. 1992, p. 27.

1337 Richardson, Justin, and Peter Parnell. *And Tango Makes Three.* Simon. Moved from the children's fiction section to children's nonfiction at two Rolling Hill's Consolidated Library's branches in Savannah and St. Joseph, Mo. (2006) after parents complained it had homosexual undertones. The illustrated book is based on a true story of two male penguins that adopted an abandoned egg at New York City's Central Park in the late 1990s. Challenged at the Shiloh, Ill. Elementary School library (2006). A committee of school employees and a parent suggested the book be moved to a separate shelf, requiring parent permission before checkout. The school's superintendent, however, rejected the proposal and the book remained on the library shelf. Pulled from four elementary-school libraries in the Charlotte-Mecklenburg, N.C. (2007) after a few parents and Mecklenburg County Commissioner Bill James questioned the controversial but true story. The books were returned after the local paper questioned the ban. It should be noted that there was no formal request for the book's removal. Source: 11, May 2006, p. 129; Jan. 2007, p. 9; Mar. 2007, pp. 71–72.

1338 Richardson, Samuel. *Pamela.* Houghton; Penguin; Norton. Condemned by the Roman Catholic Church in 1744 and was prohibited reading for Catholics. It appeared on the *Index Librorum Prohibitorum* mainly because it was a novel that related a suggestively romantic relationship. The work appears on the Index of Benedict XIV, issued in 1758, and the Indexes of Pope Leo XIII, issued in 1881 and 1900 and still in force in 1906. Source: 3, p. 135; 6, pp. 2,039–40; 8, pp. 371–72.

1339 Rigaud, Milo. *Secrets of Voodoo.* Arco. Challenged, but retained, at the Madison Elementary School in Cedar Rapids, Iowa (1998). Source: 11, May 1998, pp. 87–88.

1340 Riker, Andrew, et al. *Married Life.* Bennett. Challenged in Collinsville, Ill. (1981), in Jefferson County, Ky. (1982) because it "pushes women's lib which is very degrading to women and will destroy the traditional family." Source: 11, May 1981, p. 68; Mar. 1983, p. 41.

1341 Riker, Andrew. *Finding My Way.* Bennett. Challenged in Tell City, Ind. (1982). Challenged in Walker County, Ga. (1982) by the Eagle Forum because its "treatment of sexual matters was too explicit and its method of presentation faulty." Challenged at the Laramie, Wy. Junior High School (1987) because the book "doesn't stress saying 'No.'" Challenged at the Grove, Okla. High School (1991) because it was "too graphic for presentation in the classroom." Source: 11, May 1982, p. 85; July 1982, p. 142; Sept. 1987, p. 177; Sept. 1991, p. 179.

1342 Riker, Audrey Palm, and Holly Brisbane. *Married and Single Life.* Bennett. Returned to the Racine, Wis. Unified School District (1984) curriculum just one week after the school board voted to ban it. The home economics text was criticized for encouraging premarital sex and advocating that unmarried couples live together. Source: 11, Sept. 1984, p. 158; Jan. 1985, p. 10.

1343 Ringgold, Faith. *Tar Beach.* Crown. Challenged in the Spokane, Wash. elementary school libraries (1994) because it stereotypes African Americans as eating fried chicken and watermelon and drinking beer at family picnics. The book is based on memories of its author's family rooftop picnics in 1930s Harlem. The book won the 1992 Coretta Scott King Illustrator Award for its portrayal of minorities. Source: 11, Jan. 1995, p. 9; Mar. 1995, p. 54.

1344 Robbins, Harold. *The Carpetbaggers.* Trident; Pocket Bks. Sales restricted in Warwick, R.I.; Rochester, N.Y.; Mesquite, Tex.; Waterbury, Conn.; and Bridgeport, Conn. (1961). Banned in South Africa (1965). In Oct. 1982, Malaysian police confiscated the works of Robbins because they were considered "prejudicial to the public interest." Source: 4, p. 88; 5, Jan. 1983, p. 45; 13, p. 40.

1345 _____. *The Lonely Lady.* Pocket Bks.; Simon & Schuster. Challenged in Abingdon, Va. (1980) because of the book's "pornographic" nature. Source: 11, Jan. 1981, p. 5.

1346 _____. ***Never Love a Stranger.*** Knopf. Identified, along with eight other novels, as obscene in criminal proceedings in the Court of Quarter sessions in Philadelphia County, Pennsylvania (1949). The court refused to declare the novel "obscene" and in Robbin's novel, references to sexual activity are brief and general, and the main character's language is important to developing that character. Source: 14, pp. 236–37.

1347 **Robbins, Russell H.** ***Encyclopedia of Witchcraft and Demonology.*** Outlet Bk. Co. Removed from the Detroit, Mich. public school libraries (1994) after a complaint that the book was "obscene, perverse, and immoral." Source: 11, Mar. 1994, p. 51.

1348 **Roberts, J. R.** ***Ambush Moon: Gunsmith Series 148.*** Berkley; Jove. Challenged, but retained, in the Fairfield County District Library in Lancaster, Ohio (1995) because it includes profanity and explicit sex scenes. Source: 11, Nov. 1995, p. 184; Jan. 1996, p. 29.

1349 _____. ***The Gunsmith: Hands of the Strangler.*** Jove. Challenged, but retained, at the Selby, S.Dak. Library (1994) because of an inappropriate sex scene. Source: 11, July 1994, p. 129.

1350 **Roberts, Willo Davis.** ***The View from the Cherry Tree.*** Macmillan. Retained in Elko County, Nev. classrooms (1995) despite the complaint of the elementary school student. School officials said parents complained that the book contains language inappropriate for sixth-graders, including a cat named S.O.B. Source: 11, Sept. 1995, p. 160.

1351 **Robinson, David.** ***Herbert Armstrong's Tangled Web.*** Interstate. A suit was filed in Tulsa, Okla. (1981) alleging that the book was based on privileged communications, whose secrecy is protected by law. A restraining order temporarily stopped the release of this book. Source: 11, Jan. 1982, p. 23.

1352 **Rock, Gail.** ***The House without a Christmas Tree.*** Bantam. Challenged in the Des Moines, Iowa schools (1983) due to the use of the word "damn." Source: 11, May 1983, p. 73.

1353 **Rockwell, Thomas.** ***How to Eat Fried Worms.*** ABC-CLIO; Dell; Watts. Retained in the Middletown, N.J. elementary school libraries (1988)

despite a parent's objection that the book contains violence and vulgar language. Removed from the LaVille Elementary School library in LaPaz, Ind. (1991) by a library user because the book contains the word "bastard." Source: 11, May 1988, p. 103; Sept. 1991, p. 153.

1354 **Rodgers, Mary.** ***Freaky Friday.*** Harper; ABC-CLIO. Pulled, but later returned to the library shelves of Hernando County, Fla. schools (2001) after a parent's complaint about the book's references to drinking and smoking, characters who take God's name in vain, and the claim it advocates violence. Source: 11, Mar. 2001, p. 53; May 2001, p. 123.

1355 **Rodriguez, Abraham, Jr.** ***The Boy without a Flag: Tales of the South Bronx.*** Milkweed Ed. Retained in the Rosemount, Minn. High School (1994) after a complaint about "profane language and promiscuity in the stories." Source: 11, July 1994, p. 130.

1356 **Rodriguez, Luis J.** ***Always Running.*** Curbstone Pr. Challenged as an optional reading at the Guilford High School in Rockford, Ill. (1996) because it is "blatant pornography." Challenged, but retained, on the San Jose, Calif. Unified School District optional reading list at district high schools (1998) despite complaints that the book is "pornographic and offensive in its stereotyping of Latinos." The book will be kept in libraries, but students must have parental consent to check it out. Removed from the Santa Rosa, Calif. high school reading lists (1998). Removed, pending review, at the Fremont, Calif. schools (1998). Challenged, but retained in three Beyer High School classrooms in Modesto, Calif. (2003) despite complaints that the book is "pornographic." The decision reversed the actions of district administrators who had removed the book in early November 2003. The book won the Chicago Sun Times Carl Sandburg Literary Award and was designated as a *New York Times* notable book. Pulled from the Santa Barbara, Calif. schools (2004) after a parent complained about graphic passages depicting violence and sex. Source: 11, July 1996, p. 118; Sept. 1998, pp. 142–43; Jan. 2003, pp. 27–28; Mar. 2004, pp. 51–52; Jan. 2005, p. 7; 13, pp. 8–11.

1357 **Rojas, Don.** ***One People, One Destiny: The Caribbean and Central America Today.*** Pathfinder Pr. Confiscated by custom officials in Grenada along with *Maurice Bishop Speaks; Thomas Sankara Speaks: The Burkina Faso Revolution, 1983-87,* and other books by Nelson Mandela, Karl Marx,

Che Guevara, Fidel Castro, and Malcom X. The books were labeled as "subversive to the peace and security of the country." Source: 11, Mar. 1989, pp. 49–50; July 1989, pp. 141–42.

1358 **Roman, Jo. *Exit House.*** Bantam. Challenged at the Springdale, Ark. Public Library (1994) because it presented suicide as "a rational and sane alternative." Source: 11, July 1994, p. 128.

1359 **Ronan, Margaret, and Eve Ronan.** ***Astrology and Other Occult Games.*** Scholastic. Challenged in the Akron, Ohio school system (1982) because the book promotes Satan. Source: 11, Mar. 1983, p. 38.

1360 **Roquelaire, A. E. [Anne Rice].** ***Beauty's Punishment.*** NAL. Removed from the shelves of the Lake Lanier Regional Library system in Gwinnett County, Ga. (1992) following complaints that centered on sexuality. Removed from the Columbus, Ohio Metropolitan Library (1996) as hard-core pornography. Source: 11, Jan. 1993, p. 7; July 1996, pp. 119–20.

1361 _____. ***Beauty's Release.*** NAL. Removed from the shelves of the Lake Lanier Regional Library system in Gwinnett County, Ga. (1992) following complaints that centered on sexuality. Removed from the Columbus, Ohio Metropolitan Library (1996) as hard-core pornography. Source: 11, Jan. 1993, p. 7; July 1996, pp. 119–20.

1362 _____. ***The Claiming of Sleeping Beauty.*** NAL. Removed from the shelves of the Lake Lanier Regional Library system in Gwinnett County, Ga. (1992) following complaints that centered on sexuality. Removed from the Columbus, Ohio Metropolitan Library (1996) as hard-core pornography. Source: 11, Jan. 1993, p. 7; July 1996, pp. 119–20.

1363 **Roth, Philip. *Goodbye, Columbus.*** Bantam; Houghton. Challenged in Abingdon, Va. (1980) because of the book's "pornographic" nature. Source: 11, Jan. 1981, p. 5.

1364 _____. ***Portnoy's Complaint.*** Bantam; Random. Many libraries were attacked for carrying this novel, and some librarians' jobs were threatened. Source: 4, p. 99.

1365 **Rounds, Glen. *Wash Day on Noah's Ark.*** Holiday. Challenged at the Hubbard, Ohio

Public Library (1991) because the book alters the story of Noah's Ark, making it secular and confusing to children. Source: 11, Sept. 1991, p. 153.

1366 **Rousseau, Jean-Jacques. *Confessions.*** Penguin. Placed the book on the list of prohibited books of the Roman Index of 1806 by Pope Pius VII and later renewed the prohibition because of the sexual adventures that Rousseau recounted. Banned by the U.S. Customs Department for being injurious to public morals (1929); banned in the USSR (1935). Source: 4, p. 30; 8, pp. 325–26.

1367 _____. ***Emile.*** Penguin. Condemned by the archbishop and Parlement of Paris, the Sorbonne, and the Inquisition (1762). Rousseau fled France to avoid arrest (1762). In 1763, his novel and The Social Contract were banned in Geneva. Both books were placed on the Spanish and Roman (1766) Index of Forbidden books and remained forbidden to Catholics until 1966. Source: 1, pp. 88–90.

1368 **Rowling, J. K. *Harry Potter and the Chamber of Secrets.*** Scholastic. Challenged in South Carolina schools (1999) because "the book has a serious tone of death, hate, lack of respect, and sheer evil." Parents have also objected to the book's use in the Douglas County, Colo. schools (1999); two Moorpark, Calif. elementary schools (1999); and in suburban Buffalo, N.Y. (1999), among other districts. Restricted to fifth- through eighth-graders who have written parental permission in the Zeeland, Mich. schools (2000). No future installments can be purchased and teachers are prohibited from reading the books aloud in class. The book was considered objectionable because of the intense story line, the violence, the wizardry, and the sucking of animal blood. Removed from the Bridgeport Township, Mich. public school (2000) because it promotes witchcraft. Challenged, but retained in Frankfort, Ill. School District 157-C (2000). Parents were concerned that the book contains lying and smart-aleck retorts to adults. Challenged in Bend, Oreg. at the Three Rivers Elementary School (2000) due to references to witchcraft and concerns the book will lead children to hatred and rebellion. Challenged in the Salamanca, N.Y. elementary school libraries (2000) because a family complained about the book's dark themes. Retained at Orange Grove Elementary School in Whittier, Calif. (2000); it was challenged for dealing with magic and bad experiences. Challenged in six Santa Rosa County schools in Pace, Fla. (2000) for its presentation of witchcraft. Retained in the Durham School District, Ontario, Canada (2000) after a challenge of the

138

series because of concerns about witchcraft. Challenged, but retained in Arab, Ala. school libraries and accelerated reader programs (2000) over objections that the author "is a member of the occult and the book encourages children to practice witchcraft." Challenged in the Fresno, Calif. Unified School District classrooms (2000) by a religious group voicing concerns about sorcery and witchcraft. Restricted to students with parental permission in the Santa Fe, Tex. School District (2000) because critics say the book promotes witchcraft. Challenged, but retained in the Newfound Area School District in Bristol, N.H. (2000) despite an objection the book "is scary." Banned from the Christian Outreach College library in Queensland, Australia (2000) because the book was considered violent and dangerous. Challenged in the Owen J. Roberts School District classrooms in Bucktown, Pa. (2001) because the "books are telling children over and over again that lying, cheating, and stealing are not only acceptable, but that they're cool and cute." Burned in Alamagordo, N.Mex. (2001) outside Christ Community Church because the Potter series is "a masterpiece of satanic deception." Challenged, but retained in the Duval County, Fla. school libraries (2001) despite a complaint about witchcraft depicted in the book. Proposed for removal, along with more than fifty other titles, by a teachers' prayer group at the high school in Russell Springs, Ky. (2002) because the book deals with ghosts, cults, and witchcraft. A federal judge overturned restricted access to the Harry Potter book after parents of a Cedarville, Ark. (2002) fourth-grader filed a federal lawsuit challenging the restrictions, which required students to present written permission from a parent to borrow the book. The novel was originally challenged because it characterized authority as "stupid" and portrays "good witches and good magic." In December 2002, a representative of the International Foundation for Slavic Writing and Culture criminal hate-crime charges against Rosman Publishing in Moscow for publishing a Russian translation of the novel, claiming that "it instilled religious extremism and prompted students to join religious organizations of Satanist followers." After an investigation, the Moscow City Prosecutor's Office decided that there were no grounds for a criminal case. Challenged, but retained in the New Haven, Conn. schools (2003) despite claims the series "makes witchcraft and wizardry alluring to children." The Gwinnett County, Ga. school board (2006) rejected a parent's pleas to take Harry Potter books out of school libraries, based on the claim they promote witchcraft. The Georgia Board of Education ruled December 14 that the parent had failed to prove her contention that the series

"promote[s] the Wicca religion," and therefore that the book's availability in public schools does not constitute advocacy of a religion. Source: 11, Jan. 2000, pp. 1, 26; Mar. 2000, pp. 46, 48, 50, 63; May 2000, p. 77; July 2000, p. 124; Sept. 2000, pp. 165–66; Nov. 2000, pp. 193–94, 216; Jan. 2001, pp. 11, 12, 13, 15; Mar. 2001, pp. 43, 62, 75; July 2001, p. 146; Jan. 2002, p. 49; Mar. 2002, p. 61; May 2002, p. 116; Sept. 2002, p. 197; Mar. 2003, p. 77; May 2003, p. 95; July 2003, pp. 137, 159; July 2006, pp. 207–8; Sept. 2006, p. 231; Nov. 2006, p. 289; Mar. 2007, pp. 72–73.

1369 _____. *Harry Potter and the Goblet of Fire.* Scholastic. Challenged in six Santa Rosa County schools in Pace, Fla. (2000) for its presentation of witchcraft. Retained in the Durham School District, Ontario, Canada (2000) after a challenge of the series because of concerns about witchcraft. Challenged, but retained in Arab, Ala. school libraries and accelerated reader programs (2000) over objections that the author "is a member of the occult and the book encourages children to practice witchcraft." Challenged in the Fresno, Calif. Unified School District classrooms (2000) by a religious group voicing concerns about sorcery and witchcraft. Restricted to students with parental permission in the Santa Fe, Tex. school district (2000) because critics say the book promotes witchcraft. Challenged, but retained in the Newfound Area School District in Bristol, N.H. (2000) despite an objection the book "is scary." Banned from the Christian Outreach College library in Queensland, Australia (2000) because the book was considered violent and dangerous. Challenged in the Owen J. Roberts School District classrooms in Bucktown, Pa. (2001) because the "books are telling children over and over again that lying, cheating, and stealing are not only acceptable, but that they're cool and cute." Burned in Alamagordo, N.Mex. (2001) outside Christ Community Church because the Potter series is "a masterpiece of satanic deception." Challenged, but retained in the Duval County, Fla. school libraries (2001) despite a complaint about witchcraft depicted in the book. Proposed for removal, along with more than fifty other titles, by a teachers' prayer group at the high school in Russell Springs, Ky. (2002) because the book deals with ghosts, cults, and witchcraft. Challenged in Moscow, Russia (2002) by a Slavic cultural organization that alleged the stories about magic and wizards could draw students into Satanism. A federal judge overturned restricted access to the Harry Potter book after parents of a Cedarville, Ark. (2002) fourth-grader filed a federal lawsuit challenging the restrictions, which required students to present written permission

139

from a parent to borrow the book. The novel was originally challenged because it characterized authority as "stupid" and portrays "good witches and good magic." Challenged, but retained in the New Haven, Conn. schools (2003) despite claims the series "makes witchcraft and wizardry alluring to children." The Gwinnett County, Ga. school board (2006) rejected a parent's pleas to take Harry Potter books out of school libraries, based on the claim they promote witchcraft. The Georgia Board of Education ruled December 14 that the parent had failed to prove her contention that the series "promote[s] the Wicca religion," and therefore that the book's availability in public schools does not constitute advocacy of a religion. Source: 11, Nov. 2000, pp. 193–94, 216; Jan. 2001, pp. 11, 12, 13, 15; Mar. 2001, pp. 43, 62, 75; July 2001, p. 146; Jan. 2002, p. 49; Mar. 2002, p. 61; May 2002, p. 116; Sept. 2002, p. 197; Mar. 2003, p. 77; May 2003, p. 95; July 2003, pp. 137, 159; July 2006, pp. 207–8; Sept. 2006, p. 231; Nov. 2006, p. 289; Mar. 2007, pp. 72–73.

1370 _____. *Harry Potter and the Half-Blood Prince.* Scholastic. Removed by the Wilsona School District trustees from a list recommended by a parent-teacher committee for the Vista San Gabriel, Calif. Elementary School library (2006) along with twenty-three other books. Trustees said one rejected book contained an unsavory hero who made a bad role model for children; another was about a warlock, which they said was inappropriate; and others were books with which they were unfamiliar and didn't know whether they promoted good character or conflicted with textbooks. Rejected titles included three bilingual *Clifford the Big Red Dog* books, *Disney's Christmas Storybook*, two books from the Artemis Fowl series, *Beauty is a Beast, California (Welcome to the USA)*, and *The Eye of the Warlock*. The Wilsona School District board approved new library book-selection guidelines in wake of the trustees' controversial decision. Books now cannot depict drinking alcohol, smoking, drugs, sex, including "negative sexuality, implied or explicit nudity, cursing, violent crime or weapons, gambling, foul humor, and dark content." The Gwinnett County, Ga. school board (2006) rejected a parent's pleas to take Harry Potter books out of school libraries, based on the claim they promote witchcraft. The Georgia Board of Education ruled December 14 that the parent had failed to prove her contention that the series "promote[s] the Wicca religion," and therefore that the book's availability in public schools does not constitute advocacy of a religion. Source: 11, May 2006, p. 127; July 2006, pp. 207–8; Sept. 2006, pp. 229–31; Nov. 2006, pp. 287–88; Mar. 2007, pp. 72–73.

1371 _____. *Harry Potter and the Prisoner of Azkaban.* Scholastic. Challenged in South Carolina schools (1999) because "the book has a serious tone of death, hate, lack of respect, and sheer evil." Parents have also objected to the book's use in the Douglas County, Colo. schools (1999); two Moorpark, Calif. elementary schools (1999); and in suburban Buffalo, N.Y. (1999), among other districts. Restricted to fifth- through eighth-graders who have written parental permission in the Zeeland, Mich. schools (2000). No future installments can be purchased and teachers are prohibited from reading the books aloud in class. The book was considered objectionable because of the intense story line, the violence, the wizardry, and the sucking of animal blood. Removed from the Bridgeport Township, Mich. public school (2000) because it promotes witchcraft. Challenged, but retained in Frankfort, Ill. School District 157-C (2000). Parents were concerned that the book contains lying and smart-aleck retorts to adults. Challenged in Bend, Oreg. at the Three Rivers Elementary School (2000) due to references to witchcraft and concerns the book will lead children to hatred and rebellion. Challenged in the Salamanca, N.Y. elementary school libraries (2000) because a family complained about the book's dark themes. Retained at Orange Grove Elementary School in Whittier, Calif. (2000); it was challenged for dealing with magic and bad experiences. Challenged in six Santa Rosa County schools in Pace, Fla. (2000) for its presentation of witchcraft. Retained in the Durham School District, Ontario, Canada (2000) after a challenge of the series because of concerns about witchcraft. Challenged, but retained in Arab, Ala. school libraries and accelerated reader programs (2000) over objections that the author "is a member of the occult and the book encourages children to practice witchcraft." Challenged in the Fresno, Calif. Unified School District classrooms (2000) by a religious group voicing concerns about sorcery and witchcraft. Restricted to students with parental permission in the Santa Fe, Tex. School District (2000) because critics say the book promotes witchcraft. Challenged, but retained in the Newfound Area School District in Bristol, N.H. (2000) despite an objection the book "is scary." Banned from the Christian Outreach College library in Queensland, Australia (2000) because the book was considered violent and dangerous. Challenged in the Owen J. Roberts School District classrooms in Bucktown, Pa. (2001) because the "books are telling children over and over again that lying, cheating, and stealing are not only acceptable, but that they're cool and cute." Burned in Alamagordo, N.Mex. (2001) outside

Christ Community Church because the Potter series is "a masterpiece of satanic deception." Challenged, but retained in the Duval County, Fla. school libraries (2001) despite a complaint about witchcraft depicted in the book. Proposed for removal, along with more than fifty other titles, by a teachers' prayer group at the high school in Russell Springs, Ky. (2002) because the book deals with ghosts, cults, and witchcraft. Challenged in Moscow, Russia (2002) by a Slavic cultural organization that alleged the stories about magic and wizards could draw students into Satanism. A federal judge overturned restricted access to the Harry Potter book after parents of a Cedarville, Ark. (2002) fourth-grader filed a federal lawsuit challenging the restrictions, which required students to present written permission from a parent to borrow the book. The novel was originally challenged because it characterized authority as "stupid" and portrays "good witches and good magic." Challenged, but retained in the New Haven, Conn. schools (2003) despite claims the series "makes witchcraft and wizardry alluring to children." The Gwinnett County, Ga. school board (2006) rejected a parent's pleas to take Harry Potter books out of school libraries, based on the claim they promote witchcraft. The Georgia Board of Education ruled December 14 that the parent had failed to prove her contention that the series "promote[s] the Wicca religion," and therefore that the book's availability in public schools does not constitute advocacy of a religion. Source: 11, Jan. 2000, pp. 1, 26; Mar. 2000, pp. 46, 48, 50, 63; May 2000, p. 77; July 2000, p. 124; Sept. 2000, pp. 165–66; Nov. 2000, pp. 193–94, 216; Jan. 2001, pp. 11, 12, 13, 15; Mar. 2001, pp. 43, 62, 75; July 2001, p. 146; Jan. 2002, p. 49; Mar. 2002, p. 61; May 2002, p. 116; Sept. 2002, p. 197; Mar. 2003, p. 77; May 2003, p. 95; July 2003, pp. 137, 159; July 2006, pp. 207–8; Mar. 2007, pp. 72–73.

1372 _____. *Harry Potter and the Sorcerer's Stone.* Scholastic. Challenged in South Carolina schools (1999) because "the book has a serious tone of death, hate, lack of respect, and sheer evil." Parents have also objected to the book's use in the Douglas County, Colo. schools (1999); two Moorpark, Calif. elementary schools (1999); and in suburban Buffalo, N.Y. (1999), among other districts. Temporarily restricted to fifth- through eighth-graders who have written parental permission in the Zeeland, Mich. schools (2000). The Zealand school superintendent overturned most of the restriction including that no future installments could be purchased. One restriction remains is that teachers are prohibited from reading the books aloud in kindergarten through fifth grade classes. The book was considered objectionable because

of the intense story line, the violence, the wizardry, and the sucking of animal blood. Removed from the Bridgeport Township, Mich. public school (2000) because it promotes witchcraft. Challenged, but retained in the Simi Valley, Calif. School District (2000). A parent complained that the book was violent, anti-family, had a religious theme, and lacked educational value. Challenged, but retained in Frankfort, Ill. School District 157-C (2000). Parents were concerned that the book contains lying and smart-aleck retorts to adults. Challenged in the Cedar Rapids, Iowa school libraries (2000) because the book romantically portrays witches, warlocks, wizards, goblins, and sorcerers. Challenged in Bend, Oreg. at the Three Rivers Elementary School (2000) due to references to witchcraft and concerns the book will lead children to hatred and rebellion. Challenged in the Salamanca, N.Y. elementary school libraries (2000) because a family complained about the book's dark themes. Retained at Orange Grove Elementary School in Whittier, Calif. (2000). It was challenged for dealing with magic and bad experiences. Challenged in six Santa Rosa County schools in Pace, Fla. (2000) for its presentation of witchcraft. Retained in the Durham School District, Ont., Canada (2000) after a challenge of the series because of concerns about witchcraft. Challenged, but retained in Arab, Ala. school libraries and accelerated reader programs (2000) over the objections the author "is a member of the occult and the book encourages children to practice witchcraft." Challenged in the Fresno, Calif. Unified School District classrooms (2000) by a religious group voicing concerns about sorcery and witchcraft. Restricted to students with parental permission in the Santa Fe, Tex. School District (2000) because critics say the book promotes witchcraft. Challenged, but retained in the Newfound Area School District in Bristol, N.H. (2000) despite an objection that the book "is scary." Banned from the Christian Outreach College library in Queensland, Australia (2000) because the book was considered violent and dangerous. Challenged in the Owen J. Roberts School District classrooms in Bucktown, Pa. (2001) because the "books are telling children over and over again that lying, cheating, and stealing are not only acceptable, but that they're cool and cute." Burned in Alamagordo, N.Mex. (2001) outside Christ Community Church because the Potter series is "a masterpiece of satanic deception." Challenged, but retained in the Duval County, Fla. school libraries (2001) despite a complaint about witchcraft depicted in the book. Proposed for removal, along with more than fifty other titles, by a teachers' prayer group at the high school in Russell Springs, Ky. (2002) because the book deals with ghosts, cults, and witchcraft.

Challenged in Moscow, Russia (2002) by a Slavic cultural organization that alleged the stories about magic and wizards could draw students into Satanism. A federal judge overturned restricted access to the Harry Potter book after parents of a Cedarville, Ark. (2002) fourth-grader filed a federal lawsuit challenging the restrictions, which required students to present written permission from a parent to borrow the book. The novel was originally challenged because it characterized authority as "stupid" and portrays "good witches and good magic." In February 2002, board of education officials in the United Arab Emirates banned twenty-six books from the schools, including Rowling's novels because "they have written or illustrated material that contradicts Islamic and Arab values." Challenged, but retained in the New Haven, Conn. schools (2003) despite claims the series "makes witchcraft and wizardry alluring to children." The Gwinnett County, Ga. school board (2006) rejected a parent's pleas to take Harry Potter books out of school libraries, based on the claim they promote witchcraft. The Georgia Board of Education ruled December 14 that the parent had failed to prove her contention that the series "promote[s] the Wicca religion," and therefore that the book's availability in public schools does not constitute advocacy of a religion. Source: 8, pp. 240–43; 11, Jan. 2000, pp. 1, 26; Mar. 2000, pp. 46, 48, 50, 63; May 2000, p. 77; July 2000, pp. 104, 124; Sept. 2000, pp. 165–66; Nov. 2000, pp. 193–94, 216; Jan. 2001, pp. 11, 12, 13, 15; Mar. 2001, pp. 43, 62, 75; July 2001, p. 146; Jan. 2002, p. 49; Mar. 2002, p. 61; May 2002, p. 116; Sept. 2002, p. 197; Mar. 2003, p. 77; May 2003, p. 95; July 2003, pp. 137, 159; July 2006, pp. 207–8; Nov. 2006, p. 289; Mar. 2007, pp. 72–73.

1373 Royko, Mike. *Boss: Richard J. Daley of Chicago.* NAL. Barred from the Ridgefield, Conn. High School reading list (1972) because it "downgrades police departments." Challenged in the Hannibal, N.Y. High School (1983) because the book is "detrimental to students and contributed to social decay because it contains rough language." Source: 4, p. 99; 5; 11, May 1983, p. 74; July 1983, p. 123.

1374 Ruby, Laura. *Lily's Ghosts.* HarperCollins. Removed from the Pinellas, Fla. school district and Hillsborough County, Fla. fourth-grade reading list (2006), although the book is on the Sunshine State Young Reader's Award list of books for third- through fifth-graders. Source: 11, Nov. 2006, pp. 290–91.

1375 Ruddell, Robert B., et al. *Person to Person.* Bennett. Challenged in the Jefferson County, Ky. School District (1982) because the book "confuses sex roles." The Evergreen School Board in Vancouver, Wash. (1985) banned the textbook because some members said it is too favorable to alternative lifestyles. The controversy centered on a chapter titled "Changing Life Styles," in which the book describes relationships other than the traditional family. Source: 11, Mar. 1983, p. 41; May 1985, p. 79; July 1985, p. 115.

1376 Rushdie, Salman. *The Satanic Verses.* Viking. Banned in Pakistan, Saudi Arabia, Egypt, Somalia, Sudan, Bangladesh, Malaysia, Qatar, Indonesia, South Africa, and India because of its criticism of Islam. Burned in West Yorkshire, England (1989) and temporarily withdrawn from two bookstores on the advice of police who took threats to staff and property seriously. In Pakistan five people died in riots against the book. Another man died a day later in Kashmir. Ayatollah Khomeini issued a fatwa or religious edict, stating, "I inform the proud Muslim people of the world that the author of the Satanic Verses, which is against Islam, the prophet, and the Koran, and all those involved in its publication who were aware of its content, have been sentenced to death." Challenged at the Wichita, Kans. Public Library (1989) because the book is "blasphemous to the prophet Mohammed." In Venezuela, owning or reading it was declared a crime under penalty of 15 months' imprisonment. In Japan, the sale of the English-language edition was banned under the threat of fines. The governments of Bulgaria and Poland also restricted its distribution. In 1991, in separate incidents, Hitoshi Igarashi, the Japanese translator was stabbed to death and its Italian translator, Ettore Capriolo, was seriously wounded. In 1993, William Nygaard, its Norwegian publisher, was shot and seriously injured. Source: 3, pp. 269–70; 6, pp. 2,071–75; 8, pp. 291–96; 11, Mar. 1989, p. 47; July 1989, p. 125; Sept. 1989, p. 185.

1377 Russell, Bertrand. *What I Believe.* Dutton. Banned in Boston, Mass. (1929). Source: 4, p. 62.

1378 Russo, Vito. *The Celluloid Closet: Homosexuality in the Movies.* Harper. Challenged at the Deschutes County Library in Bend, Oreg. (1993) because it "encourages and condones" homosexuality. Source: 11, Sept. 1993, pp. 158–59.

1379 Sachar, Louis. *The Boy Who Lost His Face.* Knopf. Challenged at the Thousand Oaks, Calif. Library (1991) because of inappropriate language. Removed from the Cuyler Elementary

142

School library in Red Creek, N.Y. (1993) because "the age level and use of some swear words may make it inappropriate to younger children." Challenged at the Golden View Elementary school in San Ramon, Calif. (1993) because of its profanity, frequent use of obscene gestures, and other inappropriate subject matter. Removed from the Jackson Township Elementary School in Clay City, Ind. (1993) due to "unsuitable words." Source: 11, Mar. 1992, p. 39; May 1993, p. 71; July 1993, p. 97; Sept. 1993, p. 157; Mar. 1994, p. 51.

1380 _____. *Marvin Redpost: Is He a Girl?* Random. Challenged in Chapman Elementary School libraries in Huntsville, Ala. (2000) because it contains a fantasy about kissing your elbow and changing sexes. Challenged in the New Lenox, Ill. elementary school (2000) because its young hero plays with girls and dreams that he wears a dress to baseball practice. Source: 11, Mar. 2000, p. 47; July 2000, p. 104.

1381 _____. *Sideways Stories from Wayside Schools.* Avon; McKay. Challenged at the Neely Elementary School in Gilbert, Ariz. (1992) because the book shows the dark side of religion through the occult, the devil, and satanism. Source: 11, May 1992, p. 78; July 1992, p. 124.

1382 _____. *There's a Boy in the Girls' Bathroom.* Knopf. Challenged, but retained, in the fifth-grade Pea Ridge, Ark. curriculum (1998) after objections to "inappropriate language." Source: 11, May 1998, p. 89.

1383 _____. *Wayside School Is Falling Down.* Avon. Removed from the list of suggested readings from the Antigo, Wis. elementary reading program (1995) because the book included passages condoning destruction of school property, disgraceful manners, disrespectful representation of professionals, improper English, and promotion of peer pressure. Source: 11, July 1995, p. 100.

1384 Sade, Marquis de. *Juliette.* Grove. Author imprisoned much of his life in France; still on the *Index Librorum Prohibitorum* in Rome (1948); seized by British Customs (1962). In Sept. 1982, Greek police confiscated thousands of books by Marquis de Sade. The publisher, Themis Banousis, was sentenced to two years' imprisonment for violating the laws on indecent literature by translating and publishing the works of de Sade. Forty-seven other publishers were reported arrested in mid-Sept. 1982 for denying the ban.

In Oct. 1982, Malaysian police confiscated the works of de Sade because they were considered "prejudicial to the public interest." Source: 4, p. 34; 5, Jan. 1983, pp. 44–45.

1385 _____. *Justine or the Misfortunes of Virtue.* Grove. Author imprisoned much of his life in France; still on the *Index Librorum Prohibitorum* in Rome (1948); seized by British Customs (1962). Source: 4, p. 34.

1386 Said, Edward W. *The Politics of Dispossession: The Struggle for Palestinian Self-Determination.* Vintage. Removed from West Bank and Gaza bookstores, the confiscation reportedly having been ordered by the Ministry of Information. The first raid occurred on a small bookstore in central Ramallah. Sales of the book were banned (1996). Source: 7, p. 411.

1387 Salinger, J. D. *Catcher in the Rye.* Bantam; Little. Since its publication, this title has been a favorite target of censors. In 1960, a teacher in Tulsa, Okla. was fired for assigning the book to an eleventh grade English class. The teacher appealed and was reinstated by the school board, but the book was removed from use in the school. In 1963, a delegation of parents of high school students in Columbus, Ohio, asked the school board to ban the novel for being "anti-white" and "obscene." The school board refused the request. Removed from the Selinsgrove, Pa. suggested reading list (1975). Based on parents' objections to the language and content of the book, the school board voted 5-4 to ban the book. The book was later reinstated in the curriculum when the board learned that the vote was illegal because they needed a two-thirds vote for removal of the text. Challenged as an assignment in an American literature class in Pittsgrove, N.J. (1977). After months of controversy, the board ruled that the novel could be read in the Advanced Placement class, but they gave parents the right to decide whether or not their children would read it. Removed from the Issaquah, Wash. Optional High School reading list (1978). Removed from the required reading list in Middleville, Mich. (1979). Removed from the Jackson-Milton school libraries in North Jackson, Ohio (1980). Removed from two Anniston, Ala. high school libraries (1982), but later reinstated on a restrictive basis. Removed from the school libraries in Morris, Manitoba (1982) along with two other books because they violate the committee's guidelines covering "excess vulgar language, sexual scenes, things concerning moral issues, excessive violence, and anything dealing with the occult." Challenged at the Libby, Mont.

High School (1983) due to the "book's contents." Challenged, but retained for use in select English classes at New Richmond, Wis. (1994). Banned from English classes at the Freeport High School in De Funiak Springs, Fla. (1985) because it is "unacceptable" and "obscene." Removed from the required reading list of a Medicine Bow, Wyo. Senior High School English class (1986) because of sexual references and profanity in the book. Banned from a required sophomore English reading list at the Napoleon, N.Dak. High School (1987) after parents and the local Knights of Columbus chapter complained about its profanity and sexual references. Challenged at the Linton-Stockton, Ind. High School (1988) because the book is "blasphemous and undermines morality." Banned from the classrooms in Boron, Calif. High School (1989) because the book contains profanity. Challenged at the Grayslake, Ill. Community High School (1991). Challenged at the Jamaica High School in Sidell, Ill. (1992) because the book contains profanities and depicted premarital sex, alcohol abuse, and prostitution. Challenged in the Waterloo, Iowa schools (1992) and Duval County, Fla. public school libraries (1992) because of profanity, lurid passages about sex, and statements defamatory to minorities, God, women, and the disabled. Challenged at the Cumberland Valley High School in Carlisle, Pa. (1992) because of a parent's objections that it contains profanity and is immoral. Challenged, but retained, at the New Richmond, Wis. High School (1994) for use in some English classes. Challenged as required reading in the Corona-Norco, Calif. Unified School District (1993) because it is "centered around negative activity." The book was retained and teachers selected alternatives if students object to Salinger's novel. Challenged as mandatory reading in the Goffstown, N.H. schools (1994) because of the vulgar words used and the sexual exploits experienced in the book. Challenged at the St. Johns County Schools in St. Augustine, Fla. (1995). Challenged at the Oxford Hills High School in Paris, Maine (1996). A parent objected to the use of "the 'F' word." Challenged, but retained, at the Glynn Academy High School in Brunswick, Ga. (1997). A student objected to the novel's profanity and sexual references. Removed because of profanity and sexual situations from the required reading curriculum of the Marysville, Calif. Joint Unified School District (1997). The school superintendent removed it to get it "out of the way so that we didn't have that polarization over a book." Challenged, but retained on the shelves of Limestone County, Ala. school district (2000) despite objections about the book's foul language. Banned, but later reinstated after community protests at the Windsor Forest High School in

Savannah, Ga. (2000). The controversy began in early 1999 when a parent complained about sex, violence, and profanity in the book that was part of an Advanced Placement English class. Removed by a Dorchester District 2 school board member in Summerville, S.C. (2001) because it "is a filthy, filthy book." Challenged by a Glynn County, Ga. (2001) school board member because of profanity. The novel was retained. Challenged, but retained as an assigned reading in the Noble High School in North Berwick, Maine (2004). Teachers will provide more information to parents about why certain books are studied. Source: 8, pp. 436–38; 9; 11, Nov. 1978, p. 138; Jan. 1980, pp. 6–7; May 1980, p. 51; Mar. 1983, pp. 37–38; July 1983, p. 122; July 1985, p. 113; Mar. 1987, p. 55; July 1988, p. 123; Jan. 1988, p. 10; Sept. 1988, p. 177; Nov. 1989, pp. 218–19; July 1991, pp. 129–30; May 1992, p. 83; July 1992, pp. 105, 126; Jan. 1993, p. 29; Jan. 1994, p. 14, Mar. 1994, pp. 56, 70; May 1994, p. 100; Jan. 1995, p. 12; Jan. 1996, p. 14; Nov. 1996, p. 212; May 1997, p. 78; July 1997, p. 96; May 2000, p. 91; July 2000, p. 123; Mar. 2001, p. 76; Nov. 2001, pp. 246–47; 277–78; Jan. 2005, pp. 8–9; Mar. 2005, pp. 73–74.

1388 _____. *Nine Stories.* Bantam; Little. Removed from the reading list of a writing class at Franklin, Va. High School (1987) after a parent of one student was offended by some of the language in a story. Source: 11, July 1987, p. 131.

1389 **Salinger, Margaretta M.** *Great Paintings of Children.* Abrams. Retained at Maldonado Elementary School in Tucson, Ariz. (1994) after being challenged by parents who objected to nudity and "pornographic," "perverted," and "morbid" themes. Source: 11, July 1994, p. 112.

1390 **Salomon, George, and Feitelson, Rose.** *The Many Faces of Anti-Semitism.* Am. Jewish Comm. Banned from the 1983 Moscow International Book Fair along with more than fifty other books because it is "anti-Soviet." Source: 11, Nov. 1983, p. 201.

1391 **Sams, Ferrol.** *Run with the Horsemen.* Viking; Penguin. Challenged in the Rockingham County, Va. schools (1995) because of sexual content. Source: 11, Nov. 1995, p. 188; Jan. 1996, p. 18.

1392 **Samuels, Gertrude.** *Run, Shelley, Run.* Harper; Crowell; NAL. Removed and destroyed from the Hot Springs, Ark. Central Junior High School library (1977) because of objectionable

144

language; challenged at the Ogden, Utah School District (1979) and placed in a restricted circulation category; removed from the Onida and Blunt, S.Dak. High Schools (1981) due to "objectionable" language; removed from the Troutman, N.C. Middle School library (1982). Challenged at Alexander Central High School and East Junior High School libraries in Taylorsville, N.C. (1987) because of "foul language." Removed from the Palmyra, Pa. middle school classroom (1995) because of its language and the portrayal of incidents involving nudity, lesbianism, and prostitution. Source: 9; 11, Mar. 1977, p. 36; May 1979, p. 49; May 1981, pp. 65–66; Mar. 1982, p. 45; May 1987, p. 87; July 1987, p. 149; July 1995, pp. 98–99; Jan. 1996, p. 17.

1393 Sanchez, Alex. *Rainbow Boys.* Simon. Challenged at the Montgomery County, Tex. Memorial Library System (2004) along with fifteen other young-adult books with gay-positive themes. The objections were posted at the Library Patrons of Texas Web site. The language describing the books is similar to that posted at the Web site of the Fairfax County, Virginia-based Parents Against Bad Books in Schools, to which Library Patrons of Texas links. The language describing the books is similar to that posted at the Web site of the Fairfax County, Virginia-based Parents Against Bad Books in Schools, to which Library Patrons of Texas links. Challenged in the Fayetteville, Ark. High School library (2005). The complainant also submitted a list of more than fifty books, citing the books as too sexually explicit and promoting homosexuality. Removed from the Webster, N.Y. Central School District summer reading list for high-school students (2006) after receiving complaints from parents. The book won the International Reading Association's 2003 Young Adults' Choice Award, and the American Library Association selected it as a Best Book for Young Adults. Source: 11, Nov. 2004, pp. 231–32; Nov. 2006, pp. 291–92.

1394 Sanders, Lawrence. *The Seduction of Peter S.* Putnam. Banned from the Stroudsburg, Pa. High School library (1985) because it was "blatantly graphic, pornographic, and wholly unacceptable for a high school library." Source: 11, May 1985, p. 78.

1395 Sanford, John. *Winter Prey.* Putnam. Expurgated by an apparent self-appointed censor at the Coquille, Oreg. Public Library (1994) along with several other books. Most were mysteries and romances in which single words and sexually explicit passages were whited out by a vandal who left either dots or solid ink pen lines where the words had been. Source: 11, Sept. 1994, p. 148.

1396 Santiago, Esmeralda. *When I Was Puerto Rican.* Addison-Wesley; Vintage. Challenged in the Newark, Calif. Unified School District (2001) because the book is sexually explicit. Challenged, along with seventeen other titles by the Fairfax County, Va. elementary and secondary libraries (2002), in a group called Parents Against Bad Books in Schools. The group contends the books "contain profanity and descriptions of drug abuse, sexually explicit conduct, and torture." Source: 11, Mar. 2001, p. 55; Jan. 2003, p. 10.

1397 Sapphire. *Push.* Vintage. Challenged, but retained at Fayetteville High School in Fayetteville, Ark. (2005) despite a parent's complaint that it was sexually explicit. The complainant also submitted a list of more than fifty books, citing the books as too sexually explicit and promoting homosexuality. Source: 11, May 2005, p. 135; Sept. 2005, p. 215; Nov. 2005, pp. 295–96.

1398 Sarton, May. *The Education of Harriet Hatfield.* Norton. Removed from the Mascenic Regional High School in New Ipswich, N.H. (1995) because it is about gays and lesbians. An English teacher was fired for refusing to remove the book. Source: 11, Sept. 1995, p. 166; Jan. 1996, p. 15.

1399 Sartre, Jean-Paul. *Age of Reason.* Random. On Feb. 21, 1973, eleven Turkish book publishers went on trial before an Istanbul martial law tribunal on charges of publishing, possessing, and selling books in violation of an order of the Istanbul martial law command. They faced possible sentences of between one month's and six months' imprisonment "for spreading propaganda unfavorable to the state" and the confiscation of their books. Eight booksellers also were on trial with the publishers on the same charge involving the *Age of Reason.* Source: 5, Summer 1973, xii.

1400 _____. *Saint Genet.* French & European. Seized (1984) by the British Customs Office as "indecent and obscene." Source: 11, Jan. 1985, p. 26.

1401 Saunders, Richard, and Brian Macne. *Horrorgami.* Sterling. Removed from the Glendale school libraries in Grants Pass, Oreg. (1993) for its alleged "satanic" content. The book is a craft book on origami, but incorporates stories about werewolves and vampires, and is allegedly illustrated with satanic symbols. Source: 11, July 1993, p. 101.

1402 **Savonarola, Girolamo.** *Writings.* After a ceremony of degradation, the author was hung on a cross and burned with all his writings, sermons, essays, and pamphlets (1498). Source: 1, pp. 53–55; 4, p. 8.

1403 **Schechter, Harold, and David Everitt.** *The A-Z Encyclopedia of Serial Killers.* Pocket Bks. Challenged and retained in the Hillsborough County, Fla. School District (2002) because of a parent's objection to the book's "gruesome details." Source: 11, July 2002, p. 179.

1404 **Schnitzler, Arthur.** *Casanova's Homecoming.* AMS Pr. Seized by the New York Society for the Suppression of Vice (1922). Simon & Schuster was brought to court for publishing this work (1930); banned by Mussolini (1939). Source: 4, p. 57; 13, pp. 42–43; 15, Vol. III, p. 636.

1405 **Schnitzler, Arthur.** *Reigen.* AMS Pr. A bookseller was convicted by the Court of Special Sessions for selling a copy of *Reigen* (1929). Source: 4, p. 57; 15, Vol. III, p. 420.

1406 **Schouweiler, Thomas.** *The Devil: Opposing Viewpoints.* Greenhaven Pr. Challenged at the Chestnut Ridge Middle School in Washington Township, Pa. (2004). The complainants want the school district to seek parental approval before elementary and middle school students can check out books related to the occult. Source: 11, May 2004, pp. 117–18.

1407 **Schreier, Alta.** *Vamos a Cuba (A Visit to Cuba).* Heinemann. Removed from all Miami-Dade County schools libraries (2006) because a parent's complaint that the book does not depict an accurate life in Cuba. The American Civil Liberties Union (ACLU) of Florida filed a lawsuit challenging the decision to remove this book and the twenty-three other titles in the same series from the district school libraries. In granting a preliminary injunction in July 2006 against the removal, Judge Alan S. Gold of U.S. District Court in Miami characterized the matter as a "First Amendment issue" and ruled in favor of the ACLU of Florida, which argued that the books were generally factual and that the board should add to its collection, rather than removing books it disagreed with. Source: 11, July 2006, p. 207; Sept. 2006, pp. 230–31; Nov. 2006, p. 288; Jan. 2007, p. 8; May 2007, pp. 91–92.

1408 **Schusky, Ernest L.** *Introduction to Social Science.* Prentice-Hall. Challenged in the South Umpqua, Oreg. School District (1985) because the book presents a variety of concepts that are "controversial and inappropriate for seventh graders. The book's sections on death education, extrasensory perception, genetic planning, group therapy, and religious values had little to do with the teaching of basic social studies." Source: 11, Mar. 1986, p. 42.

1409 **Schwartz, Alvin.** *And the Green Grass Grew All Around.* HarperCollins. Removed from elementary and middle school library shelves by the Central Dauphin school board in Harrisburg, Pa. (2000) due to its explicit language. Source: 11, Sept. 2000, p. 144.

1410 **_____.** *Cross Your Fingers, Spit in Your Eye.* Harper. Challenged at the Neely Elementary School in Gilbert, Ariz. (1992) because the book shows the dark side of religion through the occult, the devil, and satanism. Source: 11, May 1992, p. 78; July 1992, p. 124.

1411 **_____.** *Ghosts!* Ghost Stories in Folklore. HarperCollins. Challenged, but retained in the Campbell County, Wyo. School District (1998) despite the claims that "the book misleads the reader—that ghosts are actually possible. . . This book blurs the line between fantasy and reality for younger children." Source: 11, Mar. 1999, p. 38; May 1999, p. 84.

1412 **_____.** *In a Dark, Dark Room and Other Scary Stories.* Harper. Challenged at the Jefferson County school libraries in Lakewood, Colo. (1986) because the book is "too morbid for children." The Jefferson County School Board refused to ban the book. Source: 11, Sept. 1986, p. 173; Nov. 1986, p. 224.

1413 **_____.** *More Scary Stories to Tell in the Dark.* Harper; Lippincott. Challenged at the Dry Hollow Elementary School in The Dalles, Oreg. (1988) because it is too scary and violent. Challenged at the Neely Elementary School in Gilbert, Ariz. (1992) because the book shows the dark side of religion through the occult, the devil, and satanism. Challenged at the Lake Washington School District in Kirkland, Wash. (1992) as unacceptably violent for children. Restricted access at the Marana, Ariz. Unified School District (1993) because of complaints about violence and cannibalism. Removed from Vancouver, Wash. School District elementary school libraries (1994) after surviving two previous attempts (1991,

1993). Also challenged at neighboring Evergreen School District libraries in Vancouver, Wash. (1994) because "This book. . . is far beyond other scary books." Challenged, but retained, at the Whittier Elementary School library in Bozeman, Mont. (1994). The book was challenged because it would cause children to fear the dark, have nightmares, and give them an unrealistic view of death. Challenged in the Tracy, Calif. school libraries (1995) because of the book's violent content and graphic nature. Challenged as "objectionable" and "disgusting", but retained on Harper Woods, Mich. school district reading lists (1995). Retained in the Greater Clark County, Ky. elementary-school libraries (2006) despite a grandmother's request to ban the Scary Stories books written by Alvin Schwartz. She wanted all four or five volumes in the series banned because, she said, they depict cannibalism, murder, witchcraft and ghosts, and include a story about somebody being skinned. Source: 11, Jan. 1989, p. 3; May 1992, pp. 78, 94–95; July 1992, p. 124; Sept. 1993, p. 143; July 1994, p. 111; Sept. 1994, pp. 148–49, 166; May 1995, p. 65; July 1995, p. 111; Nov. 2006, pp. 317–18.

1414 _____. *More Tales to Chill Your Bones.* Harper. Challenged at the Lake Washington School District in Kirkland, Wash. (1992) as unacceptably violent for children. Challenged at the West Hartford, Conn. elementary and middle school libraries (1992) because of violence and the subject matter. Removed from Vancouver, Wash. School District elementary school libraries (1994) after surviving two previous attempts (1991, 1993). Challenged at neighboring Evergreen School District libraries in Vancouver, Wash. (1994) because "This book. . . is far beyond other scary books." Source: 11, May 1992, pp. 94–95; Sept. 1992, p. 137; July 1994, p. 111; Sept. 1994, pp. 148–49.

1415 _____. *Scary Stories to Tell in the Dark.* Harper. Challenged in the Livonia, Mich. schools (1990) because the poems frightened first grade children. Challenged at the Neely Elementary School in Gilbert, Ariz. (1992) because the book shows the dark side of religion through the occult, the devil and satanism. Challenged at the Lake Washington School District in Kirkland, Wash. (1992) as unacceptably violent for children. Challenged at the West Hartford, Conn. elementary and middle school libraries (1992) because of violence and the subject matter. Challenged at the elementary school library in Union County, Ind. (1992). Restricted access at the Marana, Ariz. Unified School District (1993) because of complaints about violence and cannibalism. Challenged by a parent of a student

at Happy Valley Elementary School in Glasgow, Ky. (1993) who thought it was too scary. Removed from Vancouver, Wash. School District elementary school libraries (1994) after surviving two previous attempts (1991, 1993). Also challenged at neighboring Evergreen School District libraries in Vancouver, Wash. (1994) because "This book. . . is far beyond other scary books." Source: 11, Mar. 1991, p. 62; May 1992, pp. 78, 94–95; July 1992, p. 124; Sept. 1992, p. 137; Jan. 1993, p. 27; Sept. 1993, pp. 143, 158; July 1994, p. 111; Sept. 1994, pp. 148–49.

1416 _____. *Scary Stories.* Harper. Challenged at the South-Western, Ohio elementary school libraries (1993) because children shouldn't be "scared by materials that they read in schools." Restricted to students in fourth grade or higher in the Enfield, Conn. elementary schools (1995). The school board was petitioned to remove all "horror" stories from the elementary schools. Source: 11, May 1993, pp. 85–86; May 1995, p. 69.

1417 _____. *Telling Fortunes: Love Magic, Dream Signs, and Other Ways to Learn the Future.* Lippincott. Challenged at Hightower Elementary School in Rockdale, Ga. (1998) because the "book involves instructions and teaches young kids how to tell the future by reading tea leaves, tarot cards, palms, crystal balls, by interpreting dreams, and by looking at an egg." Source: 11, Mar. 1999, p. 35.

1418 **Schwartz, Joel L. *Upchuck Summer.*** Dell; Delacorte. Removed from the Winslow, N.J. Elementary School No. 4 (1988) because of "age inappropriateness." The specific problem was the explicitness of scenes in the protagonist recounts a fantasy about two "older kids" kissing while nude. Source: 11, Jan. 1989, p. 8.

1419 **Schwartz, Joel L., Aidan Macfarlane, and Ann McPherson. *Will the Nurse Make Me Take My Underwear Off?*** Laurel-Leaf Bks. Challenged at the Chestatee Regional Library in Gainesville, Ga. (1994). Source: 11, Nov. 1994, p. 187.

1420 **Scoppettone, Sandra. *Happy Endings Are All Alike.*** Harper. Removed from the Evergreen School District of Vancouver, Wash. (1983) along with twenty-nine other titles. The American Civil Liberties Union of Washington filed suit contending that the removals constitute censorship, a violation of plaintiff's rights to free speech and due process, and the acts are a violation of the state Open Meetings Act because the removal decisions were made behind closed doors. Source: 11, Nov. 1983, pp. 185–86.

1421 Sebold, Alice. *The Lovely Bones.* Little. Challenged at the Coleytown Middle School library in Westport, Conn. (2007). The school superintendent acknowledged that the book is "for mature readers" and also acknowledged "the book is appropriate to be part of a middle school library collection serving students from ages 11-14, many of whom possess the maturity level to read this book." Source: 11, Mar. 2007, p. 71.

1422 Seeley, Robert A. *A Handbook for Conscientious Objectors.* Central Committee for Conscientious Objectors. Access restricted in Coleman, Wis. (1982) due to the book's alleged political overtones. Source: 11, July 1982, p. 126.

1423 Segel, Elizabeth. *Short Takes.* Dell; Lothrop. Challenged at the Cecil County Board of Education in Elkton, Md. (1994). Many deemed the text controversial because it included essays dealing with issues of abortion, gay rights, alcohol, and sex education. Source: 11, Mar. 1995, p. 55.

1424 Selby, Hubert, Jr. *Last Exit to Brooklyn.* Grove. A local Boston city attorney sought an injunction against the book (1965), but the complaint was dismissed. A circuit court in Conn. (1966) issued a temporary injunction against the book, "as obscene and pornographic." The injunction was overturned and sales were permitted again. Judged obscene by jury in England (1967). Banned in Italy and Ireland, and placed on a restricted list in Russia. Source: 4, p. 98; 6, pp. 2,187–88; 8, pp. 462–63.

1425 Sendak, Maurice. *In the Night Kitchen.* Harper. Removed from the Norridge, Ill. school library (1977) due to "nudity for no purpose." Expurgated in Springfield, Mo. (1977) by drawing shorts on the nude boy. Challenged at the Cunningham Elementary School in Beloit, Wis. (1985) because the book desensitizes "children to nudity." Challenged at the Robeson Elementary School in Champaign, Ill. (1988) because of "gratuitous" nudity. Challenged at the Camden, N.J. elementary school libraries (1989) because of nudity. Challenged at the Elk River, Minn. schools (1992) because reading the book "could lay the foundation for future use of pornography." Challenged at the El Paso, Tex. Public Library

(1994) because "the little boy pictured did not have any clothes on and it pictured his private area." Challenged in the Wake County, N.C. schools (2006). Parents are getting help from Called2Action, a Christian group that says its mission is to "promote and defend our shared family and social values." Source: 9; 11, May 1977, p. 71; Sept. 1977, p. 134; July 1985, p. 134; Mar. 1989, p. 43; Nov. 1989, p. 217; Mar. 1993, p. 41; Sept. 1994, p. 148; Sept. 2006, p. 231.

1426 _____. *Some Swell Pup.* Farrar; Random. Challenged at the Multnomah County Library in Portland, Oreg. (1988) because in it a dog urinates on people, and children abuse animals. Source: 11, Jan. 1989, p. 3.

1427 Servetus, Michael. *Christianity Restored.* The publication in 1531 of *On the Errors of the Trinity* made Servetus notorious and a haunted man, threatened by both the French and Spanish Inquisitions and the Protestants, who banned his book and closed cities to him. In 1532, the Inquisition in Toulouse issued a decree ordering his arrest. He went underground in Paris and assumed a new identity. On October 27, 1553, Servetus was burned at the stake. Almost two centuries later, Richard Mead, the physician to the king of England, tried to publish Servetus's work. In 1723, the government seized and burned the whole printing and imprisoned Mead and his printer. Source: 8, pp. 221–23.

1428 Seth, Roland. *Witches and Their Craft.* Taplinger. Challenged at the Plymouth-Canton school system in Canton, Mich. (1987) because the book contains information about witches and the devil. Source: 11, May 1987, p. 110; Jan. 1988, p. 11.

1429 Seuss, Dr. *The Lorax.* Random. Challenged in the Laytonville, Calif. Unified School District (1989) because the book "criminalizes the foresting industry." Source: 11, Nov. 1989, p. 237; Jan. 1990, pp. 32–33.

1430 Shafak, Elif. *The Bastard of Istanbul.* Viking. Prize-winning novelist went on trial in Istanbul, Turkey (2006), accused of belittling Turkishness. The novel had been at the top of Turkish bestsellers lists since its publication, but its treatment of the mass murder of Ottoman Armenians in 1915 angered government officials. Source: 11, Jan. 2007, pp. 35–36.

1431 Shakespeare, William. *Hamlet.*

Airmont; Cambridge Univ. Pr.; NAL; Norton; Penguin; Methuen. Banned in Ethiopia (1978). Source: 5, Sept./Oct. 1978, p. 66.

1432 _____. *King Lear.* Airmont; Methuen; NAL; Penguin; Pocket Bks. Prohibited on the English stage until 1820. Source: 4, p. 18.

1433 _____. *The Merchant of Venice.* Airmont; Cambridge Univ. Pr.; Methuen; NAL; Penguin; Pocket Bks.; Washington Square. Eliminated from the high school curricula of Buffalo and Manchester, N.Y. (1931). A group of Jewish parents in Brooklyn, N.Y. (1949) went to court claiming that the assignment of Shakespeare's play to senior high school literature classes violated the rights of their children to receive an education free of religious bias in *Rosenberg v. Board of Education of the City of New York*, 196 Misc. 542, 92 N.Y. Supp.2d 344. The King County Supreme Court decided not to ban Shakespeare's play stating, "Except where a book has been maliciously written for the apparent purpose of fomenting a bigoted and intolerant hatred against a particular racial or religious group, public interest in a free and democratic society does not warrant or encourage the suppression of any book at the whim of any unduly sensitive person or group or person, merely because a character described in such book as belonging to a particular race or religion is portrayed in a derogatory or offensive manner." Removal of the play "will contribute nothing toward the diminution of anti-religious feeling," the court said. Banned from classrooms in Midland, Mich. (1980). Banned from the ninth-grade classrooms in Kitchener-Waterloo, Ontario, Canada, until the Ontario Education Ministry or Human Rights Commission (1986) rules whether the play is anti-Semitic. Source: 4, p. 19; 11, July 1980, p. 76; Sept. 1986, p. 154; 12, pp. 23, 230.

1434 _____. *Tragedy of King Richard II.* Airmont; Methuen; NAL; Penguin; Pocket Bks.; Washington Square. Contains a scene in which the King was deposed, and it so infuriated Queen Elizabeth that she ordered it eliminated from all copies (1597). Source: 4, p. 18.

1435 _____. *Twelfth Night.* Airmont; Cambridge Univ. Pr.; Methuen; NAL; Penguin; Pocket Bks.; Washington Square. Removed from a Merrimack, N.H. high school English class (1996) because of a policy that bans any instruction that has "the effect of encouraging or supporting homosexuality as a positive lifestyle alternative." Source: 11, May 1996, p. 96.

1436 **Shannon, George.** *Unlived Affections.* Harper. Removed from the library at the Lundahl Junior High School in Crystal Lake, Ill. (1993) because the book is unfit for sixth grade. Source: 11, July 1993, p. 98; 14, pp. 281–82.

1437 **Sharpe, Jon.** *Trailsman Series.* NAL; Penguin. Challenged, but retained at the Springdale, Ark. Public Library (2001) along with all other "western" novels because the writings include "pornographic, sexual encounters." Source: 11, Nov. 2001, p. 277.

1438 **Sharpio, Amy.** *Sun Signs: The Stars in Your Life.* Contemporary Perspective. Pulled, but later placed on reserve to children with parental permission, at the Forrest Elementary School library in Hampton, Va. (1992). Source: 11, July 1992, p. 108; Sept. 1992, p. 139.

1439 **Shaw, George Bernard.** *Man and Superman.* Airmont; Penguin. The New York Public Library withdrew it from public shelves (1905) because books "calculated to make light of dishonesty and criminality were worse than books merely indecent in statement"; banned from all public libraries in Yugoslavia (1929). Source: 2, p. 87; 4, p. 55; 15, Vol. II, p. 625.

1440 _____. *Mrs. Warren's Profession.* Garland. Suppressed in London (1905); banned from all public libraries in Yugoslavia (1929). Source: 4, p. 55.

1441 **Shaw, Irwin.** *Beggarman Thief.* Dell. Banned from the Stroudsburg, Pa. High School library (1985) because it was "blatantly graphic, pornographic, and wholly unacceptable for a high school library." Source: 11, May 1985, p. 79.

1442 **Shaw, Irwin.** *Nightwork.* Dell. Banned from the Stroudsburg, Pa. High School library (1985) because it was "blatantly graphic, pornographic and wholly unacceptable for a high school library." Source: 11, May 1985, p. 79.

1443 **Sheehan, Kathryn, and Mary Waidner.** *Earth Child.* Coun. Oak Bks. Challenged at the Tulsa County, Okla. schools (1992) because the book promotes the Hindu religion and other religious rituals. Opponents also claimed the book is a manual for altering children's minds through psychological games and hypnotic techniques. Source: 11, Nov. 1992, p. 187.

1444 Sheffield, Margaret, and Sheila Bewley. *Where Do Babies Come From?* Knopf; Stuart. Moved from the children's section to the adult section of the Tampa-Hillsborough, Fla. County Public Library (1981) by order of the Tampa City Council. Placed on restricted shelves at the Evergreen School District elementary school libraries in Vancouver, Wash. (1987) in accordance with the school board policy to restrict student access to sex education books in elementary school libraries. Source: 11, Jan. 1982, p. 4; July 1986, p. 118; Sept. 1986, p. 172; May 1987, p. 87.

1445 Sheldon, Sidney. *Bloodline.* Morrow; Warner. Challenged in Abingdon, Va. (1980) and Elizabethton, Tenn. (1981). Source: 11, Jan. 1981, p. 5; May 1981, p. 66.

1446 Shengold, Nina, ed. *The Actor's Book of Contemporary Stage Monologues.* Penguin. Challenged at the Salem Junior High School in Virginia Beach, Va. (1988) because it contains racial slurs, profanity, and lewd descriptions. Source: 11, Mar. 1989, p. 43.

1447 Sherman, Josepha, and T. K. F. Weisskopf. *Greasy Grimy Gopher Guts.* August House Pubs. Retained in the collection of the Kingston Frontenac Public Library in Kingston, Ontario, Canada (2000). It had been challenged as unsuitable for children. Source: 11, Sept. 2000, p. 165.

1448 Shoup, Barbara. *Wish You Were Here.* Hyperion. Removed from the Jackson County, W.Va. school libraries (1997) along with sixteen other titles. Source: 11, Jan. 1998, p. 13.

1449 Showers, Paul, and Kay Sperry Showers. *Before You Were a Baby.* Crowell. Placed on restricted shelves at the Evergreen School District elementary school libraries in Vancouver, Wash. (1987) in accordance with the school board policy to restrict student access to sex education books in elementary school libraries. Source: 11, May 1987, p. 87.

1450 Showers, Paul. *A Baby Starts to Grow.* Crowell. Placed on restricted shelves at the Evergreen School District elementary school libraries in Vancouver, Wash. (1987) in accordance with the school board policy to restrict student access to sex education books in elementary school libraries. Source: 11, May 1987, p. 87.

1451 Shreve, Susan. *Masquerade.* Knopf. Removed from the Grants Pass, Oreg. middle school libraries (1982) because of the profanity, violence, and sexual innuendos in the book. Source: 11, Mar. 1983, p. 39.

1452 Shulman, Irving. *The Amboy Dukes.* Bantam; Doubleday. Book under fire by local authorities in Milwaukee, Wis.; Detroit, Mich.; Newark, N.J. (1949-1951); and cleared of obscenity charges in Brantford, Ontario, Canada (1949). Source: 4, p. 89.

1453 Shyer, Marlene Fanta. *Welcome Home, Jellybean.* Macmillan. Challenged, but retained, in the Carroll County, Md. schools (1991). Two school board members considered the book depressing. Source: 11, Mar. 1992, p. 64.

1454 Sidhwa, Bapsi. *Cracking India.* Milkweed Eds. Challenged at Deland High School, near Daytona Beach, Fla. (2005) as part of the school's International Baccalaureate Program, whose curriculum is college-level. In a letter sent home, parents were offered the option of having their children assigned an alternate book. A parent objected to a two-page scene in which the narrator brushes off an older cousin's attempt to trick her into performing oral sex. Source: 11, Jan. 2006, pp. 13–14.

1455 Sijie, Dai. *Balzac and the Little Chinese Seamstress.* Knopf; Chatto. Pulled from the Federal Way's, Wash. Todd Beamer High School English classes and library (2004) by the superintendent, who overruled a committee of educators and parents that unanimously recommended keeping the book. The novel about censorship was considered sexually explicit and inappropriate for high-school students. Source: 11, July 2004, p. 139.

1456 Silko, Leslie Marmon. *Ceremony.* Viking; Penguin. Removed at the Nease High School in St. Augustine, Fla. as a required summer reading book for honors English students (1995) because of its language, sexual descriptions, and subject matter. The National Council of Teachers of English recommended the book for honor students. Retained on the Round Rock, Tex. Independent High School reading list (1996) after a challenge that the book was too violent. Source: 11, Nov. 1995, p. 184; Jan. 1996, p. 14; May 1996, p. 99.

1457 Silverstein, Alvin, and Virginia B. Silverstein. *The Reproductive System: How Living Creatures Multiply.* Prentice-Hall. Placed on restricted shelves at the Evergreen School District elementary school libraries in Vancouver, Wash. (1987) in accordance with the school board policy to restrict student access to sex education books in elementary school libraries. Source: 11, May 1987, p. 87.

1458 Silverstein, Charles, and Edmund White. *The Joy of Gay Sex.* Crown; Simon & Schuster/Fireside. Confiscated from three Lexington, Ky. bookstores (1977) by the local police and challenged at the San Jose, Calif. Public Library (1981). Seized and shredded (1984) by the British Customs Office. Challenged at the Belmont, Calif. Public Library (1997) because it is "pornographic." Challenged, but retained in the Marple Public Library in Broomall, Pa. (2004) along with several sexual instruction manuals including: *Sex Toys 101: A Playfully Uninhibited Guide*, by Rachel Venning; *Great Sex Tips*, by Anne Hooper; *Ultimate Guide to Fellatio*, by Violet Blue; and *The Illustrated Guide to Extended Massive Orgasm*, by Steve Bodansky because the books are "seriously objectionable in text and pictures due to the sexually explicit material." Challenged, but retained at the Nampa, Idaho Public Library (2006) along with seven other books, including *The Joy of Sex* despite the complaint that, "they are very pornographic in nature and they have very explicit and detailed illustrations and photographs which we feel doesn't belong in a library." Source: 11, Mar. 1978, p. 40; Jan. 1982, p. 9; Jan. 1985, p. 26; Sept. 1997, p. 125; Mar. 2004, p. 50; May 2004, p. 117; July 2006, p. 183.

1459 Silverstein, Charles, and Felice Picano. *The New Joy of Gay Sex.* Harper. Challenged, but retained, at the Lewis and Clark Library in Helena, Mont. (1993). Challenged at the River Bluffs Regional Library in St. Joseph, Mo. (1994) as "pornography." The controversy began after a patron removed a copy of the book from the library and refused to return it, submitting instead a petition with 700 signatures calling for its permanent removal. Challenged at the Kansas City, Mo. Public Library (1995). The complainants asked the Jackson County prosecutor's office to ban the book under state's obscenity and sodomy laws. Restricted to patrons over eighteen years of age at the Main Memorial Library in Clifton, N.J. (1996). The book is hidden behind the checkout counter and on the shelves is a dummy book jacket. The book was described as hard-core pornography by the complainant. Source: 11, July 1993, p. 100; Sept. 1993, p. 158; Nov. 1994, p. 188; Jan. 1995, p. 7; July 1995, p. 94; Mar. 1996, p. 63; May 1996, p. 83.

1460 Silverstein, Charles. *Man to Man.* Morrow. Seized in London, United Kingdom (1986) as "indecent or obscene" and "contrary to the

prohibition contained in Section 42 of the Customs Consolidation Act, 1876." Source: 5, May 1986, p. 38.

1461 Silverstein, Shel. *The Giving Tree.* Harper. Removed from a locked reference collection at the Boulder, Colo. Public Library (1988). The book was locked away originally because the librarian considered it sexist. Source: 11, Jan. 1989, p. 27.

1462 _____. *A Light in the Attic.* Harper. Challenged at the Cunningham Elementary School in Beloit, Wis. (1985) because the book "encourages children to break dishes so they won't have to dry them." Removed from the shelves of the Minot, N.Dak. Public School libraries (1986) by the assistant superintendent "in anticipation of a parent's complaint." The superintendent found "suggestive illustrations" on several pages of Silverstein's work. Upon the recommendation of a review committee, the book was returned to the shelves. Challenged at the Big Bend Elementary School library in Mukwonago, Wis. (1986) because some of Silverstein's poems "glorified Satan, suicide and cannibalism, and also encouraged children to be disobedient." Challenged at the West Allis-West Milwaukee, Wis. school libraries (1986) because the book "suggests drug use, the occult, suicide, death, violence, disrespect for truth, disrespect for legitimate authority, rebellion against parents," and because it inspires young people to commit "acts of violence, disbelief, and disrespect." Challenged at the elementary schools in the Papillion-LaVista School District in Omaha, Nebr. (1986) because the book promotes "behavior abusive to women and children, suicide as a way to manipulate parents, mockery of God, and selfish and disrespectful behavior." Challenged at the Appoquinimink schools in Middletown, Del. (1987) because the book "contains violence, idealizes death, and makes light of manipulative behavior." Challenged at the Moreno Valley, Calif. Unified School District libraries (1987) because it "contains profanity, sexual situations, and themes that allegedly encourage disrespectful behavior." The poem "Little Abigail and the Beautiful Pony" from this award-winning children's book was banned from second grade classes in Huffman, Tex. (1989) because a mother protested that it "exposes children to the horrors of suicide." Challenged at the Hot Springs, S.Dak. Elementary School (1989) as suitable classroom material because of its "objectionable" nature. Challenged at the South Adams, Ind. school libraries (1989) because the book is "very vile" and "contains subliminal or underlying messages and anti-parent material." Restricted to students with parental permission at the Duval County, Fla. public school libraries (1992) because the book features a caricature of a person whose nude behind has been stung by a bee. Challenged at the West Mifflin, Pa. schools (1992) because the poem "Little Abigail and the Beautiful Pony" is morbid. Challenged at the Fruitland Park Elementary School library in Lake County, Fla. (1993) because the book "promotes disrespect, horror, and violence." Challenged, but retained, on the Webb City, Mo. school library shelves (1996). A parent had protested that the book imparts a "dreary" and "negative" message. Source: 11, July 1985, p. 134; May 1986, p. 80; Sept. 1986, p. 172; Nov. 1986, p. 224; Jan. 1987, p. 12; Mar. 1987, pp. 51, 67–68; May 1987, p. 101; July 1987, p. 125; May 1989, p. 80; July 1989, p. 129; Jan. 1990, p. 32; July 1992, p. 105; Mar. 1993, p. 45; July 1993, p. 97; Sept. 1993, p. 157; May 1996, p. 97.

1463 _____. *Where the Sidewalk Ends.* Harper. Challenged at the Xenia, Ohio school libraries (1983) because the book is "anti-Christian, against parental and school authorities, and emphasized the use of drugs and sexual activity." Removed from the shelves of the Minot, N.Dak. public school libraries (1986) by the assistant superintendent "in anticipation of a parent's complaint." Upon the recommendation of a review committee, the book was returned to the shelves. Challenged at the Big Bend Elementary School library in Mukwonago, Wis. (1986) because some of Silverstein's poems "glorified Satan, suicide and cannibalism, and also encouraged children to be disobedient." Challenged at the West Allis-West Milwaukee, Wis. school libraries (1986) because the book "suggests drug use, the occult, suicide, death, violence, disrespect for truth, disrespect for legitimate authority, rebellion against parents," and because it inspires young people to commit "acts of violence, disbelief, and disrespect." Challenged at the Moreno Valley, Calif. Unified School District libraries (1987) because it "contains profanity, sexual situations, and themes that allegedly encourage disrespectful behavior." Reversing an earlier decision to remove the poem "Dreadful" from the library's copy of this book in a Riverdale, Ill. elementary school (1989), the school board retained the book and poem, which was challenged for bad taste. Retained in the Modesto, Calif. district libraries and classrooms (1990) after being challenged as inappropriate for young readers. Challenged at the Central Columbia School District in Bloomsburg, Pa. (1993) because a poem titled "Dreadful" talks about how "someone ate the baby." Challenged at the Fruitland Park Elementary School library in Lake County, Fla. (1993) because the book "promotes disrespect, horror, and violence." Source: 11, Sept. 1983, p. 139; Nov.

1983, p. 197; May 1986, p. 80; Sept. 1986, p. 172; Nov. 1986, p. 224; Mar. 1987, p. 51; May 1987, p. 101; July 1987, p. 125; Mar. 1990, p. 61; May 1990, p. 105; May 1993, p. 86; July 1993, p. 97; Sept. 1993, p. 157.

1464 **Simon, Neil.** *Brighton Beach Memoirs.* NAL; Random. Challenged at the Grayslake, Ill. Community High School (1991). Removed from the required reading and optional reading lists from the Dallas, Tex. schools (1996) because of passages containing profanity and sexually explicit language. Source: 11, July 1991, pp. 129–30; May 1996, p. 88.

1465 **Simon, Sidney.** *Values Clarification.* Hart. Burned in Warsaw, Ind. (1979). Source: 9; 11, Mar. 1980, p. 40.

1466 **Sinclair, April.** *Coffee Will Make You Black.* Hyperion. Removed from the curriculum at the Julian High School in Chicago, Ill. (1996) because the book was not appropriate for freshman as required reading because of sexually explicit language. Source: 11, May 1996, p. 87.

1467 **Sinclair, Upton.** *The Jungle.* Airmont; Bantam; Bentley; NAL; Penguin. Banned from public libraries in Yugoslavia (1929). Burned in the Nazi bonfires because of Sinclair's socialist views (1933). Banned in East Germany (1956) as inimical to Communism. Banned in South Korea (1985). Source: 4, p. 63; 5, April 1986, pp. 30–33.

1468 _____. *Oil!* Airmont; Bantam; Bentley; NAL; Penguin. Forbidden in Boston, Mass. (1927) because of its comments on the Harding Administration—although Harding had died in 1923 and his cronies were long dispersed. Sinclair defended the case himself, at a cost of $2,000, and addressed a crowd of some 2,000 people on Boston Commons, explaining at length the character and intent of his book. The court suppressed nine pages of the book, including a substantial portion of the Biblical "Song of Solomon." The bookseller from whose store the book had been seized was fined $100 and the offending pages were blacked out. Banned from public libraries in Yugoslavia (1929); burned by the Nazi bonfires because of Sinclair's socialist views (1933); banned in East Germany (1956) as inimical to Communism. Source: 2, p. 133; 3, pp. 282–83; 4, p. 63.

1469 _____. *Wide Is the Gate.* Airmont; Bantam; Bentley; NAL; Penguin. Banned from public libraries in Yugoslavia (1929); burned in the Nazi bonfires because of Sinclair's socialist views (1933); banned in East Germany (1956) as inimical to Communism; banned in Ireland (1953). Source: 4, p. 63.

1470 **Sioux City Community School District.** *Sioux City, Past and Present.* Sioux City Community School District. Banned from the Sioux City, Iowa schools (1984) because the textbook is "racist and offensive." Source: 11, Mar. 1985, p. 43.

1471 **Sissley, Emily L., and Bertha Harris.** *The Joy of Lesbian Sex.* Crown; Simon & Schuster. Seized (1984) by the British Customs Office. Source: 11, Jan. 1985, p. 26.

1472 **Sizer, Frances Sienkiewicz, et al.** *Making Life Choices: Health Skills and Concepts.* West Pub. Co. The Franklin County, N.C. school board (1997) ordered three chapters cut out of the ninth-grade health textbooks. Those chapters dealt with AIDS, HIV, and other sexually transmitted diseases; pairing, marriage, and parenting; and sexual behavior and contraception. Source: 11, Nov. 1997, p. 169.

1473 **Skarmeta, Antonio.** *Burning Patience.* Graywolf. Challenged as required reading in a freshman English class Orono, Maine High School (1995) because of the book's sexual content. The book was made into the successful film *The Postman.* Source: 11, Nov. 1995, p. 186.

1474 **Slepian, Jan.** *The Alfred Summer.* Macmillan. Challenged in Charlotte County, Va. (1983) due to "objectionable" words in the text. Pulled, but later restored to the language arts curriculum at four Cheshire, Conn. elementary schools (1991) because the book is "filled with profanity, blasphemy and obscenities, and gutter language." Source: 11, Nov. 1983, p. 197; Mar. 1992, p. 42; May 1992, p. 96; July 1992, pp. 109–10.

1475 **Slier, Deborah, ed.** *Make a Joyful Sound.* Checkboard. Challenged at the Deer Park, Wash. elementary schools (1992) because the poetry collection contains the poem, "The Mask," by Dakari Kamaru Hru. A Deer Park parent complained that, "This is religious indoctrination. We in the Western World would refer to it as devil worship. It also smacks of New Age religion." Source: 11, May 1992, pp. 84–85.

1476 **Small, Beatrice.** *To Love Again: A Historical Romance.* Ballantine. Challenged at the Pocatello, Idaho Public Library (1993) because a patron considered the romance novel "pornographic." Source: 11, Mar. 1994, p. 69.

1477 **Smiley, Jane.** *A Thousand Acres.* Fawcett; Knopf; Thorndike Pr. Banned at the Lynden, Wash. High School (1994). Winner of the Pulitzer Prize for fiction in 1991, it was described as having "no literary value in our community right now." School officials note that the protestors have tried to block an anti-drug program, a multicultural program, and a Valentine's Day dance, saying that they did not reflect the values parents want taught. Retained on the Round Rock, Tex. Independent High School reading list (1996) after a challenge that the book was too violent. Source: 11, May 1994, p. 88; May 1996, p. 99.

1478 **Smith, Betty.** *Joy in the Morning.* Harper. Removed from the Jackson County, W.Va. school libraries (1997) along with sixteen other titles. Source: 11, Jan. 1998, p. 13.

1479 **Smith, Lillian.** *Strange Fruit.* Harcourt. Majority of bookstores in Boston, Mass. and Detroit, Mich. (1944) removed the book from sale. The book's distributor was charged in 1945 under the Massachusetts laws governing obscene material, in that he had distributed a publication that was "obscene, indecent, impure, or manifestly tends to corrupt the morals of youth." The court found the bookseller guilty and fined him $200, later reduced to $25. The fact that the novel might promote "lascivious thoughts and . . . . arouse lustful desire" outweighed any artistic merit that the novel might possess. Banned in Ireland (1953). Source: 3, p. 305; 4, pp. 78–79; 15, Vol. IV, p. 698.

1480 **Smith, Patrick.** *A Land Remembered.* Pineapple Pr. Challenged, but retained in the Indian River County Schools in Vero Beach, Fla. (2003) despite two parents' complaints about racially offensive language. One of the parents said the book's use of the 'N-word' created a hostile learning environment for his children. Source: 11, Jan. 2004, p. 28.

1481 **Smith, Rebecca M.** *Family Matters: Concepts in Marriage and Personal Relationships.* Butterick; Glencoe. Challenged as proposed ninth-grade curriculum textbook in the Buffalo, N.Y. schools (1986) because it promotes "secular humanism." In particular, the complainant objected

153

to references to the psychological theories of Erik Erikson, Sigmund Freud, Abraham Maslow, and Jean Piaget. Source: 11, Mar. 1987, p. 68.

1482 Smith, Robert Kimmell. *Chocolate Fever.* Dell. Challenged at the Gahanna-Jefferson, Ohio Public Schools (1992) because it contains the words "damn" and "sucks." Source: 11, Jan. 1993, p. 12.

1483 _____. *Jelly Belly.* Delacorte. Challenged at the Gahanna-Jefferson, Ohio Public Schools (1992) because it contains the words "damn" and "sucks." Source: 11, Jan. 1993, p. 12.

1484 _____. *Mostly Michael.* Delacorte. Challenged at the Gahanna-Jefferson, Ohio Public Schools (1992) because it contains the words "damn" and "sucks." Source: 11, Jan. 1993, p. 12.

1485 Smith, Wallace. *Bessie Cotter.* Heinemann. Charged with selling an "obscene book" and "intent to corrupt" and was ordered to appear before the Bow Street magistrate in London (1935). The court fined Heinemann "for publishing an allegedly indecent American book" and ordered the book to be removed from distribution. Source: 13, pp. 25–26.

1486 Smucker, Barbara. *Runaway to Freedom.* Harper. Challenged, but retained, in the Carroll County, Md. schools (1991). Two school board members were offended by its allegedly coarse language. Challenged at the West Dover, Del. Elementary School (1993) because it is offensive to African Americans. The objectionable passage reads, "Massa lay on the feather bed and nigger lay on the floor." Source: 11, Mar. 1992, p. 64; Jan. 1994, p. 15.

1487 Snepp, Frank. *A Decent Interval.* Random; Vintage. The U.S. Justice Department filed a civil complaint in 1978 against the author demanding a lifetime ban on his writing or speaking about the CIA. Source: 4, p. 100; 8, pp. 36–39; 15, Vol. IV, p. 717.

1488 Snow, Edgar. *Red Star over China.* Bantam; Grove. Banned in South Korea (1985). Source: 5, April 1986, pp. 30–33.

1489 Snyder, Jane McIntosh. *Sappho.* Chelsea House Pubs. Removed from the Anaheim, Calif. school district (2000) because school officials said the book is too difficult for middle school students and that it could cause harassment against students seen with it. The American Civil Liberties Union (ACLU) of Southern California filed suit in *Doe v. Anaheim Union High School District* alleging that the removal is "a pretext for viewpoint-based censorship." The ACLU claims no other books have been removed from the junior high library for similar reasons, even though several, such as works by Shakespeare and Dickens, are more difficult reading. The ACLU contends that the school officials engaged in unconstitutional viewpoint discrimination by removing the book because it contains gay and lesbian material. In March 2001, the school board approved a settlement that restored the book to the high school shelves and amended the district's policy to prohibit the removal of books for subject matter involving sexual orientation, but the book will not be returned to the middle school. Source: 11, Mar. 2001, p. 53; May 2001, p. 95; July 2001, p. 173.

1490 Snyder, Zilpha Keatley. *The Egypt Game.* Dell; Macmillan. Challenged in the Richardson, Tex. schools (1995) because it shows children in dangerous situations, condones trespassing and lying to parents, and teaches children about the occult. The school board declined to ban the award-winning novel but did decide that parents should be notified when it is used in class. Source: 11, Mar. 1995, p. 56.

1491 _____. *The Headless Cupid.* Atheneum; Random. Challenged at the Hays, Kans. Public Library (1989) because the book "could lead young readers to embrace satanism." Retained in the Grand Haven, Mich. school libraries (1990) after a parent objected to the book because it "introduces children to the occult and fantasy about immoral acts." The Newbery Award-winning book was retained on the approved reading list at Matthew Henson Middle School in Waldorf, Md. (1991) despite objections to its references to witchcraft. Challenged in the Escondido, Calif. school (1992) because it contains references to the occult. Source: 11, July 1989, p. 143; May 1990, p. 106; Sept. 1991, pp. 155–56; Sept. 1992, p. 161.

1492 _____. *The Witches of Worm.* Atheneum. Restricted in Escambia County, Fla. (1982) to sixth graders and above because "it contains 183 pages of rejection, fear, hatred, occult ritual, cruel pranks, lies and even an attempted murder by arson all perpetrated by a twelve-year-old girl." Challenged at the Kennedy High School in Mt. Angel, Oreg. (1988) for its witchcraft theme and scary illustrations. Retained in the Grand Haven, Mich. school libraries (1990) after a parent objected to the book because it "introduces children to the occult and fantasy about immoral acts." Source: 11, July 1982, p. 123; Jan. 1989, p. 3; May 1990, p. 106.

1493 Solotareff, Gregoire. *Don't Call Me Little Bunny.* Farrar. Challenged at the Douglas County Library in Roseburg, Oreg. (1989) because the character gets away with bad behavior. Challenged in the Cook Memorial Library in Libertyville, Ill. (1995) because the actions taken by the bunny character in the book were anti-social and inappropriate for children's reading. Source: 11, Jan. 1990, pp. 4–5; Jan. 1996, p. 29.

1494 Solzhenitsyn, Aleksandr Isayevich. *August 1914.* Bantam; Farrar. Barred from publication in the USSR; the author was stripped of Soviet citizenship and deported (1974). Source: 4, p. 9.

1495 _____. *Cancer Ward.* Bantam; Farrar. Barred from publication in the USSR; the author was stripped of Soviet citizenship and deported (1974). Source: 4, p. 91.

1496 _____. *Candle in the Wind.* Univ. of Minn. Pr. Barred from publication in the USSR; the author was stripped of Soviet citizenship and deported (1974). Source: 4, p. 91.

1497 _____. *The First Circle.* Bantam. Barred from publication in the USSR; the author was stripped of Soviet citizenship and deported (1974). Source: 4, p. 91.

1498 _____. *The Gulag Archipelago.* Harper. Barred from publication in the USSR; the author was stripped of Soviet citizenship and deported (1974). Source: 4, p. 91; 8, pp. 76–77.

1499 _____. *The Love Girl and the Innocent.* Farrar. Barred from publication in the USSR; the author was stripped of Soviet citizenship and deported (1974). Source: 4, p. 91.

1500 _____. *One Day in the Life of Ivan Denisovich.* Dutton; Farrar; NAL. Barred from publication in the USSR; the author was stripped of Soviet citizenship and deported (1974). Removed from the Milton, N.H. High School library (1976) due to objectionable language. Challenged in Mahwah, N.J. (1976); Omak, Wash. (1979) and at the Mohawk Trail Regional High School in Buckland, Mass. (1981)

because of profanity in the book. Removed from the Lincoln County, Wyo. high school curriculum (1995) because of "considerable obscenities." Retained at the Storm Lake, Iowa High School (1999) despite objections to the novel's profanity. Source: 4, p. 91; 11, May 1976, p. 61; Jan. 1977, p. 8; July 1979, pp. 10–11; July 1995, p. 100; July 1999, p. 105.

1501 _____. *Stories and Prose Poems.* Farrar. Barred from publication in the USSR; the author was stripped of Soviet citizenship and deported (1974). Source: 4, p. 91.

1502 Sones, Sonya. *What My Mother Doesn't Know.* Simon. Removed from the library shelves of the Rosedale Union School District in Bakersfield, Calif. (2003) because of discomfort with Sones's poem, "Ice Capades"—a teenage girl's description of how her breasts react to cold. Challenged at the Bonnette Junior High School library in Deer Park, Tex. (2004) because the book includes foul language and references to masturbation. The book was selected as a "Best Book for Young Adults," by ALA in 2002; "Young Adults Choice," by the International Reading Association in 2003; and included on the Texas Lone Star State Reading List. Source: 11, Nov. 2003, p. 227; Jan. 2005, p. 7.

1503 Soyinka, Wole. *The Man Died: Prison Notes of Wole Soyinka.* Harper. Banned in Nigeria (1984). The 1984 Public Officers Decree—Protection Against False Accusation—"made it a criminal offence to publish any article that brought the government or any public official into disrepute." Thus, any published statement, true or false, that could embarrass any government official was forbidden. Soyinka received the Nobel Prize in literature in 1986. Source: 7, p. 321.

1504 Spargo, Edward. *Topics for the Restless.* Jamestown Pub. Challenged at the Jefferson County school libraries in Lakewood, Colo. (1986). The textbook is a collection of stories and essays designed to promote critical thought among high school students. Parents found "most objectionable" selections from the *Feminine Mystique*, which they said was too favorable to the Equal Rights Amendment; a story on Marilyn Monroe; "Death with Dignity," which addresses what children should be taught about death; and "Hiroshima—Death and Rebirth I and II," stories they claimed "make Americans feel guilty about bombing Hiroshima." The Jefferson County School Board refused to ban the book. Source: 11, May 1986, p. 82; Sept. 1986, p. 173; Nov. 1986, p. 224.

155

1505 **Sparks, Beatrice.** *Jay's Journal.* Times Bks. Challenged for use in the Richland, Wash. high school English classes (1998) along with six other titles because the "books are poor-quality literature and stress suicide, illicit sex, violence, and hopelessness." Source: 11, Mar. 1999, p. 40.

1506 **Speare, Elizabeth George.** *The Sign of the Beaver.* Houghton. Challenged in a Pinellas County, Fla. elementary school (2000) for use of the word "squaw" to refer to Native American women. Source: 11, May 2000, p. 76.

1507 **_____.** *Witch of Blackbird Pond.* Houghton. Challenged in the middle school curriculum in Cromwell, Conn. (2002) based on concern that it promotes witchcraft and violence. The book is the recipient of the 1959 Newbery Medal for children's literature. Source: 11, Sept. 2002, p. 197; Nov. 2002, pp. 257–58.

1508 **Spencer, Scott.** *Endless Love.* Ballantine; Knopf. Banned from the Berkeley County, S.C. High School media center (1991) because of "explicit pornographic passages and adult material for teenage readers." Source: 11, Mar. 1992, p. 41.

1509 **Spiegelman, Art, and Francoise Mouly.** *Raw.* Viking Penguin. Challenged at the Douglas County Library in Roseburg, Oreg. (1992) because "it's full of cartoon pornography." Source: 11, Jan. 1993, p. 9.

1510 **Spies, Karen Bornemann.** *Everything You Need to Know about Incest.* Rosen. Pulled from the Ouachita Parish School library in Monroe, La. (1996) because of sexual content. The Louisiana chapter of the ACLU filed a lawsuit in the federal courts on October 3, 1996, claiming that the principal and the school superintendent violated First Amendment free speech rights and also failed to follow established procedure when they removed the book. The three-year-old school library censorship case headed to court after the Ouachita Parish School Board made no decision to seek a settlement at a special meeting April 12, 1999. On August 17, 1999, the Ouachita Parish School Board agreed to return the book to the library and to develop a new book-selection policy that follows state guidelines for school media programs. Source: 11, Sept. 1996, pp. 151–52; Jan. 1997, p. 7; July 1999, p. 93; Jan. 2000, p. 27.

1511 **Spinelli, Jerry.** *Jason and Marceline.* Dell. Challenged at the Pitman, N.J. Middle School library (1992) because the book promotes stealing, drinking, profanity, and premarital sex. Challenged at the Pitman, N.J. school libraries (1992) because "it's not a positive book about life. Jason smokes and drinks and there are absolutely no repercussions." Challenged, but retained, as part of the curriculum at Hughes Junior High School in Bismarck, N.Dak. (1993). The controversy centered on the use of profanity and sexually explicit language. Source: 11, July 1992, p. 106; Jan. 1993, p. 27; Sept. 1993, p. 145; Jan. 1994, p. 38.

1512 **_____.** *Space Station, Seventh Grade.* Dell; Little. Challenged at the La Grande, Oreg. Middle School library (1988) because "profanity, sexual obscenity, immoral values are throughout the book." Source: 11, May 1989, p. 93.

1513 **Spinoza, Baruch.** *Ethics.* Citadel; Penguin. His writings were widely banned in Holland as atheistic and subversive, and in 1679, the Catholic Church placed all of his work on the Index of Forbidden books. His works remained listed until 1966. Source: 1, pp. 101–3.

1514 **Spraggett, Allen.** *Arthur Ford: The Man Who Talked with the Dead.* NAL. Challenged at the Plymouth-Canton school system in Canton, Mich. (1987) because the book deals with witchcraft. Source: 11, May 1987, p. 110.

1515 **Stadtmauer, Saul.** *Visions of the Future: Magic Boards.* Raintree. Removed from the Philomath, Oreg. Middle School library (1984) because it was "badly written." Challenged at the Dallas, Oreg. school library (1991) because the book entices impressionable or emotionally disturbed children into becoming involved in witchcraft or the occult. Pulled, but later placed on reserve to children with parental permission at the Forrest Elementary School library in Hampton, Va. (1992). Source: 11, Sept. 1984, p. 138; Jan. 1992, p. 26; July 1992, p. 108; Sept. 1992, p. 139.

1516 **Stamper, J. P.** *More Tales for the Midnight Hour.* Scholastic. Challenged at the Neely Elementary School in Gilbert, Ariz. (1992) because the book shows the dark side of religion through the occult, the devil, and satanism. Source: 11, May 1992, p. 78; July 1992, p. 124.

1517 **Stanislawski, Michael.** *Tsar Nicholas I and the Jews: The Transformation of Jewish*

Society in Russia, 1825-1855. Jewish Pubn. Banned from the 1983 Moscow International Book Fair along with more than fifty other books because it is "anti-Soviet." Source: 11, Nov. 1983, p. 201.

1518 **Stanley, Lawrence A., ed. *Rap, The Lyrics.*** Viking. Parent requested that all offensive materials be labeled at the Sno-Isle Regional Library in Marysville, Wash. (1993). Source: 11, July 1993, p. 103.

1519 **Stanway, Andrew. *The Lovers' Guide.*** St. Martin. Removed from the Clifton, N.J. Public Library (1996) and replaced with a dummy book made of styrofoam. The library's new policy restricts to adults any material containing "patently offensive graphic illustrations or photographs of sexual or excretory activities or contact as measured by contemporary community standards for minors." Source: 11, July 1996, pp. 118–19.

1520 **Starhawk, and Hilary Valentine. *The Twelve Wild Swans: A Journey to the Realm of Magic, Healing, and Action: Rituals, Exercises and Magical Training in the Reclaiming Tradition.*** Harper. Challenged, but retained at the Springdale, Ark. Public Library (2001) despite a complaint that the book is a "witchcraft manual" and "turns people away from God and Bible scriptures." Source: 11, Nov. 2001, p. 277.

1521 **Stark, Evan, ed. *Everything You Need to Know about Sexual Abuse.*** Rosen. Challenged at the Arcadia, Wis. schools (1991) because the book presents sexual abuse situations too descriptively. Source: 11, Sept. 1991, p. 154.

1522 **Starkey, Marion Lena. *The Tall Man from Boston.*** Crown. Challenged at the Sikes Elementary School media center in Lakeland, Fla. (1985) because the book "would lead children to believe ideas contrary to the teachings of the Bible." Source: 11, July 1985, p. 133.

1523 **Steel, Danielle. *Changes.*** Delacorte; Dell. Banned from the Stroudsburg, Pa. High School library (1985) because it was "blatantly graphic, pornographic and wholly unacceptable for a high school library." Source: 11, May 1985, p. 79.

1524 **_____. *Crossings.*** Delacorte; Dell. Banned from the Stroudsburg, Pa. High School library (1985) because it was "blatantly graphic, pornographic and wholly unacceptable for a high school library." Source: 11, May 1985, p. 79.

1525 **_____. *The Gift.*** Delacorte. Challenged at a Coventry, Ohio school (1996) because "the schools had no business teaching his children about sex, that it was the job of the parents." Source: 11, Jan. 1997, p. 11.

1526 **Steer, Dugald. *Wizardology: The Book of the Secrets of Merlin.*** Candlewick Pr. Challenged at the West Haven's, Conn. Molloy Elementary School library (2007) because the book exposes children to the occult. Source: 11, May 2007, p. 91.

1527 **Steig, William. *Abel's Island.*** Farrar. Pulled from the fifth- and sixth-grade optional reading lists in Clay County, Fla. schools (1990) because of references to drinking wine, which administrators determined violated the district's substance abuse policy. The objectionable passage reads: "At home he had to drink some wine to dispel the chill in his bones. He drank large draughts of his wine and ran about everywhere like a wild animal, shouting and yodeling." Source: 11, Jan. 1991, p. 16.

1528 **_____. *The Amazing Bone.*** Farrar; Penguin. Challenged at the West Amwell school libraries in Lambertville, N.J. (1986) because a parent objected to "the use of tobacco by the animals." Challenged at the Discovery Elementary School library in Issaquah, Wash. (1993) because of the graphic and detailed violence. Source: 11, Mar. 1987, p. 65; Mar. 1994, p. 70.

1529 **_____. *Caleb and Kate.*** Farrar. Pulled from the Boyertown, Pa. elementary school library shelves (1992) because the book "depicts a dismal outlook on marriage and life." The book was eventually returned. Source: 11, Mar. 1993, p. 42; May 1993, p. 86.

1530 **_____. *Sylvester and the Magic Pebble.*** Simon & Schuster. Book receives the Randolph J. Caldecott Medal for the best-illustrated book of 1969. In 1970, a nationwide campaign began to remove the book from schools and public libraries across the United States. Challenged in Lincoln, Nebr., Queens, N.Y., Palto Alto, Calif., Md., Ohio, Pa., Kans., S.C., Wyo., and Ill. Removed "for reevaluation" in Toledo, Ohio, and East Alton and Woodriver, Ill. Libraries in Prince George's County and Wicomico County, Md., however, retained the book. The board of directors of the International Conference of Police Associations declared the book "contained a dangerous slur against policemen," the board members decided to call attention to the book. The Illinois Police Association wrote (1971) to librarians asking them to remove the book because its characters, all shown as animals, present police as pigs—although in favorable portrayals. The controversial page showing police officers as pigs removed from the Freeport, Ill. (1971). Source: 4, p. 87; 7, pp. 477–80.

1531 **Steiger, Brad.** *Beyond Belief: True Mysteries of the Unknown.* Scholastic. Challenged at the Hemet, Calif. Elementary School (1995). The teacher was placed on paid administrative leave after a parent complained that the book deals with the supernatural and the occult. Source: 11, May 1995, p. 65.

1532 **Stein, Sol.** *The Magician.* Delacorte; Dell. Challenged in Montello, Wis. (1981). Source: 11, May 1981, p. 73.

1533 **Steinbeck, John.** *East of Eden.* Penguin. Removed from two Anniston, Ala. high school libraries (1982) because it is "ungodly and obscene," but later reinstated on a restrictive basis; removed from school libraries in Morris, Manitoba (1982). Challenged in the Greenville, S.C. schools (1991) because the book uses the name of God and Jesus in a "vain and profane manner along with inappropriate sexual references." Source: 11, Mar. 1983, p. 37; July 1991, p. 130.

1534 _____. *Grapes of Wrath.* Penguin; Viking. Burned by the East St. Louis, Ill. Public Library (1939) and barred from the Buffalo, N.Y. Public Library (1939) on the grounds that "vulgar words" were used. Banned in Kansas City, Mo. (1939); Kern County, Calif., the scene of Steinbeck's novel, (1939); Ireland (1953); Kanawha, Iowa High School classes (1980); and Morris, Manitoba (1982). On Feb. 21, 1973, eleven Turkish book publishers went on trial before an Istanbul martial law tribunal on charges of publishing, possessing and selling books in violation of an order of the Istanbul martial law command. They faced possible sentences of between one month's and six months' imprisonment "for spreading propaganda unfavorable to the state" and the confiscation of their books. Eight booksellers were also on trial with the publishers on the same charge involving the Grapes of Wrath. Challenged in Vernon-Verona-Sherill, N.Y. School District (1980); challenged as required reading for Richford, Vt. (1981) High School English students due to the book's language and portrayal of a former minister who recounts how he took advantage of a young woman. Removed from two

Anniston, Ala. high school libraries (1982), but later reinstated on a restrictive basis. Challenged at the Cummings High School in Burlington, N.C. (1986) as an optional reading assignment because the "book is full of filth. My son is being raised in a Christian home and this book takes the Lord's name in vain and has all kinds of profanity in it." Although the parent spoke to the press, a formal complaint with the school demanding the book's removal was not filed. Challenged at the Moore County school system in Carthage, N.C. (1986) because the book contains the phase "God damn." Challenged in the Greenville, S.C. schools (1991) because the book uses the name of God and Jesus in a "vain and profane manner along with inappropriate sexual references." Challenged in the Union City, Tenn. High School classes (1993). Source: 4, p. 82; 5, Summer 1973, p. xii; 8, pp. 61–70; 9, p. 142; 11, May 1980, pp. 52, 62; Jan. 1982, p. 18; Mar. 1983, p. 37; July 1986, p. 120; Nov. 1986, p. 210; Jan. 1987, p. 32; July 1991, p. 130; Mar. 1994, p. 55; 15, Vol. III, pp. 651–52.

1535 _____. *In Dubious Battle.* Penguin. Banned in Ireland (1953). Source: 4, p. 83.

1536 _____. *Of Mice and Men.* Bantam; Penguin; Viking. Banned in Ireland (1953); Syracuse, Ind. (1974); Oil City, Pa. (1977); Grand Blanc, Mich. (1979); Continental, Ohio (1980) and other communities. Challenged in Greenville, S.C. (1977) by the Fourth Province of the Knights of the Ku Klux Klan; Vernon-Verona-Sherill, N.Y. School District (1980); Saint David, Ariz. (1981) and Tell City, Ind. (1982) due to "profanity and using God's name in vain." Banned from classroom use at the Scottsboro, Ala. Skyline High School (1983) due to "profanity." The Knoxville, Tenn. School Board chairman vowed to have "filthy books" removed from Knoxville's public schools (1984) and picked Steinbeck's novel as the first target due to "its vulgar language." Reinstated at the Christian County, Ky. school libraries and English classes (1987) after being challenged as vulgar and offensive. Challenged in the Marion County, W.Va. schools (1988), at the Wheaton-Warrenville, Ill. Middle School (1988), and at the Berrien Springs, Mich. High School (1988) because the book contains profanity. Removed from the Northside High School in Tuscaloosa, Ala. (1989) because the book "has profane use of God's name." Challenged as a summer youth program reading assignment in Chattanooga, Tenn. (1989) because "Steinbeck is known to have had an anti-business attitude." In addition, "he was very questionable as to his patriotism." Removed from all reading lists and collected at the White Chapel High School in Pine Bluff, Ark. (1989) because of objections to language. Challenged as appropriate for high school reading lists in the Shelby County, Tenn. school system (1989) because the novel contained "offensive language." Challenged, but retained in a Salina, Kans. (1990) tenth-grade English class despite concerns that it contained "profanity" and "takes the Lord's name in vain." Challenged by a Fresno, Calif. (1991) parent as a tenth-grade English college preparatory curriculum assignment, citing "profanity" and "racial slurs." The book was retained, and the child of the objecting parent was provided with an alternative reading assignment. Challenged in the Riveria, Tex. schools (1990) because it contains profanity. Challenged as curriculum material at the Ringgold High School in Carroll Township, Pa. (1991) because the novel contains terminology offensive to blacks. Removed and later returned to the Suwannee, Fla. High School library (1991) because the book is "indecent." Challenged at the Jacksboro, Tenn. High School (1991) because the novel contains "blasphemous" language, excessive cursing, and sexual overtones. Challenged as required reading in the Buckingham County, Va. schools (1991) because of profanity. In 1992 a coalition of community members and clergy in Mobile, Ala., requested that local school officials form a special textbook screening committee to "weed out objectionable things." Steinbeck's novel was the first target because it contained "profanity" and "morbid and depressing themes." Temporarily removed from the Hamilton, Ohio High School reading list (1992) after a parent complained about its vulgarity and racial slurs. Challenged in the Waterloo, Iowa schools (1992) and the Duval County, Fla. public school libraries (1992) because of profanity, lurid passages about sex, and statements defamatory to minorities, God, women, and the disabled. Challenged at the Modesto, Calif. High School as recommended reading (1992) because of "offensive and racist language." The word "nigger" appears in the book. Challenged at the Oak Hill High School in Alexandria, La. (1992) because of profanity. Challenged as an appropriate English curriculum assignment at the Mingus, Ariz. Union High School (1993) because of "profane language, moral statement, treatment of the retarded, and the violent ending." Pulled from a classroom by Putnam County, Tenn. school superintendent (1994) "due to the language." Later, after discussions with the school district counsel, it was reinstated. Challenged at the Loganville, Ga. High School (1994) because of its "vulgar language throughout." Challenged in the Galena, Kans. school library (1995) because of the book's language and social implications.

Retained in the Bemidji, Minn. schools (1995) after challenges to the book's "objectionable" language. Challenged at the Stephens County High School library in Toccoa Falls, Ga. (1995) because of "curse words." The book was retained. Challenged, but retained in a Warm Springs, Va. High School (1995) English class. Banned from the Washington Junior High School curriculum in Peru, Ill. (1997) because it was deemed "age inappropriate." Challenged, but retained, in the Louisville, Ohio high school English classes (1997) because of profanity. Removed, restored, restricted, and eventually retained at the Bay County schools in Panama City, Fla. (1997). A citizen group, the 100 Black United, Inc., requested the novel's removal and "any other inadmissible literary books that have racial slurs in them, such as the using of the word 'Nigger.'" Challenged as a reading list assignment for a ninth-grade literature class, but retained at the Sauk Rapids-Rice High School in St. Cloud, Minn. (1997). A parent complained that the book's use of racist language led to racist behavior and racial harassment. Challenged in O'Hara Park Middle School classrooms in Oakley, Calif. (1998) because it contains racial epithets. Challenged, but retained, in the Bryant, Ark. school library (1998) because of a parent's complaint that the book "takes God's name in vain 15 times and uses Jesus's name lightly." Challenged at the Barron, Wis. School District (1998). Challenged, but retained in the sophomore curriculum at West Middlesex, Pa. High School (1999) despite objections to the novel's profanity. Challenged in the Tomah, Wis. School District (1999) because the novel is violent and contains obscenities. Challenged as required reading at the high school in Grandville, Mich. (2002) because the book "is full of racism, profanity, and foul language." Banned from the George County, Miss. schools (2002) because of profanity. Challenged in the Normal, Ill. Community High School (2003) because the book contains "racial slurs, profanity, violence, and does not represent traditional values." An alternative book, Steinbeck's *The Pearl*, was offered but rejected by the family challenging the novel. The committee then recommended The House on Mango Street and The Way to Rainy Mountain as alternatives. Retained in the Greencastle-Antrim, Pa. tenth-grade English classes (2006). A complaint was filed because of "racial slurs" and profanity used throughout the novel. The book has been used in the high school for more than thirty years, and those who object to its content have the option of reading an alternative reading. Source: 8, pp. 474–76; 9; 11, Mar. 1975, p. 41; Nov. 1977, p. 155; Jan. 1978, p. 7; Mar. 1979, p. 27; May 1980, p. 62; July 1980, p. 77; May 1982, pp. 84–85; July 1983, p. 198; July 1984, p. 104; May

1988, p. 90; July 1988, p. 140; Sept. 1988, pp. 154, 179; Nov. 1988, p. 201; Jan. 1989, p. 28; Nov. 1989, p. 162; Jan. 1990, pp. 10–12; Mar. 1990, p. 45; Mar. 1991, p. 62; July 1991, p. 110; Jan. 1992, p. 25; Mar. 1992, p. 64; July 1992, pp. 111–12, 126; Sept. 1992, pp. 140, 163–64; Jan. 1993, p. 29; Mar. 1994, p. 53; Mar. 1995, pp. 46, 53; May 1995, p. 84; July 1995, pp. 93, 111–12; Sept. 1995, pp. 157–58; Jan. 1996, p. 29; Mar. 1996, pp. 50, 63; May 1997, pp. 63, 79; Nov. 1997, pp. 167–69; Jan. 1998, pp. 28–29; July 1998, pp. 107, 120; Jan. 1999, p. 9; July 1999, p. 105; Jan. 2000, p. 16; Mar. 2000, p. 52; Nov. 2002, p. 280; Mar. 2003, p. 55; Jan. 2004, p. 11; Sept. 2004, pp. 177–78; Jan. 2007, pp. 29–30.

1537 _____. **The Red Pony.** Viking. Challenged at the Vernon-Verona-Sherill, N.Y. School District (1980) as a "filthy, trashy, sex novel." Challenged in the Oconee County, Ga. school libraries (1994) because a parent complained the book contained profanity. The Oconee School Board voted to evaluate all 40,000 volumes in the system's library and remove any books and teaching materials from the public school that contain "explicit sex and pornography." Challenged, but retained, on a recommended reading list, at Holmes Middle School in Eden, N.C. (1996). A parent complained that there were curse words on ten different pages of the book. Challenged in the Attalla, Ala. school system (1997) because the book contains "profanity and violence." Source: 11, May 1980, p. 62; Sept. 1994, p. 145; Sept. 1996, p. 170; May 1997, p. 62.

1538 _____. **The Wayward Bus.** Penguin. Placed on list of books disapproved (1953) by the Gathings Committee (a House of Representatives select committee on indecent literature); banned in Ireland (1953). Source: 4, p. 83.

1539 **Stendhal (Marie-Henri Beyle).** *The Red and the Black.* Longman; Chelsea House Pubs. Placed on the Index of Forbidden Books (1864) and confirmed by the Index of Pope Leo XIII in 1897. The novel and all of Stendhal's "love stories" remained on the list through the last edition compiled in 1948 and in effect until 1966. Banned in Russia (1850) by Czar Nicholas I, whose motto in a campaign to suppress liberal thought was "autocracy, orthodoxy, and nationality." Purged from Spanish libraries (1939) by the dictatorship of Francisco Franco. Source: 8, pp. 284–85.

1540 **Stern, Howard.** *Miss America.* Regan. Challenged at the Prince William County, Va. Library (1996). Two newly appointed members of the library

board want to limit young people's access to books by removing them from the collection or by creating an "adults-only" section of the library. Challenged in the Pikes Peak Library District in Colorado Springs, Colo. (1997) because the book is considered "obscene." Source: 11, Nov. 1996, p. 194; July 1997, p. 93.

1541 _____. *Private Parts.* Simon & Schuster; Pocket Bks. Challenged at the Weslaco, Tex. Public Library (1994). A petition, with more than 300 signatures, was presented to city officials asking them to more closely monitor what books the library purchases. The librarian labeled as "too liberal" subsequently resigned. Challenged, but retained, at the Scott Public Library in Alabaster, Ala. (1994). The Shelby County District Attorney called the book "obscene" and threatened to prosecute the library for circulating it, although no action was taken. Former Weslaco, Tex. (1995) librarian filed a federal lawsuit charging that she was fired for publicly discussing that city's efforts to ban Stern's work from the library. Source: 11, Nov. 1994, p. 189; Mar. 1995, p. 53; Sept. 1995, p. 153.

1542 **Stewart, Jon, Ben Karlin, and David Javerbaum.** *America (The Book): A Citizen's Guide to Democracy Inaction.* Warner. Returned to circulation at the Jackson-George Regional Library System in Pascagoula, Miss. (2004). The library board had banned the best-selling satirical book because the book contained an image of Supreme Court judges' faces superimposed on naked bodies. The book was named a Book of the Year by *Publishers Weekly,* the industry trade magazine. Source: 11, Mar. 2005, p. 73; 13, pp. 15–17.

1543 **Stillman, Peter R.** *Introduction to Myth.* Hayden. Challenged as a text for an elective course for junior and senior high school students in Renton, Wash. (1982) because it was considered anti-Christian by some parents. Source: 11, Sept. 1982, p. 171.

1544 **Stine, R. L.** *Beach House.* Pocket Bks. Challenged at the Pulaski Heights Elementary School library in Little Rock, Ark. (1996) along with similar Stine titles. The book, part of the "Fear Street" series, includes graphic descriptions of boys intimidating and killing girls. Source: 11, Nov. 1996, p. 211.

1545 _____. *Double Date.* Scholastic. Removed from the Crawford County, Ga. Middle School library (2003) because the book deals with

160

complex issues teenagers confront. Source: 11, Jan. 2004, p. 9.

1546 _____. *Ghost Camp.* Scholastic. Challenged, but retained, at the Jackson Elementary School library in Gwinnett County, Ga. (1997). A concerned parent complained because of graphic content and references to the occult. Source: 11, Sept. 1997, p. 148.

1547 _____. *Goosebumps.* Scholastic. Challenged at the Bay County, Fla. elementary schools (1996) because of "satanic symbolism, disturbing scenes and dialogue." *The Barking Ghost*, for satanic symbolism and gestures, possession and descriptions of dogs as menacing and attacking; *Night of the Living Dummy II*, for spells or chants, violence and vandalism; *The Haunted Mask*, for graphic description of the ugly mask, demonic possession, violence, disturbing scenes and dialogue; *The Scarecrow Walks at Midnight*, for satanic acts and symbolism, and disturbing scenes; and *Say Cheese and Die!*, for promoting mischief, demonic possession, a reference to Satan and his goals, a disturbing scene describing a death, and a scene that tells of a child disappearing from a birthday party. Challenged, but retained, in the Anoka-Hennepin, Minn. school system (1997) because "children under the age of twelve may not be able to handle the frightening content of the books." Source: 11, July 1996, p. 134; Mar. 1997, p. 35; May 1997, p. 77.

1548 _____. *The Haunted Mask.* Scholastic. Challenged, but retained, at the Battle Creek, Mich. Elementary School library (1994) despite protests from a parent who said the book is satanic. Source: 11, Nov. 1994, p. 200.

1549 Stirling, Nora. *You Would If You Loved Me.* Avon. Removed from the Utah State Library bookmobile (1980). Source: 11, Nov. 1980, p. 128.

1550 Stock, Gregory. *The Kid's Book of Questions.* Workman Pub. Challenged in the Albemarle County schools in Charlottesville, Va. (1990) because it is "inappropriate in an academic class." One parent cited a question from the book, which asked whether a child had ever farted and blamed someone else. Source: 11, Jan. 1991, p. 18.

1551 Stoker, Bram. *Dracula.* Airmont; Bantam; Delacorte; Dell; NAL; Puffin; Random; Scholastic; Viking. Eliminated from required reading lists for juniors and seniors in advanced English classes at the Colony High School in Lewisville, Tex. (1994) because "the book contains unacceptable descriptions in the introduction, such as 'Dracula is the symptom of a wish, largely sexual, that we wish we did not have.'" Source: 11, July 1994, p. 116.

1552 Stopes, Marie. *Married Love.* Fifield; Critic and Guide Co. Declared "not obscene or immortal" in Philadelphia after two social workers imported copies of the book to use in their work (1930). The case went before Judge Kirkpatrick, U.S. District Judge for the Eastern District of Pennsylvania. Despite the judge's decision, the book was again seized later that year and again went to court, where it was determined was not obscene. Banned in Ireland (1931) by the Irish Censorship Board for its discussion of contraception. Source: 14, pp. 225–26.

1553 Stoppard, Miriam. *The Magic of Sex.* Newspaper Guild. Restricted to patrons over 18 years of age at the Main Memorial Library in Clifton, N.J. (1996). The book is hidden behind the checkout counter and on the shelves is a dummy book jacket. The book was described as hard-core pornography by the complainant. Challenged, but retained at the Auburn-Placer County, Calif. Library (1999) because of sexually explicit material. Source: 11, Mar. 1996, p. 63; May 1996, p. 83; Nov. 1999, p. 171.

1554 _____. *Woman's Body.* Dorling Kindersley. Challenged at the Gwinnett-Forsyth, Ga. Regional Library (1995) because it is "too sexually explicit to be on regular library shelves." Source: 11, Jan. 1996, p. 29.

1555 Storm, Hyemeyohsts. *Seven Arrows.* Harper. Challenged at the Creswell, Oreg. High School (1985) because the book contains references to masturbation, rape, and incest. Source: 11, Mar. 1985, p. 45; May 1985, p. 81.

1556 Stowe, Harriet Beecher. *Uncle Tom's Cabin.* Airmont; Bantam; Harper; Houghton; Macmillan; NAL. Banned in Russia (1852) and prohibited in Italy and all papal states (1855). Challenged in the Waukegan, Ill. School District (1984) because the novel contains the word "nigger." Source: 8, pp. 185–87; 11, July 1984, p. 105.

1557 Strasser, Todd. *Angel Dust Blues.* Coward. Challenged as reading material for the Manhasset, N.Y. Public Library's young adult Popsicle series (1983) because of "explicit and graphic sex scenes of a most crude and exploitative nature" and "blasphemy." Challenged at Alexander Central High School and East Junior High School libraries in Taylorsville, N.C. (1987) because of "sexually explicit passages." Challenged at the Crook County Middle School in Prineville, Oreg. (1989) because of explicit language. Source: 11, Nov. 1983, p. 185; May 1987, p. 87; July 1987, p. 149; Jan. 1990, pp. 4–5.

1558 _____. *Friends 'til the End.* Dell. Challenged at the Arlington, Tex. junior high school libraries (1985) because of "sexually descriptive words." Source: 11, Mar. 1985, p. 60.

1559 *Street Law.* West Pub. Challenged in Linthicum Heights, Md. (1983) because it is "biased and pressures teenagers to make moral judgments." Source: 11, Nov. 1983, p. 186; Mar. 1984, p. 53.

1560 **Sturges, Jock.** *Radiant Identities.* Aperture. Despite pressure from protestors demanding that Barnes & Noble face child pornography charges, a prosecutor in Cobb County, Ga. (1998) declined to take the nation's largest bookstore chain to court for carrying Sturges's book. Activists from Operation Rescue claimed the book contains children in sexually suggestive positions and should be deemed illegal. Barnes & Noble officials noted that the decision follows similar rulings by prosecutors in Texas, Maryland, Kansas, and Wisconsin. Source: 11, Jan. 1999, p. 20.

1561 **Stwertka, Eve and Albert.** *Marijuana.* Watts. Challenged at the Stanwood Elementary School in Hempfield, Pa. (1997) because its chapters on purchasing related paraphernalia and marijuana recipes were considered inappropriate. Source: 11, July 1997, p. 94.

1562 **Styron, William.** *The Confessions of Nat Turner.* Bantam; Random. Removed from the Thompson High School library in Mason City, Iowa (1987) after a parent objected to some "sexual materials" in the book. Source: 11, July 1987, p. 126; Sept. 1987, p. 174.

1563 _____. *Sophie's Choice.* Bantam; Random. Banned in South Africa in Nov. 1979. Won the National Book Award (1980). Removed, but later returned to La Mirada, Calif. High School library (2002) despite a complaint about its sexual content, which prompted the school to pull the award-winning novel about a tormented Holocaust

survivor. Source: 5, Apr. 1980, p. 72; 8, pp. 384–85; 11, Mar. 2002, p. 105.

1564 **Sullivan, Tim, ed.** *Cold Shocks.* Avon. Challenged at the Montclair, N.J. Public Library (1993) because the language in the collection of horror stories "was not conducive to a sixth grader." The complainant demanded that books with possibly offensive contents be labeled with warnings and kept in a limited-access section. Source: 11, July 1993, p. 100.

1565 **Sullivan, Tom, and Derek Gill.** *If You Could See What I Hear.* Harper. Removed from the Utah State Library bookmobile (1980). Source: 11, Nov. 1980, p. 128.

1566 **Summers, Montague.** *The Popular History of Witchcraft.* Causeway Bks. Challenged by the "God Squad," a group of three students and their parents, at the El Camino High School in Oceanside, Calif. (1986) because the book "glorified the devil and the occult." Source: 11, Sept. 1986, p. 151; Nov. 1986, p. 224; Jan. 1987, p. 9.

1567 **Suzuki, D. T.** *Zen Buddhism: Selected Writings.* Doubleday. Challenged at the Plymouth-Canton school system in Canton, Mich. (1987) because "this book details the teachings of the religion of Buddhism in such a way that the reader could very likely embrace its teachings and choose this as his religion." Source: 11, May 1987, p. 109.

1568 **Swarthout, Glendon.** *Bless the Beasts and the Children.* Pocket Bks. Banned in the Dupree, S.Dak. High School English classes (1987) because of what the school board called "offensive language and vulgarity." Source: 11, Jan. 1988, p. 12.

1569 **Swedenborg, Emanual.** *Arcana Coelesta.* North Atlantic Bks. Banned as heretical for contradicting Lutheran doctrine in Sweden (1747-58). His most notable scientific volume, Principia (1721), which proposed a rational mathematical explanation of the universe, was placed on the Catholic Church's Index of Forbidden books and remained listed for more than two centuries. Source: 1, pp. 16–18.

1570 **Sweedloff, Peter.** *Men and Women.* Time-Life. Banned from the Brighton, Mich. High School library (1977) along with all other sex education materials. Source: 11, Sept. 1977, p. 133.

1571 Sweeney, Joyce. *Shadow.* Delacorte. Challenged, but retained, on the Anderson County Junior/Senior High School library shelves in Garnett, Kans. (1997). A parent objected to the book's "graphic language." Source: 11, July 1997, p. 109.

1572 Swift, Jonathan. *Drapier's Letters.* Airmont; Bantam; Bobbs-Merrill; Dell; Grosset; Houghton; NAL; Norton; Oxford Univ. Pr.; Pocket Bks. All attempts to prosecute the printer or to identify the anonymous writer were frustrated by the aroused Irish nation (1724). Source: 4, p. 25.

1573 _____. *Gulliver's Travels.* Airmont; Bantam; Bobbs-Merrill; Dell; Grosset; Houghton; NAL; Norton; Oxford Univ. Pr.; Pocket Bks. Denounced as wicked and obscene in Ireland (1726). Source: 4, p. 25.

1574 _____. *Tale of a Tub.* AMS Pr.; Oxford Univ. Pr. Placed on the *Index Librorum Prohibitorum* in Rome (1734). It was listed until 1881. Source: 1, pp. 324–25; 3, p. 135.

1575 Talbert, Marc. *Dead Birds Singing.* Dell; Little. Challenged, but retained, as part of the curriculum, at Hughes Junior High School in Bismarck, N.Dak. (1993) because it is "offensive." Source: 11, Sept. 1993, p. 145; Jan. 1994, p. 38.

1576 *The Talmud.* Soncino Pr. The history of suppression of the *Talmud* is many centuries long. Early attempts to ban it date at least to the seventh and eight centuries. During the Middle Ages, with the revival of learning and the appearance of books of theological speculation, the Roman Catholic Church began to adopt a more severe attitude toward suspect books. It began to examine Jewish literature and the *Talmud* more intensively. Burned in Cairo, Egypt (1190); Paris, France (1244); and Salamanca, Spain (1490). Burned (1239) on the orders of Pope Gregory IX. Pope Innocent IV ordered Louis IX of France to burn all copies. This order, which met great opposition from the Jewish community, was repeated in 1248 and 1254. Pope Benedict XIII ordered all copies to be delivered to the bishops of the Italian dioceses (1415) and held by them, subject to further instruction. Jews were forbidden to possess any material that was antagonistic to Christianity. On the instruction of the Inquisition of Rome (1555) the houses of the Jewish community were searched and all copies seized. Pope Julius III ordered that no Christian might own or read the *Talmud*, nor might they print such material, on pain of excommunication. After the publication of the Roman Index of 1559, which prohibited the *Talmud* and all other works of Jewish doctrine, some 12,000 volumes of Hebrew texts were burned after the Inquisitor Sixtus of Siena destroyed the library of the Hebrew school at Cremona. Pope Clement VIII forbade (1592) both "Christians and Jews from owning, reading, buying or circulating Talmudic or Cabbalistic books or other godless writing," either written or printed, in Hebrew or in the other languages, which contained heresies or attacks on the church, its persons or practices. Any such work, ostensibly expurgated or not, was to be destroyed. The prohibitions of Jewish doctrinal material as set out in 1559, 1564, and 1592 were all repeated by Pope Clement XIV. No Hebrew books were to be bought or sold until they had been submitted to the papal chaplain charged with administering the censorship system. In the 20th century, the most extensive censorship was reported in Europe under the Communist Party in the Soviet Union and under the Nazis during the Holocaust. For Western Civilization, a change in attitudes toward the *Talmud* was brought about by the Second Vatican Council in 1965, which deplored anti-Semitism and the persecution of Jews, emphasizing the church's biblical connection to Judaism and the common religious heritage of Christians and Jews. Source: 3, pp. 55–56; 4, p. 5; 6, p. 844; 8, pp. 300–303.

1577 Tamar, Erika. *Fair Game.* Harcourt. Challenged at the Springdale, Ark. Public Library (1995) because "ethics take a back seat to graphic sexual material. Perhaps there is a less prurient work that explores the issue of rape vs. consensual sex or date rape." Source: 11, Sept. 1995, p. 157.

1578 Tan, Amy. *The Joy Luck Club.* Putnam. Banned from the Lindale, Tex. Advanced Placement English reading list (1996) because the book "conflicted with the values of the community." Challenged at the Arrowhead High School in Waukesha, Wis. (2004) as an elective reading list assignment by a parent because the book contains "sexually explicit and inappropriate material." Source: 11, Nov. 1996, p. 199; Jan. 2005, p. 11.

1579 Tax, Meredith. *Families.* Little. Challenged in Mosinee, Wis. (1982) because it teaches family living. Eliminated from the Fairfax County, Va. School's Family Life Education program (1994) after "parents complained that it glorifies divorce and shows two women living together." Source: 9; 11, May 1982, p. 87; May 1994, p. 88; Sept. 1994, p. 153.

1580 **Taylor, Mildred D.** *The Friendship.* Dial. Challenged, but retained, in the Prince George's County, Md. school system (1997) after a parent claimed the book has "no redeeming value." Source: 11, Sept. 1997, p. 149.

1581 _____. *Mississippi Bridge.* Dial. Challenged, but retained at the Donahoe Elementary School library in Sandston, Va. (2001) despite objections of its "negative content and [that] it's riddled with prejudice." The novel by the Newbery Medal-winning author tells the story of a young black man who tries to save white passengers in a bus accident, despite being ordered earlier to give up his seat to "white folks." Source: 11, May 2001, p. 97; July 2001, p. 174.

1582 _____. *Roll of Thunder, Hear My Cry.* Bantam; Dell. Removed from the ninth-grade reading list at the Arcadia, La. High School (1993). The 1976 Newbery Medal-winning book was charged with racial bias. Challenged in O'Hara Park Middle School classrooms in Oakley, Calif. (1998) because it contains racial epithets. Challenged in Chapman Elementary School libraries in Huntsville, Ala. (2000) because it uses racial slurs in dialogue to make points about racism. Challenged, but retained as a part of the Seminole County, Fla. school curriculum (2004) despite the concerns of an African American couple who found the book inappropriate for their thirteen-year-old son. The award-winning book depicts the life of an African American family in rural Mississippi in the 1930s and uses the word "nigger." Source: 11, May 1993, p. 72; July 1998, p. 107; Mar. 2000, p. 47; Mar. 2004, pp. 75–76.

1583 **Taylor, Theodore.** *The Cay.* Avon; Doubleday. Challenged as required reading at the Moorpark, Calif. schools (1992) because it allegedly maligns African Americans. Removed from the Oak Grove School District's core reading list for seventh-graders in San Jose, Calif. (1995) because of offensive, racist language. Placed on an "extended" list for use in the eighth grade. Challenged, but retained, at the Prince George's County, Md. school system (1997) after a parent claimed the book has "no redeeming value." Source: 11, May 1992, p. 95; July 1995, p. 96; Sept. 1997, p. 149.

1584 **Taylor, William.** *Agnes the Sheep.* Scholastic. Removed from the Nesbit Elementary School in Gwinnett County, Ga. (1995) because it overused the words "hell, damn, and God." Although other parents wanted the book restored in the elementary school, the County Board of Education refused to reinstate the book. Source: 11, Jan. 1996, p. 11; Mar. 1996, p. 64.

1585 **Tchudi, Stephen.** *Probing the Unknown: From Myth to Science.* Scribner. Challenged in the West Branch-Rose City, Mich. school district (1995) because it discusses occult beliefs. Source: 11, Jan. 1996, p. 15.

1586 **Telander, Rick.** *Heaven Is a Playground.* Grosset. Removed from the Evergreen School District of Vancouver, Wash. (1983) along with twenty-nine other titles. The American Civil Liberties Union of Washington filed suit contending that the removals constitute censorship, a violation of plaintiff's rights to free speech and due process, and the acts are a violation of the state Open Meetings Act because the removal decisions were made behind closed doors. Source: 11, Nov. 1983, pp. 185–86.

1587 *Teleny: A Novel Attributed to Oscar Wilde.* Gay Sunshine; Warner. Seized (1984) by the British Customs Office as "indecent and obscene." Source: 11, Jan. 1985, p. 26.

1588 **Terkel, Studs.** *Working: People Talk about What They Do All Day and How They Feel about What They Do.* Pantheon. Challenged in Wales, Wis. (1978) due to the book's "obscene language." Challenged in the senior vocational-technical English class in Girard, Pa. (1982) because some parents and students considered the book obscene. Removed from an optional reading list at the South Kitsap, Wash. High School (1983) because the chapter "Hooker" demeaned marital status and degraded the sexual act. Deleted from the seventh- and eighth-grade curriculum in the Washington, Ariz. School District (1983) due to "profane language. When we require idealistic and sensitive youth to be burdened with despair, ugliness and hopelessness, we shall be held accountable by the Almighty God." Source: 9; 11, July 1978, p. 89; Sept. 1978, p. 123; July 1982, p. 143; Nov. 1983, p. 187; Jan. 1984, pp. 10–11.

1589 **Terris, Susan.** *Stage Brat.* Four Winds Pr. Removed from, but later reinstated at, the Pine Middle School library in Gibsonia, Pa. (1990) because "it talks of adults slithering around in hot tubs, abortions, palm reading and horoscopes as ways of making life decisions, anti-religious language, and four-letter words." Source: 11, Nov. 1990, pp. 209–10; Jan. 1991, pp. 28–29.

1590 Terry, Wallace. *Bloods: An Oral History of the Vietnam War by Black Veterans.* Ballantine; Random. Banned from the West Hernando Middle School library in Spring Hill, Fla. (1987) because of "harsh language and presents a moral danger to students." The librarian filed a grievance, and the book was returned to the shelves following a ruling by the American Arbitration Association. Forty minutes after the book was returned, the book was removed again, pending a review by an advisory committee. The advisory committee recommended the book be removed from middle school library and placed in the high school library. Source: 7, pp. 60–61; 11, May 1987, p. 85; Sept. 1987, pp. 173–74; Jan. 1988, p. 9.

1591 Thom, James Alexander. *Follow the River.* Mass Market. Removed from the tenth grade curriculum at the high school in Noblesville, Ind. (2002) after a parent objected to passages about an imagined rape; the book remains in the library collection. Source: 11, May 2002, p. 117.

1592 Thomas, Piri. *Down These Mean Streets.* Knopf; Random. Removed from the junior high school library Community School Board 1250, Queens, N.Y. (1972). Decision upheld by the court's ruling in *President's Council, District 25 v. Community School Board No. 25*, 457 F.2d 289 (2d Cir. 1972), 409 U.S. 998 (1972). Removed from the Island Trees, N.Y. Union Free School District High School library in 1976 along with nine other titles because they were considered "immoral, anti-American, anti-Christian, or just plain filthy." Returned to the library after the U.S. Supreme Court ruling on June 25, 1982 in *Board of Education, Island Trees Union Free School District No. 26 et al. v. Pico et al.*, 457 U.S. 853 (1982). Source: 11, July 1973, p. 115; Nov. 1982, p. 197; 12, pp. 142–44, 239.

1593 Thompson, Charlotte E. *Single Solutions: An Essential Guide for the Career Woman.* Branden. Challenged for technical errors, but retained at the Multnomah, Oreg. County Library (1991). Source: 11, Jan. 1992, p. 6.

1594 Thompson, Craig. *Blankets.* Top Shelf. Challenged in the Marshall, Mo. Public Library (2006) because the book was deemed "pornographic" by some members of the community. The book was moved to the adult book section, rather than the young-adult area where it had been shelved before. Source: 11, Nov. 2006, p. 289; Jan. 2007, pp. 9–10; May 2007, p. 115.

1595 *The Three Billy Goats Gruff.* Harcourt. Challenged at the Eagle Point, Oreg. Elementary School library (1984) because the story was too violent for children. Source: 11, Sept. 1984, p. 155.

1596 Tindal, Matthew. *Rights of the Christian Church Asserted.* Kessinger Pub. In 1707, an English grand jury made a presentation against the book, and in 1710, it was proscribed by Parliament and burned. Source: 1, pp. 287–88.

1597 Toer, Pramoedya Ananta. *The Fugitive.* Morrow. Banned in Indonesia. The author has spent much of his life imprisoned for political reasons for fourteen years and on house or city (Jakarta) arrest for an additional twenty years, from 1979 to 1999. Toer wrote the novel in 1949 while he was imprisoned by the Dutch from 1947 to 1950 for his role in Indonesia's anticolonial revolution. With the success of the revolution in 1949, the novel was published in 1950, was acclaimed and then banned because it contained elements of class conflict and was perceived as a potential threat to society. In the following years, his works—thirty novels and books—were burned and banned in Indonesia because they were considered "subversive." Ownership of his books led some to imprisonment and torture. Toer has won many national and international awards for this works. Source: 8, pp. 55–57.

1598 Toland, John. *Christianity Not Mysterious.* Kessinger Pub. Presented by an English grand jury (1696) and ordered burned for heresy by the Irish Parliament (1697). Toland escaped arrest by fleeing to Holland. Source: 1, pp. 39–40.

1599 Tolkien, J. R. R. (John Ronald Reuel). *Lord of the Rings.* Ballantine; Houghton. Burned in Alamagordo, N.Mex. (2001) outside Christ Community Church along with other Tolkien novels as satanic. Source: 11, Mar. 2002, p. 61.

1600 Tolstoy, Leo. *The Kreutzer Sonata.* AMS Pr. Publication forbidden in Russia (1880) for "immoral content." Banned by the U.S. Post Office Department (1890) from general distribution and mailing. As soon as the ban was enacted, street vendors in New York loaded pushcarts with copies and large signs stating "Suppressed." They were arrested and the book was confiscated. A Philadelphia vendor was indicted (1890) for selling a translation of the novel and taken to court. The court declared the novel to possess "very little dramatic interest or literary merit" and

165

acknowledged as bizarre Tolstoy's recommendation of complete celibacy for all people, married or otherwise, but he also stated that "it cannot, on that account, be called an obscene libel." Banned in Hungary (1926), and Italy (1929). Source: 4, p. 49; 10, p. 144; 13, pp. 134–35; 15, Vol. II, pp. 621–22.

1601 Touchette, Charleen. *It Stops with Me: Memoir of a Canuck Girl.* Touch Arts Bks. Removed from the Woonsocket Harris, R.I. Public Library shelves (2005) after the author's father challenged the book. He wrote, "If members of a family wish to harm one another, those actions should be kept private and should not draw in others by involving matters of public policy." The book was later returned to the shelves. Source: 11, March 2006, p. 91.

1602 *The Treasury of American Poetry.* Doubleday. Challenged at the Gretna, Va. High School library (1981) because it contained eight objectionable words. The review committee recommended to cut out pages or ink over the offending words. Source: 11, May 1981, p. 66.

1603 Trocchi, Alexander. *Cain's Book.* Grove. Police in Sheffield, England, raided a number of bookstores and confiscated the novel (1964). Eventually, the court ruled that the book was obscene marked the first time a judgment of obscenity had been made based not on the vulgar language, depiction of sexual activity, or depravity in a work but on the lifestyle it advocated. Lord Chief justice Parker determined that the narrator's heroin addiction was the reason for censoring the book. Source: 14, p. 72.

1604 Trotsky, Leon. *Report of the Siberian Delegation.* New Park Pub. Banned by the imperial government in 1903 and by the government of the Soviet Union in 1927. In the 1930s, Trotsky's works were banned in quite disparate venues: Boston, Mass. (1930); Soviet Union (1933); Germany (1933); and Italy (1934). Source: 7, pp. 426–27.

1605 Trueman, Terry. *Stuck in Neutral.* HarperCollins. Challenged, but retained on the reading list for eighth-graders at the Evansville, Wis. High School (2003) despite concerns about profanity, sexual imagery, and violence. Source: 11, Jan. 2004, p. 13.

1606 Trumbo, David. *Johnny Got His Gun.* Lippincott. Challenged and/or censored in schools: in Michigan (1977) for too much profanity, too gruesome details of a human being, expressing unpatriotic and anti-American ideas, and sexual passages; in Wisconsin (1977) for too much profanity; in Texas (1977) as unpatriotic and anti-American; in Colorado (1977) for the description of the main character after he had been maimed in the war; in California (1977) for the language and for several passages describing sexual encounters; in Wisconsin (1982) as antiwar; in Vermont and Illinois (1982) as too violent. Source: 8, pp.107–9.

1607 Tryon, Thomas. *The Other.* Knopf. Challenged at the Merrimack, N.H. High School (1982). Source: 11, Sept. 1982, p. 170.

1608 Turkle, Brinton. *Do Not Open.* Dutton. Challenged at the Jackson, Calif. Elementary School (1990) because of objections to its pictures of supernatural beings. Source: 11, May 1990, p. 105.

1609 Twain, Mark [Samuel L. Clemens]. *The Adventures of Huckleberry Finn.* Bantam; Bobbs-Merrill; Grosset; Harper; Holt; Houghton; Longman; Macmillan; NAL; Norton; Penguin; Pocket Bks. Banned in Concord, Mass. (1885) as "trash and suitable only for the slums"; excluded from the children's room of the Brooklyn, N.Y. Public Library (1905) on the grounds that "Huck not only itched but scratched, and that he said sweat when he should have said perspiration"; confiscated at the USSR border (1930); dropped from the New York City (1957) list of approved books for senior and junior high schools, partly because of objections to frequent use of the term "nigger." Removed from the Miami Dade, Fla. Junior College required reading list (1969) because the book "creates an emotional block for black students that inhibits learning." Challenged as a "racist" novel in Winnetka, Ill. (1976); Warrington, Pa. (1981); Davenport, Iowa (1981); Fairfax County, Va. (1982); Houston, Tex. (1982); State College, Pa. Area School District (1983); Springfield, Ill. (1984); Waukegan, Ill. (1984). Removed from the required reading in the Rockford, Ill. public schools (1988) because the book contains the word "nigger." Challenged at the Berrien Springs, Mich. High School (1988). Removed from a required reading list and school libraries in Caddo Parish, La. (1988) because of racially offensive passages. Challenged at the Sevier County High School in Sevierville, Tenn. (1989) because of racial slurs and dialect. Challenged on an Erie, Pa. High School supplemental English reading list (1990) because of its derogatory references to African Americans. Challenged in Plano, Tex. Independent School District (1990) because the novel is "racist." Challenged in the Mesa, Ariz. Unified School District (1991) because the book repeatedly

uses the word "nigger" and damages the self-esteem of black youth. Removed from the required reading list of the Terrebone Parish public schools in Houma, La. (1991) because of the repeated use of the word "nigger." Temporarily pulled from the Portage, Mich. classrooms (1991) after some black parents complained that their children were uncomfortable with the book's portrayal of blacks. Challenged in the Kinston, N.C. Middle School (1992) when the superintendent told the novel could not be assigned because the students were too young to read the book because of its use of the word "nigger." Challenged at the Modesto, Calif. High School as a required reading (1992) because of "offensive and racist language." The word "nigger" appears in the book. Challenged at the Carlisle, Pa. area schools (1993) because the book's racial slurs are offensive to both black and white students. Challenged, but retained on high school reading lists, by the Lewisville, Tex. school board (1994). Challenged in English classes at Taylor County High School in Butler, Ga. (1994) because it contains racial slurs and bad grammar and does not reject slavery. The book will be taught in the tenth rather than the ninth grade. Challenged at the Santa Cruz, Calif. Schools (1995) because of its racial themes. Removed from the curriculum of the National Cathedral School in Washington, D.C. (1995) because of the novel's content and language. Removed from the eighth-grade curriculum at a New Haven, Conn. middle school (1995) because parents complained it undermined the self-esteem of black youth. Removed from the required reading lists in East San Jose, Calif. high schools (1995) in response to objections raised by African-American parents. They said the book's use of racial epithets, including frequent use of the word "nigger," erodes their children's self-esteem and affects their performance in school. Challenged in the Kenosha, Wis. Unified School District (1995). The complaint was filed by the local NAACP, which cited the book as offensive to African-American students. Challenged as required reading in an honors English class at the McClintock High School in Tempe, Ariz. (1996) by a teacher on behalf of her daughter and other African-American students at the school. In May 1996, a class-action lawsuit was filed in U.S. District Court in Phoenix, alleging that the district deprived minority students of educational opportunities by requiring racially offensive literature as part of class assignments. In January 1997, a federal judge dismissed the lawsuit stating he realized that "language in the novel was offensive and hurtful to the plaintiff," but that the suit failed to prove the district violated students' civil rights or that the works were assigned with discriminatory intent. The U.S. Court of Appeals for the Ninth Circuit in San Francisco ruled that requiring public school students to read literary works that some find racially offensive is not discrimination prohibited by the equal protection clause or Title VI of the 1964 Civil Rights Act. The ruling came in the case *Monteiro v. Tempe Union High School District*. Dropped from the mandatory required reading list at the Upper Dublin, Pa. schools (1996) because of its allegedly insensitive and offensive language. Banned from the Lindale, Tex. Advanced Placement English reading list (1996) because the book "conflicted with the values of the community." Challenged for being on the approved reading list in the Federal Way, Wash. schools (1996) because it "perpetuates hate and racism." Challenged in the South Euclid-Lyndhurst, Ohio City Schools (1997) because a student complained that some classmates snickered and giggled as the word "nigger" was read aloud by students. Challenged at the Columbus, Ind. North High School (1997) because the book is "degrading, insensitive, and oppressive." Challenged, but retained, at McLean High School in Fairfax, Va. (1997) despite a parent's complaint that the book offends African Americans. Removed from classrooms in the Cherry Hill, N.J. schools (1997) in January 1997 after concerns were raised about its racial epithets and the depiction of its African-American characters. In December 1997, however, the school board approved a new curriculum that places the book in the context of nineteenth-century racial relations and presents the works of African-American writers, including Frederick Douglass, Maya Angelou, and Langston Hughes. The Pennsylvania NAACP called for the removal of the book from required reading lists (1998) in school districts across the state because of its offensive racial language. Challenged in the Dalton and Whitfield County, Ga. schools (1998) because the book's language is offensive. Recommended for removal from the Fairbanks, Alaska North Star Borough School District's required reading lists (1999) because of its frequent use of the word "nigger." Challenged, but retained in the Enid, Okla. schools (2000). The novel was previously removed from the curriculum in Enid in 1977 after similar protests. It was returned to the required reading list in 1991. Challenged in the Kankakee, Ill. School District (2001) because the book uses the word "nigger." Challenged in the Portland, Oreg. schools (2002) by an African-American student who said he was offended by an ethnic slur used in the 1885 novel. Challenged in the Normal, Ill. Community High School sophomore literature class (2003) as being degrading to African Americans. *The Chosen* was offered as an alternative to Twain's novel. Pulled from the reading lists at the three Renton, Wash. high schools (2004) after an African American student said the book degraded her and her culture. The novel, which is not required

reading in Renton schools but is on a supplemental list of approved books, was eventually retained for classroom usage. Challenged as required reading at Cactus High in Peoria, Ariz. (2006). The student and mother have threatened to file a civil-rights complaints because of alleged racial treatment, the segregation of the student, and the use of a racial slur in the classroom. Pulled from classes in Taylor, Mich., schools (2006) because of complaints about its liberal use of common racial slurs. Challenged in the Lakeville, Minn. High School (2007) and St. Louis Park High School in Minneapolis, Minn. (2007) as required reading for sophomores. Source: 2, pp. 86–87; 4, pp. 49–50; 6, pp. 398–400; 11, May 1969, p. 52; July 1976, p. 87; Sept. 1976, p. 116; Nov. 1981, p. 162; Jan. 1982, pp. 11, 18; May 1982, p. 101; July 1982, p. 126; Sept. 1982, p. 171; Jan. 1984, p. 11; May 1984, p. 72; July 1984, pp. 121–22; Nov. 1984, p. 187; 8, Sept. 1988, pp. 152–53; Nov. 1988, p. 201; Jan. 1989, p. 11; Mar. 1989, p. 43; May 1989, p. 94; Jan. 1991, pp. 17–18; Mar. 1991, pp. 44–45; May 1991, pp. 90–92; Mar. 1992, pp. 43, 64; July 1992, p. 126; Sept. 1992, p. 140; May 1993, p. 73; May 1994, pp. 99–100; Mar. 1995, p. 42; May 1995, pp. 68, 69, 83; July 1995, pp. 96–97; Jan. 1996, p. 13; Mar. 1996, pp. 64–65; May 1996, p. 98; July 1996, p. 120; Sept. 1996, p. 153; Nov. 1996, pp. 198–99; Jan. 1997, p. 12; Mar. 1997, p. 40; May 1997, pp. 65–66, 72; July 1997, pp. 95–98; Sept. 1997, p. 149; Nov. 1997, p. 182; Mar. 1998, p. 56; May 1998, pp. 72–73; Nov. 1998, p. 182; Jan. 1999, pp. 13–15; July 1999, pp. 93–94; Mar. 2000, p. 52; July 2000, p. 125; Mar. 2001, p. 57; Jan. 2003, pp. 11–12; Jan. 2004, p. 11; May 2004, p. 91; Jan. 2007, pp. 14–15; Mar. 2007, pp. 50–52; May 2007, pp. 121–22; 15, Vol. II, p. 617.

1610 _____. *The Adventures of Tom Sawyer.* Airmont; And/Or Press; Bantam; Grosset; Longman; NAL; Pocket Bks. Excluded from the children's room in the Brooklyn, N.Y. Public Library (1876) and the Denver, Colo. Public Library (1876). Confiscated at the USSR border (1930). Removed from London, United Kingdom school libraries by education officials (1985) who found it "racist" and "sexist." Challenged in the Plano, Tex. Independent School District (1990) because the novel is racist. Retained in the O'Fallon, Ill. schools (1992), but parents will be able to request that their children not be required to read the book. A parent had sought the book's removal, charging that its use of the word "nigger" is degrading and offensive to black students. Challenged in the Columbus, Ind. schools (1997) because the book is "degrading, insensitive, and oppressive." It was suggested that middle school students in the district might use an edited version that deletes controversial language. Source: 4, pp. 49–50; 11, Sept. 1985, p. 156; Jan. 1991, p. 18; Mar. 1991, pp. 45–46; May 1991, p. 92; May 1992, p. 97; Sept. 1994, p. 152; July 1997, pp. 97–98.

1611 _____. *Eve's Diary.* Arden Lib. Removed from circulation at the Charlton Library in Worcester, Mass. (1906) because the "Edenic costumes" worn by Eve in the book's fifty illustrations had created an inordinate demand for it among the library's patrons. Source: 15, Vol. II, p. 626.

1612 Ungerer, Tomi. *Beast of Monsieur Racine.* Farrar. Challenged at the Rogers-Hough, Ark. Memorial Library (1989) because the book is violent. Source: 11, Sept. 1991, p. 151.

1613 Ungerer, Tomi. *Zeralda's Ogre.* Harper; Penguin. Removed from the Cascades Elementary School in Lebanon, Oreg. (1989) because the book had frightening illustrations. Source: 11, Jan. 1990, pp. 4–5.

1614 Updike, John. *Rabbit Is Rich.* Knopf. Removed from the library at Sun Valley High School in Aston, Pa. (1996) because it contains "offensive language and explicit sexual scenes." The novel won the Pulitzer Prize for fiction in 1982. Source: 11, May 1996, pp. 83–84.

1615 _____. *Rabbit Run.* Fawcett. Banned in Ireland in 1962 because the Irish Board of Censors found the work "obscene" and "indecent," objecting particularly to the author's handling of the characters' sexuality, the "explicit sex acts" and "promiscuity." The work was officially banned from sales in Ireland until the introduction of the revised Censorship Publications Bill in 1967. Restricted to high school students with parental permission in the six Aroostock County, Maine community high school libraries (1976) because of passages in the book dealing with sex and an extramarital affair. Removed from the required reading list for English class at the Medicine Bow, Wyo. Junior High School (1986) because of sexual references and profanity in the book. Source: 8, pp. 376–77; 11, Mar. 1977, p. 36; Mar. 1987, p. 55; 13, pp. 196–97.

1616 Valentine, Johnny. *The Daddy Machine.* Alyson Pubns. Challenged in the Wicomico County Free Library in Salisbury, Md. (1993) along with three other books on homosexuality intended for juvenile readers. Source: 11, Jan. 1994, p. 35.

1617 _____. **The Duke Who Outlawed Jelly Beans.** Alyson Pubns. Moved from the children's section to the adult section at the Elizabethtown, N.C. library (1993). Challenged in the Wicomico County Free Library in Salisbury, Md. (1993) along with three other books on homosexuality intended for juvenile readers. Retained at the Dayton and Montgomery County, Ohio Public Library (1993). Challenged at the Brevard County, Fla. Library (1998). When the request failed to have the book banned, the complainant kept the book from other patrons by keeping it checked out for a year. Source: 11, May 1993, p. 71; July 1993, pp. 100–101; Jan. 1994, p. 35; Mar. 1994, p. 69; July 1998, p. 105.

1618 **Van Devanter, Lynda, and Christopher Morgan.** **Home before Morning.** Warner. Challenged at the Esperanza Middle School library in Lexington, Md. (1988) because the book's "liberal use of profanity and explicit portrayals of situations." Source: 11, Nov. 1988, p. 201.

1619 **Van Lustbader, Eric.** **White Ninja.** Fawcett. Challenged at the Prince William County, Va. Library (1995) because of passages that describe the vicious rape and flaying of a young woman. Source: 11, Jan. 1996, p. 12; Nov. 1996, pp. 194, 211; Jan. 1997, p. 26.

1620 **Van Slyke, Helen.** **Public Smiles, Private Tears.** Bantam; Thorndike Pr. Challenged at the Public Libraries of Saginaw, Mich. (1989) because the book is "pornographic" with no redeeming value. Source: 11, May 1989, p. 77.

1621 **Van Vooren, Monique.** **Night Sanctuary.** Summit. Challenged at the White County Library in Searcy, Ark. (1983) by a local parent, a minister and a group called the Institute for American Ideals. Source: 11, Nov. 1983, p. 185; Jan. 1984, p. 25.

1622 **Vasilissa the Beautiful: Russian Fairy Tales.** Progress Pubns. Challenged at the Mena, Ark. schools (1990) because the book contains "violence, voodoo, and cannibalism." Source: 11, July 1990, p. 147.

1623 **Vergil, Polydore.** **De Inventoribus Rerum.** Included in a 1551 list of books condemned by the Sorbonne, then in the Spanish Index of Forbidden books in 1559, the Roman Index of Forbidden books issued by Pope Paul IV in 1564, and the Liege Index of 1569. Source: 1, pp. 69–70.

1624 **Vidal, Gore.** **Live from Golgotha.** Random. Challenged at the Carrollton, Tex. Public Library (1992) because the book is "offensive and pornographic." Source: 11, Mar. 1993, p. 42.

1625 **Vinge, Joan D.** **Catspaw.** Warner. Restricted to Mediapolis, Iowa junior high students (1995) with parental consent because it was "unredeeming and destructive" as well as "morally decadent." Source: 11, May 1994, p. 83; July 1995, p. 109.

1626 **Voigt, Cynthia.** **David and Jonathan.** Scholastic. Placed on the teacher reserve shelf, available for students to check out after they consult with a teacher, at the Colleyville Middle School in Grapevine-Colleyville, Tex. (1998). The novel, which chronicles the effects of the Holocaust on a group of adolescent boys in the 1950s, was found "to be disturbing and full of sexual references, crude language and adult themes such as suicide, masturbation, and abortion." Source: 11, May 1998, p. 88; July 1998, p. 106.

1627 _____. **Homecoming.** Fawcett; Macmillan. Challenged at the Lynchburg, Va. middle and high school English classes (1992) because it presents readers with negative role models and values. Source: 11, Sept. 1992, p. 164.

1628 _____. **Tell Me If the Lovers Are Losers.** Atheneum. Removed from the Jackson County, W.Va. school libraries (1997) along with sixteen other titles. Source: 11, Jan. 1998, p. 13.

1629 _____. **When She Hollers.** Scholastic. Removed from the Jackson County, W.Va. school libraries (1997) along with sixteen other titles. Source: 11, Jan. 1998, p. 13.

1630 **Voltaire, Francois M. [Francois-Marie Arouet].** **Candide.** Bantam; Holt. Placed the book on the list of prohibited books of the Roman Index of 1806 by Pope Puis VII. Seized by U.S. Customs in Boston, Mass. (1929) and declared as obscene; suppressed in the USSR (1935). Voltaire's best-known work remained anathema to American authorities as late as 1944 when Concord Books, issuing a sale catalog that included the book, was informed by the Post Office that such a listing violated U.S. postal regulations on sending obscene matter through the mails. Source: 2, p. 137; 3, p. 354; 4, p. 27; 8, pp. 323–24; 15, Vol. III, pp. 418–19.

Caution! Some People Consider These Books Dangerous

1631 _____. ***Letters Concerning the English Nation.*** Oxford Univ. Pr. Printed clandestinely, banned by the French Parlement (1734), burned by the public executioner, and placed on the Catholic Church's Index of Forbidden books (1752), along with thirty-eight other books by Voltaire. The Spanish Index also prohibited all of his writings. Source: 1, pp. 185–86.

1632 Vonnegut, Kurt. *Breakfast of Champions.* Dell. Challenged in the Monmouth, Ill. School District Library (1995) because it is "pornographic trash." Source: 11, Mar. 1996, p. 45.

1633 _____. ***Cat's Cradle.*** Delacorte; Dell. The Strongsville, Ohio School Board (1972) voted to withdraw this title from the school library; this action was overturned in 1976 by a U.S. District Court in *Minarcini v. Strongsville City School District*, 541 F.2d 577 (6th Cir. 1976). Challenged at the Merrimack, N.H. High School (1982). Source: 4, p. 95; 11, Sept. 1982, p. 170; 12, pp. 145–48.

1634 _____. ***God Bless You, Mr. Rosewater.*** Delacorte; Dell. The Strongsville, Ohio School Board (1972) voted to withdraw this title from the school library; this action was overturned in 1976 by a U.S. District Court. Source: 4, p. 95.

1635 _____. ***Slaughterhouse-Five.*** Dell; Dial. Challenged in many communities, but burned in Drake, N.Dak. (1973). Banned in Rochester, Mich. because the novel "contains and makes references to religious matters" and thus fell within the ban of the establishment clause. An appellate court upheld its usage in the school in *Todd v. Rochester Community Schools*, 41 Mich. App. 320, 200 N.W.2d 90 (1972). Banned in Levittown, N.Y. (1975), North Jackson, Ohio (1979), and Lakeland, Fla. (1982) because of the "book's explicit sexual scenes, violence, and obscene language." Barred from purchase at the Washington Park High School in Racine, Wis. (1984) by the district administrative assistant for instructional services. Challenged at the Owensboro, Ky. High School library (1985) because of "foul language, a section depicting a picture of an act of bestiality, a reference to 'Magic Fingers' attached to the protagonist's bed to help him sleep, and the sentence: 'The gun made a ripping sound like the opening of the fly of God Almighty.'" Restricted to students who have parental permission at the four Racine, Wis. Unified District high school libraries (1986) because of "language used in the book, depictions of torture, ethnic slurs, and negative portrayals of women." Challenged at the LaRue County, Ky. High School library (1987) because "the book contains foul language and promotes deviant sexual behavior." Banned from the Fitzgerald, Ga. schools (1987) because 'it was filled with profanity and full of explicit sexual references." Challenged in the Baton Rouge, La. public high school libraries (1988) because the book is "vulgar and offensive." Challenged in the Monroe, Mich. public schools (1989) as required reading in a modern novel course for high school juniors and senior because of the book's language and the way women are portrayed. Retained on the Round Rock, Tex. Independent High School reading list (1996) after a challenge that the book was too violent. Challenged as an eleventh-grade summer reading option in Prince William County, Va. (1998) because the book "was rife with profanity and explicit sex." Removed as required reading for sophomores at the Coventry, R. I. High School (2000) after a parent complained that it contained vulgar language, violent imagery, and sexual content. Retained on the Northwest Suburban High School District 214 reading list in Arlington Heights, Ill. (2006), along with eight other challenged titles. A board member, elected amid promises to bring her Christian beliefs into all board decision-making, raised the controversy based on excerpts from the books she'd found on the Internet. Challenged in the Howell, Mich. High School (2007) because of the book's strong sexual content. In response to a request from the president of the Livingston Organization for Values in Education, or LOVE, the county's top law enforcement official reviewed the books to see whether laws against distribution of sexually explicit materials to minors had been broken. "After reading the books in question, it is clear that the explicit passages illustrated a larger literary, artistic or political message and were not included solely to appeal to the prurient interests of minors," the county prosecutor wrote. "Whether these materials are appropriate for minors is a decision to be made by the school board, but I find that they are not in violation of the criminal laws." Source: 8, pp. 165–70; 11, Jan. 1974, p. 4; May 1980, p. 51; Sept. 1982, p. 155; Nov. 1982, p. 197; Sept. 1984, p. 158; Jan. 1986, pp. 9–10; Mar. 1986, p. 57; Mar. 1987, p. 51; July 1987, p. 147; Sept. 1987, pp. 174–75; Nov. 1987, p. 224; May 1988, pp. 86–87; July 1988, pp. 139–40; July 1989, p. 144; May 1996, p. 99; Nov. 1998, p. 183; Jan. 2001, p. 14; July 2006, pp. 210–11; May 2007, p. 116; 12, pp. 78–79.

1636 _____. ***Welcome to the Monkey House.*** Delacorte; Dell. A Montgomery, Ala., teacher was dismissed for assigning this title to her eleventh-grade English class because the book

170

promoted "the killing off of elderly people and free sex." The teacher brought suit and won in *Parducci v. Rutland*, 316 F.Supp. 352, (M. D. Ala 1970). Pulled from the high school classes in Bloomington, Minn. (1977). Source: 11, Jan. 1970, p. 28; July 1977, p. 101; 12, pp. 126–27, 238.

1637 **Wagner, Jane.** *J. T.* Dell. Removed from classroom use in Raleigh, N.C. (1981) due to book's racial stereotyping, but later reinstated by an ad hoc review committee. Source: 11, Nov. 1981, p. 170.

1638 **Walker, Alice.** *The Color Purple.* Harcourt. Challenged as an appropriate reading for Oakland, Calif. High School honors class (1984) due to the work's "sexual and social explicitness" and its "troubling ideas about race relations, man's relationship to God, African history, and human sexuality." After nine months of haggling and delays, a divided Oakland Board of Education gave formal approval for the book's use. Rejected for purchase by the Hayward, Calif. school trustees (1985) because of "rough language" and "explicit sex scenes." Removed from the open shelves of the Newport News, Va. school library (1986) because of its "profanity and sexual references" and placed in a special section accessible only to students over the age of 18 or who have written permission from a parent. Challenged at the public libraries of Saginaw, Mich. (1989) because it was "too sexually graphic for a 12-year-old." Challenged as a summer youth program reading assignment in Chattanooga, Tenn. (1989) because of its language and "explicitness." Challenged as an optional reading assignment in the Ten Sleep, Wyo. schools (1990). Challenged as a reading assignment at the New Bern, N.C. High School (1992) because her stepfather raped the main character. Banned in the Souderton, Pa. Area School District (1992) as appropriate reading for tenth graders because it is "smut." Challenged on the curricular reading list at Pomperaug High School in Southbury, Conn. (1995) because sexually explicit passages aren't appropriate high school reading. Retained as an English course reading assignment in the Junction City, Oreg. high school (1995) after a challenge to Walker's Pulitzer Prize-winning novel caused months of controversy. Although an alternative assignment was available, the book was challenged due to "inappropriate language, graphic sexual scenes, and book's negative image of black men." Challenged at the St. Johns County Schools in St. Augustine, Fla. (1995). Retained on the Round Rock, Tex. Independent High School reading list (1996) after a challenge that the book was too violent. Challenged, but retained, as part of the reading list for Advanced Placement English classes at Northwest High School in High Point, N.C. (1996). The book was challenged because it is "sexually graphic and violent." Removed from the Jackson County, W.Va. school libraries (1997) along with sixteen other titles. Challenged, but retained as part of a supplemental reading list at the Shawnee School in Lima, Ohio (1999). Several parents described its content as vulgar and "X-rated." Removed from the Ferguson High School library in Newport News, Va. (1999). Students may request and borrow the book with parental approval. Challenged, along with seventeen other titles in the Fairfax County, Va. elementary and secondary libraries (2002), by a group called Parents Against Bad Books in Schools. The group contends the books "contain profanity and descriptions of drug abuse, sexually explicit conduct, and torture." Source: 11, July 1984, p. 103; Sept. 1984, p. 156; Mar. 1985, p. 42; May 1985, pp. 75, 91; July 1985, p. 111; Nov. 1986, p. 209; May 1989, p. 77; Sept. 1989, p. 162; May 1990, p. 88; Sept. 1992, p. 142; Mar. 1993, p. 44; May 1993, p. 74; July 1995, p. 98; Sept. 1995, pp. 135, 160–61; Jan. 1996, p. 14; May 1996, p. 99; Mar. 1997, p. 50; May 1997, pp. 78–79; Sept. 1997, p. 149; Jan. 1998, p. 13; Sept. 1999, pp. 131–32; Nov. 1999, p. 163; Jan. 2003, p. 10.

1639 _____. *The Temple of My Familiar.* Harcourt. Removed from the Jackson County, W.Va. school libraries (1997) along with sixteen other titles. Source: 11, Jan. 1998, p. 13.

1640 _____. *Warrior Marks: Female Genital Mutilation and the Sexual Blinding of Women.* Harcourt. Former Weslaco, Tex. (1995) librarian filed a federal lawsuit charging that she was fired for publicly discussing that city's efforts to ban Walker's work from the library. Source: 11, Sept. 1995, p. 153.

1641 **Walker, Barbara G.** *The Woman's Encyclopedia of Myths and Secrets.* Harper. Restricted to non-required assignments at the North Bend, Oreg. (1988) High School library because the book "is of no benefit to anyone." Source: 11, Jan. 1990, pp. 4–5.

1642 **Walker, Kate.** *Peter.* Houghton. Challenged at the Barron, Wis. School District (1998). Challenged at the Montgomery County, Tex. Memorial Library System (2004) along with fifteen other young-adult books with gay-positive themes. The objections were posted at the Library Patrons of Texas Web site. The language describing the books is similar to that posted at the Web site of the Fairfax County, Virginia-based Parents Against Bad Books in Schools, to which Library Patrons of Texas links. Source: 11, Jan. 1999, p. 9; Nov. 2004, pp. 231–32.

1643 Walker, Margaret. *Jubilee.* Houghton; Bantam. Challenged in the Greenville, S.C. County school libraries (1977) by the Titan of the Fourth Province of the Knights of the Ku Klux Klan because the novel produces "racial strife and hatred." Source: 11, May 1977, p. 73.

1644 Wallace, Daisy, ed. *Witch Poems.* Holiday. Challenged at the Bozeman, Mont. elementary school libraries (1993) because it scared a kindergartner. Source: 11, Sept. 1993, p. 158.

1645 Wallace, Irving. *The Fan Club.* Bantam. The twenty-six branch librarians of Riverside County, Calif. (1974) were advised that the book was not selected for circulation, and patrons should be told the county selection committee could not in good conscience spend tax money on it; further, that it was not their policy to purchase "formula-written commercial fiction." In Oct. 1982, Malaysian police confiscated the works of Wallace because the books were considered "prejudicial to the public interest." Destroyed in Beijing, China (1988) and legal authorities threatened to bring criminal charges against the publishers. Source: 4, p. 91; 5, Jan. 1983, p. 45; 11, Jan. 1989, p. 15.

1646 Wambaugh, Joseph. *The Black Marble.* Dell. Banned from the Stroudsburg, Pa. High School library (1985) because it was "blatantly graphic, pornographic and wholly unacceptable for a high school library." Source: 11, May 1985, p. 79.

1647 _____. *The Delta Star.* Bantam; Morrow. Banned from the Stroudsburg, Pa. High School library (1985) because it was "blatantly graphic, pornographic and wholly unacceptable for a high school library." Source: 11, May 1985, p. 79.

1648 _____. *The Glitter Dome.* Bantam. Banned from the Stroudsburg, Pa. High School library (1985) because it was "blatantly graphic, pornographic and wholly unacceptable for a high school library." Source: 11, May 1985, 79.

1649 _____. *The New Centurions.* Dell; Little. Banned from the Stroudsburg, Pa. High School library (1985) because it was "blatantly

graphic, pornographic and wholly unacceptable for a high school library." Source: 11, May 1985, p. 79.

1650 Warren, Patricia Nell. *The Front Runner.* Bantam. Challenged at the Three Rivers, Mich. Public Library (1982) because it "promotes homosexuality and perversion." Source: 11, Mar. 1983, p. 29.

1651 Warren, Robert Penn. *All the King's Men.* Harcourt; Random. Challenged at the Dallas, Tex. Independent School District high school libraries (1974). Source: 11, Jan. 1975, pp. 6–7.

1652 Watkins, Yoko Kawashima. *So Far from the Bamboo Grove.* HarperTeen. Removed from the sixth-grade English curriculum at Dover-Sherborn, Mass. Middle School (2006) due to scenes hinting at rape, violence against women by Korean men, and a distorted presentation of history. It is part of the state's recommended reading list for the grade level. The book is based on the real-life experiences of Watkins, whose father was a Japanese government official. In a reversal of its decision made, the Dover-Sherborn Regional School committee voted unanimously to keep the book as part of a sixth-grade language arts unit on survival. The school is exploring other texts to bring balance to the unit in response to the criticism leveled against the book by some parents and community members. Source: 11, Jan. 2007, pp. 13–14; Mar. 2007, pp. 73–74.

1653 Watson, Jane Werner, and Sol Chambers. *The Golden Book of the Mysterious.* Golden. Challenged at the Winchester, Md. Elementary School (1988) because of the book's reference to witchcraft, sorcery, spells, fortune telling, reincarnation, werewolves, vampires, and ghosts. Source: 11, July 1988, p. 120; Sept. 1988, p. 178.

1654 Waugh, Evelyn. *Brideshead Revisited.* Chapman & Hall Ltd. Alabama Representative Gerald Allen (R-Cottondale) proposed legislation (2005) that would prohibit the use of public funds for the "purchase of textbooks or library materials that recognize or promote homosexuality as an acceptable lifestyle." The bill also proposed that novels with gay protagonists and college textbooks that suggest homosexuality is natural would have to be removed from library shelves and destroyed. The bill would impact all Alabama school, public, and university libraries. While it would ban books like *Heather Has Two Mommies*, it could also include classic and popular novels with gay characters such as Evelyn Waugh's *Brideshead Revisited*, *The Color Purple* or *The Picture of Dorian Gray*. Source: 11, Jan. 2005, p. 5.

1655 Waxman, Stephanie. *What Is a Girl? What Is a Boy?* Peace Pr. After the Minnesota Civil Liberties Union sued the Elk River, Minn. School Board (1983), the board reversed its decision to restrict this title to students who have written permission from their parents. Challenged at the Blue Mountain schools in Wells River, Vt. (1991). Placed in a special nonfiction section where an adult must request it for a child at the Lake Lanier Regional Library in Lawrenceville, Ga. (1994) after a group of parents complained that the book is not appropriate for young children. Moved to the nonfiction section of the Gwinnet-Forsyth, Ga. (1994) Regional Library. Source: 11, Sept. 1982, pp. 155–56; May 1983, p. 71; Sept. 1983, p. 153; Sept. 1991, p. 178; Nov. 1994, p. 187; Jan. 1995, p. 6.

1656 *We the People–History of the U.S.* D.C. Heath. Removed from the Mississippi state-approved textbook list (1981). Source: 11, July 1981, p. 93.

1657 Webb, James. *Fields of Fire.* Bantam. Challenged at the Fort Mill, S.C. High School (1988) because the book contains "offensive language and explicit sex scenes." School officials decided to retain the novel, but to explore the possibility of setting up a "restricted" shelf for "controversial" books. Source: 11, July 1988, p. 122; Sept. 1988, pp. 178–79.

1658 Wei Hui, Zhou. *Shanghai Baby.* Simon. Banned in China (2001) because it contains "too much decadence and too much sexual description" and officials believed that it would "give a bad influence to a new generation." Police publicly raided book fairs and confiscated and burned copies of the novel. Source: 13, p. 217.

1659 Welch, James. *Fools Crow.* Doubleday; Viking; Penguin. Banned from Laurel, Mont. High School classrooms (1999) because the contents are "objectionable, inappropriate, disgusting, and repulsive." Two copies remain in the library. Challenged, but retained at the Bozeman, Mont. High School (2000) despite objections to its descriptions of rape, mutilation, sex, and violence. Source: 11, July 1999, p. 96; Mar. 2000, p. 51; July 2000, p. 125.

1660 Welch, James. *Winter in the Blood.* Harper. Retained on the Round Rock, Tex. Independent High School reading list (1996) after a challenge that the book was too violent. Source: 11, May 1996, p. 99.

1661 Wells, Rosemary. *Shy Charles.* Dial. Challenged because the mother allegedly is portrayed too negatively, but retained at the Multnomah, Oreg. County Library (1991). Source: 11, Jan. 1992, p. 6.

1662 Wentworth, Harold, and Stuart B. Flexner. *Dictionary of American Slang.* Crowell. Returned to the publisher after a parent complained to the Stuart, Fla. Middle School (1979); removed from the Westminster, Colo. elementary and secondary school libraries (1981). Source: 11, July 1979, p. 75; Mar. 1982, pp. 42–43.

1663 Wersba, Barbara. *Whistle Me Home.* Holt. Banned in Carroll County, Md. schools (2005). No reason stated. Source: 11, Mar. 2006, pp. 70–71.

1664 Wertenbaker, Lael Tucker. *The World of Picasso.* Time-Life. Retained at Maldonado Elementary School in Tucson, Ariz. (1994) after being challenged by parents who objected to nudity and "pornographic," "perverted," and "morbid" themes. Source: 11, July 1994, p. 112.

1665 Westheimer, David. *Von Ryan's Express.* Doubleday; NAL. Challenged at the North Suburban District Library in Loves Park, Ill. (1977) because the novel contains "vulgar sexual expressions, profanity, and a discussion of a scene of gross immorality." Source: 11, July 1977, p. 99.

1666 Wharton, William. *Birdy.* Knopf; Penguin. Banned, but later returned to the shelves of the Mary E. Taylor Middle School in Camden, Maine (1988). The book was originally removed because it contained ten phrases and sentences that contain sexual material and "offensive" language. Source: 11, Jan. 1988, pp. 8, 28.

1667 White, Edmund, and Adam Mars-Jones. *The Darker Proof: Stories from a Crisis.* NAL. Challenged at the Deschutes County Library in Bend, Oreg. (1993) because it "encourages and condones" homosexuality. Source: 11, Sept. 1993, pp. 158–59.

1668 **White, Edmund, ed.** *Faber Book of Gay Short Fiction.* Faber. Challenged in the Charlotte, N.C. Public Library (2000) because of its sexual content. Source: 11, Sept. 2000, p. 143.

1669 **White, Ellen Emerson.** *Long Live the Queen.* Scholastic. Challenged in the Mount Vernon, Wash. school libraries (1991) because it contained a word they found objectionable. Source: 11, Mar. 1992, p. 41.

1670 **White, Ryan, and Ann Marie Cunningham.** *Ryan White: My Own Story.* Dial. Removed from the curriculum, but placed on library shelves, with restricted access, at the Stroudsburg, Pa. middle school (1996) because a section "uses a gutter term for sodomy and another approves of teen smoking." Source: 11, Mar. 1997, p. 37.

1671 **Whitlock, Katherine.** *Bridge of Respect: Creating Support for Lesbian and Gay Youth.* American Friends Service Committee. Challenged at the Muscatine, Iowa Public Library (1990) because it is "wrong to promote immorality." Source: 11, Nov. 1990, p. 225.

1672 **Whitman, Walt.** *Leaves of Grass.* Adler; Doubleday; Holt; Norton; Penguin. Banned, informally, in New York and Philadelphia bookstores in the 1870s and legally in Boston in the 1880s. As per their usual practice, the Watch and Ward Society in Boston and the New York Society for the Suppression of Vice placed pressure on booksellers to suppress the sale of the book in their shops. Booksellers agreed neither to advertise the book nor to suggest its sale to customers. Source: 2, p. 38; 4, p. 45; 8, pp. 465–67; 15, Vol. I, p. 562, II, p. 610.

1673 **Wiebe, Rudy.** *The Story-Makers: A Selection of Modern Short Stories.* Gage; Macmillan. Removed from the Halton County, Ontario, Canada, School District (1984) because the short story anthology contains "The Sins of Jesus," by Isaac Babel. According to the complainants, some Christians consider the story "blasphemous because the Lord Jesus appears as a slightly confused comic character who in the end seems to accept that he has made a mistake." Source: 11, Nov. 1984, p. 188.

1674 **Wieler, Diane.** *Bad Boy.* Delacorte. Challenged at the State College, Pa. area middle school libraries (1996). Three parents requested the book's removal, charging that it was full of profanity and portrayed underage drinking and other problems. In addition, the portrayal of the homosexual relationship between two secondary characters "conveys a wrong message." Source: 11, Nov. 1996, p. 211; Jan. 1997, p. 9.

1675 **Wilde, Oscar.** *The Happy Prince and Other Stories.* Penguin. Challenged at the Springfield, Oreg. Public Library (1988) because the stories were "distressing and morbid." Source: 11, Jan. 1989, p. 3.

1676 _____. *Salome.* Collins. Lord Chamberlain withheld the play license on the grounds that it introduced biblical characters (1892); book banned in Boston, Mass. (1895). Source: 4, p. 55.

1677 **Wilder, Laura Ingalls.** *Little House in the Big Woods.* Buccaneer; Harper; Transaction. Removed from the classrooms, but later reinstated, for third-graders at the Lincoln Unified School District in Stockton, Calif. (1996). Complainants also want the book removed from the library because it "promotes racial epithets and is fueling the fire of racism." Source: 11, Jan. 1997, p. 9; Mar. 1997, p. 50.

1678 _____. *Little House on the Prairie.* Buccaneer; Harper; Transaction. Challenged at the Lafourche Parish elementary school libraries in Thibodaux, La. (1993) because the book is "offensive to Indians." Banned in the Sturgis, S.Dak. elementary school classrooms (1993) due to statements considered derogatory to Native Americans. Temporarily removed at the Yellow Medicine East Elementary School near Granite Falls, Minn. (1998) due to the book's racist statements against Native Americans. Source: 11, July 1993, pp. 124–25; Mar. 1994, p. 55; Mar. 1999, p. 36.

1679 **Willhoite, Michael.** *Daddy's Roommate.* Alyson Pubns. Removed from the Brooklyn, N.Y. School District's curriculum (1992) because the school board objected to words that were "age inappropriate." Challenged at the Timberland Regional Libraries in Olympia, Wash. (1992) because the book promotes homosexuality and is offensive. Challenged at the Roswell, N.Mex. Public Library (1992) and the Dauphin County, Pa. Library System (1992) because the book's intent "is indoctrination into a gay lifestyle." Challenged at the Wayne County Public Library in Goldsboro, N.C. (1992), Grand Prairie, Tex. Memorial Library (1992), Fayetteville, N.C. (1992) and Tillamook, Oreg. (1992) because it "promotes a dangerous and ungodly lifestyle from which children must be protected." Restricted to adults at the Lake Lanier Regional Library System in Gwinnett County, Ga. (1992). Moved from the children's section to the adult section at the Manatee, Fla. Public Library (1993) and the Elizabethtown, N.C. library (1993). Challenged as a reading in the Rosemount-Apple Valley-Eden, Minn. School District (1993). Moved from the children's section to the adult section of the Mercer County Library System in Lawrence, N.J. (1993). Challenged at the Alachua County Library in High Springs, Fla. (1993), Seekonk, Mass. library (1993), the North Brunswick, N.J. Public Library (1993), the Cumberland County Public, N.C. Library (1993), Chattanooga-Hamilton County, Tenn. Bicentennial Library (1993), Wicomico County Free Library in Salisbury, Md. (1993), Sussex, Wis. Public Library (1993) and Juneau, Alaska school libraries (1993). Challenged at the Mesa, Ariz. Public Library (1993) because it "is vile, sick and goes against every law and constitution." Retained at the Dayton and Montgomery County, Ohio Public Library (1993). Removed by Lane County Head Start officials in Cottage Grove, Oreg. (1994) from its anti-bias curriculum. Challenged at the Chandler, Ariz. Public Library (1994) because the book is a "skillful presentation to the young child about lesbianism/homosexuality." Removed from the children's section of the Fort Worth, Tex. Public Library (1994) because critics say it legitimizes gay relationships. Challenged at the Brevard County, Fla. Library (1998). When a request to ban the book failed, the complainant kept the book from other patrons by keeping it checked out for a year. Challenged, but retained, at the Hays, Kans. Public Library (1998). A resident objected to "the teaching of the homosexual lifestyle as another way to show love." Challenged at the Wichita Falls, Tex. Public Library (1998) when the request to have the book banned failed, the complainant kept the book from other patrons by keeping it checked out for a year. The deacon body of the First Baptist Church requested that any literature that promotes or sanctions a homosexual lifestyle be removed. The Wichita Falls City Council established a policy that allows library cardholders who collect 300 signatures to have children's books moved to an adult portion of the library. U.S. District Court Judge Jerry Buchmeyer struck down the library resolution as unconstitutional and the books were returned. Challenged, but retained in the juvenile non-fiction section of the Nampa, Idaho Public Library (1999). Challenged, but retained at the Ada, Idaho Community Library (2000). Source: 11, May 1992, pp. 83, 95; Sept. 1992, p. 162; Nov. 1992, pp. 197–99; Jan. 1993, pp. 7, 9, 10, 28; May 1993, pp. 69–71; July 1993, pp. 101, 106–7, 123–26; Sept.

1993, pp. 143–46; Nov. 1993, p. 179; Jan. 1994, pp. 13, 34–36; Mar. 1994, p. 69; July 1994, p. 115; Sept. 1994, pp. 147–48, 166; Nov. 1994, p. 187; Jan. 1995, pp. 4, 6, 8; Sept. 1995, p. 159; May 1998, pp. 69, 88; July 1998, pp. 105–7; Jan. 1999, pp. 8–9; Mar. 1999, p. 36; May 1999, p. 67; Sept. 1999, p. 131; Nov. 1999, p. 172; Mar. 2000, pp. 44, 61; Nov. 2000, pp. 201–2.

1680 **Williams-Garcia, Rita. *Like Sisters on the Homefront.*** Lodestar Bks. Removed from Central Dauphin school district, Harrisburg, Pa., elementary and middle school library shelves (2000) due to explicit language. Source: 11, Sept. 2000, p. 144.

1681 **Williams, Chancellor. *The Destruction of African Civilization and the Origin of African Civilization.*** Third World. Challenged at the Prince George County, Md. high school libraries (1993) because the two volumes promote "racism against white people." In a complaint filed with the state, the works were called "racist pornography" written "to provoke emotions and actions of racial prejudice, bias, hatred and hostility towards citizens and students in Maryland." Source: 11, Nov. 1993, p. 177.

1682 **Williams, Garth. *The Rabbit's Wedding.*** Harper. Removed from the "open" shelves to the "reserved" shelves at the Montgomery, Ala. Public Library (1959) because an illustration of the lapin couple, the buck was black while the doe was white. Such miscegenation, stated an editor in Orlando, Fla., was "brainwashing. . . . as soon as you pick up the book and open its pages you realize these rabbits are integrated." The Home News of Montgomery, Ala., added that the book was integrationist propaganda obviously aimed at children in their formative years. Source: 3, p. 250.

1683 **Williams, Jaston; Joe Sears; and Ed Howard. *Greater Tuna.*** Samuel French. Challenged at the Grayslake, Ill. Community High School (1991). Source: 11, July 1991, pp. 129–30.

1684 **Williams, Jay. *The Magic Grandfather.*** Macmillan. Challenged at the Little Butte Intermediate School in Eagle Point, Oreg. (1989) because the book used swear words, and deals with magic and witches. Source: 11, Jan. 1990, pp. 4–5.

1685 **Williams, Roger. *The Bloudy Tenent of Persecution.*** Burned publicly (1644) by order of the British Parliament. Source: 8, pp. 215–16.

1686 Willingham, Calder. *End as a Man.*
Vanguard. New York Society for Suppression of Vice sought a ban (1947). In *People v. Vanguard Press, Inc.*, 192 Misc. 127, 84 N.Y.S.2d 427, Magistrate Strong dismissed the case and concluded that, "its effect on the reasonably normal reader would not be sexually demoralized." The following year the novel was again in court, this time in the Court of Quarter Sessions in Philadelphia County, Pennsylvania. Seized in Philadelphia raid (1948). Criminal proceedings were brought against five booksellers who were charged with possessing and intending to sell nine novels identified as obscene. Judge Bok concluded, "I hold that the books before me are not sexually impure and pornographic, and are therefore not obscene, lewd, lascivious, filthy, indecent, or disgusting." The judgment was later sustained in the Superior and Supreme Courts of Pennsylvania. Source: 4, p. 96; 14, pp. 129–30.

1687 Wilson, August. *Fences.* NAL.
Challenged in the honors and academic English classes in Carlisle, Pa. schools (1993) because it is "demeaning to women." Teachers must send parents a letter warning about the work's content and explaining that their children may read alternate selections. Source: 11, July 1993, p. 127.

1688 Wilson, Colin. *The Sex Diary of Gerard Orme.* Dial; Pocket Bks. A bookseller in New Britain, Conn. (1964) was arrested for selling this title. Source: 4, p. 99.

1689 _____. *Witches.* A & W Pub.
Challenged at the Albany, Oreg. Library (1986) because the book "is satanic in nature, thereby having tremendous drawing power to the curious and unsuspecting." Source: 11, July 1986, p. 136.

1690 Wilson, Edmund. *Memoirs of Hecate County.* Godine; Octagon. Confiscated by the New York City police from four Doubleday bookshops after the New York Society for Suppression of Vice charged that it was salacious and lascivious (1946). In 1946, booksellers in San Francisco and New York City were arrested for selling the work and taken to trial. That same year, copies of the book were confiscated in Philadelphia and he publisher ceased shipment to Massachusetts because of its censorship laws. In San Francisco, a bookseller was charged with selling an "obscene" book, but the first trail was dismissed because it resulted in a hung trail. In the second trial of *People v. Wepplo*, 78 Cal.App.2d 959, 178 P.2d 853 (1947), the jury acquitted the bookseller. Banned from the U.S. mail

(1956). Source: 4, pp. 76–77; 8, pp. 365–66; 15, Vol. IV, pp. 697–99.

1691 Winship, Elizabeth; Frank Caparulo, and Vivian K. Harlin. *Human Sexuality.*
Houghton. Challenged in the Fulton County, Ga. schools (1992) because the "book is a 'how-to' book. It's not only explicit, but it promotes promiscuity in a subtle way that the determined abstainer would have second thoughts about their position." The group alleged that the text "undermines parents' authority, encourages breaking the law, and tears down normal sexual barriers by co-ed, hard-core, adult subject matter covered." Removed from use in health classes by the Belleville, Mo. School District School Board (1994) after parents had complained that the book "didn't stress abstinence from sex by high school students," and because "it didn't say whether sexual relations before marriage, homosexuality, masturbation, or abortion are right or wrong." Banned in the Fulton County, Ga. high schools (1994) because the book was too graphic, out-of-date, and did too little to persuade students not to have sex. Source: 11, May 1992, pp. 82–83; May 1994, p. 87; Sept. 1994, p. 150.

1692 Winship, Elizabeth. *Perspectives on Health: Human Sexuality.* D. C. Heath. Retained by unanimous school board vote, two mothers nevertheless protested by removing their daughters from classes at an Argos, Ind. Community School (1994) using this textbook because they felt it is too explicit and sends mixed messages about abstinence." They also objected to treatment of abortion and homosexuality. Source: 11, May 1994, p. 99.

1693 Winsor, Kathleen. *Forever Amber.*
NAL. Temporary injunction issued against sale of the book in Springfield, Mass. (1946). Attorney General George Rowell cited as due cause for banning the book some seventy references to sexual intercourse; thirty-nine illegitimate pregnancies; seven abortions; ten descriptions of women undressing, dressing or bathing in the presence of men; five references to incest; thirteen references ridiculing marriage; and forty-nine "miscellaneous objectionable passages." Rowell lost his case, and Judge Donahue of the Massachusetts Supreme Court defined the book as "a soporific rather an aphrodisiac. . . . while the novel was conducive to sleep, it was not conducive to a desire to sleep with a member of the opposite sex." Copies burned at British ports and by the public library in Birmingham, England (1946); banned in Ireland (1953). Banned in New Zealand (1952) after

the Minister of Customs, reviewed a copy seized by Customs officers. Source: 3, p. 95; 4, p. 93; 8, pp. 336–38; 15, Vol. IV, pp. 696–98.

1694 **Winthrop, Elizabeth.** *The Castle in the Attic.* Bantam; Dell; Fawcett; Greenwillow. Challenged at the Medway, Maine schools (1995) because the book uses swear words and deals with sorcery. Source: 11, July 1995, p. 97.

1695 **Witt, Mary A., et al.** *The Humanities: Cultural Roots and Continuities.* Heath. Banned from classroom use, but returned to the Columbia High School library in Lake City, Fla. (1986) because of "offensive" language. The school board banned two sections of the text that contained modern adaptation of *The Miller's Tale*, by Chaucer and *Lysistrata*, by Aristophanes. In December 1986, four parents filed a lawsuit charging that their children's rights were violated when the textbook was banned from classroom use. On January 30, 1988, the U.S. District Court for the Middle District of Florida ruled that in *Virgil v. School Board of Columbia County* "the school board acted within its broad range of discretion in determining educational suitability" and thus may constitutionally ban a textbook because of sex and vulgarity. Upholding this ruling, the U.S. Court of Appeals for the Fourth Circuit ruled on January 16, 1989, that the school board did not violate students' constitutional rights when it removed the textbook. Source: 11, July 1986, p. 119; Nov. 1986, p. 207; Mar. 1987, p. 51; Nov. 1987, p. 223; May 1988, pp. 81, 98; Sept. 1988, p. 150; Mar. 1989, p. 52.

1696 **Wolf, Eric.** *Peasant Wars of the Twentieth Century.* Harper. Banned in South Korea (1985). Source: 5, April 1986, pp. 30–33.

1697 **Wolfe, Daniel.** *T. E. Lawrence.* Chelsea House Pubs. Removed from the Anaheim, Calif. school district (2000) because school officials said the book is too difficult for middle school students and that it could cause harassment against students seen with it. The American Civil Liberties Union (ACLU) of Southern California filed suit in *Doe v. Anaheim Union High School District* alleging that the removal is "a pretext for viewpoint-based censorship." The ACLU claims no other books have been removed from the junior high library for similar reasons, even though several, such as works by Shakespeare and Dickens, are more difficult reading. The ACLU contends that the school officials engaged in unconstitutional viewpoint discrimination by removing the book because it contains gay and lesbian material. In March

2001, the school board approved a settlement that restored the book to the high school shelves and amended the district's policy to prohibit the removal of books for subject matter involving sexual orientation, but the book will not be returned to the middle school. Source: 11, Mar. 2001, p. 53; May 2001, p. 95; July 2001, p. 173.

1698 **Wolfe, Thomas.** *Of Time and the River.* Scribner. Removed from four high school libraries in the Amarillo, Tex., area (1963) after parents of students raised charges of obscenity against the book. Four members of the Alabama State Textbook Committee (1983) called for the rejection of Wolfe's work for use in Alabama public schools. Source: 11, Mar. 1983, p. 39; 14, pp. 242–43.

1699 **Wolff, Tobias.** *This Boy's Life: A Memoir.* Atlantic Monthly Pr.; Perennial Library. Removed from the Blue Valley School District's high school curriculum in Overland Park, Kans. (2005). The book was challenged by parents and community members because of "foul language, and references to alcohol and sexual activity." Source: 11, Nov. 2005, pp. 282–83.

1700 **Wolk, Robert L., and Arthur Henley.** *The Right to Lie.* Wyden. Challenged at the Plymouth-Canton school system in Canton, Mich. (1987) because the book is "a psychological guide to everyday deceit." Source: 11, May 1987, p. 110.

1701 **Wood, Audrey.** *Elbert's Bad Word.* Harcourt. Challenged in the Columbia County, Ga. school libraries (1992) because Elbert visits a friendly gardener who is a "practicing wizard." Source: 11, Nov. 1992, p. 197.

1702 **Wood, Bari.** *Amy Girl.* NAL. Removed from the shelves of the Northern Burlington County, N.J. Regional High School library (1988) because of its "descriptions of underage drinking and teenage sex." Source: 11, Mar. 1988, p. 46.

1703 **Wood, Maryrose.** *Sex Kittens and Horn Dawgs Fall in Love.* Delacorte. Removed along with nine other titles from a library order at the Hernando County, Fla. (2006) schools. Among the other books culled from Nature Coast Technical High School's order were Barbara Kingsolver's first novel, *The Bean Trees*; *The Clan of the Cave Bears*, by Jean Auel; *Boy's Life*, by Robert McCammon; and the abridged young-adult version of *The Power of One*, by Bryce Courtenay. A board member led the charge against those books, reading profanity-laced passages and castigating the school officials who placed the order. Other books the school system wants to have reviewed are: *Are You in the House Alone?*; *Rainbow Boys*; *Rats Saw God*; and *The King Must Die.* Source: 11, July 2006, p. 182.

1704 Woodroofe, Patrick. *The Second Earth: The Pentateuch Retold.* Avery Pub. Removed from the Warrenton, Va. Junior High School library (1992) because a single parent complained about its "anti-Christian" ideas and its illustrations. Source: 11, May 1992, pp. 81–82.

1705 Woolley, Persia. *Queen of the Summer Stars.* Pocket Bks. Challenged, but retained, at the Case Junior High School Library in Watertown, N.Y. (1995) because, although the book contains scenes of sex, kidnapping, rape and incest, the themes of love, loyalty, honor and trust are more obvious to the reader. Source: 11, May 1995, p. 66; July 1995, pp. 109–10.

1706 Worth, Valerie. *Imp and Biscuit: The Fortune of Two Pugs.* Farrar. Challenged at the Mena, Ark. schools (1990) because the book contains "violence, voodoo and cannibalism." Source: 9, July 1990, p. 147.

1707 Wright, Peter. *Spycatcher.* Viking; Penguin. Banned in England (1987) because the author had violated his secrecy oath under the Official Secrets Act. After a two-and-a-half-year battle, the courts determined that three London newspapers could publish excerpts from the former intelligence agent's memoirs. Banned in India (1987). Source: 8, pp. 173–76; 11, Nov. 1987, p. 229; May 1988, p. 93; Jan. 1989, p. 15.

1708 Wright, Richard. *Black Boy.* Harper. Removed from classroom use in Michigan (1972) after parents objected to the book's sexual overtones and claimed that it was unsuitable for impressionable sophomores. Removed from Tennessee schools (1975) for being obscene, instigating hatred between the races and encouraging immorality. Challenged, but retained in the East Baton Rouge, La. schools (1975) despite claims the book contains obscenity, filth or pornography. Restricted to students with parental approval at the Island Trees, N. Y. Union Free School District High School library in 1976; restriction lifted after the U.S. Supreme Court ruling on June 25, 1982, in *Board of Education, Island Trees Union Free School District No. 26 et al. v. Pico et al.*, 457 U.S. 853 (1982). Nebraska Governor Kay Orr's "kitchen cabinet" (1987) called for the novel's removal asserting it had a "corruptive obscene nature" and citing the use of profanity throughout and the incidents of violence. The book was removed from library shelves, and then returned after the controversy abated. Challenged in the Lincoln, Nebr. school libraries (1987) because of the novel's "corruptive, obscene nature." Retained on the Round Rock, Tex. Independent High School reading list (1996) after a challenge that the book was too violent. Challenged in the Jacksonville, Fla. public schools (1997) by a minister who said the book contains "profanity and may spark hard feelings between students of different races." Challenged in the Howell, Mich. High School (2007) because of the book's strong sexual content. In response to a request from the president of the Livingston Organization for Values in Education, or LOVE, the county's top law enforcement official reviewed the books to see whether laws against distribution of sexually explicit materials to minors had been broken. "After reading the books in question, it is clear that the explicit passages illustrated a larger literary, artistic or political message and were not included solely to appeal to the prurient interests of minors," the county prosecutor wrote. "Whether these materials are appropriate for minors is a decision to be made by the school board, but I find that they are not in violation of the criminal laws." Source: 8, pp. 23–28; 11, May 1978, p. 57; Nov. 1982, p. 197; Nov. 1987, p. 225; May 1996, p. 99; Sept. 1997, p. 127; Mar. 2007, pp. 51–52; May 2007, p. 116.

1709 _____. *Native Son.* Harper. Challenged in Goffstown, N.H. (1978); Elmwood Park, N.J. (1978) due to "objectionable" language; and North Adams, Mass. (1981) due to the book's "violence, sex, and profanity." Challenged at the Berrien Springs, Mich. High School in classrooms and libraries (1988) because the novel is "vulgar, profane, and sexually explicit." Retained in the Yakima, Wash. schools (1994) after a five-month dispute over what advanced high school students should read in the classroom. Two parents raised concerns about profanity and images of violence and sexuality in the book and requested that it be removed from the reading list. Challenged as part of the reading list for Advanced Placement English classes at Northwest High School in High Point, N.C. (1996). The book was challenged because it is "sexually graphic and violent." Removed from Irvington High School in Fremont, Calif. (1998) after a few parents complained the book was unnecessarily violent and sexually explicit. Challenged in the Hamilton High School curriculum in Fort Wayne, Ind. (1998) because of the novel's graphic language and sexual content. Source: 11, May 1978, p. 57; July 1978, p. 98; Sept. 1981, p. 125; Nov. 1981, p. 170; Jan. 1989, p. 28; Nov. 1994, pp. 202–3; Mar. 1997, p. 50; Sept. 1997, p. 149; Sept. 1998, p. 142; Mar. 1999, p. 39.

1710 **Wycliffe, John.** *On Civil Lordship.* Condemned by the pope (1377). A Council at Oxford prohibited his work as heretical and forbade him from preaching or lecturing (1381). In 1415, a church council in Germany ordered his bones exhumed and burned and his ashes thrown into a running stream. Source: 1, pp. 228–29.

1711 **Wyden, Peter, and Barbara Wyden.** *Growing Up Straight: What Every Thoughtful Parent Should Know about Homosexuality.* New American Library; Stein and Day. Challenged at the Deschutes County Library in Bend, Oreg. (1993) because it "encourages and condones" homosexuality. Source: 11, Sept. 1993, pp. 158–59.

1712 **Yashima, Taro.** *Crow Boy.* Puffin; Viking Child. Challenged by a school board member in the Queens, N.Y. school libraries (1994) because it "denigrate[s] white American culture, 'promotes racial separation, and discourages assimilation.'" The rest of the school board voted to retain the book. Source: 11, July 1994, pp. 110–11; Sept. 1994, p. 166.

1713 **Yates, Elizabeth.** *Amos Fortune, Free Man.* Dutton; Penguin. Temporarily removed from the classrooms as an optional reading assignment in the Montgomery County, Md. schools (1989) because the 1950 Newbery Award-winning book contained "racist dialogue, fostered stereotypes, and could be degrading to black children who read it." Source: 11, Mar. 1990, p. 62.

1714 **Yep, Laurence.** *Dragonwings.* Harper. Challenged at the Apollo-Ridge schools in Kittanning, Pa. (1992) because of the frequent use of the word "demon" in the book. The Newbery Award-winning book might encourage children to "commit suicide because they think they can be reincarnated as something or someone else." On Sept. 15, 1992, Judge Joseph Nickleach denied a request seeking to ban the book from the district's curriculum. In his opinion, Nickleach wrote: "The fact that religions and religious concepts are mentioned in school does not automatically constitute a violation of the establishment clause." Challenged at the Henryville, Ind. schools (1999) because of graphic violence, profanity, references to

demons and prostitution, and alcohol and drug use depicted in a positive light. Source: 11, Sept. 1992, pp. 142–43; Jan. 1993, p. 18; Nov. 1999, p. 164.

1715 **Young, Lawrence A.** *Recreational Drugs.* Macmillan. Challenged in the Alameda County, Calif. Library (1982) because it allegedly encourages drug use. Source: 11, Sept. 1982, p. 169.

1716 **Zacks, Richard.** *History Laid Bare: Love, Sex, and Perversity from the Ancient Etruscans to Warren G. Harding.* HarperCollins. Challenged, but retained at the Cumberland County Library in Fayetteville, N.C. (1999) despite a complaint that the book deals with sexual history and customs. In addition, the complainant suggested that the library move sexually explicit materials, as well as ones about homosexuality, into an adult section and establish a review committee to screen materials. Source: 11, July 1999, p. 94; Jan. 2000, pp. 27–28.

1717 **Zacks, Richard.** *An Underground Education: The Unauthorized and Outrageous Supplement to Everything You Thought You Knew about Art, Sex, Business, Crime, Science, Medicine, and Other Fields of Human Knowledge.* Doubleday. Challenged, but retained at the Cumberland County Library in Fayetteville, N.C. (1999) despite a complaint that the book deals with sexual history and customs. In addition, the complainant suggested that the library move sexually explicit materials, as well as ones about homosexuality, into an adult section and establish a review committee to screen materials. Source: 11, July 1999, p. 94; Jan. 2000, pp. 27–28.

1718 **Zemach, Margot.** *Jake and Honeybunch Go to Heaven.* Farrar. The public libraries in Chicago, Milwaukee, and San Francisco, after surveying librarians employed in their public libraries, refused to acquire the book because it is "racially offensive." The *New York Times* stated, "In this case, librarians are deliberately keeping a widely acclaimed book by a major author-artist off their shelves in the name of morality." Source: 14, pp. 189–90.

1719 **Zindel, Paul.** *Loch.* HarperCollins. Challenged due to explicit language, but retained at the Lander County, Nev. School District (1997). Source: 11, Mar. 1998, p. 56.

1720 **_____.** *My Darling, My Hamburger.* Bantam; Harper. Removed from the Frazee, Minn. School library (1973); Lyons, N.Y. Elementary School

179

library (1976); and Hiawatha, Iowa Public Library (1979). Challenged in Champaign, Ill. (1980) and Jefferson County, Ky. (1982). Banned in the Dupree, S.Dak. High School English classes (1987) because of what the school board called "offensive language and vulgarity." Source: 11, Nov. 1973, p. 135; July 1976, p. 86; Mar. 1979, p. 27; May 1980, p. 61; Mar. 1983, p. 41; Jan. 1988, p. 12.

1721 _____. *Pigman.* Bantam; Harper. Challenged at the Hillsboro, Mo. School District (1985) because the novel features "liars, cheaters and stealers." Challenged as suitable curriculum material in the Harwinton and Burlington, Conn. schools (1990) because it contains profanity and subject matter that set bad examples and give students negative views of life. Challenged at the Lynchburg, Va. middle and high school English classes (1992) because the novel contains twenty-nine instances of "destructive, disrespectful, antisocial and illegal behavior . . . placed in a humorous light, making it seem acceptable." Source: 11, Mar. 1985, p. 44; Mar. 1991, p. 44; May 1991, p. 90; Sept. 1992, p. 164.

1722 **Zola, Emile.** *J'Accuse.* French & European. Listed on the *Index Librorum Prohibitorum* in Rome (1894); banned in Yugoslavia (1929) and in Ireland (1953). Source: 4, pp. 51–52.

1723 _____. *Nana.* Airmont; French & European; Penguin. In 1888, an English court agreed that all of Zola's works must be withdrawn from circulation, making Zola the only writer to have his works outlawed in England in the nineteenth century. Listed on the *Index Librorum Prohibitorum* in Rome (1894); banned in Yugoslavia (1929) and in Ireland (1953). The major complaints centered on the perception that Zola had made a heroine of a prostitute and had discussed "debased man's nature" by uncovering the often sordid sexuality of the period. Source: 4, pp. 51–52; 6, pp. 2,718–20; 14, pp. 234–35.

1724 **Zwerman, Gilda.** *Martina Navratilova.* Chelsea House Pubs. Removed from the Anaheim, Calif. school district (2000) because school officials said the book is too difficult for middle school students and that it could cause harassment against students seen with it. The American Civil Liberties Union (ACLU) of Southern California filed suit in *Doe v. Anaheim Union High School District* alleging that the removal is "a pretext for viewpoint-based censorship." The ACLU claims no other books have been removed from the junior high library for similar reasons, even though several, such as works by Shakespeare and Dickens, are more difficult reading. The ACLU contends that the school officials engaged in unconstitutional viewpoint discrimination by removing the book because it contains gay and lesbian material. In March 2001, the school board approved a settlement that restored the book to the high school shelves and amended the district's policy to prohibit the removal of books for subject matter involving sexual orientation, but the book will not be returned to the middle school. Source: 11, Mar. 2001, p. 53; May 2001, p. 95; July 2001, p. 173.

Attic

The Giving Tree

Huck Finn

Harry Potter

Notable
First Amendment
Court Cases

The Lorax

Mother Goose

Notable First Amendment Court Cases

This section contains summaries of frequently cited First Amendment cases. Arranged by topic, they cover case law issued by a variety of courts: the Supreme Court of the United States, the Court of Appeals of different Federal circuits, and the District Court of several Federal districts as well as the highest court of several states and particular appellate courts of action.

The standard citation is given to indicate where to find the complete text of a decision. For example, *Kreimer v. Bureau of Police for Morristown*, 958 F.2d 1241 (3d Cir. 1992), tells the names of the main parties in the case ("Kreimer," who sued the "Bureau of Police for Morristown"), the abbreviated title of the case reporter where the decision is published ("F.2d" for *Federal Reporter, Second Series*)—which is preceded by the particular volume number ("958") of the reporter and followed by the page number ("1242") where the decision begins—and, in parentheses, the name of court that issued the decision ("3d Cir." for Circuit of Appeals for the Third Circuit) and the year ("1992"). Other conventions may apply, depending on which case reporter is involved.

Abbreviations:

U.S.	*United States Reports*
S.Ct	*Supreme Court Reporter*
L.Ed.	*United States Supreme Court Reports Lawyers' Edition*
L.Ed.2d.	*United States Supreme Court Reports Lawyers' Edition, Second Series*
F.2d	*Federal Reporter Second Series*
F.3d	*Federal Reporter Third Series*
F.Supp.	*Federal Supplement*
F.Supp.2d	*Federal Supplement Second Series*
N.W.	*North Western Reporter*
N.W.	*North Western Reporter, Second Series*
N.Y.S.	*New York Supplement*
N.Y.S.	*New York Supplement, Second Series*
P.	*Pacific Reporter*

Foundations of Free Expression: Historic Cases

Schenck v. United States
249 U.S. 47, 39 S.Ct. 247, 63 L.Ed.2d (1919)

Justice Oliver Wendell Holmes stated in this case his famous aphorism about "falsely shouting fire in a theatre" and set forth a "clear and present danger test" to judge whether speech is protected by the First Amendment. "The question," he wrote, "is whether the words are used in such circumstances and are of such a nature as to create a clear and present danger that they will bring about the substantive evils that Congress has the right to prevent. It is a question of proximity and degree." The Supreme Court affirmed the convictions of the defendants for conspiring to violate certain federal statutes by attempting to incite subordination in the armed forces and interfere with recruitment and enlistment. During wartime, the defendants mailed to new recruits and enlisted men leaflets that compared military conscription to involuntary servitude and urged them to assert constitutional rights.

Near v. Minnesota
283 U.S. 697, 51 S.Ct. 625, 75 L.Ed. 1357 (1931)

In this case, the Supreme Court interpreted the First and Fourteenth Amendments to forbid "previous restraints" upon publication of a newspaper. "Previous restraints"—or in current terminology, "prior restraints"—suppress the freedom of the press to publish without obstruction, and recognize that lawsuits or prosecutions for libel are "subsequent punishments." The Court invalidated as an infringement of constitutional guarantees a Minnesota statue allowing specified government officials or private citizens to maintain a lawsuit in the name of the State to suppress a public nuisance and enjoin the publication of future issues of a "malicious, scandalous and defamatory newspaper, magazine or other periodical," unless the publisher can prove "the truth was published with good motives and for justifiable ends."

Brandenburg v. Ohio
395 U.S. 444, 89 S.Ct. 1827, 23 L.Ed.2d 430 (1969)

The Supreme Court established the modern version of the "clear and present danger" doctrine, holding that states only could restrict speech that "is directed to inciting or producing imminent lawless action, and is likely to incite or produce such action."

The Right to Read Freely

Evans v. Selma Union High School District of Fresno County
222 P. 801 (Ca. 1924)

The California State Supreme Court held that the King James version of the Bible was not a "publication of a sectarian, partisan, or denominational character" that a State statute required a public high school library to exclude from its collections. The "fact that the King James version is commonly used by Protestant Churches and not by Catholics" does not "make its character sectarian," the court stated. "The mere act of purchasing a book to be added to the school library does not carry with it any implication of the adoption of the theory or dogma contained therein, or any approval of the book itself, except as a work of literature fit to be included in a reference library."

Rosenberg v. Board of Education of City of New York
92 N.Y.S.2d 344 (Sup. Ct. Kings County 1949)

After considering the charge that *Oliver Twist* and the *Merchant of Venice* are "objectionable because they tend to engender hatred of the Jew as a person and as a race," the Supreme Court, Kings County, New York, decided that these two works cannot be banned from the New York City schools, libraries, or classrooms, declaring that the Board of Education "acted in good faith without malice or prejudice and in the best interests of the school system entrusted to their care and control, and, therefore, that no substantial reason exists which compels the suppression of the two books under consideration."

Todd v. Rochester Community Schools
200 N.W.2d 90 (Mich. Ct. App. 1972)

In deciding that *Slaughterhouse-Five* could not be banned from the libraries and classrooms of the Michigan schools, the Court of Appeals of Michigan declared: "Vonnegut's literary dwellings on war, religion, death, Christ, God, government, politics, and any other subject should be as welcome in the public schools of this state as those of Machiavelli, Chaucer, Shakespeare, Melville, Lenin, Joseph McCarthy, or Walt Disney. The students of Michigan are free to make of *Slaughterhouse-Five* what they will."

Minarcini v. Strongsville (Ohio) City School District
541 F.2d 577 (6th Cir. 1976)

The Strongsville City Board of Education rejected faculty recommendations to purchase Joseph Heller's *Catch-22* and Kurt Vonnegut's *God Bless You, Mr. Rosewater* and ordered the removal of *Catch-22* and Vonnegut's *Cat's Cradle* from the library. The U.S. Court of Appeals for the Sixth Circuit ruled against the School Board, upholding the students' First Amendment right to receive information and the librarian's right to disseminate it. "The removal of books from a school library is a much more serious burden upon the freedom of classroom discussion than the action found unconstitutional in *Tinker v. Des Moines School District*."

Right to Read Defense Committee v. School Committee of the City of Chelsea
454 F. Supp. 703 (D. Mass. 1978)

The Chelsea, Massachusetts, School Committee decided to bar from the high school library a poetry anthology, *Male and Female Under 18*, because of the inclusion of an "offensive" and "damaging" poem, "The City to a Young Girl," written by a fifteen-year-old girl. Challenged in U.S. District Court, Joseph L. Tauro ruled: "The library is 'a mighty resource in the marketplace of ideas.' There a student can literally explore the unknown, and discover areas of interest and thought not covered by the prescribed curriculum. The student who discovers the magic of the library is on the way to a life-long experience of self-education and enrichment. That student learns that a library is a place to test or expand upon ideas presented to him, in or out of the classroom. The most effective antidote to the poison of mindless orthodoxy is ready access to a broad sweep of ideas and philosophies. There is no danger from such exposure. The danger is mind control. The committee's ban of the anthology *Male and Female* is enjoined."

Salvail v. Nashua Board of Education
469 F. Supp. 1269 (D. N.H. 1979)

MS magazine was removed from a New Hampshire high school library by order of the Nashua School Board. The U.S. District Court decided for the student, teacher, and adult residents who had brought action against the school board, the court concluding: "The court finds and rules that the defendants herein have failed to demonstrate a substantial and legitimate government interest sufficient to warrant the removal of *MS* magazine from the Nashua High School library. Their action contravenes the plaintiffs' First Amendment rights, and as such it is plainly wrong."

Loewen v. Turnipseed
488 F. Supp. 1138 (N.D. Miss. 1980)

When the Mississippi Textbook Purchasing Board refused to approve *Mississippi: Conflict and Change* for use in Mississippi public schools, on the grounds that it was too concerned with racial matters and too controversial, the authors filed suit. U.S. District Judge Orma R. Smith ruled that the criteria used were not justifiable grounds for rejecting the book. He held that the controversial racial matter was a factor leading to its rejection, and thus the authors had been denied their constitutionally guaranteed rights of freedom of speech and the press.

Kreimer v. Bureau of Police for Morristown
958 F.2d 1242 (3d Cir. 1992)

In detailed analysis, the court of appeals held

183

that a municipal public library was a limited public forum, meaning open to the public for the specified purposes of exercising their First Amendment rights to read and receive information from library materials. Such exercise could not interfere with or disrupt the library's reasonable rules of operation. The court then upheld three library rules that: 1) required patrons to read, study, or otherwise use library materials while there; 2) prohibited noisy or boisterous activities which might disturb other patrons; and 3) permitted the removal of any patron whose offensive bodily hygiene was a nuisance to other patrons.

Case v. Unified School District No. 233
908 F. Supp. 864 (D. Kan. 1995)
When the Olathe, Kansas, School Board voted to remove the book *Annie on My Mind*, a novel depicting a lesbian relationship between two teenagers, from the district's junior and senior high school libraries, the federal district court in Kansas found they violated the students' rights under the First Amendment to the United States Constitution and the corresponding provisions of the Kansas State Constitution. Despite the fact that the school board testified that they had removed the book because of "educational unsuitability," which is within their rights under the Pico decision, it became obvious from their testimony that the book was removed because they disapproved of the book's ideology. In addition, it was found that the school board had violated their own materials selection and reconsideration policies, which weighed heavily in the judge's decision.

Campbell v. St. Tammany Parish School Board
64 F.3d 184 (5th Cir. 1995)
Public school district removed the book *Voodoo and Hoodoo*, a discussion of the origins, history, and practices of the voodoo and hoodoo religions that included an outline of some specific practices, from all district library shelves. Parents of several students sued and the district court granted summary judgment in their favor. The court of appeals reversed, finding that there was not enough evidence at that stage to determine that board members had an unconstitutional motivation, such as denying students access to ideas with which board members disagreed; the court remanded the case for a full trial at which all board members could be questioned about their reasons for removing the book. The court observed that "in light of the special role of the school library as a place where students may freely and voluntarily explore diverse

topics, the school board's non-curricular decision to remove a book well after it had been placed in the public school libraries evokes the question whether that action might not be an attempt to 'strangle the free mind at its source.'" The court focused on some evidence that school board members had removed the book without having read it or having read only excerpts provided by the Christian Coalition. The parties settled the case before trial by returning the book to the libraries on specially designated reserve shelves.

Sund v. City of Wichita Falls, Texas
121 F.Supp.2d 530 (N.D. Texas, 2000)
City residents who were members of a church sought removal of two books, *Heather Has Two Mommies* and *Daddy's Roommate*, because they disapproved of the books' depictions of homosexuality. The Wichita Falls City Council voted to restrict access to the books if three hundred persons signed a petition asking for the restriction. A separate group of citizens filed suit after the books were removed from the children's section and placed on a locked shelf in the adult area of the library. Following a trial on the merits, the District Court permanently enjoined the city from enforcing the resolution permitting the removal of the two books. It held that the City's resolution constituted impermissible content-based and viewpoint based discrimination; was not narrowly tailored to serve a compelling state interest; provided no standards or review process; and improperly delegated governmental authority over the selection and removal of the library's books to any three hundred private citizens who wish to remove a book from the children's area of the library.

Counts v. Cedarville School District
295 F.Supp.2d 996 (W.D. Ark. 2003)
The school board of the Cedarville, Arkansas, school district voted to restrict students' access to the Harry Potter books, on the grounds that the books promoted disobediance and disrespect for authority and dealt with witchcraft and the occult. As a result of the vote, students in the Cedarville school district were required to obtain a signed permission slip from their parents or guardians before they would be allowed to borrow any of the Harry Potter books from school libraries. The District Court overturned the Board's decision and ordered the books returned to unrestricted circulation, on the grounds that the restrictions violated students' First Amendment right to read and receive information. In so doing, the Court noted that while the Board necessarily performed highly discretionary functions related to the operation of the schools, it was still

bound by the Bill of Rights and could not abridge students' First Amendment right to read a book on the basis of an undifferentiated fear of disturbance or because the Board disagreed with the ideas contained in the book.

See also:

Board of Education, Island Trees Union Free School District No. 26 v. Pico, 457 U.S. 853, 102 S.Ct. 2799, 73 L.Ed.2d 435 (1982)

Smith v. Board of School Commissioners of Mobile (Ala.) County, 827 F.2d 684 (11th Cir. 1987)

Mozert v. Hawkins County Board of Education, 827 F.2d 1058 (6th Cir. 1987)

Virgil v. School Board of Columbia County, 862 F.2d 1517 (11th Cir. 1989)

American Library Association v. U.S. Department of Justice and Reno v. American Civil Liberties Union, 521 U.S. 844, 117 S.Ct. 2329, 138 L.Ed.2d 874 (1997)

Mainstream Loudoun, et al. v. Board of Trustees of the Loudoun County Library, 24 F.Supp.2d 552 (E.D. of Va. 1998)

Freedom of Expression in Schools

Tinker v. Des Moines Independent Community School District

393 U.S. 503, 89 S.Ct. 733, 21 L.Ed.2d 731 (1969)

In this seminal case considering the First Amendment rights of students who were expelled after they wore black armbands to school in symbolic protest of the Vietnam War, the Supreme Court held that students "do not shed their constitutional rights at the schoolhouse gate" and that the First Amendment protects public school students' rights to express political and social views.

Zykan v. Warsaw (Indiana) Community School Corporation and Warsaw School Board of Trustees

631 F.2d 1300 (7th Cir. 1980)

A student brought suit seeking to reverse school officials' decision to "limit or prohibit the use of certain textbooks, to remove a certain book from the school library, and to delete certain courses from the curriculum." The district court dismissed the suit. On appeal, the Court of Appeals for the Seventh Circuit ruled that the school board has the right to establish a curriculum on the basis of its own discretion, but it is forbidden to impose a "pall of orthodoxy." The right of students to file complaints was recognized, but the court held that the students' claims "must cross a relatively high threshold before entering upon the field of a constitutional claim suitable for federal court litigation."

Board of Education, Island Trees Union Free School District No. 26 v. Pico

457 U.S. 853, 102 S.Ct. 2799, 73 L.Ed.2d 435 (1982)

In 1975, three school board members sought the removal of several books determined objectionable by a politically conservative organization. The following February, the board gave an "unofficial direction" that the books be removed from the school libraries, so that board members could read them. When the board action attracted press attention, the board described the books as "anti-American, anti-Christian, anti-Semitic, and just plain filthy." The nine books that were the subject of the lawsuit were *Slaughterhouse-Five,* by Kurt Vonnegut, Jr.; *The Naked Ape,* by Desmond Morris; *Down These Mean Streets,* by Piri Thomas; *Best Short Stories of Negro Writers,* edited by Langston Hughes; *Go Ask Alice,* by Anonymous; *Laughing Boy,* by Oliver LaFarge; *Black Boy,* by Richard Wright; *A Hero Ain't Nothin' But a Sandwich,* by Alice Childress; and *Soul on Ice,* by Eldrige Cleaver.

The board appointed a review committee that recommended that five of the books be returned to the shelves, two be placed on restricted shelves, and two be removed from the library. The full board voted to remove all but one book.

After years of appeals, the U.S. Supreme Court upheld (5-4) the students' challenge to the board's action. The Court held that school boards do not have unrestricted authority to select library books and that the First Amendment is implicated when books are removed arbitrarily. Justice Brennan declared in the plurality opinion: "Local school boards may not remove books from school library shelves simply because they dislike the ideas contained in those books and seek by their removal to prescribe what shall be orthodox in politics, nationalism, religion, or other matters of opinion."

Smith v. Board of School Commissioners of Mobile (Ala.) County

827 F.2d 684 (11th Cir. 1987)

Parents and other citizens brought a lawsuit against the school board, alleging that the school system was teaching the tenets of an anti-religious religion called "secular humanism." The complainants asked that forty-four different elementary- through high school-level textbooks be removed from the curriculum. After an initial ruling in a federal district court in favor of the plaintiffs, the U.S. Court of Appeals for the Eleventh Circuit ruled that as long as the school was motivated by a secular purpose, it didn't matter whether the curriculum and texts shared ideas held by one or more religious groups. The Court found that the texts in question promoted important secular values (tolerance, self-respect, logical decision making) and thus the use of the textbooks neither unconstitutionally advanced a nontheistic religion nor inhibited theistic religions.

Mozert v. Hawkins County Board of Education
827 F.2d 1058 (6th Cir. 1987)

Parents and students brought this action challenging the mandatory use of certain textbooks on the ground that the texts promoted values offensive to their religious beliefs. The U.S. Court of Appeals for the Sixth Circuit rejected the plaintiffs' claim, finding that the Constitution does not require school curricula to be revised substantially in order to accommodate religious beliefs.

Hazelwood School District v. Kuhlmeier
484 U.S. 260, 108 S.Ct. 562, 98 L.Ed.2d 592 (1988)

After a school principal removed two pages containing articles, among others, on teenage pregnancy and the impact of divorce on students from a newspaper produced as part of a high school journalism class, the student staff filed suit claiming violation of their First Amendment rights. The principal defended his action on the grounds that he was protecting the privacy of the pregnant students described, protecting younger students from inappropriate references to sexual activity and birth control, and protecting the school from a potential libel action.

The Supreme Court held that the principal acted reasonably and did not violate the students' First Amendment rights. A school need not tolerate student speech, the Court declared, "that is inconsistent with its 'basic educational mission,' even though the government could not censor similar speech outside the school." In addition, the Court found the newspaper was part of the regular journalism curriculum and subject to extensive control by a faculty member. The school, thus, did not create a public forum for the expression of ideas, but instead maintained the newspaper "as supervised learning experience for journalism students." The Court concluded that "educators do not offend the First Amendment by exercising editorial control over the style and content of student speech in school-sponsored expressive activities so long as their actions are reasonably related to legitimate pedagogical concerns." The Court strongly suggested that supervised student activities that "may fairly be characterized as part of the school curriculum," including school-sponsored

publications and theatrical productions, were subject to the authority of educators. The Court cautioned, however, that this authority does not justify an educator's attempt "to silence a student's personal expression that happens to occur on the school premises."

Virgil v. School Board of Columbia County
862 F.2d 1517 (11th Cir. 1989)

This case presented the question of whether the First Amendment prevents a school board from removing a previously approved textbook from an elective high school class because of objections to the material's vulgarity and sexual explicitness. The U.S. Circuit Court of Appeals concluded that a school board may, without contravening constitutional limits, take such action when the removal decision was "reasonably related" to the "legitimate pedagogical concern" of denying students access to "potentially sensitive topics." The written "stipulation concerning Board Reasons" cites explicit sexuality and excessively vulgar language in two selections contained in *Volume 1, The Humanities: Cultural Roots and Continuities* as the basis for removal of this textbook. The two selections are Chaucer's *The Miller's Tale* and Aristophanes's *Lysistrata*.

Romano v. Harrington
725 F.Supp. 687 (E.D. N.Y. 1989)

The U.S. District Court found in favor of a faculty adviser to a high school newspaper who claimed a violation of the First and Fourteenth Amendments when fired following the newspaper's publication of a student's article opposing the federal holiday for Martin Luther King, Jr. The Court held that educators may exercise greater editorial control over what students write for class than what they voluntarily submit to extracurricular publications.

Cohen v. San Bernardino Valley College
92 F.3d 968 (9th Cir. 1996)

A tenured professor of English was disciplined for violating the college's sexual harassment policy against creating a "hostile learning environment" for his in-class use of profanity, and discussions of sex, pornography, obscenity, cannibalism, and other controversial topics in a confrontational, devil's advocate style. The court held the policy unconstitutionally vague as applied to Cohen's in-class speech, calling it a "legalistic ambush." In-class speech did not fall within the policy's core definition of sexual harassment and Cohen, who had used this apparently sound and proper teaching style for years, did not know the policy would be applied to him or his teaching methods.

Notable First Amendment Court Cases

See also:

Evans v. Shelma Union High School District of Fresno County, 222 P. 801 (Ca. 1924)

West Virginia State Board of Education v. Barnette, 319 U.S. 624 (1943)

Rosenberg v. Board of Education of City of New York, 92 N.Y.S.2d 344 (Sup. Ct. Kings County 1949)

Todd v. Rochester Community Schools, 200 N.W.2d 90 (Mich. Ct. App. 1972)

Minarcini v. Strongsville (Ohio) City School District, 541 F.2d 577 (6th Cir. 1976)

Right to Read Defense Committee v. School Committee of the City of Chelsea, 454 F.Supp. 703 (D. Mass. 1978)

Salvail v. Nashua Board of Education, 469 F.Supp. 1269 (D. N.H. 1979)

Loewen v. Turnipseed, 488 F.Supp. 1138 (N.D. Miss. 1980)

Case v. Unified School District No. 233, 908 F.Supp. 864 (D. Kan. 1995)

Campbell v. St. Tammany Parish School Board, 64 F.3d 184 (5th Cir. 1995)

Counts v. Cedarville School District, 295 F.Supp.2d 996 (W.D. Ark. 2003)

Minors' First Amendment Rights

American Amusement Machine Association, et al., v. Teri Kendrick, et al.

244 F.3d 954 (7th Cir. 2001); cert. denied, 534 U.S. 994; 122 S.Ct. 462; 151 L.Ed.2d 379 (2001).

Enacted in July 2001, an Indianapolis, Indiana, city ordinance required video game arcade owners to limit access to games that depicted certain activities, including amputation, decapitation, dismemberment, bloodshed, or sexual intercourse. Only with the permission of an accompanying parent or guardian could children seventeen years old and younger play these types of video games. On March 23, 2001, a three-judge panel of the Seventh Circuit Court of Appeals reversed and remanded the trial court's decision stating that "children have First Amendment rights." On Monday, October 29, 2001, the U.S. Supreme Court denied certiorari.

Interactive Digital Software Association, et al., v. St. Louis County, Missouri, et al.

329 F.3d 954 (8th Cir. 2003)

St. Louis County passed an ordinance banning selling or renting violent video games to minors, or permitting them to play such games, without parental consent, and video game dealers sued to overturn the law. The Court of Appeals found the ordinance unconstitutional, holding that depictions of violence alone cannot fall within the legal definition of obscenity for either minors or adults, and that a government cannot silence protected speech for children by wrapping itself in the cloak of parental authority. The Court ordered the lower court to enter an injunction barring enforcement of the law, citing the Supreme Court's recognition in *Erznoznik v. Jacksonville, 422 U.S. 205, 213-14, 45 L.Ed.2d 125, 95 S.Ct. 2268 (1975)* that "speech that is neither obscene as to youths nor subject to some other legitimate proscription cannot be suppressed solely to protect the young from ideas or images that a legislative body thinks unsuitable for them. In most circumstances, the values protected by the First Amendment are no less applicable when the government seeks to control the flow of information to minors."

See also:

West Virginia State Board of Education v. Barnette, 319 U.S. 624 (1943)

Ginsberg v. New York, 390 U.S. 629 (1968)

Tinker v. Des Moines Independent Community School District, 393 U.S. 503, 89 S.Ct. 733, 21 L.Ed.2d 731 (1969)

Board of Education, Island Trees Union Free School District No. 26 v. Pico, 457 U.S. 853, 102 S.Ct. 2799, 73 L.Ed.2d 435 (1982)

Free Press

New York Times Company v. United States

403 U.S. 713, 91 S.Ct. 2140, 29 L.Ed.2d 822 (1971)

In the "Pentagon Papers" case, the U.S. government attempted to enjoin the *New York Times* and the *Washington Post* from publishing classified documents concerning the Vietnam War. Applying the doctrine of prior restraint from *Near v. Minnesota,* the Court found that the claims that publication of the documents would interfere with foreign policy and prolong the war were too speculative, and could not overcome the strong presumption against prior restraints.

Hustler Magazine, Inc. v. Falwell

485 U.S. 46, 108 S.Ct. 876, 99 L.Ed.2d 41 (1988)

Hustler magazine published a parody of a liquor advertisement in which Rev. Jerry Falwell described his "first time" as a drunken encounter with his mother in an outhouse. A unanimous Supreme Court held that a public figure had to show actual malice in order to recover for intentional infliction of emotional distress as a result of a parody in a magazine. The Court held that political cartoons

187

and satire such as this parody "have played a prominent role in public and political debate." And although the outrageous caricature in this case "is at best a distant cousin of political cartoons," the Court could see no standard to distinguish among types of parodies that would not harm public discourse, which would be poorer without such satire.

Simon & Schuster, Inc. v. Members of New York State Crime Victims Board
502 U.S. 105, 112 S.Ct. 501, 116 L.Ed.2d 476 (1991)

The Supreme Court struck down New York's "Son of Sam Law," which required book publishers to turn over to the state any proceeds from a book written by any person convicted of a crime, related to, or about that crime. The Court said the law impermissibly singled out income only from the prisoner's expressive activity, and then only expressive activity relating to his crime, without necessarily compensating any victims of those crimes. The Court agreed that many important books—including *The Autobiography of Malcolm X*, Thoreau's *Civil Disobedience*, and works by Martin Luther King—perhaps might not have been published with such a law in place.

See also:

The New York Times v. Sullivan, 376 U.S. 254, 84 S.Ct. 710, 11 L.Ed.2d 686 (1964)

Gertz v. Robert Welch, Inc., 418 U.S. 323, 94 S.Ct. 2997, 41 L.Ed.2d 789 (1974)

The Right to Dissent

West Virginia State Board of Education v. Barnette
319 U.S. 624, 87 L.Ed. 1628, 63 S.Ct. 1178 (1943)

In 1940, the West Virginia Board of Education issued regulations requiring every schoolchild to participate daily in a salute to the flag of the United States. The Barnette children, all members of the Jehovah's Witnesses, refused to participate in the flag salute, consistent with the tenets of their religious beliefs, and were expelled from school. The Supreme Court struck down the regulation on the grounds that the First Amendment barred any rule compelling an individual to salute the flag or participate in the Pledge of Allegiance. In strong language, the Court affirmed the right to dissent: "But freedom to differ is not limited to things that do not matter much. That would be a mere shadow of freedom. The test of its substance is the right to differ as to things that touch the heart of the existing order. If there is any fixed star in our constitutional constellation, it is that no official, high

or petty, can prescribe what shall be orthodox in politics, nationalism, religion, or other matters of opinion, or force citizens to confess by word or act their faith therein. If there are any circumstances which permit an exception, they do not now occur to us."

Texas v. Johnson
491 U.S. 397, 109 S.Ct. 2533, 105 L.Ed.2d 342 (1989)

In this case the Supreme Court held that burning the United States flag was a protected form of symbolic political speech, concluding that there is no legitimate government interest in protecting the U.S. flag where the sole act in question is destroying the flag in its symbolic capacity. "A bedrock principle underlying the First Amendment is that Government may not prohibit the expression of an idea simply because society finds the idea itself offensive or disagreeable."

U.S. v. Eichman and U.S. v. Haggerty
496 U.S. 310, 110 S.Ct. 2404, 110 L.Ed.2d 287 (1990)

The Supreme Court struck down a federal statute designed to allow the government to punish persons who burn United States flags. The Court held that the plain intent of the statute was to punish persons for political expression and that burning the flag inextricably carries with it a political message.

City of Ladue v. Gilleo
512 U.S. 43, 114 S.Ct. 2038, 129 L.Ed.2d 36 (1994)

A federal court struck down a local ordinance banning the placement of signs on private property, in a challenge brought by a woman who had posted a sign on her lawn protesting the Persian Gulf War. The Court said lawn signs were a "venerable means of communication that is both unique and important," for which "no adequate substitutes exist."

R.A.V. v. St. Paul
505 U.S. 377, 112 S.Ct. 2538, 120 L.Ed.2d 305 (1992)

St. Paul, Minnesota, passed an ordinance that banned "hate speech," any expression, such as a burning cross or swastika, that might arouse anger, alarm, or resentment in others on the basis of race, color, religion, or gender. The Supreme Court struck the ordinance down as unconstitutionally discriminating based on the content of expression: the law banned only fighting words that insult based on race, religion, or gender, while abusive invective aimed at someone on the basis of political affiliation or sexual orientation would be permissible. The law thus reflected only the city's special hostility towards certain biases and not others, which is what the First Amendment forbids.

See also:

Tinker v. Des Moines Independent Community School District, 393 U.S. 503, 89 S.Ct. 733, 21 L.Ed.2d 731 (1969)

The Right to Free Association and the Freedom of Religion

Concerned Women for America, Inc. v. Lafayette County

883 F.2d 32 (5th Cir. 1989)

The County library that had permitted various groups to use its auditorium had created a designated public forum and thus could not deny access to groups whose meetings had political or religious content. Such a denial would be based on the content of speech and would be permissible only as the least restrictive means to serve a compelling interest. Preventing disruption or interference with general use of the library could be such an interest; library officials' first step to controlling such disruptions would be to impose reasonable regulations on the time, place, or manner of the auditorium's use, provided the regulations apply regardless of the subject matter of the speech.

Lamb's Chapel v. Center Moriches Union Free School Dist.

508 U.S. 384, 113 S.Ct. 2141, 124 L.Ed.2d 352 (1993)

The Court held that a school district that opened its classrooms after hours to a range of groups for social, civic, and recreational purposes, including films and lectures about a range of issues such as family values and child-rearing, could not deny access to a religious organization to discuss the same, permissible issues from a religious point of view. Whether or not the classrooms were public fora, the school district could not deny use based on the speaker's point of view on an otherwise permissible topic.

Right to Privacy and Anonymity

Stanley v. Georgia

394 U.S. 55, 22 L.Ed. 2d 542, 89 S.Ct. 1243 (1969)

A man found to possess obscene materials in his home for his private use was convicted of possessing obscene materials in violation of the state laws of Georgia. The Supreme Court overturned the conviction, holding that Constitution protects the right to receive information and ideas, regardless of their social worth, and to be generally free from governmental intrusions into one's privacy on the grounds that the government "cannot constitutionally premise legislation on the desirability of controlling a person's private thoughts."

McIntyre v. Ohio Election Commission

514 U.S. 334, 115 S.Ct. 1511, 131 L.Ed.2d 426 (1995)

The Supreme Court struck down a state law banning distribution of anonymous campaign literature, emphasizing the long tradition of anonymous and pseudonymous political and literary speech and recognizing the right to exercise First Amendment rights anonymously as an "honorable tradition of advocacy and dissent."

Tattered Cover, Inc. v. City of Thornton

44 P.3d 1044 (Colo. Sup. Ct., 2002)

The Colorado Supreme Court reversed a court decision that required Denver's Tattered Cover Book Store to turn over information about books purchased by one of its customers. As part of an investigation, officers of the City of Thornton (Colo.) discovered two books on the manufacture of amphetamines in a suspect's residence and found a Tattered Cover mailer in the garbage. The officers, seeking to tie the books to the suspect directly, served a Drug Enforcement Agency subpoena on the Tattered Cover. The subpoena demanded the title of the books corresponding to the order and invoice numbers of the mailer, as well as information about all other books ever ordered by the suspect. The Tattered Cover then brought suit to litigate the validity of the search warrant. The court began its opinion by stating that both the First Amendment to the U.S. Constitution and Article II, Section 10 of the Colorado Constitution protect an individual's fundamental right to purchase books anonymously, free from governmental interference.

When Is Speech Unprotected?

OBSCENITY AND INDECENCY

Butler v. Michigan

352 U.S. 380, 1 L.Ed.2d 412, 77 S.Ct. 524 (1957)

A man convicted of selling "a book containing obscene, immoral, lewd, lascivious language, or descriptions, tending to incite minors to violent or depraved or immoral acts, manifestly tending to the corruption of the morals of youth" to a police officer appealed his conviction to the Supreme

189

Court. The Court overturned the conviction and struck down the law, holding that the state's attempt to quarantine the general reading public against books not too rugged for grown men and women to read in order to shield juvenile innocence "is to burn the house to roast the pig." Famously, the Court ruled that the state of Michigan could not "reduce the adult population of Michigan to reading only what is fit for children."

Ginsberg v. New York

390 U.S. 62, 20 L.Ed.2d 195, 88 S.Ct. 1274 (1968)

The Supreme Court upheld a New York State statute barring retailers from selling sexually explicit publications to minors under the age of seventeen. Noting that the statute did not interfere with the right of adults to purchase and read such materials, it found that it was not constitutionally impermissible for New York to restrict minors rights to such publications in light of the state's interest in safeguarding children's welfare and supporting parents' claim to authority in the rearing of their children.

Miller v. California

413 U.S. 15, 93 S.Ct. 2607, 37 L.Ed.2d 419 (1973)

In this case, the U.S. Supreme Court mapped out its famous three-part definition of obscenity. First, the average person, applying contemporary community standards, must find that the work, taken as a whole, appeals to prurient interests; second, that it depicts or describes, in a patently offensive way, sexual conduct as defined by state law; and third, that the work, taken as a whole, lacks serious literary, artistic, political, or scientific value. The Court ruled that community standards and state statutes that describe sexual depictions to be suppressed could be used to prosecute Miller, who operated one of the largest West Coast mail order businesses dealing in sexually explicit materials.

New York v. Ferber

458 U.S. 747, 102 S.Ct. 3348, 73 L.Ed.2d 1113 (1982)

In July 1982, the U.S. Supreme Court added child pornography as another category of speech excluded from First Amendment protection. The other categories excluded are obscenity, defamation, incitement, and "fighting words." The ruling came in the case when the U.S. Supreme Court affirmed a conviction against Ferber for showing a movie depicting two young boys masturbating. The film itself was not seen as obscene for adults, but the Court made the distinction between what was obscene if children were the participants compared with if adults were the leading actors.

American Booksellers Assoc., Inc. v. Hudnut

771 F.2d 323 (7th Cir. 1985) (Easterbrook, J.), aff'd, 475 U.S. 1001, 106 S.Ct. 1172, 89 L.Ed.2d 291 (1986)

The city of Indianapolis passed a statute outlawing pornography, defined as the graphic, sexually explicit subordination of women, presenting women as sex objects, or as enjoying pain, humiliation, or servility. The court of appeals struck the law down, saying it impermissibly established an "approved" view of women and how they react in sexual encounters. The law therefore allowed sexually explicit words and images that adhered to that approved view, but banned sexually explicit words and images that did not adhere to the approved view. The court called this "thought control," saying the "Constitution forbids the state to declare one perspective right and silence opponents."

National Endowment for the Arts, et al. v. Finley, et al.

524 U.S. 569, 118 S.Ct. 2168, 141 L.Ed.2d 500 (1998)

In 1990, homoerotic photographs by Robert Mapplethorpe and blasphemous ones by Andres Serrano created a furor on Capitol Hill because both artists had received grants from the National Endowment for the Arts (NEA). As a consequence, the NEA governing statute was amended to require the NEA to consider "decency" and "respect" for American "values" when selecting future grant recipients. Shortly thereafter, performance artists Karen Finley, John Fleck, Holly Hughes, and Tim Miller were denied fellowships because of the "decency and respect" clause, they alleged. They made this allegation in a federal court lawsuit seeking to have the clause declared unconstitutional; and they were successful at the district court and court of appeals level. The U.S. Supreme Court ruled, however, that the statute is constitutional "on its face." Writing for the court, Justice Sandra Day O'Connor did not "perceive a realistic danger that it will be utilized to preclude or punish the expression of particular views," nor did she think that the statute would "significantly compromise First Amendment values."

John D. Ashcroft, Attorney General, et al. v. Free Speech Coalition, et al.

535 U.S. 234, 122 S.Ct. 1389, 152 L.Ed.2d 403, (2002)

The U.S. Supreme Court affirmed the Ninth Circuit's judgment invalidating the Child Pornography Prevention Act of 1996 on the grounds that the act's ban on any depiction of pornographic images of children, including computer-generated images, was overly broad and unconstitutional under the First Amendment. Supreme Court Justice

Anthony M. Kennedy wrote: "First Amendment freedoms are most in danger when the government seeks to control thought or to justify its laws for that impermissible end. The right to think is the beginning of freedom, and speech must be protected from the government because speech is the beginning of thought."

See also:

Stanley v. Georgia, 394 U.S. 55, 22 L.Ed.2d 542, 89 S.Ct. 1243 (1969)

LIBEL

The New York Times v. Sullivan

376 U.S. 254, 84 S.Ct. 710, 11 L.Ed.2d 686 (1964)

To protect "uninhibited, robust, and wide-open" debate on public issues, the Supreme Court held that no public official may recover "damages for a defamatory falsehood relating to his official conduct unless he proves that the statement was made with 'actual malice'—that is, with knowledge that it was false or with reckless disregard of whether it was false or not." The Court stated that the First and Fourteenth Amendments require that critics of official conduct have the "fair equivalent" to the immunity protection given to a public official when he is sued for defamatory speech uttered in the course of his duties.

Gertz v. Robert Welch, Inc.

418 U.S. 323, 94 S.Ct. 2997, 41 L.Ed.2d 789 (1974)

The Court applied the rule in the *New York Times* case to public figures, finding that persons who have special prominence in society by virtue of their fame or notoriety, even if they are not public officials, must prove "actual malice" when alleging libel. Gertz was a prominent lawyer who alleged that a leaflet defamed him.

See also:

Hustler Magazine, Inc. v. Falwell, 485 U.S. 46, 108 S.Ct. 876, 99 L.Ed.2d 41 (1988)

The First Amendment and New Technologies

BROADCAST AND CABLE COMMUNICATIONS

FCC v. Pacifica Foundation

438 U.S. 726, 57 L.Ed.2d 1073, 98 S.Ct. 3026 (1978)

In a case that considered the First Amendment protections extended to a radio station's daytime broadcast of comedian George Carlin's "Seven Filthy Words" monologue, the Supreme Court held that Section 326 of the Telecommunications Act, which prohibits the FCC from censoring broadcasts over radio or television, does not limit the FCC's authority to sanction radio or television stations broadcasting material that is obscene, indecent, or profane. Though the censorship ban under Section 326 precludes editing proposed broadcasts in advance, the ban does not deny the FCC the power to review the content of completed broadcasts. In its decision, the Court concluded that broadcast materials have limited First Amendment protection because of the uniquely pervasive presence that radio and television occupy in the lives of people, and the unique ability of children to access radio and television broadcasts.

Denver Area Educational Telecommunications Consortium, Inc. v. FCC

518 U.S. 727, 116 S.Ct. 2374, 135 L.Ed.2d 288 (1996)

In a decision that produced six opinions, the Supreme Court upheld a federal law permitting cable system operators to ban "indecent" or "patently offensive" speech on leased access channels. The Court also struck down a similar law for non-leased, public access channels, and struck down a law requiring indecent material to be shown on separate, segregated cable channels. The case is significant in that the Court affirmed that protecting children from some speech is a compelling state interest.

United States, et al. v. Playboy Entertainment Group, Inc.

529 U.S. 803, 120 S.Ct. 1878, 146 L.Ed.2d 865 (2000)

On May 22, in a 5-4 decision, the U.S. Supreme Court upheld a U.S. District Court decision that Section 505 of the Telecommunications Act of 1996 violated the First Amendment when it sought to restrict certain cable channels with sexually explicit content to late night hours unless they fully scrambled their signal bleed. In an opinion written by Justice Anthony Kennedy, the court ruled that the government may have a legitimate interest in protecting children from exposure to "indecent material." Section 505, however, is a content-based speech restriction and, therefore, must be the least restrictive means for meeting the governmental interest. The court found that Section 505 is not the least restrictive means.

TELECOMMUNICATIONS

Sable Communications of California, Inc. v. FCC

492 U.S. 115, 106 L.Ed.2d 93, 109 S.Ct. 2829 (1989)

The Supreme Court overturned a Telecommunications Act ban on indecent telephone messages, concluding the law violates the First Amendment because the statute's denial of adult access to such messages far exceeds that which is necessary to serve the compelling interest of preventing minors from being exposed to the messages. Unlike broadcast radio and television, which can intrude on the privacy of the home without prior warning of content and which is uniquely accessible to children, telephone communications require the listener to take affirmative steps to receive the communications. The failure of the government to show any findings that would justify a conclusion that there are no constitutionally acceptable less restrictive means to achieve the government's interest in protecting minors, such as scrambling or the use of access codes, demonstrates that a total ban on such communications goes too far in restricting constitutionally protected speech. To allow the ban to stand would have the effect of "limiting the content of adult telephone communications to that which is suitable for children to hear."

THE INTERNET

American Library Association v. U.S. Department of Justice and Reno v. American Civil Liberties Union
521 U.S. 844, 117 S.Ct. 2329, 138 L.Ed.2d 874 (1997)
In a 9–0 decision, the U.S. Supreme Court on June 26, 1997, declared unconstitutional a federal law making it a crime to send or display indecent material online in a way available to minors. The decision in the consolidated cases completed a successful challenge to the so-called Communications Decency Act by the Citizens Internet Empowerment Coalition, in which the American Library Association and the Freedom to Read Foundation played leading roles. The Court held that speech on the Internet is entitled to the highest level of First Amendment protection, similar to the protection the Court gives to books and newspapers.

Mainstream Loudoun, et al. v. Board of Trustees of the Loudoun County Library
24 F.Supp.2d 552 (E.D. of Va. 1998)
Adopted in 1997, the Loudoun County, Virginia, Library Board's "Policy on Internet Sexual Harassment" was designed to prevent adult and minor Internet users from accessing illegal pornography and to avoid the creation of a sexually hostile environment. To accomplish these goals, the board contracted with Log-On Data Corporation, a filtering software manufacturer that offers a product called "X-Stop." Though Log-On Data Corp. refused to divulge the method by which X-Stop filters sites, it soon became apparent that the software blocks some sites that are not prohibited by the policy. Shortly after the adoption of the policy, People for the American Way Foundation commenced litigation on behalf of several Loudoun County residents and members of a nonprofit organization, claiming the policy violates the right to free speech under the First Amendment. The suit was predicated on the theory that the policy is unnecessarily restrictive because it treats adults and children similarly, and precludes access to legitimate as well as pornographic material. On November 23, 1998, Judge Leonie Brinkema declared that the highly restrictive Loudoun County Internet policy was invalid under the free speech provisions of the First Amendment.

United States, et al. v. American Library Association, Inc. et al.
539 U.S. 194, 123 S.Ct. 2297, 156 L.Ed.2d 221 (2003)
The Supreme Court upheld the Children's Internet Protection Act, which requires libraries receiving federal funds for Internet access to install filters so that both adult and child patrons cannot access materials considered obscene, child pornography, or "harmful to minors." Chief Justice Rehnquist announced the judgment of the court that the law, on its face, is constitutional. Speaking for a plurality of four justices, Rehnquist held that CIPA was a valid exercise of Congress' spending power and did not impose an unconstitutional condition on public libraries that received federal assistance for Internet access because Congress could reasonably impose limitations on its Internet assistance, and because any concerns over filtering software's alleged tendency to erroneously "overblock" access to constitutionally protected speech were dispelled by the ease with which library patrons could have the filtering software disabled. Justices Kennedy and Breyer concurred with the judgment, holding that CIPA, while raising First Amendment concerns, did not violate the First Amendment as long as adult library users could request that the Internet filter be disabled without delay.

Quotes on the First Amendment

Attic
The Giving Tree
Harry Potter
Huck Finn
The Lorax
Mother Goose

"The public library is the most dangerous place in town."

John Ciardi

"Censorship is telling a man he can't have a steak just because a baby can't chew it."

Mark Twain

193

Quotes on the First Amendment

"Freedom of thought and freedom of speech in our great institutions of learning are absolutely necessary . . . the moment that either is restricted, liberty begins to wither and die and the career of a nation after that time is downwards."

John Peter Altgeld,
Governor of Illinois, 1893–1897 (1847–1902).

"Intellectual freedom, the essence of equitable library services, promotes no cause, furthers no movements, and favors no viewpoints. It only provides for free access to all expressions of ideas through which any and all sides of a question, cause, or movement may be explored. Toleration is meaningless without tolerance for what some may consider detestable. Librarians cannot justly permit their own preferences to limit their degree of tolerance in collection development, because freedom is indivisible."

American Library Association. Office for Intellectual
Freedom. Intellectual Freedom Manual, seventh ed.
Chicago: ALA, 2006, p. 126.

"The use of 'religion' as an excuse to repress the freedom of expression and to deny human rights is not confined to any country or time."

Margaret Atwood. Letter.
Index on Censorship. 1995.

"The freedom to share one's insights and judgments verbally or in writing is, just like the freedom to think, a holy and inalienable right of humanity that, as a universal human right, is above all the rights of princes."

Carl Friedrich Bahrdt.
On Freedom of the Press and Its Limits. 1787.

"The oppression of any people for opinion's sake has rarely had any other effect than to fix those opinions deeper, and render them more important."

Hosea Ballou, U.S. educator (1796–1861).

"To permit every interest group, especially those who claim to be victimized by unfair expression, their own legislative exceptions to the First Amendment so long as as they succeed in obtaining a majority of legislative votes in their favor demonstrates the potentially predatory nature of what defendants seek through this Ordinance and defend in this lawsuit.

"It ought to be remembered by defendants and all others who would support such a legislative initiative that, in terms of altering sociological patterns, much as alteration may be necessary and desirable, free speech, rather than being the enemy, is a long-tested and worthy ally. To deny free speech in order to engineer social change in the name of accomplishing a greater good for one sector of our society erodes the freedoms of all and, as such, threatens tyranny and injustice for those subjected to the rule of such laws. The First Amendment protections presuppose the evil of such tyranny and prevent a finding by this Court upholding the Ordinance."

U.S. District Court Southern District of Indiana
Judge Sarah Evans Barker. American Booksellers
Association, Inc. et al. v. William H. Hudnut III. U.S.
District Court, 598 F. Supp. 1316 (S.D. Ind. 1984).

"Thought that is silenced is always rebellious. Majorities, of course, are often mistaken. This is why the silencing of minorities is necessarily dangerous. Criticism and dissent are the indispensable antidote to major delusions."

Alan Barth. The Loyalty of Free Men.
London: Gollancz, 1951.

"As long as I don't write about the government, religion, politics, and other institutions, I am free to print anything."

Pierre-Augustin Caron de Beaumarchais,
French writer (1732–1799).

"I'm in favour of free expression provided it's kept rigidly under control."

Alan Bennett, British playwright (1934–).

"Political correctness is really a subjective list put together by the few to rule the many—a list of things one must think, say, or do. It affronts the right of the individual to establish his or her own beliefs."

Mark Berley. Argos, Spring 1998.

"In order to get the truth, conflicting arguments and expression must be allowed. There can be no freedom without choice, no sound choice without knowledge."

David Knipe Berninghausen. Arrogance of the
Censor, 1982, quoted from Mike Reed, "Scientology,
Censorship, President."

"The layman's constitutional view is that what he likes is constitutional and that which he doesn't like is unconstitutional."

U.S. Supreme Court Justice Hugo L. Black.
New York Times, February 26, 1971.

Quotes on the First Amendment

"I fear more harm from everybody thinking alike than from some people thinking otherwise."

Charles G. Bolte, U.S. publisher and Carnegie Endowment for International Peace (1920–1994).

"Censorship is the mother of metaphor."

Jorge Luis Borges, Argentine novelist and poet (1899–1986).

"Without free speech no search for truth is possible. . . . no discovery of truth is useful. Better thousandfold abuse of free speech than denial of free speech. The abuse dies in a day, but the denial slays the life of the people, and entombs the hope of the race."

Charles Bradlaugh, British freethinker and reformer (1833–1891).

"Correctly applied, (the clear and present danger test) . . . will preserve the right of free speech from suppression by tyrannous majorities and from abuse by irresponsible, fanatical minorities."

U.S. Supreme Court Justice Louis Dembitz Brandeis, Schaefer v. U.S., 251 U.S. 466, 40 S.Ct. 259, 64 L.Ed. 360 (1920).

"Those who won our independence by revolution were not cowards. They did not fear political change. They did not exalt order at the cost of liberty. . . . If there be time to expose through discussion the falsehood and fallacies, to avert the evil by the processes of education, the remedy to be applied is more speech, not enforced silence."

U.S. Supreme Court Justice Louis Dembitz Brandeis, Whitney v. California, 274 US 357, 47 S.Ct. 641, 71 L.Ed. 1095 (1927).

"Experience teaches us to be most on our guard to protect liberty when the government's purpose is beneficent. The greatest dangers to liberty lurk in insidious encroachments by men of zeal, well-meaning but without understanding."

U.S. Supreme Court Justice Louis Dembitz Brandeis, dissenting, Olmstead v. United States, 277 U.S. 438, 48 S.Ct. 564, 72 L.Ed. 944 (1928).

"Debate on public issues should be uninhibited, robust, and wide-open and that . . . may well include vehement, caustic, and sometimes unpleasantly sharp attacks on government and public officials."

U.S. Supreme Court Justice William Brennan, New York Times v. Sullivan, 376 U.S. 254, 84 S.Ct. 710, 11 L.Ed.2d 686 (1964).

"If there is a bedrock principle underlying the First Amendment, it is that the Government may not prohibit the expression of an idea simply because society finds the idea itself offensive or disagreeable."

U.S. Supreme Court Justice William Brennan, Texas v. Johnson, 491 U.S. 397, 109 S.Ct. 2533, 105 L.Ed.2d 342 (1989).

"Everybody favours free speech in the slack moments when no axes are being ground."

Heywood Broun, U.S. journalist (1888–1939).

"Censorship is the tool of those who have the need to hide actualities from themselves and others. Their fear is only their inability to face what is real. Somewhere in their upbringing they were shielded against the total facts of our experience. They were only taught to look one way when many ways exist."

Charles Bukowski, U.S. writer and poet (1920–1994).

"The only thing necessary for the triumph of evil is for good men to do nothing."

Edmund Burke, British orator, philosopher, and politician (1729–1797).

"Freedom of expression is the matrix, the indispensible condition, of nearly every other form of freedom."

U.S. Supreme Court Justice Benjamin Nathan Cardozo, Palko v. Connecticut, 302 U.S. 319, 58 S.Ct. 149, 82 L.Ed. 288 (1937).

"If we don't believe in freedom of expression for people we despise, we don't believe in it at all."

Noam Chomsky, U.S. professor of linguistics (1928–).

"From a comparative perspective, the United States is unusual if not unique in the lack of restraints on freedom of expression. It is also unusual in the range and effectiveness of methods employed to restrain freedom of thought... Where the voice of the people is heard, elite groups must insure their voice says the right things."

Noam Chomsky, Index on Censorship, July/August 1986.

Quotes on the First Amendment

"Everyone is in favor of free speech. Hardly a day passes without it being extolled, but some people's idea of it is that they are free to say what they like, but if anyone says anything back, that is an outrage."

Sir Winston Churchill,
British statesman and author (1874–1965).

"You see these dictators on their pedestals, surrounded by the bayonets of their soldiers and the truncheons of their police. Yet in their hearts there is unspoken—unspeakable!—fear. They are afraid of words and thoughts! Words spoken abroad, thoughts stirring at home, all the more powerful because they are forbidden. These terrify them. A little mouse—a little tiny mouse!—of thought appears in the room, and even the mightiest potentates are thrown into panic."

Sir Winston Churchill.

"The public library is the most dangerous place in town."

John Ciardi, U.S. poet and critic (1916–1986).

"The fact is that censorship always defeats its own purpose, for it creates, in the end, the kind of society that is incapable of exercising real discretion. . . . In the long run it will create a generation incapable of appreciating the difference between independence of thought and subservience."

Henry Steel Commager, U.S. historian (1902–1998).

"The irony of book-banning attempts is that the publicity often causes people to read the books for the wrong reasons. If a book is controversial, perhaps the best place for it is the classroom where, under the guidance of a teacher, the book can be discussed and evaluated, where each student will be free to proclaim how he or she feels about the book and, in fact, can even refuse to read the book. The point is that free choice must be involved."

Robert Cormier, in Foerstel, Herbert N. **Banned in the U.S.A.: A Reference Guide to Book Censorship in Schools and Public Libraries.** *Westport, Conn.: Greenwood Press, 2002, p. 156.*

"The library is not a shrine for the worship of books. It is not a temple where literary incense must be burned or where one's devotion to the bound book is expressed in ritual. A library, to modify the famous metaphor of Socrates, should be the delivery room for the birth of ideas—a place where history comes to life."

Norman Cousins,
U.S editor and essayist (1912–1990).

"What censorship accomplishes, creating an unreal and hypocritical mythology, fomenting an attraction for forbidden fruit, inhibiting the creative minds among us and fostering an illicit trade. Above all, it curtails the right of the individual, be he creator or consumer, to satisfy his intellect and his interest without harm. In our law-rooted society, we are not the keeper of our brother's morals—only of his rights."

Judith Crist. **Censorship: For and Against, 1971.**

"Freedom of the press is not just important to democracy, it is democracy."

Walter Leland Cronkite, U.S. journalist and radio and television news broadcaster (1916–).

"Students throughout the totalitarian world risk life and limb for freedom of expression, many American college students are demanding that big brother restrict their freedom of speech on campus. This demand for enhanced censorship is not emanating only from the usual corner—the know-nothing fundamentalist right—it is coming from the radical, and increasingly not-so-radical left as well."

Alan Dershowitz. **Shouting Fire: Civil Liberties in a Turbulent Age.** *Boston: Little, Brown, 2002.*

"The function of free speech under our system of government is to invite dispute. It may indeed best serve its high purpose when it invites a condition of unrest, creates dissatisfaction with conditions as they are, or even stirs people to anger. Speech is often provocative and challenging. It may strike at prejudices and preconceptions and have profound unsettling effects as it passes for acceptance of an idea."

U.S. Supreme Court Justice William O. Douglas,
Terminello v. Chicago, 337 U.S. 1,
69 S.Ct. 894, 93 L.Ed. 1131 (1949).

"It is our attitude toward free thought and free expression that will determine our fate. There must be no limit on the range of temperate discussion, no limits on thought. No subject must be taboo. No censor must preside at our assemblies."

U.S. Supreme Court Justice William O. Douglas,
address, Author's Guild, December 3, 1952, on receiving the Lauterbach Award.

"Restriction of free thought and free speech is the most dangerous of all subversions. It is the one un-American act that could most easily defeat us."

U.S. Supreme Court Justice William O. Douglas,
address, Author's Guild, December 3, 1952, on receiving the Lauterbach Award.

Quotes on the First Amendment

"One has the right to freedom of speech whether he talks to one person or to 1,000."

U.S. Supreme Court Justice William O. Douglas, United States v. International Union Auto. Workers, 352 U.S. 567, 77 S.Ct. 529, 1 L.Ed.2d 563 (1957).

"[T]he ultimate welfare of the single human soul (is) the ultimate test of the vitality of the First Amendment."

U.S. Supreme Court Justice William O. Douglas, Gillette v. United States, 401 U.S. 437, 91 S.Ct. 828, 28 L.Ed.2d 168 (1971).

"A government that can give liberty in its constitution ought to have the power to protect liberty in its administration."

Frederick Douglass, U.S. abolitionist and journalist (1817–1895).

"When books are challenged, restricted, removed, or banned, an atmosphere of suppression exists. . . . The fear of the consequences of censorship is as damaging as, or perhaps more damaging than, the actual censorship attempt. After all, when a published work is banned, it can usually be found elsewhere. Unexpressed ideas, unpublished works, unpurchased books are lost forever."

Robert P. Doyle. Banned Books: 1998 Resource Guide. Chicago: ALA, 1998, p. ii.

"Free speech has been on balance an ally of those seeking change. Governments that want stasis start by restricting speech. . . . Change in any complex system ultimately depends on the ability of outsiders to challenge accepted views and the reigning institutions. Without a strong guarantee of freedom of speech, there is no effective right to challenge what is."

U.S. Court of Appeals for the Seventh Circuit Judge Frank H. Easterbrook, American Booksellers Association, Inc. et al. v. William H. Hudnut III, 771 F.2d 323 (7th Cir. 1985).

"It is evident that any restriction of academic freedom acts in such a way to hamper the dissemination of knowledge among the people and thereby impedes national judgment and action."

Albert Einstein, U.S. (German-born) physicist (1879–1955).

"Don't join the book burners. Don't think you are going to conceal thoughts by concealing evidence that they ever existed."

Dwight D. Eisenhower, speech at Dartmouth College, June 14, 1953.

"The libraries of America are and must ever remain the home of free, inquiring minds. To them, our citizens—of all ages and races, of all creeds and political persuasions—must ever be able to turn with clear confidence that there they can freely seek the whole truth, unwarped by fashion and uncompromised by expediency. For in such whole and healthy knowledge alone are to be found and understood those majestic truths of man's nature and destiny that prove, to each succeeding generation, the validity of freedom."

Dwight D. Eisenhower, letter to the American Library Association's Annual Conference, Los Angeles, 1953.

"Censorship is advertising paid by the government."

Federico Fellini, Italian film director (1920–1993).

"If the human body's obscene, complain to the manufacturer, not me."

Larry Flynt, Hustler magazine publisher (1942–).

"Students in school as well as out of schools are 'persons' under our Constitution. They are possessed of fundamental rights which the state must respect. . . . It can hardly be argued that either students or teachers shed their constitutional rights to freedom of speech or expression at the schoolhouse gate."

U.S. Supreme Court Justice Abe Fortas, Tinker et al. v. Des Moines Independent Community School District et al., 393 U.S. 503, 89 S.Ct. 733, 21 L.Ed.2d 731 (1969).

"Liberty is always dangerous, but it is the safest thing we have."

Harry Emerson Fosdick, U.S. clergyman (1878–1969).

"Freedom of the press is not an end in itself but a means to the end of [achieving] a free society."

U.S. Supreme Court Justice Felix Frankfurter, Pennekamp et al. v. Florida, 328 U.S. 331, 66 S.Ct. 1029, 90 L.Ed. 1295 (1946).

Quotes on the First Amendment

"Whoever would overthrow the liberty of a nation must begin by subduing the freeness of speech."

Benjamin Franklin,
U.S. author, diplomat, inventor, physicist, politician, and printer (1706–1790).

"They that can give up essential liberty to obtain a little temporary safety deserve neither liberty nor safety."

Benjamin Franklin.
Historical Review of Pennsylvania, 1759.

"If all printers were determined not to print anything till they were sure it would offend nobody, there would be very little printed."

Benjamin Franklin, 1730.

"What progress we are making. In the Middle Ages they would have burned me. Now they are content with burning my books."

Sigmund Freud,
Austrian psychologist (1856–1939).

"To suppress free speech in the name of protecting women is dangerous and wrong."

Betty Friedan (Betty Naomi Goldstein), U.S. women's rights activist and author (1921–2006).

"We must learn to welcome and not to fear the voices of dissent. We must dare to think about 'unthinkable things' because when things become unthinkable, thinking stops and action becomes mindless."

James William Fulbright,
U.S. senator, D-Ark. (1905–1995).

"Whenever I notice that my name isn't on the list of banned and challenged authors, I feel faintly like I'm letting the side down. Although I suspect all I'd have to do to get on the list is to write a book about naked, bisexual, hard-swearing wizards who drink a lot while disparaging the Second Amendment, and I'd be home and dry."

Neil Gaiman,
The Badger Herald, September 27, 2004.

"Freedom is not worth having if it does not include the freedom to make mistakes."

Mahatma Gandhi,
Indian ascetic, peace activist (1896–1948).

"The First Amendment was designed to protect offensive speech, because nobody ever tries to ban the other kind."

Mike Godwin,
staff counsel, Electronic Freedom Foundation.

"The First Amendment does not require silence in the face of outrage. On the contrary, freedom demands a constant assertion of values."

Richard Goldstein.

"When there is official censorship it is a sign that speech is serious. When there is none, it is pretty certain that the official spokesmen have all the loudspeakers."

Paul Goodman. **Growing Up Absurd. New York: Vintage Books, 1960.**

"Censorship is never over for those who have experienced it. It is a brand on the imagination that affects the individual who has suffered it, forever."

Nadine Gordimer,
South African novelist (1923–).

"Books won't stay banned. They won't burn. Ideas won't go to jail. In the long run of history, the censor and the inquisitor have always lost. The only sure weapon against bad ideas is better ideas. The source of better ideas is wisdom."

Alfred Whitney Griswold. *Essays on Education.* **New Haven: Yale University Press, 1954.**

"[O]ne man's vulgarity is another's lyric."

U.S. Supreme Court Justice John Marshall Harlan, Cohen v. California, 403 U.S. 15, 91 S.Ct. 1780, 29 L.Ed.2d 284 (1971).

"Where they have burned books, they will end in burning human beings."

Heinrich Heine, **Almansor, 1823; German critic and poet (1797–1856).**

"I cannot and will not cut my conscience to fit this year's fashions."

Lillian Hellman, subpoenaed to appear before the House Un-American Activities Committee, 1952.

"To prohibit the reading of certain books is to declare the inhabitants to be either fools or slaves."

Claude Adrien Helvetius. **De l'Homme, Vol. 1, sec. 4.**

Quotes on the First Amendment

"Our Constitution was not intended to be used by . . . any group to foist its personal religious beliefs on the rest of us."

Katherine Hepburn, U.S. actress (1907–2003).

"The only difference between the expression of an opinion and an incitement in the narrower sense is the speaker's enthusiasm for the result. Eloquence may set fire to reason."

U.S. Supreme Court Justice Oliver Wendell Holmes, Gitlow v. People of State of New York, 268 U.S. 652, 45 S.Ct. 625, 69 L.Ed. 1138 (1924).

"The best test of truth is the power of the thought to get itself accepted in the competition of the market. . . . We should be eternally vigilant against attempts to check the expression that we loathe."

U.S. Supreme Court Justice Oliver Wendell Holmes, dissenting, Abrams v. United States, 250 U.S. 616, 40 S.Ct. 17, 63 L.Ed. 1173 (1919).

"The right to be heard does not automatically include the right to be taken seriously."

Vice President Hubert H. Humphrey, speech to National Student Association, Madison, Wis., August 23, 1965.

"The vast number of titles which are published each year—all of them are to the good, even if some of them may annoy or even repel us for a time. For none of us would trade freedom of expression and of ideas for the narrowness of the public censor. America is a free market for people who have something to say, and need not fear to say it."

Vice President Hubert Humphrey, as reported by the New York Times, March 9, 1967, p. 42. Humphrey addressed the National Book Awards ceremony in New York City, March 8, 1967, where during his speech more than fifty people walked out to protest the U.S. role in Vietnam.

The Freedom to Read Statement

"We state these propositions neither lightly nor as easy generalizations. We here stake out a lofty claim for the value of the written word. We do so because we believe that it is possessed of enormous variety and usefulness, worthy of cherishing and keeping free. We realize that the application of these propositions may mean the dissemination of ideas and manners of expression that are repugnant to many persons. We do not state these propositions in the comfortable belief that what people read is unimportant. We believe rather that what people read is deeply important; that ideas can be dangerous; but that the suppression of ideas is fatal to a democratic society. Freedom itself is a dangerous way of life, but it is ours."

Concerned about threats to free communication of ideas, more than thirty librarians, publishers, and others conferred at Rye, New York, May 2–3, 1953. A committee was appointed to prepare a statement to be made public. This was endorsed officially by the American Library Association Council on June 25, 1953, and subsequently by the American Book Publishers Council (ABPC), American Booksellers Association, Book Manufacturers' Institute, and other national groups. In the light of later developments, a somewhat revised version was prepared after much consultation, and was approved in 1972 by the ALA Council, Association of American Publishers (successor to ABPC and American Educational Publishers Institute), and subsequently by many other book industry, communications, educational, cultural, and public service organizations. The statement was revised in 1991, 2000, and 2004, and is available at http://www.ala.org/oif/policies/freedomtoread.

Quotes on the First Amendment

"Fear of corrupting the mind of the younger generation is the loftiest form of cowardice."

Holbrook Jackson,
English writer and critic (1874–1948).

"Did you ever hear anyone say 'That work had better be banned because I might read it and it might be very damaging to me?'"

Joseph Henry Jackson,
American critic, travel-writer (1894–1955).

"The First Amendment grew out of an experience which taught that society cannot trust the conscience of a majority to keep its religious zeal within the limits that a free society can tolerate. I do not think it any more intended to leave the conscience of a majority to fix its limits. Civil government cannot let any group ride roughshod over others simply because their consciences tell them to do so."

U.S. Supreme Court Justice Robert H. Jackson,
Douglas et al. v. City of Jeannette et al., 319 U.S. 157, 63 S.Ct. 877, 87 L.Ed. 1324 (1943).

"If there is any fixed star in our constitutional constellation, it is that no official, high or petty, can prescribe what shall be orthodox in politics, nationalism, religion, or other matters of opinion or force citizens to confess by word or act their faith therein."

U.S. Supreme Court Justice Robert H. Jackson, West Virginia State Board of Education v. Barnette, 63 S.Ct. 1178, 87 L.Ed. 1628 (1943), 319 U.S. 624.

"The very purpose of the Bill of Rights was to withdraw certain subjects from the vicissitudes of political controversy, to place them beyond the reach of majorities and officials and to establish them as legal principles to be applied by the courts."

U.S. Supreme Court Justice Robert H. Jackson, West Virginia State Board of Education et al. v. Barnette et al., 319 U.S. 624, 63 S.Ct. 1178, 87 L.Ed. 1628 (1943).

"The First Amendment says nothing about a right not to be offended. The risk of finding someone else's speech offensive is the price each of us pays for our own free speech. Free people don't run to court— or to the principal—when they encounter a message they don't like. They answer it with one of their own."

Jeff Jacoby. "A Little Less Freedom of Speech," Townhall.com, January 26, 2004.

"A democratic society depends upon an informed and educated citizenry."

Thomas Jefferson, U.S. President (1743–1826).

"If the book be false in its facts, disprove them; if false in its reasoning, refute it. But for God's sake, let us hear freely from both sides."

Thomas Jefferson, A Bookman's Weekly.

"Books and ideas are the most effective weapons against intolerance and ignorance."

Lyndon Baines Johnson, commenting as he signed into law a bill providing increased Federal aid for library service, February 11, 1964.

"The First Amendment is often inconvenient. But that is besides the point. Inconvenience does not absolve the government of its obligation to tolerate speech."

U.S. Supreme Court Justice Anthony M. Kennedy, International Society for Krishna Consciousness, Inc., and Brian Rumbaugh, Petitioners v. Walter Lee, Walter Lee, Superintendent of Port Authority Police v. International Society for Krishna Consciousness, Inc., et al., 505 U.S. 672, 112 S.Ct. 2711, 120 L.Ed.2d 541 (1992).

"The Constitution exists precisely so that opinions and judgments, including aesthetic and moral judgments about art and literature, can be formed, tested, and expressed. What the Constitution says is that these judgments are for the individual to make, not for the Government to decree, even with the mandate or approval of a majority. Technology expands the capacity to choose; and it denies the potential of this revolution if we assume the government is best positioned to make these choices for us."

U.S. Supreme Court Justice Anthony M. Kennedy, United States, et al. v. Playboy Entertainment Group, Inc., 529 U.S. 803, 120 S.Ct. 1878, 146 L.Ed.2d 865 (2000).

"We are not afraid to entrust the American people with unpleasant facts, foreign ideas, alien philosophies, and competitive values. For a nation that is afraid to let its people judge the truth and falsehood in an open market is a nation that is afraid of its people."

John F. Kennedy. Remarks made on the twentieth anniversary of the Voice of America at H.E.W. Auditorium, February 26, 1962.

Quotes on the First Amendment

"People hardly ever make use of the freedom they have, for example, freedom of thought; instead they demand freedom of speech as a compensation."

Søren Kierkegaard,
Danish philosopher (1813–1855).

"A library's role never has been, is not currently and will not be in the future to keep people from the information they need and want. If the United States is to continue to be a nation of self-governors, the people must have available and accessible the information they need to make decisions."

Judith F. Krug, "Intellectual Freedom 2002: Living the Chinese Curse," Luminary Lectures at the Library of Congress, May 23, 2002.

"The first step in liquidating a people is to erase its memory. Destroy its books, its culture, its history. Then have somebody write new books, manufacture a new culture, invent a new history. Before long the nation will begin to forget what it is and what it was. The world around it will forget even faster."

Milan Kundera, from "Memories of a Wistful Amnesiac," by Walter Goodman, The New Leader, Vol. 63, No. 23, December 15, 1980, p. 26ff.

"I am absolutely convinced that the most important perspective is that people are obligated to respect opposing views. . . . If we are a poor respecter of other people's thoughts, our thoughts are not going to be well-received at another time."

Jim Leach, U.S. representative, R-Iowa, 2003.

"Why should freedom of speech and freedom of the press be allowed? Why should a government which is doing what it believes to be right allow itself to be criticized? It would not allow itself to be criticized? It would not allow opposition by lethal weapons. Ideas are much more fatal things than guns."

V. I. Lenin, speech in Moscow, 1920. From H. L. Mencken, ed., A New Dictionary of Quotations on Historical Principles from Ancient and Modern Sources. New York: Knopf, 1991, p. 966.

"The burning of an author's books, imprisonment for opinion's sake, has always been the tribute that an ignorant age pays to the genius of its time."

Joseph Lewis, U.S. film director (1907–)

"Where all men think alike, no one thinks very much."

Walter Lippmann,
U.S. author and journalist (1889–1974).

"Censorship, like charity, should begin at home; but unlike charity, it should end there."

Clare Booth Luce, U.S. diplomat, dramatist, journalist, and politician (1903–1987).

"Every American librarian worthy of the name is today the champion of a cause. It is, to my mind, the noblest of all causes for it is the cause of man, or more precisely the cause of the inquiring mind by which man has come to be. But noblest or not, it is nevertheless a cause—a struggle—not yet won: a struggle which can never perhaps be won for good and all. There are always in any society, even a society founded in the love of freedom, men and women who do not wish to be free themselves and who fear the practice of freedom by others—men and women who long for the comfort of a spiritual and intellectual authority in their own lives and who would feel more comfortable if they could also impose such an authority on the lives of their neighbors. As long as such people exist—and they show no sign of disappearing from the earth, even the American earth—the fight to subvert freedom will continue. And as long as the fight to subvert freedom continues, libraries must be strong points of defense."

Archibald MacLeish. Champion of a Cause. Chicago: ALA, 1971, pp. 228–29.

"A popular government, without popular information, or the means of acquiring it, is but a prologue to a farce or a tragedy; or perhaps both. Knowledge will forever govern ignorance; and a people who mean to be their own governors, must arm themselves with the power which knowledge gives."

James Madison, letter to W. T. Barry, August 4, 1782, in The Complete Madison. New York: Harper, 1953, p. 337.

"It is impossible for ideas to compete in the marketplace if no forum for their presentation is provided or available."

Thomas Mann, German writer (1875–1955).

"Thanks to television, for the first time the young are seeing history made before it is censored by their elders."

Margaret Mead,
U.S. anthropologist (1901–1978).

"One cannot and must not try to erase the past merely because it does not fit the present."

Golda Meir, Israeli political leader (1898–1978).

Quotes on the First Amendment

"If all mankind minus one were of one opinion, and only one person were of the contrary opinion, mankind would be no more justified in silencing that one person, than he, if he had the power, would be justified in silencing mankind."

John Stuart Mill. On Liberty.
Girard, Kan.: Haldeman-Julius Co., 1925.

"Who can compute what the world loses in the multitude of promising intellects combined with timid characters, who dare not follow out any bold, vigorous, independent train of thought, lest it should land them in something which would admit of being considered irreligious or immoral? . . . No one can be a great thinker who does not recognize that as a thinker it is his first duty to follow his intellect to whatever conclusions it may lead."

John Stuart Mill. On Liberty.

"As good almost kill a man as kill a good book; who kills a man kills a reasonable creature, God's image; but he who destroys a good book kills reason itself."

John Milton. Aeropagitica.
Christchurch, New Zealand: Caxton Pr., 1941.

"Give me the liberty to know, to utter, and to argue freely according to conscience, above all liberties."

John Milton. Aeropagitica.

"To forbid us anything is to make us have a mind for it."

Michel de Montaigne. Essays, 1595.

"You have not converted a man because you have silenced him."

John Lord Morley,
English politician and writer (1838–1923).

"Senator Smoot (Republican, Ut.)

Is planning a ban on smut

Oh rooti-ti-toot for Smoot of Ut.

And his reverent occiput.

Smite. Smoot, smite for Ut.,

Grit your molars and do your dut.,

Gird up your l--ns,

Smite h-p and th-gh,

We'll all be Kansas

By and By."

Ogden Nash, "Invocation," 1931.

"When voices of democracy are silenced, freedom becomes a hollow concept. No man or woman

should be sentenced to the shadows of silence for something he or she has said or written."

Allen H. Neuharth, U.S. journalist (1924–).

"When information which properly belongs to the public is systematically withheld by those in power, the people will soon become ignorant of their own affairs, distrustful of those who manage them, and—eventually—incapable of determining their own destinies."

Richard M. Nixon.
Washington Post, January 23, 1996, p. D16.

"Censorship of anything, at any time, in any place, on whatever pretense, has always been and always be the last resort of the boob and the bigot."

Eugene Gladstone O'Neill,
American playwright (1888–1953).

"The First Amendment forbids any law 'abridging the freedom of speech.' It doesn't say, 'except for commercials on children's television' or 'unless somebody says 'cunt' in a rap song or 'chick' on a college campus.'"

P. J. O'Rourke. Parliament of Whores: A Lone
Humorist Attempts to Explain the Entire U.S.
Government. New York: Vintage Books, 1992.

"Who controls the past controls the future, and who controls the present controls the past."

George Orwell, English essayist,
novelist, and satirist (1903–1950).

"That is what pluralism is: a nation where people who are different from one another are all entitled to the same rights and opportunities; the same standing before the law; the same respect, given to and received from each other.

"The First Amendment's value is linked directly to its use. To preserve it, it must be shared. Unless it is everyone's, it can be no one's."

Jean Hammond Otto. U.S. journalist (1925–).

"It is shared values, not shared opinions, that keep a diverse and pluralistic nation from splintering. It is tolerance for our differences that binds us. It is the First Amendment that protects the individual mind and conscience against the authority of government and the tyranny of the majority."

Jean Hammond Otto.
Social Education, October 1990, p. 356.

Quotes on the First Amendment

"He that would make his own liberty secure, must guard even his enemy from opposition; for if he violates this duty he establishes a precedent that will reach to himself."

Thomas Paine. Dissertation on First Principles of Government. London: D. I. Eaton, 1795.

"A censor is an expert in cutting remarks. A censor is a man who knows more than he thinks you ought to."

Dr. Laurence Peter. Peter's Quotations: Ideas for Our Time. New York: Morrow, 1977, p. 97.

"Now that eighteen-year-olds have the right to vote, it is obvious that they must be allowed the freedom to form their political views on the basis of uncensored speech before they turn eighteen, so that their minds are not a blank when they first exercise the franchise. And since an eighteen-year-old's right to vote is a right personal to him rather than a right to be exercised on his behalf by his parents, the right of parents to enlist the aid of the state to shield their children from ideas of which the parents disapprove cannot be plenary either. People are unlikely to become well-functioning, independent-minded adults and responsible citizens if they are raised in an intellectual bubble."

Seventh District Judge Richard Posner, American Amusement Machine Association, et al., Plaintiffs-Appellants, v. Teri Kendrick, et al., 244 F.3d 954 (7th Cir. 2001).

"A free press is a cornerstone of our democracy. In the First Amendment to the Constitution, our Founding Fathers affirmed their belief that competing ideas are fundamental to freedom. We Americans cherish our freedom of expression and our access to multiple sources of news and information."

Ronald Reagan, message of the President for National Newspaper Week, October 10–16, 1982.

"Indeed, perhaps we do the minors of this country harm if First Amendment protections, which they will with age inherit fully, are chipped away in the name of their protection."

Judge Lowell A. Reed, Jr., American Civil Liberties Union, et al. v. Janet Reno, 931 F. Supp. 2d 473 (E.D. Pa. 1999).

"Where, after all, do universal human rights begin? In small places, close to home—so close and so small that they cannot be seen on any maps of the world. Yet they are the world of the individual persons; the neighborhood he lives in; the school or college he attends; the factory, farm, or office where he works. Such are the places where every man, woman and child seeks equal justice, equal opportunity, equal dignity without discrimination. Unless these rights have meaning there, they have little meaning anywhere. Without concerned citizen action to uphold them close to home, we shall look in vain for progress in the larger world."

Eleanor Roosevelt, U.S. diplomat and reformer (1884–1962).

"If in other lands the press and books and literature of all kinds are censored, we must redouble our efforts here to keep it free. Books may be burned and cities sacked, but truth, like the yearning for freedom, lives in the hearts of humble men and women. No people in all the world can be kept eternally ignorant or eternally enslaved."

Franklin Delano Roosevelt, speech before the National Education Association, 1938.

"Free societies . . . are societies in motion, and with motion comes tension, dissent, friction. Free people strike sparks, and those sparks are the best evidence of freedom's existence."

(Ahmed) Salman Rushdie, British (Indian-born) author (1947–).

"What is freedom of expression? Without the freedom to offend, it ceases to exist."

(Ahmed) Salman Rushdie.

"Men fear thoughts as they fear nothing else on earth—more than ruin—more even than death . . . Thought is subversive and revolutionary, destructive and terrible, thought is merciless to privilege, established institutions, and comfortable habit. Thought looks into the pit of hell and is not afraid. Thought is great and swift and free, the light of the world, and the chief glory of man."

Betrand Russell, English author, mathematician, and philosopher (1872–1970).

"Intellectual freedom is essential to human society. Freedom of thought is the only guarantee against an infection of people by mass myths, which, in the hands of treacherous hypocrites and demagogues, can be transformed into bloody dictatorships."

Andrei Dmitrievich Sakharov, Russian physicist (1921–1989).

Quotes on the First Amendment

"The First Amendment cases of the 1990s and the twenty-first century will pit powerful emotional interests—such as privacy or nationalism—against our intellectual commitment to the value of information and the right of the public to freely receive information."

Bruce W. Sanford, U.S. attorney (1945–).

"All truth passes through three stages: first it is ridiculed, second it is violently opposed, third it is accepted as being self-evident."

Arthur Schopenhauer,
German philosopher (1788–1860).

"All censorships exist to prevent anyone from challenging current conceptions and existing institutions. All progress is initiated by challenging current conceptions, and executed by supplanting existing institutions. Consequently the first condition of progress is the removal of censorship."

George Bernard Shaw.
Preface to Mrs. Warren's Profession.
Studio City, Calif.: Players Press, 1991.

"The war between the artist and writer and government or orthodoxy is one of the tragedies of humankind. One chief enemy is stupidity and failure to understand anything about the creative mind. For a bureaucratic politician to presume to tell any artist or writer how to get his mind functioning is the ultimate in asininity. The artist is no more able to control his mind than is any outsider. Freedom to think requires not only freedom of expression but also freedom from the threat of orthodoxy and being outcast and ostracized."

Helen Foster Snow, U.S. writer promoting American-Chinese understanding (1908–1997).

"The ultimate result of shielding men from the effects of folly is to fill the world with fools."

Herbert Spencer,
British philosopher (1820–1903).

"Our nation's understanding and appreciation of the First Amendment is not passed along genetically. It must be reaffirmed and defended, over and over. Keep fighting and keep winning."

Paul Steinle, U.S. journalist.

"The interest in encouraging freedom of expression in a democratic society outweighs any theoretical but unproven benefit of censorship."

U.S. Supreme Court Justice John Paul Stevens,
Janet Reno, Attorney General of the United States, et al., Appellants v. American Civil Liberties Union et al., 521 U.S. 844, 117 S.Ct. 2329, 138 L.Ed. 2d 874 (1997).

"The sound of tireless voices is the price we pay for the right to hear the music of our own opinions."

Adlai Stevenson, U.S. politician (1900–1965).

"Freedom rings where opinions clash."

Adlai Stevenson.

"You see, boys forget what their country means by just reading 'the land of the free' in history books. When they get to be men, they forget even more. Liberty is too precious a thing to be buried in books, Miss Saunders. Men should hold it up in front of them every single day of their lives and say 'I'm free—to think and speak. My ancestors couldn't, I can. And my children will.'"

James Stewart, Mr. Smith Goes to Washington.

"Censorship reflects a society's lack of confidence in itself. It is the hallmark of an authoritarian regime."

U.S. Supreme Court Justice Potter Stewart,
dissenting, Ginzberg v. United States, 383 U.S. 463, 86 S.Ct. 942, 16 L.Ed.2d 31 (1966).

"The ultimate expression of free speech lies not in the ideas with which we agree, but in those ideas that offend and irritate us."

Chuck Stone, U.S. journalist.

"There is no more fundamental axiom of American freedom than the familiar statement: In a free country we punish men for crimes they commit but never for the opinions they have."

Harry S. Truman, U.S. President (1884–1972).

"Once a government is committed to the principle of silencing the voice of opposition, it has only one way to go, and that is down the path of increasingly repressive measures, until it becomes a source of terror to all its citizens and creates a country where everyone lives in fear."

Harry S. Truman,
message to Congress, August 8, 1950.

Quotes on the First Amendment

"Censorship is telling a man he can't have a steak just because a baby can't chew it."

Mark Twain [Samuel Langhornne Clemens],
U.S. author and humorist (1835–1910).

"In America, as elsewhere, free speech is confined to the dead."

Mark Twain.

"It is by the goodness of God that in our country we have those three unspeakable precious things: freedom of speech, freedom of conscience, and the prudence never to practice either."

Mark Twain, Pudd'nhead Wilson's Calendar.

"Everyone has the right to freedom of opinion and expression; this right includes freedom to hold opinions without interference and to seek, receive, and impart information and ideas through any media regardless of frontiers."

United Nations Universal
Declaration of Human Rights, Article 19.

"The basis of the First Amendment is the hypothesis that . . . free debate of ideas will result in the wisest governmental policies."

United States Supreme Court Justice Fred M.
Vinson, Dennis et al. v. United States, 341 U.S. 494,
71 S.Ct. 857, 95 L.Ed. 1137 (1951).

"I may disagree with what you have to say, but I shall defend to the death, your right to say it."

Voltaire [François Marie Arouet],
French writer (1694–1778).

"It is the characteristic of the most stringent censorships, that they give credibility to the opinions they attack."

Voltaire [François Marie Arouet].
Poeme sur le desastre de Lisbonne, 1958.

"If I open my mouth to speak, must I always be correct, and by whose standards."

Alice Walker, In Search of Our Mothers' Gardens.
San Diego: Harcourt, 1983.

"Teachers and students must always remain free to inquire, to study and to evaluate, to gain new maturity and understanding; otherwise our civilization will stagnate and die."

U.S. Supreme Court Chief Justice Earl Warren,
Sweezy v. New Hampshire, 354 U.S. 234, 77 S.Ct.
1203, 1 L.Ed.2d 1311 (1957).

"The values embodied in the First Amendment are not indigenous only to the USA. The drive of the human spirit to be free—and to be able to express that freedom—is a worldwide hope."

Christine Wells.

"I believe in censorship. I made a fortune out of it."

Mae West, U.S. movie actress (1892–1980).

"There were a lot of things the censors wouldn't let me do in the movies that I did on stage. They wouldn't even let me sit on a guy's lap and I'd been on more laps than a napkin."

Mae West, Index on Censorship.

"The books that the world calls immoral are the books that show the world its own shame."

Oscar Wilde, Irish dramatist,
novelist, and poet (1854–1900).

"An idea that is not dangerous is unworthy of being called an idea at all."

Oscar Wilde.

"I believe in America because in it we are free—free to choose our government, to speak our minds, to observe our different religions. Because we are generous with our freedom, we share our rights with those who disagree with us."

Wendell Lewis Willkie,
U.S. politician (1892–1944).

"To suppress minority thinking and minority expression would tend to freeze society and prevent progress. . . . Now more than ever we must keep in the forefront of our minds the fact that whenever we take away the liberties of those whom we hate, we are opening the way to loss of liberty for those we love."

Wendell Lewis Willkie. One World.
New York: The Limited Editions Club, 1944.

"I have always been among those who believed that the greatest freedom of speech was the greatest safety, because if a man is a fool the best thing to do is to encourage him to advertise the fact by speaking."

Woodrow Wilson, U.S. President (1856–1924).

Quotes on the First Amendment

"The wisest thing to do with a fool is to encourage him to hire a hall and discourse to his fellow citizens. Nothing chills nonsense like exposure to the air."

Woodrow Wilson, 1908. From: Inglehart, Louis Edward, ed., First Amendment: What Americans Have Said about Freedom of Expression. Reston, Va.: Newspaper Association of America, p. 14.

"The trouble with free speech is that it insists on living up to its name."

Jonathan Yardley.
Washington Post, June 17, 1996, p. CO2.

"Every dogma has its day, but ideals are eternal."

Israel Zangwill, English novelist (1864–1926).

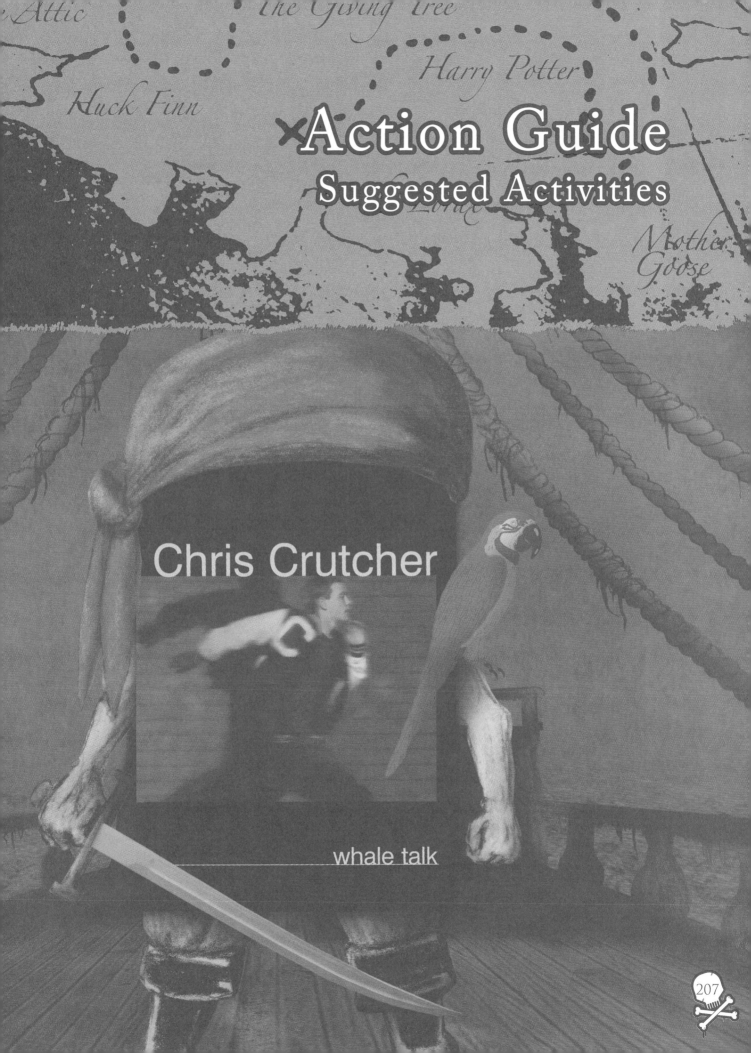

Action Guide
Suggested Activities

Chris Crutcher

whale talk

VISIT our Web site at www.ala.org/bbooks.

PRINT the message of Banned Books Week on bags to use during the week. The Camden County (New Jersey) College Library Learning Resource Center and the Merrick (New York) Library used the bag to enclose all materials checked out that week.

ORGANIZE a reading and discussion series. Your series could focus on books banned in the past year, or it might examine banned books throughout history or by topic (religion, politics, sex, etc.).

ASSIGN a research paper for students, such as: "Censorship and the Democratic Society"; "Banned Authors"; "The Various Forms of Censorship." Make arrangements for the local or school newspaper to print the best paper.

ASK the student or community newspaper to devote an issue to Banned Books Week. Suggest editorials on the importance of the Bill of Rights, the Constitution, and students' rights.

ILLUSTRATE flyers, posters, newsletters, and booklets with the clip art in this book, which can be enlarged, reduced, or duplicated. Local print shops can assist you with printing specifications. There are essentially two kinds of printers: instant printers and commercial printers. Instant printers, usually able to do a job in a few days, are best used for simple, small jobs. Ask to see paper samples and, to save money, try to use what is in stock. Show the printer a sample of a comparable finished piece showing the quality you're looking for. For larger orders, it may be more economical to use a commercial printer. To find a good commercial printer, ask local businesses whose printed pieces you admire which printer they use. Call the recommended printers and ask for a representative to call. Again, show them samples of comparable finished products and give them a budget range. The representatives will be able to advise you on paper stock, size, and color. Commercial printers require more lead time, so plan ahead.

HOLD a film festival of movies depicting censorship. *Storm Center*, a Bette Davis classic, is the story of a small-town librarian (Davis) who refuses to remove a book on communism. The

I read banned books.
www.ala.org/bbooks

Available from the American Library Association

flaming conclusion should generate discussion and interest (1965, bw, 87m, Columbia/Phoenix). *Fahrenheit 451* shows a futuristic fascist society where the fireman's job is to burn books (1966, color, 112m, Rank/Anglo Enterprise/Vineyard). *1984* is the George Orwell classic about Big Brother and the subordination of the individual to the state (1955, bw, 91m, Holiday). *The Seven Minutes,* based on the Irving Wallace novel of the same title, tells the story of a bookseller arrested for distributing an "obscene" novel (1971, col., 102m, TCF). *Inherit the Wind* is a fictionalized account of the famous Scopes "monkey trial" starring Spencer Tracy as Clarence Darrow and Matthew Harrison Brady as William Jennings Bryan (1960, bw, 127m, United Artists/Lomitas). *South Park: Bigger, Longer and Uncut,* when the boys see an R-rated movie, they are pronounced "corrupted," and their parents pressure the United States to wage war against Canada (1999).

Banned Films: Movies, Censors, and the First Amendment, by Edward de Grazia and Roger K. Newman (New York: Bowker, 1982) provides 122 examples of American and foreign films banned in the U.S., including *The Birth of the Nation, The Exorcist*, and *Carnal Knowledge.*

Forbidden Films: Censorship Histories of 125 Motion Pictures, by Dawn Sova (New York: Facts on File, 2001) traces the efforts to censor 125 films, ranging from the silent *Birth of a Nation* to *Schlindler's List*. Entries are arranged alphabetically by film title and include production details such as country and date of production, distribution, format, running time, director, writer, awards, genre, and cast. A summary of the film's plot is followed by a description of its censorship history. Each entry concludes with a short bibliography for further reading.

STAGE a mock trial or moot court. Put a banned book on trial and have students argue for and against the book. Select a jury that has not read the book. For mock trial materials and technical assistance, contact the following organizations:

1) The Constitutional Rights Foundation, 601 South Kingsley Drive, Los Angeles, CA 90005; phone: (213) 487-5590; fax: (213) 386-0459; www.crf-usa.org, has packets of mock trial material available for $5.95 each, and will send you a free catalog

on request, or you can download it directly from the Web site.

2) Street Law Inc., 1010 Wayne Ave., Suite 870, Silver Spring, MD 20910; phone: (301) 589-1130; fax: (301) 589-1131; www.streetlaw.org, has many mock trial scenarios compiled into case packets; they are available free from their Web site at www.streetlaw.org/mockt2.html, or you can purchase paper copies for $10. Note that the mock trials they have are not on censorship, but can be used as examples.

3) The Center for Civic Education, 5145 Douglas Fir Road, Calabasas, CA 91302-1440; phone: (818) 591-9321; fax: (818) 591-9330; www.civiced.org; e-mail: cce@civiced.org, develops curriculum materials to teach about the Constitution in upper elementary grades, and will send a catalog of items free upon request. They also have Constitution Day and Citizenship Day lessons for kindergarten through high school available for download at www.civiced.org/byrd2006.

MARCH in a community parade. Staff at the Parlin-Ingersoll Library in Canton, Illinois, celebrated Banned Books Week by marching in the Friendship Festival parade dressed as famous banned books; Dawn Ward is pictured as *Charlotte's Web*. Other Banned Books Week activities included the creation of a Banned Book Club, book discussions for children, and the distribution of an annotated list of banned books with the "hot books" logo.

GIVE away gags imprinted with the titles of banned books. The gags also could be worn as mourning armbands, e.g., "Censorship=the death of ideas."

WEAR this bright red button sold by the American Society of Journalists and Authors, 1501 Broadway, Suite 302, New York, NY 10036; phone: (212) 997-0947; fax: (212) 937-2315; www.asja.org. 1–10, $1 each; 11–50, 75¢ each; 51–100, 50¢ each; 101–1,000, 40¢ each; 1,001+, 30¢ each. Or wear the First Amendment on a T-shirt. Cranberry lettering on unbleached cotton, sizes L, XL, XXL; $10 each. Add $3 postage and handling each.

SPONSOR a poster contest for children illustrating the concept of free speech. Display the posters in your bookstore or library during Banned Books Week—Celebrating the Freedom to Read.

GET a daily dose of freedom from this thought-provoking desktop calendar. Each day's page features words of wisdom about the freedoms guaranteed to Americans in the First Amendment to the U.S. Constitution. You'll find quotes from everyone from Napoleon Bonaparte, Henry David Thoreau, and Thurgood Marshall to Woody Allen, Maureen Dowd, and Bill Gates. A perfect gift for the New Year! Price: $9. There is also a First Amendment poster available from the store, which features the full text of the First Amendment and highlights the amendment's five freedoms. $8. The Freedom Forum, 1101 Wilson Blvd., Arlington, VA 22209; phone: (703) 528-0800; fax: (703) 284-3770; www.freedomforum.org; e-mail: newseumstore@ freedomforum.org. There are also several publications available to download free of charge.

CREATE radio spots. Improve the spot with music! Ask the radio station's technician, engineer, or disc jockey to help you select music and dub it into the radio spot. For example, one library used the theme from Dragnet for an effective, attention-grabbing spot.

WEAR a T-shirt with a clever anti-censorship message. The Washington Coalition Against Censorship has developed five different designs available in various colors and sizes. All profits support public education efforts by the coalition. T-shirts are $20 each, plus $2 shipping per order. Contact the Washington Coalition Against Censorship, 6201 15th NW #640, Seattle, WA 98107; phone: (206) 784-6418; e-mail: wcac-help@ comscast.net, to get ordering information.

REENACT the signing of the Constitution. Follow with a discussion of the First Amendment and the rights it ensures.

Available from the American Library Association

PRINT annotated, Freedom to Read bookmarks. The Serra Cooperative Library System in California and the San Diego Booksellers Association printed bookmarks that included a short summary of banned books with a history of censorship efforts against them.

CO-SPONSOR an essay contest with the state library association, local school, or community group. Possible topics include "What the First Amendment means to me" or "What does freedom to read mean?" Contestants can include junior or senior high students. Use local newspaper editors and journalists or university faculty as judges, and award banned books as prizes.

USE readership surveys to point out the hazards of censorship. A serendipitous combination of promotions for a week-long literacy celebration at the Carroll County Public Library, Maryland, and Banned Books Week resulted in an unprompted editorial in the local newspaper. As part of the literacy celebration, the library surveyed prominent citizens in the community on books that influenced their lives. When the list was published in the newspaper, it coincided with publicity on Banned Books Week from the People for the American Way. The editor noted that many of the "influential" books also were on the banned books list. His editorial "Literature's Worst Obscenity Is Banning, Burning Books" gave the library an added P.R. effort.

SPONSOR a contest. Possibilities include matching quotes and titles of the banned books; matching titles and authors; selecting banned authors or titles from lists or displays of books. Make sure your selections reflect the literary quality of the works and inspire contestants to read them. Award banned books to the winners.

BLOW UP Banned Books Week balloons. Print your message on helium-strength balloons. Use for decoration or distribute at schools, shopping areas, programs, etc.

COMMISSION a local storyteller or theater group to prepare a dramatic rendition of banned or challenged books. Provide printed lists of appropriate material (books, videotapes, etc.) and take the show on the road—to schools, libraries, and community centers.

PRINT the easily removable, camera-ready clip art to promote Banned Books Week. Ask local newspaper and magazine editors to use the public service advertisements as fillers whenever space is available. Community newsletters and staff newsletters also are good places to run the ads. You may want to duplicate the ads for distribution to several sources. Be sure the duplication process (use photostats or print on heavy, enamel paper) produces good camera-ready art.

SCHEDULE provocative speakers to focus on intellectual freedom issues. The Merrick Library, New York, scheduled the Honorable James Buchanan, former chairman of People for the American Way, to speak during Banned Books Week. Also during the week, a librarian from a nearby community spoke on her experience with the Secret Service. The ALA Office for Intellectual Freedom can provide suggestions for speakers; phone: 800-545-2433, ext. 4223; e-mail: oif@ala.org.

SPONSOR a day at the state capitol for students, teachers, community leaders, seniors, or other people to learn about the democratic process—work with organizations such as the League of Women Voters.

PRESENT "Banned." Sigma Tau Delta, the International Honor Society at the University of Northern Colorado, created a collaboration of six directors and their individual ideas about censorship. It presents literature, poetry, musical lyrics, and drama that has been banned, censored, or deemed dangerous by certain individuals.

INCLUDE a study of banned books in your school's curriculum. Ruth Bauerle, Assistant Professor of English at Ohio Wesleyan University, planned a fall semester seminar on "Banned Books: From Judy Blume to Molly Bloom." The coursework consisted of six reading units and several individual and group projects. The six-week seminar began with a background lecture on laws (Constitution, court cases) governing censorship, and case histories of book withdrawals from libraries.

The reading units were followed by class discussion of the controversial elements in each book, the positive or negative merits in each work, and whether each book met the court test of having social value. Role-playing was used in the first reading unit, with students assuming the roles of a parent complaining about the book, a parent defending the right to read, the high school librarian, the high school English teacher, school board members, and high school students for and against the book.

Suggested Activities

The unit "themes" and titles were:

1) Young adult fiction—Judy Blume's *Are You There God? It's Me, Margaret*; *Deenie*; and *Tiger Eyes* and J. D. Salinger's *The Catcher in the Rye*.

2) Studs Terkel's *Working* was the second unit. As part of the study of this work, students were asked to "test" the common complaint of many dictionaries—including (or excluding) "bad" language. Students listed dirty, profane, and obscene expressions and then looked the words up in a variety of dictionaries.

3) National security censorship readings included: Victor Marchetti and John D. Marks, *The CIA and the Cult of Intelligence*; Philip Agee, *Inside the Company: CIA Diary*; and Frank Snepp, *Decent Interval*.

4) The fourth reading unit was on censored black writers. Bauerle explains this somewhat "illogical" grouping—the books were challenged or banned due to their content, not the color of the author—stating that the books provide realistic portrayals of the black experience and may have been censored because of the sordidness of that experience. Readings included Ralph Ellison, *Invisible Man*; Maya Angelou, *I Know Why the Caged Bird Sings*; Richard Wright, *Native Son*; and Gordon Park, *The Learning Tree*.

5) The class examined school texts (elementary through high school) for slanting, factual completeness, omissions in science and social science; e.g., creationism vs. evolution; controversial topics—women, minorities, Vietnam War, Watergate.

6) "Literary classics" that have been banned was the final unit, and James Joyce's *Ulysses* was used. Group projects included interviewing librarians, county school superintendents, curriculum supervisors, and principals to see what censorship problems or complaints they've encountered and how the complaint was handled.

Individual projects included researching a particular author or book (What has been the writer's experience with censorship? What was the writer's reaction? How many times has the book been challenged? Why was the book banned?). Students also could study a single censorship incident; e.g., the Island Trees case, the Louisiana creationism case, the Scopes trial, the Kanahwa County, the West Virginia controversy. In addition, students could examine positions taken by particular advocacy groups—People for the American Way, the ACLU, the American Family Association, the Family Research Council, the American Library Association, the American Booksellers Association, the Association of American Publishers, etc.

CONTACT the Constitutional Rights Foundation, 601 South Kingsley Drive, Los Angeles, CA 90005; phone: (213) 487-5590; fax: (213) 386-0459; www. crf-usa.org, for a catalog of materials on the U.S. Constitution and Bill of Rights, or visit the Web site for a series of free online lessons.

COMBINE the message of Banned Books Week with your bookstore catalog. The Carleton College Alumni Bookstore in Minnesota added interesting reading to its catalog by including "Faculty Favorites," a list of five most meaningful or most highly treasured books in the lives of the faculty. *The Adventures of Huckleberry Finn* was one of the top ten, and clip art from the 1988 Resource Book was used as the cover of the catalog.

ENCOURAGE your governor, city council, and mayor to proclaim "Banned Books Week—Celebrating the Freedom to Read" in your state or community. For example, the state of Ohio and city of St. Louis did for the purpose of "informing our citizens as to the nature and magnitude of the threat censorship poses to our First Amendment rights of freedom of speech and press, the cornerstone of American liberty."

CREATE an interesting photo for publicity. The North Salem (N.Y.) Free Library dressed three library employees in "prison garb" borrowed from the local barbershop chorus. The "prisoners" were shown reading banned books.

SPONSOR a readout. The American Society of Journalists and Authors supported a spirited public rally on the steps of the New York Public Library. Members of the society dramatized the dangers of book censorship by reading selections from banned books. The American Center of Poets, Playwrights, Editors, Essayists and Novelists, or P.E.N. (www. pen.org), sponsored a "Forbidden Books" evening, where well-known writers and actors read sections from banned books. In Virginia Beach, the public library led a storytelling and audience discussion program about banned children's books. In planning these programs, determine your audience, select a well-known place and time for the readout, provide some musical link between the readings, and make it visually interesting by, for instance, enlarging the jackets of banned books.

PARTICIPATE—Big Banned Books was the name of the Missoula Public Library's float, as Banned Books Week coincided with the University of Montana's homecoming parade, "The Big Band Era." The anti-censorship float featured library staff and friends dressed as characters from books that have been banned.

HOLD—At the Ossining (N.Y.) Public Library, actor Alan Arkin and author Sol Stein participated in an evening of celebrity readings. Arkin read from *Catch 22* to a crowd of 250. At the Merrick (N.Y.) Public Library patrons were invited to speak out against censorship by writing their own comments on sheets of newsprint beneath some famous quotes about censorship.

ORGANIZE a slide show that introduces Banned Books Week. Collect slides that help teach and explain the meaning of freedom. The slides can show books written by or about persons who valued intellectual freedom. Examples could include Thomas Jefferson, Benjamin Franklin, Maya Angelou, John Peter Zenger, Henry Thoreau, Judy Blume, James Baldwin, and Susan B. Anthony. Slides also could include clip art and book jackets. A short slide show can easily be shown during a class or at a library. These shows are especially effective for large group presentations.

SPONSOR a community forum. The forums serve both educational and participatory purposes. They allow the public to examine various aspects of the Constitution, its evolution, the underlying values involved, and its significance in contemporary society and to the individual citizen. By encouraging the audience to speak out on the constitutional issues, these sessions emphasize the citizen's role in the continuing development of the law. Organizers may choose from several different model formats; for example, mock legislative hearing, town hall meeting (Socratic discussion), mock trial, and debate. For planning assistance, use *Speaking & Writing Truth: Community Forums on the First Amendment*, by Robert S. Peck and Mary Manemann, published by the American Bar Association. The guide contains information on planning mock legislative hearings, mock trials or debates and provides detailed suggestions on getting started and six First Amendment issues with scripts and legal memoranda.

GIVE AWAY a banned book! Parents and students from the Goochland (Va.) High School were offered free copies of Stephen King's *Salem's Lot* after the school board banned it. The bookstore, Volume I, created a front window display featuring *Salem's Lot* and twenty other banned books. The Richmond *Times-Dispatch* published a photograph of the display and interviewed the bookstore owner. In the first week, twenty-two copies were given away.

EXAMINE the role of the free press in contemporary society by hosting a community discussion. The Society of Professional Journalists' Project Sunshine will help with suggestions on topics and speakers for your area. For more information, contact Society of Professional Journalists' Project Sunshine, Eugene S. Pulliam National Journalism Center, 3909 N. Meridian St., Indianapolis, IN 46208; phone: (317) 927-8000; fax: (317) 920-4789; e-mail: spj@spj.org; www.spj.org.

JOIN the Freedom to Read Foundation. The Foundation is dedicated to the legal and financial defense of intellectual freedom, especially in libraries. Since its establishment in 1969, the foundation has stood at the forefront of nearly all major battles to defend the right to read. Your contribution will help the Freedom to Read Foundation preserve First Amendment freedoms by challenging those who would remove or ban materials from library collections, and establishing, through the courts, legal precedents on behalf of intellectual freedom principles. For more information, contact the Freedom to Read Foundation, 50 E. Huron St., Chicago, IL 60611; phone: 800-545-2433, ext. 4226; e-mail: ftrf@ala.org.

GO FOR THE "BURN" and kick off Banned Books Week with a fun run in your community. Print "Banned Books Week—The Censorship Challenge" race T-shirts for participants, volunteers, and for sale to spectators. Keep the race distance short (less than three miles) to involve as many people as possible. Check with your local running club on how to promote and organize the event. Or pick up a copy of the *Road Runners Club of America Handbook*, available for $28.50 member rate or $33.50 for nonmember (postage included) from RRCA, 8965 Guilford Rd., Ste. 150, Columbia, MD 21046; phone: (410) 290-3890; fax: (410) 290-3893; e-mail: office@rrca.oeg; www.rrca.org.

HOLD—Brown and Clark Booksellers in Mashpee, Massachusetts, held a "Whodunit/Duzzit" forum on censorship and book banning. Four local authors made presentations on self-censorship by authors, the role of "bestseller" lists and chain stores, and the future of electronic books. Coffee and snacks—e.g., *Chocolate War* Brownies and Uncensored Salsa—were served after the program. The bookstore had both in-store and window displays profiling banned books.

HOLD a book discussion group with teenagers and their parents. Select banned titles that deal realistically with teens' issues. Have several people read each book. At the book discussion, have the teens discuss the book, followed by parents' reactions to the books and discussion by the teens. End the sessions with a brief description of the book selection policies and procedures for teens, stressing the importance of free access for young adults.

PETITION your neighbors and politicians to challenge censorship and cooperate with all persons or groups that resist abridgment of free expression and free access to ideas. In Connecticut, several hundred signatures were obtained on a petition protesting censorship, which was then sent to the governor, state representatives, and members of the U.S. Congress.

DISTRIBUTE and place table tent cards that promote the freedom to read in cafeterias, reading rooms, and study halls in schools and libraries. The cards could even be personalized with a statement or story.

CREATE a year-long public awareness campaign like the one developed at the After-Words new and used bookstore in Chicago. A shelf of banned books is on permanent display in a prominent area. In each of these books—and in many other banned books throughout the store--are custom-made bookmarks with the author and title of the book, reasons why the book was banned, and in what year. These citations are referenced from the Banned Books Week Resource Book. According to the owner, Beverly Dvorkin these "banned books" sell very, very well.

SELECT a video. *The Video Sourcebook*, 33rd ed., features programs currently available on video and lists a variety videotapes on censorship. Those videos are *Books Under Fire; Censorship in a Free Society; Censorship or Selection: Choosing Books for Public Schools; The Designated Mourner; Dirty Pictures; Free Press, Fair Trial: Inside the Anonymous Source; Is It Easy to Be Young?; It's Only Rock and Roll; Legacy of the Hollywood Blacklist; Life and Liberty . . . For All Who Believe; See Evil;* and *What Johnny Can't Read.* The *Sourcebook* gives complete ordering information, program description, release date, and other information.

PURCHASE a variety of promotional materials (T-shirts, bumper stickers, and buttons) from the American Booksellers Foundation for Free Expression and speak your mind every time you use them. Contact the American Booksellers Foundation for Free Expression, 275 7th Ave., 15th Fl., New York, NY 10001; phone: (212) 587-4025; fax: (212) 587-2436; www.abffe.org.

CONTACT your college public relations department. Let them know about your Banned Books Week activities. Their media contacts are well-established, and their help usually will result in better coverage.

PUBLICIZE the Bill of Rights with camera-ready art available from the Newspaper Association of America Foundation, NAA, P.O. Box 2527, Kearneysville, WV 25430; phone: 800-651-4622, fax: 800-525-5562, Order Fulfillment Department, Item #80079. The foundation's pamphlet "First Things First: Using the Newspaper to Teach the Five Freedoms of the First Amendment" is available for download at www.naafoundation.org/pdf/FirstAmendmentBooklet.pdf.

REWARD patrons who check out banned books during the week. The staff at the Dallas (Tex.) Public Library gave library patrons gift certificates redeemable at a local bookstore each time a banned book was checked out.

ENLIST the help of a local business that has an electronic bulletin board on its property. The Algona (Iowa) Public Library asked the Iowa State Bank to run a weeklong info-notice about Banned Books Week, and it agreed.

HUNT for banned books throughout the business community. The Bernardsville (N.J.) Public Library worked with local retail businesses of all kinds to develop a "treasure" hunt of banned books, hiding the titles in plain sight in the display windows and areas of the stores. Patrons were invited to make the rounds of the stores and list all titles they discovered. Participating businesses included flower shops, paint stores, jewelry stores, travel agencies, and many others.

WORK with the local arts council to develop a proposal for Banned Books Week. Present the proposal well in advance of Banned Books Week to potential supporting agencies that might provide some funds for Banned Books Week programs and activities, especially if Banned Books Week is communitywide in focus, and multi-disciplinary in nature. The Hartland Art Council in Michigan successfully combined an "Authors Live at the Library" program with a banned books theme.

RUN a raffle that can be entered only by visiting your Banned Books display. The Honolulu (Hawaii) Community College bookstore donated a backpack for the raffle; students checked out the display and entered the contest.

WORK with other libraries in your area to develop a united front for Banned Books Week; have each library responsible for one event, and schedule them to complement each other. A letter to the editor from four or five libraries, especially representing different constituencies, will be more effective than your library going it alone. Develop information packets that are available at all participating libraries, and say so in your press releases.

USE the public address system in your school or library to communicate about Banned Books Week. A First Amendment quote at the beginning of the day, or at peak times, would certainly give your patrons something to think about. This idea was submitted by Shannon Van Kirk, who successfully used a public address announcement at the St. Cecilia Academy in Nashville, Tennessee.

PRINT a Banned Books Week calendar. The Merrick (N.Y.) Library observed Banned Books Week by printing a calendar showing activities in the library as well as holidays, events, etc. Each month of the calendar was illustrated with a quotation by a prominent artist, poet, philosopher, scientist, or statesman on the importance of the freedom to read. This Resource Book is a good source for quotations and clip art for your calendar.

DISTRIBUTE materials to high school students. The Paulsboro (N.J.) High School librarian compiled a list of challenged and banned books that the students would recognize. These were distributed to English, history, and civics classes along with a copy of the First Amendment and the editorial from the Banned Books Week kit.

SUPPORT the legal battle of the Little Sisters Bookstores and other gay and lesbian Canadian stores. Since the 1980s, the stores have been waging an expensive legal battle with the Canadian government for seizing and confiscating books at the Canadian borders. To raise funds, they have published *Forbidden Passages: Writings Banned in Canada*, excerpts from a number of the confiscated materials. In the United States, the book can be obtained from Cleis Press, P.O. Box 14684, San Francisco, CA 94197; phone: 800-780-2279 or (415) 575-4700; fax: (415) 575-4705; www.cleispress.com.

PLAN a quiz. In Bound Brook, New Jersey, middle school and high school librarian Lillian Keating planned a contest to commemorate the week—a daily quiz from a list of books that have been challenged or removed from libraries. The winner of the quiz received a gift certificate to a local bookstore.

The high school questions were:

Monday: What is a popular book in many high school English classes by Harper Lee that has been banned or challenged?

Tuesday: What is the part of the *Bill of Rights* that guarantees the freedom of religion, speech, press, assembly, and petition?

Wednesday: Who is the author of *The Chocolate War*, a novel about peer pressure which was banned and challenged?

Thursday: What was one of the most challenged titles in 1995? The *Adventures of _____*.

Friday: John _____, one of America's most famous novelists, has had many titles, banned and challenged, and continues to be challenged frequently.

Suggested Activities

The middle school questions were:

Monday: What was S. E. Hinton's famous novel? *The* _____.

Tuesday: *A Light in the Attic* and *Where the Sidewalk Ends* are frequently challenged. Who is the author?

Wednesday: Who wrote Matilda, a book found offensive for its disrespect for adults?

Thursday: What is the title of a spooky series that is often challenged? You may have read the stories when you were younger.

Friday: Who is the popular author of novels for young adults, such as *Forever* and *Deenie*?

Answers to Plan a Quiz

The high school answers are:
Monday: *To Kill a Mockingbird*
Tuesday: First Amendment
Wednesday: Robert Cormier
Thursday: *The Adventures of Huckleberry Finn*
Friday: Steinbeck

The middle school answers are:

Monday: *The Outsiders*
Tuesday: Shel Silverstein
Wednesday: Roald Dahl
Thursday: *Scary Stories to Tell in the Dark*
Friday: Judy Blume

CONDUCT a poll. The Goosebumps and Fear Street series by R. L. Stine are among the most censored books in the United States today. Conduct a poll of twenty-five adults asking them if and why they feel scary stories are harmful to children and teenagers. Then, poll twenty-five teenagers, asking them the same question. Make a visual contrasting the results of each poll.

PREPARE a speech. Many parents believe that Halloween promotes "evil" and should not be celebrated in schools. Research the origin of Halloween and prepare a persuasive speech about why it should or should not be celebrated by children.

USE a periodical index to locate as many articles as possible regarding book challenges in schools in the United States in the past five years. Draw a map of the United States and color in the states where you found challenges. Which state has the most challenges? How have each of the cases been resolved?

WRITE a ballad or a legend. Ballads and legends are often written about heroic people. For example, research John Peter Zenger's historic fight for First Amendment rights, or select your favorite First Amendment advocate and write a ballad or a legend about him.

FORM a banned books book club. The Malverne (N.Y.) Public Library celebrated Banned Books Week by starting a Banned Books Book Club. Patrons were asked to discuss books from around the world that have been banned in the author's country of origin. The reading list included *One Day in the Life of Ivan Denisovich* by Aleksandr Isayevich Solzhenitzyn for Russia; *This Earth of Mankind* by Ananta Pramoedya Toer for Indonesia; *Spycatcher* by Peter Wright for England; *Madame Bovary* by Gustave Flaubert for France; *Brave New World* by Aldous Huxley for England; *The Sorrows of Young Werther* by Goethe for Germany; *Blood Wedding* by Federico Garcia Lorca for Spain; and *Ulysses* by James Joyce for Ireland.

SPONSOR a program on the importance of privacy in libraries and bookstores, particularly in light of the USA PATRIOT Act. Show the video, "Reading Your Rights," a twenty-six minute documentary on the fight waged by Denver's Tattered Cover Bookstore against a search warrant for customer records. Contact the American Booksellers Foundation for Free Expression, 275 7th Ave., 15th Fl., New York, NY 10001; phone: (212) 587-4025; fax: (212) 587-2436; www.abffe.org to order the $35 video.

TEACH a Banned Books Course. Rebecca Godin at Alternative Community School in Ithaca, New York, uses First Amendment rights as a centerpiece for a course called "Banned Books." Each student younger than eighteen takes home a parent permission slip along with a syllabus describing course expectations, a list of books recommended for independent reading, assignments, and discussion topics. Although the course focuses on books banned in public schools, First Amendment issues in the arts and in society at large are explored.

Can citizens always exercise their First Amendment rights in our country today? Can students always exercise their First Amendment rights? Can these rights be taken too far? Should pornography be outlawed? Should violence and sex be limited on television or in the movies? Should rock music be censored? Should we allow advertisements for all products, even those that are harmful? Discussing these questions helps students find their own voices and sharpen their critical inquiry.

Some of the works discussed are *Howl* by Allen Ginsberg, *The Catcher in the Rye*, some of Whitman's *Leaves of Grass*, *Soul on Ice* by Eldridge Cleaver, Alice Walker's *The Color Purple*, and excerpts from the Bible. From the list of books banned in public schools and elsewhere, students choose one book to read independently for their position paper. They write a synopsis, then an analysis of why the book was banned using the 1957 Supreme Court Roth-decision (*Lady Chatterley's Lover*) triple test for prurient interest: 1) What is its effect on the average person? 2) Does it appeal to prurient or lustful interests? 3) Does it offend in the light of community standards?

The best approaches for teaching sexually explicit literature are the same ones used in any good teaching: critical thinking, enthusiasm, humor, and trust in each student's intelligence.

DEDICATE one day's programming on your National Public Radio (NPR) station to Banned Books Week. For example, "Today's programming on [the name of the radio station] is made possible in part by [your name], who is celebrating this Banned Books Week by re-reading their favorite banned or frequently challenged book.

TOP TEN Justin Richardson and Peter Parnell's award-winning *And Tango Makes Three*, about two male penguins parenting an egg from a mixed-sex penguin couple, tops the list of most challenged books in 2006 by parents and administrators due to the issues of homosexuality.

The list also features two books by author Toni Morrison. *The Bluest Eye* and *Beloved* are on the list due to sexual content and offensive language.

The ALA Office for Intellectual Freedom (OIF) received a total of 546 challenges in 2006. A challenge is defined as a formal, written complaint filed with a library or school, requesting that materials be removed because of content or appropriateness. Public libraries, schools and school libraries report the majority of challenges.

"The number of challenges reflects only incidents reported," said Judith F. Krug, director of the ALA Office for Intellectual Freedom. "For each reported challenge, four or five likely remain unreported."

The "10 Most Challenged Books of 2006" reflect a range of themes, and consist of the following titles:

- *And Tango Makes Three* by Justin Richardson and Peter Parnell, for homosexuality, anti-family, and unsuited to age group;
- *Gossip Girls* series by Cecily Von Ziegesar, for homosexuality, sexual content, drugs, unsuited to age group, and offensive language;
- *Alice* series by Phyllis Reynolds Naylor, for sexual content and offensive language;
- *The Earth, My Butt, and Other Big Round Things* by Carolyn Mackler, for sexual content, anti-family, offensive language, and unsuited to age group;
- *The Bluest Eye* by Toni Morrison, for sexual content, offensive language, and unsuited to age group;
- *Scary Stories* series by Alvin Schwartz, for occult/Satanism, unsuited to age group, violence, and insensitivity;
- *Athletic Shorts* by Chris Crutcher, for homosexuality and offensive language.
- *The Perks of Being a Wallflower* by Stephen Chbosky, for homosexuality, sexually explicit, offensive language, and unsuited to age group
- *Beloved* by Toni Morrison, for offensive language, sexual content, and unsuited to age group;
- *The Chocolate War* by Robert Cormier, for sexual content, offensive language, and violence.

Off the list this year, but on for several years past, are the *Catcher in the Rye* by J. D. Salinger, *Of Mice and Men* by John Steinbeck and *The Adventures of Huckleberry Finn* by Mark Twain.

USE the Illinois First Amendment Center's (IFAC) First Amendment Materials. IFAC produces First Amendment materials to cover grades kindergarten through twelve (some materials are also appropriate for the college level).

The IFAC's First Amendment campaign began in 2002 with the production of "The First Amendment—Keep It Strong" posters. When the U.S. Congress issued a federal mandate in 2005 that all schools (including grades kindergarten though

  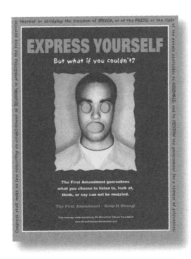

college) receiving federal monies must teach about the U.S. Constitution on September 17 of each year, the IFAC significantly ramped up its First Amendment educational campaign.

Currently, the IFAC's First Amendment materials include the following:

First Amendment Coloring Books
Five books individualized for each of grades kindergarten through four. The kindergarten and first grade books contain English and Spanish side by side; the books for grades two, three, and four are English-only and Spanish-only, due to lengthier content. May be viewed on the IFAC Web site at www.illinoisfirstamendmentcenter.com.

First Amendment Flash Cards
For grades three through eight. Currently available in English and Spanish. May be viewed on the IFAC Web site.

First Amendment Curriculum Guide on CD-ROM
For grades five through seven containing sixty-nine pages, including reproducible activity pages for students. Currently available in English. Available in Spanish after May 1, 2007. (Also available from Web site in e-mailable PDF format at no cost.)

First Amendment's Five Freedoms Posters
Set of five, depicting each of the Five Freedoms contained in the First Amendment. Appropriate for grades kindergarten through eight or above. Currently available in English. Available in Spanish after May 1, 2007. May be viewed on the IFAC Web site.

First Amendment Classroom Video on DVD
Four minutes in length. Appropriate for grades two through eight. May be viewed on the IFAC Web site.

First Amendment—Keep It Strong posters
For eighth grade through adult. Currently available in English. Available in Spanish after May 1, 2007. May be viewed on the IFAC Web site.

First Amendment Curriculum Guide on CD-ROM
For grades eight through twelve containing seventy-nine pages, including reproducible activity pages for students. Currently available in English. Available in Spanish after May 1, 2007. (Also available from Web site in e-mailable PDF format at no cost.)

TV Spots on DVD featuring the First Amendment—Keep It Strong posters.
May be viewed on the IFAC Web site. Currently available in English. Available in Spanish after May 1, 2007. May be viewed on the IFAC Web site.

Newspaper print campaign on CD-ROM—featuring the First Amendment—Keep It Strong posters
For use in school or professional newspapers.

First Amendment Teen Video on DVD
For grades nine and above. Will be available after May 1, 2007.

IFAC's materials are free to educators and carry only a nominal shipping charge. All items may be ordered online at www.illinoisfirstamendmentcenter. com or by contacting IFAC, located within and affiliated with the Illinois Press Association, 900

Community Dr., Springfield, IL 62703; phone: (217) 241-1300; fax: (217) 241-1301. All materials are copyrighted and cannot be reproduced with the exception of the curriculum guides.

WRITE an editorial for your local newspaper. Pat Scales, Library Media Specialist at the Greenville (S.C.) Middle School, wrote the following op-ed piece for publication:

"According to statistics gathered by the ALA Office for Intellectual Freedom and the National Coalition Against Censorship, book challenges are at an epidemic level in school and public libraries across the United States. What is amiss in this 'land of the free?'

"Is this 'censorship war' about fear? control? power? How does this battle affect the education of our children? What kind of messages are we sending to them regarding their constitutional rights?

"When I was in library school, there was a course called 'Censorship.' This course surveyed books such as *Portnoy's Complaint, Of Mice and Men*, and *The Catcher in the Rye*. This was in the days before Judy Blume, Robert Cormier, Stephen King, R.L. Stein, Katherine Paterson, and Alvin Schwartz. It was in the days when public libraries had more challenges than school libraries.

"Most library school students took this censorship course for personal enjoyment. They never realized that fighting censorship could become a very real part of their job.

"Today, the battle is raging, and public librarians and school media specialists are stumbling in their fight to win the war. Their enemies are organized groups of people, from the right and the left, who are determined to gain power over what students read and learn.

"In some cities, library boards are under pressure to place ratings on books. In other places, students' names are tagged, at parental request, for restricted use of certain library materials. Frightened librarians are limiting young students to the 'easy' books section, and they are requiring older students to bring written parental permission to read books such as Judy Blume's *Forever*, Katherine Paterson's *Bridge to Terabithia*, Mark Twain's *The Adventures of Huckleberry Finn*, Harper Lee's *To Kill a Mockingbird*, and Alice Walker's *The Color Purple*.

"Professionals are self-censoring in the selection process, making every effort to make 'safe' book choices. These practices, however, aren't eliminating the problem; they are only amplifying the issue.

"The problem is obvious. Censors want to control the minds of the young. They are fearful of the educational system because students who read learn to think. Thinkers learn to see. Those who see often question.

"The answer is the classroom. As educators, we cannot, for the sake of the students, allow ourselves to be bullied into diluting the curriculum into superficial facts. We must talk about the principles of intellectual freedom. We must challenge students to think about the intent of our forefathers when they wrote the Bill of Rights.

"We must teach students about their First Amendment rights rather than restrict their use of particular books and materials. As educators, we must encourage students to express their own opinions while respecting the views of others.

"Teachers, through interdisciplinary units of study, can lead students toward understanding the implications of the First Amendment for all Americans. As librarians and library media specialists, we must realize that our professional role extends beyond removing all restrictions and barriers from the library collection.

"We can go into the classroom and engage students in activities and discussion that will enable them to think about their personal rights and responsibilities provided by the Constitution. The appropriate time to make this connection is when students are already engaged in a study of the Constitution.

"Ask students to read and react to a contemporary young adult novel like Richard Peck's *The Last Safe Place on Earth*, Julian Thompson's *The Trials of Molly Sheldon*, or Stephanie Tolan's *Save Halloween* that deals with censorship issues. Invite them to apply the situations in the novel to real life.

"Encourage them to debate the conflict presented in each novel. Provide a forum in which they can express their views regarding the subject of intellectual freedom. And, help them understand their personal options regarding the use of books and materials that might offend them. Above all, grant them the opportunity to think, to speak, and to be heard.

218

Suggested Activities

"Classrooms and schools that foster this type of open atmosphere are sending a clear message: The First Amendment is important in school as well as in society at large.

"The Censorship War Memorial, an exhibit prepared for Banned Books Week by Jill Sekula, a student in Education at Bowling Green State University, Ohio, lists books challenged or banned. The bottom of the 'wall' reads 'Dedicated to those wounded or killed in the war against Free Speech in the United States, which has been taking place since our country was born and will continue until we stop the madness.'"

PRINT and **DISTRIBUTE** the Internet Safety Bookmarks by MySpace and Illinois Library Association.

The bookmarks are printed as a series, each aimed at a specific audience including kids, teens, and parents to help educate youth and parents to make safe and informed decisions online. The Internet Safety bookmarks contain information on the safety topics below, as well links to additional online resources.

Dealing with Cyberbullies: Tips for Kids
Safe Blogging: Tips for Teens
Social Networking: Tips for Parents

The Internet Safety Bookmarks are available to download and print locally at the Illinois Library Association Web site (www.ila.org/netsafe).

DEALING WITH CYBERBULLIES
TIPS FOR KIDS

▶ **Don't reply.** You may want to respond, but this is exactly what cyberbullies want. They want to know they've got you scared, worried and upset. Don't give them that satisfaction.

▶ **Don't keep this to yourself!** You are not alone, and you did not do anything to deserve bullying. Tell an adult you trust about the situation. Don't try and solve this on your own.

▶ **Don't delete messages.** You don't have to read them, but you should keep them. They are your evidence. You may unfortunately get similar messages again, perhaps from other accounts. The police and your ISP, and/or your telephone company can use these messages to help you.

▶ **Do get a trusted adult's help.** If you are getting physical threats:
  ▶ **Call** your local police.
  ▶ **Inform** your Internet service provider (ISP) or cell phone service.
  ▶ **Protect** yourself.

▶ Never arrange to meet with someone you met online unless your parents, friends, or a trusted adult go with you. If you are meeting them, make sure it is in a public place.

For more information, go to
http://www.cyberbullying.org/

SPONSORED BY
 Illinois Library Association  myspace.com a place for friends

---

SAFE BLOGGING
TIPS FOR TEENS

▶ **Be anonymous.** Avoid postings that could help a stranger to locate you. This includes your last name, address, phone numbers, sports teams, the town you live in, and where you hang out.

▶ **Protect your info.** Check to see if your service has a "friends" list that allows you to decide who can visit your profile or blog. If so, allow only people you know and trust.

▶ **Avoid in-person meetings.** don't get together with someone you "meet" in a profile or blog unless you are certain of their actual identity. Talk it over with an adult first. Although it's still not risk-free, arrange any meetings in a public place and bring along some friends, your parents, or a trusted adult.

▶ **Think before you post.** What's uploaded to the net can be downloaded by anyone and passed around or posted online pretty much forever. Avoid posting photos that allow people to identify you, especially sexually suggestive images.

▶ **Check comments regularly.** don't respond to mean or embarrassing comments.

▶ **Be honest about your age.** Membership rules are there to protect people. If you are too young to sign up, don't lie about your age.

© 2006 ConnectSafely.org   SPONSORED BY
Illinois Library Association myspace.com a place for friends

SOCIAL NETWORKING
TIPS FOR PARENTS

▶ **Be reasonable and try to set reasonable expectations.** pulling the plug on your child's Internet activities is rarely a good first response to a problem—it's too easy for them to "go underground" and establish accounts at a friend's house or many other places.

▶ **Be open with your children.** encourage them to come to you if they encounter a problem online—cultivate trust and communication because no rules, laws or filtering software can replace you as their first line of defense.

▶ **Talk with your children.** Find out how they use the services. Make sure they understand basic Internet safety guidelines, including privacy protection and passwords, the risks involved in posting personal information, avoiding in-person meetings, and not posting inappropriate photos.

▶ **Consider requiring that all online activity take place in a central area of the home, not in a child's bedroom.** be aware that there are also ways children can access the Internet away from home.

▶ **Try to get your children to share their blogs or online profiles with you.** be aware that they can have multiple accounts on multiple services. Use search engines and the search tools on social-networking sites to search for your child's identifying information.

© 2006 ConnectSafely.org   SPONSORED BY
Illinois Library Association   myspace.com a place for friends

Action Guide
Annotated Bibliography of
First Amendment Resources

Adams, Thelma, ed. *Censorship and First Amendment Rights: A Primer.* Tarrytown, New York: American Booksellers Foundation for Free Expression, 1992. Case studies and resources for handling censorship, working with lawyers and lobbyists, etc., with an introduction by Anthony Lewis.

Article 19 Freedom of Expression Handbook: International and Comparative Law, Standards and Procedures. London: ARTICLE 19, Int. Centre Against Censorship, 1996. The handbook brings together, by topic, summaries and analysis of relevant international jurisprudence as well as decisions from national courts around the world that declare strong protections of the rights to freedom of expression and access to information. The handbook's aims are: 1) to enable lawyers around the world to use international and comparative freedom of expression law in cases before national courts and to assess whether their client's case would be advanced by filing an application with an international body; 2) to inform journalists, writers, and human rights campaigners and provide access to information under international and comparative law and standards, and to provide them with examples of how courts from a diversity of legal traditions have protected and promoted freedom of expression, often in the face of repressive government practices; 3) to provide a resource for academics, lawyers, and others interested in comparative and international freedom of expression law and jurisprudence. Updates to the handbook are available at www.article19.org.

Bollinger, Lee C., and Geoffrey R. Stone. *Eternally Vigilant: Free Speech in the Modern Era.* Chicago, Univ. of Chicago Pr., 2002. While freedom of speech has been guaranteed us for centuries, the First Amendment as we know it today is largely a creation of the past eighty years. Eternally Vigilant brings together a group of distinguished legal scholars to reflect boldly on its past, its present shape, and what forms our understanding of it might take in the future.

Brown, Jean E. *Preserving Intellectual Freedom: Fighting Censorship in Our Schools.* Urbana, Ill.: National Council of Teachers of English, 1995. The author sheds light on the ways in which censorship arises; how it affects curricula, students, and teachers; and how it can be fought. The book also takes a comprehensive look at the provisions and implications of the 1988 U.S. Supreme Court decision in *Hazelwood v. Kuhlmeir*, which held that a high school principal's censorship of a student newspaper did not violate students' First Amendment rights, because the paper was not a public forum.

Censorship or Selection: Choosing Books for Public Schools. A dynamic, hour-long videotape of a twenty-two member panel responding to issues of how books get into classrooms and libraries and how they are sometimes removed. Encourage your local television station to screen the tape, or use it to create your own program. Available for $79.95 plus $6.00 for shipping and handling from PBS Video, 1320 Braddock Place, Alexandria, VA 22314; (800) 424-7963.

Cloonan, Martin, and Reebee Garofalo, eds. *Policing Pop.* Philadelphia: Temple Univ. Press, 2003. A fascinating survey of the ways in which pop music has been censored and restricted, it also makes an eloquent argument for the political and social importance of popular music. The essays collected here focus on the forms of censorship as well as specific instances of how the state and other agencies have attempted to restrict the types of music produced, recorded and performed within a culture. Several show how even unsuccessful attempts to exert the power of the state can cause artists to self-censor. Others point to material that taxes even the most liberal defenders of free speech. Taken together, these essays demonstrate that censoring agents target popular music all over the world, and they raise questions about how artists and the public can resist the narrowing of cultural expression.

Coetzee, J. M. *Giving Offense: Essays on Censorship.* Chicago: Univ. of Chicago Pr., 1996. South African writer J. M. Coetzee presents a coherent, unorthodox analysis of censorship from the perspective of a writer who has lived and worked under its shadow.

Cole, David, and James X. Dempsey. *Terrorism and the Constitution: Sacrificing Civil Liberties in the Name of National Security*. New York: New Press, 2002. Tracing the history of government intrusions on Constitutional rights in response to threats from abroad, Cole and Dempsey warn that a society in which civil liberties are sacrificed in the name of national security is in fact less secure than one in which they are upheld. In a vivid and important critique of our government's response to threats —real and perceived — from communists in the 1950s, Central American activists in the 1980s, Palestinians in the 1990s, and now Islamic terrorists in the twenty-first century, the authors warn that

many of our government's anti-terrorism efforts sacrifice civil liberties without effectively protecting national security.

Curtis, Michael Kent. *Free Speech, "the People's Darling Privilege:" Struggles for Freedom of Expression in American History.* Durham, N.C.: Duke Univ. Pr., 2001. Modern ideas about the protection of free speech in the United States did not originate in twentieth-century U.S. Supreme Court cases, as many have thought. Free Speech, "The People's Darling Privilege" refutes this misconception by examining popular struggles for free speech that stretch back through American history. Curtis focuses on struggles in which ordinary and extraordinary people, men and women, black and white, demanded and fought for freedom of speech during the period from 1791— when the Bill of Rights and its First Amendment bound only the federal government to protect free expression—to 1868, when the Fourteenth Amendment sought to extend this mandate to the states. A review chapter is also included to bring the story up to date. Curtis analyzes three crucial political struggles: the controversy that surrounded the 1798 Sedition Act, which raised the question of whether criticism of elected officials would be protected speech; the battle against slavery, which raised the question of whether Americans would be free to criticize a great moral, social, and political evil; and the controversy over anti-war speech during the Civil War. Many speech issues raised by these controversies were ultimately decided outside the judicial arena—in Congress, in state legislatures, and, perhaps most importantly, in public discussion and debate.

DelFattore, Joan. *What Johnny Shouldn't Read: Textbook Censorship in America.* New Haven, Conn.: Yale Univ. Pr., 1992. An enlightening treatise on how pressure groups affect textbook publishing, influencing schools throughout the country. The stories behind recent lawsuits show how local communities' concerns become national issues because of sophisticated pressure group tactics.

Demac, Donna A. *Liberty Denied: The Current Rise of Censorship in America.* 2nd ed. New Brunswick, N.J.: Rutgers Univ. Pr., 1992. Shows the extent of the assault on free expression in the past decade, making the point that the quiet eroding of individual rights poses a threat to the principles Americans hold dear.

Foerstel, Herbert N. *Banned in the Media.* Westport, Conn.: Greenwood, 1998. Herbert Foerstel traces the history of media censorship in the United States, from colonial times to the present day, keeping an eye on the future. This comprehensive reference guide to media censorship provides in-depth coverage of each media format--newspapers, magazines, motion pictures, radio, television, and the Internet. Each format is examined in-depth, from its origins and history through its modern development, and features discussion of landmark incidents and cases.

_____. *Banned in the U.S.A.: A Reference Guide to Book Censorship in Schools and Public Libraries.* Westport, Conn.: Greenwood, 2002. Almost every aspect of book censorship is examined in this comprehensive source. Included in this readable survey of major book-banning incidents, legal cases surrounding censorship, interviews with the most censored authors, and an annotated list and discussion of the fifty most frequently challenged books for 1996 through 2000.

_____. **Free Expression and Censorship in America: An Encyclopedia.** Westport, Conn.: Greenwood, 1997. This comprehensive encyclopedia includes analysis of the First Amendment implications of major political issues of the 1990s including abortion, campaign finance, violence on television, homosexuality, and the Internet.

_____. **Freedom of Information and the Right to Know: The Origins and Applications of the Freedom of Information Act.** Westport, Conn.: Greenwood, 1999. Foerstel examines the Freedom of Information Act (FOIA) and explores its importance as a tool in guaranteeing an informed citizenry and an open government.

_____. **Refuge of a Scoundrel: The PATRIOT Act in Libraries.** Westport, Conn.: Greenwood, 2004. The USA PATRIOT Act may be the most complex and controversial federal statute in American history, argued to undercut American civil liberties in countless ways, including a dramatic extension of domestic surveillance. The author convincingly proves that under this act and FBI guidelines, libraries and bookstores--long subject to FBI surveillance--are more vulnerable than ever before.

For Freedom's Sake, ALA Video/Library Video Network, 1996. The first part of this tape presents an overview of intellectual freedom in libraries today. *The Library Bill of Rights* is examined and library administrators discuss their experiences when facing challenges to their collections. The second part of the tape presents vignettes to which viewers can react. After the vignette is depicted, viewers are asked to stop the tape and react to the scene; possible solutions are then presented.

Garbus, Martin. **Tough Talk: How I Fought for Writers, Comics, Bigots, and the American Way.** New York: Times Books, 1998. As one of America's leading First Amendment attorneys, Martin Garbus' clients have included Lenny Bruce, Daniel Ellsberg, Kathy Boudin, Jeffrey Toobin, William B. Shockley, Peter Matthiessen, Spike Lee, Prodigy, Robert Redford, Chuck D, Al Goldstein, and major publishers. What is clear from the many accounts of Garbus's battles for freedom of speech is that the struggle to be free or to remain free will never end.

Garbus also shows how one person (or a few) can make a huge difference in the free society we enjoy today.

Haynes, Charles, et al. **The First Amendment in Schools: A Guide from the First Amendment Center.** Alexandria, Va.: Association for Supervision and Curriculum Development, 2003. A rich resource, the book includes: an explanation of the origins of the First Amendment; a concise, chronological history of fifty legal cases, including many landmark decisions, involving the First Amendment in public schools; and answers to frequently asked questions about the practice of the First Amendment in schools, covering specific issues of religious liberty, free speech, and press as they affect school prayer, use of school facilities, dress and speech codes, student press, book selection, and curriculum.

Heins, Marjorie. **Not in Front of the Children: "Indecency," Censorship, and the Innocence of Youth.** New York: Hill & Wang, 2001. Heins investigates the origins of conjecture regarding child and adolescent innocence and the history of "harm to minors" censorship beginning with the "virtuous thoughts" espoused by Plato's *Republic* on through to the installation of Internet filters in schools and libraries. With legal and social examples taken from cultures around the world, the author provides evidence that the "harm to minors" argument lies on unstable ground.

_____. **Sex, Sin, and Blasphemy: A Guide to America's Censorship Wars.** New York: New Press, 1998. Heins has been on the front lines of the "wars" as director of the Arts Censorship Project of the American Civil Liberties Union. She uses many examples to identify the legal themes and strategies of the adversaries, to elucidate the importance of artistic free expression, and to explain why suppression will not solve the problems that beset society.

Hentoff, Nat. **Free Speech for Me but Not for Thee: How the American Left and Right Relentlessly Censor Each Other.** New York: HarperCollins, 1993. Hentoff explores not only the "traditional" sources of censorship--religious fundamentalists and political right-wingers--but also censorship from the left, e.g., feminists who tried to prevent a pro-life women's group from participating in Yale University's Women's Center. He also takes on proponents of "hate speech" regulations as enemies of free expression.

_____. ***Living the Bill of Rights: How to Be an Authentic American.*** New York: HarperCollins, 1998. Through portrayals of the famous (Supreme Court Justices William O. Douglas and William Brennan) and the not-so-famous (Anthony Griffin, a black lawyer and ACLU volunteer who defended the First Amendment rights of the Ku Klux Klan), Nat Hentoff pays tribute to American citizens whose lives embody the values and principles of the U.S. Constitution.

_____. ***The War on the Bill of Rights and the Gathering Resistance.*** Rev. ed. New York: Seven Stories Pr., 2004. This concise manifesto by a longtime defender of constitutional liberties is a blistering attack on the Bush administration, and on U.S. Attorney General John Ashcroft in particular, who Hentoff says has "subverted more elements of the Bill of Rights than any attorney general in American history." Hentoff berates the U.S. Congress for its "supine" acquiescence to the USA PATROIT Act, and the media for slack coverage of these issues and raises the specter of J. Edgar Hoover's goon squads.

Index on Censorship; c/o Mercury Airfreight Int./ Ltd. Inc., 2323 Randolph Ave., Avenue, NJ 07001; indexoncenso@gn.apc.org; http://www.oneworld.org/index_oc/. This bimonthly publication examines censorship from an international perspective. Special issues have been devoted to subjects such as film censorship, art censorship, and libraries.

Intellectual Freedom Manual, Seventh Edition. Compiled by the Office for Intellectual Freedom, American Library Association. Chicago: ALA, 2006. Completely revised, the manual is designed to answer practical questions that confront librarians in applying the principles of intellectual freedom to library service. It provides guidance on developing a materials selection policy and public library Internet use policy, dealing with the political strategies of organized pressure groups, and promoting access to all types of information for all types of users. New features include new interpretations to the *Library Bill of Rights*, plus guidelines for the development of policies and procedures regarding user behavior and library usage. It is an indispensable reference tool.

Jones, Barbara M. ***Libraries, Access and Intellectual Freedom: Developing Policies for Public and Academic Libraries.*** Chicago: ALA, 1999. Jones describes the affirmative steps libraries can take before a challenge happens. She identifies potential areas of conflict, legal issues, and the need for strong intellectual freedom policies. Written in clear, concise language, this volume is essential for all libraries seeking to develop intellectual freedom policies.

Jones, Derek, ed. ***Censorship: A World Encyclopedia.*** 4 vols. Chicago: Fitzroy Dearborn, 2001. This work provides a wide-ranging view of censorship, spanning ancient Egypt to present times and covering art, literature, music, newspapers and broadcasting, and the visual arts, among many other topics. In addition, the work provides country surveys and discussions of major controversies for specific movies, books, and television shows. Some 1,550 entries, arranged alphabetically order by subject, were written by about 600 contributors from fifty countries. Entries are enhanced by occasional illustrations, a name-subject index, and an alphabetical and thematic list of entries at the beginning of each volume.

Karolides, Nicholas J., Margaret Bald, and Dawn B. Sova. ***120 Banned Books: Censorship Histories of World Literature.*** New York: Checkmark Books, 2005. This reference book contains extensive information about books that have been banned, suppressed, or censored for religious, political, sexual, or social reasons across twenty centuries and in many. Each entry contains the author's name, original date and place of publication and literary form, as well as a plot summary. A separate section of each entry provides details of the censorship history of the work, followed by a list of further readings for a more in-depth examination of the challenges.

Bald, Margaret. ***Literature Suppressed on Religious Grounds, Rev. ed.*** New York, N.Y.: Facts on File, 2006.

Karolides, Nicholas J. ***Literature Suppressed on Political Grounds, Rev. ed.*** New York, N.Y.: Facts on File, 2006.

Sova, Dawn B. ***Literature Suppressed on Sexual Grounds, Rev. ed.*** New York, N.Y.: Facts on File, 2006.

_____. ***Literature Suppressed on Social Grounds, Rev. ed.*** New York, N.Y.: Facts on File, 2006.

The aim of this four-volume set is to spotlight some 400 works that have been censored, banned, or condemned because of their political, social, religious, or sexual content. The entries, which include a summary, censorship history, and brief bibliography, range widely from Aristotle through Galileo and on up to Adolf Hitler and Judy Blume.

225

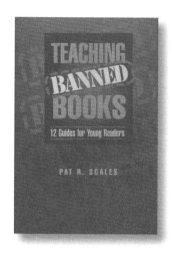

Such well-known prohibited works as de Sade's 120 Days of Sodom, the Communist Manifesto, and Huckleberry Finn are included here, but so are many other works that are now less controversial, e.g., Milton's *Areopagitica* and *Uncle Tom's Cabin*. Some of the censorship histories are several pages long, but others are very short.

Krull, Kathleen. ***A Kids' Guide to America's Bill of Rights: Curfews, Censorship, and the 100-Pound Giant.*** New York: Avon, 1999. Examines the ten amendments to the United States Constitution that make up the Bill of Rights, explaining what the amendments mean, how they have been applied, and the rights they guarantee.

Minow, Mary, and Thomas A. Lipinski. ***The Library's Legal Answer Book.*** Chicago: ALA, 2003. Containing answers to more than 600 legal questions, the work tackles topics and concerns as diverse as copyright, Web page design, filters and other restrictions on Internet access, privacy, library spaces as "public forums," professional liability, ADA compliance, library employment, and lobbying by nonprofit organizations, foundations, associations, and others. An index and the occasional case study enhance the guide's usability and thoroughness.

Newsletter on Intellectual Freedom. Chicago: ALA. This ALA bimonthly publication reports censorship incidents across the country, summarizes recent court cases on the First Amendment, and includes a bibliography on intellectual freedom. It

is the best source of information on the continuing battle to defend and extend First Amendment rights.

Noble, William. ***Bookbanning in America: Who Bans Books?—And Why?*** Middlebury, Vt.: Paul S. Eriksson, 1992. Anecdotes, interviews, trial transcripts, and case histories show how and why bookbanning happens, beginning in 1650, through the Salman Rushdie affair.

Nuzum, Eric D. ***Parental Advisory: Music Censorship in America.*** New York: Perennial, 2001. This thorough history of music censorship — case by case and fight by fight— focuses on the 1950s to the present, but includes incidents dating back to the 19th century. Part one is organized thematically, with chapters on the main hot-potato issues that music (especially rock, heavy metal, and gangsta rap) has drawn fire for: "excessive" violence, sex, and drugs; political protests perceived as threatening; and religious "blasphemy." Part two is a nearly year-by-year chronology, beginning in 1865, of notable censorship cases.

O'Harrow, Robert. ***No Place to Hide: Behind the Scenes of Our Emerging Surveillance Society.*** New York: Free Press, 2005. Detail the post-9/11 marriage of private data and technology companies and government anti-terror initiatives to create something entirely new: a security-industrial complex. Drawing on his years of investigation, O'Harrow shows how the government now depends on burgeoning private reservoirs of information about almost every aspect of our lives to promote homeland security and fight the war on terror. In this new world of high-tech domestic intelligence, the author contends there is literally no place to hide.

Peck, Robert. **Libraries, the First Amendment and Cyberspace.** Chicago: ALA, 2000. This handbook answers the questions librarians have about the First Amendment and provision of library services. It addresses basic First Amendment principles and their applicability to libraries and the Internet. Information on the application of the First Amendment to children and schools is also included. Appendixes include copies of ALA policies and guidelines.

Phillips, Peter and Project Censored. **Censored 2006: The Top 25 Censored Stories.** New York: Seven Stories Press, 2006. This annual publication of Project Censored presents a report card for the American press, listing the least-reported news stories of the past year. In addition to summarizing the year's twenty-five most censored stories, the volume includes Censored Déjà Vu, censored stories from past years that have since reached the mainstream media; Censored Resource Guide, a directory of media and anti-censorship organizations; and reprints of the top ten censored stories.

Ravitch, Diane. **The Language Police: How Pressure Groups Restrict What Students Learn.** New York: Knopf, 2003. Describes in copious detail how pressure groups from the political right and left have attempted to wrest control of the language and content of textbooks and standardized exams, often at the expense of the truth (in the case of history), of literary quality (in the case of literature), and of education in general.

Reichman, Henry F. **Censorship and Selection: Issues and Answers for Schools, 3rd ed.** Chicago: ALA, 2001. The manual contains clear, concise, and useful information on the issues and solutions to censorship. Though its focus is primarily for schools, information is sufficiently general so libraries will find it useful. Censorship and Selection addresses how to develop viable policies ranging from how to handle complaints to the selection of learning materials. Specific recommendations for how to plan for potential crises also are included.

Robbins, Louise S. **Censorship and the American Library: The American Library Association's Response to Threats to Intellectual Freedom, 1939-1969.** Westport, Conn.: Greenwood, 1996.

A study of the development of the American Library Association's intellectual freedom policies from 1939, when ALA first articulated its commitment to providing diverse viewpoints to library users, to 1969, when the Freedom to Read Foundation was founded.

Scales, Pat. R. **Teaching Banned Books: 12 Guides for Young Readers.** Chicago: ALA, 2001. This book can serve as a springboard for class discussions, staff development for administrators and teachers, and for parent groups. It can also reinforce the courage of those who work with young people to provide avenues for them to practice this important right.

Simmons, John S. and Eliza Dresang. **School Censorship in the 21st Century: A Guide for Teachers and School Library Media Specialists.** Newark, Del.: International Reading Association, 2001. This book offers insights into the nature of current censorship challenges, the historical and cultural context in which they occur in the United States, and the resources that exist for meeting these increasingly complex challenges.

Smith, Robert Ellis. **Ben Franklin's Web Site: Privacy and Curiosity from Plymouth Rock to the Internet.** Providence, R.I.: Privacy Journal, 2004. Smith explores the hidden niches of American history to discover the tug between Americans' yearning for privacy and their insatiable curiosity. The book describes Puritan monitoring in Colonial New England, then shows how the attitudes of the founders placed the concept of privacy in the Constitution. This panoramic view continues with the coming of tabloid journalism in the Nineteenth Century, and the reaction to it in the form of a new right—the right to privacy. The book includes histories of wiretapping, of credit reporting, of sexual practices, of Social Security numbers and ID cards, of modern principles of privacy protection, and of the coming of the Internet and the new challenges to personal privacy it brings.

Stone, Geoffrey R. **Perilous Times: Free Speech in Wartime from the Sedition Act of 1787 to the War on Terrorism.** New York: Norton, 2004. Stone investigates how the First Amendment and other civil liberties have been compromised in America during wartime. He delineates the consistent suppression of free speech in six historical periods from the Sedition Act of 1798 to the Vietnam War, and ends with a coda that examines the state of civil liberties in the Bush era. Full of fresh legal and historical insight, Perilous Times magisterially presents a dramatic cast of characters who influenced the course of history over a two-hundred-year period: from the presidents—Adams, Lincoln, Wilson, Roosevelt, and Nixon—to the Supreme Court justices—Taney, Holmes, Brandeis, Black, and Warren—to the resisters—Clement Vallandingham, Emma Goldman, Fred Korematsu, and David Dellinger. Filled with dozens of rare photographs, posters, and historical illustrations, Perilous Times is resonant in its call for a new approach in our response to grave crises.

Sova, Dawn. **Banned Plays: Censorship Histories of 125 Stage Dramas.** New York: Facts on File, 2004.

_____. **Forbidden Films: Censorship Histories of 125 Motion Pictures.** New York: Facts on File, 2001. Since the earliest days of the film industry, mainstream films have been banned for their sexual, religious, social, and political content. Forbidden Films traces the efforts to censor 125 films, ranging from the silent Birth of a Nation to Schlindler's List. Entries are arranged alphabetically by film title and include production details such as country and date of production, distribution, format, running time, director, writer, awards, genre, and cast. A summary of the film's plot is followed by a description of its censorship history. Each entry concludes with a short bibliography for further reading.

Wachsberger, Ken, ed. **Literature Suppressed on Political Grounds** by Nicholas J. Karolides; **Literature Suppressed on Religious Grounds**, by Margaret Bald; **Literature Suppressed on Sexual Grounds**, by Dawn B. Sova; and **Literature Suppressed on Social Grounds**, by Dawn B. Sova. Banned Books Series. New York: Facts on File, 2006. The aim of this four-volume set is to spotlight some 400 works that have been censored, banned, or condemned because of their political, social, religious, or sexual content. The entries, which include a summary, censorship history, and brief bibliography, range widely from Aristotle through Galileo and on up to Adolf Hitler and Judy Blume. Such well-known prohibited works as de Sade's *120 Days of Sodom*, the Communist Manifesto, and *The Adventures of Huckleberry Finn* are included here, but so are many other works that are now less controversial, e.g., Milton's *Areopagitica* and *Uncle Tom's Cabin*.

Teaching Students about the First Amendment: A Bibliography. Compiled by Pat Scales, South Carolina Governor's School for the Arts

FICTION

Christian, Peggy. **The Bookstore Mouse.** Illus. by Gary A. Lippincott. San Diego: Harcourt Brace, 1995. Cervantes, a mouse who lives in an antiquarian bookstore, embarks on a great adventure while trying to elude Milo the cat. When Cervantes discovers the power of words, he finds a special way to deal with Milo, and they both live a more enlightened life.

Diaz, Jorge. **The Rebellious Alphabet.** Illus. by Oivind S. Jorfald. New York: Henry Holt & Company, 1993. For older readers, this illustrated fable tells the story of an illiterate dictator who bans reading and writing, but is outwitted by an old man who trains canaries to deliver printed messages to people.

Facklam, Margery. **The Trouble with Mothers.** New York: Clarion, 1989. Eighth-grader Luke Troy is devastated when his Mother, a teacher, writes an historical novel that is considered pornography by some people in the community where they live.

Hentoff, Nat. **The Day They Came to Arrest the Book.** New York: Dell, 1985. Students in a high school English class protest the study of Huckleberry Finn until the editor of the school newspaper uncovers other cases of censorship and in a public hearing reveals the truth behind the mysterious disappearance of certain library books and the resignation of the school librarian.

Lasky, Kathryn. *Memoirs of a Bookbat.* San Diego: Harcourt, Brace, 1994. Fourteen-year-old Harper Jessup, an avid reader, runs away because she feels that her individual rights are threatened when her parents, born again fundamentalists, lodge a public promotion of book censorship.

Meyer, Carolyn. *Drummers of Jericho.* San Diego: Harcourt Brace, 1995. When a fourteen-year-old Jewish girl joins the high school marching band and discovers that the band will play hymns and stand in the formation of a cross, she objects and major issues of individual rights are raised.

Miles, Betty. *Maudie, and Me and the Dirty Book.* New York: Knopf, 1994. Eleven-year-old Kate Harris volunteers to read to first graders but her choice of book, The Birthday Dog, causes the children to ask questions about how puppies are born. When parents of the younger children raise objection, the principal suspends the reading project, and Kate and her friends learn first-hand about censorship.

Peck, Richard. *The Last Safe Place on Earth.* New York: Delacorte, 1995. The Tobin family is satisfied that Walden Woods is a quiet, safe community to rear three children. Then, seven-year-old Marnie begins having nightmares after a teenage babysitter tells her that Halloween is "evil," and Todd and Diana, sophomores in high school, witness an organized group's attempt to censor books in their school library.

Thompson, Julian F. *The Trials of Molly Sheldon.* New York: Henry Holt, 1995. When high schooler Molly Sheldon begins working for her father in his eclectic general store in central Vermont, she faces First Amendment issues for the first time in her life. Moralists try to censor the books that her father sells, and Molly is accused of being a witch.

Tolan, Stephanie S. *Save Halloween!* New York: William Morrow, 1993. When sixth-grader Johnna Filkings gets caught up in researching and writing a class pageant about Halloween, her father and uncle, fundamentalist ministers, disrupt the entire community by declaring Halloween evil.

NONFICTION

Faber, Doris, and Harold Faber. *We The People: The Story of the United States Constitution since 1787.* New York: Scribner's, 1987. An historical account of the writing of the Constitution and the adoption of the Bill of Rights, including a discussion of the responsibility of the Supreme Court as an interpreter of this important document.

Gold, John C. *Board of Education v. Pico (1982).* New York: Twenty-First Century Books, 1994. Traces the Pico case from its beginning in 1975 to the 1982 final Supreme Court decision that ordered the school board of the Island Trees Union Free School District No. 26 on Long Island, New York, to return nine books to the library shelves.

Gottfried, Ted. *The American Media.* New York: Franklin Watts, 1997. Focusing on the history of the media in the United States, this book explores topics such as yellow journalism, censorship, and freedom of the press. Index.

Greenberg, Keith, and Jeanne Vestal. *Adolescent Rights: Are Young People Equal under the Law?* New York: Twenty-First Century Books, 1995. Details adolescent rights from an historical and contemporary perspective and invites readers to form their own conclusions regarding specific issues.

Meltzer, Milton. *The Bill of Rights: How We Got It and What It Means.* New York: Crowell, 1990. A comprehensive discussion of the history of the Bill of Rights with specific references to contemporary challenges of the ten amendments.

Monroe, Judy. *Censorship.* New York: Crestwood House, 1990. An overview, in simple language, of the problems of censorship with textbooks, movies, music, and children's books.

Pascoe, Elaine. *Freedom of Expression: The Right to Speak out in America.* Brookfield, Conn.: Millbrook Press, 1992. Traces the First Amendment's roots in earlier societies, and examines how it has been tested and interpreted from colonial times to the present.

Rappaport, Doreen. *Tinker vs. Des Moines: Student Rights on Trial.* New York: HarperCollins, 1993. Part of the Be The Judge, Be The Jury series, this book deals with students' First and Fourteenth Amendment rights by recreating the trial of John Tinker and his classmates who were suspended from school in 1965 for protesting the Vietnam War by wearing black armbands.

Sherrow, Victoria. **Censorship in Schools.** Springfield, N.J.: Enslow Publishers, 1996. well-documented text that clearly defines censorship and traces the development of censorship in schools throughout history. There is detailed discussion of problems of free expression in schools today, including censorship of literature, textbooks, student newspapers, etc. Index.

Steele, Philip. **Censorship.** New York: New Discovery Books, 1992. A short (seven chapters) book that looks at the history of censorship in all forms--its religious, political and moral--aspects, and its impact on American society.

Stein, Richard, and Jeanne Vestal. **Censorship: How Does It Conflict with Freedom?** New York: Twenty-First Century Books, 1995. In six quick chapters, this easy-to-read text explains the First Amendment and applies the meaning of free expression to the use of printed materials, the arts, and the Internet. Glossary. Index.

Attic

The Giving Tree

Harry Potter

Huck Finn

Action Guide
Suggestions for Dealing with
Concerns about Library Resources

The Lorax

Goose

Introduction

Libraries are often challenged by individuals and groups concerned about the availability of a wide variety of library materials to everyone.

Addressing these challenges requires a balance of carefully crafted library policy, knowledge and understanding of intellectual freedom principles, and sensitivity to community needs and concerns. It also requires effective communication.

Communicating Effectively

A few simple communication techniques can go a long way toward defusing emotion and clearing up misunderstanding. Make sure your staff is trained in procedures for handling complaints and understands the importance of treating all people with respect. The goal is to resolve complaints informally whenever possible.

ONE ON ONE

- Greet the person with a smile. Communicate your openness to receive inquiries and that you take them seriously. Listen more than you talk.

- Practice "active listening." Take time to really listen and acknowledge the individual's concern. This can be as simple as "I'm sorry you're upset. I understand your concern."

- Stay calm and courteous. Upset parents are not likely to be impressed by talk about the First Amendment or *Library Bill of Rights*. Talk about freedom of choice, the library's role in serving all people and the responsibility of parents to supervise their own children's library use. Avoid library jargon.

- Distribute facts, policy and other background materials in writing to all interested parties. Avoid giving personal opinions.

- Be prepared to give a clear and non-intimidating explanation of the library's procedure for registering a complaint and be clear about when a decision can be expected.

DEALING WITH THE MEDIA

When a challenge occurs, realize this may attract media attention. How effectively you work with the media may well determine how big the story becomes and will help to shape public opinion.

Some suggestions:

- Have one spokesperson for the library. Make sure that reporters, library staff and the members of the board know who this is. Make it clear that no one other than this spokesperson should express opinions on behalf of the library.

- Prepare carefully for any contacts with the media. Know the most important message you want to deliver and be able to deliver it in 25 words or less. You will want to review your library's borrowing and collection development policies and the American Library Association's *Library Bill of Rights*.

- Practice answering difficult questions and answers out loud. You may wish to invest in a session with a professional media consultant. ALA offers this training at Annual Conferences.

- Keep to the high ground—no matter what. Don't mention the other side by name, either personal or corporate. Be careful to speak in neutral terms. Name calling and personalization are great copy for reporters but create barriers to communication.

- Do not let yourself be put on the defensive. Stay upbeat, positive—"Libraries are vital to democracy. We are very proud of the service our library provides." If someone makes a false statement, gently but firmly respond: "That's absolutely incorrect. The truth is the vast majority of parents find the library an extremely friendly, safe place for their children. We receive many more compliments from parents than we do complaints."

- Be prepared to tell stories or quote comments from parents and children about how the library has helped them.

- Be strategic in involving others. For instance, board members, friends of libraries, community leaders, teachers and other supporters can assist by writing letters to the editor or an opinion column and/or meeting with a newspaper editorial board or other members of the media.

MORE TIPS

The following tips apply both when dealing with the media and when speaking to other audiences—community groups, trustees, staff:

- Never repeat a negative. Keep your comments upbeat and focused on service.

- Keep it simple. Avoid professional jargon. Try to talk in user-friendly terms your audience can relate to: Freedom of choice—not the Library Bill of Rights. "People with concerns" or "concerned parents"—not censors.

- Ask questions. Find out what the approach is, whether there will also be someone with an opposing view present. If you do not feel qualified to address the question or are uncomfortable with the approach, say so. Suggest other angles ("The real issue is freedom of choice. . .")

- Be clear who you represent—yourself or your library.

- Know your audience. Make sure you know which newspaper, radio or TV station you're dealing with and who the audience is—whether they're parents, seniors, teenagers, their ethnic background, religious affiliation and anything else that will help you focus your remarks.

- Anticipate the standard "Who-What-When-Where-and-Why" questions and develop your answers beforehand. Keep your answers brief and to the point. Avoid giving too much information. Let the reporter ask the questions.

- Beware of manipulation. Some reporters may ask leading questions, something like "Isn't it true that . . . ?" Make your own statement.

- Don't rush. Pause to think about what you want to say and the best way to say it. Speak deliberately. It will make you sound more thoughtful and authoritative.

- Don't be afraid to admit you don't know. "I don't know" is a legitimate answer. Reporters do not want incorrect information. Tell them you'll get the information and call back.

- Provide hand-outs with copies of relevant policies, statistics, other helpful information. You also may want to provide a written copy of your statement.

- Never say "No comment." A simple "I'm sorry I can't answer that" will suffice.

- Remember, nothing is "off the record." Assume that anything you say could end up on the front page or leading the news broadcast.

IT'S NOT JUST WHAT YOU SAY

How you look and the tone of your voice can be as important as what you say—especially on radio and TV or before a live audience.

You want to sound and look professional, but also friendly and approachable. Studies have shown

audiences are more likely to trust and believe you if they like how you look and sound.

- Smile when you're introduced, if someone says something funny, if you want to show your enthusiasm for all the good things that your library is doing. On the flip side, be sure not to smile when others are making a serious point.

- Dress and make up appropriately. There are many articles and books on what works for TV and speaking appearances. On radio, use your voice as a tool to express your feelings—concern, enthusiasm, empathy. A smile can be "heard" on the radio.

Don't panic if you misspeak. Simply say "I'm sorry, I forgot what I was going to say." Or, "I'm sorry I was confused. The correct number is..." To err is human, and audiences are very forgiving of those who confess—but don't agonize over—their mistakes.

KEY MESSAGES

When responding to a challenge, you will want to focus on three key points:

- Libraries provide ideas and information across the spectrum of social and political views.

- Libraries are one of our great democratic institutions. They provide freedom of choice for all people.

- Parents are responsible for supervising their own children's library use.

These simple, but sometimes overlooked essentials, are the bulwark against challenges.

SAMPLE QUESTIONS AND ANSWERS

The following questions provide sample language to use when answering questions from the media and other members of the public. You will want to personalize your remarks for your library and community. Remember, keep it simple. Keep it human.

What is the role of libraries in serving children?
The same as it is for adults. Libraries provide books and other materials that will meet a wide range of ages and interests. Many libraries have special areas for children and teenagers. They also have many special programs, such as preschool storyhour,

movies, puppet shows, term paper clinics. In fact, more children participate in summer reading programs at libraries than play Little League baseball!

Why don't libraries restrict certain materials based on age like movie theaters or video stores?

Movie theaters and video stores are private businesses and can make their own policies. Libraries are public institutions. They cannot limit access on the basis of age or other characteristics. Our library does provide copies of movie reviews and ratings, and we encourage parents to use them in guiding their children's library use.

How do libraries decide what to buy?

Every library has its own policies, which are approved by its board. Our library has adopted the *Library Bill of Rights*. We also have a mission statement that says our goal is to serve a broad range of community needs. Librarians are taught as part of their professional education to evaluate books and other materials and to select materials based on library policies.

What is the Library Bill of Rights?

The *Library Bill of Rights* is a policy statement adopted by the American Library Association to protect the right of all library users to choose for themselves what they wish to read or view. The policy is more than 50 years old and has been adopted voluntarily by most libraries as a way of ensuring the highest quality library service to their communities.

Does that mean a child can check out Playboy or other materials intended for adults?

We believe in freedom of choice for all people but we also believe in common sense. It would be extremely unusual for a young child to check out that type of adult material. Most libraries are designed with special areas for children and teenagers. And there are librarians to provide assistance. We also provide suggested reading lists to help them make appropriate choices. Our goal is to provide the best possible service for young people, and we are very proud of what we offer. If you haven't been to our library recently, we encourage you to come and see for yourself!

What should I do if I find something I don't approve of in the library?

Libraries offer a wide range of materials, and not everyone is going to like or approve of everything. If you have a concern, simply ask to speak to a

librarian. We do want to know your concerns, and we're confident we have or can get materials that meet your needs. The library also has a formal review process if you wish to put your concern in writing.

What does the library do if someone complains about something in its collection?

We take such concerns very seriously. First, we listen. We also have a formal review process in which we ask you to fill out a special form designed to help us understand your concerns. Anyone who makes a written complaint will receive a response in writing.

What can parents do to protect their children from materials they consider offensive?

Visit the library with your children. If that's not possible, ask to see the materials your children bring home. Set aside a special shelf for library materials. If there are materials on it you don't approve of, talk with your children about why you would rather they not read or view them. Most libraries provide suggested reading lists for various ages. And librarians are always glad to advise children and parents on selecting materials we think they would enjoy and find helpful.

I pay tax dollars to support the library. Why shouldn't I be able to control what my kids are exposed to?

You can control what your children are exposed to simply by going with them to visit the library or supervising what they bring home. The library has a responsibility to serve all taxpayers, including those you may not agree with—or who may not agree with you. We believe parents know what's best for their children, and each parent is responsible for supervising his or her child.

Public Libraries

An ounce of prevention is worth a pound of cure. Make sure all library staff and board members understand the library's policies and procedures for dealing with challenges. Provide customer service and other human relations training that will help staff deal effectively with sensitive matters.

TIPS FOR DIRECTORS

- Make sure you have an up-to-date selection policy, reviewed regularly by your library board, which includes a request for reconsideration form.

Suggestions for Dealing with Concerns about Library Resources

- As a public institution, the library must develop and implement all policies within the legal framework that applies to it. Have your policies reviewed regularly by the library's legal counsel for compliance with federal and state constitutional requirements, federal and state civil rights legislation, other applicable federal and state legislation, including confidentiality legislation and applicable case law.

- Have the request for reconsideration form available at your major service desks and at all your branch facilities.

- Work with your trustees to ensure that they know and understand the library's policies. Institute formal education procedures so all library trustees have the same information.

- Model the behavior you want your staff to practice. When confronted by an individual or representative of an organization that wants an item or items removed or reclassified, listen closely and carefully to what is being said (and what is not). Respect that person's right to have an opinion, and empathize. Keep the lines of communication open to the greatest possible extent.

- Work with your frontline staff (children's librarians, reference librarians, circulation, branch, bookmobile and support staff) to make sure they understand the library's policies. Help them to understand that they are responsible for implementing the library's policy, not their personal beliefs, while they are on duty. Make this a part of customer service training for your staff.

- Have an ongoing public relations program to communicate the many ways your library serves all members of the community, especially families.

- Build a solid working relationship with your local media before controversy arises. Provide them with upbeat, positive stories about what the library is doing, especially in the area of children's services.

- Put key contacts on your library mailing list. The time to build these relationships is before you need them.

- Hit the talk circuit. Every social, fraternal and religious organization that meets regularly needs speakers for its meetings. This is your opportunity to reach leaders and opinion makers in your community and to build a support network.

TIPS FOR TRUSTEES

- First, remember your role. As a library trustee, you have a responsibility to speak your mind, and to argue forcibly for your point of view within the forum of the board. Once the board has made a decision, it is your responsibility to support the decision of the majority. If you disagree for whatever reason, do not speak out publicly. If, for reasons of conscience, you feel you cannot be silent, it is best to resign from the board before making your opposition public.

- Work with your library director to ensure that the necessary policies are in place and that they are reviewed regularly and thoroughly. Review and affirm your library's selection policy annually and make sure it is followed carefully.

- Insist that the entire board understands the library's collection policy and that it be involved in reviewing and reaffirming this policy annually.

- Be an effective advocate for the library. Use your contacts in the community to educate and mobilize others in support of the library.

- Bring what you hear back to the library director. Your roots in the community may be much deeper and of longer duration that those of the director. The things that people will tell you what they won't tell a director can provide valuable feedback.

- Be involved with the professional state and national organizations serving library trustees.

- Remember the roots of the word "trustee." The community has placed its trust in you to act as an effective steward for the library. This means representing the interests of the entire community, not just a vocal minority.

TIPS FOR CHILDREN'S AND YOUNG ADULT LIBRARIANS

- Make sure you and your staff are familiar with the library's collection policy and can explain it in a clear, easily understandable way.

- Take time to listen to and empathize with a parent's concern. Explain in a non-defensive way the need to protect the right of all parents to determine their own children's reading.

- Keep your director informed of any concerns expressed, whether you feel they have been successfully resolved or not.

- Join professional organizations to keep abreast of issues and trends in library service to children and families.

235

- Encourage parents or guardians to participate in choosing library materials for their young people and to make reading aloud a family activity. Host storytelling, book discussion groups and other activities that involve adults and youth.

- Offer "parent education" programs/workshops throughout the year. National Library Week in April, Teen Read Week in October and Children's Book Week in November provide timely opportunities. Suggested topics: how to select books and other materials for youth; how to raise a reader; how books and other materials can help children and teens cope with troubling situations; the importance of parents being involved in their children's reading and library use; concepts of intellectual freedom.

- Reach out to the media. Offer to write a newspaper column or host a radio or TV program discussing good books and other materials for children and teens. Give tips for helping families get the most from libraries.

- Build bridges. Offer to speak to parent and other groups on what's new at the library, good reading for youth, how to motivate children and teens to read, how to make effective use of the library and other topics of special interest.

School Libraries

School librarians play a key role in making sure that students have the broad range of resources and ideas they need to develop critical thinking skills. Challenges to materials provide a "teachable moment" that can help you build understanding and support for the principles of intellectual freedom, including First Amendment rights, student rights of access and professional ethics.

APPLYING THE PRINCIPLES OF INTELLECTUAL FREEDOM

- Connect academic freedom with intellectual freedom. Academic freedom guarantees the teacher's right to teach and to select classroom and library resources for instruction.

- Make sure everyone involved understands the right of people in a democratic society to express their concerns and that all people have the right to due process in the handling of their complaints.

- Explain the obligation of the school district to provide intellectual and physical access to resources that provide for a wide range of abilities and differing points of view.

- Define intellectual and physical access when appropriate. Intellectual access includes the right to read, receive and express ideas and the right to acquire skills to seek out, explore and examine ideas. Physical access includes being able to locate and retrieve information unimpeded by fees, age limits, separate collections or other restrictions.

- Emphasize the need to place the principles of intellectual and academic freedom above personal opinion, and reason above prejudice, when selecting resources.

- Connect intellectual freedom and access. The freedom to express your beliefs or ideas becomes meaningless when others are not allowed to receive or have access to those beliefs or ideas.

- Stress the need for teachers and librarians to be free to present students with alternatives and choices if students are to learn and use critical thinking and decision-making skills.

PROTECTING STUDENTS AND STAFF WITH A MATERIALS SELECTION POLICY

- Update your materials selection policy. Include a formal reconsideration process for textbooks, gift materials, electronic and other resources used in classrooms, laboratories and libraries. Seek board of education approval.

- Be sure to include the educational goals of the school district and to relate the selection policy to these goals.

- Emphasize the positive role of the selection policy in clarifying the use of educational resources and in ensuring stability and continuity regardless of staff change.

- To ensure uniformity and fairness in dealing with complaints, delegate the responsibility for dealing with complaints and requests for reconsideration to the principal in each school.

- Inform all your school staff (including nurses, secretaries, cafeteria workers and custodians) about the materials selection policy and reconsideration process. Review the policy with staff at the beginning of each school year.

- Distribute a copy of the policy with a simple statement that explains its importance in protecting students, teachers and librarians against censorship.

Suggestions for Dealing with Concerns about Library Resources

PREPARING FOR CHALLENGES

- Develop rationales for the use of required materials in each department and/or grade.

- Introduce the rationales at Parent's Night or open houses or through the school newsletter to help parents understand what materials are being taught and why.

- Work with administrators, teachers and librarians to prepare a list of alternative materials for instructional activities.

- Prepare a packet of materials, including the school district's educational goals and materials selection policy, to give to those registering concerns.

- Review all policies dealing with access to ensure that school rules are conducive to free and open access to the library.

- Prepare an audiocassette that explains principles of intellectual and academic freedom contained in the materials selection policy and reconsideration process for staff members to listen to at home or in their car.

- Inform staff and board members that complaints and requests for reconsideration made by them will get the same due process as from a parent or community member.

- Engage students in discussions and activities related to intellectual freedom. An educated and informed student body can provide a strong support group for the school when educational resources are challenged.

- Remind school administrators that to ignore or override a board-approved materials selection policy can place them in legal jeopardy.

- Unite with other groups in your community that are concerned with intellectual freedom issues. Make them aware of the rights of children and young adults.

- Educate administrators, teachers and other school personnel to the importance of the school library and the role it plays in the education of the student as part of in-service training.

HELPING EVERYONE UNDERSTAND THE RECONSIDERATION PROCESS

- Be clear that materials under reconsideration will not be removed from use, or have access restricted, pending completion of the reconsideration process.

- Emphasize that parents can request only that their child be denied access to materials being reconsidered.

- Develop a time frame to guide the reconsideration process. For example, the building principal should act within 20 working days.

- Emphasize that the reconsideration process is to collect information in order to make thoughtful decisions.

- Keep careful and accurate records of all requests for reconsideration, even those settled informally.

- Report all requests for reconsideration to the superintendent and other staff members. It is important to demonstrate the ability and commitment to protect the rights of students and staff and still provide due process for those registering their concern.

- Provide clear instruction to the appointed reconsideration committee. Have the committee focus on principles rather than attempt to define or interpret materials or parts of materials.

- Keep the request for reconsideration form uncomplicated and non-threatening.

- Direct the reconsideration committee to prepare a report presenting both majority and minority opinions. Present the report to the principal when the process is completed.

- Keep staff and administrators informed about the reconsideration process and progress toward resolution. Rumors and speculation can distort everyone's perceptions of the situation.

- Explain the benefits of a board-approved materials selection policy, which guides staff in the selection of materials and minimizes the arbitrary and personal element. Such a policy also clarifies to the community how the school decides what materials will be used.

Attic

The Giving Tree

Huck Finn

The Lorax

Mother Goose

Maya Angelou
I Know Why the Caged Bird Sings

Sandra Cisneros
The House on Mango Street

"Sandra Cisneros is one of the most brilliant of today's young writers. Her work is sensitive, alert, masterful... rich with music and picture."—Gwendolyn Brooks

John STEINBECK

Of Mice and Men

NINE MONTHS ON THE NEW YORK TIMES BESTSELLER LIST

The JOY LUCK CLUB

AMY TAN
Author of THE HUNDRED SECRET SENSES

Title Index

Note: The bibliographic entries are numbered sequentially and the entry number, rather than the page number, is listed below.

Title Index

Title Index

Title Index

243

Title Index

Title Index

Title Index

Title Index

Title Index

Title Index

Title Index

253

Title Index

Topical Index

Topical Index

Note: The bibliographic entries are numbered sequentially and the entry number, rather than the page number, is listed below.

Selected titles in this book have been indexed in the following categories: Art Books, Biographical Works, Black Literature, Children's Literature, Folk Tales, Gay and Lesbian Literature, Nonfiction, Novels, Occult Books, Philosophical Treatises,

Plays, Poetry, Political Works, Reference Books, Religious Titles, Sex Education Titles, Short Stories, Textbooks, and Young Adult Literature.

Neither this list nor any of the categories is all-inclusive and comprehensive. Rather, this index is meant to assist in the development of displays, articles, editorials, and presentations.

Topical Index

Children's Literature

Topical Index

Topical Index

Folk Tales

Gay and Lesbian Literature

Nonfiction

Novels

Topical Index

Topical Index

Occult Books

Philosophical Treatises

Plays

Topical Index

Poetry

Political Works

Reference Books

Religious Titles

Sex Education Titles

Topical Index

Topical Index

Topical Index

Attic

The Giving Tree

Harry Potter

Huck Finn

Geographical Index

The Lorax

Mother Goose

IN THE NIGHT KITCHEN
MAURICE SENDAK

CAPTAIN UNDERPANTS
AND THE PREPOSTEROUS
PLIGHT OF THE PURPLE
POTTY PEOPLE

EVIL

HORROR

LAFFS

It's Perfectly Normal

CHANGING BODIES, GROWING UP,
SEX & SEXUAL HEALTH

Geographical Index

Note: The bibliographic entries are numbered sequentially and the entry number, rather than the page number, is listed below. This index is meant to assist in the development of displays, articles, editorials, and presentations. For example, a display of titles challenged or banned within your state.

Geographical Index

Geographical Index

Geographical Index

278

Geographical Index

Geographical Index

Geographical Index

Gibsonia, 750, 1589
Girard, 64, 327, 328, 906, 962, 1588
Greencastle, 1536
Grove City, 114
Hanover, 155, 156, 160, 163, 166, 888
Harrisburg, 138, 725, 1116, 1409, 1680
Hempfield, 60, 1561
Hershey, 628
Horsham, 22
Kittanning, 1714
Loysburg, 531
Marple, 93
Mechanicsburg, 1239
Mifflinburg, 914, 1135
Montour, 779
Morrisville, 1138
Muhlenburg, 1319
Muncy, 83
Newville, 320
Norwin, 364
Oil City, 1536
Palmyra, 296, 1392
Pennridge, 1195
Philadelphia, 489, 497, 500, 502, 748, 1346, 1552, 1600, 1672, 1686, 1690
Pulaski, 41
Pulaski Township, 571, 1239
Richland, 171
Saint Mary's, 591
Scranton, 157
Selinsgrove, 1387
Sharon, 910
Shenandoah Valley, 446
Shippensburg, 902
Souderton, 1638
State College, 1609, 1674
Stroudsburg, 82, 328, 918, 1157, 1302, 1394, 1441, 1442, 1523, 1524, 1646, 1647, 1648, 1649, 1670
Tamaqua, 333, 961, 1090
Tyrone, 165, 1189
Upper Dublin, 1609
Upper Moreland, 78
Warrington, 1609
Washington Township, 87, 1406
Weatherly, 1271
West Chester, 844, 1066, 1138, 1153
West Middlesex, 687, 1116, 1536
West Mifflin, 1462
Williamsport, 793
Rhode Island, 1110
Coventry, 1635
Great Bend, 13
Providence, 959
Richmond, 50, 52, 54, 328
Tiverton, 64
Warwick, 773, 1344
Westerly, 1230
Woonsocket, 1601
South Carolina, 35, 1368, 1371, 1372, 1530
Anderson, 89, 1250

Berkeley County, 340, 923, 1298, 1335, 1508
Charleston, 511
Charleston County, 351
Chester, 884
Columbia, 298, 328
Conway, 335
Darlington, 255, 558
Easley, 587
Fort Mill, 1657
Greenville, 299, 795, 988, 1533, 1534, 1536, 1643
Greenville County, 106, 296, 319, 636
Horry County, 610
Saint Andres Parish, 318
Seneca, 1228, 1277
Spartanburg, 204
Summerville, 1387
West Columbia, 460, 1006
South Dakota, 1069
Blunt, 1392
Box Elder, 172
Dupree, 1568, 1720
Faulkton, 635
Hot Springs, 1462
Huron, 916
Onida, 1392
Selby, 1349
Sioux Falls, 95
Sturgis, 1678
Sully Buttes, 590
Tennessee, 383, 1708
Brentwood, 950
Chattanooga, 987, 1536, 1638
Chattanooga-Hamilton County, 1679
Church Hill, 484
Claxton, 87, 278
Cleveland, 133, 553, 746, 763, 792, 811, 879, 882, 979, 1027, 1028, 1029, 1073
Elizabethton, 1445
Gatlinburg-Pittman, 181
Hendersonville, 59
Jacksboro, 1536
Knoxville, 1110, 1536
Murfreesboro, 1210
Nashville, 172, 312, 709, 1151
Putnam County, 1536
Sevierville, 1609
Shelby County, 902, 1536
Union City, 1534
Texas, 654, 1560, 1606
Alamo Heights, 114, 1240
Aledo, 64
Amarillo, 640, 641, 816
Arlington, 155, 333, 1153, 1558
Austin, 37, 1031, 1305
Bastrop, 82
Bedford, 38
Boerne, 639
Boling, 610
Brazoria, 953, 1248
Carrollton, 1624
Cleburne, 1239
Cleveland, 863
Colleyville, 1626

Colony, 559
Commerce, 655, 883
Conroe, 180, 549
Corpus Christi, 534, 686
Dallas, 3, 103, 590, 696, 703, 1117, 1311, 1464, 1651
Deer Park, 1502
Del Valle, 155
Dripping Springs, 78
Eagle Pass, 64
Ector County, 786, 1172, 1173, 1174
El Paso, 1425
Ennis, 1107
Fort Worth, 1311, 1679
Galveston, 646
Garland, 72
Granbury, 1334
Grand Prairie, 1679
Grapevine, 1626
Greenville, 328
Hooks, 59
Houston, 426, 782, 1031, 1609
Huffman, 1462
Hurst-Euless-Bedford, 597
Irving, 77
Judson, 78
LaPorte, 881
Lewisville, 1551, 1609
Lindale, 687, 950, 1102, 1578, 1609
Lufkin, 369
Mercedes, 695, 759
Mesquite, 1165, 1344
Montgomery County, 235, 247, 251, 350, 385, 442, 508, 510, 542, 560, 561, 610, 675, 685, 845, 933, 1393, 1642
Olney, 590
Page, 1284
Plano, 1609, 1610
Richardson, 1490
Richmond, 675
Riveria, 1536
Round Rock, 35, 59, 338, 948, 1131, 1137, 1456, 1477, 1635, 1638, 1660, 1708
San Antonio, 255
Santa Fe, 1368, 1369, 1371, 1372
Southlake, 1019, 1076
Weslaco, 1255, 1541, 1640
Wichita Falls, 7, 278, 1181, 1679
Wimberley, 59
Utah, 156, 240, 821, 1549, 1565
Davis County, 260, 405
Farmington, 564
Ogden, 64, 129, 661, 1392
Orem, 209
Payson, 1250
Provo, 675
Salt Lake County, 796
Vermont, 440, 1606
Bennington, 205
Chester, 1079
Goochard, 863
Richford, 1534
Rutland, 1679
Shaftsbury, 1256

281

Geographical Index